KHRUSHCHEV
REMEMBERS

KHRUSHCHEV REMEMBERS

with an Introduction, Commentary and Notes by

Edward Crankshaw

Translated and Edited by

Strobe Talbott

Illustrated with Photographs

LITTLE, BROWN AND COMPANY · BOSTON · TORONTO

Publisher's Note

THIS book is made up of material emanating from various sources at various times and in various circumstances. The publisher is convinced beyond any doubt, and has taken pains to confirm, that this is an authentic record of Nikita Khrushchev's words. Whether the author intended or expected his words ever to find their way into print, either in his own country or in the West, is a matter of speculation. The publisher takes full responsibility for the manner in which Nikita Khrushchev is represented here. Moreover, he does so with confidence that the genuineness as well as the significance of these reminiscences speak for themselves.

Introduction

by EDWARD CRANKSHAW

WHEN I was told of the existence of Nikita Khrushchev's reminiscences, my first thought was that they would prove to be a
forgery. There have been a number of such documents which were in
fact manufactured in the West for political or commercial reasons.

I did not have to read very far, however, to feel pretty well sure that
these were the real thing; and by the time I had finished I was convinced. Here was Khrushchev himself, quite unmistakably speaking,
a voice from limbo, and a very lively voice at that. To anyone who
had listened to him in the days of his prime, or read his speeches in
Russian, there was no mistaking the authentic tone. I have read almost
every word of Khrushchev's that has been published since the late
1920's. On a number of occasions I have met him face to face, and I
have listened to him speaking publicly and privately inside and outside
the Soviet Union. For just on fifteen years, from his recall by Stalin
from Kiev to Moscow in the winter of 1949 to his eclipse in October,
1964, it was my constant task to study him and try to penetrate his
character and motives. And I am as sure as it is possible to be sure of
anything that cannot be scientifically proved that the man who speaks
in these pages is the man I came to know in all his public aspects and
in the largely hidden processes (still hidden, alas, as far as these reminiscences are concerned) of his struggle to seize power and retain it. He
is older now, tired, diminished by sickness, his vitality no longer what
it was — but in some ways all the more self-revealing because of that.

So what we have is an extraordinary, a unique personal history.

With all its limitations, its evasions, concealments, deceptions, omissions (some deliberate, some due clearly to the forgetfulness of the old), it is the first thing of its kind to come from any Soviet political leader of the Stalin and post-Stalin eras. It takes us straight into what has been hitherto a forbidden land of the mind. And for me the supreme interest and value of this narrative lies in the unconscious revelation of the underlying attitude: the assumptions, the ignorances, the distorted views, which must be shared to a greater or lesser degree by all those Soviet leaders who came to maturity under Stalin and were favored by him for their macabre combination of perfect ruthlessness and almost perfect obedience.

How was this remarkable document assembled, and why? Here I have to say at once that I do not know. My own personal decision as to its authenticity had to be based on the evidence of a Russian typescript and nothing else at all. This, on the face of it, extremely unsatisfactory situation is not so strange to me (though sufficiently bizarre) as it would be to those who work in and with open societies and have no experience of the inhibitions, the conspiratorial procedures, which surround all but the most elementary human activities in the Soviet Union. Often enough in the past I have had to rely on nothing but my own judgment and experience in determining the truth or falsity of this or that Russian-language document. Conversely, there have been occasions when I have handled and published such documents knowing where they came from but pledged not to divulge their provenance to any other person. So I was not surprised or shocked to discover that there would be no answer to any of my questions.

There was still one question, nevertheless, which I had to ask myself. Were those responsible for conveying this material to the West exploiting it as a weapon in political warfare? Particularly, were they working for the final ruin of its author? The first thought, again, was that some faction in or around the Kremlin, might be interested in compromising Khrushchev himself, or alternatively, in undermining individuals or a group in the present Soviet leadership. Careful reading of the whole scotched any such idea. Khrushchev does not emerge very well from these pages, but by Soviet governmental standards he does not emerge all that badly either: there is much self-justification, and the really damaging admissions are the unconscious ones — and the omissions and evasions. More importantly, nobody now active and in office is attacked directly. The main target of criticism is Stalin himself, and after him, Beria; a long way after Beria, Kaganovich and Malenkov. All are either dead or retired. I think it may be assumed that the chief concern of the person, or persons, responsible for releasing these reminiscences to the West — it certainly appears to be one of Khrushchev's chief concerns — was to counter the current attempts to rehabilitate Stalin.

As for the book itself, what we have are the thoughts and memories, highly selective, of an old man trying to justify himself. The material adds up to a rambling, repetitive, sometimes self-contradictory, sometimes inaccurate, usually tendentious narrative in no sort of order and full of gaps. Mr. Talbott has taken this fragmentary record and put it into a coherent narrative in more or less chronological order.

Now a word about the ground that is covered in this book — and the ground that is not covered. There will be two main categories of readers: the general reader who has heard a good deal and read a little about Russia under Stalin and Khrushchev but has not had occasion to penetrate deeply; and the specialist reader who is familiar with the whole story and will be looking for confirmation, correction, and above all, amplification of what he already knows.

For the general reader, many episodes in this narrative, indeed perhaps the whole tone of it, will come, I believe, as a revelation. And it is for him that I have written the short introduction to each chapter and section, and added the notes, putting the various parts into the larger context, pointing to omissions and suppressions, correcting demonstrable misstatements, false implications, and so on, indicating who was who, and generally trying to put the record straight.

For the specialist reader on the other hand, there are no major surprises. He knows the whole story and he does not need me, or anybody else, to signpost the narrative and comment on it point by point. But he will find valuable confirmation of many facts already suspected or established by deduction, innumerable new details and vivid pictures from the life which will fill out and illuminate his existing picture, and above all, the re-creation of the mood and atmosphere of Stalin's court. The picture of Stalin himself confirms and amplifies the picture given us first by Milovan Djilas in his superb *Conversations with Stalin*, then by Svetlana Alliluyeva in *Twenty Letters to a Friend*. It is a picture so different from the conventional image which held the stage for some thirty years, from Stalin's seizure of power until some years after his death, that we cannot have too much of it.

Khrushchev also illuminates himself. From his early days to the death of Stalin he enables us to trace his development as a human being and a Party boss. From 1955, when he began to assume supreme power, until 1964 when he fell, he gives us a great deal of insight into his thinking and activity as a world statesman. What is missing is any sort of account of the power struggle inside the Kremlin which ended in his victory and subsequent defeat. There is a hair-raising account of the arrest of Beria, three months after Stalin's death. But after that, apart from a very personal version of the Twentieth Party Congress and the genesis of the Secret Speech denouncing Stalin, early in 1956, we are told next to nothing directly about the domestic scene during the Khrushchev era — neither the large policy conflicts affecting industry, agriculture, and the government structure, nor the power game in which Khrushchev was so deeply involved and which he played so skillfully. It is necessary to make this clear from the start. The general reader with no particular interest in the detailed maneuvers in the higher echelons of the Soviet Communist Party will scarcely be affected by this blank. The specialist can only hope, as I do, that it will be at least partly filled one day.

Meanwhile we must make do with what we have, which is a great deal. The narrative has two major themes: the self-presentation of a very remarkable man who rose from the humblest peasant background to be master of one of the two greatest powers in the world, and an exposure of Stalin designed to reinforce and elaborate the revelations of the famous Secret Speech (the text of which is given in Appendix 4). Khrushchev is deeply concerned at the attempts of the past few years to rehabilitate Stalin and is doing his best to make this as hard as possible.

As far as Stalin's actual crimes are concerned, Khrushchev has little to add to the revelations of the Secret Speech, and indeed, in some particulars that speech went into fuller detail. It has to be remembered, however, that the Secret Speech has never been published inside the Soviet Union: copies of it were circulated to Party secretaries all over the country and read aloud, in whole or in part, to assemblies of the Party rank and file. These could carry away as much as they could remember. But the Soviet people at large have never been able to read it for themselves, and Khrushchev's account of how he came to make it, though questionable, embodies in fact the first public admission on his part that such a speech was ever made. Given all this, it is natural enough that these recollections should offer, as though for the first time, facts long familiar to the outside world. As in so many matters, the West is still, as it has been for many years, better informed about the details of Stalin's crimes than the Russians themselves.

But the emphasis here is less on Stalin's crimes, though there is a good deal about some of these, than on his general attitude and behavior in his private circle — his way of doing business; and on his relations with his immediate subordinates — and their relations with him.

It is here that Khrushchev finds himself in difficulties. Because in condemning Stalin he is condemning himself. In the Secret Speech he was able to skate around this problem with more or less success because he was concerned not with presenting his own life story but rather with a highly selective exposure of Stalin's own excesses. In this personal narrative, however, he is compelled to tread quite large expanses of very thin ice indeed. And although he manages to conceal or blur his own contribution to the horror of those days' activities — for example, his ardent and vociferous support of Stalin at the height of the purges and the treason trials in 1936–37 and his personal purge of the Ukraine in 1938 — what he does say is quite enough to constitute the most damaging direct admission of complicity, over a long period, with Stalin at his worst. He is plainly aware of this, though even now, recollecting in troubled tranquillity the savagery and viciousness of the past, he seems to be very largely unconscious of the depth of corruption into which he and all his colleagues plunged themselves by the very act of surviving in positions of authority under Stalin.

In condemning Stalin in the Secret Speech, and therefore, by implication, himself, Khrushchev was also condemning the whole system of government that had made Stalin possible. In the Secret Speech, of course, there was not the faintest suggestion of this: it was Stalin who, from the middle 1930's, had perverted the system. And any foreign Communist, most notably the Italian Party Secretary Togliatti, who suggested that any system which had permitted Stalin to behave as he did must be in need of radical overhaul, was brushed aside. This was understandable. Khrushchev had inherited the system from Stalin and made it his own. He could conceive of no other. But now, in his old age, there are flashes here and there which suggest that he has had second thoughts about a number of things. In this connection perhaps the most interesting feature is the short section on the collectivization of agriculture in which he states astonishingly but with perfect accuracy that "the Stalin brand of collectivization brought us nothing but misery." He is speaking of that fearful, man-made catastrophe which caused the deaths of millions, virtually halved the agricultural production of the Soviet Union, and contributed more than any other single factor to the reduction of the Soviet people to thralldom and to the economic imbalance which threatens the leadership to this day. If Khrushchev had been able to bring himself to this admission when he still held power, heaven knows what might not have happened. Scattered about the narrative there are other observations with implications scarcely less explosive.

I should like to say here that I have not seen it desirable to challenge and counter all the assumptions, statements, arguments from which I dissent. My own views on Khrushchev, his failures and achievements, are copiously on record. Here he is speaking for himself. And I have done no more in my own commentary than indicate omissions in his narrative and point out important discrepancies between the facts as presented by him and as generally accepted in the West.

Nor is this the place to recapitulate Khrushchev's career in outline. A detailed record of the main events, many of which he does not touch upon at all, may be found in Appendix 1. Each separate section is prefaced by a short explanation, or clarification, of what follows — and an indication of what has been passed over in silence. This process of clarification is continued in greater detail in the footnotes, which also identify the chief characters referred to, except for a few internationally famous names. Mr. Talbott has provided fuller biographies of Khrushchev's most prominent or enduring colleagues in Appendix 3.

But with all that the fact remains that Khrushchev does not do himself justice in this narrative. In one sense, of course, in the sense that he suppresses a great deal of his own past and presents his own swift rise under Stalin in an altogether too rosy light, he does himself much more than justice. But what he does not do, perhaps cannot do, is provide the clue to his own astonishing transformation from one of Stalin's most reliable henchmen into the international figure who, toward the end of his career, was showing, his temperament and prejudices notwithstanding, signs of wisdom of a really superior kind.

Of course, he remained a prisoner of his past until the end. In some ways he transcended the system which made him and which he helped to make. But he could never escape it entirely, and in the end it destroyed him. His achievement was extraordinary all the same. And the qualities which he began to exhibit toward the end of his career were not suddenly added to him: they must have been latent all the time, when, to all appearance, as a determinedly ambitious Party professional, sycophantic toward his master, bullying toward his subordinates, maneuvering around his rivals with deep peasant cunning, he was simply a thug among other thugs, visibly distinguished from the others only by a certain liveliness of imagination, a warmth of feeling, a sturdy self-reliance, and at times the recklessness of a born gambler. Paradoxically, in one so committed to the Stalinist bandwagon, he had about him, I should think from the earliest days, a certain quality of apartness. He mixed with others of all kinds far more than any Soviet leader before or since. Unlike any other Party official known to me (or any Soviet factory or collective farm manager, if it comes to that) he was not afraid to get mud on his boots. He was always happiest from his earliest days laying down the law and telling people what to do and how to do it and where they were wrong. Even at the summit of his glory he would stand in the middle of a muddy field expounding to an audience of deeply skeptical peasants the proper way to plant potatoes. But he was also a great listener, and he was a very quick learner to the end of his career. I have seen him listening to a group of factory managers when his silence and stillness was so absolute that it seemed to be drawing the virtue out of them and into himself, to be stored up and transformed into his own energy. I have seen him, particularly on his early excursions outside the Soviet Union, making mistake after mistake in rapid succession — but never the same mistake twice. And all the time when he was not himself holding forth, sometimes roughly, sometimes with avuncular benevolence, punctuating his talk with Biblical phrases and allusions which must have burned very deep into him in childhood, those small angry eyes were fixed in the faraway look of a man seeing visions. He did, indeed, see visions.

One of the most disconcerting aspects of this narrative, the narrative of a man who went after power because it was irresistible but who also dreamed of a better world for the Soviet people, was his apparently unquestioning acceptance of some of the vilest of the vile. Their names keep turning up in these pages. He seems to have liked the police chief Yagoda and the still more loathsome Yezhov: they were "honest fellows" before they went wrong. So, in his eyes, was his own chief policeman, Ivan Serov, who was nice to children and could be charm-

ing to his friends when he wasn't rounding up whole nations to be sent
to Siberia or put to death. The answer is, I suppose, that Khrushchev
himself was a naturally violent man (his violence would still break out
even when he had become an international statesman), and violence
was the mood of the times. He and his colleagues were engaged in
the desperate labor of coercing the Soviet people into building a new
Russia, and this could not be done without tears. Anyone — the great
mass of the people in effect — who resisted this transformation had to
be compelled, and the means of compulsion were brutal and summary.
But what he came to object to was arresting people without what
appeared to him good reason. Above all, he objected to Stalin's destruction of "honest Communists." The stress he lays here, as in the
Secret Speech of 1956, on Stalin's crimes against the Party and his
silence about his crimes against the ordinary people is thus quite logical. He really believed that the Party represented a higher form of life.

There is another consideration. Khrushchev was evidently so full
of the sense of his own abilities that other people did not count: at
best, they were useful colleagues and subordinates engaged with him
in the great task. The others were children to be bullied, coaxed, flattered, smiled on, punished. This is not to suggest that Khrushchev in
his early career had his eye on the highest peaks. He was obviously
ambitious. But he had a sharp sense of his own limitations (he was, for
example, very conscious indeed of his lack of formal education). It is
probable that even in the early 1930's, when he found himself touching
the periphery of Stalin's circle, it did not cross his mind that he might
soon be within that circle. He was the sort of man who begins to rise in
a large organization, and continues rising, because he is driven to
dominate all those who happen to be around him — then to look upward. And at each stage in the upward journey he finds, perhaps rather
to his surprise, that he can do much better than the men who were
lately set above him. It was in this way that Khrushchev progressed
from his first post as a very minor provincial Party functionary in
Yuzovka in 1926 to become the Party chieftain of all Moscow precisely ten years later. By then, of course, the feeling that he could do
any job better than anyone he knew, and could outmaneuver his rivals
into the bargain, must have become a certainty. It was a certainty he
would have been at pains to conceal.

Even so, the way to further promotion was effectively barred by a
host of senior figures. These were not the old oppositionists, who for

all practical purposes were already finished though not yet shot, but Stalin's own men, who had supported him against Trotsky, against Zinoviev and Kamenev, against Rykov and Bukharin. These now filled the highest Party appointments in Moscow and all over the Soviet Union, and Stalin, who owed so much to them, had for some time been regarding most of them with a jealous eye. In 1935 it must have seemed to Khrushchev that his rapid upward progress would be checked more or less indefinitely by a massive promotion block. But quite suddenly, in the next three years, the way was cleared by the mass destruction of the very men (among at least seven million others) who stood between him and the inner circle of power. In 1938 he found himself a candidate member of the Politbureau, a year later a full member.

The Politbureau (renamed the Party Presidium in 1952) presented itself to the outer world as an all-powerful committee of hard-faced men who had done well out of the purges and who arrived at policy decisions of great moment after prolonged deliberation. But for some time it has been clear—above all, through the memories of Milovan Djilas and Svetlana Alliluyeva — that it was nothing of the kind. Stalin and Stalin alone made the decisions and told his henchmen to get on with the job. Although Khrushchev's picture of Stalin would have been better for more insight into the qualities of mind and nerve which enabled this sinister man first to maneuver himself into a position where his word was law, then to hold his own with a Churchill, bamboozle a Roosevelt, and play them off against each other (neither of them, after all, was afraid of being clapped into jail and shot), the hair-raising picture of his way of doing business in his later years is evidently true as far as it goes — which is quite a long way. There were no formal meetings. Stalin could still show devastating qualities of insight and coolness — as in his characteristic decision to keep Russia out of North Korea — but for the most part he ran his vast realm, as it were, off the cuff: sitting up half the night watching some idiotic film, carousing, terrified of being alone yet making life intolerable for the men he had in to keep him company, throwing out in his thick Georgian tones casual instructions and threats (but all his instructions were threats) to a sycophantic group the worse for drink and lack of sleep. At a word from him they would go off and set in motion the requisite machinery — for the arrest of an individual none of them had ever heard of, for the rounding up and forcible deportation of a whole people (the Chechens of the Caucasus, the Tartars of the Crimea), for the shooting of one of their own closest colleagues, for the complete rewriting of the history of the Soviet Communist Party, for the introduction of a new style of agriculture guaranteed to produce a ruined harvest over an area the size of Western Europe.

The salvation of Khrushchev was his promotion to be Stalin's viceroy over the Ukraine in 1938. For twelve years he was away from Moscow, from the daily maneuvering for position, from the intrigue, the flattery, and the backbiting that went on in Stalin's shadow, enervating even able men like Malenkov. For three years before the war, and for five years after 1944, he was master of forty million souls — Little Russians, dourer, more practical, harder-working than the dominant Great Russians of Muscovy — who inhabited the borderland which was then the granary of the Soviet Union and its main industrial base. Here, as far as it was possible to be under Stalin, Khrushchev was his own man, able to develop his gifts and also his character, which otherwise must have been corrupted beyond redemption. At first he ruled with all the blinkered arrogance of the worst kind of colonial governor. Then came the war. In uniform now as political advisor to some of the most able generals, he had his first induction into a world far removed from the enclosed circle of the Kremlin. He found himself siding with the soldiers against his fellow Party thugs. He also experienced at first hand the bitter hatred of the regime, the regime to which he belonged, exhibited by the common people of the Ukraine in the early days of the war. Finally he saw, also at first hand, the fearful suffering they were called upon to endure and the way in which, despite that suffering, they turned against the Germans, seen at first as liberators, and fought them to the death — making a demigod out of Stalin, who was unworthy of their trust. There was no other Party chieftain, with the exception of A. A. Kuznetzov who went through the siege of Leningrad and was quite soon afterward shot by Stalin, who experienced for so long and so vividly the realities of life in Soviet Russia under Stalin. I think it changed him. And I think the self-reliance he developed as master of the Ukraine and the patient cunning he developed in keeping Stalin at arm's length, served him well when he was recalled to Moscow at the end of 1949 and when, with Stalin's death in 1953, he saw his chance of getting to the top.

He went very carefully at first. For a time, after he had combined with his colleagues to kill Beria (his account of Beria's arrest, though not of the process which led up to it, is likely to remain the definitive one) he entered into the farce of collective government. But all the time he was working to undermine Malenkov, his most powerful and able rival, who was trying to base his power not on the reactionary Party apparatus but on the new generation of managerial technocrats. Khrushchev first watched in silence as Malenkov put forward all sorts of schemes for domestic reform and international cooperation. Then he struck, invoking the forces of reaction in the name of Lenin, to bring his rival down. Then, without turning a hair, he proceeded to adopt the ideas of reform and coexistence as his own. Thus, even in the struggle to seize the power, which would enable him to break with Stalinism, he employed the techniques he had learned from Stalin.

It was a brilliant performance, culminating in the Twentieth Party Congress and the de-Stalinization in 1956. And although it was touch and go for Khrushchev when the de-Stalinization led directly to the revolts in Poland and Hungary — and to the demoralization of the Soviet people, from which they have not yet recovered — he managed to survive, refused to submit to a majority vote of the Party Presidium calling for his resignation, demanded to be heard by the full Central Committee in accordance with the Party Statutes to which nobody had paid any attention for many years past, had his supporters on the Central Committee flown into Moscow from all over the Soviet Union in a spectacular airlift laid on by Marshal Zhukov, stated his case, took the vote, and won. Malenkov, Molotov, Kaganovich, and others were stripped of their offices and sent off to eat humble pie in the remote provinces. But they were not imprisoned and they were not shot.

Khrushchev was now, in 1957 at the age of sixty-three, on the way to becoming a statesman. But he was still very much a split personality. He could dream great dreams, he could genuinely seek for universal peace and the prosperity of the Soviet Union as part of a peaceful world; but equally, when crossed, he could revert disconcertingly to violence and chicanery. He saw the necessity for a lasting detente between the Soviet Union and the U.S.A. if only to avoid an atomic holocaust; but he still believed that it was a reasonable thing to work for the collapse of the capitalist world while expecting that world to behave in a neutral manner toward the Soviet empire. Just as he could never escape from his Stalinist past, so he could never transcend the suffocating half-truths of his kindergarten Marxism. And his increasing power and experience of the world gave scope not only to his genuinely questing mind, to his deep but intermittent and unregulated insights into reality, but also, alas, to his impatience with restraint and his megalomaniacal predilection for wholesale and ill-prepared schemes for the reform of this or that symptomatic manifestation of a diseased regime. In all this, perhaps, Khrushchev was not so very different from many Western politicians operating on our side of the hill — except for the violence and lawlessness which was his natural air. It is a large exception, of course. What was saddening was that he had in his make-up so many of the attributes of a great statesman. On the other hand, what was astonishing was that in the context of post-Stalin Russia these attributes could make themselves felt at all.

Although he has little to say about his domestic policies, his struggle for supremacy, his fall, the last section of the book, which deals, sometimes in a perfunctory manner, sometimes in enthralling detail, with his contacts with the world outside the Soviet Union, tells us a great deal about his mature outlook and his general state of mind. We see the incessant and unresolved conflict between the habits of thought and action of more than forty years and the lessons derived from a newly perceived reality. Indeed, the contradictions are such that it is insufficient to call him a split personality: his personality was fragmented. Nowhere, it seems to me, are the contradictions more clearly exposed than in the chapter on the quarrel with China, with its lapse into strident chauvinism, and the chapter on Nasser and Egypt, in which all the warmth of his sympathy comes to the surface and yet still finds itself at odds with his calculating eye for personal and national advantage.

Taking the narrative as a whole, every reader must determine for himself the balance between self-deception and deliberate falsification. There is a good deal of both. The problem is at its most acute in those chapters which deal with the Soviet seizure of eastern Poland and the Baltic States. How much did Khrushchev realize what he was doing when he presided over the arrest, imprisonment, or deportation to Siberia of practically the whole of the middle and lower-middle classes of what is now called the Western Ukraine? To what extent did he really believe, in his ignorance of life outside the Soviet Union, that he was conferring immeasurable privilege and benefit on the toiling masses of an alien society? Judgment is not made easier by the fact that in one breath he speaks of this crime as an act of liberation, in the next as an annexation. Again, in his early days he quite evidently believed, with millions of others, that in rallying around Stalin he was assisting in the glorious, if harsh and painful, transformation of the old Russia into a society more just and equitable than any seen on earth. Soon, of course, he became interested in achieving power for its own sake, then in hanging onto it. But how much of the old dream remained, and how deeply did it color his views on the Soviet mission, first in Eastern Europe, then farther afield? There can, of course, be no firm answers to these questions. But they are important ones. And in considering them, it is as well to remember how indelibly our own views may be colored by self-deception, prejudice, and ignorance. It was one of Khrushchev's greatest achievements that with all his intermittent saber-rattling, his threats, his deceptions, his displays of violence, he nevertheless broke out of the Stalinist mold and made it possible for the Western world to hope that a measure of coexistence more complete than he himself was yet ready to conceive might one day be realized.

Translator-Editor's Note

I HAVE attempted here to render Nikita Khrushchev's reminiscences into a coherent, if informal, narrative. The original material, when it came into my hands, was quite disorganized. In trying to turn it into a readable English book, I have had to take certain liberties with the structure. However, I have also taken pains not to misrepresent Khrushchev, even when drawing together diverse fragments into what are here presented as chapters. Except for an occasional paraphrase or improvised transitional sentence, Khrushchev has said everything attributed to him in this book. I have endeavored to preserve the letter and spirit of what he says as well as a suggestion, across the language barrier, of how he says it.

Khrushchev's discourse is characterized by a curious and often intentional alternation between cautious insinuation and bold revelation, apparent indiscretion and deft evasion, earthy vulgarism and stilted euphemism. One moment he sounds like the stereotype of the retired politician, boring anyone who will listen with tales of his greatest moments; the next, he sounds like a crusty propagandist reeling off the Party Line; then like a blusterous bumpkin describing with great relish and embellishment a barroom brawl. And often he sounds like one of modern history's most perceptive insiders. The language of the material on which this book is based abounds with the playful colloquialisms, pet phrases, Marxian rhetorical flourishes, histrionic outbursts, and the odd Biblical archaism that were trademarks of Khrushchev's distinctive oratorical style during his years on the Party podium.

These are the recollections of an old man with much to remember, and seemingly inexhaustible resources of bombast and intelligence, thuggish toughness and instinctive humanity. They comprise an important historical document, particularly for the depositions Khrushchev makes to history's prosecution of Stalin. Khrushchev's reminiscences add up to the most devastating and authoritative case for de-Stalinization ever made, and it is all the more convincing coming from a loyal Soviet citizen and devout Marxist-Leninist. But the book is also an important personal document, a vivid self-portrait by the man who emerged from Stalin's shadow to challenge Stalin's ghost. It can, I think, be taken as a deliberate and revealing exercise in self-rehabilitation, the final testament of a clever peasant-turned-*apparatchik* who rose from the coal mines of the Donets Basin to be one of the most powerful men in the world.

— STROBE TALBOTT

Contents

Illustrations

KHRUSHCHEV
REMEMBERS

Since Khrushchev's narrative abounds with official titles and references to government and Party administrative units, the reader is urged at the outset to consult Appendix 2 (page 535) for a capsule explanation of the structure and terminology of the Soviet Government and the Communist Party.

Prologue

I now live like a hermit on the outskirts of Moscow. I have practically no communication with other people. I communicate only with those who guard me from others — and who guard others from me. I suppose the people around me spend most of their time guarding others from me.[1]

In looking back over the years I emphasize the most striking events of Stalin's rule which damaged the fabric of our Soviet society. There's no point in dwelling on the positive side of Stalin's leadership because that side has already been amply treated at government meetings, in the press, and in our literature. You might even say Stalin's image has been polished and embellished. In fact, if everything positive that has ever been said about Stalin were diminished by eighty percent, enough would remain to praise a thousand great men. Besides, the very history of our Soviet State and the victory of our Communist Party are sufficient testimony to our virtues and our achievements. If we look down the road of the past fifty years, we can see where we started and how far we have come. We have astonished even our enemies.

Even today you can find people who think that we have Stalin to thank for all this progress. Even after his massive crimes were exposed and his guilt indisputably proved at the Twentieth Party Congress,[2]

1. Khrushchev appears to exaggerate his present isolation. In fact he is closely attended by his family and often visited by friends, including foreigners of various nationalities, even Americans. Although "accompanied," he occasionally visits Moscow, where he has an apartment.

2. Khrushchev's Secret Speech on the crimes of the Stalin era was delivered to the Twentieth Party Congress on the night of February 24–25, 1956. The version issued by the US State Department has never been seriously challenged. It was published the next year under the title *Khrushchev and Stalin's Ghost*, with an exhaustive commentary and analysis by Bertram D. Wolfe.

there are those who still quake before Stalin's dirty underwear, who stand at attention and salute it, never questioning that all the deaths caused by Stalin were historically inevitable and relatively insignificant compared to the greatness of our leader, "the Dear Father of the Soviet People," the Genius and Master. There are still those who use the term "Stalinist" for someone who did what Stalin said — and consider this to be a good quality. I consider Stalinism a bad quality.

How much of a genius was Stalin really? What sort of a "Dear Father" was he to us? How much blood shed by our country was Stalin personally responsible for? The covers over the answers to these and other questions should be ripped away. Stalin should be shown to the Soviet people naked, so that he can occupy his proper place in history.

Of course, credit is due Stalin, and it is considerable. But our overall success has mostly been the success of the people, and the strength that sustains us has been derived from the ideas of Lenin. Lenin was the founder of our Party and the creator of our system. He developed the theory on which our State has been built. His ideas form the bedrock of all we have accomplished. Moreover, Lenin explicitly warned us about Stalin. At the very beginning of Stalin's rise to power, Lenin told us about his faults. Subsequent events proved how right Lenin was. As long as Lenin's own ideas were properly applied, they gave us positive results. Even despite Stalin's perversions of Lenin's positions and directives, Marxist-Leninist theory is still the most progressive doctrine in the world. It has enriched, fortified, and armed our people, and it has given us the strength to achieve what we have.

Everyone knows about Stalin's own revolutionary spirit and about his other virtues which have been cited by the Party over and over again. His pretensions to a very special role in our history were well founded, for he really was a man of outstanding skill and intelligence. He truly did tower over everyone around him, and despite my implacable condemnation of his methods and his abuses of power, I have always recognized and acknowledged his strengths. But Stalin's strengths have to be appraised in a number of different respects. It was one thing when they were devoted to consolidating the gains of the Revolution. It was another thing when, under the guise of impassioned slogans about defending our Party against its enemies, his strength was turned against the Revolution. Stalin's vengeance against his own enemies, who he claimed were enemies of the Party, cost us incalculable losses. His intolerance, which the Great Lenin himself had warned us

The young Khrushchev

about, led to the annihilation of thousands of people, devoted in the depths of their souls to the Marxist-Leninist cause.

I will give Stalin credit for one thing: he didn't simply come with a sword and conquer our minds and bodies. No, he demonstrated his superior skill in subordinating and manipulating people — an important quality necessary in a great leader. In everything about Stalin's personality there was something admirable and correct as well as something savage. Nothing about him fitted into its own frame. Everything has to be seen in the light of his very complex personality.

Nevertheless, if he were alive today and a vote were taken, I would vote that he should be brought to trial and punished for his crimes.

I've often been asked, "What was it about Stalin? How could an intelligent man like him do all those terrible things?" I've often asked myself the same thing. I think Lenin had the answer. As early as 1923, when he was writing his Testament, Lenin already saw clearly where Stalin might lead the Party if he kept the post of General Secretary. Lenin understood the basic reasons for Stalin's tyranny long before the executions and other crimes began. He wrote that while Stalin possessed the qualities necessary for leadership, he was basically brutish and not above abusing his power. He suggested transferring Stalin and promoting into his place someone more moderate and conscientious, someone more tolerant in his relations with his comrades, someone who would be sure not to abuse his high position.[3] The Central Committee gave no heed to Lenin's words, and consequently the whole Party was punished.

There was unquestionably something sick about Stalin. I think there's a similar case of this sickness in the present day which should be mentioned. People of my generation remember how the glorification of Stalin grew and grew, and everyone knows where it led. I often see films about China on television, and it seems to me that Mao Tse-tung

---

3. The document commonly referred to as Lenin's Testament was one of several letters Lenin wrote in 1923, when he was trying to head off a split in the Party after his death. The relevant passages: "Comrade Stalin, having become General Secretary, has concentrated enormous power in his hands; and I am not sure that he always knows how to use that power with sufficient caution. . . . Stalin is too rude, and this fault, entirely supportable in relations among us Communists, becomes insupportable in the office of General Secretary. Therefore, I propose to the comrades to find a way to remove Stalin from that position and appoint to it another man who in all respects differs from Stalin in one superiority — namely, that he be more tolerant, more loyal, more polite, and more considerate to comrades, less capricious, etc." (The full text of this and other documents are included in Bertram Wolfe's *Khrushchev and Stalin's Ghost*.)

is copying Stalin's personality cult. He's even echoing some of the same slogans. If you close your eyes, listen to what the Chinese are saying about Mao, and substitute "Comrade Stalin" for "Comrade Mao," you'll have some idea of what it was like in our time. Huge spectacles were organized in Moscow in much the same way they're being organized in Peking today. I used to think that this urge to glorify himself was a weakness unique to Stalin, but apparently men like Stalin and Mao are very similar in this respect: to stay in power, they consider it indispensable for their authority to be held on high, not only to make the people obedient to them, but to make the people afraid of them as well.

I stress the negative side of the Stalin years to show that if Stalin hadn't committed such terrible abuses, we would have achieved even more than we have. I give an account of his crimes in order to help prevent a repetition of the damage he did to the working class, the peasantry, the intelligentsia—to all the laboring peoples of the Soviet Union and of other Socialist countries as well.

Unfortunately much remains a carefully guarded secret. Much is still unknown or unrevealed, some of it weighted down under heavy suppression. But its time will come. It will all come out in the end. Even the best-kept secrets will be brought out into the open.

Perhaps other comrades of mine, men with whom I worked in the leadership under Stalin, will leave their memoirs behind them. If they do, I hope they'll be objective and won't be afraid to tell history what they know about Stalin's faults. They witnessed the same things I did. I was very seldom alone with Stalin. Usually there were five or six, and sometimes as many as ten, other people present when I was with Stalin.

Anyone who really wants to reestablish Leninist norms in the Party must do everything he can to expose Stalin and to condemn Stalinist methods. In order to prevent the ghosts of those years from coming back from their graves to haunt us, we have no choice but to rehabilitate *all* of Stalin's victims. Many of his victims were returned to their rightful places in history by the Twentieth Party Congress; but many more still await rehabilitation, and the reasons for their deaths are still hidden. This is shameful — it's absolutely disgraceful! And now they're starting to cover up for the man guilty of all those murders. I know it doesn't make any sense, but it's a fact nonetheless.

I wonder particularly about a few of our influential military leaders who in their speeches and memoirs are trying to whitewash Stalin and to put him back on his pedestal as the Father of the People. They're trying to prove that if it hadn't been for Stalin, we would never have won the war against Hitlerite Germany and would have fallen under the yoke of fascism. The reasoning behind this sort of claim is stupid. It reflects a slavish mentality. Just because Stalin isn't around any more, does that mean we will succumb to German or English or American influence? Of course not. The Soviet people will always be able to produce leaders and to defend our country against invaders, just as we've always defended ourselves in the past.

I hope I don't even need to point out the absurdity of those military leaders who are trying to rehabilitate Stalin and his victims at the same time. Once when I was in Bulgaria, I made a speech in which I quoted from Pushkin's verse play *Mozart and Salieri,* from the episode in which Mozart, who doesn't suspect that Salieri intends to poison him, says, "Genius and crime are incompatible." [4] The same goes for Stalin. One man can't be both a genius and a murderer. Regardless of his motives, Stalin still committed a horrible crime when he had thousands executed. There are those who argue that Stalin was motivated by his concern for the well-being of the people and not by selfishness. This is crazy. While concerned for the interests of the people, he was exterminating the best sons of the people! The logic here is fairly original. But then, it's always a complicated thing to argue for the acquittal of a mass murderer.

Even now people sometimes say to me, "Comrade Khrushchev, perhaps you shouldn't be telling all these stories about Stalin." The people who say this sort of thing aren't necessarily former accomplices in Stalin's villainy. They're just old, simple folk who became accustomed to worshiping Stalin and who can't give up the old concepts of the Stalinist period. It's hard for them to adjust to the truth. They are the product of defects in the way Party members were trained and conditioned while Stalin was alive. Stalin adapted all methods of indoctrination to his own purposes. He demanded unthinking obedience and unquestioning faith. To go to your death without a single doubt in your mind about what you're dying for is all right, of course, in wartime, but there's another side to that coin: absolute devotion will become bitter hatred if a man discovers his trust has been betrayed. This can become a vicious circle. A country's leaders can't just assume that the people

4. Pushkin's verse play was based on the legend that the fashionable composer Salieri poisoned Mozart out of jealousy.

will close their eyes and never realize what's happening to them. Such an assumption on the part of men in responsible positions will have the effect of undermining the people's confidence in the Party and the Government.

That's why I've always stood for complete truthfulness before the Party, before the Lenin League of Communist Youth [the Komsomol], and before the people — and I stand for truthfulness all the more now. Only through truthfulness can we win the confidence of the people. The truth has always been an inexhaustible source of strength for the Party, and it must continue to be so.

There may still be some who will ask why do I discuss the events that did such terrible harm to our Party and why do I delve into the motivations which led Stalin to do things which cost the lives of tens of thousands of our best sons, the best sons of our Party and of our country. The answer is this: I do it because, unpleasant as these revelations may be, they contribute to the self-purification of our Party. It is no disgrace when the Party questions itself and scrutinizes its own history. Besides, even more people will come over to the side of our Party when they realize that the abuses of Stalin's rule were not committed *by* the Party but were inflicted *on* the Party.

The Party has already begun to correct its mistakes and to guarantee that what happened under Stalin will never happen again. That's why I'm not afraid to tell all. What I have to say is not slander, and it's not malicious gossip. It is meant to serve the important and constructive function of our Party's self-purification. I speak as a man who spent his whole life in close touch with the Soviet people and who also stood for many years at Stalin's side in the leadership of the Party and the country. As a witness to those years, I address myself to the generations of the future, in the hope that they will avoid the mistakes of the past.

ONE

From the Coal Mines to the Kremlin

I

Early Career

Years of Hardship

Khrushchev was twenty-four when he joined the Bolshevik Party in 1918, some months after the October Revolution. Until then, after his peasant childhood, he had worked as a mechanic in the mining town of Yuzovka (renamed Stalino, now Donetsk) in the Donbass region of the Ukraine. As such, he was in a reserved occupation, exempt from military service in World War I. But early in 1919 he joined the Red Army and played his part in the Civil War. It was not until 1922 that he returned to Yuzovka, now a hardened Party activist, to help get the mines working again in a starving and devastated land. Here he provides an insight into the mood of those difficult days when uneducated peasants and workers were put into positions of responsibility only because they had demonstrated their devotion to the Bolshevik cause. It was at this time, from 1921 onward, that Lenin was forced to retreat from socialism and develop his New Economic Policy, which encouraged private enterprise and conceded privileges to bourgeois merchants, traders, and specialists of all kinds as the only way to rebuild the ruined economy. The NEP, of course, aroused great bitterness among the Party faithful. It remained in force until Stalin put an end to it in 1926, two years after Lenin's death.

Nor too long ago many of my old comrades called me up to exchange greetings on the anniversary of the creation of the Soviet Army. It was a great occasion, a day of celebration, devoted to honor-

Khrushchev (third from left in front row) with fellow students at the
Yuzovka Workers' Faculty in the early 1920's

ing our armed forces. Created under the leadership of Lenin, our army won many important victories against our White-Guardist class enemies in the first years of the Revolution. Later, in the Great Patriotic War, we turned back the invasion launched by the fascists against our Marxist-Leninist way of life. Thanks to our army, we met head-on Hitler's threat to the country of soviets and to the Russian people. We have crushed our enemies. Our armed forces have always held high the Banner of the Struggle, the Red Banner of the Working Class, stained with the blood of the Soviet people in its battle against our class enemies.

Our armed forces have come a long way, a very long way. I'm proud to say that it was my privilege to serve in our glorious armed forces in the first, most dangerous years of our young Soviet Republic. From January, 1919, until the end of the Civil War I underwent many severe hardships in the ranks of the Red Army. I happened to serve in the Ninth Rifle Division. We were first driven back from Orel to Mtsensk. We then took the offensive and marched right through a hail of enemy bullets, reaching Taganrog by Christmas of 1919. By that time our rifle division had been attached to the First Mounted Army under the command of Semyon Mikhailovich Budyonny.[1] We pursued the retreating Whites and by April, 1920, completed a long march to the Black Sea. We captured Anapa and drove the White-Guardist bands into the sea. Our division occupied Anapa and rested for five or six days, then moved on down the Taman Peninsula. I remember we celebrated the great proletarian holiday, May First, in Taman.

When I returned from the Front to the Donbass at the beginning of 1922, hard times had set in. Lenin was striving to use the respite at the end of the Civil War to build up our industry, our economy, and the living standard of our people. Armed with our staunch devotion to the ideas of Lenin, we set about to accomplish in a few years what had taken the capitalist countries decades. We had to pull in our belts and we suffered cold, hunger, and deprivation. We spared no sacrifice to build up our heavy industry and our army so that no enemy would ever be able to threaten our borders again.

There was famine in the mines of the Donbass in 1922, and even iso-

1. Khrushchev was a junior political commissar attached to the fighting troops. S. M. Budyonny, a sergeant major in the Tsarist cavalry, who became a hard-drinking crony of Stalin's, was operating against General Denikin's army, which at one time offered the most dangerous threat to the new Bolshevik regime. It was this Budyonny, now a marshal and hopelessly out of his depth in modern warfare, who led his army to disaster in the Ukraine when Hitler invaded in 1941.

Krasin, Molotov, and A. S. Yenukidze with bust of Lenin, December, 1924

lated incidents of cannibalism. The villages were even more ravaged than the mines. My first wife, Galina, died during the famine in 1921. Her death was a great sadness to me. I was left with two children to look after, my son Leonid and my daughter Julia. In 1924 I married again, to Nina Petrovna. Those first years of Soviet Power were years of struggle and hardship and self-sacrifice. But the people still believed in the Party; even the most illiterate of our citizens understood the Party's slogans and rallying cries. The people knew that these hardships were being thrust upon us by the bourgeoisie — both by our own bourgeoisie and by the bourgeoisie of the world at large, which was instigating counterrevolution and intervention against us. We told ourselves that no matter how bad things were, they had been worse in the old days, before the Revolution.

Actually, this wasn't true for everyone. The most highly skilled miners in the pits where I worked in the Donbass had been better off before the Revolution than immediately after it. As far as my own material condition was concerned, I'd say I lived worse after the Revolution when I was a deputy manager of mining operations than before the Revolution when I was a simple metalworker.

Most of us willingly submitted to privation because, as we saw it, we had to squeeze the last drop of productivity out of our resources in order to industrialize the country as quickly as possible. If we were to survive, we had to catch up with the capitalists. Sometimes achieving this goal required sacrificing moral principles as well as material comfort. But on the whole the people gladly underwent these sufferings for the Party's sake. And in the space of a few years we brought a modern industrial society into being.

In those days, in order to be a Communist you couldn't expect to be rewarded for your sacrifices with eventual blessings. It's not like that nowadays. Of course, there are still people of principle among Communists, but there are also many people without principle, lickspittle functionaries and petty careerists. Nowadays a Party card all too often represents nothing more than its bearer's hope of finding a comfortable niche for himself in our Socialist society. Shrewd people these days manage to get much more out of our society than they put into it. Their attitude is a violation of the principle that a citizen should be compensated according to the quantity and quality of labor which he expends in the building of Communism. It's sad but true. This state of affairs is one of the scourges of our time.

I don't mean to say that there wasn't a certain amount of opportunism among would-be Communists in the first years of the Revolution, too. It existed, but to nowhere near the same extent. I remember during the Civil War when we attacked and occupied the city of Malo-arkhangelsk, a dim-witted schoolteacher asked me what post he would be given if he joined the Communist Party. This question immediately put me off, but I restrained myself and said: "You'll be given the most responsible and prestigious of all posts."

"Which one is that?"

"You'll be given a rifle and sent to fight the White-Guardists. You'll have a chance to help decide whether Soviet Power will prevail in our country. What greater responsibility is there?"

"And what if I don't want to join the Party?"

"It's just as well you don't. The Party will be better off without you."

It was during this period of the Civil War and the years of hardship immediately afterward that Stalin earned his reputation as a "specialist-eater." A specialist-eater was someone who refused to trust the bourgeois specialists whose help Lenin had enlisted, particularly in the formation of the Red Army. In those days Trotsky was head of the People's Commissariat of Defense.[2] Naturally Trotsky followed the directive he got from Lenin to seek out commanders for the Red Army from among the bourgeois officers who had been trained in tsarist military academies. In later years Stalin used to enjoy telling us that he refused to have anything to do with the bourgeois officers whom Trotsky dispatched to Tsaritsyn and that they invariably turned out to be traitors.

Admittedly, during this period, a certain amount of distrust of the bourgeois intelligentsia was justified. In the first days of the Revolution most intellectuals failed to make clear where they stood. Some of them emigrated at the very beginning of the Revolution. Some of them waited to see what would happen. Some of them tried to sabotage us, and the rest actively joined the struggle against Soviet Power, organizing armed resistance. Hence the strong antispecialist or "specialist-eater's" attitude among the people. Party organizations, acting on

2. Trotsky, of course, as Lenin's Commissar (or Minister) of Defense, was the creator of the Red Army. It is interesting to find Khrushchev giving him credit for this after forty years of total rejection. It was at Tsaritsyn (later Stalingrad; now Volgograd) that Stalin had his first major quarrel with Trotsky, which was to have such tremendous consequences. Budyonny and Voroshilov objected strongly to Trotsky's commissioning of young Tsarist officers who were ready to fight in the Red Army. Stalin supported them.

Lenin's instructions, were hard pressed to control and restrain this attitude.

In addition to distrust, there was also much resentment against the special privileges which accrued to the specialists. Unavoidable but very embarrassing developments in our society aggravated the people's hostility to the bourgeois intellectuals whom Lenin recruited. The country was ravaged. Many workers were worse off than they'd ever been under capitalism. They were starving. Although the workers were willingly making great sacrifices for the sake of industrializing and fortifying our country, they were under the impression that with the victory of the Revolution their lives would improve materially. Therefore they resented the fact that the bourgeois specialists weren't having to suffer the same hardships as everyone else. After all, if people were going to be equal before the law, they should be equal in terms of material security as well. We had been taught by the Party to believe that once we set about building Communism, the means of consumption would be evenly distributed among all those who toiled. Yet here were bourgeois specialists being singled out for special privileges and high wages while the workers were being paid less than in the old pre-Revolutionary times.

The reason for this was as follows: under capitalism, specialists had private apartments with all the necessary conveniences, while the workers had nothing. For the workers, "communal services" meant wells or water barrels which were usually a long way from where they lived and worked. The workers had always had to trudge to and from the market through the mud, while the specialists had ridden on horseback. There was terrible animosity among the people toward the specialists, and toward their wives and servants especially.

Despite these obvious injustices, Lenin and the Party understood that it was vitally important to enlist the bourgeois specialists to the cause because, without their scientific expertise, it would have been impossible to build our society on the foundation of technology. The building of a Communist society requires extensive and profound scientific knowledge. Lenin and the Party also understood that the only way to enlist the specialists to the cause was to appeal to their material interests. This meant they had to be given certain privileges which at least partially corresponded to the privileges they had enjoyed under the capitalists. They had to be given passable apartments and adequate transportation. A chief engineer would have a pair of horses and a driver, while a regular engineer would have only one horse and a driver. Of course, this wasn't exactly luxury, but in the workers' minds it seemed to be.

In order to enlist bourgeois officers into the Red Army, Lenin knew he would have to give them the freedom to make decisions on their own. Commissars were to watch over the bourgeois officers but not to interfere with them. Just imagine: a former colonel of the old tsarist army would suddenly be given a command in the Red Army. During the Civil War, I saw many misunderstandings arise between officers and the commissars who were standing over them. As Stalin was later to remind us so frequently, there were many instances of treason among the bourgeois officers. A certain amount of treason had to be expected. These people had been brought up under the old capitalist regime. Some came over to our side out of fear, some came for the novelty, others came because they had no alternative — they had to earn a living. And some came out of treachery.

But the Party had no choice. We had to win over as many specialists as possible to our cause. It was part of Lenin's genius that at such a critical moment he was able to learn some lessons from the capitalists and take advantage of their experience and expertise.

Stalin, for his part, remained a specialist-eater all his life.

Another of Lenin's measures that proved to be very controversial was the New Economic Policy. This was a bold, decisive, and dangerous — but absolutely necessary — step for him to take. It was another example of Vladimir Ilyich's wisdom and foresight. In essence the New Economic Policy meant the restoration of private property and the revival of the middle class, including the kulaks. The commercial element in our society was put firmly back on its feet. Naturally this was, to some extent, a retreat on the ideological front, but it helped us to recover from the effects of the Civil War. As soon as the NEP was instituted, the confusion and famine began to subside. The cities came back to life. Produce started to reappear in the market stalls, and prices fell.

The Party slogan at the time was "Learn Commerce!" We were supposed to defeat the private merchants and NEP men not by taking administrative measures against them, but by beating them at their own game. We tried to take over as much commerce as possible and put it in state hands. We tried hard to underprice the NEP men in state cooperatives and also to offer higher quality and better service. But we didn't have much success. Merchants who were in business for themselves could put up better displays of their products and give their customers more personal attention. Private stores catered to housewives, who like to have a choice when they shop; they like to browse around and examine everything carefully.

I remember that when I lived and worked in Yuzovka I went around to the marketplace almost every day. I always went straight to the workers' cooperative. As soon as I stepped into the store, my old friend Vanya [Ivan] Kosvinsky, who was chairman of the cooperative, would say, "Well, I suppose you've come by to scold me again, haven't you? What can I do? We're doing everything we can to compete with the NEP men, but the private merchants still seem to be attracting more customers."

In the southwest corner of the Yuzovka industrial area, at the very edge of the mining fields, there were many Greek settlements which raised livestock. They sold their meat cheaply — and privately. By the fall of 1925 there was an abundance of vegetables, watermelons, and poultry, and meat cost only fifteen kopeks a pound. We had returned to prewar standards. Fortunately, the political situation at the time was favorable. The workers understood the Party guidelines and followed them. But it was still difficult and even painful for us to adapt ourselves to the New Economic Policy.

First Rungs on the Party Ladder

Khrushchev's rise in the Party apparatus was very swift. Although here and throughout his reminiscences he insists that he was reluctant to accept promotion, it is clear that very soon after his return to Yuzovka he decided that his future lay in full-time Party work rather than industrial management as such. And although at first he did not understand the real significance of Stalin's vicious and successful campaign against Trotsky, he owed his early career to Lazar Kaganovich (see Appendix 3), who was very close to Stalin, and more immediately, to the Yuzovka Party Secretary, K. V. Moiseyenko, who was a committed Stalinist. Here and later it becomes obvious that Khrushchev had no clear idea of the policy differences between the various groups of opposition Communists. His Marxism was received doctrine of a fairly primitive kind — slogan-Marxism, or hurrah-Marxism, it might justly be called. The heretic, the enemy, was anyone who questioned Stalin. Temperamentally, Khrushchev was on the side of Stalin's thugs and bullies, the practical men who got things done, ruthlessly and without counting the cost; and he was against the intellectuals, largely from bourgeois backgrounds, often Jews, often with years of foreign exile behind them, whom Stalin was soon to destroy. After Lenin's death in 1924, Stalin combined with G. E. Zinoviev (head of the Comintern and Leningrad Party chief) and L. B. Kamenev (head of the Moscow Party apparatus) to defeat Trotsky. Their victory was celebrated at the Fourteenth Party Congress in December, 1925, which Khrushchev attended as a provincial delegate. It was now that the slogan "Socialism in One Country" was proclaimed. And it was this Congress that saw the final suppression of free debate within the Party. Stalin then combined with Rykov and Bukharin to put down Zinoviev and Kamenev. In 1927, while Khrushchev was holding Yuzovka for Stalin, Trotsky was expelled from the Party. When Khrushchev arrived in Moscow in 1929, the First Five-Year Plan had been launched and the country stood on the eve of the terrible events which ensued from the forced collectivization of agriculture.

I SUPPOSE you could say my political education began during my boyhood in the little village of Kalinovka where I was born. My schoolteacher there was a woman named Lydia Shchevchenko. She was a revolutionary. She was also an atheist. She instilled in me my first political consciousness and began to counteract the effects of my strict religious upbringing. My mother was very religious, likewise her father — my grandfather — who as a serf had been conscripted into the tsarist army for twenty-five years. When I think back to my childhood, I can remember vividly the saints on the icons against the wall of our wooden hut, their faces darkened by fumes from the oil lamps. I remember being taught to kneel and pray in front of the icons with the grown-ups in church. When we were taught to read, we read the scriptures. But Lydia Shchevchenko set me on a path which took me away from all that.

Well before the Revolution I became an avid reader of proletarian and Social-Democrat newspapers. I read *Pravda* as soon as it started coming out regularly in 1915, when I was a metal fitter at the genera-

tor plant of the Pastukhov mine near Yuzovka. My job at the Pastukhov mine was one of a series of jobs I had after being fired for taking
part in a strike in 1912. I had some of my first serious political conversations at the pit in 1915. We had many prisoners of war from the Aus-
tro-Hungarian army working there, mostly Austrians but some Czechs,
too. I got on very well with the Czechoslovaks. They used to tell us
Russians that we Slavs were all brothers. They said they didn't want to
make war on us, they only wanted to live in peace and friendship. I remember two Czechs in particular. I used to invite them back to my
quarters for tea with jam. In return, they gave me lessons in mechanical drawing, which was very useful to me in my profession. The
Czechs used to tell me about the Pan-Slavist movement and about how
we were united by our common Slavic blood. I admit this was the first
I'd ever heard of Pan-Slavism, and I was very impressed. The fact that
I was so fascinated by what those Czechs had to tell me about the so-
called Pan-Slavist brotherhood shows that I was still a long way away
from understanding the Marxist-Leninist concept of class solidarity.

When I read Emile Zola's *Germinal,* I thought that he was writing
not about France, but about the mine in which my father and I
worked. The worker's lot was the same both in France and in Russia.
When, later on, I listened to lectures on political economy and the lec-
turer spoke about the wage system under capitalism, about the exploitation of the workers, it seemed to me as though Karl Marx had been
at the mine where my father and I had worked. It seemed as if it were
from observing our life as workers that he had deduced his laws and
scientifically proved why and how the workers must liberate themselves from capitalist slavery and build a Socialist society.

I became a Bolshevik and a member of the Communist Party after
the Revolution and a short time later joined the Red Army as a political worker and propagandist. As soon as I returned from the Front
after the Civil War, the Yuzovka Party organization made me a deputy
manager of the Ruchenkov mines. I'd worked there ten years before,
when the mines belonged to a French company. The manager in 1922
was my close friend Yegor [Georgi] Trofimovich Abakumov. This was
the Abakumov who later became Minister of the Coal Industry, not the
one who was to be Minister of Internal Affairs under Stalin.

I was offered the directorship of the Pastukhov mines but I asked instead to be released from my Party duties so that I could study at the
Yuzovka Workers' Faculty. After persistent requests, I finally prevailed

With his colleagues in the Donbass when he was a metal fitter

upon Abram Pavlovich Zavenyagin, the Secretary of the local Party committee, to send me to the Workers' Faculty.

Subsequently I held various posts in the Yuzovka Party organization, and in 1925 I was elected a delegate to the Fourteenth Party Congress in Moscow. The head of the Yuzovka organization at that time was a medical student named Kostyan Moiseyenko. He had a petty-bourgeois streak in him, and he had contacts with people who were little better than NEP men. Later we were to remove him from the secretariat of our organization, causing an uproar that went all the way to the Central Committee of the Ukrainian Communist Party, which sent a commission out to Yuzovka to investigate Moiseyenko's removal. In the end the commission supported us against him. But Moiseyenko was an excellent orator and a good organizer — you couldn't take that away from him — and at the time of the Fourteenth Party Congress he still had a firm grip on the minds of Communists in our area. He was head and shoulders above anyone else in the local active Party membership.[3]

There were four voting delegates and four consulting delegates chosen to go to the Congress. I was a consulting delegate. We were chosen democratically, on the basis of the size of our respective Party constituencies. I was head of the Petrovsko-Marinsk District, which was only the sixth or seventh largest Yuzovka district in terms of the number of Party members, so it was fitting that I should have been a consulting rather than a voting delegate.

I was overjoyed to have an opportunity to see Moscow and to attend an All-Union Congress. We lived in the House of Soviets at Number 3, Karetny Row. Our quarters were very simple and crowded. We slept on plank beds and were all stacked together like logs. I remember that Postyshev, the Secretary of the Kharkov organization, used to sleep with his wife in a row with some of the rest of us.[4] This arrangement made for some jokes at Postyshev's expense, but it was all in good fun. We were young, and besides, Postyshev was well respected in the Party. The first morning after we got to Moscow I tried to take a streetcar to the Kremlin, but I didn't know which number to take and ended up getting lost. From then on I woke up early and walked to the Kremlin. It took longer, but at least I learned my way around. I

3. It was at the Fourteenth Party Congress that Moiseyenko distinguished himself by helping to shout down the opposition to Stalin. Moiseyenko was demoted in the following year, one of many provincial secretaries who were purged for corruption.

4. This was Pavel Postyshev, a devoted Stalinist, who was to rise to the top in the Ukraine, only to be arrested and executed in the purges.

even skipped breakfast in order to be sure of arriving in time to get a good seat.

Each delegation had a block of seats assigned to it, but within each block it was first come, first served. I always tried to find a seat right in front of the podium. The Congress was held in the hall where the Supreme Soviet now sits. At that time it hadn't yet been rebuilt, and it was still called Vladimir Hall. The Ukrainian delegations sat in the center of the hall, and the Yuzovka delegation had the first rows in the center section. The proletarian Donbass organization was given the best seats in recognition of its strategic position in the Party organization of the Ukraine.

The head of the Ukrainian organization was Lazar Moiseyevich Kaganovich, and his Politbureau included Petrovsky, Chubar, Shikhter, and Skrypnik. Kaganovich was First Secretary of the Central Committee of the Ukrainian Communist Party, and Chubar was Chairman of the Ukrainian Council of Ministers.[5]

The Fourteenth Party Congress made a lasting impression on me. Here I was, only a few feet from the leaders of our State and our Party! I had my first chance to see Stalin in the flesh. I was very impressed by him, and I think I can explain why by mentioning an incident which occurred during the Congress.

At one point the head of our Regional Party organization, Comrade Moiseyenko, requested that Comrade Stalin permit himself to be photographed with our delegation. We were informed that Stalin would be willing to join us when our group photograph was taken and that he would let us know when he would be free. We waited and waited. Finally we were told to gather in Catherine Hall during a recess of the Congress. Stalin arrived and sat down. We all took our places around him. The photographer, whose name was Petrov, went to his camera and started to arrange the group for the picture. Petrov was a respected specialist in his trade. He had worked around the Kremlin for years and was well known among Party workers. He started giving us instructions on which way to look and how to turn our heads. Suddenly Stalin remarked in a voice everyone could hear, "Comrade Petrov loves to order people around. But now that's forbidden here. No

5. The important names here, apart from Kaganovich, are V. Y. Chubar and N. Skrypnik. Chubar was Prime Minister of the Ukraine; Skrypnik was Minister of Education. Skrypnik, after bravely opposing Postyshev's first major purge of the Ukraine, which was designed to subdue Ukrainian national consciousness, committed suicide in 1933. The fate of these and other personalities is described in Chapter 3.

one may order anyone else around ever again." Even though he said this jokingly, we all took him seriously and were heartened by the democratic spirit he displayed.

A similar incident occurred a few years later when my friend Lev Abramovich Rimsky took a group of students to Moscow to see the sights of the capital. Rimsky decided to ask Stalin if he would receive a delegation of these students. As Lev Abramovich told me, "I called the Kremlin and was put straight through to Stalin. What accessibility! Stalin agreed to receive us. When we arrived at Stalin's office, I said, 'Comrade Stalin, we've come from the city formerly called Yuzovka which now bears your name. It's called Stalino. Therefore we'd like to ask you to send a letter of greeting back with us to the Stalino workers.'" And here is how Stalin answered this request: "What do you think I am? A big landowner? The workers in the factories aren't serfs on my farm. It would be insulting and completely unsuitable for me to write them a letter of greeting. I won't do it myself, and I don't like it when other people do that sort of thing." Lev Abramovich was pleasantly surprised. When he got home he spread this story around to illustrate Stalin's democratic spirit, his accessibility, and his proper understanding of his place.

Most of what I saw and heard of Stalin during these early years pleased me very much. In the twenties transcripts of Politbureau sessions were distributed to Party organizations throughout the country, where they were read and studied by active Party members. I remember reading in one of these transcripts an argument between Stalin and either Trotsky or Zinoviev. One phrase that Stalin used stuck in my memory. He said something like this: "I'll do everything in my power to preserve unity in the Party and to fortify the monolithic solidarity of our movement. Don't you see what you're doing? Good God,[6] man, don't you see what you're saying? But — God be with you, God be with you!" Now, even though he'd once studied in a seminary, Stalin certainly wasn't a religious man, and an expression like that wasn't at all characteristic of him. I took his saying "God be with you" to mean: "There's nothing more I can do to help you. I don't wish you evil. May God be with you, and may He help you to see the error of your ways." While naturally I'm not a religious man either, and never have been, I was glad to see this evidence of Stalin's tolerance for his opponents.

6. Atheism is an article of Marxist faith, and therefore Khrushchev, as a doctrinaire Marxist, would not capitalize the g of God.

In 1925 the public hadn't yet gotten wind of the fierce struggle going on inside the Party. Stalin had emerged as General Secretary while Lenin was still alive and while Trotsky was still active. However, years were to go by before the very special nature of Stalin's role became known in Party circles, to say nothing of among the masses.

In 1927 I attended — again, as a delegate from the Yuzovka Party organization — the Fifteenth Party Congress, at which Stalin and his supporters squared off against the Zinovievites, or "Leningrad opposition," as they were then called. I remember we used to say that even the sparrows were chirping the news to the man in the street that a schism had formed in the Party.

Our delegation was again quartered in the House of Soviets at Number 3, Karetny Row. Shortly after we arrived in Moscow, we were told that Yakov Arkadyevich Yakovlev was coming by to talk to us about certain developments in the Party and to warn us about the situation which was likely to arise at the Congress.[7] I think Yakovlev was one of Sergo Ordzhonikidze's deputies.[8] We knew Yakovlev must be coming to see us on factional business because we were told not to let anyone into the meeting except members of the Ukrainian delegations.[9] We also realized that Yakovlev was passing on to us confidential information and instructions directly from Stalin himself. Yakovlev explained where we differed with the Zinovievites and told us what we were to do. In other words, he prepared us to carry out factional work against the Zinoviev-Kamenev opposition which was then gathering force. Zinoviev was Chairman of the Comintern, the international Communist organization which steered the course of the world revolution. As the main person in the international Communist movement, Zinoviev commanded much authority and prestige. Yakovlev explained that Zinoviev was to be co-speaker with Stalin at the Congress. (He had given the General Report after Lenin's death and had been co-speaker with

7. Y. A. Yakovlev, a onetime People's Commissar of Agriculture, was deeply involved in the excesses of collectivization and was on many occasions used by Stalin as a trusted strong-arm man. This did not save him from being condemned as a right-wing oppositionist in 1938 and subsequently shot. The irony was that the real "right" oppositionists had been opposed to the collectivization.

8. "Sergo" Ordzhonikidze was, like Stalin, a Georgian. For years he was very close to Stalin.

9. This segregation of the various delegations to the Fifteenth Party Congress is exceptionally interesting. It shows us that as early as 1927 Stalin refused to allow devoted Party delegates from different Republics even to talk to each other. So a long-lived tradition started. At the Moscow Congress of world Communist Parties in 1960, the foreign delegates complained bitterly that the Soviet comrades (headed by Khrushchev himself) refused to allow them to meet and talk together.

Stalin at the previous Party Congress, the Fourteenth, in 1925.) Yakovlev told us that the Leningrad delegation to the Fifteenth Congress had written a letter to the Congress Presidium demanding, on the basis of the Party Statutes, that Zinoviev once again be given equal time with Stalin.

When the Congress began we found that once again we had the central place in the hall. On our left were the Leningraders, and on our right was the Moscow delegation. We were in contact with the Moscow Party workers, coordinating with them our activities against the Leningrad opposition. Discussions and arguments were going on everywhere, formal and informal, in large groups and small, during the sessions and during the recesses, inside St. George's Hall and out in the corridors.

I was distressed to find my old comrade Abramson in the enemy camp. He had been the editor of the newspaper *The Dictatorship of Labor* in Yuzovka when I returned from the army in 1922. Now he was working in Leningrad as the secretary of some district committee. He was a good Communist, but like all Leningraders, he was a Zinovievite. The Zinovievites had also added Badayev and Nikolayeva[10] to their delegation, so that the opposition might swing more weight at the Congress. These were good active Party members. They're all dead now.

Stalin, Rykov, and Bukharin spoke for the Central Committee line — that is, Stalin's line. There was the Central Committee line on one side and the opposition on the other. There was nothing in between.

A word about Bukharin. He was much respected and very popular. I had seen him and heard him speak back in 1919 when I was serving in the Red Army. As Secretary of our unit's Party cell I had been invited to a meeting of the active Party members in Kursk Province at which Bukharin gave a speech. Everyone was very pleased with him, and I was absolutely spellbound. He had an appealing personality and a strong democratic spirit. Later I met some comrades who had worked with him — simple, progressive Communists from Moscow who were more or less at my level of political development. They told me how Bukharin had lived with them in their dormitory and eaten with them

10. K. I. Nikolayeva was, apart from Nadezhda Krupskaya, Lenin's widow, the only woman who was a full member of the Central Committee on the eve of the great purge. Although she had indeed supported Zinoviev, she survived the purges and still held her position when the Terror subsided.

at their mess at the same table. This impressed me very much. Bukharin was also the editor of *Pravda*. He was the Party's chief theoretician. Lenin always spoke affectionately of him as "Our Bukharchik." On Lenin's instructions he wrote *The A-B-C of Communism*, and everyone who joined the Party learned Marxist-Leninist science by studying Bukharin's work. In short, Bukharin was much beloved in the Party.

During the Fifteenth Party Congress some delegation or other presented the Congress Presidium with a steel broom. Rykov, who was Chairman of the Presidium, made a speech, saying, "I hereby present this steel broom to Comrade Stalin so that he may sweep away our enemies." There was a burst of appreciative applause and laughter. Rykov himself broke into a smile and then laughed, too. He obviously trusted Stalin to use the broom wisely, for the good of the Party, against anti-Party elements and opponents of the General Line. Rykov could hardly have foreseen that he, too, would be swept away by this same broom which he handed over to Stalin in 1927.[11]

At the time of the Fifteenth Party Congress we had no doubt in our minds that Stalin and his supporters were right, and that the opposition was wrong. I still think that Stalin's ideological position was basically correct. We realized that a merciless struggle against the opposition was unavoidable. We justified what was happening in a lumberjack's terms: when you chop down a forest, the chips fly. After all, it was no accident that Stalin held the leading position in the Party, and it was no accident that the Party supported him against such powerful opponents as the Trotskyites, Zinovievites, and later the right-left bloc of Syrtsov and Lominadze.[12] Stalin was a powerful personality, and he had contributed greatly to the mobilization of the Party's forces for the reconstruction of our industry and agriculture and the strengthening of our army. It shouldn't be overlooked that Stalin's

11. A. Rykov, Prime Minister of the Soviet Union in succession to Lenin, and N. Bukharin, the great Party intellectual and beloved friend of Lenin's, had helped Stalin defeat Zinoviev and Kamenev. Very soon they were themselves to be condemned as right oppositionists. They were to be tried at the third and most celebrated of the great treason trials in 1938, condemned, and shot.

12. S. Syrtsov, who became a candidate member of the Politbureau, and Prime Minister of the Russian Federal Republic, and V. V. Lominadze, one of Stalin's closest friends, had both helped Stalin, first against Trotsky, and then against Bukharin. In the early thirties they turned against him actively and openly urged his deposition as General Secretary of the Party. They were arrested and imprisoned. They were named as conspirators in the Bukharin trial. Their precise fate has never been revealed. Khrushchev's odd-sounding reference to "the right-left" bloc was evidently inspired by the fact that the trials of Bukharin, et al., in 1938, was officially known as "the Case of the Anti-Soviet Bloc of Rightists and Trotskyites."

name hadn't been very widely known among the masses in the first years of the Revolution. He had come a long way in a short time, and he had brought our Party and our people with him.

In 1928 Kaganovich called me to Kharkov [then the capital of the Ukraine] and offered me a post as Deputy Chief of the Organizational Section of the Ukrainian Party Central Committee. As Kaganovich explained, there were very few workers on the Ukrainian Central Committee, which was then based in Kharkov, and he wanted to bring me from Stalino [Yuzovka] in order to equalize the representation of workers in the Party apparatus. I was reluctant to accept the offer. I'd already had enough contact with the Kharkov organization to know that it was filled with people who weren't to be trusted. I was pretty sure that I would run into trouble if I took the job. People in Kharkov tended to be jealous of the Yuzovka organization, and not without reason: we were miners and metalworkers; we were the real proletariat, the salt of the earth and the bedrock of the Party. Therefore I told Kaganovich, "I think you're quite right to want to bring more workers into the Central Committee apparatus, but I don't want to leave Stalino. I'm very much at home there; I know the procedures and the personnel of the Stalino organization. I'm completely unfamiliar with the setup here in Kharkov and I doubt I could adapt myself to the Organizational Section of the Central Committee."

"Well," said Kaganovich, "if you put it that way, I guess the Central Committee can do without you. There's no need to transfer you from Stalino if you feel so strongly against it."

I went home and began to reconsider Kaganovich's offer. I reviewed in my mind my past relationship with Kaganovich and the prospect of working with him. Kaganovich liked me very much. We met in the first days of the February Revolution at a meeting in Yuzovka, which I attended as a representative of the workers at the Ruchenkov mines. Then a week or two later we met again. In those days I knew him not as Kaganovich, but as Zhirovich. I trusted and respected him one hundred percent. I knew that Kaganovich needed all the help he could get in Kharkov. He wasn't considered much of an administrator, to say nothing of being a real leader. Kaganovich's position in the collective leadership of the Ukraine was shaky, and his relations with the other members of the Central Committee were complicated at best. The old men in the collective were constantly trying to undercut his authority.

Petrovsky wasn't behind him, and neither was Chubar. Generally speaking, the group from the Dniepropetrovsk area was against him. Kaganovich leaned very heavily on the Donbass, and particularly on the Yuzovka organization, for support.

There was something else that made me think seriously about going to Kharkov. People were beginning to lose confidence in Stroganov, the Secretary of the Yuzovka committee, and they were starting to come to me rather than to him. This was partly because I'd lived in Yuzovka since my childhood. My father had worked in the pit at Uspensk, four versts [two and two-thirds miles] south of Yuzovka. I had learned my own trade as a metal fitter at the Bosse factory and had a wide circle of friends whom I'd known since I was a boy. As people started to turn to me and bypass Stroganov, my relations with him became more and more strained, since I was nominally his deputy. By the way, he perished later on. (Poor fellow, he certainly didn't deserve to be shot.) In any event, in order to avoid getting into a fight with Stroganov, I thought it might be best for me to get out of Yuzovka before my relations with him became any worse.

After carefully weighing all these considerations, I decided to accept Kaganovich's offer after all. I told Kaganovich that I'd changed my mind and agreed to being transferred to Kharkov — but only on one condition: that I be sent somewhere else as soon as there was an opening; I didn't care where as long as it was in an industrial area. I didn't have much experience in farming and would have been out of my element in an agricultural area.

I went to Kharkov and was confirmed as Deputy Chief of the Organizational Section under Nikolai Nesterovich Demchenko.[13] He was a good man and a good Communist, devoted to the General Line of the Party, to the Central Committee, and to Stalin. But he, too, later perished at Stalin's hand.

As I had expected, my job in Kharkov turned out to be most disagreeable. It was nothing but paper work. I'm a man of the earth, a man of action, a miner; I'm used to working with metal and chemicals. I have a constitutional block against clerical work — it's completely alien to me. I hate having to look over a stack of forms and files to see the flesh-and-blood world. My job in Kharkov was a dead end; I felt stifled and trapped. I went to Kaganovich two or three times and re-

13. Petrovsky, Stroganov, Demchenko — three individuals among the countless Party officials unknown to the West who were to "perish at Stalin's hand."

minded him that he'd promised to get me out of Kharkov as soon as there was an opening somewhere else.

Then one day he called me up and said, "I've got a job opening for you in Kiev. Demchenko has gone there as Secretary of the District Committee, and he's asked that you be sent to head up the Organizational Section in Kiev. If you agree to the transfer, you can get yourself a ticket and leave today."

I accepted without thinking twice. This was on a Sunday. I was on a train that evening and in Kiev the next morning. I'd never been to Kiev before. My own hometown of Yuzovka was a tiny village compared to Kiev. As soon as I arrived I went straight to the banks of the Dnieper and gazed at the famous river with my suitcase still in hand.

The Kiev organization was not considered a very secure outpost of the Party. In fact, the area was notorious as a stronghold of Ukrainian nationalist elements, and its reputation was well deserved. The local proletariat was weak and unstable; and the intelligentsia, which was centered around the Ukrainian Academy of Sciences, was led by Grushitsky, a nationalist and a follower of Petlura.[14] There was also a formidable contingent of Trotskyites in the area. I knew that the Ukrainian nationalists in Kiev were sure to regard me as a hopeless "Rusak" [derisive Ukrainian term for Russian].

Despite my forebodings, I must admit that my year in Kiev turned out to be very satisfactory. I have many pleasant memories of that period. I found it easy to work there. The people seemed to like me and trust me. I'd even say they respected me.

I'm not saying there weren't some difficulties. Far from it. The Mensheviks, Social-Revolutionaries, Ukrainian nationalists, and Trotskyites all tried to take advantage of the troubles we were having in Kiev. There were many people out of work, and they used to demonstrate in the streets, parading around with red banners. We had a large meeting in the old Kiev City Soviet Council building to discuss the problem. I told the people who came to this meeting, "I know where there's great demand for workers, and I can easily find work for you there."

They seemed pleased. "Where?" they asked.

"In the Donbass."

"We'd rather be out of work here than go to the Donbass for jobs," they said.

14. S. V. Petlura was the most celebrated of the Ukrainian nationalist leaders who were dedicated to an independent Ukraine and fought against incorporation into the new Soviet Union.

This infuriated me because my own roots were in the Donbass, and I missed the miners whom I'd grown up with very much. As far as these Kievans were concerned, the Donbass meant the backward provinces. Besides, it was mining country, and they had no training for that kind of work.[15]

In 1929 I reached the age of thirty-five. I realized this was my last chance to think seriously about going to an institution of higher learning. I had never gotten further than the Yuzovka Workers' Faculty, and time was weighing on me heavily. I decided to try and get a leave of absence to complete my education. At first I encountered some resistance from my superiors. Kaganovich by now had been transferred to the Central Committee in Moscow, and Comrade Kossior had been sent to take his place.[16] I was widely regarded as someone who had been very close to Kaganovich, and it's true, I had been. But people also assumed that the real reason I was asking permission to go back to school was that I didn't want to work with Kossior, which wasn't true. I didn't know Kossior very well, but I respected him. He was a fairly mild-mannered person, pleasant and intelligent. I would have put him on a higher level than Kaganovich as regards his ability to get along with people, but he couldn't compete with Kaganovich as an organizer. Kaganovich was a man who got things done. If the Central Committee put an ax in his hands, he would chop up a storm; unfortunately he often chopped down the healthy trees along with the rotten ones. But the chips really flew — you couldn't take that away from him.

Anyway, I went to Kharkov and explained my position to Kossior, man to man: "Look, I'm already thirty-five years old. I want to finish my education. Will you write me a recommendation? I want to apply for admission to the Industrial Academy in Moscow and I'd like to ask for the Central Committee's support. I want to become a metallurgist."

Kossior was very understanding. He heard me out and gave me his personal consent. Demchenko, however, was very upset and tried to persuade me to stay, although he, too, could understand how a man might want to continue his studies. The Bureau met to decide whether

15. Here and in subsequent chapters Khrushchev can never make up his mind whether to admit the very real strength of Ukrainian nationalism or pretend that it was unimportant.
16. S. V. Kossior, a member of Stalin's Politbureau, remained as First Secretary of the Ukrainian Communist Party until his recall in 1938 and subsequent arrest. It was Khrushchev who then took over his job in the Ukraine.

to grant me a leave of absence. Some of them thought that I was trying to get away from Demchenko, and they hinted that they would support me if that was the reason I wanted to be released from my job in Kharkov. I had to convince them that my request for leave had nothing to do with my relations with Demchenko and that I simply wanted to complete my education. Finally, after a number of sessions, the Bureau decided to release me from my Party responsibilities in the Ukraine so that I could enter the Industrial Academy. I soon left for Moscow.

2

Party Work in Moscow

From Industrial Academy to Politbureau

In the light of subsequent events it seems more than probable that the thirty-five-year-old Party functionary from the Ukraine was brought up to the Industrial Academy in Moscow not primarily to study but to prove himself in political work and at the same time turn the academy into a Stalinist stronghold. For in 1929 and 1930 this forcing house of the new Communist elite was in fact a focus of anti-Stalinism. Be that as it may, Khrushchev did very soon win control of the Party cell and beat down the opposition by the use of methods that were both rough and devious. So successful was he that within two years he was able to leave the academy behind him and start, in the shadow of Kaganovich, on the swift career that was soon to make him the Party chieftain of all Moscow. The larger background to this chapter was the first frenzied and violent campaign for the rapid industrialization of the Soviet Union represented by the First Five-Year Plan and the collectivization of agriculture, about which Khrushchev has something to say later.

I RAN into some difficulties during my first year at the Industrial Academy. I was told that I didn't have enough experience in executive management to be a student there. "This is a school for managers and directors," the comrades said, "and you're just not ready for the course here. Maybe you should switch to the Central Committee's course in Marxism-Leninism." I finally had to get Kaganovich's help. Lazar Moiseyevich was a Secretary of the Central Committee. With his backing, I was able to remain at the academy. There were all sorts of people there. The students varied greatly in their political and educational backgrounds. Many had never gone any further than the village school and knew nothing but the four basic operations of arithmetic. Then there were also people who had gone through secondary school. Having completed the Workers' Faculty in Yuzovka, I was considered in that category.

The classroom building of the academy was located on the Novo-Bassmannaya, not far from the dormitory where I lived at Number 40, Pokrovka. I had a room of my own. It was an ideal setup. My daily routine was to walk to the academy. I never took the streetcar.

The overseer was Comrade Kuibyshev, the Chairman of the State Planning Commission.[1] Who could have been better? He was a respected and influential figure, and he gave the academy all his support. Our director was G. M. Kaminsky, an Old Bolshevik and a good comrade.[2] I remember that in 1930 we asked him to see if Comrade Stalin would receive some representatives of the first graduating class. We were planning a commencement celebration in the Hall of Columns,[3] and we wanted to ask Comrade Stalin to give the valedictory address on the great occasion. We were informed that Stalin would receive a delegation of six or seven people. Even though I wasn't a member of the graduating class myself, I was included in the group because I was Secretary of the academy Party organization. During our meeting with Stalin he gave us some advice along the following lines: he told us to master our studies, and to make ourselves experts in our fields; naturally we should be versatile in the general area of management, but we should also be specialists. This was good counsel, even though we'd heard it before. I'd been told the same thing back at the Yuzovka Workers' Faculty. As Stalin was speaking I thought to myself, "Here is a man who knows how to direct our minds and our energies toward the priority goals of industrializing our country and assuring the impregnability of our Homeland's borders against the capitalist world; the well-being of the people is obviously in firm hands!"

1. V. V. Kuibyshev, senior Bolshevik and head of the State Planning Commission (Gosplan), aligned himself early on with Stalin but was a comparative moderate. He died suddenly in January, 1935, and may have been killed on Stalin's orders. At the great trial of Bukharin et al. in 1938, the two doctors (Levin and Pletnev) accused of murdering the writer Maxim Gorky and others were also accused of murdering Kuibyshev.

2. G. M. Kaminsky, onetime People's Commissar for Health, signed Kuibyshev's death certificate and also Ordzhonikidze's. His fate is described in Chapter 3.

3. This was the ornate hall of the Tsarist Noblemen's Club in Moscow.

When he finished giving us his advice, Stalin said, "I'm afraid I won't be able to attend your celebration this evening myself, but Comrade Kalinin will be there." Our interview with Stalin had taken longer than expected. We had to run to the Hall of Columns. By the time we got there Kaminsky had already finished speaking, but we didn't miss Mikhail Ivanovich Kalinin's speech. We all respected him very much and listened to him attentively.

I should explain how I came to be chosen Secretary of the Party organization at the academy. It's a fairly long story, but it's worth telling.

When I first came to Moscow in 1929, the student body at the academy was full of unstable and undesirable elements. There were a lot of people who for one reason or another had abandoned their Party, trade union, or managerial duties and had settled into cozy niches. They did nothing but loaf. We had two days off a week — Sunday, and then another day which we were supposed to use for "assimilating" what we had learned that week. Well, I used to notice how these good-for-nothings would leave the dormitory early in the morning and not come back until late at night. I don't know what they did all day, but it's a sure thing they weren't "assimilating" their studies. Most of them hadn't come to the academy to study at all; they had come because it was a good place to lie low and wait for the political storm to blow over. They made themselves snug little nests in the academy and avoided political involvement altogether. This practice led to an ironic state of affairs: the political enemies of the Central Committee were just about the only people in the country who were able to take advantage of our institutions of higher learning. I remember Molotov once asked me, "Comrade Khrushchev, do you have much time to read?"

"Very little," I replied.

"It's the same with me. My job never lets up. Much as I'd like to sit down and read a book, and much as I know I should, I never have a chance."

I knew what he meant. Ever since I'd returned from the army in 1922, I'd been too busy to read. I was an active Party member, and therefore all my time was taken up with fighting for the General Line of the Central Committee. My life wasn't my own. If someone did have a chance to appreciate literature, he was likely to be reproached for shirking his civic and Party duties. I remember Stalin once put it very well: "So this is how it's turned out! The Trotskyites and the rightists have been rewarded for their activities with the privilege of higher education! The Central Committee doesn't have confidence in them so it removes them from their Party posts, and they rush straight into our scientific and technological institutes. And meanwhile, the people who've stood firmly for the General Line and done the day-to-day practical work of the Party never have an opportunity to advance their education and their professional training."

As a result of this situation, the Industrial Academy was teeming with rightists, and they'd gotten control of the Party cell. When I arrived in 1929 the Secretary of the Party organization was Khakharev. He was fairly influential and had pre-Revolutionary Party experience, dating, I think, from about 1906. He had what we called the Old Guard around him of men who supported the rightists Rykov, Bukharin, and Uglanov [4] against Stalin and the General Line of the Party. The Old Guard at the academy consisted of Old Bolsheviks, former plant directors, and trade union leaders — in short, respectable men who were attending the academy ostensibly to refresh their technical skills.

There was a group of us at the academy who stood for the General Line and who opposed the rightists: Rykov, Bukharin, and Uglanov, the Zinovievites, the Trotskyites, and the right-left bloc of Syrtsov and Lominadze. I don't even remember exactly what the differences were between Bukharin and Rykov on the one hand and Syrtsov and Lominadze on the other. Rightists, oppositionists, right-leftists, deviationists — these people were all moving in basically the same political direction, and our group was against them. We all came from the South — from the Donbass, from Dniepropetrovsk, and from Kharkov. Furthermore, we had all joined the Party after the Revolution. When someone's candidacy to a post in the academy organization was proposed at a meeting, he had to go to the podium and say where he was from and when he had joined the Party. This made it easy for the Old Guard in the Party cell to recognize and vote down anyone who was likely to oppose them. [5]

My election to the academy presidium was blocked two or three

4. N. A. Uglanov was First Secretary of the Moscow Party Committee and thus responsible for the Industrial Academy. When he was purged in 1928 he was succeeded first by K. Y. Bauman, who did not last long, then by Molotov, then by Kaganovich, and after that by Khrushchev himself.

5. Khrushchev here makes an interesting point: the Party intellectuals and moderates, most of them Old Bolsheviks, were confronted by Stalin with a phalanx of ruthless toughs, particularly Khrushchev's colleagues from the industrial complex of the Ukraine, comparative newcomers to the Party.

times, and I wasn't even nominated as a delegate to the Sixteenth Party Congress. However, even though I was new in Moscow, my name was already beginning to emerge as an active Party member on the side of the General Line, and therefore the Central Committee gave me a permanent guest pass to the Congress. That's how I was able to hear Stalin's General Report. I didn't attend all of the Congress sessions, and even though my pass was supposed to be nontransferable, I let some of my comrades use it so that they could get into the Congress, too. I'm glad I wasn't discovered sharing my pass because people were punished if they were caught.

At the time of the Sixteenth Party Congress the tide began to turn in our struggle against the rightists at the academy, and I took a position of leadership in the campaign to make the academy a stronghold for the Central Committee. My role in the struggle for the Party Line was not insignificant. Modesty aside, I'd say mine was the leading role. The bureau of the academy Party cell knew this and tried to get me out of town so that I wouldn't interfere with its plan to elect a rightist delegation to the Bauman District Party Conference in 1930. I was sent out into the country to inspect a collective farm which the academy Party organization sponsored.

When I got back to Moscow the Bauman Conference was already in full swing, and the academy was being represented largely by rightists. Comrade Tabakov came and told me everything that had happened while I was away. He was a Jew by nationality. He was one of my staunchest supporters in the academy, a politically sophisticated comrade and a Communist of the highest order. He was later shot. Tabakov told me that the Party cell had put up a slate of somewhere between ten and thirteen delegates to the Conference, including Stalin, Rykov, Bukharin, and, I think, Uglanov. This tactic was devised by the rightists to make it impossible to support Stalin's candidacy without also supporting Rykov and Bukharin.

Later that evening I was called to the telephone. I didn't have many acquaintances in Moscow, and I couldn't imagine who would be calling me. I picked up the phone, and a voice said, "This is Mekhlis, the editor of *Pravda*, speaking.[6] Can you come over to my office right

6. L. Z. Mekhlis, one of Nature's secret-policemen, was put in charge of *Pravda* to make it safe for Stalin. Later, he proved to be a particularly unpleasant and treacherous NKVD general who achieved high military rank after the great purge of the Red Army and cost his country dear by his incompetence in battle. He survived to become Minister of State Control and died, naturally by all reports, in 1953.

away? I'll send my car for you. I have an urgent matter I want to discuss with you."

A few minutes later his car pulled up outside the dormitory where I lived. I got in and was driven to the *Pravda* editorial offices. I'd never met Mekhlis before. He read me a letter from the academy complaining about political machinations and illegal procedures which had been used to select a rightist delegation to the Bauman District Conference.

"Are you in agreement with the contents of this letter?" Mekhlis asked me.

"Yes, absolutely. It accurately reflects the situation we're facing at the academy."

"Would you be willing to put your signature on it?"

"How can I do that? I didn't have anything to do with drafting the letter. I don't even know who the author is."

"That's not important. Your name and the author's name won't figure in this business at all. I'm asking you to sign it because I trust you; I've heard a lot about you and the role you've been playing, and your signature would assure me that the letter is a fair reflection of what's happening."

"Very well. I'll sign." I did so and was driven straight back to my dormitory in Mekhlis's car.

The next day *Pravda* carried the letter in its correspondence column.[7] It was like a clap of thunder out of a clear blue sky. The academy was immediately thrown into a turmoil. Classes were suspended, and the Party group organizers called a meeting at which all the academy delegates to the Bauman District Conference were recalled except Stalin. Perhaps we got orders from above not to recall Bukharin, but I don't remember. In any case, Rykov, Uglanov, and the other rightist representatives of the academy were all recalled, and new delegates were chosen. I was made chairman of the meeting and was put on the new delegation.[8]

These changes were made so hurriedly that there wasn't even time to print new credentials, so we were simply given the credentials of the old delegates. This aroused a certain amount of curiosity at the Confer-

7. The letter appeared on May 30, 1930. It has long been obvious that Khrushchev was a key figure behind it. It is interesting that he should admit it. His story, even so, may be oversimplified.
8. The story was more complicated than that. The Bukharinites fought back almost recklessly. But their cause was forlorn.

ence. Once I was even challenged because someone else's name was on my credentials. "I know," I explained. "These papers were issued originally to the person whose name is on them, but now they're mine." That's all I said. Most of the other delegates seemed to understand.

Our delegation decided that I should report to the Conference on where we stood. As I started my speech, there were voices that shouted disapprovingly, "We know all about you and your Industrial Academy!" The academy was notorious as a hotbed of rightists, so my first task was to prove that we represented a position different from the one taken by the previous delegates. Only after I made clear that we stood firmly for the Party Line did the other delegates to the Conference begin to trust us.

After I became Secretary of the Party organization at the academy, we began to crack down on the loafers and good-for-nothings who were using the academy as a place to sit out the political struggle which was going on in the Party. We reminded the students that they hadn't come there to see the sights of Moscow; they'd come to study and to equip themselves with theoretical and practical knowledge so that they could be more productive in the building of Socialism. Soon the academy began to play a leading role in the struggle against the opposition. Resolutions passed at our meetings were often published the next day in *Pravda* as guidelines for other Party organizations.

That's how my Party activity in Moscow got under way. As a result of my leadership of the academy organization, my name became even better known to the Moscow Party organization and to the Central Committee. During those years there was a District Party conference every six or twelve months. Another conference of the Bauman District Party was held in January, 1931, and I was elected Secretary of the District Party Committee, replacing Shirin — who only a year before had opposed my candidacy to the Sixteenth Party Congress. Shirin was politically immature. I'm sure he'd had his own reasons for voting against me in 1930, but all that was over and done with. My future as a Party worker now looked very bright.[9]

At first I thought I had Kaganovich to thank for my advancement in the Moscow apparatus, but I soon began to realize that my promotion was due not so much to Kaganovich as to Stalin himself. Stalin had ap-

9. This was in fact the moment of Khrushchev's breakthrough and the end of the Bukharinites in the academy. A. P. Shirin was broken and Khrushchev stepped into his shoes, the first of many such promotions.

parently been keeping an eye on me through his wife, Nadezhda Sergeyevna Alliluyeva. She sang my praises to Stalin, and Stalin told Kaganovich to help me along.

Nadezhda Sergeyevna and I were fellow students at the academy. She studied chemistry in the textile faculty, specializing in artificial fibers. She was a Party group organizer, and I used to meet with her regularly in my capacity as Secretary of the Party organization.[10] I had to give her instructions, and I knew that she went home and told Stalin about my performance. I felt just like Pinya, the hero of the story by Vinchenko.[11]

However, Nadezhda Sergeyevna was careful never to abuse her connection with Stalin. Only a limited circle of people even knew she was Stalin's wife. She was Alliluyeva, and that's all. We had another Alliluyev at the academy, a mining engineer from the Far East. He sat on the bureau of the Party cell. Nadezhda Sergeyevna let people assume that she was his wife or sister. She never took advantage of the privileges available to her as Stalin's wife. She never traveled between the academy and the Kremlin by car, but always came and went by streetcar. Nothing singled her out from the mass of students around her. It was very shrewd of her not to show that she was close to the person who was considered the Big Man by both her friends and her enemies in the political world.

In those days I called her Nadya. Later we started calling her Nadezhda Sergeyevna. It wasn't until I began to work in the Moscow City Party Committee and started going regularly to Stalin's for family dinners that I realized how much Nadya had told Stalin about my activities at the Industrial Academy in the struggle for the General Line. Sometimes Stalin would remind me of incidents which I had forgotten myself.

During the years that followed I stayed alive while most of my contemporaries, my classmates at the academy, my friends with whom I had worked in the party organization, lost their heads as enemies of

10. Nadezhda Sergeyevna Alliluyeva, Stalin's unhappy second wife, the mother of Svetlana Stalin, indeed knew Khrushchev well at the Industrial Academy. It seems odd that such a sensitive creature should have liked a rough, half-educated peasant as Khrushchev was in those days.

11. Khrushchev has on more than one occasion compared himself to the hero of Vinchenko's story. Pinya was a puny little Jew elected as their headman by a number of very tough prisoners as a gesture of contempt. When the proving time came — a prison breakout — he put them all to shame by rising to the occasion as a born and sacrificial leader.

the people. I've often asked myself, how was I spared? The fact that I am truly devoted to the Party has always been beyond doubt. But those comrades who perished were also devoted to the Party, and they, too, contributed to the struggle for Stalin's General Line. Why did I escape the fate which they suffered? I think part of the answer is that Nadya's reports helped determine Stalin's attitude toward me. I call it my lottery ticket. I drew a lucky lottery ticket when it happened that Stalin observed my activities through Nadezhda Sergeyevna. It was because of her that Stalin trusted me. In later years he sometimes attacked and insulted me, sometimes made rude remarks about me; but he always got over it, and right up until the last day of his life he liked me. It would be stupid and sentimental to talk about this man loving anyone, but there's no doubt that he held me in great respect.

Stalin had very little respect for Nadezhda Konstantinovna Krupskaya and Maria Ilinichna Ulyanova [Lenin's widow and sister respectively]. He used to say that he didn't think either of these women was making a positive contribution to the Party's struggle for victory.

After Stalin's death we found an envelope in a secret compartment, and inside the envelope was a note written in Lenin's hand. Lenin accused Stalin of having insulted Nadezhda Konstantinovna. Vladimir Ilyich demanded that Stalin apologize for insulting her — otherwise Lenin would no longer consider Stalin his comrade. I was astonished that this note had been preserved. Stalin had probably forgotten all about it.[12]

It was always very upsetting to see how disrespectfully Stalin behaved toward Nadezhda Konstantinovna while she was still alive. She opposed Stalin during the struggle against the rightists and made a speech defending Bukharin and Rykov at the Bauman District Party

---

12. The contents of this note were revealed for the first time by Khrushchev in the Secret Speech. Lenin had suffered more than one stroke and was desperately trying to warn his colleagues against Stalin's overweening ambition. The distinguished scholar, the late Boris Nicolaevsky, believed that Stalin deliberately insulted Krupskaya, knowing that this would get back to Lenin and so upset him that his death would be accelerated. The text of Lenin's note to Stalin (with copies to Kamenev and Zinoviev) reads: "Dear Comrade Stalin! You permitted yourself a rude summons of my wife to the telephone and a rude reprimand of her. . . . I have no intention to forget so easily that which is being done against me, and I need not stress here that I consider as directed against me that which is being done against my wife. I ask you, therefore, that you weigh carefully whether you are agreeable to retracting your words and apologizing or whether you prefer the severance of relations between us. Sincerely: Lenin. (5 March, 1923)." See Appendix 4.

Conference in 1930. As a result she came under attack from most of the delegates at the Conference; and afterward, without any publicity, the word went out to Party cells to give her a working-over. As for Maria Ilinichna Ulyanova, everyone knew she was a good friend of Bukharin's; she had been secretary of *Pravda* when he was editor.

For my part, as a young Communist with a record of experience dating from after the October Revolution, I had always revered Lenin as our great leader and therefore had the utmost respect for Nadezhda Konstantinovna. She had been Vladimir Ilyich's inseparable companion. It was a bitter thing for me to watch her at these sessions of the Bauman District Conference when everyone started coming out against her. I remember her as a broken old woman. People avoided her like the plague. On Stalin's instructions, she was kept under close surveillance because she had strayed from the Party Line.

As I analyze now what happened during that period, I think Nadezhda Konstantinovna was correct in the stand she took. But I say that with the benefit of hindsight. At the time, everything was mixed up in one pile, and everyone was slinging mud at Nadezhda Konstantinovna and Maria Ilinichna.

Later, when I was working on the Moscow City Party Committee, Nadezhda Konstantinovna was in charge of dealing with citizens' complaints. Anyone who had been dealt with unjustly by the Moscow City Soviet took his grievance to her. Undoubtedly there were many faults in the way the Moscow City Soviet worked. Conditions were especially hard for workers, office employees, and intellectuals. Whenever someone ran up against a brick wall in the bureaucracy, he would appeal to Nadezhda Konstantinovna as a last recourse. She was limited in what she could do to help. She didn't have enough influence to redress even the most valid grievances that were brought to her. She often forwarded them to me at the Moscow City Committee. Unfortunately, even though I held a high post, there wasn't much I could do to help, either. We had a widespread shortage of apartments in Moscow. The whole housing situation was a nightmare. We were industrializing the country and building new factories everywhere, but the expansion of Moscow's worker population wasn't taken into account. Only the barest minimum of housing facilities were being built, and these new apartment buildings didn't begin to compensate for all the houses that were being torn down to make room for factories.

I did whatever I could when Nadezhda Konstantinovna sent people

to me with complaints. I would always report to her what had been
done, or else I would tell her that we were powerless. Occasionally I
met with her. She was perfectly correct about where I stood. She knew
that I toed the General Line of the Party and that I was a product of
Stalin's generation. She treated me accordingly.

Nadezhda Konstantinovna Krupskaya was absolutely right: I was a
hundred percent faithful to Stalin as our leader and our guide. I believed that everything Stalin said in the name of the Party was inspired by genius, and that I had only to apply it to my own life.

Nevertheless I felt divided against myself when Nadezhda Konstantinovna fell into disfavor in the Party. I felt a basic human sympathy for
her.

Stalin used to tell his inner circle that there was some doubt as to
whether Nadezhda Konstantinovna was really Lenin's widow at all,
and that if the situation continued much longer we would begin to express our doubts in public. He said if necessary we would declare that
another woman was Lenin's widow, and he named a solid and respected Party member. This person is still alive; I don't want to try to
comment on such matters.[13]

I think Stalin's attitude toward Krupskaya was just another instance
of his disrespect toward Lenin himself. Nothing was sacred to Stalin,
not even Lenin's good name. Stalin never let himself breathe a word
against Krupskaya in public, but in his inner circle he allowed himself
to say all sorts of outrageous things about her. He wasn't just indulging
in frivolous gossip, either. He wanted to influence us psychologically,
to undermine our limitless love for Lenin, and to increase his own stature as the uncontested leader and great thinker of our era. To this end
he cautiously but deliberately sprinkled into the consciousness of those
around him the idea that privately he wasn't of the same opinion about
Lenin that he professed publicly.

I have to mention Kaganovich in this regard. His behavior disgusted
me, and it disgusted others, too. He was nothing but a lackey. All Stalin had to do was scratch Kaganovich behind the ears to send him
snarling at the Party.

Kaganovich used to throw back his chair, bring himself up to his full

13. According to Alexander Orlov, a high-ranking NKVD officer who defected to
the West, the substitute widow was to have been Elena Stasova, who later spent
years in labor camps and was rehabilitated after Stalin's death. A rumor still current in Moscow identifies the candidate for "official widow" as R. S. Zemlyachka, an
Old Bolshevik and onetime colleague of Bela Kun in the Crimea.

height, and bellow: "Comrades! It's time for us to tell the people the truth. Everyone in the Party keeps talking about Lenin and Leninism. We've got to be honest with ourselves. Lenin died in 1924. How many years did he work in the Party? What was accomplished under him? Compare it with what has been accomplished under Stalin! The time has come to replace the slogan 'Long Live Leninism' with the slogan 'Long Live Stalinism.' "

While he would rant on like this, we would all keep absolutely silent and lower our eyes. Stalin was always the first and only one to dispute Kaganovich.

"What are you talking about?" he would say, "How dare you say that?!" But you could tell from the tone in Stalin's voice that he was hoping someone would contradict him. This device is well known among village folk. When a mother is about to go off with someone on a visit to another village and wants her little child to come with her, she scolds, "Now, you stay here! Don't you dare follow me, you little devil!" and she wags her finger at the child. Then, when the person who has come to fetch her isn't looking, the mother beckons to the child and whispers, "Come on, follow me!" So the little child runs along behind her. I've often witnessed this scene myself, and it was in just this way that Stalin would start scolding Kaganovich.

Stalin liked to rebuke Kaganovich with the following comparison: "What is Lenin? Lenin is a tall tower! And what is Stalin? Stalin is a little finger!" Sometimes when he made this remark he substituted an analogy which, shall we say, isn't suitable for recording here. Kaganovich was encouraged all the more, and he persistently repeated his claim about Stalin. Kaganovich was a master at sensing when Stalin's indignation was false.

This "dispute" between Kaganovich and Stalin became more and more frequent, right up until Stalin's death. No one ever interfered and Stalin always had the last word in settling the matter.

This routine of theirs was typical of both Stalin and Kaganovich. Kaganovich was unsurpassed in his viciousness. Stalin used to hold him up as an example of a man "resolute in his class consciousness" and "implacable toward his class enemies." Later we found out all too well how resolute and implacable Kaganovich really was. He was the kind of man who wouldn't say a single word on behalf of his own brother, Mikhail Kaganovich, who was accused of being a German spy planted by Hitler to form a puppet Russian government after the Germans captured Moscow. What could be more absurd? Hitler was planning to put Mikhail Kaganovich, a *Jew*, in a *fascist* Russian government? From the standpoint of the Nazis, this would have been criminal! But nonetheless, that was the charge made against Mikhail Kaganovich; and when he had no other way out, he committed suicide. I never heard anyone mention this incident after it happened, and Lazar Moiseyevich himself seemed to ignore his brother's tragedy. As far as he was concerned, it was all quite simple: once there was a man named Mikhail Kaganovich, People's Commissar of the Aviation Industry; then Mikhail Kaganovich was no more; he might as well have never existed. And all the while, Lazar Moiseyevich never stopped groveling before Stalin.[14]

But I'm getting ahead of myself . . .

After working for six months as Party Secretary of the Bauman District, I became Secretary of the Red Presnya District in 1931. It was definitely a step up the Party ladder. In view of its historical importance in the 1905 uprising, the Red Presnya was politically more important than the Bauman District. Actually, it was the leading Party district committee in Moscow. After another six months I was elected Second Secretary of the Moscow City Party Committee at a city conference. Much as I appreciated the honor and the responsibility that went with this promotion, I was sorry to have to leave the Industrial Academy without graduating. Taking the job on the Moscow City Committee meant giving up my hopes of ever completing my higher education. Furthermore, as I confided to Kaganovich, I was apprehensive about the difficulties I was sure to encounter in the city apparatus. But I proved up to the challenge, and a year later I became Second Secretary of the Moscow Regional Committee.

I was elected to the Central Committee of the All-Union Communist Party (Bolsheviks) at the Seventeenth Party Congress in 1934. The election procedure impressed me as being very democratic. Here's how it worked: Candidates were nominated and their names put on a ballot, which was then passed around to all the delegates. Admittedly, there wasn't much choice left to the delegates because the number of names on the ballot was just enough to fill the staff of the Central

14. Lazar Kaganovich indeed took his brother's disgrace and suicide without apparently turning a hair. Khrushchev throughout his narrative has difficulty in arranging his ideas about his onetime sponsor and protector, to whom he owed so much, and whom he finally ruined in 1957 (see Appendix 3.)

Committee, including members and candidate members, plus the staff of the Inspection Commission. However, every delegate was given a chance to express his opinion about each candidate either by leaving his name on the ballot or striking it off. Stalin then made the rounds of the delegates to collect the ballots, looking each delegate squarely in the eye so as not to see his ballot. (It was only later that I found out that nobody's name was ever put on the ballot without Stalin's approval.) Then the ballots were counted, and the number of votes for and against each candidate was announced.

I remember that at the Seventeenth Party Congress Stalin didn't receive a unanimous vote. Six people voted against him. Why do I remember this so well? Because when my name was announced — "Khrushchev!" — I also was only six votes short of unanimous election to the Central Committee! This meant I was in a position comparable to Stalin's. Other candidates often received twenty or thirty or even a hundred votes against them. It took a majority of the votes cast for a candidate to be elected.

In 1935 Kaganovich was appointed People's Commissar of Transport and released from his duties in the Moscow organization. I was promoted to take his place as First Secretary of the Moscow Regional and City committees.[15]

At the very next plenum of the Central Committee I was elected a candidate member of the Politbureau. I was pleased and flattered, but I was also terrified by the onerous responsibility that went with this job. I was now a full-fledged professional Party worker, but I kept with me the tools of my trade — calipers, markers, a try square, a ruler, and a liter measure. I was reluctant to sever my ties with my old profession. The way I looked at it, a Party job was elective, and if I weren't reelected, I might any day have to return to my original career as a metal fitter.

I started attending Politbureau sessions regularly. In those days Stalin was still, to a certain extent at least, observing Leninist traditions. Members of the Central Committee who happened to be in Moscow were entitled to attend Politbureau sessions, as long as they sat quietly and didn't disrupt the work. I learned a lot at these sessions about how the leadership of the Party made decisions.

To be able to sit with the Politbureau, to be able to work side by

15. This meant that Khrushchev was absolute master, under Stalin, of the city of Moscow and the surrounding Region.

side with the leaders of our Party, and to be close to Stalin — this seemed like the crowning opportunity of my career. For years I had been devoted with all my soul to the Central Committee and to Stalin. Ever since first coming to Moscow and hearing him speak at mass meetings, I had admired Stalin for his clearness of mind and the conciseness of his formulations. I had been equally impressed by this same succinctness and lucidity in his address to a smaller group, at a closed meeting of industrial managers in 1932, when he was formulating his Six Great Conditions. And now that I was a candidate member of the Politbureau, I had an opportunity to watch Stalin in action at close quarters, regularly. My admiration for him continued to grow. I was spellbound by the patience and sympathy for others that he showed at Politbureau meetings in the middle thirties.

I can think of various examples of what I mean, but I'll single out just one. It was a fairly unusual case, involving a young diplomat who had gone to some Latin American country with one of our trade missions and let himself be compromised by the local press. He was brought in to testify during a Politbureau meeting and was obviously very embarrassed and upset. Stalin opened the discussion.

"Tell me, please, everything that happened. Don't hold anything back."

The young diplomat explained that just after he arrived in the Latin American country, he went to a restaurant to get something to eat. "I was shown to a table, and I ordered dinner. A man came up and sat down at my table. He asked me if I were from Russia. I said, yes, I was. Then he started asking all sorts of questions — what did I come to buy, had I served in the army, did I know how to shoot? I told him that I'd been in the cavalry, that I wasn't a bad shot — things like that. Then, to my horror, an article appeared in the newspaper the very next day. It was full of all kinds of nonsense about how I was a real Caucasian cowboy and a crack shot; it was also full of lies about why I'd come, what I was going to buy, what prices I was going to pay, and so on. Shortly afterward the embassy told me I'd better return to the Homeland and report to you. That's what happened. I only ask you to take into account that I committed this blunder out of inexperience, and without any malicious intent."

I felt very sorry for this young man. He had obviously been a victim of his own naïveté. Everyone squirmed in his seat and whispered to his neighbor — we were all waiting to see what would happen.

Stalin, 1931

Khrushchev as a rising politico in the early 1930's. Below: with Party delegates from the Red Presnya District of Moscow, 1931

Khrushchev and Stalin,
May 1, 1932

Sergo Ordzhonikidze (left) and Stalin (right)

Stalin, Molotov, Kaganovich, and Ordzhonikidze

Kalinin, Kaganovich, Ordzhonikidze, Stalin, and Voroshilov

Voroshilov and Stalin

Suddenly Stalin said, "Well, as far as I can see, a trusting fellow was taken advantage of by a bunch of rascals. Is there anything more to it than that?"

"No."

"Then the incident is closed." Stalin looked the young diplomat in the eye and said, "See that you're more careful in the future." The poor fellow just sat there with his mouth open as the meeting was adjourned. He was so surprised by his good fortune that he couldn't move. Then he grabbed his briefcase and scurried out.

I was very impressed by the simplicity and compassion with which Stalin had handled the case. So was everyone else.

City Father

From 1932, when he became Second Secretary (under Kaganovich) of the Moscow City Party Committee, to 1938, when he was appointed to be First Secretary of the Ukraine, Khrushchev was primarily concerned with the management of Moscow. In 1935, he was in absolute control of the <u>Moscow Regional and City Party organizations</u>. It was in these years that he made his reputation as a hard and ruthless driver of men who, unlike so many Russians in exalted positions, was not afraid to get mud on his boots. His most spectacular operation was the construction of the Moscow Metro, that celebrated showpiece of the Soviet regime, with its gilded and marble underground halls which were to become a wonder of the world. The Metro was named after Kaganovich, who initiated it, with Khrushchev as his assistant. But soon Khrushchev himself took over and brought it to a successful conclusion. Khrushchev gives us an account of those feverish days. He did, indeed, work without ceasing. He had under his command not only bands of enthusiastic young Communist volunteers, but also a large forced-labor contingent at the disposition of G. G. Yagoda, the NKVD chieftain. From 1936 onward, it was also Khrushchev's job to help make Moscow safe for Stalin during the terrible purge years. It was then that he distinguished himself, though he does not mention this, by addressing mass meetings in which he praised Stalin in more high-flown terms than any of his colleagues and demanded death for the victims of the treason trials.

From the beginning of my Party activities in the Moscow organization, there was a lot to be done in a short time. I played a central role in the management and reconstruction of our Soviet capital through the early and middle thirties. My comrades and I worked with enthusiasm and self-sacrifice. Our jobs consumed our whole lives. We knew no such thing as rest. We frequently called mass meetings or had consultations among ourselves on our days off, and we worked long hours, often well into the night. In our eyes, there was something romantic about our task. Everyone lived to see the day when Lenin's words would come true: after the first ten years of its existence, Soviet Power would be invincible! Nowadays, unfortunately, a lot of that spirit of idealism and self-sacrifice has gone out of the Party; many of the attitudes that seem all too prevalent today have a touch of bourgeois pettiness about them. Back when I helped run the city of Moscow, no one would have permitted himself so much as a single thought about having his own dacha [country house]. After all, we were Communists! We always went around in plain work clothes. None of us ever wore suits. Our uniform was a field shirt with an open collar or a white peasant smock. Stalin set a good example for us in this regard.

While Kaganovich was First Secretary of the Moscow City and Regional committees, he was also Second Secretary of the Central Committee. That made him Stalin's deputy. Therefore he had to devote most of his time to the Central Committee, and the lion's share of the responsibility for getting things done in Moscow fell on my shoulders, since I was Second Secretary of the City and Regional committees. This job required effort, industriousness, and great care on my part. I had to make up in diligence what I lacked in experience. I enjoyed good relations with my comrades in the Moscow Party organization. Apparently my performance justified the trust and responsibility which had been invested in me when I had been promoted from the district level.

Of course, there were trying moments. I remember the following episode which occurred in 1932: People were going hungry in Moscow, and as Second Secretary, I devoted much of my energy to finding the means to feed the citizenry — or "working class," as we used to say.[16]

16. Moscow was now feeling the effects of the famine resulting from collectivization. Although the main Political Directorate and the army forced the peasants to give up their produce for the benefit of the urban workers, there was still not enough to go around. The state of the peasantry at this time is described in the following chapter.

Stalin had suggested the idea of raising rabbits for food. I was all for this plan and worked zealously to carry out his instructions. Almost every factory, plant, and workshop started raising rabbits to help stock its own kitchen. Then we began pushing a plan to raise mushrooms in cellars and ditches around Moscow. Some establishments contributed their share, but every mass movement has its bad elements and some factory directors didn't support the cause. We ran into more trouble when it came to distributing ration cards. There were never enough cards, and a certain amount of swindling was inevitable. The card shortage tempted some people, especially the unstable ones, to play fast and loose with the law or to steal outright. There were different ration cards for people who worked and people who didn't, and among those who worked, cards varied in exchange value. This state of affairs, too, made for all sorts of irregularities and abuses, and even thievery.

Kaganovich called me in one day and said, "You'd better make a report to the Politbureau on what you're doing to keep people from getting hold of ration cards illegally."

This assignment worried me. I'd go so far as to say that I was really frightened by the prospect of delivering a speech to our most prestigious body; Stalin would be there, judging my report.

Actually, in those days, Stalin never chaired the Politbureau sessions himself. He always left that job to Molotov. Molotov was Stalin's oldest friend. They had known each other from the pre-Revolutionary underground. Molotov had always been promoted as Stalin's most faithful, most unshakable comrade-in-arms. They say he claimed this himself when he was nominated for the chairmanship of the Council of People's Commissars at a Central Committee plenum toward the end of 1930. After I started working as Secretary of the Moscow City and Regional committees, I often went by Stalin's office, and Molotov was almost always with Stalin when I got there. They regularly went on vacation together, too. Molotov was Stalin's right hand in the battle against the opposition. That's why the oppositionists called him Stalin's bludgeon. Stalin used Molotov to strike out at any member of the Politbureau who opposed him. But in those days, Molotov impressed me as a strong-willed, independent man who thought for himself.[17]

I presented myself at a Politbureau meeting and delivered a speech listing all the measures we were taking to liquidate abuses of the ration card system. I claimed we had already been very successful.

17. See Molotov's biography, Appendix 3.

Molotov and Stalin

Molotov, Khrushchev, and Stalin on the Lenin Mausoleum during a May
Day parade (1934?)

Greeting the people

"Stop bragging, Comrade Khrushchev," said Stalin. "There are still many thieves left — very many — don't think you've caught them all."

Stalin's remark was made in a fatherly tone and it didn't upset me at all. He was right. I had convinced myself that we had rounded up all the ration card swindlers, and I was astounded that Stalin — who hardly ever left the confines of the Kremlin — was so all-seeing that he probably knew exactly how many thieves were still at large! This raised Stalin all the more in my eyes.

Some time afterward I found out that a delegation from Leningrad was going to deliver a report to the Politbureau on the same problem of ration cards. I was interested to hear how the Leningraders were doing because we were in competition with them in every area, particularly confidential ones. Sergei Mironovich Kirov was First Secretary of the Leningrad organization. He assigned the report on rationing to one of the other secretaries — someone with a Lettish name. As far as I could tell, the Leningraders' report spoke well for the amount of headway they had made in building up their economy so that they could cut back on rationing.

When the Leningraders finished presenting their report, a recess was called and people filed out of the hall to go into a nearby lounge where refreshments were served. There was hunger in the land, and even people in high positions like myself lived modestly, to put it mildly, and we often didn't have enough to eat at home. Therefore we used to gorge ourselves on sandwiches, sausages, sour cream, and sweet tea between working sessions at the Kremlin. While everyone else stormed the buffet next door, I stayed behind for a moment, waiting until everyone in the back of the room had left. Unintentionally, I was witness to an exchange of sharp words between Stalin and Sergei Mironovich Kirov. Sergei Mironovich said something favorable about his delegation's report on rationing, and Stalin shot back with some insulting remark about the Secretary who had delivered the report.[18] I was shocked. In those days I was very idealistic about Party morale. I couldn't believe that Stalin, the leader of our Party, would behave disrespectfully toward another Party member. The way I looked at it, if someone carried a Party card and was a true Communist, then he was my brother — he was really more than that. We were bound together

18. In the late twenties and early thirties, S. M. Kirov was as close as anyone to Stalin. Already here we see the first signs of that independence of mind which was to end in his murder and the launching of the great purge. (Chapter 3).

by the invisible threads of our shared belief in the lofty struggle. The building of Communism was something almost sacred to me. If I may use the language of religious believers, I'd say that every participant in the Communist movement was to me an apostle, ready to sacrifice himself in the name of our common cause.[19]

At the time, the incident I overheard between Stalin and Kirov struck me as an inexplicable departure from Stalin's usual conduct.

I started seeing more of Stalin in informal circumstances after I began to work in the Moscow city Party Organization. Along with Bulganin, who was Chairman of the Moscow City Soviet [in effect, mayor], I used to be invited regularly to family dinners at Stalin's apartment. Stalin and Nadezhda Sergeyevna were always host and hostess. Nadezhda Sergeyevna's parents, Mama and Papa Alliluyev, were often there, too. So were Nadezhda's brother and his wife, and her sister Anna Sergeyevna and her husband Redens. Redens was Chief of the Moscow Regional office of the NKVD. Stalin would always seat Bulganin and me next to him and pay close attention to us during the meal. He was fond of saying, "Well, how's it going, City Fathers?"

At first it was strange to hear Stalin make light conversation at the dinner table. Worshiping him as I did, I couldn't get used to being with him in relaxed surroundings: here was a man not of this world, laughing and joking like the rest of us! After a while I began to admire him not only as a political leader who had no equal, but simply as another human being.

Sometimes when there was something he wanted to talk over with us pertaining to the administration of the city, Stalin would instruct someone to call up Bulganin and myself and have us join him at the theater. We always concentrated hard on what he was saying and then tried to do exactly as he had advised us.

Once — I think it was before the Seventeenth Party Congress — I got a message to call a phone number which I immediately recognized as Stalin's apartment. Stalin answered when I called.

"Comrade Khrushchev," he said, "rumors have reached me that you've let a very unfavorable situation develop in Moscow as regards public toilets. Apparently people hunt around desperately and can't find anywhere to relieve themselves. This won't do. It puts the citizens

---

19. This is a little high-flown. Nevertheless, for all their brutality, men like Khrushchev at this time did feel they were building a new world.

in an awkward position. Talk this matter over with Bulganin and do something to improve these conditions."

This may seem like a trivial subject for Stalin to have brought to our attention, but I was impressed nonetheless. Bulganin and I began to work feverishly. We personally inspected buildings and courtyards. We also booted the militia [uniformed police] off their behinds and got them to help. Later Stalin assigned us the task of installing clean, modern pay toilets. This also was done. I remember when I was at a conference with comrades from the provinces, the Party Secretary of Novosibirsk Eikhe asked me, with typical Lettish simplicity, "Comrade Khrushchev, is it true what people are saying? Are you really busying yourself about toilets in Moscow, and is this really on Stalin's instructions?" [20]

"Yes, that's perfectly true," I answered, "and I think it proves our concern for the citizens. A big city like Moscow can't get along without enough decent toilets."

This episode, trivial as it may seem, shows how Stalin, the leader of the world's working class, wasn't too busy to bother himself over as important a detail of city life as public toilets.

In 1934 Kaganovich, Bulganin, and I worked together on the reconstruction of Moscow and supervised the erection of many new buildings. I remember that once when we were standing around in a group, inspecting a new complex that had been built around the Moscow Soviet, Kaganovich pointed at the Marx-Engels Institute and said, "Who the hell designed *that* monstrosity?"

The architects who were with us glanced around nervously, and the city's chief architect, Chernyshev, became extremely embarrassed. "Lazar Moiseyevich," he said, "I designed that building." Kaganovich smiled, apologized, and qualified his observation. Actually, the flat, squat, gray concrete mass of the Marx-Engels Institute was indeed a very gloomy-looking structure.

It was a period of feverish activity, and stupendous progress was made in a short time. A hundred important projects seemed to be proceeding all at once: the construction of a ball-bearing factory, the enlargement of the Dux Number One aviation factory, the installation of

20. R. I. Eikhe. Khrushchev made much in his Secret Speech of Eikhe's fate during the purges. A candidate member of the Politbureau, he was arrested in April, 1938, and forced under torture to sign a confession. He repudiated the confession and appealed to Stalin for a Central Committee investigation of his case. He was shot in February, 1940.

oil, gas, and electricity plants, the excavation of the Moscow-Volga Canal, and the reconstruction of the bridges over the Moscow River — to name just a few. The huge task of overseeing all this was largely mine because Kaganovich was up to his ears in work outside the Moscow Party organization.

In addition to putting up new buildings, there was a lot to be done in the way of modernizing the most basic metropolitan services. Moscow's sewage and water drainage systems were long out of date, and there were no water mains at all in the city. Most streets were cobblestone, and some were completely unpaved. Much of the city's transport was still horsedrawn. It's incredible to look back on it all now, but things really were that primitive.

During the reconstruction of Moscow I had the honor of setting up the first trolley lines in the Soviet Union. It took a lot of effort for me to convince people that trolleybuses were a good idea. There were many opponents of this means of transport. For example, my late friend Aleksei Ivanovich Likhachev was in love with the internal combustion engine and fought tooth and nail against the installation of a trolley system. I even ran into some resistance from Stalin himself. After we'd put up the wires and were getting ready to test the system, I got a call from Kaganovich, who said we had to call the whole thing off. Apparently Stalin was sure that the trolley cars would overturn on the slope in front of the Central Telegraph building. But it was already too late to call off the test, and fortunately everything went smoothly. We reported to Stalin that because a trolley worked on electricity, it didn't make much noise or pollute the air. In short, it was the most progressive mode of transport, and a trolley system would definitely contribute to the advancement of the city. Stalin supported my recommendation. It's true that later, when we bought doubledecker trolleys, Stalin absolutely refused to let us use them. He was afraid that they would tip over, and nothing we could say would change his mind. Generally speaking, though, Stalin supported modern improvements and progressive developments of all kinds.

When we started building the Moscow Metro, we had only the vaguest idea of what the job would entail. We were very unsophisticated. We thought of a subway as something almost supernatural. I think it's probably easier to contemplate space flights today than it was for us to contemplate the construction of the Moscow Metro in the early 1930's.

It was recommended that we put Pavel Pavlovich Roter in charge of the project. He was reputed to be the best builder in Moscow. He was a Russian of German extraction who had supervised one of the State's most ambitious construction projects — the Government House on Dzerzhinsky Square in Kharkov.

At first I had nothing to do with the Metro myself. Then, after some time passed, Kaganovich said, "Things aren't going very well. Since you've had some experience with mining, you'd better take charge and supervise the building of the Metro. I suggest you put aside all your work in the City Committee. You'll have to go down into the shafts to familiarize yourself with what's being done. Bulganin should do the same." Kaganovich's suggestion made sense. At the time I still held Lazar Moiseyevich in high esteem. There was no question about his devotion to the Party and to the cause. In the course of chopping firewood he sent a lot of chips flying, as they say, but he never flagged in strength or energy. He was as stubborn as he was devoted.

After I'd spent some time down in the shafts, I had a better idea of exactly what the Metro was all about. I realized that things were done much as they were in the mines where I'd worked in my youth. As for Bulganin, he developed a sciatic condition on the project and was laid up in bed for a long time. That's how the supervision of the Metro fell on my shoulders. I started giving regular progress reports to Kaganovich, stressing that we didn't have enough skilled personnel to do the job quickly and properly. At my urging, we started looking for experienced mining engineers to supervise the work in the shafts.

About this time things were going badly in the coal industry in the Donbass. We weren't able to mine coal fast enough to meet the country's growing demand. Molotov was sent to the Donbass to look into the situation. He wasn't able to do much good because he didn't know the first thing about mining. Yegor Trofimovich Abakumov was head of coal works in the Donbass. We'd been friends since we worked in the same pit back in 1912; after the Civil War I'd worked as his deputy. He was a good administrator and widely recognized as an experienced miner. Molotov made a report to the Politbureau recommending that we release Abakumov from his post in the Donbass. Kaganovich called me and told me about this.

"Do you know this Abakumov?"

"Yes, I know him well."

Supervising the construction
of the Moscow Metro
in the 1930's

On an inspection tour

Wearing his first Order of Lenin, awarded for his work on the Moscow
Metro, Khrushchev delivers an address into an early microphone

At a Party meeting
in the 1930's

"What would you think if Abakumov were made deputy director of the construction of the Metro under Roter?"

"A better deputy we'd never find," I said. "He'd even make an excellent director."

"I didn't ask you about that," snapped Kaganovich. "We've already got Roter as our director."

So Abakumov was assigned to us. My job became easier after he arrived. We knew and trusted each other. We started right away to recruit experienced mining engineers.

One day Kaganovich asked me, "What if we were to make you chief of construction work for the Metro?"

"I wouldn't want that."

"Why not? You've demonstrated the necessary ability and experience. Frankly, we've already started looking to you as the manager of day-to-day operations around here. What difference would it make to you if we made it official and put you in charge?"

"If that's what you decide to do," I said, "then I'll do everything in my power to justify your confidence in me. I would only ask that you release me from my duties as Secretary of the City Committee. I couldn't possibly hold both jobs at once."

"Oh, no, that would be out of the question."

I later found out that it had been Stalin's idea to make me manager of the Metro construction. Kaganovich never told me this himself, but apparently Stalin had instructed him to see if I would take on the Metro job in addition to my Moscow City Committee duties. The suggestion was dropped when I said I couldn't hold both positions at the same time.

As it turned out, even though I formally kept my job at the City Committee, I gave eighty percent of my time to the Metro. I went to and from the Moscow Committee through the shafts. In the morning I climbed down a shaft near where I lived and came up out of a shaft near the Party office building. It would be hard for me to describe how strenuous a working day we put in. We slept as little as possible so that we could give all our time to the cause.

One day a young engineer who worked in the planning section came to me with an idea of how we might improve the Metro. His name was Makovsky. I liked him immediately. He was sharp and handsome, one of our Socialist era's new generation of specialists. Here is what he said:

"Comrade Khrushchev, we're building the Metro according to the so-called German, or open-trench, method. This method is very unsuitable for a city. I propose that we switch to the English, or closed-tunnel, method. We'd have to build the Metro deeper, and it would be a little more expensive. But if you keep in mind the possibility of war, you'll see that the tunnels, with their reinforced shielding and buttressed walls, would make excellent bomb shelters. There's another advantage to the English method: we wouldn't have to build along the main transport lines; we could tunnel right under buildings. Then there's also the matter of how we're going to get passengers down into the Metro and up and out again. Pavel Pavlovich Roter has already given instructions for us to build elevators. That's also the German method. I propose that we build escalators instead." I admit this was the first time I'd ever heard this word "escalator." I asked him what it meant. He explained, and I followed him as best I could. It sounded extremely complicated. Makovsky finished by saying, "I ask you please to think over my proposals. If you want, I can make a report explaining exactly what I have in mind. However, please don't tell Pavel Pavlovich that I've been to see you. He's very jealous and very strict. I've brought this idea to you without his permission. It would have been fruitless for me to have spoken to him first. He's awfully opinionated, and he would have knocked my proposal down without even listening to me."

"All right," I said, "I'll talk it over with Comrade Kaganovich, and we'll let you know what we decide."

I reported to Kaganovich. He answered curtly, "Why don't you get Makovsky to tell you in more detail about these escalators of his, and then you'll see why we have to build elevators instead. We'd have to order the escalators from England or Germany, and we can't afford to spend our gold reserves abroad, even for the sake of the Metro."

I decided to call a meeting with both Makovsky and Pavel Pavlovich Roter present. I wanted to get the whole question settled once and for all. There were some other people invited, too. Try to imagine the scene: Makovsky, young and handsome and delicate-looking; and Roter, old and fat, scowling at Makovsky from under his craggy brows like a crocodile at a rabbit. Makovsky was obviously very nervous, but he handled himself well. He argued convincingly that we were using an outmoded system and that he was proposing a progressive alternative. He kept citing England as an example: Piccadilly station — the best station in London, right in the heart of the most aristocratic section of the city — was built deep in the ground, and it had escalators rather than elevators. Roter kept spewing contempt on Makovsky, calling him an irresponsible young whippersnapper. But Makovsky had made his point. I took his side when we made our report to the Central Committee. Roter was very stubborn. He was determined to defend his position to the bitter end. Kaganovich, who was on Makovsky's side with me, was embarrassed about this impasse because it meant we'd have to take the dispute to the Politbureau. Roter would present his case against us, and there was a chance Stalin might support him. However, we had no choice.

Roter gave his report at the Politbureau meeting, and then it was our turn to speak. An argument broke out. At one point Roter said, "What you're proposing is much too expensive . . ."

But Stalin cut him off sharply. "Comrade Roter, the question of what is expensive and what is inexpensive will be left up to the Government to decide. Your job is to let us know what is technically feasible, not what is financially feasible. Now, tell us, is the proposal of this young engineer Makovsky technically feasible?"

"Yes, but it will be much too expensive."

"I just told you, Comrade Roter, the Government will decide that. We will go ahead and accept Comrade Makovsky's plan for deep tunneling."

I was delighted. Stalin showed great wisdom and boldness. He had taken into account the long-range factor of civil defense, and he decided on that basis that tunnels merited the extra expense. Sure enough, in the first part of the war, the city's command post was situated in the Myasnitsky Gates Metro station, and the tunnels were used as bomb shelters.

In 1935 the citizens of Moscow celebrated the completion of the first stage of the Metro. Many people received government awards. I was decorated with the Order of Lenin. This was my first such honor. Bulganin received the Order of the Red Star. And the Metro was named after Kaganovich. A competition had already begun among Politbureau members to see who could "claim" the most factories, collective farms, towns, and so on. This regrettable practice had come into being under Stalin, and Kaganovich was already adept at it.

3

The Terror

Collectivization

What came to be known as the Great Terror did not start until 1935. But the use of terror in principle, to shatter opposition to the regime, had been a feature of Bolshevik rule since its formal invocation by Lenin in 1918. Collectivization (1928–33) was the wholesale application of terror to the countryside, and nobody knows, or ever will know, how many millions perished in a madhouse operation which, years later, Stalin himself in conversation with Winston Churchill described as being more critical for the Soviet Union than any of the crises of World War II. In 1933, when it was all over, the agricultural production and the livestock population of the Soviet Union had been diminished by more than half. On the eve of the German invasion in 1941 they had still not returned to their 1928, precollectivization levels. What makes this section of outstanding interest is that Khrushchev for the first time admits that "the Stalin brand of collectivization brought us nothing but misery." For nearly forty years the Soviet leadership, Khrushchev included, have pretended that the collectivization, bitterly opposed at the time by Bukharin and others, was a necessary and brilliantly successful operation. In fact it was an atrocity on a colossal scale, the consequences of which have been permanently damaging to the Soviet economy.

COLLECTIVIZATION was begun the year before I was transferred from the Ukraine, but it wasn't until after I started work in Moscow that I began to suspect its real effects on the rural population —

and it wasn't until many years later that I realized the scale of the starvation and repression which accompanied collectivization as it was carried out under Stalin.

My first glimpse of the truth was in 1930, when the bureau of the Party cell at the Industrial Academy tried to get rid of me by sending me out into the country on a business trip. The academy sponsored the Stalin Collective Farm in the Samara [later named Kuibyshev] Region, to which I was supposed to deliver money we had collected for the purchase of agricultural implements. Sasha [Aleksandr] Sdobnov, another student at the academy, accompanied me on that trip. He was a good comrade from the Urals. Later he got caught in the meat-mincer of 1937.

We spent only a few days at the collective farm and were appalled at the conditions we found there. The farmers were starving to death. We called a meeting to present the money we'd brought them. Most of the workers on this collective farm were drawn from the Chuvash population, so we had to speak to them through an interpreter. When we told them that the money was allocated for farm equipment, they told us they weren't interested in equipment — what they wanted was bread. They literally begged us to give them food. Sdobnov and I were put up in the hut of an old widow who was so poor that she had nothing to give us; we shared with her the food we'd brought along for the trip.

I'd had no idea that things were this bad. At the Industrial Academy we'd been living under the illusion promoted by *Pravda* that collectivization was proceeding smoothly and everything was fine in the countryside.

Then, without warning, Stalin delivered his famous "Dizzy with Success" speech, laying the blame for the excesses of the collectivization on active local Party members.[1] The same people who had been conducting the collectivization with such reckless, bestial fervor, suddenly found themselves under *Pravda*'s lash. At the time we considered Stalin's speech a masterpiece, a bold blow struck by the Party leadership against the men responsible for the excesses.[2] But I remember being

1. The speech was delivered on March 2, 1930. Stalin insisted that his perfectly straightforward instructions had been misunderstood. This was the master denouncing his own instruments for carrying out his orders.

2. "At the time we considered Stalin's speech a masterpiece . . ." But who was "we"? Stalin spoke without warning to the Politbureau and the Central Committee. The Central Committee actually found the courage to protest at being saddled with the blame for Stalin's crime.

bothered by the thought: if everything has been going as well on the collective farms as Stalin has been telling us up until now, then what's the reason for the "Dizzy with Success" speech all of a sudden?

The controversy over collectivization sparked a rapid turnover in the Moscow Party leadership. Uglanov, who was an opponent of collectivization, was replaced by Bauman.[3] Then Bauman was caught in the crackdown on excesses, and he was replaced by Molotov, who in turn was replaced by Kaganovich. It was when Kaganovich was the leader of the Moscow organization that word began to leak out that there was trouble on the collective farms, although I never had any idea that trouble meant peasant uprisings and that people were sent out from Moscow to put them down.

I remember that while I was working on the Moscow City Committee in 1932, Kaganovich suddenly announced that he had to go on a business trip to Krasnodar. He was away for a week or two. He didn't tell us at the time, but it later came to light that he'd gone to quell a strike — or "sabotage," as it was then called — of Kuban Cossacks who refused to cultivate their land. As a result of Kaganovich's trip, whole Cossack settlements were picked up and moved forcibly to Siberia.

One of my friends was Veklishev, the Chief of the Political Directorate [armed forces "security"] of the Moscow Military District. He told me that strikes and sabotage were going on all over the place in the Ukraine, and that Red Army soldiers had to be mobilized to weed the sugar beet crop. I was horrified. I knew from my own experience with agriculture that sugar beets are very delicate; they have to be weeded at the right time and with the proper care. You couldn't expect Red Army soldiers, most of whom had never seen a sugar beet and didn't give a damn if they ever saw one again, to be able to do the job right. Naturally, the sugar beet crop was lost.

Subsequently the word got around that famine had broken out in the Ukraine. I couldn't believe it. I'd left the Ukraine in 1929, only three years before, when the Ukraine had pulled itself up to prewar living standards. Food had been plentiful and cheap. Yet now, we were told, people were starving. It was incredible.

It wasn't until many years later, when Anastas Ivanovich Mikoyan

---

3. It was against the collectivization drive that the "rightists," above all Bukharin, made their last fight. The irony was that Trotsky and the "leftists" had first advocated collectivization, which Stalin had opposed at the time. Molotov was Moscow Party chieftain from 1928–30, when he became Prime Minister.

told me the following story, that I found out how bad things had really been in the Ukraine in the early thirties. Mikoyan told me that Comrade Demchenko, who was then First Secretary of the Kiev Regional Committee, once came to see him in Moscow. Here's what Demchenko said: "Anastas Ivanovich, does Comrade Stalin — for that matter, does anyone in the Politbureau — know what's happening in the Ukraine? Well, if not, I'll give you some idea. A train recently pulled into Kiev loaded with corpses of people who had starved to death. It had picked up corpses all the way from Poltava to Kiev. I think somebody had better inform Stalin about this situation."

You can see from this story that an abnormal state of affairs had already developed in the Party when someone like Demchenko, a member of the Ukrainian Politbureau, was afraid to go see Stalin himself. We had already moved into the period when one man had the collective leadership under his thumb and everyone else trembled before him. Demchenko decided to tell Mikoyan about what was happening in the Ukraine because he knew Mikoyan was close to Stalin and might be able to get something done. Active Party members in those days often referred to Stalin, Ordzhonikidze, and Mikoyan as the Caucasian clique. I've always held Anastas Ivanovich Mikoyan in high esteem. We all have our faults and Anastas Ivanovich certainly has his, but he's an honest, intelligent, and capable comrade who has made a large contribution to the Party and the State.

The conditions that existed under collectivization have been described by Sholokhov in *Virgin Soil Upturned*. Sholokhov wrote his book while Stalin was still alive, so he had no choice but to describe collectivization according to the Stalinist interpretation. When the failure of the collectivization became widely known, we were all taught to blame scheming kulaks, rightists, Trotskyites, and Zinovievites for what was happening. There was always the handy explanation of counterrevolutionary sabotage.

But now that Stalin's abuses of power have been exposed, a more searching, objective analysis of collectivization is in order if we're ever going to understand what really happened. Perhaps we'll never know how many people perished directly as a result of collectivization, or indirectly as a result of Stalin's eagerness to blame its failure on others. But two things are certain: first, the Stalin brand of collectivization brought us nothing but misery and brutality; and second, Stalin played the decisive role in the leadership of our country at the time. Rykov,

Bukharin, Zinoviev, and Kamenev had already been removed from their posts, and Trotsky was in exile. Therefore, if we were looking for someone to hold responsible, we could lay the blame squarely on Stalin's own shoulders.

But all this is hindsight. At the time, we didn't know the truth. We still believed in Stalin and trusted him.

The Purge Years

Here we have an inevitably selective and distorted account of the most terrible period in the history of the Soviet Union. Unlike Molotov and Malenkov, Khrushchev was not actively involved in the excesses of the purge years until he was sent out to the Ukraine in 1938 to finish off the great purge there before reconstructing the shattered Party apparatus. But he knew a great deal of what was going on; he profited directly by the shooting of his senior colleagues; and he says enough (as in the affair of Yaroslavsky) to indicate that, like every other senior Party functionary at that time, he himself performed some vile actions, even before he arrived in Kiev. This chapter should be compared with the passages in the Secret Speech which deal with the arrest, torture, and execution of men wholly guiltless of the charges preferred against them — though far from innocent in other ways. The whole appalling story was known in very great detail in the West, but it was not until the Secret Speech that the horrors were confirmed by an official Soviet source. Even then it has to be remembered that Khrushchev gives no idea of the sheer scale of the butchery. At the same time, he limited his revelations to the crimes committed by Stalin against the Party and the army: he had not a word to say about the effect of the terror on millions of rank-and-file Party members and ordinary unpolitical citizens. In a word, he is speaking throughout of Stalin's crimes against the Party, not of his crimes against the Soviet people as a whole. The most usual estimate of the number of Party members arrested is close on one million. Non-Party citizens arrested were at least seven times this number. It is worth mentioning that the deliberate torturing of prisoners under interrogation (as distinct from spontaneous kicking, punching, and the like) was forbidden under the regulations until 1937. Early in 1937 or late in 1936 secret instructions were issued saying that torture might be used. It was finally approved by the Central Committee in 1939. (The Great Terror by Robert Conquest is incomparably the best and most complete study of the purges as a whole, and essential for a proper understanding of their range. Perhaps the most revealing account of what it was like to be a Party member caught up in the purges is Into the Whirlwind by Yevgenia S. Ginzburg.)

In giving an objective, concentrated analysis of Stalin's negative side, I must say something about the practice Stalin instituted of ruthlessly branding Party members as enemies of the people, then bringing them to trial and having them eliminated. Our Party is still scarred by the damage done during the purges. The attitudes which Stalin inculcated in the minds of many Party members left a kind of encrustation on the consciousness of many people, especially dull, limited people. Even today you'll find those who think that Stalin's way was the only right way to build Socialism and to get things done in our country. As far as I'm concerned, it reflects a fairly primitive, slavish mentality to say that people won't work unless there's someone standing over them, cracking a whip above their heads. If you believe in the psychology of a slave society — that people have to be kept in line by force or else they'll revolt — then maybe you're one of those who thinks the repression inflicted on the Soviet people by Stalin was historically inevitable. But I think that claim is nonsense. Moreover, it contradicts one of the basic tenets of our Marxist-Leninist doctrine: namely, it's the people who make history, not a single powerful personage. The October Revolution was achieved in response to Lenin's compelling rational leadership, not under his whip. The people followed Lenin because they believed in him, not because they feared him. Lenin raised and unified the aspirations of the people. Stalin tried to bully the people and the Party into obedience.

It all started one evening in 1934. The telephone rang and I picked it up. It was Kaganovich. "I'm calling from the Politbureau. Come over here right away. It's urgent."

I went straight to the Kremlin. Kaganovich met me. He had a frightful look about him. I was immediately on my guard, ready for anything. "What's happened?" I thought to myself.

"There's been a terrible tragedy," he said. "Kirov has been murdered in Leningrad. I'll tell you about it in more detail later. Right now the

Politbureau is discussing the matter. We're putting together a delegation to go to Leningrad — Stalin, Voroshilov, Molotov, plus a delegation of sixty people from the Moscow Party organization and the Moscow worker class. You'll lead the delegation. You'll be in the honor
guard there and then accompany Kirov's body back to Moscow."

"Very well."

I went straight to the Moscow Committee. I put together a delegation and left for Leningrad that same night. I didn't see Stalin, Voroshilov, and Molotov. They were traveling separately, in special railroad cars. It seemed to me that the whole city of Leningrad was in a
state of mourning, although maybe I was just projecting my own feelings onto everyone else.

We were all completely in the dark about what had happened. We
knew only that Kirov's murderer was someone named Nikolayev, who
had been expelled from the Party for taking part in the Trotskyite
opposition — which indicated that the Trotskyites were behind the
whole thing. We all felt sincere outrage and indignation.[4]

I don't remember how long we spent in Leningrad — two or three
days, I think. We took turns standing around the coffin in an honor
guard as the Leningraders said their last farewells to the body of Sergei Mironovich. I could see that Kaganovich was badly shaken, even
frightened. I can't say how the other leaders felt about Kirov's death. I
watched Stalin closely when he stood in the honor guard. He had
enormous self-control, and his expression was absolutely impenetrable.

4. S. M. Kirov, already referred to in Chapter 2, for long a devoted Stalinist,
had built up a very strong position as the Leningrad Party chieftain in succession
to Zinoviev. Having helped Stalin defeat the opposition, he challenged the idea
that it was necessary and desirable to pursue a policy of revengeful persecution —
particularly insofar as this involved killing. He was the only man close to Stalin
who was strong enough to say what he felt and to be regarded by others who
thought like him as an alternative leader. He was shot in his Leningrad office on
December 1, 1934, by a disgruntled ex-Bolshevik, L. Nikolaev, who had been expelled from the Party not, as Khrushchev says, because he was a Trotskyite but because he had quarreled with the Party bureaucracy. Kirov was given a state funeral with all honors and Stalin appeared to be deeply affected. But there were
many who believed that Stalin himself was behind the murder: certainly Nikolaev
was acting for no opposition faction. Later, in 1938, the deposed police chief Yagoda, on trial for his life, was accused of facilitating the murder. In the Secret
Speech, and subsequently, Khrushchev himself suggested that Stalin had inspired
the murder and promised a full judicial investigation. If this took place it has
never been reported. It was the Kirov murder which triggered off the great purge
which, starting in Leningrad, spread under successive police chiefs to the whole
country, stifled it in terror, and reduced the surviving population to a state of
cowed and frightened apathy.

It didn't even occur to me that perhaps he had other things on his mind besides Kirov's death.

Part of my job as Secretary of the Moscow Committee was to supervise the activity of the Moscow office of the NKVD. The chief of the office was Comrade Redens.[5] He was Stalin's brother-in-law, a Pole by nationality. He was a good comrade and had been a member of the Party since 1914. Stalin later had him shot. I found out from Comrade Redens that the operation of the NKVD changed drastically after Kirov's murder.

Before the murder, the Cheka rarely resorted to administrative methods for dealing with people. By administrative methods, I mean arrest and trial. Such methods were used only in cases involving activities of an overtly anti-Soviet character.[6] For example, we had always tried to deal with work stoppages and strikes in Moscow by going to the barracks or factories and explaining to the workers that we had to raise production quotas in order to catch up with our enemies. The workers who had been recruited from the villages lived in unspeakable conditions — filth, bedbugs, cockroaches, bad food, and inadequate clothing. It tended to aggravate their discontent when their collective agreements on output norms were revised in favor of the State. We would sit down with them and try to explain that sometimes the interests of the State superseded those of the individual. Usually the workers were very understanding and eager to get on with the job, even if their output norm was raised ten or fifteen percent while their wages were left the same. If certain individuals refused to adapt themselves to the necessary conditions, they would be openly denounced by the Party. But we almost always stopped short of using administrative methods against them.

All that suddenly changed after Kirov's murder. Redens told me he had received instructions to "purge" Moscow. Moscow unquestionably needed a purgative. It was constipated with many undesirable

5. S. Redens was uncle by marriage to Svetlana Alliluyeva. Very active in the purge years, he vanished when Beria assumed control of the NKVD in 1939.
6. There were plenty of arrests, with or without trial, before the Kirov murder: "anti-Soviet" activity was a very broad term. But Party unity was a holy concept, and it was not until the Kirov murder that it became in effect a crime for Party members to diverge, or to have diverged in the past, even fractionally from Stalinist orthodoxy.
The NKVD, or People's Commissariat of Internal Affairs, had been established in July, 1934, to take over from the GPU, which itself had been created by Lenin in 1921 to take over from the Cheka, also created by Lenin. (See Appendix 2.)

elements — nonworkers, parasites, and profiteers. A list was put together of the people who should be exiled from the city. I don't know where these people were sent. I never asked. We always followed the rule that if you weren't told something, that meant it didn't concern you; it was the State's business, and the less you knew about it the better. Anyway, the deportation of criminal elements from Moscow was the first stage of the repression which began after Kirov's murder.[7]

Soon the political terror started. I caught only an occasional, accidental glimpse of its inner workings.

While the trial of the Leningrad oppositionists was going on, Kaganovich and Sergo Ordzhonikidze were left in charge whenever Stalin and Molotov were out of Moscow. Once I went by the Central Committee office to see Kaganovich about some matter relating to city administration. When Kaganovich was informed that I was outside, he asked me to come into his study. He had Sergo Ordzhonikidze and Demyan Bedny with him. They were conferring about the trial of the oppositionists and the presentation of the trial in the press. A series of articles condemning the oppositionists was being published in order to prepare public opinion for the harsh sentences which actually had already been decided upon.

I remember the scene very well. Sergo and Kaganovich asked Demyan Bedny, "Well, Comrade Demyan, have you written a poem that we can use?"

"Yes," said Demyan, and he recited the poem.

When he finished, there was an awkward pause. Kaganovich spoke up first: "That's not quite what we had in mind, Comrade Demyan." Sergo, who had a fiery temper, didn't beat around the bush. He heatedly exhorted Demyan to do better. Demyan Bedny was an obese man, and he was completely bald. His head looked like a huge copper cauldron. He looked at them with his good-natured eyes and said, "I'm afraid I can't do any better. Much as I've tried, this is all I've been able to squeeze out. I just can't raise my hand against the oppositionists. I can't do it. I'm impotent toward them." Actually, he used a cruder, more manly expression.

I don't know if what Demyan wrote was ever published. He obviously wasn't completely convinced that the oppositionists were

7. The first stage of the repression which began after Kirov's murder was in fact a wave of political arrests in Leningrad itself. Khrushchev's so-called "criminal elements" in Moscow had nothing to do with the case.

criminals. That's why he couldn't muster the inspiration and the Party spirit to rip them apart in his poem. He just wasn't sure they were enemies. To mention my own attitude, naturally I was on Kaganovich's side — that is, on Stalin's side. Therefore, at the time I glared at Demyan disapprovingly. But now I understand why Demyan had his doubts.[8]

The flower of the Party was stamped out in the savage violence which erupted shortly after that scene I witnessed in Kaganovich's office. Many of the original leaders of our Party and our country were wiped out. Where had men like Molotov or Kaganovich or Voroshilov or Mikoyan been when Zinoviev, Kamenev, Trotsky, Bukharin, and Rykov were running the country? Almost the whole Politbureau which had been in office at the time of Lenin's death was purged. Take for example Zinoviev and Kamenev, who were eliminated as leaders of the opposition: they had made some errors during the Revolution. Everyone knows that. But everyone also knows something else, too. After they saw the error of their ways, Lenin himself enlisted them to work in the leadership. At Lenin's side, Zinoviev and Kamenev gave worthy guidance to the Party. When the Government moved from Leningrad to Moscow, Zinoviev stayed in Leningrad. He was entrusted with the supervision of our original capital, our most revolutionary city, which had raised the banner of insurrection in the October Revolution. And Moscow had been entrusted to Kamenev. Yet now these men were in the dock as criminals and were soon to be eliminated as enemies of the people!

Stalin's purge of the Party swept from the oppositionists in 1936 to the rightists in 1938, when Rykov, Bukharin, and other leaders of the people and the Party were brought to trial. It is fitting that these men should be called leaders. Take Rykov for example. He became Chairman of the Council of People's Commissars after Lenin's death. He was a man of merit in the eyes of the Party and a worthy representative of Soviet Power. Yet he was shot. As for Bukharin, Lenin had called him "our Bukharchik," and his *A-B-C of Communism* was a primer of Marxist-Leninist wisdom for the entire older generation. He, too, was brought to trial and eliminated.[9]

8. D. Bedny, a hack versifier, may have had his doubts at this time. He soon recovered, however, and produced a series of nauseating "poems" vilifying the accused (including the main victims of the subsequent purge of the Red Army) and demanding savage punishment.

9. To establish the main chronology: While the purge gathered force in 1935,

During that period the Party started to lose its authority and to be subservient to the NKVD. I remember the following state of affairs at the Moscow Party Conference of 1937. All candidates nominated for membership on the Moscow City and Regional committees had to be screened and "sanctioned" by the NKVD. Neither the Central Committee nor the Party at large could promote its own members. The NKVD had the last word in assessing the activities of any Party member and in deciding whether or not he could be elected to top Party posts. We had been conditioned to believe that this practice helped local Party organizations expose enemies who had penetrated the ruling Party organizations. I remember one incident in particular that occurred during the 1937 Moscow Party Conference. There was a commissar from

---

Stalin was preparing the first great show trial, which Khrushchev here refers to as the trial of the Leningrad oppositionists. His instrument was G. G. Yagoda, head of the NKVD, who had first inaugurated the Soviet system of forced labor. This trial, held in August, 1936, was officially called the Trial of the Trotsky-Zinoviev Terrorist Center, and it ended with the shooting of Lenin's close colleagues, G. E. Zinoviev and L. B. Kamenev, together with fourteen others.

Immediately afterward, Yagoda was removed for lack of zeal and replaced by N. Yezhov, a pathological case, a dwarf, with whom Khrushchev had worked on the Moscow Party Committee. It was under Yezhov that the purge ran wild and the terror became universal. The second show trial, prepared by Yezhov, took place in January, 1937, and was known as the Trial of the Anti-Soviet Trotskyite Center. Khrushchev scarcely mentions this. The chief victims were G. L. Pyatakov, a protégé of Lenin's who had earlier been pressured into demanding the death penalty for Zinoviev; G. Sokolnikov, a member of Lenin's first Politbureau; K. Radek, the brilliant journalist; and fourteen others.

The third great treason trial, and the most spectacular, occurred in March, 1938, also prepared by Yezhov. This was the Trial of the Anti-Soviet Bloc of Rightists and Trotskyites. There were twenty-one accused, headed this time by Bukharin himself; Rykov, Lenin's successor as Prime Minister of the Soviet Union; and Yagoda, Yezhov's predecessor as head of the NKVD.

In all these trials the accused were charged with conspiring to murder Stalin, with being agents of foreign intelligence services, and many other things besides.

In the summer of 1937, between the show trials of 1937 and 1938, occurred the secret trial and execution of the cream of the Red Army high command, headed by Marshal Tukhachevsky, Deputy People's Commissar of Defense, an action which preceded the unpublicized liquidation of approximately half the entire officers' corps.

The purge continued in a lunatic progression until the end of 1938, when it was Yezhov's turn to be liquidated. He was succeeded by Lavrenty Pavlovich Beria, head of the Georgian NKVD, whose first task it was to purge the purgers (incidentally paying off any old scores of his own). The great mass of victims, including many of the most ardent Stalinists in high positions who had thrown themselves into the early purges with enthusiasm, were arrested, tortured, and shot without trial and without publicity. They simply vanished from the scene. Khrushchev was head of the Moscow Party organization throughout the blood purge until January, 1938, when he went off to rule the Ukraine. He was taken into the Politbureau at the height of the *Yezhovshchina*.

the Frunze Military Academy who, from the standpoint of the Moscow Party Committee, was a good Communist and a good comrade. When it was moved that his name be put on the ballot, the delegates to the Conference were clearly enthusiastic about his candidacy. His nomination was greeted by thunderous applause. Suddenly I got a message from the NKVD: "Do everything you can to bring that man down. He's not to be trusted. He's connected with enemies of the people and will be arrested." We obeyed and defeated his nomination, but it was a distressing experience for all the delegates. The very next night that commissar was arrested.

The case of Emelyan Yaroslavsky was much the same.[10] He was an Old Bolshevik and much respected in the Party. He was Secretary of the Party Collegium of the Central Control Commission, which means he was considered beyond reproach from the Party's standpoint. He was nominated as a candidate for election to the Moscow Regional Committee. Suddenly I got a call saying that Yaroslavsky had to be brought down. This order was very hard on me personally, but I had to obey. I passed the word around to the other secretaries of the Regional Committee to launch an agitation campaign against Yaroslavsky among the delegates without letting it reach Yaroslavsky himself. But it was too late. Despite our activity, he was elected by a margin of something like one vote. After the Conference, Comrade Zemlyachka, whom I respected very much, went so far as to write a letter to the Central Committee blaming me, as Secretary of the Moscow City Committee, for the disrespect shown to Yaroslavsky during the Conference. Of course, at the time I couldn't explain to her that I had just been following orders. Naturally, her letter didn't have any effect.

The point of these stories is that since every promotion or transfer of Party personnel had to be made in accordance with directives from the NKVD, the Party lost its guiding role. It was disgraceful.[11]

I was personally acquainted with many victims of the political terror. Some of them I'd known from my days in the Donbass. Take Ivan Tarasovich Kirilkin, for instance. He was manager of the Ruchenkov mines in 1925–26 and later was made the director of the Makeyev metal works, which he ran very competently. Then there was Vasily

10. E. Yaroslavsky had earned notoriety as head of the League of the Militant Godless, the spearhead of the Bolshevik attack on religion.

11. For all practical purposes the original Bolshevik Party had been destroyed by 1937. What remained was Stalin, his police chief of the moment, and his closest colleagues, of whom Khrushchev was one.

Bazulin. He did a pretty good job supervising a factory near Yuzovka. Both men perished in 1937. They disappeared off the face of the earth, without leaving so much as a trace. Nobody would tell me what had happened to either of them. I don't know how many factory directors and engineers perished in just the same way. In those days it was easy enough to get rid of someone you didn't like. All you had to do was submit a report denouncing him as an enemy of the people; the local Party organization would glance at your report, beat its breast in righteous indignation, and have the man taken care of.

I also knew Treivas.[12] His name had been widely known in the twenties as a prominent figure in the Lenin League of Communist Youth [Komsomol]. He was an intelligent, capable, decent man. I got to know him through the Moscow Party organization when Treivas and I worked for six months together in the Bauman District. Kaganovich once took me aside and warned me that Treivas's political record had a black mark on it. Apparently he had been among the so-called Youth League Ninety-Three, who had once signed a declaration in support of Trotsky. He came to a tragic end. When Stalin proposed that regional committee secretaries should go around and inspect Chekist prisons in their areas, I found Treivas in jail during my rounds. He didn't escape the meat-mincer when the butchery began in 1937.

Sometimes you hear the name of Lomov mentioned on the radio. They tell you how Lenin instructed Lomov to do such-and-such. Where is this Lomov now? I knew him well. I met him frequently when I was working in the Donbass after the Civil War. He was put in charge of coal output in the Ukraine, and I used to see him frequently at his office in Kharkov. He was much respected in the Party as a man with a Party record going back to the days of the pre-Revolutionary underground. But you still want to know, where is this Lomov now? The answer is — shot! No more Lomov.[13]

Even the people closest to Stalin were swept up in the frenzy of the hunt. Take Ordzhonikidze's fate.[14] Comrade Sergo, as we always called him, was a popular figure. He enjoyed well-deserved respect

12. Kirilkin, Basulin, and Treivas were minor figures who shared the fate of tens of thousands like them.

13. G. I. Lomov (real name, Oppokov) was a member of the Control Commission of the Council of People's Commissars of the USSR. He was arrested and shot on Molotov's orders.

14. "Sergo" Ordzhonikidze, having been very close to Stalin, took exception to his excesses and quarreled personally with his master. Immediately afterwards he

throughout the Party. The three Caucasians—Stalin, Mikoyan, and Sergo—were inseparable for many years. But even though Stalin and Sergo were both Georgians and Old Bolsheviks, they were completely unlike. Despite his explosive temper, Sergo was a man of chivalrous character, much respected for his accessibility, his humanity, and his sense of justice. Sergo by no means approved of the butchery that was going on in the Party. I remember, for example, that he felt great respect and sympathy for Lominadze.[15] Once he even called me at the Moscow Committee and asked, in his thick Georgian accent, if I would intervene on Lominadze's behalf. I told him there wasn't much I could do since Lominadze was an active oppositionist and had given the Party ample reason for denouncing him. Sergo pressed me to do whatever I could to see that Lominadze was left in peace. However, his own efforts notwithstanding, people continued to be rounded up as enemies of the people, and finally Sergo couldn't stand it any more. At the beginning of 1937 he shot himself. It wasn't until many years later that I found out the real story behind his death. Stalin covered up the whole affair very cleverly. I first heard Sergo was dead when Abel Sofrenovich Yenukidze called me on my day off and said, "Comrade Khrushchev, come to my office right away. It's urgent." [16]

I went straight to the Kremlin and asked, "What's this all about, Abel Sofrenovich?"

"Sergo is dead."

"*What?* I just saw him a little while ago."

"He died very suddenly. You must not have known that he was a sick man. The Government has set up a commission to arrange his funeral, and you've been appointed to it."

All the procedures for an appropriately solemn State funeral were followed. I gave a funeral oration on behalf of the Moscow Committee during the ceremony at the Lenin Mausoleum. I mourned Sergo sin-

---

died in circumstances that are still a mystery. He was not formally executed. He was honored after his death. Khrushchev said in the Secret Speech that he was forced to commit suicide. But nobody knows to this day exactly what happened.

15. V. V. Lominadze, an early supporter of Stalin's, more independent-minded than most, was named as a conspirator in the first and third show trials.

16. A. S. Yenukidze, another Georgian, was a Stalinist who, like Kirov and Ordzhonikidze, objected to Stalin's increasing brutality. Since he was deprived of his posts and outlawed in 1935 it is hard to see how this conversation could have taken place.

cerely. He had always been particularly kind to me. I had benefited greatly from his fatherly protection.

I didn't find out that he had committed suicide until during the war, when I was at a dinner with Stalin and some of the other comrades and just happened to bring up the subject of Sergo:

"Sergo! Now there was a real man. What a pity he died before his time. What a loss!"

There was an embarrassed silence. I sensed that I had said something wrong. I asked Malenkov as we were leaving after dinner, "What did I say that I shouldn't have said?"

"Don't you know?"

"No."

"You mean you thought Sergo died a natural death? You didn't know he shot himself? Stalin won't forgive him for that. You saw how awkward it was when you mentioned Sergo's name. That was pretty careless of you."

Of course, at the time Sergo died, Malenkov didn't know anything about the suicide either. He wasn't as close to Stalin as I was. He'd only found out about it indirectly.

After Stalin's death Anastas Ivanovich Mikoyan, who had been very close to Sergo, told me he had had a talk with him on the very eve of his suicide. On a Saturday evening they had gone for a walk together around the Kremlin. Sergo told Anastas Ivanovich that he couldn't go on living. He said it was impossible to tolerate what Stalin was doing to the Party, and he didn't have the strength to fight it any more. The next day, Sunday, he shot himself. Comrade Sergo was a singularly honorable man.

Shortly after Sergo's death Stalin struck against the Old Guard of the Red Army. I can't enumerate all the generals he eliminated, but I would like to single out a few.

Tukhachevsky's arrest came like a thunderbolt out of a clear blue sky. He was our brilliant Deputy People's Commissar of Defense. At the age of twenty-six he had commanded the Western Front in the Civil War. Lenin entrusted the Kronstadt operation to him, as well as the operations against Antonov and Kolchak. When Tukhachevsky was executed, there was a lot of cackling from men who had been connected with him in the Civil War — men who couldn't reach up to his knees, much less to his navel. They started kicking his corpse around and blaming him for their own failures in the Civil War. But in the opinion of experts, those failures had occurred only because Tukhachevsky hadn't been placed high enough in the command. And the fact remains that Lenin entrusted Tukhachevsky with many critical operations on which the life or death of the country depended.

I had known Tukhachevsky slightly and used to meet with him when I worked as First Secretary of the Moscow City and Regional committees. We used to talk on the telephone and see each other at plenums. He occasionally took me out into the field to show me some new weapon or new piece of engineering equipment. He had a deep understanding of military innovations and a high regard for them. I'm convinced that if he hadn't been executed, our army would have been much better trained and better equipped when Hitler attacked.

Then there was Gamarnik. He was Chief of the Red Army Political Directorate, so he was an important political figure as well as a good soldier. He had played a significant part in the creation of the Red Army. They'll tell you Gamarnik wasn't executed. True enough. He shot himself. He foresaw that he would be arrested, and when they came pounding on his door, he put a pistol to his head and pulled the trigger. The executioners arrived to drag him to the block, but he decided it would be better to end his life by his own hand. Gamarnik was a very honorable man.

Other victims were Yegorov [17] — one of our greatest military leaders, our commander on the Southern Front in the Civil War — and Yakir.[18] General Yakir was a relatively young fellow. He hadn't taken part in World War I or the Revolution. His career began during the Civil War, when he joined a newly formed detachment. In those days we were armed with anything we could get our hands on, but our main weapon was our hatred of the old bourgeois capitalistic regime and our devotion to the new Socialist way of life for which the Civil War was being fought. Yakir's detachment grew to a division, and he was put in command. He and his troops were cut off from the Red Army in the South, but he managed to break out of the encirclement and lead his division right through the White-Guardist lines to rejoin our main forces. After the Civil War, Yakir commanded the troops in the

17. Marshal A. Yegorov was arrested and shot comparatively late in the army purge, having briefly succeeded Tukhachevsky as Deputy People's Commissar for Defense.

18. General Yakir, an army commander in charge of the Kiev Military District, was the father of the historian Peter Yakir, a leader of the dissident Soviet intelligentsia today.

Ukraine and the Crimea. Suddenly he was arrested and executed. So was Eideman — a poet as well as a soldier, one of our outstanding military leaders.[19]

Now about Blücher.[20] The newspapers often talk about Blücher: Blücher received the First Order of the Red Banner, Blücher did this, Blücher did that, Blücher, Blücher, Blücher. Blücher was a proletarian, a worker, a plumber by trade. He was a self-made military man. He got his first experience in World War I, and then commanded entire formations in the Civil War. Later he was sent to China as our consultant to Chiang Kai-shek. He also commanded the troops of the Far Eastern Military District. We trusted him both as a military leader and as a political figure. So where was Blücher when we really needed him in the war against Hitler? He was already dead. But how? Did he die a natural death? No, he was executed. He was arrested and shot as an enemy of the people.

Now they're putting up a monument to Blücher, as well they should. But the monument should tell the whole truth about him, and those people who don't want the whole truth to be told should be ashamed. Any monument to Blücher should let the people know that it wasn't a natural death that deprived us of his talents in the war against the Germans; no, Blücher fell by the hand of someone who Lenin said shouldn't be trusted.

In recent years I've seen the film *The Iron Torrent* a number of times, and it always affects me very deeply. *The Iron Torrent* was also a book. It was the first book about the Civil War that I ever read. It was written by our talented writer Serafimovich. Now it has come out on the screen. Whenever I see this movie, I'm always haunted by the thought, "Where have I seen this brave, clever general who commands the Taman army?" In the film and in the book he's called Kozhukh, but his real name was Kovtyukh.[21] This was the man who displayed such brilliance, skill, and courage when he broke an encirclement by the Whites and led the Taman army through enemy lines. Everyone who saw this general in action has nothing but praise for him. You might ask, "Where is this Kozhukh-Kovtyukh now? What happened to

19. General R. P. Eideman had been an army commander in the Civil War. He was head of the civil defense organization when he was arrested and shot.
20. Marshal Blücher was commander of the Far Eastern troops and perhaps the ablest Red Army commander. Arrested in August, 1938, he was interrogated personally by Beria, who had just succeeded Yezhov.
21. General Kovtyukh, corps commander, was shot in July, 1938.

him? What did he do during the war against Hitler? Kovtyukh was gone when World War II broke out. He had been rounded up with the enemies of the people and shot.

I was personally very close to Ivan Naumovich Dubovoy.[22] He came from a proletarian family. His father was a miner on the Don. Dubovoy finished officers' school during World War I. When the Civil War broke out, he was made deputy commander of a division commanded by Shchors. Later I used to see Dubovoy at congresses of the Ukrainian Communist Party. I got to know him particularly well in 1928–29, when I ran the Organizational Section of the Kiev Regional Committee. Dubovoy commanded the Kiev Military District. I used to go out with him to inspect the troops. I was very pleased that we had commanders like him in the Red Army — men devoted body and soul to the Revolution, to Soviet Power, and to Socialism.

When the enemies of the people were exposed, Stalin distributed the testimonies of Tukhachevsky, Yakir, and the others to the Politbureau. Among these testimonies was a confession written in Ivan Naumovich Dubovoy's own handwriting. He wrote that he had killed his commander Shchors during the Civil War. Here is what he said in his confession:

"Shchors and I were lying on the ground watching the battle. Suddenly an enemy machine gunner opened fire in our direction. The bullets sprayed all around us. Shchors was in front of me. He turned his head and said, 'Vanya, Vanya, the Whites have a good machine gunner. Look how accurately he's firing on us.' A few moments later he turned around again and started to say something else. Then and there I killed him. I shot him in the head. I killed him in order to take his place as commander of the division."

You can imagine how disgusted I was when I first read this confession. I had always respected Dubovoy, and suddenly I discovered he had done something as vile as that. I rebuked myself: how could I have been so blind? Why hadn't I known that Dubovoy was Shchors's murderer?

But at the time of the Twentieth Party Congress in 1956 — when we opened the archives and looked into the files of all the people who had been declared enemies of the people and shot or strangled — I found out that Dubovoy's testimony was all a lie. I had been deceived a second time. The first time was when my regard for Dubovoy as an honest

22. I. N. Dubovoy, another army commander, was shot in July, 1938.

man was shattered by his confession to Shchors's murder. Now I had been deceived again, this time by Dubovoy's own murderer — Stalin himself.

In the late thirties Hitler was preparing his attack and doing everything he could to undermine our military leadership. We helped him along considerably by destroying the cream of our executive personnel, our Party leadership, and our scientific intelligentsia. The blood bath reached a red-hot frenzy in 1937. It was no accident that 1937 was the first year we didn't fulfill our Industrial Plan. All this has to be taken into account in making an objective analysis of the beginning of the war. But for years nobody raised the curtain on these facts. The extermination of the Old Guard of the army was for a long time considered a credit to the men responsible rather than a crime for which they should have been punished. And who paid for the crime? The army, the people, and the country paid for it.

You could put together a whole book consisting of nothing but the names of the important military, Party, administrative, and diplomatic leaders — all men of the Leninist school — who were Stalin's first victims. Honest, loyal Leninists, devoted to the cause of the Revolution — they were the first to go when Stalin imposed his arbitrary rule on the Party.

Most of the generals who perished by Stalin's hand have been given back their good names. They were rehabilitated at the Twentieth Party Congress. But more recently, many things about them have been silenced. All those who perished should not only be given back their names: they should also be presented to the people as martyrs of the terror waged by Stalin under the slogan of the struggle against the enemies of the people.

Why did Stalin commit these crimes? Was he deceived? If he was deceived, then by whom? And with how many lives did we pay for this deception?

Beria's Rise to Power

In this section Khrushchev moves from the early days of his assignment in the Ukraine, at the beginning of 1938, back to Moscow under the great purge, and forward again to Kiev. By the time of Khrushchev's appointment as the Ukrainian First Secretary, it might have

*been thought that the purge in the Ukraine had been completed. This
is not unnaturally the way Khrushchev himself likes to see it in retrospect. But in fact his first action in Kiev was to preside over a new
purge of his own. By the summer of 1938 there were only three survivors of the Central Committee, eighty-six strong, of the previous year.
Khrushchev was building a new Party apparatus, a new government,
in his own image. "I pledge myself to spare no effort in seizing and annihilating all agents of fascism, Trotskyites, Bukharinites, and all those
despicable bourgeois nationalists on Ukrainian soil," he publicly declared in May, 1938. Later that summer the Ukrainian Party organ carried the following eulogy: "The merciless uprooting of the enemies of
the people — the Trotskyites, Bukharinites, bourgeois nationalists, and
all other spying filth — began only after the Central Committee of the
All-Union Communist Party sent the unswerving Bolshevik and Stalinist, Nikita Sergeyevich Khrushchev, to the Ukraine to lead the Central
Committee of the Ukrainian Communist Party." This was a gross exag-
geration. But it was the way Khrushchev liked to be regarded at the
time. This should be remembered when contemplating his strictures on
Stalin in general, and now, in particular, as he turns to consider the
rise of Lavrenty Pavlovich Beria, the notorious Georgian police chief,
who was to hold sinister sway at Stalin's elbow for so many years.*

EARLY in 1938 Stalin offered me the post of First Secretary of the
Ukrainian Central Committee. He said that Kossior wasn't doing a
good job. I went to Kiev and took over from Kossior.[23] He was brought
back to Moscow and made Deputy Chairman of the Council of People's Commissars under Molotov. About a year later the question came
up of making me Molotov's deputy. Molotov himself first mentioned
this possibility to me. Then, during one of my visits to Moscow for consultations, Stalin took me aside and said, "Molotov insists on having
you as his deputy. I think he should have his way. What do you
think?" I objected strongly because I had only just settled in Kiev. The

23. S. V. Kossior had been First Secretary of the Ukrainian Party since 1928. A
Stalinist, he was also, like so many of the Ukrainian Party leaders, not untouched
by Ukrainian national feeling, resenting and trying to resist absolute domination by
Moscow. This included a vain attempt to moderate the effects of the great purge.
In 1937 his like-minded Second Secretary, Postyshev, was arrested. And at the be-
ginning of 1938 he himself was removed from the First Secretaryship, called to
Moscow, and given the job of first deputy to Molotov, still Prime Minister. But he
was soon arrested, tortured (according to Khrushchev in the Secret Speech), and in
February, 1939, sentenced to be shot.

Voroshilov and Beria

In the Hall of Columns,
Moscow

In Mongolian national dress, with Bulganin

people had accepted me and I was just beginning to build up a strong Party organization in the Ukraine. Most important, it was clear that we were heading toward war; if a new man were brought into the Ukraine at that late date, he might run into trouble when war broke out. I convinced Stalin that it wouldn't be in the interests of the cause to transfer me from Kiev after I'd just been installed there; someone else could easily be found to be Molotov's deputy in Moscow. Stalin agreed: "That's the end of this discussion. Khrushchev stays in the Ukraine." [24]

Sometimes if you persistently opposed Stalin and if he became convinced you were right, he would retreat from his position and accept yours. Of course, such flexibility and reasonableness is a positive quality in any man. But unfortunately, you could count on the fingers of one hand the number of times he displayed this virtue. More often than not, if Stalin decided you should do something — intelligent or stupid, helpful or harmful — he made you do it. And you did it.

In any case, that's how I came to remain in the Ukraine.

But before telling of my years as First Secretary of the Ukrainian Communist Party, I should talk about some important developments in Moscow that began before my transfer to Kiev and continued after I left. I want particularly to explain the growth of Lavrenty Beria's role in the Party.

In order to analyze how and why Beria came to hold a position of such influence, I have to go back to the period when the butchery of the purges was in full swing. Six months before Tukhachevsky's group had been exposed, Stalin had declared that People's Commissar of Internal Affairs Yagoda wasn't doing an adequate job and should be replaced. In those days we still had absolute faith in Stalin. We blamed ourselves for being blind to the presence of enemies all around us. We thought we lacked Stalin's deep understanding of the political struggle and were therefore unable to discern enemies in our midst the way Stalin could.

Stalin named Yezhov to replace Yagoda.[25] Yezhov had been in

24. The story of Khrushchev's being offered the deputy premiership of the USSR is new.

25. This was the occasion of the famous telegram of September 25, 1936, from Stalin and Zhdanov, on vacation at Sochi on the Black Sea, to Kaganovich, Molotov, "and other members of the Politbureau," instructing them to replace Yagoda with Yezhov because the secret police had fallen "four years behind" in its work of "unmasking the Trotskyite-Zinoviev bloc." It was the signal for the redoubling of the terror.

charge of personnel for the Central Committee. Malenkov had been his first deputy and took over his Central Committee job when Yezhov was transferred to the NKVD. But Yezhov kept his seniority over Malenkov, which explains why the supervision of Central Committee personnel fell under the control of the NKVD.

I had always liked Yagoda. Personally, I saw nothing anti-Party in his behavior. I couldn't understand Stalin's outward rationale, much less his hidden motives, for replacing Yagoda. On the other hand, I certainly had no objections to Yezhov.[26] He was diligent and reliable. I knew he'd been a Petrograd worker and a Party member since 1918, which was a mark in his favor. He'd been my own supervisor after I was elected Secretary of the Party organization at the Industrial Academy because the academy came under the authority of the Personnel Section of the Central Committee. The Personnel Section would assign me to mobilize students for a work project or a political campaign, and I would frequently make progress and status reports to Yezhov.

After Yezhov was put in charge of the NKVD in 1936, the repressions became worse than ever. A literal slaughter began, and masses of people were caught up in the meat-mincer.

Some time later, Stalin said that Yezhov needed help and should be given a deputy. He asked Yezhov who should be his deputy. Yezhov suggested Malenkov, since Malenkov had previously been his deputy in the Personnel Section of the Central Committee. I believe that there were several such conversations, but the question wasn't decided finally until one day Stalin said, "No, it looks like we'd better not reassign Malenkov to you. We'd better leave him where he is, in the Central Committee Secretariat." [27]

Stalin eventually suggested to Yezhov that he appoint Beria as his deputy. By this time Stalin's dissatisfaction with Yezhov had become apparent. Gone were the days when placards were carried at demonstrations with chain-mail gauntlets drawn on them; Stalin no longer

---

26. It is interesting to see how Khrushchev always seems to have found successive secret police chiefs to be friendly and honest fellows. Yagoda's chief claim to fame, apart from his management of the first great treason trial (Zinoviev, Kamenev, et al.) was his introduction of the system of organized forced labor with the construction of the White Sea Canal.

27. The association of Malenkov with Yezhov is deliberately intended to blacken Malenkov. The two men were in fact very close. Malenkov in the Personnel Section of the Central Committee handed over his fellow Party members to Yezhov for liquidation.

In the Ukraine in the 1930's

At the time he was a member of the Moscow City Soviet (before 1938)

called Yezhov "Our Mailed Fist" and "Our Blackberry" [puns on Yezhov's name].

When Stalin assigned Beria to be Yezhov's deputy, it was clear that
Yezhov's removal was imminent. Yezhov himself understood this. He
knew his star was in decline. His career was over, and perhaps he even
sensed that his very existence was coming to an end. He said to Stalin,
"Comrade Beria is unquestionably a most worthy person. In fact, he
could be more than just a deputy. Perhaps he could be a full-fledged
People's Commissar."

"I doubt that," said Stalin, "but he'll make a good deputy."

So Beria was confirmed as Yezhov's deputy.[28] Since I was then on
good terms with Beria, I went up to him after the meeting and half-
seriously, half-jokingly congratulated him on his new post.

"I don't accept your congratulations," he said.

"Why not?"

"You didn't accept the assignment to be Molotov's deputy, so why
should I be glad that they've assigned me to be Yezhov's deputy? It
would be better for me to remain in Georgia."

I think Beria was probably sincere when he said this. In any event,
he was transferred from Georgia to the central NKVD offices in Moscow. At first his activities seemed to be turning out promisingly. During my visits to Moscow Beria often said to me, "What's going on
here? We're arresting and imprisoning people right and left, even secretaries of Regional committees. This whole business has gone much
too far. We've got to stop it before it's too late."

Meanwhile Yezhov's position was more and more precarious all the
time. An episode — which centered around Uspensky, the People's
Commissar of Internal Affairs in the Ukraine — presaged Yezhov's
downfall.[29] Stalin phoned me one day in Kiev and said, "There's evidence against Uspensky which leaves us with no doubts as to his guilt.
Can you take care of arresting him yourselves?"

"Of course we can, if those are your instructions."

28. Beria was appointed Yezhov's deputy in July, 1938.
29. It was Yezhov's man A. I. Uspensky, head of the Ukrainian NKVD, who carried out the purge over which Khrushchev himself presided in the Ukraine. "I consider myself a pupil of Nikolai Ivanovich Yezhov," Uspensky declared in June,
1938. And: "Only after the faithful Stalinist, Nikita Sergeyevich Khrushchev, arrived in the Ukraine did the smashing of the enemies of the people begin in earnest." Within weeks of this declaration Uspensky vanished without trace. Khrushchev's account of his end is therefore news. Beria finally took over from Yezhov
in December, 1938.

"Then arrest him." At first it sounded over the telephone as though Stalin were talking about Usenko and not Uspensky. There was a Usenko in Kiev, a Youth League worker. It so happened there was also incriminating evidence against him. But when Stalin began to specify the details of the case, I realized he was talking about Uspensky, the Ukrainian Commissar of Internal Affairs. A few moments after I hung up Stalin called back and said, "Forget what I told you about Uspensky. Now there's nothing for you to do. We'll take care of it ourselves. We'll call him back to Moscow and have him arrested along the way."

I had already planned a trip to Dniepropetrovsk. I left before Uspensky was summoned to Moscow. I had a premonition that he wouldn't actually go to Moscow. He must have guessed why he'd been called back and known that he was in danger of being arrested. Therefore as I was leaving, I told Korotchenko,[30] who was Chairman of the Ukrainian Council of People's Commissars, "Keep an eye on Uspensky while I'm gone."

The next morning, when I arrived in Dniepropetrovsk, I got a call from Beria — *not Yezhov, but Beria!* — who said, "While you've been traveling around the countryside, Uspensky has gotten away."

"What?"

"That's right, he's escaped."

I went straight back to Kiev. Sure enough, Uspensky was gone. He had left a note saying he was going to commit suicide by throwing himself into the Dnieper. We searched for him with fishing nets and divers, but there was no trace of him. He seemed to have disappeared into thin air. Later they caught him somewhere — in Voronezh, I think — and he was shot.

When I was in Moscow soon after this, Stalin told me that it looked as though Yezhov had warned Uspensky of what was in store for him: "Yezhov overheard us when we were talking," said Stalin, "and instead of ordering Uspensky to Moscow as he was supposed to, Yezhov tipped him off that he would be arrested along the way."

So Stalin had already come to the conclusion that Yezhov was an enemy of the people and wasn't to be trusted. Shortly afterwards Ye-

30. D. S. Korotchenko was not a Ukrainian at all. He was born Korotchenkov. He served on the Moscow Party Committee under Khrushchev and was sent to Smolensk in Belorussia at the height of the purge, where he distinguished himself by his extreme rigor. Khrushchev took him to the Ukraine with him in 1938, and he was to rise to great heights under his new master, becoming in due course a member of the Central Committee Secretariat.

zhov was arrested and Beria took his place. Beria immediately started consolidating his forces. Now that Uspensky was gone, the Ukraine didn't have a People's Commissar of Internal Affairs, so Beria sent Kabulov down to Kiev. This was the younger brother of the Kabulov who was Beria's deputy in the NKVD and who had worked with Beria in Georgia.[31]

In the aftermath of Yezhov's arrest, all his deputies and everyone who was connected with him were arrested. This cloud hung over Malenkov, too, because Yezhov had requested that Malenkov be appointed his first deputy. Moreover, everybody knew Malenkov was a close friend of Yezhov's. I'd also been a friend of Malenkov's for many years. We'd worked together on the Moscow Committee. I drew my own conclusions about the suspicions surrounding Malenkov after the following incident.

One day I arrived in Moscow from Kiev, and Beria invited me to his dacha. "Let's go out to my place," he said, "I'm alone. No one else is around. We'll take a stroll and you can spend the night there."

"That's fine with me," I said, "I'm alone, too."

We drove out to his dacha and went for a walk in the woods. Beria started talking:

"Listen, what do you think about Malenkov?"

"What should I think?"

"I mean now that they've arrested Yezhov."

"So what if Malenkov and Yezhov were friends? You were Malenkov's friend, too, and so was I. I think Malenkov is honest and irreproachable."

"That's beside the point. You're still friends with Malenkov. Listen, think about it some more. Just think it over."

So I thought it over. I didn't reach any particular conclusion, and I continued to be friendly with Malenkov. When I returned to Moscow, I often stayed with him at his dacha on our days off. I think maybe Stalin was trying to warn me about Malenkov through Beria. However, this cup passed from Malenkov, and later he and Beria became inseparable friends.

At the beginning of 1939, in February, a Central Committee plenum was convened to discuss a resolution condemning excesses and abuses

31. Nothing is known of this Kabulov, who did not last long in this job. He was to be succeeded very soon by I. A. Serov, who was to become notorious (see Chapter 4).

in the NKVD. The slackening of the terror which had reigned for the past three years was attributed largely to Beria's influence. People concluded that Beria had made an investigation of NKVD practices after he took over as commissar and then convinced Stalin to approve a series of recommendations. However, there were a number of incidents at the February Central Committee Plenum of 1939 indicating that the terror was by no means over — it had just become more subtle and discriminating.

The February Plenum was a very self-critical meeting. Everybody had something critical to say about everybody else. The only person highly placed in the Party leadership who seemed to be escaping criticism was myself, Khrushchev. Then suddenly Yakovlev, whose real name was Yakov Arkadyevich Epstein, made a very unusual and original accusation against me. He criticized me for the fact that everyone in the Moscow organization called me Nikita Sergeyevich. That's all he said. I took the floor and replied that it was true my comrades called me by my name and patronymic. I hinted that his own name was not Yakovlev at all, but Epstein. After the session, Mekhlis, who was still running *Pravda*, took me aside. He was indignant about Yakovlev's speech. Even though Mekhlis himself was a Jew, he said, "Yakovlev is a Jew and doesn't understand that among Russians it's acceptable to call people by their name and patronymic." [32]

Later, after an all-day session of the Central Committee Plenum, everybody dispersed for dinner. I stayed behind for a moment. When I was getting up to go, Stalin suddenly shouted at me, "Khrushchev, where are you going?"

"I'm going to have dinner."

"Come with me. We'll eat together."

I wondered to myself, "Why is he inviting me to have dinner with him?" As we were leaving, Yakov Arkadevich Yakovlev, who had been hovering around nearby, followed Stalin to his apartment uninvited. The three of us ate dinner together. Stalin did most of the talking. Epstein-Yakovlev was in a very agitated state. You could see he was undergoing some sort of inner turmoil. He feared that he was about to be

32. Y. A. Yaklovev, onetime People's Commissar for Agriculture (see Chapter 2). This is a remarkable example (there are others to follow) of the way in which Khrushchev, though professing to abhor anti-Semitism, seems nevertheless unable to resist denigrating individual Jews. Russian Jews use "name and patronymic" like all other Russians. Yaklovev in his speech was probably in fact accusing Khrushchev of self-glorification.

arrested. He wasn't mistaken in his forebodings. Shortly after Stalin's friendly chat with him over dinner, Yakovlev was arrested and eliminated. I'm telling this story to show how even someone as close to Stalin as Yakovlev — who was head of the Agricultural Section of the Central Committee and who had been one of Stalin's most trusted supporters during the struggle against the opposition — could suddenly find his life hanging by a thread. The episode was typical of Stalin's treacherous character.

Another incident at that same February Plenum indicated that even though Beria had initiated the investigation into the abuses and excesses of the NKVD, he was capable of great treachery himself. In the course of the Plenum, Grisha [Grigory] Kaminsky gave a speech. He was People's Commissar of Health for the Russian Federation, a highly respected comrade with pre-Revolutionary Party experience. I first knew him at the beginning of my work in the Moscow organization. He was very straightforward, very sincere and honest. I would say his Party conduct had always been impeccable. Here's what he said in his speech to the Central Committee:

"Comrades! Everyone is making a speech saying what he knows about everyone else. I also have something I want to say for the information of the Party. When I worked in Baku, there were rumors rampant that during the occupation of Baku by English troops, Beria worked for the counterintelligence service of the Mussavat government. Since the Mussavat counterintelligence service was under the control of the English, it was said that Beria must be an English intelligence agent operating through the Mussavatists." [33]

Kaminsky finished his speech and sat down. No one came forward with either refutation or clarification, nor did Beria himself offer any comment. Immediately after that session of the Plenum, Kaminsky was arrested and disappeared without a trace. I've always been tormented by his case because I completely trusted him. I knew he would never make up something like that. He always told the truth.[34]

I remember Malenkov's speech, too. He criticized both the secretary of a Central Asian bureau and Beria for self-glorification. Malenkov

33. The Mussavats were Transcaucasian nationalists (Moslems), fighting the Bolsheviks in Baku at the time of the British intervention.
34. G. M. Kaminsky, People's Commissar for Health. Earlier he had been one of those who had put his signature to the death certificate which stated that Sergo Ordzhonikidze had died of natural causes.

said that some mountain climbers had conquered one of the highest peaks in Central Asia and then named it after this Party secretary. The man was later arrested. Beria was also accused of self-glorification. There was already plenty of cause for criticizing him in this regard.

At the end of the Plenum the Central Committee passed a resolution condemning the excesses of the NKVD. This gave us some hope that the arbitrary rule which had prevailed in the Party would be ended. For over three years a man had had no way of knowing from one moment to the next whether he would survive or disappear into thin air. This fear and uncertainty had undermined the morale of the Party. After the February Plenum the brakes were applied to the purges, but the repressions weren't brought to a complete halt by any means: people continued to sink out of sight forever just as though the ice had broken beneath them and swallowed them up.

Beria and I started to see each other frequently at Stalin's.[35] At first I liked him. We had friendly chats and even joked together quite a bit, but gradually his political complexion came clearly into focus. I was shocked by his sinister, two-faced, scheming hypocrisy. Soon after his transfer to Moscow, the atmosphere in the collective leadership and in Stalin's inner circle took on an entirely different character from what it had been before. It changed very much for the worse. Stalin himself once even confided to me his own unhappiness with Beria's influence: "Before Beria arrived, dinner meetings used to be relaxed, productive affairs. Now he's always challenging people to drinking contests, and people are getting drunk all over the place." [36]

Even though I agreed with Stalin completely, I knew I had to watch my step in answering him. One of Stalin's favorite tricks was to provoke you into making a statement — or even agreeing with a statement — which showed your true feelings about someone else. It

35. As already noted, Beria did not take up his appointment as Yezhov's deputy in Moscow until July, 1938, when Khrushchev had already left for the Ukraine. But the two men would have met long before this on Beria's frequent visits to Moscow, and they went on meeting when Khrushchev came to Moscow from Kiev.

36. Both here and later, with special reference to Zhdanov and Shcherbakov, Khrushchev speaks very disparagingly of the drunken habits of certain of his colleagues. Drunkenness of the most thoroughgoing kind was in fact de rigueur not only in Stalin's circle but also in the army high command. Khrushchev himself was a very heavy drinker and frequently appeared drunk in public, at least until 1956. Indeed, the Soviet attitude to drunkenness is still very like the British attitude of one hundred and fifty years ago. In fairness to Khrushchev I might mention that Beria was drunk more often than most. On the few occasions I saw him he was invariably drunk.

was perfectly clear to me that Stalin and Beria were very close. To what extent this friendship was sincere, I couldn't say, but I knew it was no accident that Beria had been Stalin's choice for Yezhov's replacement. In addition to being the potentate of a powerful commissariat, Beria also pulled a lot of weight in the collective leadership. Anyone who wanted to be sure of staying in Stalin's good graces had to fawn all over Beria, too. Kaganovich was especially adept at getting ahead by flattery. I must say, I never saw any of this kind of debasing obsequiousness on Molotov's part. Nor did I ever kowtow to Beria myself, and I often had to contend with Beria working against me as a result. Since I worked for the Party and State in a number of important posts, I had many opportunities to make recommendations for progressive improvements. I usually had Stalin's support, and when I failed to have his support, it was almost always because of Beria's and Malenkov's influence on Stalin. I'm convinced that their opposition to me was based primarily on jealousy.

Beria, particularly, was fiercely jealous of his power in the collective leadership and his influence over Stalin. A story illustrates what he was capable of:

Stalin's brother-in-law, Redens, had once been Beria's Deputy People's Commissar of State Security in Georgia.[37] Before Beria himself was transferred to Moscow, he decided to have Redens bounced out of Georgia. Why? So that Stalin would have no informer in Georgia other than Beria himself. Beria had always been hostile to Sergo Ordzhonikidze for the same reason. So what did Beria do to get rid of Redens? He instructed some of his men to lure Redens into a café, where they took advantage of his weakness for drink, got him drunk, and threw him out into the gutter. The police came along and saw him lying there in a disreputable state. Beria saw to it that Stalin found out that Redens had discredited himself. That's why Redens was sacked from his job in Georgia and ended up in the Moscow Regional office of the NKVD. You see what sort of provocateur Beria was? Many years later, after Beria's downfall, the Central Committee received a long letter from a Georgian ex-convict enumerating all the people in Georgia who had been victims of similar provocations perpetrated by Beria.

Beria was fond of telling stories about favors he had done for people

---

37. Redens was Svetlana Alliluyeva's uncle, and she has a good deal to say about him in *Twenty Letters to a Friend*.

when they were in trouble. But even these stories, and they were mostly lies, had a sinister ring to them. I remember he once told me how Marshal Meretskov was broken and forced to sign a confession admitting that he was an English agent, an enemy of the people, and so on.[38] I never read his testimony myself. Stalin didn't distribute it. It happened during the war and by that time Stalin was the only judge in the only court in the land. He decided whom to eliminate all by himself; he didn't need others to support him. Anyway, the way he told the story, Beria deserved credit for arranging Meretskov's release and return to active service:

"I went to Comrade Stalin and said, 'What's this about Meretskov being in jail as an English spy? How could he be an English spy? He's an honest man. There's a war going on, and we need him at the Front. He could be given a field command.'

"Stalin answered, 'You're probably right. Go talk to him.' So I called Meretskov in and said, 'This is nonsense you've written in your confession. You're no spy. You're an honest man, a good Russian. How could you be an English spy?'

"Meretskov looked at me forlornly and said, 'I've got nothing more to say. You have a confession written in my own handwriting. I don't know why you're interrogating me again.'

"'I'm not interrogating you, Comrade Meretskov. I just want to tell you that I know you're not a spy. Go back to your cell and think it over. Sleep on it. I'll talk to you again tomorrow.' They took him away. The next day I summoned him again and asked, 'Well, have you thought it over?'

"He started weeping and thanking me, saying, 'How could I be a spy? I'm a good Russian. I love my people. I believe in my people.' So they let him out of jail, dressed him in a general's uniform, and off he went to be a commander at the Front."

Well, I know for a fact the story wasn't that simple. Before his arrest, Meretskov had been a strapping young general, very strong and impressive-looking. After his release he was just a shadow of his former self. He'd lost so much weight he could hardly squeak. Beria's version of what happened confuses me in other ways, too. For one thing, I

38. General Meretskov was only one of a number of high-ranking Red Army commanders who escaped by a miracle and survived to be brought out of prison and sent to fight Hitler. Marshal Rokossovsky was the most famous of these. Another was General Gorbatov, who eventually became the Soviet commandant of Berlin and published an account of his experiences in prison, *Years of My Life*.

can't understand who arrested Meretskov in the first place. Beria blamed it on V. S. Abakumov, but who was Abakumov? He was one of Beria's own men. Abakumov reported to Beria before anyone else, even before Stalin. Consequently, Abakumov couldn't have arrested Meretskov unless it was on Beria's orders.[40]

While Beria was telling me the story about how he got Meretskov out of jail, another favorite remark of his kept running through my mind. It was something he used to say about anyone who had fallen under suspicion: "Listen, let me have him for one night, and I'll have him confessing he's the king of England." I never knew quite how to take that, but I had no doubt Beria knew how to get what he wanted. His arrogance and his treachery grew in direct proportion to his increasingly powerful position.

40. V. S. Abakumov, a notorious Chekist who was to become head of the Ministry of State Security in 1946. He was dismissed in 1951. In 1954, he was shot, ostensibly for having fabricated the Leningrad Case in 1949. He makes a cameo appearance in Aleksandr Solzhenitsyn's novel, *The First Circle*.

4

Return to the Ukraine

Putting the Party Together Again

*Khrushchev's first task as First Secretary of the Ukrainian Commu-
nist Party in 1938 was to build up, virtually from nothing, a brand-new
Party apparatus to succeed the one which had been presided over by
Kossior from 1929 until its destruction in the purges. But even as Khrushchev was building, the purges continued. The following section offers a revealing glimpse of the nature of this process. What Khrushchev
does not mention is that his second task was to Russify the Ukraine by
eliminating from positions of authority and trust all Ukrainians who
might be suspected of local patriotism (the so-called "bourgeois nationalists") and by discouraging the use of the Ukrainian language in
schools and elsewhere. This was an operation of extreme importance in
the eyes of Stalin. Ukrainian nationalism was very strong in this rich
land, which was not only the breadbasket of the Soviet Union but also
the most powerful industrial base. The official excuse for this policy,
which was carried out with great ruthlessness, was — as Khrushchev
himself said in the summer of 1938 — to eliminate all those who "wanted
to let in the German fascists, the landowners and bourgeois, and make
the Ukrainian workers and peasants slaves of fascism, and the Ukraine
a colony of the Polish-German fascists."*

W E want to send you to the Ukraine to head the Party organization there. Kossior doesn't seem able to manage. We'll transfer
him to Moscow to be First Deputy of the Council of People's Commissars and Chairman of the Central Committee Commission."

When Stalin offered me the top Ukrainian post in 1938, I was reluctant to accept it for three reasons: First, I liked Kossior and was un-

comfortable about taking his place. I'd known him when he succeeded Kaganovich as First Secretary of the Ukrainian Central Committee in 1929. That was the year I applied for admission to the Industrial Academy, and it had been Kossior who approved my application. Second, I doubted that I was experienced or qualified enough to take Kossior's place; I thought the cap of Ukrainian First Secretary was simply too big for my head. Finally, the nationality question entered into my thinking. It's true, I'd already worked in the Ukraine and had always gotten along well with Ukrainian Communists and non-Party members alike. Nevertheless, as a Russian, I still felt some awkwardness among Ukrainians. Even though I understand the Ukrainian language, I'd never mastered it to the extent that I could make speeches in it. I explained all these drawbacks to Stalin, and told him that I was afraid the Ukrainians, and particularly the intelligentsia, might be very cool to me: "It hardly makes sense to send me, a Russian, to the Ukraine," I told him.

"Kossior's not a Russian, is he? He's a Pole. Why should a Russian have a harder time with the Ukrainians than a Pole?"

"Kossior may be a Pole," I conceded, "but he can give speeches in Ukrainian. Moreover, Kossior is much more experienced than I am."

"No more argument. You're going to the Ukraine."

"Very well. I'll try to do everything I can to justify your confidence in me and to put the Ukrainian Party back on its feet." I was still worried that I wouldn't be able to manage the assignment, but I won't deny I was flattered that the Central Committee would entrust me with such a high post.

I knew there had been a top-to-bottom shake-up in the Ukrainian organization. Kossior's removal was an indication of how far it had gone. I also had a glimpse into the fate of Chubar, the former Chairman of the Ukrainian Council of People's Commissars, whom I'd often met in the twenties at congresses of the Ukrainian Party and at miners' convocations.[1] For a time he'd been in charge of mining in the Donbass. His Party behavior had always been excellent. Then one day when I was sitting in Stalin's office at the Kremlin, Stalin was called to the phone. He talked to someone for a few moments and hung up. Stalin said Chubar had called, in tears, trying to prove he was an honest man.

1. V. Chubar was a colleague of Khrushchev in his early days in the Ukraine. He was appointed Prime Minister of the Ukraine in 1923 and joined the Politbureau at the same time as Mikoyan in 1935, in place of the murdered Kirov. He disappeared from view in the summer of 1938 and was executed in February, 1939.

Stalin's tone of voice was almost sympathetic to Chubar. At least he seemed to understand why Chubar was so upset. The very next day Chubar was arrested and eliminated.

The Communist Party of the Ukraine was demolished partly as a consequence of the Polish and Western Ukrainian purges. It was easy for Stalin to destroy the leaders of the Polish Party because most of them lived and worked in the Comintern in Moscow.[2] The only reason Bierut and Gomulka stayed alive was that they were relatively unknown in Party circles. The Communist Party of the Western Ukraine was filled with unstable and even subversive elements, and all the personnel we could get our hands on were eliminated as provocateurs, turncoats, and agents of Pilsudski. Since the Ukrainian Central Committee was technically responsible for the Western Ukrainian Party, many Ukrainian Party leaders whom I'd known from the twenties were swept up in the purge, including Comrade Demchenko, who had been First Secretary of the Kiev Regional Committee when I was Chief of the Organizational Section there in 1928–29.[3]

When he sent me to Kiev, Stalin told me that in addition to being First Secretary of the Ukrainian Central Committee I would also be First Secretary of both the Kiev Regional and City committees. I told him it was impossible for me to hold so many positions at once, but he was insistent.

"You can manage," he said. "Just select whom you want to help you when you get there."

I asked Malenkov to assign some Ukrainians to assist me. Malenkov made one of his own deputies, Burmistenko, my Second Secretary. I liked Burmistenko the moment I met him. We were cut from the same cloth.[4] I told him to select ten or so people from the Moscow organization and the Central Committee apparatus.

2. This is a brutally casual reference to Stalin's deliberate destruction of the Polish Communist Party in 1937–39. As Khrushchev says, the purge was easy to carry out since most of the Polish Party's most prominent men had sought refuge in Moscow from the Polish dictator, Marshal Pilsudski. Many German, Spanish, and other foreign Communists then working in Moscow were executed at this time.

3. The Western Ukraine to which Khrushchev refers was then part of Poland; it was seized by the Soviet Union when Germany invaded Poland in 1939 (see Chapter 5).

4. M. O. Burmistenko distinguished himself by joining the Cheka in 1919, when he was only seventeen. He was notorious for his brutality in the destruction of resistance to the collectivization. As Malenkov's deputy in ORPO (Department of Leading Party Organs) he played an active and sinister part in purges. His appointment to be Khrushchev's deputy in Kiev was in itself enough to show that heads would soon be rolling.

When we got to the Ukraine, Comrade Kossior briefed us about the troubles they'd been having and introduced us to the few Party leaders who had survived the purge. He formally introduced us to the Ukrainian Party at a special Central Committee plenum. The Party had been purged spotless. It seemed as though not one regional or executive committee secretary, not one secretary of the Council of People's Commissars, not even a single deputy was left. The Party leadership was almost totally demolished. We had to start rebuilding from scratch.[5]

I asked Stalin for permission to bring Lukashov from Moscow. He's still alive but has been retired for a long time. He had been in charge of vegetable and fruit procurements for the workers' cooperatives in Moscow. I liked him for his efficiency and his capacity for hard work. I told Stalin I wanted to appoint Lukashov People's Commissar of Internal Trade in the Ukraine, and Stalin gave his consent.

Then suddenly Lukashov was arrested.[6] This was very unpleasant for me, first, because I liked Lukashov personally, and second, because I had requested his appointment to a responsible post. I knew it might reflect badly on me that Lukashov had been arrested as an enemy of the people. A considerable amount of time passed, and Lukashov was released. He returned to the Ukraine beaten up, crippled in body and spirit. He told me he had been tortured and ordered to denounce me as a member of a conspiracy. It had so happened that earlier, while working in Moscow, I'd once asked that Lukashov be sent to Poland and Lithuania to purchase onion seeds and vegetables. When he was arrested, he was pressured to testify that his trade mission to Poland had actually been a secret political assignment to establish contacts with anti-Soviet organizations abroad. He refused to confess and was released — a rare thing. I told Stalin about the episode.

"Yes," he said, "I know what you mean; there are these kinds of perversions. They're gathering evidence against me, too."

I began to feel even more uneasy about the activities of the NKVD after the following incident: The People's Commissar of Internal Af-

5. In the light of what happened in the Ukraine before Khrushchev got there, let alone what happened under his leadership, it is clear that he had, at least by 1938, a very clear idea of the havoc Stalin was creating. He says enough here and in the preceding section to make nonsense of his insistence at various points in this narrative that it was not until Stalin was dead that he realized that Stalin's behavior had been criminal.
6. The individuals referred to here were men of at most secondary importance, their fates characteristic of tens of thousands.

fairs, when I arrived in the Ukraine, was Uspensky. I knew him slightly and liked him. He was a Russian even though his name was Polish. He'd been a worker in Yagoda's central NKVD apparatus, then an NKVD representative for the Moscow Region, and later a commandant of the Kremlin. From that post he'd been sent to the Ukraine. The Central Committee evidently trusted him, and from what I could tell when I first arrived, this trust was well founded. But soon I started to have some doubts.

The Second Secretary of the Kiev City Committee was a man named Kostenko. I didn't know him very well, but he seemed diligent and trustworthy. He was an honest, simple person. I forget if he was a worker or a peasant by background. Suddenly he fell under suspicion and was arrested. I was sent a lengthy testimony about his connections with the enemies of the people. It perplexed me very much.

I told Uspensky, "I want to have a talk with this man Kostenko whom you've arrested."

"That can be arranged, Comrade Khrushchev."

I went to the Commissariat of Internal Affairs, and Kostenko was brought to me. He confirmed everything he'd said in his confession.

"Yes," he told me, "I did all those things. I was part of a conspiracy. I made a clean breast of everything, about everyone I knew. I didn't keep anything back."

I wasn't entirely satisfied. Kostenko's confession seemed to raise more questions than it answered, and that worried me. As I was leaving the NKVD offices I warned Uspensky, "Comrade Uspensky, if you sentence Kostenko to death as an enemy of the people, he may inform on someone else in his last words. If that happens, then I would urge you not to have him executed until we have a chance to check out his accusations. We must make sure that he doesn't incriminate anyone by slander."

Some time later Uspensky brought me a document saying that just before he was shot, Kostenko had claimed that his replacement on the Kiev Regional Committee, Cherepin, was guilty of the same crimes. I liked Cherepin. He was a simple peasant from Poltava, but a clever man. I was sure he was honest. When I heard that Kostenko had tried to implicate him, I was furious.

"How could you let this happen, Comrade Uspensky? I explicitly told you to verify any charges Kostenko made against anyone before you had him shot!"

I immediately phoned Malenkov at the Central Committee because he was in charge of personnel and might be able to help. I told him what had happened.

"Do you trust Cherepin?" Malenkov asked.

"Yes."

"Then let him keep his job."

I was relieved. However, not too long after that phone conversation Malenkov called me back and said, "Now it looks as though we'd better not keep Cherepin on the Secretariat after all. I realize you trust him, but serious evidence has been brought against him."

"What evidence? You mean Kostenko's accusation? That's not evidence, it's slander!"

But Malenkov wouldn't give in. I tried hard to arrange for Cherepin's return to good standing in the Party. We had already made him Deputy People's Commissar of Agriculture. I kept raising the question to the Central Committee about using him for Party work. My conscience tormented me about him. I kept insisting that he was beyond reproach and had been unjustly accused. Finally Malenkov gave in, and Cherepin was promoted to First Secretary of the Sumsky Regional Committee. When the war started I proposed his candidacy to the Military Council of the Coastal Army. He was killed during the German invasion. Thus he honorably gave his life for his country, his people, and for the Soviet Union.

When Stalin sent me to the Ukraine, he said, "I know you have a weakness for cities and industry, so I'd better warn you not to concentrate on industrial and municipal management at the expense of your agricultural responsibilities. And be especially careful not to spend all your time in the Donbass. You won't find as many problems in industry as in agriculture, and just remember: farming in the Ukraine is very important to the Soviet Union. Try to do something to organize our agriculture down there more efficiently."

I heeded his warning, although it wasn't always easy to resist the temptation of my first loves, mining and industry. I felt continually drawn to the factories, machine shops, and the mines. Nonetheless I tried to learn everything I could about farming. I spent a lot of time traveling around the Ukraine, visiting farms and villages, talking to agronomists and managers.

Burmistenko and I arrived in the Ukraine in January or February of 1939, just in time to start getting ready for the spring sowing. We immediately found ourselves up against a dangerous problem. Horses were dropping dead on farms all over the western sections of the Ukraine, along the Polish border. No one could figure out what was making the horses sick. During a visit to a collective farm in the Vinnitsa region, I asked a stable attendant if he had any idea why the horses were dying like flies. He told me that the horses were being poisoned:

"I saw this man administering poison to the horses," he said, "so we grabbed him and turned him in. And you know what he turned out to be? A veterinarian!"

This was plausible enough. We figured that the Germans, who were then preparing for war against us, might be trying to sabotage our economy and our military capabilities. You see, horses weren't just livestock in those days; they were what tanks, airplanes, and jeeps are today.[7]

I decided to look into the situation a little bit further. I asked Uspensky, "Do you still have in jail any of the men who were caught poisoning horses?"

"Yes, we have."

"Which ones?"

He named some professor at the Kharkov Veterinary Institute, a Jew, and the director of the Kharkov Institute of Animal Husbandry, a Ukrainian.

"I'd like to talk to them, but I'd rather not go to the prison to do so. Call them into your office, will you?"

"What's the use? They've already confessed to the NKVD that they're saboteurs and German agents. They'll just be repeating their confessions to you."

"Maybe so. But there's still something that bothers me. In their confessions they gave the chemical formula of the poison which they supposedly used. I asked our scientists to make a sample and test it. We fed it to some horses and nothing happened. I'm puzzled about why the poison they claim to have used doesn't work. That's why I want to talk to the prisoners myself."

"All right, I'll arrange an interview for you."

---

7. This may sound odd, but it is true. For example, until American trucks started arriving in their thousands by the Persian route at the time of the Battle of Stalingrad, Soviet army transport was almost entirely horsedrawn.

I went to the NKVD and the Jewish professor, a gray-haired man of about fifty, was brought to me.

"Well, what do you have to say for yourself?"

"I've already given two testimonies, and I can only confirm what I said there. Yes, we're German agents, and we were given an assignment to poison horses."

"How do you explain the fact that the chemical you say you used doesn't even make a horse sick?"

"Well, that's possible. You see, we received a prepared ingredient directly from Germany which we added to our own mixture here. We don't know what the stuff from Germany was."

I wasn't satisfied. As far as I was concerned, his testimony remained unsubstantiated, and the case was by no means closed. I'd given him a perfect chance to declare his innocence, yet he stuck to his original story. There was something else that bothered me. Why would a Jew be in the employ of his worst enemies, the anti-Semitic German fascists? It didn't make sense. Of course, you could explain it in terms of the class struggle and so on and so forth, but I still had my doubts.

I called in the second doctor, the director of the Kharkov Animal Husbandry Institute. He too repeated his confession. It was no joking matter to be accused of sabotage, and maybe they were hoping things would go easier on them if they were repentant and made a clean breast of it. But still . . .

I decided to set up a commission to look into the mysterious deaths of all the horses. I was faced with a problem here, too, because there had already been several such commissions, and when the horses kept on dying, the commissions had been dissolved and their members arrested and eliminated. Therefore, with some justification, it was widely thought that an appointment to serve on one of these commissions sealed a man's fate.

I summoned Comrade Bogomolets, the president of the Ukrainian Academy of Sciences. He was a non-Party member, but as far as I was concerned that was a matter of formality, which I never held against a good Soviet citizen and a progressive person.

"Comrade Bogomolets," I said, "you know that the horses on our farms are still dying. We have to do something."

"What's there to do?"

"I can't believe that science is absolutely helpless here. Surely if we make a concerted effort, we can isolate and identify the cause of the deaths. I think we should set up another commission to investigate. Now, I realize your colleagues are afraid of being appointed to these commissions since the members of past commissions have been arrested. But if you, the president of the Academy of Sciences, were the chairman, I'm sure other specialists would join you willingly. I promise you I'll attend all the plenary sessions of the commission myself and listen to the reports of your scientists. Comrade Uspensky, the People's Commissar of Internal Affairs, will attend, too, in order to help avoid the danger to your commission of being accused of anything. I propose we take another precaution as well: we'll set up two commissions to work in parallel with each other. That way we'll double the chances of one commission's coming up with the answer."

I actually had another reason for proposing two parallel commissions. I wasn't excluding the possibility that there were saboteurs about, and I was hoping that if a saboteur got on one of the commissions, the other commission would be made up of honest men.

Bogomolets agreed, but without much enthusiasm.

The staffs of the two commissions were approved by the People's Commissariat of Agriculture of the USSR. Just to be absolutely safe, we added a third commission made up of Russian scientists from Moscow, headed by Professor Vertinsky. All three groups went out to the stricken farms and started to work.

Sometime later one of the Ukrainian commissions, Professor Dobrotko's, came to the conclusion that the horses were being made sick by a fungus which grew in wet hay.

"When I realized this must be the cause," Comrade Dobrotko told me, "I even contaminated myself with the fungus to see what would happen, and I came down with an illness very similar to the one which is killing the horses."

Professor Vertinsky wasn't willing to accept Dobrotko's conclusions. Vertinsky was a Muscovite, and Dobrotko was a Ukrainian. At that time the difference was still very significant. In order to avoid a clash between them, I suggested that the investigation go a bit further to make absolutely certain we had found the answer.

A long time passed, and finally Vertinsky informed me that he agreed with Dobrotko's findings. The field research came to an end, and a report was made at a plenum in Kiev. The recommended method for stamping out the disease was simple — keep hay dry.

Stalin had been following the whole affair closely. He had been distressed when he heard that horses were being poisoned in the Ukraine. When I returned to Moscow and reported on the results of our commissions' work, I proposed that the various chairmen be decorated. Professor Dobrotko was awarded the Order of the Laborers' Red Banner. In my opinion he deserved the Order of Lenin. I proposed Professor Vertinsky for the Order of Honor, although he had been little more than a catalyst in the process.

We had won more than just a victory for our agriculture. It was a moral and political victory as well. But how many collective farm chairmen, cattle raisers, agronomists, animal husbandry specialists, and scientists had lost their heads as saboteurs before I stepped in and took charge of the situation?

It took a long time for the atmosphere of distrust and treachery to dissipate in the Ukraine. I was constantly running up against vestiges of the attitudes which had prevailed during the purges. We had a doctor in the Ukraine who was also a political figure. His name was Medved [a common last name which also means "bear"]. Years later he was a member of the Ukrainian delegation to the founding of the United Nations in San Francisco. He annoyed our enemies very much, and they used to say, "The Ukrainian bear is growling again!" He really did have a voice like a bear and an irascible temper to go with it. In my time there was a story in the Ukraine about this Medved which illustrates the crazy extremes which the situation reached at the height of the purges:

When Medved was Deputy Chief of the Regional Health Department either in Kiev or in Kharkov, some woman got up at a Party meeting, pointed her finger at him, and said, "I don't know that man over there but I can tell from the look in his eyes that he's an enemy of the people." [8] Can you imagine?

Fortunately Medved didn't lose control of himself. He retorted immediately, "I don't know this woman who's just denounced me, but I can tell from the look in her eyes that she's a prostitute" — only he used a more expressive word. Medved's quick comeback probably saved his life. If he'd let himself be put on the defensive and had started protesting that he wasn't an enemy of the people, he would have fallen all the more under suspicion, and the woman who denounced him would have been encouraged to press her charge against

8. This is a highly characteristic example of the sort of malicious or hysterical denunciation that sent millions to their death or to the labor camps.

him, knowing that she wouldn't have to take any responsibility for what happened.

This kind of thing happened less and less after I got settled in the Ukraine — and after Uspensky was removed as People's Commissar of Internal Affairs.

I must say something about Uspensky's successor, Serov. Serov was punished during my time. I think he was careless, but he was an honest, uncorruptible, reliable comrade despite his mistakes. I respected and trusted him. He was a simple person, simple to the point of being naïve. When I first knew him, he was still young and inexperienced. He had just graduated from an artillery academy. He was among those mobilized when we started drafting military men into the service of the NKVD. Naturally, he had no experience in security operations. This was both an advantage and a disadvantage for him. Before Serov was assigned to security duty, people had been acquiring experience which proved harmful both to the country and to the Party, as well as to themselves. They had become experienced at staging provocations, at arresting innocent people, and at extracting confessions by elaborate tortures. Serov's predecessors in the NKVD weren't necessarily cruel men, but they had been turned into automatons. They were guided by one thought only: "If I don't do this to others, then others will do it to me; better I do it than have it done to me." It's frightening to realize that in our time, in our Socialist era, Communists devoted to the Party could be dictated to, not by conscience or by reason, but by an animal-like fear for their own hides. In order to protect their lives, they snuffed out the lives of completely innocent people. Serov, fortunately, wasn't a product of that period and that mentality.[9]

With his help, I was able to put the Ukraine back on its feet. Industry started fulfilling its quotas, and the agricultural situation began to

9. I. S. Serov was a Red Army officer who was transferred from the Frunze Military Academy to the NKVD in 1938. His rise was swift and he was sent out to succeed Uspensky, after a brief interregnum, as head of the Ukrainian NKVD working alongside Khrushchev in 1939. For the nature of his activities in the Ukraine see the next chapter. He was not an enthusiastic killer. He was essentially an organization man and a gifted administrator, detached, cynical, wholly ruthless, killing without turning a hair when required to do so, organizing mass deportations as a matter of routine, then going home from his office and emerging on social occasions as an amiable, kindly, and amusing companion. When the Ministry of State Security (MGB) was transferred into the Committee of State Security (KGB) after Stalin's death, Khrushchev appointed Serov as its first head. It was now his job to behave with relative mildness where before he had behaved with absolute ruthlessness. But, as in Hungary in 1956, he could arrest and kill as efficiently as ever when the occasion arose. In 1958, for reasons unknown, he was dismissed.

stabilize. The repressions diminished, and the ranks of the Party and managerial workers were replenished until they returned to their normal size.

Academician Paton

Here we contemplate Khrushchev the practical man of action. His observations about the waste of time caused by the endless indoctrination meetings in which busy men were compelled to participate are very just. But they go on to this day. In refusing so indignantly to have the new bridge in Kiev named after him, Khrushchev may have forgotten that in the days when he ruled the Ukraine he managed to encourage a formidable "personality cult" of his own, which was deeply resented by some of his peers who were living more immediately in the shadow of Stalin in Moscow.

SHORTLY after I took up my duties in the Ukraine, a well-known mechanical engineer named Yevgeny Oskarovich Paton called my office and asked for an appointment. When he came in to see me I found him a thick-set man with gray hair, already well along in years; he had a face like a lion's and bright, piercing eyes. He greeted me and immediately produced a lump of metal from his pocket. He thrust it onto my desk in front of me.

"Look at this, Comrade Khrushchev, look what our institute can do! This is a piece of bar iron ten millimeters thick, and look how well we've been able to weld it!"

I examined the joint closely. As a metalworker myself, I'd had many occasions to inspect welded joints. Here was a seam as smooth as if the bar had been cast in a single piece.

"That's an example of fusion welding," said Academician Paton.

I'd never heard the term before and asked him what it meant. Paton, who already had a number of other inventions to his credit, explained that he'd designed a new, much improved, welding technique. He drew me a sketch showing how we could make portable fusion welders for working on ships and bridges. I was literally enchanted by Academician Paton. All my life I've been fascinated with metalworking. My father wanted me to become a shoemaker, but I chose to be a mechanic's apprentice instead. Once, as a boy, I even put together a motorbike from pieces of scrap. From the moment we met I knew that Academician Paton was a man after my own heart. I decided then and there to do what I could to see that his invention received the attention it deserved.

The next time I was in Moscow I told Stalin about Paton. Stalin was very impressed and asked if I thought Paton was up to being made a commissioner to the Council of People's Commissars: "Would he be able to handle all the bureaucrats and make them do what he said if we gave him unlimited power to introduce his new welding method in our factories and at our construction sites?"

"From what I've seen of Paton, Comrade Stalin, the bureaucrats wouldn't stand a chance against him."

So Paton was given the authority to introduce fusion welding throughout our industry. One day I broached the idea with him of using fusion welding to build tank bodies on an assembly line.

"Tell me, Comrade Paton, do you think your technique would work on tank steel?"

"I'll have to study the problem. How thick would the armor be?"

"Perhaps one hundred millimeters."

"That could make it difficult, but we'll try. I think we can do it."

I sent Paton to the Kharkov tank factory and asked the Party organizer there, Comrade Yepishev (who's now Chief of the Political Directorate of the Soviet Army), to introduce him to the designers and supervisors there. That was the beginning of an important stage in Academician Paton's career. He played an important part in the war. Thanks to the improvements he introduced in our tank production, tanks started coming off our assembly lines like pancakes off a griddle. He moved with our armor works to the Urals when we had to evacuate our industry from Kharkov early in the war.

In 1943 Paton happened to be in Moscow when Stalin called me back from the Front for consultation. Paton asked to see me and brought me a letter he'd written to the Central Committee. Here's what his letter said:

"In 1917 I failed to take the Revolution seriously. My father was a tsarist consul in Italy, and I was a product of the old regime; mine was an old-fashioned tsarist upbringing. I did not sympathize with the October Revolution, but at the same time I took no part in anti-Soviet activities of any kind. But with every passing year I have been more and more won over to the side of Soviet Power. Hitherto, I have never believed that I deserved any special confidence or recognition from the Party — I have never forgotten my shortsightedness in the first days of the Revolution. But now I have been on the side of Soviet Power for a long time, and I believe I have recently made a significant contribution to the wartime defense of our country by helping in the production of tanks. Therefore I feel I have earned the moral right to address myself to the Party with a request that I be accepted into its ranks. I enclose an application for Party membership, and I ask the Central Committee for its endorsement."

Needless to say, I was not only pleased by this letter — I was deeply moved. I told him I was sure he would be accepted. I immediately took his letter straight to Stalin. Stalin, too, was obviously very moved, although he rarely showed his emotion. He said simply, "So Paton has decided he wants to join the Party. I see no reason why he shouldn't. I propose we issue a special decree admitting Paton to full membership right away and exempting him from the usual trial period." At that time there was a compulsory trial period or "candidacy" of two years for all Party applicants who came from the bourgeoisie or intelligentsia. An exception was made in Paton's case.

After the war Paton returned to his job as a scientist at the Ukrainian Academy of Sciences. Later he became vice-president of the academy. Shortly after that, a great misfortune befell the Ukraine and the Ukrainian scientific community in particular: Comrade Bogomolets, the president of the academy, passed away. Knowing the special regard in which I, Khrushchev, held Academician Paton, many people were sure that he would be named Bogomolets' successor.

I should explain that Paton was a rather controversial figure at the academy. Opinions about him varied. I remember once the Chief of the Propaganda Section of the Ukrainian Central Committee complained to me about him. He said Paton had showed disrespect to the Central Committee by walking out of a Party meeting to which he'd been invited.

"What sort of subjects was this meeting meant to discuss?" I asked.

"Oh, various questions pertaining to ideological work."

"No wonder he walked out. Comrade Paton can't be wasting his time on meetings like that. He probably thought he should get back to his scientific work." The incident was typical of Paton. He didn't have any patience with those fruitless, abstract discussions in which a lot of silly, pretentious people sit around playing at being learned. Such people felt threatened by Paton.

We could have had him elected president of the academy if we'd wanted to apply pressure, but we decided not to. Besides, Paton had no aspirations to being president. He was wrapped up in his scientific work and in running his institute.

When Paton died, a bridge across the Dnieper was being completed in Kiev, the biggest bridge in the city. It's entirely welded — there's not a single rivet in it. The Ukrainians were thinking about naming the new bridge after me. I was shocked because we had already passed a decree forbidding the dedication of factories, public facilities, collective farms, and other enterprises to members of the Party or government leadership who were in good health. We had even changed some names we felt were inappropriate. In short, we'd cracked down on this very unhealthy competition, which had started under Stalin, of seeing who could have his name put on the most plants and towns and collective farms.

I told the Ukrainians, "If you were to put my name on this bridge, it would be in direct violation of a Central Committee decree. I'm against the idea all the more because I was the one who initiated that decree. You must realize what sort of a position you would be putting me in. Why don't you name the bridge after Academician Paton?"

And that's what they did. Today the bridge is, as they say, alive and well, and people crossing over it remember with respect and gratitude the man who made it possible, the father of industrial welding in the Soviet Union — Academician Yevgeny Oskarovich Paton!

Troubleshooting in the Tire Industry

The extended anecdote that follows shows Khrushchev happily in action as a practical industrialist, lending a hand on the shop floor, bossing people about, and teaching a factory manager his own business. It illuminates both the wastefulness of the struggle to "exceed the Plan," regardless of quality, and the extremely patchy state of Soviet industry in 1939, after the first two five-year plans, in which all the best resources of the country had been concentrated on building up heavy in-

dustry. It illustrates also the remarkably hand-to-mouth way in which Stalin used his most powerful aides for quite small tasks, plugging gaps as he became aware of them. Khrushchev at this time was a full member of the Politbureau, as well as viceroy over forty million souls in the Ukraine; yet he was called away from his own bailiwick and sent off to report on the shortcomings of a tire factory in Yaroslavl, so distrustful was Stalin, so thin on the ground were competent managers in those days.

FOR a period before the war, members of the Politbureau and Central Committee were forbidden to fly in airplanes. This started after Mikoyan let some pilot take him for a joyride in Belorussia. The incident was written up in the newspapers. When Stalin read that one of his men had been up in a plane doing all sorts of aerobatics, he gave Mikoyan a stern dressing down and promptly made a rule that Central Committee members and first secretaries of the Republics weren't allowed in airplanes. I was fairly disappointed because I loved to fly. For a while I either had to take the train between Kiev and Moscow or else drive.

Aleksandr Georgievich Zhuravlev was my chauffeur for almost thirty-three years. My children used to call him Uncle Sasha. He was good at his job, and he liked it, too. I respected and trusted him.

During a trip from Kiev to Moscow in 1939, Aleksandr Georgievich told me that the tires which were being issued for our cars were wearing out much too quickly. In fact, they were blowing out at the sides while they were still almost brand-new. When I got to Moscow, I told Stalin that this manufacturing defect was costing us a lot of time and money.

Stalin never liked to hear anyone criticize something that was Soviet-made. He listened to my complaint with obvious displeasure. Then he angrily instructed me to liquidate this situation and to find the culprits. He said, "So you're criticizing our tire industry, too? Everyone's criticizing it. We are going to instruct you to deal with this situation yourself. You are going to look into it and recommend the measures necessary to eradicate these defects and to ensure the issue of good-quality tires from our factories."

I answered, "Comrade Stalin, I would accept this assignment with pleasure, but I'm absolutely unfamiliar with the rubber industry and tire manufacturing. I've had something to do with the coal industry, with metallurgy, and with the construction business, but the tire industry is completely unfamiliar to me."

"So familiarize yourself. Take over immediately. You won't go back to the Ukraine until you've taken care of this problem."

A resolution was drawn up establishing a commission, and I was confirmed as chairman of it. I was a bit worried. I didn't know how much time it would take, and I didn't know if I would be able to cope with the problem. I convened the commission and summoned specialists from the Yaroslavl tire factory, from Leningrad, from Moscow, and from various ministries. With the help of the Central Committee apparatus, I collected everyone who knew anything about tire manufacturing. Our consultations took place in the Central Committee building. Everyone had a chance to give his views. I remember that the director of the Yaroslavl factory made a particularly good impression on me from the start.

After the first round of consultations I reported to Stalin what everyone had said and then offered my own considerations. Stalin said, "I suggest you go to Yaroslavl and work this out on the spot. The Yaroslavl tire factory is the best we have."

So I went to Yaroslavl. I took some of the specialists with me from Moscow. The Secretary of the Regional Party Committee was Comrade Patolichev, who many years later became Minister of Foreign Trade. The Chairman of the Regional Executive Committee was a young Armenian who, like Patolichev, was a metallurgical engineer. They both made a good impression on me. As soon as I arrived, I told them why I had come to Yaroslavl and asked them to give me their help.

First of all, I wanted to see how the rubber outer covering of the tires was made. I told the director of the factory, "Don't describe your whole operation to me now. That would be a waste of time. Just lead me along your assembly line. I want to start from scratch." I reviewed the whole assembly line, lingering here and there and watching any workers who were doing something that interested me. I didn't have time to see the vulcanization process, so I relied on the specialists who were reporting to me to fill me in on that subject.

I was particularly interested in the technique by which the workers applied the wire cords to the tires. I watched them for a long time. They did this deftly and quickly, not even looking at their hands as they worked. Their hands moved like musicians' hands. I admired them and later asked about the production plans for what they were doing. I was told how many layers of wire cording were applied and what purpose the cords served. On the basis of what I was told, I sensed that I had found the weak spot. I had seen how quickly the workers applied the cords, and I knew that they had to be applied and stretched evenly, so that all the strands in each layer would work together like a single strand. If the cords were applied evenly, you could multiply the durability of one strand by the total number of strands and that would be the resistance of the whole layer to rupture. However, if a layer were applied unevenly, each strand would work by itself and the cords would be torn one by one. That's why the tires were breaking down. There were other problems, too, but this was the main one.

I called over the director of the factory. "Comrade Mitrokhin, let me see the instruction manual you're using for the manufacture of tires. I want to see what sort of production process is recommended. Since we purchased the equipment for this plant from America, the Americans must have recommended a process for us to use."

"Yes, we have all the instructions."

"Then check those instructions against the process now being used and report to me exactly what changes have been made in the recommended process."

According to Mitrokhin's report, there had indeed been some departures from the instructions recommended by the American firm. One or two layers of cording had been eliminated since it was thought that the number left would be sufficient to guarantee durability. I was also told that the amount of reinforcing wire had been diminished at the edges. One or two rings had been taken out. All this had been done to make the whole process more economical. I knew immediately we had found the bug.

"When were these changes made?" I asked.

"Comrade Kaganovich came here to make an inspection tour and studied our production methods. He recommended these changes." This had been when Kaganovich was head of the People's Commissariat of Transport. Apparently he had brought Sergo Ordzhonikidze with him to Yaroslavl.

"All right," I said, "give me the official minutes of your meeting with Kaganovich so that I can report to Comrade Stalin and the Central Committee. Now you should start following exactly the production method used in America." During my tour around the factory I'd notice that in this one, as in any factory, there was an honor board with the photographs of the best producers or, as they were called, the shock-workers. I asked the manager of the factory, "How does the productivity of your workers compare with that of the workers in America who apply tire cording?" I was told that we had made a giant step forward and had surpassed the American workers.

We prepared a draft resolution based on our findings, and I returned to Moscow. When I reported to Stalin, I stressed that we were producing poor-quality tires because, in our desire to economize, we had violated the production procedure recommended by the firm from which the equipment was purchased. We had "corrected" the American manufacturers and "improved" the production process, but as a result, one of their tires lasted ten times as long as one of ours. That certainly is economizing for you!

Then I told Stalin that I considered it a mistake to try to raise the productivity and output norms too high. We should avoid trying to economize on production and to raise productivity at the expense of quality. The tire workers may have surpassed their quota, but they had overdone it. Our workers should have been encouraged to pay more attention to quality when applying the tire cording. In order to do that, we needed to lower their output norms. We were learning that if you aim for a level of productivity which deprives a worker of a chance to do quality work, the product will be spoiled. All the shock-workers on the honor board at the factory were, in actual fact, ruining what they produced, lowering the productivity of our drivers, and preventing us from getting efficient use out of our motor pool.

Stalin listened to me attentively. I could see he was terribly irritated by what I was telling him, and I understood why. Any man who cares for the welfare of the State — especially the man who holds the leading position in the State — ought well to have been disturbed by this kind of news. Stalin said, "I agree with you. Give us your recommendations and we will approve them."

In my report I introduced recommendations that output norms be lowered, that workers' wage rates be raised, and that a whole series of other measures be taken as suggested by the specialists from the factory, from the scientific research institutes, and from the People's Commissariats.

Stalin then said, "We must pass a resolution to discourage excessive

competition for quantity over quality among the workers by prohibit-
ing the posting of honor boards at the tire factory."

On general principle I would have been against this. It had always
been a Leninist contention that competition is a healthy thing for productivity, and productivity is the bedrock of industrial development.
However, I approved of Stalin's position in this particular case.

I was pleased that with the help of the specialists, I had succeeded
in pinpointing and liquidating the weak spot in the manufacture of
tires. We sensed at the time that we were heading toward war, and in
wartime the mobility of the army depends on the quality of the transport industry. I was pleased that as soon as we liquidated the defects
and restored proper production methods, high-quality durable tires
started to be issued. We conducted tests at various factories to see how
long tires could last without repair. If the results of the test were positive, a factory would receive a prize which went to all the workers
collectively for their contribution to the general good.

Shortly afterward, Mitrokhin, the director of the Yaroslavl factory,
became Commissar of the Chemical Industry. I was pleased that Stalin
hadn't forgotten my high recommendation of this man and had assigned him to such a responsible post.

In relation to the scale of our whole manufacturing industry, this episode concerned a minor matter, but it still had its significance for me.
I've told this story to illustrate how Stalin was sometimes capable of a
conscientious and statesmanly approach to problems. He was a jealous
lord and master of the State, and he fought against bureaucracy and
corruption and defects of all kinds. He was a great man, a great organizer and a leader, but he was also a despot. He often fought with
harsh methods against the primitiveness which still afflicted our industry. In his desire to look out for the welfare of the State, he was merciless in liquidating any defect that came to his attention. But it
shouldn't be forgotten that as a despot, Stalin also did much harm, especially in his treatment of the Party and military leadership. This was
all a result of his unhealthy mistrust of other people.

We still have problems of productivity and output. You have probably seen on more than one occasion how men and women are engaged in chipping ice off the pavement with crowbars. This is unproductive labor. Such a sight really makes one uncomfortable. So
much has been done in our country to mechanize complicated production processes, so many machines have been created to make

work easier, and the first artificial earth satellites have been developed, but as for replacing the crowbar and shovel with a machine — we have not yet gotten around to that. We pay too little attention to such matters and regard them as trivial. But is this trivial? No, it is "trivial matters" like this that constitute the work of many people.

5

Prelude to the War

Soviet-German Relations

It is clear that Khrushchev paid little attention to foreign affairs in the dangerous prewar years: he was wholly bound up with running first Moscow, then the Ukraine. Stalin told him little of what was going on. Thus he has nothing to say about the rise of Hitler and about Litvinov's "collective security" campaign. He starts with the Molotov-Ribbentrop Pact of August, 1939, which threw Europe into confusion and gave Hitler the green light to invade Poland. The invasion duly took place on September 1, 1939. England and France declared war on Germany on September 3. The Red Army moved into eastern Poland on September 17. In his comments on the motives and behavior of the Soviet Union, Germany, Britain, and France, Khrushchev reflects the accepted Soviet line.

THE inevitability of war had been obvious long before Hitler and our enemies actually began preparing to attack us. Ever since the fascists first came to power in Germany, we'd known that sooner or later they would wage war against us. In his book *Mein Kampf*—which disgusted me so much that I could never finish it—Hitler spelled out the aggressive designs he had on the world and the misanthropic philosophy which motivated him. He set as his sworn duty the annihilation of Communism and the storming of its citadel, the Soviet Union. When he came to power, he immediately started whipping his army into shape. This was no secret. Throughout Germany there were noisy military parades and belligerent speeches threatening the Soviet Union. *Mein Kampf* didn't say anything about peaceful coexistence with us. It talked about grinding us into the dirt. And it wasn't a change of heart that moved Hitler to send Ribbentrop to Moscow on the twenty-third of August, 1939. No, he was still the same Hitler, with the same vision of himself as a warrior and a conqueror, bent on liberating the Russian people from Bolshevism.

I first heard about Ribbentrop's visit the day before he arrived. I was at Stalin's dacha on a Saturday, and he told me that Ribbentrop was flying in the next day. Stalin smiled and watched me closely to see what sort of an impression this news would make. At first I was dumbfounded. I stared back at him, thinking he was joking. Then I said, "Why should Ribbentrop want to see us? Is he defecting to our side, or what?"

"No," said Stalin, "Hitler has sent us a message saying, 'I ask you, Herr Stalin, to receive my minister, Ribbentrop, who brings with him some concrete proposals.' We've agreed to meet with him tomorrow."

I told Stalin that I'd already planned to go hunting with Bulganin and Malenkov at Voroshilov's preserve the next day. Stalin said, "Go right ahead. There'll be nothing for you to do around here tomorrow. Molotov and I will meet with Ribbentrop and hear what he has to say. When you come back from your hunt, I'll let you know what Hitler has in mind and what the outcome of our conversation with Ribbentrop is."

That night Bulganin, Malenkov, and I left for the hunting preserve in Zavidova. When we arrived we found that Voroshilov was already there, so he couldn't have been with Stalin and Molotov for the meeting with Ribbentrop.[1] There were some other marshals and generals at the preserve, too, and we all went on a hunt together. It was a wonderful day. The weather was warm, and the hunt was a great success — for me particularly. Please don't misunderstand me: I'm not one to brag about my skill as a hunter, but that day I was able to bag one duck more than Voroshilov. I mention this only because the press had

1. When Ribbentrop flew into Moscow, delegations from Britain and France imagined that they were still negotiating with the Russians in a belated and half-hearted attempt on the part of the British and French governments to achieve an alliance with the Russians. Marshal Voroshilov, People's Commissar of Defense, was the chief Russian spokesman in the talks with the British and French. It is interesting to know that he went duck shooting on the fatal day when the Molotov-Ribbentrop Pact was signed, while the British and the French, in all ignorance, were left to kick their heels.

already begun to build up Voroshilov as our number one marksman.

When we finished the hunt we went straight back to Stalin's dacha. I knew that Stalin would call us all together for dinner, so I brought my ducks along to share with the other Politbureau members that evening. I told Stalin about the hunt and boasted jokingly about our successes of the day. He was in a very good mood and was joking a lot himself. Stalin's attitude toward hunting usually depended on what sort of mood he was in. If he were in an especially good mood, he might even think about going on a hunt himself. But there were other times when he sat at home and complained bitterly about hunters. His occasional opposition to hunting wasn't based on his conviction that all life was sacred — far from it! — but simply on his feeling that hunting was a waste of time. Of course, as far as wasting time is concerned, I don't think there has ever been a leader in a position of comparable responsibility who wasted more time than Stalin did just sitting around the dinner table eating and drinking.

Anyway, we met for dinner at Stalin's that Sunday in August, 1939, and while the trophies of our hunt were being prepared for the table, Stalin told us that Ribbentrop had brought with him a draft of a friendship and nonaggression treaty which we had signed. Stalin seemed very pleased with himself. He said that when the English and French who were still in Moscow found out about the treaty the next day, they would immediately leave for home. The English and French representatives who came to Moscow to talk with Voroshilov didn't really want to join forces with us against Germany at all. Our discussions with them were fruitless. We knew that they weren't serious about an alliance with us and that their real goal was to incite Hitler against us. We were just as glad to see them leave.

That's how the Ribbentrop-Molotov Pact, as it was called in the West, came into being. We knew perfectly well that Hitler was trying to trick us with the treaty. I heard with my own ears how Stalin said, "Of course it's all a game to see who can fool whom. I know what Hitler's up to. He thinks he's outsmarted me, but actually it's I who have tricked him!" Stalin told Voroshilov, Beria, myself, and some other members of the Politbureau that because of this treaty the war would pass us by for a while longer.[2] We would be able to stay neutral and save our strength. Then we would see what happened.

2. The war Khrushchev refers to is, of course, the "Great Patriotic War" between Russia and Germany, which did not break out until June, 1941.

Of course there were some people who thought that since Hitler wanted to negotiate with us, he must be too frightened of us to attack. This interpretation of the treaty was very flattering to us. Many people in the USSR eagerly believed it and congratulated themselves. But we, the leaders of the Government, knew better. We weren't fooling ourselves. We knew that eventually we would be drawn into the war, although I suppose Stalin hoped that the English and French might exhaust Hitler and foil his plan to crush the West first and then to turn east. This hope of Stalin's must have been part of the strategy behind our agreement to sign the treaty.

I believe that the Ribbentrop-Molotov Pact of 1939 was historically inevitable, given the circumstances of the time, and that in the final analysis it was profitable for the Soviet Union. It was like a gambit in chess: if we hadn't made that move, the war should have started earlier, much to our disadvantage. As it was, we were given a respite. I think the vast majority of the Party considered the signing of the treaty tactically wise on our part, even though nobody could say so publicly. We couldn't even discuss the treaty at Party meetings. For us to have explained our reasons for signing the treaty in straightforward newspaper language would have been offensive, and besides, nobody would have believed us. It was very hard for us — as Communists, as antifascists, as people unalterably opposed to the philosophical and political position of the fascists — to accept the idea of joining forces with Germany. It was difficult enough for us to accept this paradox ourselves. It would have been impossible to explain it to the man in the street. Therefore we couldn't admit outright that we had reached an agreement on peaceful coexistence with Hitler. Coexistence would have been possible with the Germans in general, but not with the Hitlerite fascists.

For their part, the Germans too were using the treaty as a maneuver to win time. Their idea was to divide and conquer the nations which had united against Germany in World War I and which might unite against Germany again. Hitler wanted to deal with his adversaries one at a time. He was convinced that Germany had been defeated in World War I because she had tried to fight on two fronts at once. The treaty he signed with us was his way of trying to limit the coming war to one front.

All the while the English and French and the whole bourgeois press were trying to sic Hitler on the Soviet Union, trumpeting, "Russia is nothing but a colossus with feet of clay!" England and France would have loved to have stood by and watched Germany and the Soviet Union go at each other and finish each other off. The English and French rubbed their hands in delight at the idea of lying low while Hitler's rampage took its toll of our blood, our territory, and our wealth. If you look at war as a game, you might put it like this: we were betting on the possibility that we could duck behind the treaty and escape the bullets which would soon be flying — thus avoiding the fate which the Western powers hoped would befall us. If it had worked out that way, then I believe the Ribbentrop-Molotov treaty would have been completely justified.

Hitler first approached us with his proposal for a treaty through his ambassador to Moscow, Schulenburg. As history has shown, Schulenburg was genuinely in favor of strengthening peaceful relations between Germany and the Soviet Union.[3] There's no question that he opposed Hitler's plan to go to war against us. When Molotov summoned him to discuss some matter relating to the treaty, Schulenburg was radiant. "God Himself has come to our aid!" he declared. At the time we thought he was just acting, but later we realized that his delight about the treaty was sincere. He understood the necessity for building Germany's relations with the Soviet Union on a foundation of peace, friendship, and the mutually binding principle of nonaggression. He must have reported his views to Hitler at some point but Hitler paid no attention. Schulenburg took part in the plot against Hitler in 1944. The plot failed, and he was among those executed.

During the period immediately after the treaty was signed, Stalin and Hitler fulfilled — or at least pretended to fulfill — their obligations to each other as stipulated by the treaty. There was an exchange of fairly detailed information, as I recall, with Molotov frequently reporting to Stalin, "Schulenburg has said . . . Schulenburg has transmitted . . ." and so on. Of course, Schulenburg was more interested in picking up information from us than he was in passing any to us. I remember once when I was at Stalin's, Molotov told the following story: He had summoned Schulenburg to his office, where Schulenburg noticed stenographers making transcripts of radio broadcasts and remarked, "Why do you have to make stenographic copies . . . ?" Then he cut himself short, but Molotov stored the incident away in his memory. He real-

3. Count Werner von der Schulenburg indeed did all he could to keep the peace between Germany and Russia.

ized from what Schulenburg had let slip that apparently the Germans had some sort of mechanical means of recording radio broadcasts and therefore didn't need stenographers. It was only after the war that we discovered the existence of tape recorders, which explained why German intelligence had been able to monitor radio broadcasts so much better than we could. Secret radiograms are transmitted very rapidly, and it's impossible for a stenographer to copy them down. What's more, they're in code. A tape recorder can take them down and then play them back slowly so they can be decoded. Thus, Schulenburg's offhand comment to Molotov gave us our first hint that the Germans had invented tape recorders.

According to the treaty, we were supposed to give the Germans a certain amount of wheat, oil, and other products. We made all our deliveries punctually. Hitler was supposed to compensate us with a battle cruiser. He even sent along his specialists to help us arm the cruiser. A high-ranking German naval officer arrived in Leningrad to help supervise the job of fitting out the ship. The appropriate accommodations and working conditions were arranged for him. Then a scandal broke out. It seems that our intelligence service had planted in his apartment all sorts of listening and photographic devices. Apparently this admiral was an admirer of the opposite sex, so our intelligence service obliged him with a young lovely and then tried to photograph him in an indecent pose with her. This went on for a number of nights until the admiral heard a whirring noise. He started hunting around and moved a large picture which was hanging on the wall. A little window was cut in the picture, and behind it he found a camera. He immediately registered a complaint. Our Chekists had thought they could compromise him and enlist him into their own service, but the German admiral's superiors couldn't have cared less that he had been with a woman.[4]

Hitler personally raised a rumpus about what had happened. I remember that Stalin got very angry with Beria over our Chekists' handling of the whole thing. That's how I found out about the cruiser. Later, when the war ended, the cruiser was still sitting in Leningrad unfinished. Some people thought that Hitler had given us the cruiser because he was ready to share his military might with us. Actually, Hitler believed that before the cruiser was finished, he would have crushed the Soviet Union and the cruiser would be his again.

4. This episode is characteristic of Soviet secret-police behavior, now as then. Khrushchev's only criticism appears to be that the operators were found out.

I remember another example of how Hitler tried to give the appearance of honorably abiding by the conditions of the nonaggression treaty. We had a contract with a Czechoslovakian munitions firm called Skoda, which was supposed to make some antiaircraft guns for us. These were good 88 mm. guns which were being built according to samples which we had already bought from Skoda. We were also supposed to get some 205 mm. cannons. When Hitler invaded Czechoslovakia, Skoda suspended the contract. Hitler himself intervened and ordered Skoda to go ahead and fill our order. Skoda obeyed and delivered a certain number of 205 mm. heavy cannons, but not enough to make much difference. The 88 mm. antiaircraft guns, however, were adopted for production by our factories. They played an important role in the war, both as antiaircraft and as antitank guns.

Throughout this period the Germans were assessing our technological sophistication, particularly the quality of our mechanized equipment. They sensed our weakness, and this encouraged them. Of course, as it turned out, they very much underestimated us.

From 1940 on, many controversial matters arose in our relations with Hitler. After prolonged consultation among ourselves, we decided that Molotov should go to Berlin. I came to Moscow in October or November of 1940, after Molotov had gotten back from his trip. He said that strict security measures had been taken during his train ride from the Soviet border to Berlin and that during the negotiations the English had carried out an air raid, forcing Hitler and his entourage to move to a bomb shelter. Molotov said he could tell that the bomb shelter had already been in frequent use. Molotov, himself taciturn by nature, characterized Hitler as an untalkative man who never touched a drop of drink. At an official dinner Hitler didn't even pick up his wine glass and was served tea during the meal.[5]

From Molotov's answers to Stalin's questions I concluded that his trip had strengthened our general conviction that war was inevitable and probably imminent. Stalin's face and behavior showed signs of his anxiety, but he rarely shared his anxiety with us or even asked our

5. On the night of November 13, 1940, when Ribbentrop and Molotov were at a critical point in negotiating "spheres of influence" and "territorial aspirations," the RAF paid a friendly call on Berlin. During the raid, as Stalin was later to tell Churchill at Teheran, the Germans kept insisting that Britain was finished. "If that is so," Molotov retorted, "then why are we in this shelter, and whose are these bombs that are falling on us?" The Molotov visit to Berlin was, for Hitler, the very last straw. A month later he issued Directive No. 21, headed "Operation Barbarossa," instructing his generals to prepare to crush Soviet Russia before the end of the war against England.

opinion about what should be done. I remember that when Hess flew to England and the Germans put out the canard that he had fled, I said to Stalin, "The Germans are hiding something. I don't think Hess's flight to England is really an escape from Germany at all. I think he must actually be on a secret mission from Hitler to negotiate with the English about cutting short the war in the West to free Hitler's hands for the push east." [6]

Stalin heard me out, and then said, "Yes, that's it. You understand correctly." He didn't develop his thoughts on this subject further. He just agreed. We had long since become accustomed to the practice that if you weren't told something, you didn't ask. This may be a proper way to deal with functionaries, but it's no way to treat members of the Government. To deal this way with members of the ruling body of the Party and of the country is a violation of all the norms which must be observed if the Party is to be truly democratic. But that's what happened to our Party, the Party of Lenin, in the thirties and forties. Information was carefully selected, limited, and weighed by Stalin before it was passed on to the Politbureau. He had no right to do this, according to the Party Statutes. The fact that he did it anyway was another manifestation of the arbitrary rule which acquired the aspect of law under Stalin.

I came to Moscow again in the winter, either at the end of 1940 or at the beginning of 1941. As soon as I arrived I received a message that Stalin wanted to see me at the Nearby Dacha [the stock phrase for Stalin's dacha] right away. When I got there, Stalin was lying on a couch reading. He told me he didn't feel very well. Then he started to talk to me about military matters. This was possibly the only time he ever talked about military matters when we were alone. Apparently he just needed somebody to talk to and didn't care who it was. He was always depressed when he was alone. It was as though the walls were closing in on him. I think our conversation about the coming war was just an excuse for having me around to keep him company. That's the only way I can explain it because usually he felt no urge to exchange opinions with others. He valued his own abilities and views much more than those of anyone else.

On that occasion in the winter of 1940–41, Stalin started complaining about being unable to take part in the military consultations which

6. Many Russians to this day still believe that Britain entered into some sort of a conspiracy with Hess.

were then going on. While I was with him he telephoned Timoshenko [7] and started arguing angrily with him, stressing the importance of artillery and criticizing some decision which had already been made in favor of some other sort of weaponry. He was obviously very worried about the state of our defenses. I reacted very humanly to these outward manifestations of Stalin's deep alarm. A dark cloud was indeed hanging over our country.

I remember we were all together in the Kremlin when we heard the news over the radio that the French army had capitulated and that the Germans were in Paris. Stalin's nerves cracked when he learned about the fall of France. He cursed the governments of England and France: "Couldn't they put up any resistance at all?" he asked despairingly. Molotov and I were with him at the time. Beria and Zhdanov were probably there, too.

Hitler had been stunningly successful in his conquest of Europe. He had swiftly moved his troops right up to the borders of the Soviet Union. After the fall of Poland there was only a very tentative boundary between Hitler's forces and the Soviet Union. Germany, Italy, and Japan were formidable countries, and they were united against us. The most pressing and deadly threat in all history faced the Soviet Union. We felt as though we were facing this threat all by ourselves. America was too far away to help us, and besides, it was unknown at that time how America would react if the Soviet Union were attacked. And England was hanging by a thread. No one knew if the English would be able to hold out should the Hitlerites attempt an invasion across the Channel.

Hitler knew how dangerous our situation was, and he did his best to humiliate us. I remember Stalin once told me that Hitler had sent a request for a favor through secret channels. Hitler wanted Stalin, as the man with the most authority and prestige in the Communist world, to persuade the French Communist Party not to lead the resistance against the German occupation of France. Stalin was indignant. There was no question how he would answer. Hitler had stooped to new depths of filth and vileness. How could he expect Stalin to make such a degrading deal? How could he expect him to cooperate with the fascists against the Communist Party of France! [8]

7. Marshal Semyon Timoshenko replaced Voroshilov as People's Commissar of Defense after the Finnish war in 1940. Before the Finnish war he was in the Ukraine as commander of the Kiev Military District.

8. Khrushchev in his indignation does not mention Stalin's earlier betrayal of the German Communists in the face of Hitler. Perhaps he did not know about it.

I recall another example of Hitler's brazenness. The Germans staged their capture of Danzig as though it were a cinema spectacle. They set up movie cameras in advance and filmed the battle from sea and land. They tried to distribute this film to all the countries of the world. Hitler wanted to show off his might and to paralyze his future adversaries with fear. He wanted the whole world to see what irresistible blows the fascist troops could strike and to quake in terror. Hitler proposed that Stalin take this film and have it shown in our movie theaters. Stalin agreed on one condition: "We'll distribute your film if you distribute ours." We had some very impressive films of our own, showing our troops on maneuvers and on parade. Naturally, as Stalin expected, Hitler wouldn't agree to this exchange. That's how Stalin countered Hitler's attempt to subvert our will. Hitler's film was sent to us anyway, and we watched it in the Kremlin with Stalin. It was very depressing. We knew very well that we were the next country Hitler planned to turn his army against.

At that time we had a play called *The Keys to Berlin* running in a number of theaters. It was part of our campaign to toughen the country psychologically for the coming war. The Germans were trumpeting that they were invincible and that every country on earth would soon fall under their power. This play of ours was a reminder that there had already been occasions in history when Russian troops had crushed the Germans, captured the city of Berlin, and thereby received the keys to the German capital. Unfortunately, as it turned out, we didn't succeed in getting the keys to Berlin at the end of World War II, but by rights we should have.

The Advance into Poland

Here, and in the next chapter, Khrushchev deals with one of the more obscure and terrible episodes in the history of the Soviet Union: the Soviet seizure of eastern Poland, the Polish Ukraine, in accordance with the secret provisions of the Molotov-Ribbentrop Pact. While the Polish army, facing west, was being shattered in the first German blitzkrieg, the Red Army quietly and massively took the Polish army in the rear, and meeting next to no resistance, moved up to the new frontier and agreed with the Nazis to achieve what was nothing less than the fourth partition of Poland.

Khrushchev, as viceroy of the Soviet Ukraine, was responsible for setting up a civilian administration with its capital at Lvov, and in effect, for organizing the sovietization of the annexed territory. It was an operation carried out with extreme rigor. It was the task of the Red Army, under Timoshenko, to round up whole Polish army formations and arrange for their transportation to the prisons and labor camps in the interior of the Soviet Union. Fifteen thousand Polish officers vanished from the face of the map, and the bodies of over four thousand of them were later discovered in mass graves in Katyn Forest near Smolensk, having been shot by the NKVD. Over two hundred thousand Polish prisoners, women as well as men, were taken to the camps. Many died there. Others, released in accordance with the Stalin-Sikorski agreement after the German invasion of Russia, made their way south, many dying on the way. The survivors found haven under British auspices in Persia and the Middle East, where the soldiers formed a new army which fought so bravely with the Allies at Cassino and elsewhere.

Meanwhile, the army and the bourgeoisie having been liquidated, a puppet government was set up by Khrushchev, elections being rigged in the Soviet manner, which asked for the occupied territory to be incorporated in the Soviet Union. It is impossible to tell whether Khrushchev was fully aware of the scale of this atrocity. He cheerfully talks of arrests and insists that they were necessary. But, as master of forty million souls it is improbable that he had any detailed understanding of what went on in his name. He was surrounded by sycophants and flatterers and renegades, and by some genuine enthusiasts for Russia, too (though the Communist Party of Poland had already been destroyed by Stalin). He would have beamed on cheering crowds, "spontaneously" demonstrating at carefully vetted public meetings. Having no idea of living conditions anywhere outside the Soviet Union, and believing in Leninist dogma, he would have found it easy to believe that he was really bringing comfort and light to the oppressed. The dirty work was done by the head of the Ukrainian NKVD, Ivan Serov.

In the Polish Ukraine there were indeed large numbers of oppressed. The right wing of the government of Colonel Beck had been highly dictatorial. Further, the history of the Ukraine was a muddle (Ukraine means "borderland"). The first Russian state had been based in Kiev. After the Tartar invasion in the thirteenth century Moscow won ascendancy, and by the end of the fifteenth century when the Tartars were driven back, the Great Russians of Muscovy had become in many ways different from the Little Russians of the Ukraine, which was disputed territory, with now the Poles, now the Lithuanians, the dominant power. It was not until the seventeenth century that Kiev and the Eastern Ukraine were brought back under the sway of the Muscovite Tsars. The Western Ukraine remained part of Poland, until part of it went to Russia and part to Austria with the first partition in 1772. Lvov was then known as Lemberg. The Ukrainians had developed their own characteristics and their own language — very close to Russian. Although their lands were divided among the powers, they retained a strong feeling of national consciousness and set up an independent state in 1918. This did not last. The Ukraine was divided again, now between Soviet Russia and the new Republic of Poland — until, in 1939, the Red Army under Timoshenko and the Soviet Government, represented by Khrushchev, forcibly recovered the western part and Poland once again ceased to exist as an independent power. After World War II the Russians kept their gains and compensated Communist Poland by pushing the boundaries of the new state deep into Germany — the Oder-Neisse line — driving out the German inhabitants. This chapter is interesting, valuable indeed, in that it offers a view of the Kremlin's attitude toward Eastern Europe so radically different from our own.

How did German-Soviet relations look from my position in the Ukraine?

The Germans, like all believers in bourgeois ideology, thought that since the Soviet Union was multinational, it would collapse at the first poke of a bayonet. They expected national discord to break out and the center of the people's solidarity to give way. This delusion consoled the Soviet Union's ill-wishers throughout the world, and it encouraged the Germans to concentrate pressure on the Ukraine.[9]

After the fall of Poland, Hitler moved his troops up to our border and faced them east. Since we had signed the nonaggression and friendship treaty with the Germans, Hitler's feverish efforts to fortify the border looked suspicious. We reported to Stalin what was happen-

9. The Germans were right from their point of view. When they invaded in 1941 large numbers of Ukrainians received them as liberators, before disillusionment set in.

ing. Stalin must have realized the threat, but in order to allay our fears he would usually either ignore our reports or contradict our assessments of what the Germans were up to.

One incident in particular sticks out in my mind. We were in close contact with the Germans when we began converting the railroad tracks in the Western Ukraine from the narrow European gauge to our own wide-gauge system. Germans appeared on a number of occasions and advised us against proceeding with the track conversion. I knew what they were thinking. I immediately reported to Stalin that the Germans must be planning to use our tracks for their own equipment in the near future. In this case Stalin had to agree. He cursed angrily and said, "Go ahead and give the order to convert the rest of the rails as quickly as possible." We did so, but it didn't make much difference because after their invasion the Germans simply converted the rails back to narrow gauge as they marched. Construction workers followed behind the fascist troops, ripping up spikes, moving the rails, and driving in new spikes.

Despite all the taunting haughtiness of the Germans after the fall of Poland, they took care not to provoke a military confrontation with us until they were ready for a massive invasion. I had an opportunity to keep an eye on them at close quarters. As a member of the Military Council for the Kiev District, I often went out with the commander, Timoshenko, to review our troops who were concentrated on the border. We were appalled at the complete breakdown of the Polish war machine and the Polish government after the Germans attacked on September 1, 1939. The Poles had been proud and cocky, and they had thrown back in our face our proposal that we join forces with them. And now their army was in a disgraceful shambles.[10]

The Ribbentrop-Molotov treaty set a new boundary between Poland and the Soviet Ukraine. We crossed the old border and moved west, meeting practically no resistance. First we moved our troops forward to Ternopol. We drove through Polish villages populated mostly by Ukrainians. On the second or third day of the campaign we approached Lvov. We got there just a little bit ahead of the Germans.

10. The Poles had certainly asked for trouble by refusing to consider any agreement between the Soviet Union, Britain, and France which would allow Soviet troops to pass through their territory in the event of war with Germany. Proud, cocky indeed, they also were. They were soon shattered by the German blitzkrieg. But Khrushchev should have remembered, before speaking of a "disgraceful shambles," that the Red Army itself was soon to be reduced to a disgraceful shambles by the Finns, and in June, 1941, by the same Germans.

We were anxious to avoid clashing with the Germans over who would enter Lvov, so we decided to send Yakovlev, who is now Marshal of Artillery, over to the German lines to negotiate.[11] He knew a little German. If the Germans had had their way, they would have entered Lvov first and sacked the city. But since our troops, under the command of Golikov,[12] had gotten there ahead of them, the Germans were careful not to show any hostility toward us. They stuck to the letter of the treaty and told Yakovlev in effect, "Please, be our guests! After you!" Hitler was playing for high stakes, and he didn't want to start a fight with us over small change. He wanted us to think he was a man of his word. So the German troops were pulled back to the border which had been set by the treaty.

There was great elation both among our own troops and among the local population over the annexation of the Western Ukraine to the Soviet Ukraine. Historically these lands had been populated by Ukrainians. The only exception was in the big cities. Lvov, for instance, had many more Poles than Ukrainians. But this was an artificial majority. Ukrainians were barred from jobs in the cities; they weren't even given roadwork. This discrimination had been practiced as a matter of policy to make sure that Poles dominated the cities.

If you consider the Soviet Union's acquisition of the Western Ukraine from a purely territorial point of view, you'll see that we gained practically nothing except what we were legally entitled to — that is, the Belorussian and Ukrainian lands which had been seized by Pilsudski in 1920.[13] Naturally, there were some Ukrainians who, for nationalistic reasons, weren't very happy with the Ribbentrop-Molotov treaty. They believed that the Soviet regime in the Ukraine was only temporary, and they would have preferred the Curzon Line, which was further to the west than the new border set by the Ribbentrop-Molotov treaty.

11. Lieutenant General V. F. Yakovlev, who was later to command the Soviet Fourth Army in front of Leningrad.

12. P. I. Golikov, later promoted to marshal, who became GOC Lvov Military District.

13. These lands were part of Imperial Russia until the Revolution. Poland had not existed as a sovereign state since the Third Partition between Russia, Germany, and Austria in 1863. An independent Poland was proclaimed in November, 1918. General Pilsudski became President and Paderewski, the pianist, Prime Minister early in 1919. The Bolsheviks tried to reestablish Russian ascendancy and marched on Warsaw, under Tukhachevsky. Pilsudski pushed them back and by the Treaty of Riga, in March of 1921, Polish possession of part of Belorussia and the Ukraine was conrmed.

Ukrainian nationalists gave us more trouble than anyone else between the signing of the treaty in 1939 and the outbreak of war in 1941. Indisputable documentary proof fell into our hands that they were receiving instructions and money from the Germans. This information in turn constituted the definitive proof that Hitler was getting ready to invade us. He was using Ukrainian nationalists as his agents in the Western Ukraine, and when he invaded, the nationalist packs in the area helped the German intelligence service more than once.[14]

Before the invasion, the Ukrainian nationalists looked forward eagerly to the impending war because Goebbels had duped them into believing that Hitler would drive the "Muscovites" out of the Ukraine and give the Ukrainians their independence on a silver platter. These nationalists were too blind to see what the Soviet regime — founded on Marxism-Leninism, the most advanced doctrine in the world — had to offer.

When we moved into Lvov we made the mistake of releasing the Ukrainian nationalist leader Stepan Bandera from prison. Who was this Stepan Bandera? Many people still don't know. Some even confuse him with the Ilf and Petrov character, Ostap Bender. Like his father before him, Stepan Bandera was a priest in the region of Stanislav. He once studied at the Lvov Polytechnic Institute. He was in prison in Lvov because he had been convicted in connection with the assassination of the Polish Minister of Internal Affairs. We were hardly inclined to mourn the passing of a minister of the reactionary Polish state. Nevertheless, we still showed a certain lack of judgment by freeing people like Bandera from prison without first checking up on them. We were impressed by Bandera's record as an opponent of the Polish government, but we should have taken into account the fact that men like him were also enemies of the Soviet Union. They were Ukrainian nationalists and therefore had a pathological hatred of the Soviet regime. Bandera himself was an outright agent of German fascism, and later he gave us a lot of trouble. It's true that when Bandera realized that the Hitlerites didn't intend to keep their promise to sponsor an independent Ukraine he turned his units against them. But even then he didn't stop hating the Soviet Union. During the second half of the war he fought against both us and the Germans. Later, after the war, we lost

14. Here again we see that Khrushchev finds it hard to decide whether to minimize or to stress the strength of Ukrainian nationalism when it suits him. In fact it was very strong.

thousands of men in a bitter struggle between the Ukrainian nationalists and the forces of Soviet Power.[15]

I would like to say something about a tragedy which occurred in the
Ukraine during the period just after the signing of the Ribbentrop-
Molotov Pact. I didn't have time to deal with these developments my-
self. Besides, in my very important position as Politbureau member and
Secretary of the Ukrainian Central Committee, it would have been im-
politic for me to have taken a direct hand in them. These events were
reported to me by Comrade Serov, the People's Commissar of Internal
Affairs in the Ukraine.

Serov's duties required him to have contacts with the Gestapo. A Gestapo representative used to come to Lvov on official business. I don't
know what sort of a network the Gestapo had in the Ukraine, but it
was extensive. The cover for this network was an exchange agreement
whereby people on German-occupied territory who wanted to return to
their homes in the former Polish territory now occupied by Soviet
troops were allowed to do so; and likewise, anyone in the Ukrainian
population on Soviet territory who wanted to return to German-occupied Poland could do that.

Serov described the following scene to me: "There are long lines
standing outside the place where people register for permission to return to Polish territory. When I took a closer look, I was shocked to
see that most of the people in line were members of the Jewish population. They were bribing the Gestapo agents to let them leave as soon
as possible to return to their original homes."

The Gestapo agents were eagerly accepting the bribes, getting rich,
and shipping these people straight to the gas chambers. There was
nothing we could do to stop them. They wanted to go home. Maybe
they had relatives in Poland. Maybe they just wanted to go back to
their birthplaces. They must have known how the Germans were dealing with Jews. Naturally, no better end awaited these Polish Jews who,
by the will of fate, found themselves on Soviet territory but who
wanted to get back to a land where fascism now ruled.

The Polish intelligentsia in the Western Ukraine reacted in various

15. For some years after the war, until he was killed, Stepan Bandera presented
a very serious problem to the Soviet authorities. For obvious reasons his activities
have never been publicized, but it took a large-scale military and police operation,
with all the paraphernalia of tanks, aircraft, and heavy artillery, to break up the
rebel forces, composed of dedicated Ukrainian nationalists, deserters from the Soviet armed forces, former prisoners of war, and displaced persons of all kinds and
many nationalities — all united in fear or hatred of Moscow.

ways to the arrival of the Red Army. Many intellectuals were still in a state of shock. They had been subjected to the imposition of a Hitlerite state in Poland. They had seen the Polish government liquidated. Warsaw was in ruins, and other cities had undergone vast destruction. Brought up in a bourgeois culture on bourgeois ideas, the Poles felt they were losing their national identity. Since they neither understood nor accepted Marxist-Leninist teachings, they couldn't imagine that their culture would actually be enriched by the annexation of their lands to the Soviet Union. In other words, while the Ukrainian population in the Western Ukraine felt liberated by the Red Army, the Polish population felt repressed.

Most Poles on Soviet-occupied territory were against the Soviet system, but when confronted with the alternative of what Hitler had brought to the rest of Poland, they chose what they thought was the lesser of two evils. Regrettably, some Polish intellectuals fled, and most of those perished in the Gestapo's mobile gas chambers and ovens.[16]

I remember one incident which perplexed and grieved me very much. When we moved into Lvov, there was a famous Polish opera singer there named Wanda Bandrovska. I asked our people who handled cultural matters to negotiate with her and offer her a chance to sing in the Kiev, Kharkov, or Odessa opera. I thought such an attractive opportunity would entice her to stay. I didn't want a famous singer like her to return to the Polish territory now occupied by the fascists. For her to sing in Poland would be an affront both to the Polish people and to the Soviet people. But Bandrovska outsmarted us. She pretended to be very interested in our offer, while at the same time she was conducting negotiations with the fascists behind our backs. She let them spirit her over to German-occupied territory, and one day Serov told me, "Bandrovska is gone. She is in Cracow and has already appeared in the theater there and sung to officers of the German army."

Despite setbacks like that one, we were sure that the Polish intellectuals, as well as the Polish workers and peasants, of the Western Ukraine would correctly understand the necessity for the Ribbentrop-

16. In 1939, of course, there were no gas chambers. The decision to exterminate the Jews of Europe, which led to the establishment of Auschwitz, Treblinka, and the like with their gas chambers, was not made by Hitler until 1941. In 1939 the Jews were being very actively and viciously persecuted in Germany, but Polish Jews, especially those of bourgeois origin, may well have felt, at the time, that they would stand more chance of buying their way out of Germany into Western Europe than of escaping from the Soviet labor camps.

Molotov treaty and would accept Soviet rule. It hadn't been our fault that we had had to sign the treaty. It had been the fault of an unwise Polish government — the government of the Pilsudski-ites, who were blinded by their hatred of the Soviet Union and their hostility to the workers and peasants of their own state. They were afraid that any contact with us might encourage the freedom-loving elements in their own society. More than anything else they feared the Communist Party of Poland, and they didn't want to do anything that might strengthen the Party. The Pilsudski-ites knew that if they joined forces with us their fate would depend on the will of the Polish people. So they refused our assistance, and consequently most of Poland fell to Hitler while the Western Ukraine was united with the Eastern Ukraine and its people were given an opportunity to become citizens of the Soviet Union.

Sovietizing the Western Ukraine

Here Khrushchev continues his story of the incorporation of the Polish Ukraine into the Soviet Union, referring also to the occupation of the Baltic States in 1940. The sovietization of Lithuania, Latvia, and Estonia was carried out — arrests, deportations, and all — in the manner already perfected in the Ukraine, but with the difference that these small peoples were in no sense Russians and had achieved living standards much superior to those obtaining in the Soviet Union, which proceeded to drag them down to its own level.

UNDER my leadership we got on with the job of establishing Soviet Power and normalizing the situation in the lands annexed from Poland. Assisted by Comrade Serov, I concentrated on the creation of local Party organizations in the Western Ukraine. Regional committees were formed mainly from people who came from the Soviet [Eastern] Ukraine, while district committees were drawn largely from local Party activists. Despite strong Ukrainian nationalist influences and resistance among the Polish intelligentsia, there were still plenty of people willing to recognize the Soviet reality. And even though the Communist Party of the Western Ukraine had been dissolved during the purges of

1936–37, there were many Communists in the area who still sympathized with us.

Some of the local Party workers in the Western Ukraine had their hearts in the right place but were fairly unsophisticated. I remember one amusing episode in particular. I once called at the Lvov Revolutionary Committee to see how the Chairman was getting along. His office was crowded with people who had come to see him about various matters relating to the management of the city — the condition of the trolley lines, roads which needed repair, and most important, the city's electricity and water supplies. The people who had run these services in the past were all Poles, and they were coming to the Revolutionary Committee to be certified by the new administration and to receive instructions. There, in the midst of all these people, sat the Chairman. He was a huge man, and he was wearing high felt boots and an enormous overcoat on top of his sheepskin jacket. It was late fall and beginning to turn chilly. There were two revolvers sticking conspicuously out of his overcoat. It looked as though the only reason he didn't have a cannon slung over his shoulder was that it would have been too heavy. The people sitting around waiting to see him were obviously scared of him. When his office hours were over, I told him I was horrified to find the Chairman of the Revolutionary Committee looking like that. "Listen," I said, "this will never do. You're making a terrible impression on these people; you're going to give a bad name both to yourself and to our Party. What are you going to do if a terrorist comes charging in here and tries to kill you? He'll be able to shoot you with one of your own pistols! From now on, if you want to carry a revolver, make sure that the butt isn't sticking out of your coat like that."

There was something else that surprised me in Lvov and other cities of the Western Ukraine and that was the attitude of the local Jewish population. There were many Jews among both the working class and the intelligentsia, and some of them were involved in anti-Soviet activities of one sort or another. Some Jews, along with Ukrainians, belonged to an anti-Polish, nationalist organization called the Communist Party for the Defense of the Ukraine.[17] I remember that once we invited Ukrainians, Jews, and Poles — mostly workers but some intellectuals, too — to a meeting in the Lvov opera house. It struck me as very strange to hear the Jewish speakers at this meeting refer to

17. The initials in Russian are the same as those of the Communist Party of the Western Ukraine.

themselves as "yids." They said things like, "We yids hereby declare ourselves in favor of such-and-such."

Out in the lobby after the meeting I stopped some of these men and demanded, "How dare you use the word 'yid'? Don't you know it's a very offensive term, an insult to the Jewish nation?"

"Here in the Western Ukraine it's just the opposite," they explained, "We call ourselves yids and consider the word 'Jew' an insult."

Apparently what they said was true. If you go back to Ukrainian literature — take Gogol for instance — you'll see that "yid" isn't used derisively or insultingly. But even after this custom was explained to us, it continued to grate on our sensibilities until we got used to it.[18]

While we were trying to enlist support among the intelligentsia of the Western Ukraine, I heard about a writer named Wanda Lvovna Wassilewska, whose voice carried a great deal of weight among Polish intellectuals. She and I became fast friends. She was a good person, very smart and very honest. She became a Communist of unimpeachable honor and boundless loyalty. She was later one of the few people who could talk back to Stalin and still keep in his good graces. She had fled on foot from Warsaw to the territory occupied by our troops, dressed like a simple peasant in a sheepskin coat and plain black boots. She came from a distinguished Polish family. She was the daughter of a minister in the Pilsudski government. It was even rumored that she was Pilsudski's goddaughter, although I never asked her if this was true. The important thing was that she stood clearly and firmly for the establishment of Soviet Power in the former Polish territory, and she helped us get through to those Poles in the Western Ukraine who were clinging irrationally to the idea that we had negotiated the Ribbentrop-Molotov Pact at their expense.[19] Later I came to know Wanda Lvovna's daughter Eva, who lived in the Soviet Union and worked in one of the big libraries in Moscow.

My main job was to set up organizations to represent the people of the Western Ukraine and to give them a chance to declare themselves:

18. Our own derogatory "yid" is the closest approximation to the Russian *zhid*. The Jews of the Western Ukraine do in fact refer to themselves as *zhidze*. This is so commonplace that any Ukrainian or Great Russian who has been there knows it and takes it for granted. So this seems to be yet another case of Khrushchev getting in a dig at the Jews while professing his total freedom from anti-Semitism.

19. Wassilewska rejoiced in her new Soviet citizenship and later married the no less politically minded writer Korneichuk. By the majority of Polish writers she was regarded as a traitress. As a reward for assisting in the liquidation of her own Polish colleagues, she was made a Deputy Prime Minister of the Ukraine.

did they want to join the Soviet State or not? Delegations were elected to an assembly in Lvov to decide this question. When the assembly was convened I sat in a special box and observed how the first session progressed. It was a very encouraging event. The local presidium was made up of people from the Western Ukraine. We knew where they stood politically because they had already declared themselves at public meetings and in the press. But while these men were well known to us, they were by no means our stooges or our planted agents. They were Communists by conviction.

The assembly continued for a number of days amid great jubilation and political fervor. I didn't hear a single speech expressing even the slightest doubt that Soviet Power should be established in the Western Ukraine. One by one, movingly and joyfully, the speakers all said that it was their fondest dream to be accepted into the Ukrainian Soviet Republic. It was gratifying for me to see that the working class, peasantry, and laboring intelligentsia were beginning to understand Marxist-Leninist teachings and that they all wanted to build their future on that foundation. Such was the power of Lenin's ideas! Despite all the efforts of the Polish rulers to distort our Leninist doctrine and to intimidate the people, Lenin's ideas were alive and thriving in the Western Ukraine.

At the same time we were still conducting arrests. It was our view that these arrests served to strengthen the Soviet State and clear the road for the building of Socialism on Marxist-Leninist principles; [20] but our bourgeois enemies had their own interpretation of the arrests, which they tried to use to discredit us throughout Poland. But despite this intensive slander campaign, the people of the Western Ukraine welcomed the Red Army in the way a laboring people should welcome its liberators.

20. The arrests were indeed (who would deny it?) intended to strengthen the Soviet State, which considered itself then (as today) insufficiently strong to tolerate the existence, outside prison or the labor camps, of any individual who might be expected to question the regime. In Soviet-occupied Poland and in the Soviet-occupied Baltic States the arrests of such individuals ran into many hundreds of thousands (see note 24 below). For the most moving account of what happened to civilians arrested by Serov, at Khrushchev's right hand, see the terrible story of the deportees, *The Dark Side of the Moon*, published anonymously, with a preface by T. S. Eliot. For an account of the vain search for fifteen thousand Polish officers who were taken prisoner by the Russians, see *The Inhuman Land* by Josef Gzapski, with prefaces by Maurice Halevy and Edward Crankshaw. For an account of the discovery of the bodies of some four thousand of these officers, found murdered in Katyn Forest near Smolensk, see *The Katyn Wood Murders* by Joseph Mackiewicz.

The assembly in Lvov proceeded triumphantly. Representatives made speeches with tears of joy in their eyes. They said that finally they had lived to see the day when the Ukraine was unified and when they were united with their Ukrainian brethren. The national aspirations of the Ukrainian people were being fulfilled — and at the same time the frontiers of the Soviet State were being fortified. Our borders had been pushed west, and history's injustice to the Ukrainian people was being set right. Never before had the Ukrainian people been united in a single Ukrainian state. Only now, in the Soviet era, was this dream at last coming true.[21]

However, the assembly in Lvov reflected only the feelings of the people who had been liberated from Polish oppression. Therefore the unification of the Ukraine and the official acceptance of the former Polish territory into the Soviet Union weren't yet legally accomplished. But only a formality remained. No one expected the Ukrainians of the eastern areas to object to the inclusion of the Western Ukraine in the Ukrainian Soviet State. After the representative, or founding, assembly in Lvov we transferred the discussion of all these matters to Kiev, where the delegates made an application first to the Ukrainian and then to the Soviet Government for acceptance of the Western Ukraine as part of the Soviet Ukraine. Then they made an application for inclusion in the Soviet Union at a special session of the Supreme Soviet of the USSR, which was convened in Kiev. The mood at this session was triumphant. It gave me great joy and pride to attend these meetings because from the very beginning I had organized and supervised the sovietization of the Western Ukraine.

It's true there were still some Ukrainians living on the other side of the Carpathian Mountains. After the liquidation of Czechoslovakia, the Transcarpathian Ukraine had been annexed to Hungary. Ukrainians used to say among themselves: "Well, for the time being the Transcarpathian Ukrainians aren't part of our Ukrainian state. But the hour will come when they will join us." And that's exactly what happened after the war. When Hitler was crushed, the Transcarpathian Ukraine joined the Soviet Ukraine, and all Ukrainians were at last united into one state.

Meanwhile, sovietization was also going on in Belorussia. The Belorussians, like the Ukrainians, joyfully celebrated the victory of Soviet

21. The majority of the population would have told another story.

power and the historic unification of the whole Belorussian population into a single Belorussian Soviet state.

The annexation of Lithuania, Latvia, and Estonia occurred somewhat later. When Mussolini began military actions against Greece and when Hitler attacked Yugoslavia and occupied Norway almost without a shot, moving right beside our northern frontier near Murmansk, we opened negotiations with Lithuania, Latvia, and Estonia.[22] We asked for assurance that the Baltic republics wouldn't attack us. It goes without saying that there was soon a change of government in each of these countries. I found out about what was happening there from conversations I had with Stalin when I returned to Moscow from Kiev. We were all very glad that the Lithuanians, Latvians, and Estonians would again be part of the Soviet State. This meant the expansion of our territory, the augmentation of our population, the fortification of our borders, and the acquisition of an extensive coastal frontier on the Baltic Sea.[23]

The annexation of the Baltic states also furthered our progressive aims with regard to the peoples of that area. Unlike the Belorussians and Ukrainians, who are united by strong national bonds with Russians, the Baltic peoples are of a different national stock. Yet they have still been given a chance to live in conditions equal to those of the working class, peasantry, and laboring intelligentsia of Russia. We were absolutely certain that the annexation was a great triumph for the Baltic peoples as well as for the Soviet Union. The working class and laboring peasants of the Baltic states knew that the liquidation of the exploiting classes which we had accomplished in Russia would spread to them as it would to all peoples who were to join the Soviet Union.

For a while the Lithuanians, Latvians, and Estonians were faced with a problem. Their leaders had fled with the bourgeoisie. Some leaders who didn't have time to flee were given posts in the new gov-

22. Norway was occupied in March, 1940. Mussolini attacked Greece in October, 1940. Hitler attacked Yugoslavia in April, 1941. But Russia seized the Baltic States in June, 1940.

23. An unusually cool admission of Soviet faith in Might being Right. All three countries had, after many vicissitudes, become part of Imperial Russia at various dates in the eighteenth century. In 1918 they separately declared their independence. The inhabitants of these states, unlike the Ukrainians, are not Slavs and they were all superior to the Russians in their agricultural and economic development, as well as their general cultural level. The peasants and the workers had everything to lose and nothing to gain by being sovietized.

ernments, but mostly we had to find new people.[24] We proceeded with the sovietization process more gradually than we had in the Ukraine and Belorussia. First, governments were created that were well disposed toward the Soviet Union, and local Communist Parties were granted legal status. Then progressive forces began to promote friendship with the Soviet Union among the masses. After a certain amount of time, the Baltic peoples made known their desire to become part of the Soviet Union. The establishment of Soviet rule was accomplished by democratic methods and in observance of the required judicial formalities.[25]

The Soviet people welcomed the entrance of the Baltic states into the Soviet Union with the same enthusiasm that we had welcomed the unification of the Ukraine and Belorussia. These annexations were triumphs transcending differences in nationality.

We all believed unquestioningly in the wisdom of Stalin's leadership. We glorified him for his foresight in protecting the security of our country. We had faith in his ability to assure the impregnability of our borders. It was no small thing that we had pushed west the border of the Soviet Ukraine and also secured a new access to the Baltic Sea. Before this we had only a narrow outlet through the Gulf of Finland, and now we had a wide coastal frontier. The way we looked at it, if a full-scale war broke out and if England, France, or Germany tried to launch an invasion against us, they might have tried to use the territory of Lithuania, Latvia, and Estonia as a staging area. So the annexation of the Baltic states greatly improved our defenses. This was of major importance because at that time our economy and our industry were weak, and we were encircled by the hostile — and superior — forces of the bourgeois imperialist camp.

---

24. Many did indeed flee. Others were not so lucky. It has been estimated that between the Soviet annexation and the German invasion, over 170,000 individuals were arrested, put into cattle trucks, and deported to Siberia. The list of categories to be deported, which included in principle almost everyone who was not a manual worker or a peasant or a professing Communist, was drawn up, seven months before the occupation, by I. A. Serov of the NKVD and embodied in the notorious Order No. 001223 of October 11, 1939, signed by Serov — who, almost immediately afterward joined Khrushchev in the Ukraine and put into effect the same procedure of arrests and deportations, but on a much enlarged scale.

25. A different way of putting it is to say that the puppet governments established by the Soviet overlord (Andrei Zhdanov was to the Baltic States what Khrushchev was to the Polish Ukraine) were instructed by Moscow to apply for the incorporation of their states into the Soviet Union — and obeyed.

The Winter War with Finland

*Khrushchev's story of the notorious Winter War of 1939–40, accords
fairly closely with the established facts. The best and fullest account of
the negotiations whereby Stalin tried to persuade the Finns to surrender part of Karelia in the interests of the security of Leningrad is in
Vaino Tanner's own book,* The Winter War. *Although Tanner was the
implacable opponent of Soviet expansion, he makes it plain that Stalin
was reluctant in the extreme to use force and was genuinely surprised
when the Finns would not give in to his demands. Once he decided
that force must be used, he expected the Finns to surrender at once,
and the old Finnish Bolshevik, Kuusinen, was groomed to take over
the government of the occupied territory — in effect a Finnish Quisling. As all the world knows, it did not work out like that. Marshal
Mannerheim and the Finns put up a heroic resistance and humiliated
the Red Army in its pride. It was not until Voroshilov had been superseded by Marshal Timoshenko, who brought the whole vast weight
of the Red Army to bear, that the Finns finally surrendered. It was a
traumatic experience for the Russians. After the Nazi invasion of the
Soviet Union in June, 1941, the Finns were compelled to yield to Hitler's demands and fight on the German side. It is true that after the defeat of Hitler Stalin could have taken the whole of Finland. Khrushchev's remarks about Stalin in this context are fair. Finland, apart
from Karelia, was not necessary to the Soviet Union. Further, the Russians are uncomfortable with the Finns, who make awkward subjects.
At the same time, Finland was isolated, and in the event of a major war
in Europe, could be knocked out with ease.*

As we became increasingly concerned about protecting our defenses
against attack from the north, the question of Finland arose. We had to
guarantee the security of Leningrad, which was within artillery range
of the Finnish border and could easily have been shelled from Finnish
territory. Moreover, the Finnish government was following policies
hostile to the Soviet Union. It was demonstratively flirting with Hitlerite Germany. The Finnish commander in chief, Carl Mannerheim, was

a former tsarist general and a sworn enemy of the Soviet Union.[26] Vaino Tanner was an old Social Democrat, but he remained an irreconcilable foe of our Marxist-Leninist ideology until the end of his days.[27] Consequently, Finland represented a real threat to us because its territory could be used by more powerful governments; and it was therefore sensible, indeed crucial, for the Soviet State to take steps to protect Leningrad.

First we opened negotiations with Finland in order to come to some kind of diplomatic agreement. These talks took place while I was in the Ukraine. We wanted the Finns to give up a certain amount of territory and to move the border farther away from Leningrad. This would have satisfied our need to protect the safety of Leningrad. The Finns refused to accept our conditions, so we were left with no choice but to decide the question by war.

Whenever I came to Moscow from Kiev, Stalin almost always summoned me. Occasionally I found him alone when I went to see him. It was always easier to exchange opinions with him candidly if we were alone. But much more often than not, Stalin had Molotov, Voroshilov, Kaganovich, and sometimes Zhdanov with him when I called on him. Zhdanov was the First Secretary of the Leningrad Regional Committee. Mikoyan and Beria were often there, too. One day when I came to Moscow, Stalin invited me to his apartment for dinner. He told me Molotov and Kuusinen would be there. Kuusinen was then attached to the Comintern.

When I arrived at Stalin's apartment in the Kremlin, I had the feeling that Stalin, Molotov, and Kuusinen were continuing an earlier conversation about Finland. Apparently they had already decided to present Finland with an ultimatum. It had been agreed that Kuusinen would head the government of a new Karelo-Finnish SSR. Up to that time, Karelia had been an autonomous republic annexed to the Russian

26. Marshal C. G. E. von Mannerheim was Chairman of the Finnish Defense Council when war was threatened. He was responsible for the Mannerheim line, the celebrated fortifications in depth against which the Russians beat themselves for so long in vain.

27. Vaino Tanner had been Prime Minister of Finland from 1926–27. It was he who had to negotiate with the Russians on three successive visits to Moscow in the autumn of 1939 in an effort to reach an accommodation with Stalin. He became foreign minister in the war government and subsequently the grand old man of Finnish politics. He was the bête noire of the Soviet leadership, not only because he was hated as a Social Democrat (Communists hate and fear all other kinds of Socialists far more than they hate and fear Conservatives), but also because he understood them inside out, their strength and their weakness.

Federation. Now Karelia was to be made a Union Republic. The consensus of the group was that the Finns should be given one last chance to accept the territorial demands which they had already rejected during the unsuccessful negotiations. If they didn't yield to our ultimatum, we would take military action. This was Stalin's idea. Naturally I didn't oppose him. Besides, in this case I agreed that it was the right thing to do. All we had to do was raise our voice a little bit, and the Finns would obey. If that didn't work, we could fire one shot and the Finns would put up their hands and surrender. Or so we thought. When I arrived at the apartment, Stalin was saying, "Let's get started today."

We sat around for a long time. The hour of the ultimatum had already been set. After the prescribed time had elapsed, Artillery Marshal Kulik was dispatched to supervise the bombardment of the Finnish border.[28] We waited to see what would happen. Stalin was confident. None of us thought there would be a war. We were sure that the Finns would accept our demands without forcing us to go to war. I repeat: our only goal was to protect our security in the North. Compared with our own vast territorial and natural resources, Finland had little to offer us in the way of land and forests. Our sole consideration was security — Leningrad was in danger.

Suddenly there was a telephone call. We had fired our salvo, and the Finns had replied with artillery fire of their own. De facto, the war had begun. There is, of course, another version of the facts: it's said that the Finns started shooting first and that we were compelled to shoot back. It's always like that when people start a war. They say, "You fired the first shot," or "You slapped me first, and I'm only hitting back." There was once a ritual which you sometimes see in opera: someone throws down a glove to challenge someone else to a duel; if the glove is picked up, it means the challenge is accepted. Perhaps that's how it was done in the old days, but in our time it's not always so clear-cut who starts a war.

There's some question about whether we had any legal or moral right for our actions against Finland. Of course we didn't have any legal right. As far as morality was concerned, our desire to protect ourselves was ample justification in our own eyes.

28. Marshal Kulik was an NKVD general notorious for his stupidity, brutality, incompetence, and corruptness. As Khrushchev later notes, Stalin's attachment to him was to cost the Soviet Union dearly in the early days of the German invasion.

A few days after the war began, I left for the Ukraine. Like everyone else I was confident that our advantage would prove immeasurable and that our dispute with the Finns would be solved quickly, without many casualties for us. So we thought, and so we hoped. But the history of that conflict turned out very differently.

The war dragged on stubbornly. The Finns turned out to be good warriors. They had organized their defenses brilliantly along the Mannerheim Line on the Karelian isthmus, and they thwarted our attempt to push through this strategically important passage. We soon realized we had bitten off more than we could chew. We found ourselves faced with good steel-reinforced fortifications and effectively deployed artillery. The Mannerheim Line was impregnable. Our casualties mounted alarmingly. In the winter it was decided to bypass the Karelian isthmus and to strike a blow from Lake Ladoga to the north where there were no fortifications. But when we tried to strike from the rear, we found ourselves in an even more difficult situation than before. The Finns, who are a people of the North and very athletic, can ski almost before they can walk. Our army encountered very mobile ski troops armed with automatic high-velocity rifles. We tried to put our own troops on skis, too, but it wasn't easy for ordinary, untrained Red Army soldiers to fight on skis. We started intensively to recruit professional sportsmen. There weren't many around. We had to bring them from Moscow and the Ukraine as well as from Leningrad. We gave them a splendid send-off. Everyone was confident that our sportsmen would return victorious, and they left in high spirits. Poor fellows, they were ripped to shreds. I don't know how many came back alive.

This was a terrible time — terrible because of our losses, and even more terrible in the wider perspective. The Germans were watching with undisguised glee as we took a drubbing from the Finns.

Our navy was engaged against the Finnish fleet. You wouldn't have thought that the Finns would have the advantage at sea, but our navy couldn't do anything right. I remember hearing when I was at Stalin's in Moscow that one of our submarines had been unable to sink a Swedish merchant vessel which it had mistaken for a Finnish ship. The Germans observed this incident and gave us a teasing pinch by offering their assistance: "Are things that bad? You can't even sink an unarmed ship? Maybe you need some help from us?" You can imagine how painful this was to us. Hitler was letting us know that he recognized our helplessness and was gloating over it.

I recall how Stalin spoke with bitterness and sadness about the way the war was going: "The snows are deep. Our troops are on the march. There are many Ukrainians in the units. At first they're full of spirit, saying, 'Where are those Finns? Let us at them!' Suddenly there's a burst of automatic fire, and our men fall to the ground."

The Finns used the following tactic for fighting in the forest. They would climb up into the fir trees and shoot our men at point-blank range when they came along on patrol. Covered by branches and with white cloaks over their uniforms, the Finns were completely invisible. The Ukrainian troops called the Finns "cuckoos" because of the way they perched in the trees. There was a special campaign waged against these cuckoos. But it took time, and meanwhile we lost a lot of blood.

Stalin was furious with the military, and with Voroshilov — justifiably, in my opinion. Voroshilov had held the post of People's Commissar of Defense for many years. He had been vaunted as our top marksman in order to lull the people into thinking that the country's defenses were in capable hands. Voroshilov deserved to bear the brunt of the blame for the way the Finnish war was going, but he wasn't the only guilty party. He blamed the mishandling of the war on faulty intelligence.

I remember once at the Nearby Dacha, Stalin jumped up in a white-hot rage and started to berate Voroshilov. Voroshilov was also boiling mad. He leaped up, turned red, and hurled Stalin's accusations back into his face. "You have yourself to blame for all this!" shouted Voroshilov. "You're the one who annihilated the Old Guard of the army; you had our best generals killed!" Stalin rebuffed him, and at that, Voroshilov picked up a platter with a roast suckling pig on it and smashed it on the table. It was the only time in my life I ever witnessed such an outburst. Voroshilov ended up being relieved of his duties as People's Commissar of Defense. For a long time afterward he was kept around as a whipping boy.[29]

Marshal Timoshenko, who was commander of the Kiev Military District, came to me in Kiev and said, "I've been summoned to Moscow. I'll almost certainly be going to the Finnish Front." [30] He was put in charge of our troops on the Karelian isthmus, replacing Meretskov. Our

29. See Appendix 3 for Voroshilov's biography. The incident of the suckling pig is here revealed for the first time.
30. Marshal Semyon Timoshenko was to return to Kiev after smashing the Finnish defenses and winning the war. His close association with Khrushchev was to continue in war as well as in peace.

army had learned its lesson. It was decided not to circle around and strike from the rear but to hit frontally, to crush the Finnish fortifications on the Karelian isthmus. You may rightly wonder why this strategy of an all-out frontal strike wasn't devised much earlier. In any case, the necessary artillery, air power, and infantry were concentrated for the strike. The Finnish pillboxes were wiped out. Nothing was left standing in front of our artillery.

The air force played its part in the strike, too. I remember Stalin saying, very typically, "Our air force has been called into action. The assignment is to demolish the Finnish supply lines to the Front, knock the railroads out of commission, bomb the bridges, and strafe the locomotives. Many bridges have been destroyed. Many trains have been crippled. The Finns have only their skis left. Finns can never be without their skis. Their supply of skis never runs out."

Finland called for a truce. Negotiations began. We agreed on the terms for peace and signed a treaty. The Finns pulled back about fifteen kilometers from Leningrad and gave us a base on the Hangö Peninsula.

And so the war with Finland ended. We started to analyze the reasons why we were so badly prepared and why the war had cost us so dearly. I'd say we lost as many as a million lives. Timoshenko told me that faulty intelligence hadn't been to blame after all. In fact, it was learned that our intelligence service had known about the Finnish defenses all along. The pillboxes and artillery batteries of the Mannerheim line had even been drawn on our intelligence maps before the war. The trouble was that no intelligence officers had been consulted when our first strike was planned. I can't imagine how this kind of stupidity was permitted. After all, it's a cardinal rule that a military operation should be based on a careful study of the region where it will be conducted and that strategists should cooperate closely with the intelligence service. If we had only deployed our forces against the Finns in the way even a child could have figured by looking at a map, things would have turned out differently for both the Soviet Union and Finland.

Our assumption that the government of Finland would stop at nothing and would put its territory at the disposal of our enemies was justified by later events. Even before Hitler invaded the USSR, we found out that he was amassing his troops in Finland. It could be argued that the Finns let him do this because they were furious at us and wanted to get back what they had lost in the 1940–41 war. Be that as it may, the fact remains that Leningrad had been endangered, and we had had no choice but to solve the problem by resorting to military means.

It would be wrong to claim that Stalin started the war intending to seize Finland. You might ask, why didn't we seize Finland during World War II, when the Finnish army was virtually wiped out? Stalin showed statesmanly wisdom here. He knew that the territory of Finland wasn't relevant to the basic needs of the world proletarian Revolution. Therefore when we signed a treaty with the Finns during World War II, just ending the war itself was more profitable for us than an occupation would have been. Finland's cessation of hostilities set a good example for other satellites of Hitlerite Germany, and it also made good marks for us with the Finnish people.[31]

The Winter War with Finland showed us our very serious weaknesses. It also exposed our weaknesses to Hitler. It doesn't take much imagination to guess what Hitler must have concluded after he watched us try to wage war against the Finns: "The Soviet Union has barely managed to handle a country that we could have disposed of in a few hours. What would be left of the Russians if we attacked them with our best equipment and masses of our best-trained, best-organized troops?" In short, our miserable conduct of the Finnish campaign encouraged Hitler in his plans for the blitzkrieg, his Operation Barbarossa.

In our war against the Finns we had an opportunity to choose the time and the place. We outnumbered our enemy, and we had all the time in the world to prepare for our operation. Yet even in these most favorable conditions it was only after great difficulty and enormous losses that we were finally able to win. A victory at such a cost was actually a moral defeat.

Our people never knew that we had suffered a moral defeat, of course, because they were never told the truth. Quite the contrary. When the Finnish war ended, our country was told, "Let the trumpets of victory sound!"[32]

But the seeds of doubt had been sown. The war against the Finns

31. But the Russians also imposed what they believed to be crushing reparations. Instead of subsiding into self-pity the Finns grimly set themselves to pay them off in the shortest possible time, and in so doing, at the cost of much self-sacrifice, greatly enlarged their industrial capacity, above all in shipbuilding.

32. A revealing insight into the capacity of the Soviet leadership to conceal the truth from the people.

was a dark hour for our army, whose slogan of invincibility was, "In case there's a war tomorrow, we're ready for the march today!"

The Red Army on the Eve of Barbarossa

In discussing the unpreparedness of the Red Army for war, Khrushchev is at pains to insist that, even though he was a member of the Politbureau, the supreme policy-making body, he could not have been expected to know that the vaunted Red Army was incompetently led and insufficiently equipped when the whole weight of Soviet industry had been concentrated on it for more than a decade. In the light of Stalin's way of running his government this seems reasonable enough. Khrushchev was concerned wholly with the civilian government of the Ukraine. He would have relied on his own Front commander to secure the defenses of the Ukraine, and he would have assumed that Stalin and Voroshilov (Minister of Defense) between them, would have properly organized the army as a whole and the supply of armaments and munitions. There was clearly no regular cabinet in which Khrushchev could have cross-examined the Minister of Defense, even had he been equipped to do so, which he was not. Vast expenditure was lavished on the army; maneuvers and parades were impressive in the extreme. But even Khrushchev knew that the greater part of the army high command had been liquidated by Stalin and Yezhov in 1937, though he may not have realized that some forty thousand officers of lesser rank had also been purged. He must have been alarmed by the terrible showing put up by the Red Army against the Finns. And it seems almost inconceivable that he was never warned by his military opposite number in Kiev — first, Timoshenko, then Zhukov — that there were sad deficiencies. Indeed, Timoshenko himself had been denounced as an enemy of the people and would have been shot in 1938 but for Khrushchev's personal intervention.

ALL of us — and Stalin first and foremost — sensed in our victory a defeat by the Finns. It was a dangerous defeat because it encouraged our enemies' conviction that the Soviet Union was a colossus with feet of clay. But it wasn't enough just to admit our defeat and to criticize ourselves for our mishandling of the war against Finland. Nor was it enough just to sack Voroshilov and to appoint a new People's Commissar of Defense. We had to draw some lessons for the immediate future from what had happened. We had to get a deeper and wider grasp on what had gone wrong in our preparation for the Finnish campaign. We had to locate and liquidate the flaws in our organization which had caused our defeat. We had to elevate the fighting potential of the Soviet Army. And this meant, above all, elevating the quality of leadership in our military command.

I don't know what had weakened our army more — our shortage of armaments or the inadequacy of our commanders. Undoubtedly both factors were very important. On the one hand, our military parades and troop maneuvers played a positive role in that they bolstered the morale of our people. On the other hand they played a negative role in that they covered up the faults of our army and deluded us into thinking we were safe. We should have reexamined our army, particularly our mechanized units, after the Finnish war; and we should have begun much earlier to convert our industry to our wartime needs. We didn't know how much time we had left before the enemy would attack, yet there were still many things left undone right up to the day the war began. This was an inexcusable state of affairs, and we paid for it in land and blood. The preparation for war involves more than just mapping out strategies. The foundation of military preparedness is arms production. This means airplanes, artillery, tanks, rifles, engineering equipment, chemical and bacteriological weapons — in short, all the means necessary to repulse an attack and to crush the enemy.

Part of the problem was that Stalin tried to supervise our manufacturing of munitions and mechanized equipment all by himself, with the result that no one really knew what state our arsenal was in. For example, I remember that in 1941 Stalin instructed me to look into the possibility of mounting diesel engines on airplanes. His idea was that since diesels require less fuel, they would increase the range of bombers. He told me that diesel engines were being manufactured at the Kharkov locomotive factory. Naturally I knew this factory, but this was the first I'd heard about diesels being made there. A special permit was required to get in, and Stalin made sure that nobody except those directly involved in the project went poking his nose into the factory. Even I, the First Secretary of the Ukrainian Central Committee, had known nothing of these powerful diesel engines which were being built right there in Kharkov. I didn't have time to conclude whether the engines could be mounted on bombers or not, but they did prove very effective when used to power our T-34 tanks. Unfortunately, we didn't have enough of these tanks built by the time the war broke out.

We had a terrible shortage of arms of all kinds in the first months of the war. I was a member of the Politbureau and part of Stalin's ruling circle, but I still had no way of knowing that we were woefully lacking in rifles and machine guns, not to mention tanks and heavy artillery. I couldn't imagine that we would be unprepared in such an elementary respect. Even the tsar, when he went to war against Germany in 1914, had a larger supply of rifles than we had the day after Hitler invaded. And our economic potential was incomparably higher than the tsarist government's, so we had no excuse.

I put the principal blame on Voroshilov. Until he was sacked during the Finnish war, the responsibility for the state of our armed forces was primarily his. We had set aside huge financial resources for arms, and I never heard of a single instance when Stalin refused a request for funds. Voroshilov simply didn't make the necessary requests. His negligence was criminal. His subordinates must have reported to him how bad things were, but these reports rolled off him like water off a duck's back. Oblivious of his responsibilities, he just smiled for the photographers and strutted about in front of the movie cameras. People used to say that Voroshilov spent more time posing in Gerasimov's studio than he did attending to his job at the Commissariat of Defense.[33] He also spent a lot of time in the theater world. He made quite a name for himself as a connoisseur and critic of opera. I remember once in my presence the name of some opera singer came up, and Voroshilov's wife, letting her eyes drop, remarked, "Kliment Efremovich doesn't hold a particularly high opinion of her." Voroshilov used to fancy himself quite a singer, even after his hearing started to go bad. He sang pretty well in my opinion. Just like Stalin, he'd once been in a church choir.

In short, Voroshilov was much more interested in showing off his impressive military bearing at public celebrations than he was in supervising arms procurement and organizing troop deployments. While Gamarnik, Tukhachevsky, and the other members of the Old Guard were

---

33. Gerasimov was president of the Soviet Academy of Arts and virtually Stalin's court painter. An establishment figure, he was academic in the worst sense, and the scourge of all Soviet painters with any pretensions to originality.

still around, before they were eliminated in 1937, the administrative and political business of the People's Commissariat of Defense went on without Voroshilov altogether.[34]

For his part, Stalin very much overestimated the preparedness of our army. Like so many others, he was under the spell of films showing our parades and troop maneuvers. He didn't see things as they were in real life. He rarely left Moscow. In fact, he rarely left the Kremlin except to go to his dacha or to his vacation retreat in Sochi. He got all his information from Voroshilov, who was out of touch with reality himself.

The reasons for the weakness of the military command are well known. Our best commanders were eliminated as enemies of the people. In this regard, weighing their guilt, I would say Stalin was more to blame than Voroshilov. Voroshilov sometimes defended the accused generals and argued with Stalin, but other times he deliberately goaded Stalin on. There's not much to be said about the other members of the Politbureau. Molotov stood closest to Stalin in decision-making, and even though the supervision of the military command wasn't part of Molotov's domain, he too sometimes fanned Stalin's fury against the Old Guard. However, Molotov had no responsibility in matters of arms supply.

There's no question that we would have repulsed the fascist invasion much more easily if the upper echelons of the Red Army command hadn't been wiped out. They had been men of considerable expertise and experience. Many of them had graduated from military academies and had gone through the Civil War. They were ready to discharge their soldierly duties for the sake of their Homeland, but they never had a chance. After they were eliminated, we had to appoint new commanders. The military staff underwent two, three, even four changes of command. Men who had earlier occupied third- and fourth-rank positions were promoted to the top after those in the first and second ranks were shot.

Most of the people promoted were honest and loyal, but they needed experience, and they had to acquire this experience in the war with Hitlerite Germany. Their initiation cost our people a tremendous loss of life, and it cost our country terrible ruin.

In 1940, when Timoshenko was made People's Commissar of Defense, Zhukov took his place as commander of the Kiev Military Dis-

34. This is fair comment. Voroshilov deserved all Khrushchev's strictures.

Voroshilov

trict.[35] Zhukov was more than satisfactory as Timoshenko's replacement. He was a talented organizer and a strong leader. He was to prove his mettle in the war. I still have great respect for him as a commander, despite our subsequent parting of the ways. He didn't correctly understand his role as Minister of Defense, and we were compelled to take action against him in order to prevent him from going through with certain schemes which he had concocted. But even then I valued him highly as a soldier, and I don't retreat one step today from my high evaluation of him. Nor did I disguise my admiration for Zhukov after the war when he fell out of favor with Stalin.[36]

At the end of 1940 or the beginning of 1941 Comrade Zhukov was transferred from Kiev to Moscow, where he worked in the Operational Department of General Headquarters. He was replaced in Kiev by Kirponos. Kirponos was typical of the well-intentioned but inexperienced commanders who were promoted to fill the vacuum left by the purge of the Red Army high command. Kirponos was made commander of the Kiev Military District simply because there was no one else to appoint. He had been given a division during the Finnish campaign, in which he had distinguished himself and earned the title Hero of the Soviet Union. But he wasn't prepared for the responsibility of the Kiev command.[37]

The Kiev Military District was situated directly in the path of Hitler's invasion. It had all the most favorable topographical conditions for a mechanized offensive. The roads were good, and there were hardly any swamps. In order to goad Hitler into attacking us, the foreign bourgeois press used to say that the area between Poland and Kiev was a veritable "tankodrome," where Hitler could put his tanks on display and show the world what he could do.

35. Zhukov, in fact, after brilliant operations against the Japanese in the Far East, had been appointed chief of staff to Timoshenko, who was then commanding the Kiev Military District, before the Finnish war. When Timoshenko was called in as commander in chief to smash the Finnish resistance, Zhukov went with him as his chief of staff, returning when the war was over to succeed Timoshenko in Kiev. He was promoted to the rank of army general in June, 1940, and became Deputy Minister of Defense and chief of General Staff in February, 1941, four months before the German invasion.

36. See Appendix 3 for Zhukov's further career.

37. Colonel General M. P. Kirponos, a good divisional general, was promoted above his powers as a result of the purges. He took over the Kiev Military District from Zhukov when the latter went to the Ministry of Defense. He thus found himself, four months later, in the direct path of the advancing Germans. Khrushchev's comments are fair. But he fought very bravely. In fact this front was better supplied and equipped than others.

Stalin thought Kirponos would be suitable for the Kiev command from the standpoint of honesty and devotion, and he was right. But Kirponos didn't have the necessary experience to direct such a huge number of troops. And moreover, the ill-preparedness of our country's defenses was sorely reflected in the Kiev Military District, which was supposed to guard the most dangerously exposed of our borders.

On the basis of my own observations, which I admit were fairly infrequent, it seemed to me that the Commissariat of Defense started to function better once Marshal Timoshenko took charge. I had admired Timoshenko ever since he and I had worked together in the Kiev Military District, where he was commander and I was a member of the Military Council. He was a good man and a good soldier. I got to know him even better during our liberation of Bessarabia from the Rumanian occupation in 1940.[38] I took an active part in the operation, which stemmed from our treaty with the Germans and from our desire to regain our historical rights, which had been violated by the Rumanian monarchy after the October Revolution. By this time Timoshenko was already People's Commissar of Defense. I once accompanied him on an airplane trip deep into Bessarabia behind Rumanian lines to see his relatives in the village of Furmanka where he had grown up. He hadn't been back since he was called up at the beginning of World War I. We landed in a field near Furmanka and were given a warm welcome by the villagers. Marshal Timoshenko was treated like a returning hero. I spent the night in a shed near his brother's house, while Timoshenko stayed up all night drinking wine and talking about old times with his brother and sister and his friends. Timoshenko was certainly an improvement over Voroshilov as Commissar of Defense.

Unfortunately, men like Timoshenko and Zhukov were exceptions. After the annihilation of the Old Guard, men like Mekhlis, Shchadenko and Kulik came in, and the Commissariat of Defense became like a kennel of mad dogs.[39] Once Comrade Timoshenko pulled me by the sleeve into a session of the Defense Council. He wanted me to see how

38. Bessarabia, acquired by Russia at the Congress of Berlin in 1878, went to Rumania after World War I, having first declared its independence and appealed to Rumania for help against the Bolsheviks. By agreement with Hitler, Stalin recovered it for the Soviet Union in 1940 and proceeded to sovietize it.

39. Shchadenko and Kulik were "political" generals of extreme incompetence and unpleasantness appointed by Voroshilov. Both were active in purging the Red Army in 1937. Kulik was promoted to marshal in 1940 and did all he could to lose Leningrad to the Germans. Zhukov arrived to take over in the nick of time.

these people whom he had to work with were tearing at each other's throats. Mekhlis was one of the worst.[40] He had a particularly strong influence on Stalin. He often overstepped the bounds of his office as Chief of the Political Directorate of the Red Army. Ever since Stalin had appointed him to replace Bukharin as the editor of *Pravda,* Mekhlis had been one of Stalin's right-hand men. I had once been on very good terms with him. Our friendship had grown from the soil of our common efforts in the struggle against the rightists back in 1929–30. He had given me a lot of help when I was Secretary of the Party organization at the Industrial Academy. But in the intervening years we had drifted apart. By the time he took over as Chief of the Political Directorate I considered him a nitwit, and I was appalled that someone like him could enjoy Stalin's unbounded confidence. Mekhlis often gave Stalin advice on military matters, and Stalin usually listened to him. Mekhlis's influence did the army and the country no good at all; it contributed to the inexcusably shabby state of our defenses on the eve of the war.

It's a credit to our people and our army that we survived the early disasters of the war and, in the end, prevailed. We learned from our mistakes and finally drove back the enemy and crushed him on his own ground. But at what a price! Perhaps even if Stalin hadn't eliminated our best generals, the war would still have come. But it wouldn't have cost us anywhere near as much as it cost under "Our Dear Father, the Great Genius."

40. L. Z. Mekhlis was another "political" general of the kind favored by Stalin. There is no means of determining whether he caused more death and suffering by deliberate action in the purge years and thereafter or by sheer incompetence during the war.

6

The Great Patriotic War

The Darkest Hours

Khrushchev's account of the war years, though full of revealing anecdotes and close-up views of the high command in action, is essentially impressionistic. His primary concern is evidently to show up Stalin's failures and to present himself as the man on the spot, working with the field commanders, while his colleagues sat in Moscow and allowed the fighting generals to be frustrated, obstructed, intrigued against, and starved of supplies by the "politicals." Khrushchev was, of course, a "political" himself, but with his practical nature and passion for getting things done he seems very soon to have found himself far more at home with the professional soldiers than with his colleagues in Moscow, the NKVD generals, and his fellow political advisors — and to have taken their side against the Kremlin. Certainly, throughout the greater part of the war he was indeed much nearer the guns than any other member of the Politbureau, with the exception of Zhdanov in Leningrad. As the Germans moved into the Ukraine, Khrushchev was transformed overnight from the supreme ruler, under Stalin, of that vast, rich land, the granary of the Soviet Union and its chief industrial base, into the Politbureau's representative at Front headquarters. Very soon the Front was torn to ribbons and he had the bitterness of seeing his great province swiftly overrun by the German armor, largely owing to the abject failure of one of Voroshilov's cronies, Marshal Budyonny, the almost unbelievably inept relic of the Civil War days, who was to lead a million men to total and unnecessary disaster, losing Kiev and Kharkov. Khrushchev's anecdotes and comments afford vivid glimpses of the confusion, shame, and heroism of those early days, when Stalin

was reduced to a state of breakdown while the Germans were wiping
out whole armies in vast encirclements, moving in on Leningrad and
Moscow, and overrunning the Ukraine.

DURING the years when I held a high position in the Government as
First Secretary of the Central Committee and Chairman of the
Council of Ministers, I frequently warned our military men to approach the writing of war memoirs very cautiously. I've always found
that you can't expect an objective analysis of a battle from someone
who actually took part in it. However, as a member of the Military
Council and a Politbureau representative on various fronts during the
course of the war, I think I can illuminate what happened in a number
of key operations.

Let me explain what the beginning of the war looked like from my
perspective, and also let me review the roles played by some of the
generals and government figures with whom I had to deal.

I was in Moscow just before the war broke out. I was detained there
for a long time and just sat around with nothing to do. Stalin kept telling me, "Look, what's the rush on getting back to the Ukraine? Give
them a chance to do without you for a while down there in Kiev. You
don't need to leave yet." I didn't see any sense in sticking around Moscow. I certainly wasn't learning anything new from Stalin. There was
just one long dinner after another. I'd already begun to despise those
dinners. They gave me a chance to watch Stalin closely, and I didn't
like what I saw. He'd obviously lost all confidence in the ability of our
army to put up a fight. It was as though he'd thrown up his hands in
despair and given up after Hitler crushed the French army and occupied Paris. As I've said, I was with Stalin when we heard about the
capitulation of France. He let fly with some choice Russian curses
and said that now Hitler was sure to beat our brains in.[1]

This kind of talk wasn't doing me any good at all. I kept trying to
get permission from him to return to Kiev. Finally I asked him outright,
"Comrade Stalin, war could break out any hour now, and it would be
very bad if I were caught here in Moscow or in transit when it starts.
I'd better leave right away and return to Kiev."

1. This confirms other reports of Stalin's behavior on the eve of the war. See especially *The Siege of Leningrad* by E. Harrison Salisbury.

"Yes, I guess that's true. You'd better leave." His answer confirmed what I'd suspected: that he hadn't the slightest idea why he'd been detaining me in Moscow. He knew my proper place was in Kiev. He had kept me around simply because he needed to have company, especially when he was afraid. He couldn't stand being alone.

The next morning I returned to Kiev and went straight to the Ukrainian Central Committee office to pick up the latest information. That evening I went home. At ten or eleven o'clock that night I got a call from headquarters asking me to come back to the Central Committee office to read a dispatch that had just been received from Moscow. A covering letter said that as First Secretary of the Ukrainian Party I should personally acquaint myself with the contents of the dispatch. I went over to the Central Committee office and found that the message from Moscow was cause for considerable alarm. It was a warning that we should be ready for war within the next few days or even hours.

Then we got a call from our command post at Ternopol [2] informing us that a soldier had just defected to our side from the German front lines; he claimed that Germany was going to attack the Soviet Union the next morning at three o'clock. This information seemed to confirm the dispatch we had received from Moscow. We interrogated the German soldier thoroughly, and what he said appeared to make sense. When asked how he knew that the Germans were going to attack the next day, he said he and the other troops had been issued three days' rations. And why would the attack come at three o'clock in the morning? Because, he explained, the Germans always attacked early in the morning. He said he had defected because he was a Communist, an antifascist, and an opponent of Hitler's military adventurism. We tended to believe him.

Instead of returning home that night, I waited till three o'clock to see what would happen. Sure enough, just as dawn began to break, we got word that the German artillery had opened fire. When the enemy first launched the invasion, we received orders from Moscow not to shoot back. Our leaders issued this strange command because they thought that possibly the artillery fire was a provocation on the part of some German field commander acting independently of Hitler. In other words, Stalin was so afraid of war that even when the Germans tried to take us by surprise and wipe out our resistance, Stalin convinced him-

2. Ternopol, east of Lvov, had recently been acquired by the Soviet occupation of eastern Poland.

self that Hitler would keep his word and wouldn't really attack us.[3]

But within hours our troops met the German invaders in battle and repulsed their first strike. By daylight we got word from the Military District headquarters that German planes were approaching Kiev. Soon they were over the city, bombing the airfield. Fires broke out in the hangars, but fortunately there were no planes there at the time. All our planes had been concentrated along the border under camouflage nets. Our air force, tanks, artillery, and ammunition depots were largely unscathed by the enemy's first strike.

The situation quickly turned very bad, mostly because there was so little help forthcoming from Moscow. Shortly after the war started, during the German advance on Kiev, there was a great awakening of patriotism among the people. The workers from the "Lenin Forge" and other factories around Kiev came to the Central Committee in droves asking for rifles so that they could fight back against the invaders. I phoned Moscow to arrange for a shipment of weapons with which to arm these citizens who wanted to join the Front in support of Red Power. The only person I could get through to was Malenkov.

"Tell me," I said, "where can we get rifles? We've got factory workers here who want to join the ranks of the Red Army to fight the Germans, and we don't have anything to arm them with."

"You'd better give up any thought of getting rifles from us. The rifles in the civil defense organization here have all been sent to Leningrad."

"Then what are we supposed to fight with?"

"I don't know — pikes, swords, homemade weapons, anything you can make in your own factories."

"You mean we should fight tanks with spears?"

"You'll have to do the best you can. You can make fire bombs out of bottles of gasoline or kerosene and throw them at the tanks."

You can imagine my dismay and indignation when I heard Malenkov talking this way. Here we were, trying to hold back an invasion without rifles and machine guns, not to mention artillery or mechanized weapons! I didn't dare tell anyone what Malenkov had said to me. Who knows what the reaction would have been. I certainly couldn't tell the people how bad the situation was. But the people must have figured out on their own how woefully underequipped we were. And why were we so badly armed? Because of complacency in

3. Stalin was indeed for all practical purposes prostrated during the first weeks of the war.

the Commissariat of Defense and demoralization and defeatism in the leadership. These factors had kept us from building up our munitions industry and fortifying our borders. And now it was too late.

The Germans moved swiftly into the Ukraine, Belorussia, and the Russian Federation. Their occupation of the Ukraine deprived us of our mining and agricultural heartland. We lost the European part of the Soviet Union where our industry was concentrated. A large portion of our automotive production fell into enemy hands when the Germans moved into our industrial base around Moscow. Moscow and Leningrad were our political, military, and technological brain centers, and in 1941 Leningrad was besieged. We also lost Rostov, Voronezh, Stalingrad, and the northern Caucasus.

We were forced to evacuate our industry. Our people, particularly our engineers and technicians, undertook the mammoth task of moving our manufacturing equipment out of the enemy's reach so that we could go on with the production of tanks, artillery, mechanized weapons, rifles, machine guns, mines, and so on. This required a superhuman effort and total cooperation. Ultimately the evacuation of our industry paid off, and it enabled our army to drive the enemy out of our Homeland.

Once we were at war I had to argue with Stalin many times. Even though he could have blasted me with fire and water, I doggedly tried to persuade him to my point of view. Sometimes I succeeded. I found if I kept at him, he might come around to my way of seeing things. However, it was always very difficult to argue with him — and very dangerous.

After the successful conclusion of our operation outside Moscow in which we — that is, the Southwest Front — had taken part, I was called to Moscow to consult with Stalin. I found myself confronted with a new man. He was much changed from the way he'd been at the very beginning of the war. He had pulled himself together, straightened up, and was acting like a real soldier. He had also begun to think of himself as a great military strategist, which made it harder than ever to argue with him. He exhibited all the strong-willed determination of a heroic leader. But I knew what sort of a hero he was. I'd seen him when he had been paralyzed by his fear of Hitler, like a rabbit in front of a boa constrictor. And my opinion of him hadn't changed in the meantime. During the first part of the war, when things were going badly for us, I hadn't failed to notice that Stalin's signature never appeared on a single document or order. "High Command," "General Staff," or some other term was used, but never his name. This practice didn't change even after we repulsed the Germans outside of Moscow and Stalin began to regain his confidence. Directives continued to be issued from him without his signature. Sometimes they appeared over his title, "Commander in Chief," but never over his name. And this was no accident. Nothing that Stalin ever did was an accident. His every move was deliberate and calculated. Every step he ever took, good or bad, was measured carefully.

Here is another example of Stalin's refusal to accept direct responsibility for what was happening at the Front. Many of our generals who were taken prisoner during the German advance were declared traitors on Stalin's order, and their families were sent to Siberia. I remember this practice was applied to Muzychenko and Ponedelin and their families, and to Potapov, too. Only after Stalin's death were these people allowed to return. Muzychenko, Ponedelin, and Potapov were given posts in the Soviet Army after they came back from prison camp and were rehabilitated. In short, Stalin mistreated his generals very badly.[4]

The treatment of the rank-and-file troops and junior officers was no better. I remember we had a commander named Gordov, who was generally praised for his skill, his energy, and his courage. He was a puny man, but that didn't stop him from regularly beating up his officers and his men. Later I found out that Andrei Ivanovich Yeremenko once hit a member of the Military Council. It was perfectly acceptable, even expected, for a commander to discipline his subordinates with his fists.[5] When a commander reported to Stalin about someone's incompetence or mistake, Stalin used to ask, "Did you punch him in the snout? If he does something like that again, punch him right in the snout!"

Another thing that distressed me about Stalin was his dependence

4. The three generals mentioned were commanders of mechanized corps: Major General (tank troops) M. I. Potapov, Lieutenant General I. N. Muzychenko, and Major General P. G. Ponedelin, whose formations were among those to bear the brunt of the onslaught of Kleist's and Reichenau's tanks. They fought well, but were frittered away in useless counterattacks by Kirponos. Stalin's treatment of the families of officers taken prisoner is characteristic.

5. Characteristic also was the extremely frequent use of personal violence, up to and including shooting on the spot, on the part of senior officers against offending juniors, especially in the very early days of the war when the henchmen of Stalin, Voroshilov, and Beria still had senior commands. Even Zhukov was pretty rough. Later, after the army recovered from the purges, it was commanded increasingly by able and battle-seasoned officers and developed a more civilized tradition of its own.

on the Cheka for military intelligence. On the whole the Chekists who had Stalin's confidence were a fairly despicable lot. Take Sergienko for example. He was in the Central State Security administration in Moscow. He was a resourceful fellow. I learned from experience that he was also dishonest and treacherous. It happened like this: Early in the war when things were going badly for us, the commander and I had no choice but to evacuate our headquarters from Kiev to Brovari. Suddenly I got a telegram from Stalin unjustly accusing me of cowardice and threatening to take action against me. He accused me of intending to surrender Kiev. This was a filthy lie. I was sure that no one other than that villain Sergienko had put the idea in Stalin's head. I knew Stalin considered the Chekists beyond reproach and believed anything they told him. At the time, Sergienko was behind German lines. When the Germans surrounded Kiev, he remained at the enemy's rear and sneaked out of the encirclement disguised as a peasant.

After this incident I always regarded Sergienko with deep distrust. I knew he was capable of any slander as long as it would make him out to be a hero, no matter if it were at someone else's expense.[6] But history has vindicated me from Sergienko's slanderous accusation that we planned to surrender Kiev. We inflicted heavy losses on the Germans and drove back their attempt at a frontal assault. Kiev fell, not because it was abandoned by our troops who were defending it, but because of the pincer movement which the Germans executed from the north and south in the regions of Gomel and Kremenchug.

One of the most contemptible characters around Stalin during the war was Shcherbakov.[7] He was a poisonous snake. I once heard that when Gorky was chairman of the Writers' Union, Shcherbakov was attached to him as a secretary to deal with ideological matters so that Gorky could devote himself to operational matters. Gorky wasn't the

6. Nothing much is known about this Sergienko. He appears to have been an inferior Mekhlis, which suggests the lowest form of life. In those days the Chief Directorate of State Security was a department of the NKVD, with Beria as the People's Commissar at its head. His actions as here described were characteristic of the whole race of police generals or political commissars with the army.

7. A. S. Shcherbakov, member of the Politbureau, a Moscow Party chief and head of the armed forces Political Directorate (that is, chief commissar). Fat, spectacularly gross, treacherous, and drunken, he was very close to Stalin, and during the war many in Russia believed that he was a probable successor to Stalin. If he had a redeeming feature it has yet to be discovered. He died in 1945. He·was one of the men said to have been poisoned by the Kremlin doctors in the fabricated Doctors' Plot of 1953. He may well have been poisoned, but not by Dr. Vinogradov and his colleagues.

sort of person Shcherbakov could boss around and Shcherbakov ended up being transferred at Gorky's request.

One episode was characteristic of both Shcherbakov and Stalin. It happened in 1943. Aleksandr Petrovich Dovzhenko — a remarkable film director and an excellent journalist — wrote a scenario called "The Ukraine in Flames." Many of the scenes in it were based on articles he had written exposing the faults of the Red Army. Dovzhenko, who had a sharp mind and a sharp pen, was especially critical of the people responsible for the ill-preparedness of our army on the eve of the war. He sent the scenario to the Central Committee, where Malenkov and some of the other comrades read it. During one of my trips to Moscow, Stalin asked me if I'd read it. I said, yes, I had. Actually, I hadn't really sat down and read it, but Dovzhenko himself had read it to me during the German offensive of July, 1943. Naturally three fourths of my attention had been taken up by the enemy attack, and I hadn't been able to concentrate on the text of Dovzhenko's work. I explained this to Stalin. He said I was trying to weasel out of my responsibility for what had happened, and he started a blistering denunciation of Dovzhenko, criticizing him up and down, accusing him of Ukrainian nationalism and all kinds of other sins. At that time it was very fashionable to accuse Ukrainians of nationalism, regardless of whether there was any evidence for doing so. This practice had started during Kaganovich's term in the Ukraine. He was fond of saying that every Ukrainian is potentially a nationalist — which is, of course, nonsense.

Anyway, Stalin called a meeting to discuss Dovzhenko's scenario. Shcherbakov presented the case for the prosecution. He was obviously trying hard to fan Stalin's anger against Dovzhenko by harping on the charge that the film scenario was extremely nationalistic. Malenkov sat silently through this whole discussion, even though he had already given the scenario his blessing.

Stalin didn't let the matter drop there. He told me to convene a meeting of the Ukrainian Party and government leaders, including the Central Committee secretaries in charge of propaganda. He told us to prepare a self-critical resolution about the unsatisfactory state of affairs on the ideological front in the Ukraine. Then he called Dovzhenko himself onto the carpet and gave him a fierce dressing down. Dovzhenko was put on ice as an active man in the arts for a long time afterward.

This whole disgraceful affair was mostly the doing of Shcherbakov, who had wormed his way into Stalin's confidence and did everything he could to make life miserable for everyone else. It might sound as though I'm saying all this because I have some special grudge against Shcherbakov. That's not true. I've given Shcherbakov the evaluation he deserved, and he deserved the worst. But the main culprit was Stalin. It was Stalin who made the mischievous influence of people like Shcherbakov possible.

I would like now to say something about a few of the commanders I knew during the war. I spent a lot of time with a great many generals and had excellent relations with the vast majority of them. There were, of course, occasional conflicts. A certain amount of tension is unavoidable in wartime. People make mistakes or lose their tempers. After all, nobody's perfect. I'm no saint myself. Generally speaking, though, I was impressed by the men with whom I worked on the different fronts. We almost always found a common language. There were occasional disagreements, but I won't go into them here. The war is long since over, and the enemy is crushed. Many of the commanders in question have been decorated and honorably retired. There's no point in airing dirty linen at this point.

However, before speaking about the commanders who distinguished themselves in the war, I'd like to say something about Pavlov, who was blamed for the collapse of our resistance in Belorussia at the very beginning of the war.[8] I had always had my doubts about Pavlov, even before he was given the Belorussian command. I remember in 1940 watching him, when he was commander of our armored tank forces, test our new T-34 tanks in Kharkov. On the basis of a short conversation with him, I decided he was a man of very limited scope. Even though he had been a hero of the Spanish war, he struck me as being unprepared for a position of high responsibility. I decided to pass on to Stalin my doubts about Pavlov's abilities. I broached the subject with him very cautiously:

"Comrade Stalin, do you know Pavlov well?"

8. General D. G. Pavlov was regarded as the top Soviet tank expert on the eve of the war, but he made the same mistake about tanks that so many British generals made: he did not believe they could be used as the Germans so quickly showed they could be used (taught by Captain Lidell Hart) in armored formations to cut deeply into enemy territory. The way to use tanks, he thought, was in support of the infantry. Hence the terrible wastage of Soviet armor to no purpose in the early days of the war. Pavlov commanded the Belorussian Front, which was starved of troops and supplies and collapsed with catastrophic consequences.

"Yes, very well."

"I only spoke to him a few minutes, but frankly, he made a negative impression on me. He seems fairly limited. There's no question that he knows how to handle a tank, but I don't think he's suited to a command."

Stalin was obviously agitated. "How can you say that? You don't even know the man."

"I've already admitted that I don't know him very well."

"Well, I do. He's proved himself to my satisfaction as a tank commander in Spain."

"All right. I simply wanted to let you know that he didn't make a very good impression on me. I also want to pass on to you some of my doubts about Marshal Kulik. He's responsible for all our artillery. War is imminent, and I don't think he's up to the job."

Stalin was furious. "First you complain about Pavlov, and now you're complaining about Kulik. You don't even know Kulik. I know him from the Civil War, when he commanded the artillery at Tsaritsyn [Stalingrad]. He understands artillery."

"Comrade Stalin, I don't doubt that Kulik was a good artillery officer at Tsaritsyn, but how many cannons did you have there? Two or three? And now he's in charge of all the artillery in the country."

Stalin completely lost his temper with me. He told me to shut up and stop sticking my nose into things that weren't my business. This was what I had been afraid would happen. Stalin believed that the Red Army was his baby and that nobody else was competent to comment on it. However, events proved Stalin wrong and me right about both Pavlov and Kulik.

Stalin made Pavlov commander of the Belorussian Military District. I didn't even find out about the appointment until after the fact — which was also typical. Stalin hardly ever bothered to consult with members of the Politbureau. So Pavlov was entrusted with the military district that was right in the line of attack from the west, and he did nothing to prepare his troops for Hitler's invasion. In the first days of the war Pavlov's troops were routed and his air force was destroyed on the runways. Stalin had Pavlov, his chief of staff, and the local member of the Military Council court-martialed and shot. Stalin must have realized what a mistake it had been to give Pavlov the Belorussian command, but it was already too late. The front had fallen apart, and the Germans were driving deep into our country.

As for Kulik, he proved to be totally incompetent as a military leader. I remember in 1943 Vatutin and I listened to Kulik report to Shepilov, who was a member of the Military Council for the Vorenezh Front. His report was a complete travesty. Finally, at our urging, Stalin gave in and demoted Kulik from marshal to major general. After the war Kulik was arrested and shot.

Many years later, when Stalin's abuses of power were exposed at the Twentieth Party Congress, it was decided to rehabilitate Pavlov and the other generals who were court-martialed and executed in the first days of the war. I had some reservations about rehabilitating them; I knew that there had been legitimate grounds for court-martialing Pavlov and the others. But I also knew that Stalin was the real guilty party because he had given men like Pavlov their commands in the first place. Therefore I didn't use my influence to prevent their rehabilitation.

I saw Zhukov a number of times early in the war. I was always glad when he flew in to take over the command from Kirponos. Once, after he'd been with us for a couple of days, he got a call from Stalin ordering him to drop what he was doing and return to Moscow. "Well," he said, "I'm afraid your commander here is pretty weak. But what can we do? There's nobody better available. We'll have to give Comrade Kirponos all the support we can and hope for the best." He was right; that was all we could do. I was being very sincere when I told Zhukov how sorry I was he was leaving.

People who came to the Front from Moscow early in the war were not always as helpful or as welcome as Zhukov. For example, Marshal Budyonny [9] was sent to us from Moscow when the Germans were closing in around Kiev. I sat in on a session while the Chief of our Operational Section, Colonel Bagramyan,[10] reported to Budyonny on the general situation, which was then looking grim. I don't remember exactly what was said — the whole discussion was conducted in military

9. S. M. Budyonny, the former Tsarist cavalry sergeant major who became Stalin's special friend and gave his name to the peculiar Red Army pixie hat, later abandoned. He was very dashing and brave and drunken, and totally incompetent in modern warfare. He not only lost Kiev but managed so to contrive things that an altogether disproportionate number of Russian troops were encircled and swallowed up.

10. I. K. Bagramyan, who began life as an officer cadet in the Tsarist army. He fought in the Red Army in the Civil War, served for some time in World War II as Timoshenko's chief of staff, and then distinguished himself as an army commander, finishing up as a marshal.

Voroshilov (center) and Budyonny (right)

At Voronezh, November 7, 1941. To right of Khrushchev: General Timoshenko and Colonel Bagramyan

At the Voronezh Front, July 14, 1943, with Generals Apanasenko (left) and
Rotmistrov (right)

With Generals Yepishev (center) and Moskalenko (right)

With Vasily Stalin in 1941 or 1942

With M. I. Kalinin,
President of the USSR, 1943

At the Voronezh Front, July, 1943

jargon — but I do remember how the conversation ended. Budyonny told Bagramyan in a high-pitched voice, "I've been listening to what you've been saying, and it looks to me as though you aren't even in control of your own troops. I think we'd better have you shot."

"Semyon Mikhailovich," replied Bagramyan, "why should I be shot? If I'm not fit to be Chief of the Operational Section, then give me a division to command. But what purpose would it serve to have me shot?"

Budyonny would hear nothing of a simple transfer or demotion and tried stubbornly to get Bagramyan to agree that he should be shot. Naturally, Bagramyan wasn't ready to agree to any such thing.

It should be kept in mind that this "friendly" conversation took place after a hearty dinner and a lot of brandy. Despite these extenuating circumstances, I was still shocked. It was outrageous for a representative of the Supreme High Command like Budyonny to behave this way toward a good soldier like Bagramyan. He certainly wasn't helping to solve any of the grave problems that were facing us. Our situation hadn't improved after Budyonny arrived, and it didn't get any worse after he left.

Fortunately nothing ever came of Budyonny's threat. Ivan Khristoforovich Bagramyan is still alive and well — may he live another thousand years! He's always been a decent man and a good soldier. Subsequently he was entrusted with many key sectors of the Front in our effort to repulse Hitler's invasion.

I should tell you of my association with Vlasov, who later turned traitor and betrayed his Homeland. Before the war he had commanded the heroic Ninety-ninth Division, which was to go down in history as the first division in World War II to be awarded the Order of the Red Banner. He was widely respected as a good man and a very capable commander. When Kirponos and I were looking for someone to command the Thirty-seventh Army, which we formed to defend Kiev, the Personnel Section of the Kiev Military District recommended that we appoint Vlasov. I decided to check up on him with Moscow. At that time we were still living under the suspicion that the enemies of the people were everywhere — particularly in the military — and I wanted to make sure that we could trust Vlasov with the selection of a staff for the Thirty-seventh Army and the defense of Kiev.

I called Malenkov, who was in charge of personnel for the Central Committee. Naturally I didn't expect him personally to know anything about Vlasov, but I thought he could put some of his men to work and give me an assessment of Vlasov's record. When I finally got him on the phone, I asked Malenkov, "What sort of reference can you give me on Vlasov?"

Malenkov said, "You can't imagine what it's like around here. Our whole operation has come to a standstill. I don't have anyone free to help you out. You'll have to do whatever you see fit and take complete responsibility for what you decide."

That left me with nothing to go on except the recommendations of other military men. On that basis Kirponos and I decided to go ahead and appoint Vlasov to the command. He took charge decisively and effectively. He put together his army from units that were falling back from the Front or breaking out of the German encirclement and proved himself to be a wise choice for the command. He always bore himself calmly under fire and provided firm, intelligent leadership in the defense of Kiev. He discharged his duty and kept the Germans from taking Kiev by a frontal assault. When Kiev finally fell, it was because of an encirclement and a concentration of German troops considerably to the east. It wasn't because Vlasov didn't put up a staunch defense.

Vlasov broke out of the encirclement and made it back to our lines on foot; Stalin ordered that he be flown to Moscow. I thought that General Headquarters must have had some sort of evidence against Vlasov and that he was being called back for questioning. Later we found out that he had been called to Moscow to be decorated. Stalin himself praised him and put him in command of our counteroffensive against the Germans outside Moscow, and Vlasov distinguished himself once again. Stalin then gave him the critical job of defending the Valdai sector of our Front. Again Vlasov fell into an encirclement, and again he broke out and made it back to our lines. Stalin even considered putting Vlasov in command of the Stalingrad Front. I remember Stalin once told me, in the presence of witnesses, that if Vlasov had been available he would have been given the Stalingrad command rather than Yeremenko.

When Vlasov turned traitor, Stalin called me in and reminded me in an ominous tone that I was the one who had promoted Vlasov to the command of the Thirty-seventh Army. In reply I simply reminded him that he had been the one who had put Vlasov in charge of the Moscow counteroffensive and had even suggested making Vlasov commander of the Stalingrad Front. Stalin let the subject drop and never raised it again.

Naturally the Vlasov affair was a bitter pill to swallow — for me as well as for Stalin. It was difficult to understand how a man who had displayed such devotion, bravery, and skill and who had earned such respect, could betray his country. Vlasov must have had a very unstable character to let himself be recruited as an agent by the Germans. He was supposed to be a Communist, but he must have had no real ideological substance to him at all. In civilian life he'd been a teacher. Apparently he wasn't a bad fellow. In the first years of the war he certainly seemed loyal to Soviet Power. Of course it's possible he was just following mercenary motives when he became a soldier. Maybe he was hoping to set himself up with a comfortable position as a Party official. Unfortunately, we've had such careerist types around in the past, and I'm afraid they're even more numerous nowadays. Of course Vlasov was guilty of more than just careerism. He was guilty of treason, which is a completely different order of crime.

He got the punishment he deserved. He was tried and hanged.[11]

The Kharkov Disaster

In the spring of 1942, with the Germans held in the suburbs of Leningrad and pushed back at the eleventh hour in front of Moscow, the Russians decided to mount a three-pronged offensive in the Ukraine.

11. Colonel General A. A. Vlasov, one of the most brilliant and determined of the new generation of Soviet commanders, performed prodigies in the first year of the war. Several times, by sheer courage, he extricated himself from German encirclements made possible by the incompetence of his superiors and colleagues. He was a legendary figure, a dedicated soldier, highly intelligent and conspicuous for his height. Sickened and revolted by the corruption, brutality, and incompetence of Stalin and his circle, he allowed himself to be captured by the Germans in the spring of 1942 when faced with yet another encirclement in the course of an ill-considered, inadequately prepared offensive on the river Volkhov. It seemed to him then that the only hope for Russia lay in a German victory and the destruction of the regime. He offered to turn the vast numbers of Russian prisoners of war into a fighting army and lead them into battle on the German side. But Hitler failed to seize this opportunity and the Vlasov army came to very little. Vlasov was an angry and frustrated idealist who did not understand until it was too late that there could be no salvation for Russia at the hands of the Germans. He was as far from an opportunist careerist as it is possible to be. When the Germans were defeated, his execution as a traitor was inevitable.

*The central operation was to be a major assault toward Kharkov by Ti-
moshenko, which turned out to be an unmitigated disaster for the Red
Army. Khrushchev, at Timoshenko's headquarters, was deeply involved
in the planning and execution of the offensive. Its failure was a traumatic experience for him. He went out of his way in the Secret Speech
to exculpate himself and put all the blame on Stalin. Here, he goes
over the ground once more. Zhukov, in his memoirs published after
Khrushchev's fall (Marshal Zhukov's Greatest Battles), says that the
ill-fated offensive was indeed Stalin's idea, and that he, Zhukov, opposed it for very good reasons. This is almost certainly true. But Zhukov goes on to say that Stalin was strongly supported by Timoshenko
and Khrushchev. This is also likely. He then goes on to imply (but
here the chronology is unclear, perhaps deliberately), that there was
no attempt on the part of Timoshenko and Khrushchev to have the offensive called off before disaster was upon them. Disaster came because the Germans were themselves deployed for an offensive designed
to nip out a salient in the Russian line, and it was into this salient that
Timoshenko poured his own army, which thus moved straight into the
jaws of a trap.*

STALIN's dissatisfaction with me reached its peak during the period of
our retreat, when he thought that we were going to lose the Ukraine.
He was Supreme Commander, but he didn't want to take responsibility
for the defeat. He started looking for a scapegoat. I was the obvious
candidate since I was First Secretary of the Ukrainian Central Committee and a member of the Military Council.

Perhaps my most perilous hour was during the disastrous counteroffensive toward Kharkov in 1942. The operation had begun promisingly
enough. We had broken through the enemy's front line of defense
easily — too easily. We realized that there were no forces massed
against us. We seemed to have a clear road ahead, deep into enemy
territory. This was unsettling. It meant we had stumbled into a trap.
We reconnoitered and discovered that the enemy was concentrating
his groupings in the Alvayansk sector of the Southern Front. Apparently the Germans planned to strike at our left flank and liquidate the
salient which we had formed during the winter campaign. We could
see that the deeper we penetrated to the west, the more we would
stretch our flank and the easier it would be for the Germans to cut us
off and encircle us. We had just barely figured out the enemy's scheme

before it was too late. Now it remained for us to get permission to call off the offensive altogether and to pull back.[12]

I forget who had taken the initiative for organizing the Kharkov operation in the first place. Later Stalin was to accuse me of having ordered the offensive. I don't deny that I may have had a part in it, but, as I asked Stalin, "What about the commander, Timoshenko?"

"No," said Stalin. "It was your idea and Timoshenko simply gave in to you."

"That's impossible," I replied. "You must not know Timoshenko very well. He's very strong-willed, and he would never have given his consent to the operation unless he thought it was a good idea."

As a matter of fact, it was actually Comrade Bagramyan who worked out the plan of attack for the Kharkov counteroffensive. Our own headquarters for the Southwest Front approved it, and so did General Headquarters. We had all been in on the original decision together, and now I had to persuade General Staff to call off the operation. I knew it wouldn't be easy.

As soon as we realized the danger of proceeding toward Kharkov, we ordered a halt to our offensive and took steps to build up our defenses. We moved our artillery, armor, and antitank forces around to cover our exposed left flank. When all the necessary orders had been given and we had effectively shifted from the offensive to the defensive, I returned to my quarters to get some rest. It was three o'clock in the morning and already beginning to get light. I was just taking off my clothes to lie down when Comrade Bagramyan burst in on me. He was very upset. "I'm sorry to bother you, Comrade Khrushchev," he said, "but I thought you should know that Moscow has countermanded our order halting the offensive."

"What? How can this be? Who made the decision?"

"I don't know. All I know is that if we go ahead with the offensive, we'll be heading straight for disaster. Our troops in the salient will be doomed. I implore you: speak to Comrade Stalin personally. Our only chance is that you can talk him into reversing his decision to countermand our order."

12. Timoshenko's advance started on May 12 and went all too well for several days. It was not until May 17, with the Soviet troops dangerously extended, that the real picture began to emerge. And it was only at midnight on the 17th that the telephoned appeals to Stalin were made. At dawn on the 18th the Germans launched their counteroffensive and the deadly encirclement was under way. The Russians in the pocket were out of control and desperately on the defensive.

I'd never seen Comrade Bagramyan in such a state before. He's a rational, evenhanded man. I like him. I can even say I'm very fond of him. I've always admired him for his sober mind, his Party spirit, his wide-ranging knowledge of military affairs, and his uncorruptible integrity and straightforwardness. What's more, I completely agreed with him about the need for me to talk to Stalin. I had to try to change Stalin's mind even though I expected the worst.

Comrade Bagramyan was with me when I put through a call to General Headquarters. I got Aleksandr Mikhailovich Vasilevsky on the line.[13] He already knew what had happened.

"Aleksandr Mikhailovich," I said, "as a military man who has studied maps and who understands enemy strategy, you know the situation in greater detail than Comrade Stalin does. Please take a map along and explain to Comrade Stalin what will happen if we continue this operation." Vasilevsky understood what I was getting at. We had both seen how Stalin tried to plan battle movements by tracing troop lines and the Front with his finger on a globe of the world.

"Stalin's now at the Nearby Dacha," said Vasilevsky.

"Then go talk to him there. You know he'll see you any time. After all, there's a war going on. Take a map and show him how our decision to call off the offensive is the only rational thing to do."

"No, Comrade Khrushchev. Comrade Stalin has already made up his mind. He has already issued his orders."

Anyone who has ever dealt with Vasilevsky will be able to imagine the steady, droning voice with which he said this. I was on very good terms with him; so, after hanging up, I decided to call him back and try again. This time I pleaded with him urgently to help, but he still refused: "Nikita Sergeyevich, Comrade Stalin has made up his mind and that's all there is to it." If only Zhukov had been at General Headquarters instead of Vasilevsky, I'm sure he would have driven straight out to the Nearby Dacha and intervened on our behalf.

Anyway, I had no choice but to try to call Comrade Stalin myself. This was a very dangerous moment for me. I knew Stalin by now considered himself a great military strategist. I called the Nearby Dacha and Malenkov answered. We exchanged greetings, and then I asked, "May I please speak to Comrade Stalin?" Stalin must have been there. I knew the layout of the dacha very well. I knew exactly where every-

13. Marshal A. M. Vasilevsky, chief of General Staff in succession to Marshal Shaposhnikov, who had died.

one would be sitting and how many steps it would take Stalin to reach the telephone. I had watched many times as he went to answer a phone call. I could hear Malenkov saying that I was on the phone and asking Stalin to come talk to me. Malenkov came back and told me, "Comrade Stalin says you should tell me what you want, and I'll pass on your message." This was a sure sign of trouble.

I insisted, "I want to speak with Comrade Stalin personally. I have to report to him about the situation at the Front."

Malenkov passed this on to Stalin and then came back on the line, "Comrade Stalin repeats that you should tell me what you want."

So I had to tell Malenkov that by continuing our offensive we would be playing right into the enemy's hands. We had overextended and weakened our front; we were exposing our flank to the Germans. There was another pause while Malenkov reported to Stalin. When he came back, he said, "Comrade Stalin knows you didn't get the Front commander's approval on your decision to halt the offensive; he knows that calling off the operation was your idea and your idea alone, and he's against it." I still can't believe that Timoshenko told Stalin I had forced the decision down his throat. I think Stalin was simply trying to throw me off balance and undercut my argument.

"Comrade Malenkov, you know Timoshenko's character better than that. He would never have accepted the decision unless he too were convinced that the operation must be called off."

"There's no point in discussing it further. Stalin says the offensive must continue."

"All right," I said, "orders are orders. Continuing the offensive is all too easy since we have no enemy troops in front of us. That's exactly what worries us."

Malenkov hung up. Comrade Bagramyan was with me and overheard this conversation. His nerves cracked, and he burst into tears. He foresaw what was going to happen. He was weeping for our army.[14]

Catastrophe struck a few days later, exactly as we expected. There was nothing we could do to avert it. Many generals, colonels, junior officers, and troops perished. The staff of the Fifty-seventh Army was

14. The story of the telephone conversation coincides with the account in the Secret Speech, except for a new and very odd detail: namely that Stalin, through Malenkov, accused Khrushchev of acting independently of Timoshenko. Both Timoshenko and his chief of staff, Bagramyan, were desperate for permission to break off the offensive and pull out what they could save.

wiped out completely. Almost nobody managed to escape. The army had advanced deep into enemy territory, and when our men were encircled, they didn't even have enough fuel to escape. It was too far to return on foot. Many were killed, but most were taken prisoner. General Gurov somehow managed to escape in a tank. Some people suggested that he should be court-martialed for desertion, but I told them, "Surely we've lost enough generals already. Do you want to lose the few who managed to escape as well? Have you all gone mad?!"

Naturally Stalin would never admit his mistake. A few days after the disaster I received a call from Moscow. They weren't summoning Timoshenko, the Front commander, back to Moscow, but me. As you can imagine, I was very depressed. I hardly need describe what I was feeling. We had lost many, many thousands of men. More than that, we had lost the hope we had been living by, the hope that we might be able to turn back the tide of the invasion in 1942. Suffering the defeat of the Kharkov operation was bad enough. To make matters worse, it looked as though I were going to have to take the blame for it personally. I knew it wouldn't make any difference that I had tried to call off the offensive and avert the disaster. For Stalin to have agreed that we had been right when we halted the operation would have meant admitting his own mistake. And that sort of nobility was not for him. He would stop at nothing to avoid taking the responsibility for something that had gone wrong.

As I flew toward Moscow I could see clearly the tragic aspect of my own predicament. I put myself in the hands of fate. I was ready for anything, including arrest.

At first Stalin didn't give any sign of whether he was furious with me or sympathetic toward me. He was a good actor. His face was a mask of inscrutability. Then he said, "The Germans have announced that they captured more than two hundred thousand of our soldiers. Are they lying?"

"No, Comrade Stalin, they're not lying. That figure sounds about right. We had approximately that number of troops, perhaps a few more. We must suppose that some were killed and the rest taken prisoner." [15]

Stalin didn't say anything more, but now I could now see he was seething. I didn't know when this boiling kettle would explode and

15. The official Soviet casualty list was 5,000 dead, 70,000 missing, and 300 tanks destroyed. The Germans said they had 200,000 prisoners.

who would get scalded when it did. But he restrained himself. He didn't say anything more for the moment.

Later we started to talk things over. What would we do now? What chance was there of building up our defenses along the Donets River in order to prevent the enemy from crossing? How could we contain the German advance with our limited resources? After this discussion we went in to dinner.

I stayed in Moscow for a number of days. The longer I stayed the more wearisome and painful became the process of waiting to see what would happen to me. I doubted very much that Stalin would forgive the defeat. He still must have wanted to find a scapegoat. Here was a chance to demonstrate his implacable toughness and dedication to the principle of harsh retribution when the interests of the people were at stake. I knew exactly how Stalin would formulate his revenge. He was a master at this sort of thing.

A few days after I got to Moscow we were sitting at Stalin's table having dinner. Stalin started a conversation in a calm, noncommittal tone. "You know," he said, looking at me closely, "in World War I, after our army fell into a German encirclement in East Prussia, the general commanding the troops was court-martialed by the tsar. He was condemned and hanged."

"Comrade Stalin," I answered, "I remember this event well. The tsar did the only right thing. Myasoyedov was a traitor. He was a German agent."

Stalin didn't say anything. He didn't develop his thoughts on this subject any further. But he'd already said enough to give me some idea of where I stood. You can imagine how I felt. I saw the analogy he was implying between the encirclement of our troops in East Prussia in World War I and the encirclement of our troops east of Kharkov. Stalin was reminding the member of the Military Council responsible for the Kharkov defeat that this kind of thing had happened before in history. Besides, there had already been a precedent in World War II: the arrest, court-martial, and execution of General Pavlov along with his chief of staff and the local member of the Military Council after the Germans overran Belorussia with impunity in the first days of the war.

Stalin was preparing me psychologically for understanding why, in the interests of the Fatherland and in order to mollify public opinion, he might have to punish severely all those who were responsible for the Kharkov disaster.

So there I was, waiting to see what my fate would be.

The only thing that made it difficult for Stalin to blame me for what had happened was that I had tried stubbornly to persuade him to call off the offensive — and I had done so in the presence of witnesses. I had transmitted my opinion and my advice to him through Malenkov, and I'm sure Beria, Mikoyan, Molotov, and possibly even Voroshilov were there at the dacha with Stalin when I called from the Front. Even though all these people were very close to Stalin, it was impossible for him to ignore the fact that I had vigorously opposed continuing the offensive. These men could have been very disagreeable witnesses for me if the offensive had turned out differently, but as it was, they were disagreeable witnesses for Stalin himself.

Finally Stalin called me into his office and said I could return to the Front. I was relieved, but I realized I wasn't safe yet. I knew of many cases when Stalin would reassure people by letting them leave his office with good news, and then have them picked up and taken somewhere other than the place they expected. But nothing happened to me during the night after I left his office, and the next morning I flew back to the Front.[16]

When I got back I found the situation very bad. Marshal Timoshenko told me that the army had been so utterly routed by the enemy that the only way to rally the troops was to set up mobile kitchens and hope that the soldiers would return when they got hungry. He was drawing on his Civil War experience here. We set up field kitchens and slowly but surely reorganized our defenses.

After these many years, I often look back on the Kharkov episode as an agonizing moment for our Homeland and a milestone in my own life.

Stalingrad

Stalingrad was Khrushchev's greatest hour. As political advisor to Marshal Yeremenko, who was responsible for the defense of Stalingrad until Zhukov turned to the attack, he was very much the man on the spot — although, of course, once the Germans destroyed the city and

16. Khrushchev indeed had cause to fear for his life. What he omits to say is that although he was let off lightly, Timoshenko was demoted as a consequence of the Kharkov disaster. Zhukov now took over as Deputy Supreme Commander under Stalin.

were fighting in its ruins, Yeremenko's headquarters had to be moved to the other side of the river. His account of the development of the battle furnishes illuminating firsthand glimpses of the fearful struggle which ended in the destruction of Paulus's Sixth Army and marked the turning of the tide.

WHEN the Battle of Stalingrad started, our armed forces were still very weak. We were suffering from a shortage of heavy artillery, machine guns, antiaircraft, and antitank weapons. The Germans were still pressing us hard. But by now our troops had begun to put up a stubborn resistance. There was none of the disorderly flight which had characterized the situation earlier in the war. Our troops were now fighting heroically and retreated only when there was no other way out. They retreated in a disciplined fashion from one position to another and never allowed themselves to be routed.

Our setbacks, although less frequent, were still very painful. During the battle I received a report that Rubén Ibarruri had been killed.[17] Early in the war Rubén Ibarruri and my own son Leonid were in the same casualty ward in Kuibyshev. Leonid, who was a pilot, later died in battle. Then I learned that Anastas Ivanovich Mikoyan's son, also a pilot, had perished. This was all very familiar to me. It was war, and many good men died as they do in every war. But the Red Army was suffering more than it ought to have because it was badly prepared and insufficiently armed.

I remember a tragic sight that I saw when I went out to the battle zone south of the city near the Noriman ravine. Some of our fighter-bombers flew over, heading toward the front. Suddenly German Messerschmitts appeared. Before our very eyes, our bombers were hit and caught fire one after the other. The pilots bailed out. Our own planes looked very much like the Messerschmitts. Our infantry thought the stricken fighter-bombers were German, so they opened fire on our pilots as they parachuted to the ground. I remember how one pilot screamed as he came down, "I'm one of you! I'm one of you!" Then there was a burst of machine-gun fire, and it was all over.

Our air force units were commanded by Khryukin, a young fellow who had been made a Hero of the Soviet Union for his part in the war

17. He was the son of Dolores Ibarruri, the celebrated Spanish Communist known as La Pasionaria, who still lives in Moscow.

against Japan when we were fighting in China on the side of Chiang Kai-shek.[18]

The Germans reached the Volga and half-encircled us, closing off our railroad contact with the North and stopping all navigation on the river. I got a call from Stalin. He asked me menacingly, "What's this about you starting to evacuate the city?"

"Comrade Stalin, who said anything about evacuating the city? Who reported this to you? Nothing of the kind is even planned. I don't know how you came by this information, but it's absolutely untrue."

He hung up. I began wondering, who could have concocted this filthy lie? It was obviously aimed against me personally. I decided to call Malyshev, although I didn't think he would stoop that low.[19] I told him about Stalin's call and he said, "Yes, I just got an indignant call from Stalin myself. He said the very same thing to me that he said to you. I have no idea who could have planted this lie."

Then I thought maybe it was Chuyanov, but Chuyanov was hardly the sort to stoop that low either. I called him anyway. He said that he'd had a nasty phone call from Stalin, too.

Stalin never mentioned the evacuation again. Later I realized that the rumor about an evacuation was Stalin's own doing. It was what he would have called a preventive device. For anyone else to have suggested an evacuation would have been to invite some very unpleasant consequences, so Stalin took the initiative of planting the idea himself, just to let us know how he felt about it in case the idea were ever to come up. This was typical of Stalin's conduct of the war. He wanted to regulate everything from Moscow. By carrying centralized control to such an extreme, Stalin hamstrung his commanders and commissars at the Front.

Our battle headquarters in Stalingrad was situated on the Tsaritsa River in a ravine which had been eroded by many years of rain and melting snow. When we first came to Stalingrad we were surprised to discover that there was already a command post dug into the steep

18. T. T. Khryukin commanded the Eighth Air Army. The reference is to the operations in the undeclared, small, but bloody war with the Japanese in Mongolia in the summer of 1939. It was here that Zhukov first made his name, arriving just in time to restore a dangerous situation at Halkin-Gol and shatter the Japanese. It is sometimes forgotten that the Russians then regarded Chiang Kai-shek as an ally and also supported him against Mao Tse-tung. Mao never forgot.

19. V. A. Malyshev, then People's Commissar of the Armament Industry, later became one of Malenkov's team of high-powered technocrats and a member of the enlarged Party Presidium.

At the Stalingrad Front, October, 1943, with General Yeremenko and staff

Conferring with a group of officers

slope of this ravine. It had been prepared and fortified long before the present war. The entrance was protected by baffles against shock waves from explosions, and the doors were reinforced with thick girders to keep them from being beaten in. Everything in this underground bunker on the Tsaritsa had a curiously familiar look about it. It was decorated very much according to Stalin's taste. The walls had oak plywood trimming, just like all Stalin's dachas. The place was very well equipped. It was even fitted out with a toilet. No real military man would have considered having a toilet like this under field conditions. I never heard, before or since, for whom this command post had originally been prepared.

Early in the battle the enemy subjected Stalingrad to the cruelest air raids. Wave after wave of German planes bombed the city. Stalingrad was in flames. We found ourselves cut off from the left bank of the Volga. Communication with the left bank was crucial to our supervision of the battle. The commander Yeremenko [20] and I decided that our continued presence in Stalingrad was inadvisable.

We sent off the appropriate dispatch to General Headquarters requesting permission to transfer our command post to the left bank so we could be in immediate contact with all our armies. A day passed, and there was no reply. We repeated the request. Again, there was no word from Moscow. We couldn't move the command post without permission.

Then Stalin called about something else entirely. I talked to him myself and said, "Comrade Stalin, we've already had to repeat our request for permission to transfer our command post to the left bank, but General Headquarters still hasn't answered. Time is of the essence, so I ask you to give us the go-ahead right now."

"No, that's impossible. If your troops find out that their commander has moved his headquarters out of Stalingrad, the city will fall."

I tried to explain to Stalin as best I could that his fears were unfounded: "Comrade Stalin, I don't look at it that way. The Sixty-second Army under the command of Chuikov [21] has undertaken the defense of

20. Marshal A. I. Yeremenko was commander of the Southeast Front, to which Khrushchev was attached. At this stage the Southeast Front included the city of Stalingrad. The Stalingrad Front was the designation of the group of armies to the north of the city.

21. Marshal V. I. Chuikov had succeeded General Lopatin as commander of the Sixty-second Army, which for so long bore the full brunt of the siege. Chuikov, who was later to race to Berlin and, in due course, to become commander of the Soviet forces in Germany, is not the pleasantest of men, but he was a brilliant soldier and the supreme hero of Stalingrad.

Stalingrad. We've also appointed Gurov to the Military Council and instructed him to stay in the city and strengthen the leadership of the army. We're absolutely sure that Chuikov and Gurov will do their jobs. They will keep the enemy from penetrating our defenses and capturing the city."

"Well, all right. If you're certain that the Front will hold and our defenses won't be broken, I'll give you permission to move to the left bank. Just make sure you leave a representative of the Front headquarters in Stalingrad who can report to you on the way things are going. I want to make sure that you have somebody in the city to back up Chuikov's reports."

Yeremenko and I prepared to move our command post. We asked our chief of staff, Zakharov, to help us.[22] (Zakharov and Yeremenko both used to punch people in the snout on Stalin's "instructions.") We decided to leave General Golikov in Stalingrad to keep us advised on how Chuikov was doing with the defense of the city. Golikov had been sent to us by Stalin as first deputy commander of the Front.[23] I'd known him during our occupation of Lvov in 1939 and also when he was chief of personnel for the Red Army. I'd often seen him in Stalin's presence when he was head of army intelligence, but before now I'd never had a chance to assess him as a human being and as a Communist.

We called Golikov in and Yeremenko told him, "Comrade Golikov, we've received permission to move our command post to the left bank. We want you to remain with our headquarters here and to maintain communications with Comrade Chuikov."

A look of terror came over Golikov's face, but for the moment he contained himself. As soon as Yeremenko left the room, Golikov pleaded with me not to leave him alone in the city. I never saw anyone, soldier or civilian, in such a state during the whole war. He was white as a sheet and begged me not to abandon him. He kept saying over and over, "Stalingrad is doomed! Don't leave me behind! Don't destroy me! Let me go with you!"

"What are you talking about! How dare you say Stalingrad is

22. General M. V. Zakharov, Yeremenko's chief of staff at Stalingrad. He was later an army commander.
23. Colonel General P. I. Golikov, a "political" general, was more successful in administrative and quasi-diplomatic assignments than in the field. Having barely escaped shooting by court-martial for a failure in the 1943 Kharkov offensive, he rose after the war to be head of the armed forces Political Directorate. It is not clear what he was doing in Stalingrad. He was certainly not there for long.

doomed! Can't you see that things have changed? We're no longer re-treating from the enemy. Our army is making a stand here. What's the matter with you? Pull yourself together. How dare you behave like this? You've been ordered to stay in the city, and you will obey."

A few days later we received a message from an officer in Stalingrad informing us that Golikov had gone completely off his head and was behaving like a madman. His presence in the army wasn't doing us any good, and he was even becoming a liability to us. The officer who lodged the complaint asked that appropriate measures be taken. We relieved Golikov of his duties and had him recalled.

Later he complained to Stalin about us. During one of my visits to Moscow Stalin reproached me angrily for having the wrong attitude toward our generals and for failing to give them the support they needed. I asked him, "Exactly what general do you have in mind?"

"Well, take Golikov for example. We sent him down to help you and look how you treated him." Then he launched into a tirade against Ye-remenko, calling him a worthless so-and-so. I was shocked. Before this I had often heard Stalin praising Yeremenko in the most glowing terms, virtually worshiping him as our best field general and so on. Part of the reason for Stalin's disillusionment with Yeremenko must have been that the Germans were still driving us back and had broken into Stalingrad; there were skirmishes and even pitched battles going on inside the city. But instead of telling me what was really bothering him, Stalin ranted on about Yeremenko's alleged mistreatment of Goli-kov.

"Comrade Stalin, I don't know what Comrade Golikov has told you, but if he has complained about our treatment of him, I have no choice but to tell you the reasons for our attitude." Then I told Stalin the story of how Golikov had behaved when we ordered him to stay with our headquarters in the city. From the way Stalin's expression changed I could tell that he had known nothing about the incident. "Therefore," I concluded, "we were perfectly justified in having Golikov sacked. I really don't see why you're lashing out at Yeremenko and myself like this. I will defend anyone who has been punished unfairly but Golikov got exactly what he deserved."

Then Stalin told me that the decision had already been made to re-lieve Yeremenko of the Stalingrad command. I told him I thought this would be a serious mistake. "I realize there may be varying opinions about Yeremenko around here," I said. "Like everyone, he has his ene-mies and there are those who don't respect him. But in my capacity as a member of the Military Council, I've gone through a critical period with Yeremenko, and in my opinion he's fully worthy of his rank and of his current assignment. I'm only talking about his virtues as a commander. I won't address myself to his other qualities. The important thing is that he's efficient, experienced, and a good leader of his troops."

At first, naturally, Stalin resisted stubbornly, but after a while he began to soften. Finally he said I could fly back to the Front. As we were saying good-bye, he shook my hand and said, "I'm glad we called you back for consultations. If it weren't for what you've told me, we would have sacked Yeremenko. I'd already made up my mind to do so. Your arguments have changed my mind. Yeremenko can stay at his post."

"You won't be sorry, Comrade Stalin. You're doing the right thing."

Meanwhile, the enemy pressed on, but our army made the Germans pay in blood for every inch they gained. Our slogans were "Not One Step Back!" "We Will Stand Our Ground at the Volga!" and "Fight to the Death; Don't Give Up Stalingrad!"

It seemed that whenever the situation was looking gravest Malenkov would fly in with Vasilevsky, Voronov, Novikov, or some other representative from General Staff.[24] Frankly, I was never very pleased to see them. Unless they were bringing us tangible assistance — and that would have meant troop reinforcements, air support, infantry, and artillery units — they weren't doing the cause any good by showing up when we already had our hands full. These celebrities always chose the wrong time to make a personal appearance, and they weren't very popular at our command post when they showed up. It was so crowded you could hardly move.

Always at the most critical moment, I sensed that Stalin was paying especially keen attention to me and that he had sent Malenkov to keep an eye on me. I would notice Vasilevsky and Malenkov whispering together. Malenkov would have to return to Moscow and report to Stalin

24. Marshal N. N. Voronov is the new name here. As chief of artillery he was one of the most gifted and intelligent of the Soviet generals. Khrushchev speaks as though Malenkov, Vasilevsky (chief of General Staff), Voronov, and Novikov (head of the Soviet air force) came in on a single flying visit. In fact Malenkov spent a good deal of time at Yeremenko's headquarters as Stalin's special envoy (deeply resented by Khrushchev), while the others mentioned, together with Zhukov, were frequent visitors. It was absolutely vital for the General Headquarters to know precisely what was going on at Stalingrad, how the city could be best supplied, how long the defenders could hold out with minimum reinforcements while Zhukov was preparing, steadily and with the utmost secrecy, his tremendous counteroffensive.

about why the battle was going so badly, and naturally he wanted to avoid any personal responsibility for what was happening. In his whispered talks with Vasilevsky, Malenkov was preparing to denounce someone, and I knew that I was the obvious choice. He didn't know anything about military matters, but he was more than competent when it came to intriguing.

In the end Vasilevsky and Malenkov would tell me they had received orders to return to Moscow. After they left, Yeremenko and I were left alone with a small operational staff in the command post. An eerie silence seemed to fall over the area as often happens in a forest after a storm.

At one point in the battle, Konstantin Simonov came to Stalingrad and asked where he should go on the front lines to see some action. I told him where, but warned him that it was a very dangerous sector. "That's all right," he said, and off he went.[25]

As the battle progressed, our armies of the Stalingrad Front swung south against Manstein.[26] The armies of Rokossovsky and Chistyakov began to close in on the Germans.[27] I got to know Chistyakov's chief of staff, General Penkovsky, and liked him very much. He was diligent and efficient, and later he made a substantial contribution to the performance of the Sixth Guards Army. General Penkovsky is still alive and well. I wish him a hundred years of life and happiness.[28]

25. Simonov was an establishment writer who had strong popular appeal. One of his poems, "Wait for me, I shall return," was sung and recited everywhere and stood for the will to endure. His epic novel *Victims and Heroes* is a deeply moving account of the muddle, confusion, treachery, and heroism of the great retreat.

26. This is a reference to the immense and majestic operation which resulted in the total destruction of the German Sixth Army under Paulus. At the end of October, 1942, Chuikov and his Sixty-second Army were hanging on to the right bank of the Volga and a few islands of rubble in the city by the skin of their teeth. But, secretly, Zhukov's forces were moving into position to start the great envelopment. On November 19 Voronov to the north opened the biggest artillery barrage of the war, while three armies went over to the attack in the south. Four days later, the ring around the city had been closed, but not yet firmly enough to withstand a serious attempt at a breakout or a break-in. It was not until early in December that Manstein made his great bid to break through and relieve Paulus. By then it was too late.

27. Marshal K. K. Rokossovsky and General I. M. Chistyakov. Rokossovsky, who was the great hero of the envelopment, had barely escaped with his life in the army purge of 1937. He was later to achieve ill fame as the commander who held back his army on the Vistula (on Stalin's orders) when the Warsaw Poles rose against the Germans. He was Polish Minister of Defense when the Poles rose against the Russians in 1956. Chistyakov commanded the Twenty-first Army advancing from the Kletskaya bridgehead. It was later renamed the Sixth Guards Army and fought at Kursk.

28. The great-uncle of Oleg Penkovsky, the MGB colonel who turned against the regime and became an agent of the West.

As we began to press the enemy in the direction of Kotelnikovo, it became more and more difficult for a single command to conduct two very different operations simultaneously: the Front command had to direct our armies that were holding Paulus in an encirclement in Stalingrad and at the same time direct our attack toward Rostov. Therefore General Staff proposed that we divide the Front in two, forming the troops facing Paulus into the Don Front and the troops facing Manstein into the Southern Front. I don't know if this was Stalin's idea or the idea of someone else at General Headquarters.[29]

Given the difficulties which had developed, it made sense to divide the Stalingrad Front, but nonetheless it was sad for Yeremenko and me to have to part with the armies of the new Don Front, which had already earned their place in history — armies like the Sixty-second, which had parried the enemy's main strike and taken the full brunt of Paulus's blow on its chest. Then there was the Sixty-fourth, commanded by Comrade Shumilov, and the Fifty-seventh, and others. We had grown close to all these men, but I knew it was in the interests of the cause to leave them to seal off the encirclement of Stalingrad while we pushed south. When Stalin called, I told him I agreed with the decision to split up the Front.

Then Stalin called Yeremenko. I don't know how their conversation went, but afterward I found Yeremenko literally in tears.

"Andrei Ivanovich," I said, "what on earth is wrong? Don't you see that we must split up the Front? Our armies have turned south, and our task now is to strike at the enemy's flank in the northern Caucasus. Stalingrad will manage on its own. All that remains is to surround the enemy and close him off. Then our comrades can just wait for him to run out of food and ammunition."

"Comrade Khrushchev, you don't understand. You're a civilian. You don't know how much we've been through. You forget how in the early days of the war we thought we were doomed, how Stalin used to ask

29. The nomenclature of the fronts is confusing. The term *front* was used to designate a group of armies, not a fixed location. In September the Stalingrad Front was renamed the Don Front and put under Rokossovsky. At the same time the Southeast Front became the Stalingrad Front, still under Yeremenko, while a new front was created further down the river and called the Southwest Front, under Vatutin. At the end of December it was decided at Supreme Headquarters that the Don Front and the Stalingrad Front must be coordinated by one commander for the final offensive. Rokossovsky was chosen in preference to Yeremenko, who had to surrender to him three of his armies, including the Sixty-second, which had for so long held what remained of the city. The Stalingrad Front, what was left of it, was now renamed the Southern Front and turned south to attack the Germans in the Rostov area.

us if we could hold out for three more days. We all believed that the Germans would capture Stalingrad, and we would be made scapegoats for the defeat. And now look! We've turned on the offensive. Maybe you don't foresee what will happen, but I do: the new Don Front will get all the glory for the Stalingrad victory, and our armies of the new Southern Front will be forgotten." He was still weeping bitterly.

I tried to calm him down, saying, "Of course the personal satisfaction of one soldier or one commander is important, but it isn't the main thing. The main thing is the glory of the people, the victory of our people and of our cause." But I couldn't do anything to console him. I really did feel very sorry for him. I knew how much he'd been through. He'd devoted every ounce of his strength and skill to assuring our victory. I can find no words in the Russian language that adequately express my admiration for Yeremenko's contribution to the cause as commander of the Stalingrad Front.

We encircled Paulus's army in the fall and finished it off in the winter. I saw a horrible scene when we moved into the city in the early spring. Of course, there are always horrors in time of war. Our troops were busy gathering up the corpses of German soldiers. We were afraid of what might happen if we left them lying around with spring coming on and a hot summer ahead. We knew that unless we did something quickly they would begin to decompose and an epidemic might break out. But it wasn't easy. The earth was still frozen, and it was hard to dig them out. We gathered thousands of corpses and stacked them in layers alternating with layers of railway ties. Then we set these huge piles on fire. I once went out to watch, but I didn't go back a second time. Napoleon or someone once said that burning enemy corpses smell good. Well, speaking for myself, I don't agree. It was a very unpleasant smell, and altogether a very unpleasant scene.

Around Stalingrad we found dead German soldiers who had been stripped half naked. Their trousers and boots were often missing. It wasn't the wolves who had gotten to them. It was the work of pillagers, I'm sorry to say. I think probably both soldiers and civilians had taken part in the pillaging.

As we pushed forward after the battle of Stalingrad, I saw many large heaps of German soldiers who had been shot. I asked General Volsky [30] about this: "Were these men executed?"

"No, they were all killed in battle."

Well, the enemy always sustains huge losses when an army is ad-

30. General T. V. Volsky, commanding the Fourth Mechanized Corps.

vancing, but I didn't rule out the possibility that some of our men had violated our strict instructions not to use force against prisoners. In addition to the moral consideration, we didn't want to give enemy propaganda an excuse to claim that the advancing Soviet forces were shooting their captives. However, it was perfectly understandable that some of our men might have given in to their hatred of the Germans and killed any fascist soldier they could get their hands on in revenge for the atrocities committed by the Germans on occupied Soviet territory.

General Malinovsky

Fresh light is shed here on the career of Marshal Malinovsky (see Appendix 3), who was, in due course, to become Minister of Defense under Khrushchev. The section also provides a graphic example of the atmosphere of intrigue and suspicion surrounding Stalin's court and threatening to suffocate, if not destroy, anyone who was touched by its miasma. It is worth noticing that the Larin episode occurred not in the confused and treacherous first months of the war, but after the triumph of Stalingrad.

DURING the early years of the war I got to know Rodion Yakovlevich Malinovsky very well. He fell into disfavor for a while after Rostov was surrendered to the Germans, but he was still widely acknowledged as one of our ablest commanders. He used to tell me fascinating stories about his early career. I don't think his mother was married. In any case, he'd never known his father. He was raised by his aunt and spent his childhood in Odessa. He had nothing but spite for his mother, but he always spoke with great tenderness about his aunt. He worked as an errand boy in Odessa, and then, when the First World War came along, he ran away and fell in with a regiment which took him to the Front. That's how he joined the army. He ended up as a machine gunner with a detachment of Russian troops that was sent to France as part of the Russian Expeditionary Force.

Many years later, when he was Minister of Defense of the USSR, Malinovsky accompanied me on my trip to Paris to meet with the heads of the three Great Powers. This meeting collapsed just before it was to begin because the Americans sent one of their U-2 spy planes over our territory and we shot it down — a landmark event in the

With General Malinovsky in 1943 or 1944

With two other generals in January, 1944

history of our struggle against the American imperialists who were waging the Cold War. While we were in Paris, Malinovsky suggested, "Let's go visit the village where our unit was stationed during World War I. The old peasant whose house we lived in is probably dead, but his wife was a young woman. Maybe she's still alive." We got in a car and drove along one of those beautiful French roads. Malinovsky directed us to the village without difficulty. We found the house where he had lived. The housewife and her son, who now had children of his own, welcomed us graciously. "My old man died a long time ago," she told us.

Friends started coming around, champagne was broken out, and Malinovsky started to reminisce and ask questions about people and places he had known.

"Didn't there used to be a saloon of some kind near here where the peasants used to gather?"

"You still remember?"

"Yes, I remember very well."

"Then you probably also remember that girl so-and-so."

"Yes," said Malinovsky, smiling, "of course I do."

They all laughed. "He remembers! She was our beauty! But she's been dead for a long time."

Other Frenchmen started arriving. The word spread quickly that the visitor was the Soviet Minister of Defense who had been a soldier in a Russian unit stationed in this village almost fifty years before.

"Of course we remember you!," they all said. "You had a Russian bear in your unit, didn't you?" Malinovsky laughed and explained to me that he and his comrades had picked up a bear cub on the way to France and taken it with them. Malinovsky had been in France when the Revolution broke out back home. I remember when he told me his life story, Malinovsky said, "It used to hang heavily on me that the Revolution found me serving in the Russian Expeditionary Force abroad." With great difficulty he returned to Russia via Vladivostok and made his way through Siberia, which was then under the control of Kolchak. Finally he met up with the Red Army. I'm recounting this part of Malinovsky's biography because it's important for an understanding of the Stalin period. For years suspicion hung over Malinovsky like the sword of Damocles, first because he had been part of the tsarist expeditionary force in France during World War I and second because he had been on White-occupied territory before he joined up with the Red Army.

He fell under Stalin's personal suspicion again while we were working together on the Southern Front after the Battle of Stalingrad. Here's the story of what happened:

One day Malinovsky burst in on me at my quarters in Verkhne-Tsaritsynsk. He was very upset. Tears were streaming down his face.

"Rodion Yakovlevich, what on earth is wrong? What's happened?"

"A terrible thing. Larin has shot himself!"

Larin was a member of the Military Council for the Second Guards Army. He was also a real soldier and a good general. He and Malinovsky were close friends. Larin had been his commissar when Malinovsky was given his first corps command, and since then he had more than once requested that Larin be his commissar.

Larin's adjutant later told me the circumstances of his death. It's an incredible story in itself. Apparently he purposely let himself be shot at by the enemy when he went out to inspect the lines at the Front. Instead of taking cover behind a haystack when the Germans opened fire, he strutted about, taunting the enemy with an enticing target and deliberately inviting death. He was wounded, but it wasn't serious. The bullet lodged in the soft part of his calf; the bone wasn't even damaged. When I went by to see him at his quarters, he was sitting up and chatting cheerfully with an Armenian woman doctor. He seemed in good spirits right up until he shot himself.

We know how Larin committed suicide, but we don't know why. It would have been more understandable at the very beginning of the war, when a number of generals shot themselves during our retreat. But now the tables were turned and we were on the attack. We had surrounded Paulus, and the Second Guards Army, for which Larin was a member of the Military Council, was putting up a good fight against Manstein. So there seemed to be no reason at all for his suicide—at least as far as our struggle against the Germans was concerned.

Larin left behind a note. This note, too, was very strange. The gist of it was simply that he couldn't go on living. Over his signature was the slogan, "Long Live Lenin!" We immediately sent Larin's suicide note off to Moscow where Shcherbakov got hold of it. One shouldn't say unkind things about the dead, so I won't say anything about Shcherbakov except that he was an upper-echelon Party workers for many years and Chief of the Political Directorate of the Red Army during the war [but see pages 171–173]. Shcherbakov showed his true colors when he got his hands on Larin's suicide note. He used it to fan Stalin's suspicion against Malinovsky and also to get in a dig against me, since I was a member of the Military Council for the Front where the incident had occurred.

Shortly after we sent off Larin's note, I was called back to Moscow. As usual there was an interminable dinner with all the trimmings at Stalin's. In the course of the meal Stalin turned to me and asked, "Who's this Malinovsky?"

"I've reported to you about Malinovsky more than once in the past," I replied. "He's a fairly well-known general who commanded a corps at the beginning of the war and then an army. Later he was in command of the Southern Front, where he suffered some reverses, as you know." Malinovsky had been relieved of his command after the fall of Rostov and reassigned to the rear, where he formed the Second Guards Army.

Then Shcherbakov started playing on Stalin's suspicions in a way calculated to turn Stalin against Malinovsky — and indirectly, against me as well. "You know, this whole thing is very puzzling," said Shcherbakov. "Maybe it's no accident that Larin wrote 'Long Live Lenin' and not 'Long Live Stalin.' What do you think he meant by saying Lenin instead of Stalin?"

"I have no idea," I replied. "Larin was obviously under the influence of some sort of psychological disturbance when he shot himself."

Shcherbakov was clearly trying to get me to denounce Larin and Malinovsky, too, but I had no intention of letting him use me like that.

Later Stalin asked me again, "Who is this Malinovsky?"

"Comrade Stalin, I've known Malinovsky since the beginning of the war, and I can give him only the highest recommendation, both as a general and as a human being."

I could see Malinovsky was in trouble. His early career, the failure at Rostov, and now Larin's suicide — these things were all tied up together in Stalin's mind. Evidence was piling up against Malinovsky, despite my staunch efforts to stick up for him.

"When you return to the Front," said Stalin, "you'd better keep a close watch on him. I want you to keep an eye on the Second Guards Army headquarters, too. Check up on all his orders and decisions. Follow his every move."

"Very well, Comrade Stalin. I won't let Malinovsky out of my sight."

When I got back to the Front I had to spy on Malinovsky every hour of the day. I had to watch him even when he went to bed to see if he closed his eyes and really went to sleep. I didn't like having to do this one bit.

It wasn't until after Stalin's death, when Malinovsky and I went on a hunt together, that I told him how Stalin had reacted to Larin's suicide and how I had had to report on him to General Headquarters. Malinovsky told me he had known all along why I was following him around and taking quarters next to his. He said he had understood the awkwardness of my position and hadn't held it against me. He had known that as long as he did an honest and competent job, I wouldn't interfere with him and I would give a good report on him to Stalin.

I don't know what actually saved Malinovsky from falling victim to Stalin's compulsive urge to arrest people and have them eliminated. Perhaps the practical demands of wartime reality compelled Stalin to hold his anger and his suspiciousness in check. Then again, perhaps it had something to do with my own intervention on his behalf that Malinovsky was spared. After all, my influence with Stalin was not inconsiderable.

A Visit from Comrade Ulbricht

Here we are given a first glimpse of Walter Ulbricht, the present master of the German Democratic Republic, or Communist East Germany. With other German Communists he spent the war in the Soviet Union being groomed for his future role. In Moscow he had been head of the Political Department of the German Communist Party in exile and had helped to further his own advancement by denouncing some of his most able colleagues. In 1942 the Russians set up the Free Germany Committee in Moscow to recruit German prisoners of war for political training and to conduct propaganda among the German front-line troops. After Stalingrad, a number of prominent German officers were recruited to this committee. The best account of this operation is given in The Shadow of Stalingrad *by Heinrich von Einsiedeln.*

AT one point Walter Ulbricht, along with a couple of other German Communists, came to Verkhne-Tsaritsynsk in order to broadcast propaganda to the enemy through bullhorns and loudspeakers.[31] They urged the German troops to give themselves up. This work was usually car-

31. This incident must have taken place in mid-December, 1942, when the Russians were countering Manstein's desperate attempt to relieve Paulus's Sixth Army cooped up in Stalingrad.

ried out at night. Ulbricht and I often had dinner together after he came back from the front lines. I used to joke with him a lot: "Well, Comrade Ulbricht, it doesn't look like you've earned your dinner today. No Germans have given themselves up."

Then one day I received a report that a German soldier had come over to our side. "Bring him here," I said. "We'll see what sort of man he is, and we'll also find out what he has to say about the morale of his comrades."

They brought the man to me. "Who are you?" I asked. "What nationality are you?"

"I'm a Pole."

"How did you get into the German army?"

"I'm from the part of Poland that was annexed to Germany. I was called up."

I had an uneasy feeling about this man. "We're planning to form a Polish army to liberate your country," I told him. "What do you think about that?"

"I'm pleased. Naturally I want Poland to be liberated."

"Well then, do you want to sign up for the Polish army?"

"No."

"Then how is Poland going to be liberated?"

"The Russians will liberate Poland."

I didn't like his tone of voice when he said this. I turned to Comrade Ulbricht and said, "So here's what you've managed to attract with your propaganda. He's not a German soldier at all, but a Pole who's fleeing from the Germans. And he's not even ready to join in the liberation of his own country."

Later, a few real pure-blood Germans defected and were taken prisoner. When Christmastime came around I ordered that they be offered the hospitality of our headquarters — that is, Malinovsky's headquarters. But first I instructed that they be taken to the baths, deloused, given a chance to wash, and dressed in some new clothes. Then we brought them around to our quarters and gave them each one hundred grams of vodka and something to eat. Ulbricht was there, too. During the conversation that followed, one of the German prisoners told us he was against the Nazis, against Hitler, and against the war. He stood out clearly as the best of the group. Ulbricht asked him, "Would you be willing for us to send you back to your own lines to work for our side?"

"I'd be willing," said the German. "Let us go one at a time, and we'll tell our officers that we escaped from you."

An argument broke out in the group. One of the other Germans said, "If we try to go back to our own lines, we'll be shot. No one will believe that we escaped. Nor will anyone believe any other story you come up with."

"Our" German retorted heatedly, "You coward! I'll go! Let them shoot me! I don't mind dying for the cause!"

Comrade Ulbricht and I were in complete agreement about the desirability of sending the German defectors back to their own lines. Then Tolbukhin found out about our plan.[32] He came to see me and said, "Comrade Khrushchev, don't go through with this idea of yours. These German prisoners know the location of our headquarters. If we let them go, they might give us away, and we'll be bombed."

"There's no danger," I said. "We led them to and from the headquarters blindfolded. They don't have any idea where they are."

"Nevertheless, I can't risk it. At least don't send them back until I've had a chance to move my headquarters to a new spot."

I could see there was no use in persisting. I knew Stalin wouldn't support me if Tolbukhin went over my head. I didn't tell Ulbricht about Tolbukhin's objections. I simply said, "Comrade Ulbricht, apparently we'd better put this plan aside because there's some risk that these Germans may give away the location of our headquarters if we let them go."

"Well," he shrugged, "I guess that's that." And he went on with his job of transmitting propaganda across to the German lines.

Kursk

The Battle of the Kursk Salient was by far the greatest tank battle in history. Stalingrad had been the turning of the tide, but in front of

32. There may be some confusion about the various headquarters referred to. Verkhne-Tsaritsynsk was at this time the headquarters of the Fifty-first Army under Major General N. I. Trufanov. This army was grouped with the Fifty-seventh Army under General F. I. Tolbukhin. Malinovsky was then commanding the Second Guards Army, which was transferred, under protest, from Rokossovsky's Don Front to the Stalingrad Front on December 15, in a swift move to halt the Manstein offensive (the offensive was broken on December 21). Khrushchev was certainly with Vasilevsky, Soviet chief of staff, at Fifty-first Army headquarters on December 12, when the Manstein threat was at its height.

Kursk in July, 1943, Zhukov tore the heart out of the German army and doomed it to ultimate annihilation. Some six thousand tanks and self-propelled guns were engaged, tearing up the open steppes in the nearest thing to a sea battle that could ever take place on land, freedom of maneuver was so absolute. It never caught the imagination of the West as Stalingrad had done. But it was a stupendous feat of arms, a set-piece battle on a colossal scale, which displayed to the utmost advantage the skill, nerve, and ruthlessness not only of Zhukov and Vasilevsky, who planned it, but also of Rokossovsky, in command of the Central Front, and Vatutin, in command of the newly strengthened Voronezh Front. They fought the most experienced German tank formations to a standstill and utterly destroyed them. On this extraordinary occasion Khrushchev was present as political advisor to Lieutenant General N. F. Vatutin, who had by now emerged as one of the most gifted generals on either side, highly intelligent as well as filled with boundless energy. He was killed by rebel Ukrainian nationalists in February, 1944. For a lucid account of the Battle of Kursk, as indeed of the whole war between Germany and the Soviet Union, see Barbarossa *by Alan Clark.*

OUR detractors used to say that the only reason we were able to defeat Paulus's colossal army at Stalingrad was that we had the Russian winter on our side. They had said the same thing about our defeat of the Germans outside Moscow in 1941. Ever since Russia turned back Napoleon's invasion, people claimed that winter was our main ally. However, the Germans couldn't use this excuse to explain their defeat at the Battle of the Kursk Salient in 1943. They fired the first shot; they chose the time, place, and form of the battle. All the cards were in the hands of Hitler and his cutthroats. It was high summer. If you like fancy phrases, you could say that the countryside was in full bloom, dripping with fragrant juices.

Our armies under Rokossovsky were supposed to start an offensive of their own on July 20. We were sure we would be successful, that we would crush the Germans and push west to the Dnieper. We were all driven by a single desire — to break through the German lines and to liberate Kharkov.

Suddenly, about fifteen or sixteen days before our operation was to begin, we got a call from the Sixth Army. The commander told us that a German soldier had defected from a front-line SS division and that he had some important information: "He says the Germans are going to attack tomorrow morning at three o'clock." We ordered that the prisoner be brought to us immediately. Vatutin and I interrogated him.

"What makes you think they're going to attack?" I asked.

"Naturally I didn't actually see the orders for the offensive," he answered, "but the troops can sense what's about to happen. And it's more than just intuition. First, we have been issued dry rations for three days. Second, tanks have been moved up all the way to the front lines. Third, an order has been given to stack ammunition right next to the heavy artillery and field pieces so as not to lose time loading once the artillery opens fire."

"But what makes you so sure the attack will start at three o'clock in the morning?" I asked.

"Well, figure it out yourself. At this time of year dawn begins to break at about that hour, and that's when the German command likes to open an attack."

This defector was a young fellow, handsome and elegant-looking — obviously not from worker stock. He was from one of the fairly well-known SS armored divisions — "Adolf Hitler" or "Reich" or "Death's Head." All three of these divisions were pitted against us. I used to tell Vatutin that no matter where I went on the Front, I always found the "Death's Head" division facing me.

I asked the German if he was a Nazi.

"No. I'm against the Nazis. That's why I've come over to your side."

"But you're with the SS, and they're all Nazis."

"Not any more. That was true in the first and second years of the war, but now the SS will take anyone it can get. They took me because of my height and appearance. Anyway, I'm not even the same sort of German as the Nazis. My parents came from Alsace, and I was brought up as a Frenchman. My parents are against Hitler, and they raised me accordingly. I don't want to risk my neck for Hitler. That's why I've defected. It's in the best interests of the German people for Hitler to be defeated and exterminated."

When we finished interrogating the prisoner, our intelligence officers took him away. We immediately called Moscow to warn the high command that the Germans were preparing to launch an offensive.

A short time later Stalin phoned me back. I don't know if he'd talked earlier with Vatutin or not. Whenever I say that Stalin called me, I'm not claiming that he didn't call the commander as well. I don't want people thinking, "There goes Khrushchev, building himself up again, all the time saying 'I-I-I.'" No, my esteemed friends, I'm not trying to build myself up. I'm just trying to tell you what happened as I saw it. I sat on the Military Council and the Politbureau; Stalin knew me and trusted me. Even if he did sometimes make me a scapegoat for his own mistakes and even if he did take out his frustration and anxiety on me sometimes, he still had great confidence in me. He often called and asked my opinion. He did so when I was in Stalingrad and in the South, and he did so here at the Kursk Salient.

Stalin listened calmly as I explained the situation. He wasn't rude or impatient as he had sometimes been in the past. This pleased me. I have no idea why he was so cool and controlled on this occasion, while on other occasions he flew completely off the handle. It was as though the devil himself held a string attached to Stalin's main nerve, and no one knew when the devil would give the string a jerk, sending Stalin into one of his fits of rage. Both Stalin's temper and his self-control were developed to an advanced degree. He was, in short, an overpowering personality.

After I finished briefing him on the situation, Stalin asked me, "What do you think we should do?"

"The commander and I have been exchanging opinions, and we're very optimistic. We're just as glad that the Germans are opening an offensive tomorrow."

"Why?"

"Because our defensive positions are solid, and we'll make the enemy pay in blood when he tries to break through. Even though we're still waiting for the reinforcements, we'll be able to hold our ground. It takes fewer forces to defend than it does to attack. We've already learned that in practice as well as in theory."

The enemy, too, was confident of victory. Later I saw an order we captured from a demolished German armored unit. It contained a message addressed to the German troops which went something like this: "You are now waging an offensive with tanks far superior to the Russian T-34's. Until now the T-34 has been the best tank in the world, better even than our own. But now you have our new Tiger tanks. There is no equal to them. With such a weapon you warriors of the German army cannot fail to crush the enemy."

Their new tanks were very menacing indeed, but our troops learned quickly how to deal with them. At Kursk we won a battle which tipped the balance of the war in our favor. In my opinion the Battle of Kursk Salient was the turning point of the Great Patriotic War. It was decisive in determining the defeat of Hitlerite Germany and the ultimate triumph of our Soviet Army, our ideology, and our Communist Party.

Victory

Khrushchev entered Kiev on November 21, 1943. He was a lieutenant general now and certainly felt at one with the soldiers with whom he had lived for over two years. He went on with them as far as the new Polish border, but his military days were over and he had to turn back to Kiev and face the task of rebuilding the administration of the Party and Government of the Ukraine.

AFTER their defeat at Kursk, the Germans began to stagger westward under the blows of our army. I'm not without certain human weaknesses, including pride, and I'm certainly pleased to have been a member of the Military Council for the fronts involved in the huge battles which the Red Army waged at Stalingrad and Kursk.

After Kursk I was connected first with the Voronezh Front, then with the First Ukrainian Front. We were pushing hard toward Kiev. It was a triumphal hour when we reached the west bank of the Dnieper. We were fighting for the liberation of the capital of the Ukraine, the mother of Russian cities. Everyone felt tears of joy welling up inside him. Since 1941 we had been thrown back all the way to Stalingrad. And now, tomorrow or the next day, we would be in Kiev!

While we were still outside the city, Zhukov arrived from General Headquarters.[33] An underground bunker was prepared for him and me to sleep in. During the day we sat around joking and discussing the situation. On the second or third day we didn't even bother to use the dugout any more. We had driven the Germans into the woods, and our

33. After Kursk, Vatutin, commander of the Voronezh Front, took over the First Ukrainian Front. Khrushchev stayed with him. When Vatutin was fatally wounded in February, 1944, Zhukov took over his command for a time, the first operational command he had held since the battle for Moscow in 1941.

At Rostov
on its liberation,
February 18, 1943

In the Kiev area, October, 1943

Kharkov on its liberation, August, 1943

Kiev, November, 1943

In the Ukraine, at the time of liberation, 1943

troops were skirmishing on the outskirts of the city. We were fighting from our bridgehead west of the city in order to prevent the enemy from breaking out on the Zhitomir-Kiev road.

The deputy commander of the Voronezh Front was Grechko.[34] We had sent him to arrange a field headquarters for himself in Mezhgora and to help organize the troops from there. I remember the sun was setting when Grechko arrived at our own command post outside Kiev. It was a warm evening, though autumn was already setting in. We had come outdoors with our burkas [Caucasian capes] thrown back over our shoulders. Grechko drove up and reported directly to me. I had known him for a long time and respected him very much, so I allowed myself to joke about his incredible height: "Comrade General, please stand back a bit so I can look you in the eye." He laughed. I don't remember exactly what he said in his report, but his main point was what we already knew: the enemy had been smashed.

Shortly afterward there was a sudden explosion, and a cloud of smoke went up from the city. I knew Kiev like the palm of my hand and said, "The Germans are blowing up the 'Bolshevik' factory in the western part of the city. If they've started blowing up buildings, they must be fleeing." Before our offensive I had asked that special squads be appointed to go straight to the Central Committee buildings, the headquarters of the Kiev Military District, the Council of Ministers buildings, the Academy of Sciences, and other important spots as soon as our troops broke into Kiev; these squads were to make sure that the Germans didn't have time to start fires or set explosives. They were to drive the German demolition teams away and disarm any explosives that might have been fused.

When the explosions started, I told the artillery commander, "Comrade Varentsov, give an order to cover Kiev with scattered shelling." He looked at me in surprise. He knew that I was a loyal Kievan and that I loved the city dearly. So why was I suddenly ordering him to fire on Kiev? "Comrade Varentsov, if you open fire on the city," I explained, "it will send the Germans into a panic. They'll try to clear out even faster, and they'll do less harm to the city. We can always repair the damage caused by a few scattered shells."

34. Colonel General A. A. Grechko, now Marshal Grechko and Minister of Defense, was to become commander in chief of the Warsaw Pact forces in 1960. As commander of the Kiev Military District immediately after the war he worked closely with Khrushchev for some years. It was Grechko who planned, prepared, and led the Soviet invasion of Czechoslovakia in 1968.

Our troops entered Kiev on November 6 [1943], an especially triumphal day because it was the eve of the anniversary of the Great October Revolution. It might have looked as though we deliberately arranged the liberation of Kiev as a celebration of the anniversary, but
actually it was only a happy coincidence.

Early in the morning on November 6 I sent my chauffeur, Comrade
Zhuravlev, into Kiev to check on what the road was like. He reported
that the road was perfectly clear. Some Ukrainian leaders and I drove
into the city. I can't express the emotion which overwhelmed me as I
drove along the road into Kiev. It was an old familiar one we used to
take to and from our dacha before the war. We passed through the
suburbs and came to the Kreshchatik [the main boulevard of Kiev]. I
went straight to the Council of Ministers to inspect the building. It was
all right on the outside. The Central Committee building was still
standing, too, and so were the Academy of Sciences and the theaters,
but both the "Bolshevik" and "Kreshchatik" factories had been destroyed.

There was something eerie about the city. It had been such a noisy,
lively, youthful place before the war, and now there was no one
around. As we walked along the Kreshchatik and turned onto Lenin
Street, our footsteps echoed along the empty stretch of pavement
around us. Soon people began to emerge from hiding. They appeared
as though they had come out of the ground.

As we were walking along Lenin Street in the direction of the
Opera, talking and comparing impressions, we suddenly heard a hysterical scream, and a young man came running toward us. He kept
shouting, "I'm the only Jew left! I'm the last Jew in Kiev who's still
alive!" I tried to calm him down. I could see he was in quite a state,
and I worried that maybe he had gone insane. I asked him how he had
survived. "I have a Ukrainian wife," he said, "and she kept me hidden
in the attic. She fed me and took care of me. If I'd shown myself in the
city, I would have been exterminated along with all the other Jews." [35]

Later we met an old man with a gray beard who was carrying a
lunch bag just like the one I used to take to work with me at the fac-

35. The reference is to the massacre of the Jews at Babi Yar, a ravine just outside the city. In two days 33,771 Jews were killed — lined up on the edge of great
pits and machine-gunned. The Soviet leadership, under Khrushchev as well as Stalin, refused to recognize that Soviet Jews had suffered under the Nazis more than
other Soviet citizens. The site of Babi Yar was turned into a recreation ground. It
was not until the poet Yevgeny Yevtushenko wrote his celebrated poem entitled
"Babi Yar," and got into trouble as a result, that most Russians ever heard of it.

tory at Yuzovka. He threw himself on my shoulder and kissed me on both cheeks. I was very touched. A photographer was able to get a picture of this scene, and it appeared in many newspapers and magazines.

I got my first glimpse of Americans in the late spring or early summer of 1944 near Kiev. It was a bright, warm day. Suddenly we heard a rumbling noise in the distance. We scanned the sky and saw a large formation of airplanes flying toward us. I'd never seen this type of plane before. I realized they must be Americans because we didn't have anything like them in our own air force. I certainly hoped they were American; the only other thing they could have been was German. I later found out that these planes were B-17 "flying fortresses" and were based outside of Poltava as part of our agreement with Roosevelt. They used our territory to rearm and refuel after bombing missions over Germany. We would often see them flying overhead at night, on their way to targets in Germany, and then returning at daybreak. Somehow the Germans were able to track the American bombers back to Poltava and bomb their base. I received a report that many planes had been destroyed and many lives had been lost. Most of the casualties were our own men whom we had provided as maintenance personnel at the base.[36]

As we pushed the Germans west, we encountered an old enemy — Ukrainian nationalists. We learned from Comrade Begma, the commander of our partisan headquarters in the Ukraine, that the Banderites [37] were setting up partisan detachments of their own. They were based in the forests around Rovno. Their leader was called Taras Bulba, after Gogol's hero. We instructed Begma to find out in detail what the Banderite partisans planned to do. Then we told him to give Bulba an opportunity to join forces with us against the Germans. Bulba refused. We soon realized that the Banderites were trying to conserve their strength and consolidate their forces so that they could open a

36. Apart from an RAF fighter squadron based outside Murmansk in the early days of the war, establishment of the American bomber base at Poltava represented Stalin's sole concession to his Western allies' seeking to operate military aircraft from Soviet territory. The retaliatory German raid Khrushchev mentions took place on the night of June 21–22, 1944. It destroyed fifty American bombers and killed about thirty Russians, along with two American soldiers. Despite high hopes and elaborate planning, the "shuttle bombing" of Germany, which had the apt code name Frantic, never came to much. Only eighteen missions were flown. The operation was constantly frustrated by Soviet political suspicions and bureaucratic inefficiency.

37. Followers of the Ukrainian nationalist rebel Stepan Bandera.

partisan campaign against us at our rear after we drove the Germans out of the Ukraine.

I went to Rovno myself in the winter of 1944 to consult with Comrade Begma and the commander who had captured the city and who was liberating the area. I think it was Moskalenko.[38] The ground was covered with snow, and it was bitterly cold. I decided to return to Kiev as soon as the meeting at division headquarters was over. The commander tried to persuade me to stay the night, but I insisted on getting back to Kiev right away. I headed north along our old border with Poland. I stopped for a rest at one of our rear supply bases and noticed a curiously large number of people loitering about. I wondered to myself how many of them were Banderites in disguise, eating our food, warming themselves in front of our fires, and spying on us. I was warned that the area was swarming with Banderites. Rather than spend the night at this supply base, I pushed on to a little village on the old Polish border and stopped there.

I wish I'd had more chance to visit the Front headquarters after our troops crossed over into Poland. I would have loved to see something of our pursuit of the Germans into Eastern Europe, but I had my hands full in Kiev, supervising the reconstruction of the Ukraine and the reorganization of the Party.

There was great elation in the army as we drove the enemy out of our country. The guard units particularly distinguished themselves in the last year of the war. Their slogan was "On to Berlin! From Stalingrad to Berlin!" A favorite subject for jokes and toasts was who would get to be commandant of Berlin when we finally captured the German capital. Everyone wanted the job. Any man who had seen — and personally suffered — the hardships which this war had brought to our country wanted to do his part to make sure that the Germans paid for what they had done.

I remember one day in Kiev getting a call from Zhukov. He was jubilant. "Soon I'll have that slimy beast Hitler locked up in a cage," he said. "And when I send him to Moscow, I'll ship him by way of Kiev so you can have a look at him." I wished Zhukov every success. I knew that with him commanding the front, our offensive was in good hands. Then, after Germany capitulated, Zhukov called me again and said, "I

38. Marshal K. S. Moskalenko, then an army commander of the First Ukrainian Front. He was very close to Khrushchev. In 1960 he became commander in chief of Soviet Missile Command, and later, of Strategic Missile Forces.

won't be able to keep my promise after all. That snake Hitler is dead. He shot himself, and they burned his corpse. We found his charred carcass." [39]

Thus ended the great epic of our people's war against the Hitlerite invaders. We were overjoyed at the destruction of our enemy, and we felt a lofty moral satisfaction with our victory. The words of Alexander Nevsky rang in our ears: "He who comes to us with a sword shall perish by the sword." [40]

I should have known better, but I decided to call Stalin in order to congratulate him on the capitulation of Germany. When he answered the phone, I said, "Comrade Stalin, permit me to congratulate you on the victory of our armed forces and our people over the German army." And what was his response? He cut me off rudely and said I was wasting his time. I was simply dumbfounded. I rebuked myself for having called him in the first place. I knew what sort of person he was, and I should have expected exactly what happened. As I've already said, Stalin was a good actor. He was pretending now that since the war was over and done with, he was already thinking about other, more important matters; why should I waste his time talking about yesterday when he was straining his mind, thinking about tomorrow? He acted as though he weren't in the least surprised by our victory. He wanted me to think that he had known all along how the war would turn out. But I knew better. I had watched him during moments of crisis. I knew that during the war he had been even more worried and afraid than the people around him.

Stalin and the Allies

In this chapter we have the first public acknowledgment by any Soviet politician of the immense part played by Lend-Lease and American and British aid to the Soviet army. It is a pity that Khrushchev felt unable to speak in these terms when he was in power. The Soviet people have never been told what this aid amounted to, and the whole issue has been so clouded with propaganda of one kind and another

---

39. Stalin of course for a long time insisted that Hitler was not dead at all.
40. Alexander Nevsky, the legendary Russian warrior hero, was not the first to express this sentiment.

*that there are all too many people in the West who have never prop-
erly understood the magnitude and importance of the Allied contribution. Khrushchev does not tell the half of it; but at least he has begun
to set the record straight. For the rest, we see the old agonizing about
the Second Front, the profound suspicion of Allied motives, and the
total failure to comprehend the colossal naval operation necessary to
invade across the Channel — on Russian maps so trivial an obstacle.
The section also casts further light on the almost total ignorance in
which Khrushchev was kept of the vast movements presided over by
Stalin. At this time, when all is said, he was not only master of the
Ukraine but also a long-standing member of the Politbureau, the supreme policy-making body; yet it is clear that far from being consulted
about foreign policy as it developed, he was never even informed
about Stalin's plans and his negotiations with Churchill and Roosevelt,
except casually, in the form of anecdotes told by Stalin over the supper
table. In this connection it is worth noting that in a later chapter Khrushchev remarks that until he was called back to Moscow finally, in
1950, he was not even on the distribution list of papers circulated
among his Moscow colleagues. It was a strange preparation for the
man who was in due course to become the chief architect of Soviet policy. It says a great deal for Khrushchev's basic sense and capacity to
learn that he succeeded as well as he did. It also explains in large measure his failings.*

A VICTORY Parade in Red Square was scheduled for June 24, 1945. I
came to Moscow for the occasion. I wanted to watch our troops marching and to rejoice with all our people in the capital of our Homeland.
Eisenhower came to Moscow, too. He stood with us on the Lenin Mausoleum to review the parade. This was the first time I met Eisenhower.
Stalin gave a huge banquet. All our military leaders were there. So was
Eisenhower. I don't think Montgomery, the English commander was
there. Stalin had formed good relations with Eisenhower and even better ones with Roosevelt. He had bad relations with Churchill and even
worse ones with Montgomery.

After the war, but before my transfer from the Ukraine back to Moscow [at the end of 1949], I frequently heard Stalin speak about Eisenhower's noble characteristics in conversations with his inner circle.
Stalin always stressed Eisenhower's decency, generosity, and chivalry

in his dealings with his allies. Stalin said that if it hadn't been for Eisenhower, we wouldn't have succeeded in capturing Berlin. The Americans could have been there first. The Germans had concentrated their forces against us as they prepared to surrender to the Americans and British. Stalin appealed to Eisenhower in a letter to hold back his armies; Stalin told Eisenhower that according to his agreement with Roosevelt and in view of the amount of blood our people had shed, our troops deserved to enter Berlin before the Western Allies. Eisenhower then held his troops back and halted their offensive, thus allowing our troops to take Berlin. If he hadn't done this, Berlin would have been occupied by the Americans before we reached it, in which case, as Stalin said, the question of Germany might have been decided differently and our own position might have turned out quite a bit worse. This was the sort of chivalrous generosity Eisenhower demonstrated. He was true to Roosevelt's word.

However, at this time Truman was President, and Stalin had no respect at all for Truman. He considered Truman worthless. Rightly so. Truman didn't deserve respect. This is a fact.

At the very end of the war Stalin was very worried that the Americans would cross the line of demarcation in the West. He was doubtful that they would relinquish the territory which Roosevelt had previously agreed to give us in Teheran. The Americans could have said that the line their troops reached was the new boundary dividing the zones of occupation. But the Americans pulled their troops back and deployed them along the line which had been set in Teheran. This too says something about Eisenhower's decency.

The Germans were hard pressed by our troops and couldn't resist any longer. They were supposed to throw down their arms and surrender to us. However, they refused to do this and moved west instead to surrender to the Americans. Once again, Stalin addressed himself to Eisenhower, saying that Soviet troops had shed their blood to crush the Germans and now the Germans whom they encountered were surrendering to the Americans. Stalin complained that this wasn't fair. This was on the Austrian Front, where Malinovsky was directing our advance. Eisenhower ordered the commander of the German army to surrender to the Russians who had defeated his army.

Stalin once made a similar request to Churchill. The Germans were fleeing from Rokossovsky and surrendering to the English in a region occupied by Montgomery. Stalin asked the English not to take prison-

ers and to compel the Germans to surrender to our troops. "But nothing of the sort!" said Stalin angrily. "Montgomery took them all, and
he took their arms. So the fruits of our victory over the Germans were
being enjoyed by Montgomery!"

Both General Eisenhower and Field Marshal Montgomery were representatives of the same class, the bourgeoisie. Yet they decided this
question differently. They interpreted differently the principles of part-
nership, agreement, and honor. Whenever I had dealings with Eisenhower in later years, I always remembered these actions of his during
the war. I kept in mind Stalin's words about him. Stalin could never be
accused of liking someone without reason, particularly a class enemy.
He was uncorruptible and irreconcilable in class questions. It was one
of his strongest qualities, and he was greatly respected for it.[41]

Stalin invited Eisenhower to our Victory Parade and expressed his
recognition of Eisenhower's merits by presenting him with our highest
medal, the Order of Victory. It's true the same medal was given to
Field Marshal Montgomery, but in that case it was a formal fulfillment
of our duty as an ally because the English were presenting their medals to our military leaders. It was merely reciprocity.

What were my impressions of the opinions Stalin expressed about
the interrelations of the Allies during the war and specifically about
Roosevelt and Churchill? Judging from what he said, I think Stalin
was more sympathetic to Roosevelt than Churchill because Roosevelt
seemed to have considerable understanding for our problems. Roosevelt and Stalin had a common antipathy for monarchy and its
institutions. Once he told me about the following episode. When they
were in Teheran sitting over dinner, Roosevelt raised his glass and
proposed a toast to the President of the Soviet Union: "Mr. Kalinin."
Everyone drank, and after a few moments Churchill raised his glass
and proposed a toast to the king of Great Britain. Roosevelt said he
wouldn't drink that toast. Churchill's back went up, but Roosevelt was
firm. "No," he said, "I won't drink. I cannot drink to an English king. I
can never forget my father's words." Stalin explained that when Roosevelt's father left for America from England or Ireland, he said on the

41. It is easy to believe that Stalin was more than surprised by the restraint
shown by Eisenhower and others in the matter of halting the Allied advance into
Germany. Certainly he was furious with Montgomery for taking prisoner large
numbers of Germans fleeing from the Soviet advance. He was, of course, perfectly
correct in telling Khrushchev that he got on better with Roosevelt than with
Churchill. Roosevelt held British imperialism in the deepest suspicion and was convinced that he could come to a personal understanding with Stalin.

boat to the young Roosevelt, "The king is our enemy." Roosevelt had never forgotten his father's contempt for the king of England. Despite all the requirements of etiquette, Roosevelt didn't raise his glass.[42]

In disputes during the working sessions in Teheran, Stalin often found Roosevelt siding with him against Churchill. Thus, Stalin's personal sympathies were definitely reserved for Roosevelt, although he still held Churchill in high esteem, too. Churchill was not only a great English statesman; he held one of the leading positions in the conduct of world politics. At the time of the Allies' failure in the Ardennes, which threatened their invasion landing, Churchill asked Stalin to divert the forces of the German army onto us. This required that we launch an offensive which wasn't part of our plans at the time and which shouldn't have come until considerably later, but it turned out to be most profitable for us. Stalin did well to demonstrate our goodwill toward our ally in a time of need.

Churchill certainly played an important role in the war. He understood the threat hanging over England, and that's why he did everything he could to direct the Germans against the Soviet Union — in order to pull the Soviet Union into war against Germany. When Hitler attacked us, Churchill immediately declared that England considered it necessary to make a treaty joining forces with us against Germany. Here, too, Stalin did the right thing. He accepted Churchill's proposal and signed the treaty. After a certain time America entered the war, and a coalition of the three Great Powers came into existence.

It's difficult to judge what the intentions of the Allies were toward the end of the war. I wouldn't exclude the possibility that they desired to put a still greater burden on the shoulders of the Soviet Union and to bleed us even more. Or perhaps it's as they explained: they weren't sufficiently prepared for a landing. Their arms production wasn't sufficiently developed. They needed more time, and so on. Both explanations were probably true, but I think they were mostly dictated by their desire to bleed us dry so that they could come in at the last stages and determine the fate of the world. They wanted to take advantage of the results of the war and impose their will not only on

42. It would be interesting to know whether in fact Stalin did tell the story of Roosevelt's refusal to drink to the King. If he really believed that President Roosevelt's father had emigrated to the USA from Ireland or England, he must have been very badly briefed. It seems likely that Khrushchev is confusing one of Stalin's anecdotes about the coolness between Roosevelt and Churchill at Teheran with a muddled memory about the immediate ancestry of President Kennedy.

their enemy, Germany, but on their ally, the USSR, as well. I can easily imagine how this thought played a significant role in their thinking.

To look at it from a class position, it was in the Allies' interest to rely on the Soviet Union as a wartime ally, despite the fact that our country was founded on Socialist principles. We had to unite our forces against a common enemy. None of us could have won the war singlehanded. But while exerting our collective efforts against the common enemy, each of us remained on his own class position. The Western Allies were certainly not interested in strengthening us. England and America, from their class positions, knew they had to help us to an extent, but they still wanted the Soviet Union to be considerably weaker after the war so that they could dictate their will to us.

For our part, we knew it would be useful to become considerably stronger at the end of the war in order for our voice to carry more weight in the settlement of international questions. If we had succeeded, the question of Germany wouldn't have been decided the way it was at Potsdam. The Potsdam decision was a compromise based on the distribution of power among the Allies at the end of the war. The onesidedness of the agreement was particularly reflected in the clauses concerning Berlin and Vienna. These cities were located in the zone occupied by Soviet troops, and it would have seemed that they should have been part of our zone. However, the Allies didn't give them to us. Berlin and Vienna were each divided into four sectors. We received one sector, and the Western powers — England, America, and France — received the other three. This says something about the distribution of power at the end of the war.

When we began our advance west and were approaching the border of Germany, the Allies were compelled to hurry up and launch their landing. They were afraid we might push considerably farther than the boundaries defined at Yalta.

Nevertheless, we must still give credit to the Allies for their contribution to the common cause of defeating Hitlerite Germany. In order to avoid excessive haughtiness, the people and the Party of the Soviet Union must be properly informed about the contribution of the Allies to the common cause and to the Soviet Union itself. If the past isn't analyzed objectively, the building of the future will be based on illusions and primitive patriotism instead of proved facts. Unfortunately, our historical works about World War II have perpetrated an illusion. They have been written out of a false sense of pride and out of a fear to tell the truth about our Allies' contribution — all because Stalin himself held an incorrect, unrealistic position. He knew the truth, but he admitted it only to himself in the toilet. He considered it too shameful and humiliating for our country to admit publicly.

But, telling the truth needn't have been a humiliation. Recognizing the merits of our partners in the war need not have diminished our own merits. On the contrary, an objective statement would have raised us still higher in the eyes of all peoples and it would not in the least have diminished our dignity and the importance of our victories. But in this case truthfulness was unthinkable for Stalin. He tried to cover up our weaknesses. He figured that it would make us stronger than our enemy and that we would be feared more. This was stupid. He should have known that you can't fool the enemy. The enemy can always see for himself and analyze on his own. It's also possible that Stalin feared that openness about the history of the war might backfire on him personally. That's a different matter. But I still think we should have openly admitted what happened and not tried to cover up. We would have been helping our country and our cause by not trying to hide our mistakes, by revealing them for the people to see, no matter how painful it might have been. The people would have understood and supported us. If necessary they would have forgiven the mistakes which had been committed. When I did expose the mismanagement of the war, the people were able to say, "Here Khrushchev is criticizing Stalin, but he is using Stalin only for purposes of illustration in a constructive analysis." That's perfectly true. I don't think it's ever too late for the new generation, which will soon replace the current leadership of our country, to cast objective light on the beginning of the war. We must study the past in order not to permit in our own time those mistakes which were permitted earlier. We must prevent them both in the present and in the future.

To acknowledge the material aid which we received in the past from our adversaries of the present doesn't have any bearing on the situation of today. We shouldn't boast that we vanquished the Germans all by ourselves and that the Allies moved in only for the kill. That's why I give my own view of the Allies' contribution, and I hope that my view will be confirmed by the research of historians who investigate objectively the circumstances which developed between 1941 and 1945. The English helped us tenaciously and at great peril to themselves. They shipped cargo to Murmansk and suffered huge losses. German submarines lurked all along the way. Germany had invaded Norway and moved right next door to Murmansk.

As Mikoyan confirmed after his trip to America, we received military equipment, ships, and many supplies from the Americans, all of which greatly aided us in waging the war. After Stalin's death, it seemed that all our artillery was mounted on American equipment. I remember proposing, "Let's turn all the automotive equipment we're producing over to the military so that the tractor-mounts in our parades will be Soviet-made." Almost all the artillery in the GDR [East Germany] was mounted on American Studebakers. I said, "This simply won't do. It's disgraceful. Just look how many years have passed since the war ended, and we're still driving around in American equipment!" By this I wanted only to stress how many of our cars and trucks we had received from the Americans. Just imagine how we would have advanced from Stalingrad to Berlin without them! Our losses would have been colossal because we would have had no maneuverability.[43]

In addition we received steel and aluminum from which we made guns, airplanes, and so on. Our own industry was shattered and partly abandoned to the enemy. We also received food products in great quantities. I can't give you the figures because they've never been published. They're all locked away in Mikoyan's memory. There were many jokes going around in the army, some of them off-color, about American Spam; it tasted good nonetheless. Without Spam we wouldn't have been able to feed our army. We had lost our most fertile lands — the Ukraine and the northern Caucasus.

I repeat, the Allies gave us this help neither out of compassion for our people, nor out of respect for our political system, nor out of hope for the victory of Socialism and the triumph of Marxism-Leninism. The Allies helped us out of a sober assessment of the situation. They were facing a matter of their own life or death. They helped us so that our Soviet Army would not fall under the blow of Hitlerite Germany and so that, supplied with modern weapons, we would pulverize the life force of the enemy and weaken ourselves at the same time. They wanted to wait to join the war actively against Germany at a time when the Soviet Union had already spent its might and was no longer able to occupy a decisive position in the solution of world problems.

43. The Soviet tanks were the finest in the world; but until Stalingrad the Soviet army had virtually no mechanized transport. It was with American and British trucks that it was able to advance swiftly, complete the encirclement of the German forces around Stalingrad, and sweep out rapidly across the steppe to shatter the German armor at Kursk — and on to Berlin and Vienna.

7

Famine in the Ukraine

*The great Ukrainian Famine of 1946–47 went almost completely un-
noticed in the West. It was not until December, 1947, that Andrei
Zhdanov in one of his last public speeches referred to this famine, declaring that it had been caused by the worst drought in the history of the
Ukraine, worse even than the great drought of 1890. It was not, however, as bad as the famine of the collectivization years, which has even
now never been officially admitted. The famine was due largely to
drought, but it was drought affecting a ruined agriculture. Khrushchev
has something to say about the lack of manpower on the farms (in the
immediate postwar years all over the Soviet Union, not only in the
Ukraine, there was scarcely an able-bodied man to be found on any of
the collective farms, which were cultivated by women, children, and
old men working with primitive tools). The devastation was such that
the bulk of the population in the Ukraine and Belorussia were living in
dugouts — pits dug in the ground and roughly roofed over.*

*This was the background of Khrushchev's second spell as viceroy of
the Ukraine. His accounts of hunger and cannibalism, far from being
exaggerated, give only the faintest idea of the ruinous state of affairs.
But there was one aspect, contributing to the famine, which Khrushchev does not mention: under the German occupation the collectivization had broken down, and it was one of the Party's tasks to reim-
pose it. Resistance was strong, not only from the peasants but also from
the farm managers who, in countless instances, were turning a blind
eye to the private acquisition of communal land in exchange for a
rake-off for themselves. It was this situation which Khrushchev had to
cope with, and he could not cope fast enough. It was evident at the
time that he was in trouble and that Kaganovich himself had been sent*

out from Moscow to be his superior and to bring all possible ruthless-
ness to bear on the recollectivization. The glimpse we have of Khru-
shchev fighting for his own Ukrainians against what he calls the State
(meaning the Moscow government, of which he was in fact a member)
is sufficiently revealing. In a sense it was 1930 all over again, with the
peasants being starved to feed the towns — but this time Khrushchev
was caught between two fires. He was responsible for the well-being of
the Ukraine; at the same time it was his job to carry out Stalin's orders.
We see how those orders were conceived, and we are given a close-up
of the personal intrigues among Stalin's closest colleagues in Moscow.
The great row about spring wheat versus winter wheat, about shallow
versus deep plowing, was all part and parcel of the rows between indi-
viduals, who, as always, would seize on any technicality as a weapon
in their perpetual guerrilla warfare and would play on Stalin's preju-
dices to incite him against their rivals. Malenkov was very active in all
these matters (Khrushchev does not mention it, but Malenkov had
been sent to start reconstruction work in the Ukraine as the Germans
were pushed back and while Khrushchev was still at Front headquar-
ters).

ONCE the Ukraine was liberated from the Hitlerite invaders in
1944, I worked hard reorganizing the Party and restoring the
economy. All able-bodied men had been drafted into the army. As it
battled its way forward, the Red Army reinforced itself with men who
had been in occupied territory. The recruits from the liberated areas
understood their duty and didn't need to be preached at about their
obligation to join the ranks of the Soviet Army to fight against Hitlerite
Germany.

The job of reconstructing the people's economy of the Ukraine, especially agriculture, fell upon those who were left behind the Red Army's
advance: old men, invalids, those unfit for military service, and particularly the women. Some engineers, miners, and industrial workers were
exempt from military service. Those who were mobilized into industry,
including many young girls, went willingly. Their zeal was understandable. For one thing, patriotism drew many of them to the cause.
So did the Party agitation and propaganda campaign stressing that the
restoration of industry was the only salvation from economic disaster
and the only way to raise the living standard of the people. For another thing, the areas where industry was being restored were better

supplied than rural areas. There was more food in the cities than in the villages.

In the Donbass, coal mining, steel manufacturing, machine shops, and local industries were all restored. Reconstruction progressed rapidly. It was astonishing to see how tenacious the people were and how well they understood the necessity of exerting all their power to build up industry and agriculture. Lenin's wise and forward-looking policies instituted after the October Revolution had done much to heal nationalist antagonisms between Russians and Ukrainians. Naturally, there were still problems. It will take decades to eradicate all the evils of the past. But the basic goal had already been realized. The people — the workers, peasants, and intelligentsia — all knew that only through unity could we be strong and could we achieve material as well as cultural growth. The war had united us once and for all and shattered the hopes of our enemies that we might fall prey to their divisive pressure. After the war had ended and the jubilation of the people had died down, our workers returned to the factories, the shops, the mines, the state farms, and the collective farms. Reconstruction proceeded at a still faster pace.

But 1946 was a very dry year, and the agriculture of the Ukraine suffered badly. A poor harvest was expected. Severe climatic conditions combined with the poor mechanization of our agriculture made it inevitable. We were short of tractors, horses, and oxen. In addition, our organization of manpower was still very weak. Men were coming back from the war ready to work, but no one fitted into his old place. After a long time away, some men were no longer qualified for skilled farm labor, and others had never been qualified in the first place.[1]

All possible measures were taken to supply enough grain to the State. It must be said that the Ukrainian collective farm workers understood their duty. They did everything in their power to provide the rest of the country with bread. They had suffered from hunger themselves while their own country was occupied by the Germans, and they knew what having enough bread meant. They understood that heavy industry couldn't be restored without bread. The same went for min-

1. This situation was aggravated by several factors: the appalling wartime losses, amounting to some twenty million, mainly the able-bodied; the desperate need for men to rebuild and work the factories; and Stalin's deliberate policy of directing demobilized soldiers to work far from their own homes lest they stir up discontent in their own villages with accounts of higher living standards in the West. The idea was that they would be less likely to talk to strangers about what they had seen.

On the job after the war, 1946

With Kaganovich (center) and Ukrainian Foreign Minister Manuilsky, in the Ukraine, 1946 or 1947

Visiting a metallurgical factory in occupied territory, 1944

ing, steel-making, and the chemical industry. Besides, the collective farmers had great confidence in the Party. After all, victory over the Germans had been achieved under the Party's guidance. Among the collective farm workers in the Ukraine, there was a widespread feeling of responsibility for contributing to the security of the rest of the country by providing the necessary agricultural products.

We were supposed to supply the State first and ourselves second. We had been assigned an output plan of something like 400 million pood [7.2 million tons] for the year 1946. This quota was established arbitrarily, although it was dressed up in the press with supporting scientific data. It had been calculated not on the basis of how much we really could produce, but on the basis of how much the State thought it could beat out of us. The quota system was really a system of extortion. I saw that the year was threatened with catastrophe. It was difficult to predict how it would end. I was getting letters from collective farm workers and from their chairmen. These were heart-breaking letters. A typical one comes to mind. It was from the chairman of a collective farm, who wrote, "Well, Comrade Khrushchev, we have delivered our quota to the State. But we've given everything away. Nothing is left for us. We are sure the State and the Party won't forget us and that they will come to our aid." He must have thought their fate depended on me. I was the Chairman of the Council of People's Commissars of the Ukraine and First Secretary of the Ukrainian Central Committee. He imagined that since I was the head of the Ukrainian state, I could help him. Well, he was deceiving himself. There was nothing I could do once the grain had been turned over to State receiving points. It was no longer in my power to dispose of it. I myself had to make a special request from the State for grain to feed our own people.[2]

I could already see that our output plan wouldn't be fulfilled. I assigned a group of agricultural experts and economists under Comrade Starchenko to make a realistic calculation of how much grain we really could produce. They came up with a figure of somewhere between 100 and 200 million pood. This was very little. Before the war the Ukraine had produced as much as 500 million pood, and the State had already assigned us an output plan of 400 million pood for 1946. I felt it was

2. In 1938 Khrushchev had gone to the Ukraine as Stalin's unquestioning and quite ruthless agent. His wartime experiences taken together with his close-up view of the suffering of the people had their effect. Here he emerges as a champion of the people against the State, whose representative he nevertheless was.

best to approach the problem honestly. I hoped that if I reported the situation to Stalin candidly and supported my report with facts and figures, he would believe me. I wanted to do everything in my power to make Stalin understand our position.

In the past I had sometimes succeeded in breaking through the bureaucratic resistance of the Moscow apparatus and appealed directly to Stalin on a few matters. Sometimes, if I was able to present carefully selected material with logically constructed conclusions, the facts would speak for themselves and Stalin would support me.

I hoped I could prove I was right this time, too, and that Stalin would understand that my request wasn't "sabotage." This term was always on hand as a justification for the repression and the extortion of products from the collective farms. In this case, I would be trying to convince Stalin that we couldn't supply the agricultural products we wanted and needed. Our own country needed them, and Stalin also wanted to send food to the other Socialist countries, especially Poland and Germany, which couldn't survive without our help. Stalin was already building up an alliance and fitting himself with the toga of the leader of future military campaigns. He would be very unhappy to hear that the Ukraine not only couldn't fulfill its assigned quota for delivery to the State, but in fact needed food from the State to feed its own people.

However, I had no choice but to confront Stalin with the facts: famine was imminent, and something had to be done. I gave orders for a document to be prepared for the Council of Ministers of the USSR in which I asked that the State issue us ration cards so that we could supply the farm population with a certain quantity of products and organize the feeding of the hungry. I was very doubtful of success. I was hesitant to send the document to Moscow because I knew Stalin, his rudeness and his fierce temper.. But my comrades persuaded me. They said, "We've already arranged it so that if you address this document to Stalin, it won't ever get to him personally. He'll never see it. We've talked to Kosygin, and he has agreed to give us the ration cards we need." Kosygin was then in charge of these matters.[3]

I hesitated a long time, but finally I signed the document. When the document reached Moscow, Stalin wasn't there. He was vacationing in

3. A. N. Kosygin, now Prime Minister of the USSR. During the greater part of the war he had been responsible for coordinating the various food industries, as well as what light industry there was.

Sochi. But Malenkov and Beria saw a chance to exploit my document to discredit me in Stalin's eyes. Instead of deciding the matter themselves, which they could easily have done on Stalin's behalf, they sent it on to him. All official documents to the Government were addressed personally to Stalin, but he never set eyes on most of them, just as many government decrees he'd never seen appeared over his signature. But thanks to Malenkov and Beria, this request of mine went straight to Stalin in Sochi.

In reply Stalin sent me the rudest, most insulting telegram. I was a dubious character, he said; I was writing memoranda to prove that the Ukraine was unable to take care of itself, and I was requesting an outrageous quantity of cards for feeding people. I can't express how murderously this telegram depressed me. I saw clearly the whole tragedy, which was hanging not only over me personally, but over the whole Ukrainian people. Famine was now inevitable; Stalin's response dashed our last hopes that it could be avoided.

Stalin returned from Sochi, and I immediately went from Kiev to meet him in Moscow. I was ready for the worst dressing down imaginable. In this kind of situation anything could happen. You could end up on the list of enemies of the people in no time at all. In the blink of an eye you could be thrown into the Lubyanka [the secret police headquarters and prison in the heart of Moscow]. I told Stalin that I had taken pains in my memorandum to reflect accurately the state of affairs in the Ukraine; I insisted that the Ukraine really did need help. My arguments just aggravated his anger all the more. He flatly turned down our request for ration cards.

By now, as I had predicted, famine was under way. Soon I was receiving letters and official reports about deaths from starvation. Then cannibalism started. I received a report that a human head and the soles of feet had been found under a little bridge near Vasilkovo, a town outside of Kiev. Apparently the corpse had been eaten. There were similar cases. Kirichenko,[4] who was then Secretary of the Odessa Regional Committee, told me that he had gone to a collective farm to check on how the people were surviving the winter. He was told to go

4. A. I. Kirichenko, one of Khrushchev's subordinates in the Ukrainian Party apparatus before the war; as a major general he served on the military councils of various fronts during the war. He succeeded Khrushchev as First Secretary of the Ukraine at the end of 1949 and came to Moscow as Khrushchev's right-hand man in 1957, having helped him defeat the so-called Anti-Party Group. In 1960 he was suddenly disgraced for reasons never divulged.

see a woman who worked there. Here is how he described it: "I found a scene of horror. The woman had the corpse of her own child on the table and was cutting it up. She was chattering away as she worked, 'We've already eaten Manechka [Little Maria]. Now we'll salt down Vanechka [Little Ivan]. This will keep us for some time.' Can you imagine? This woman had gone crazy with hunger and butchered her own children!" As I retell this story, my thoughts go back to that period. I can see that horrible scene vividly in my mind. There was nothing I could do. I reported all these things to Stalin, but it only fanned his anger all the more. He would say, "You're being soft-bellied! They're deceiving you. They're counting on being able to appeal to your sentimentality when they report things like that. They're trying to force you to give them all your reserves." Apparently Stalin had channels of information which bypassed me and which he trusted more than my own reports. Some people were spreading the rumor that I was giving in to local Ukrainian influences, that I was under pressure from Ukrainian interest groups, and that I was already becoming a Ukrainian nationalist myself. People were saying that I didn't deserve full confidence any more, and Stalin started to regard my reports with a certain familiar cautiousness. And where was this other information coming from? From the Chekists, of course. They were traveling around the country and reporting back to the Central Committee. Some of this information filtered up to Stalin himself. Usually people were afraid to give Stalin information because they knew that discouraging reports would displease him and jeopardize themselves. Stalin liked to think the country was thriving. He liked to think, as Taras Shevchenko [nineteenth-century Ukrainian poet] once said, "From the land of Moldavians to the land of the Finns, all tongues are silent because the times are good." The only difference was that Shevchenko was writing during the reign of Nicholas I, and this was the reign of Joseph I.

Stalin raised the question of convening a Central Committee plenum to discuss agriculture. I don't know how long it had been since a plenum had been held. There had been plenums in the late thirties, first to discuss the struggle against the enemies of the people and then to discuss the excesses which had been permitted during the struggle against the enemies of the people. At that time Stalin had played the role of a benevolent fighter against the excesses which he had initiated himself. Anyway, Stalin now raised the question of calling a plenum to discuss how to raise the productivity of our agriculture.

The question came up of who should be instructed to deliver the General Report. Stalin was thinking out loud in front of everybody. "Who should deliver the General Report?" he asked. "Malenkov? He's in charge of agricultural matters, but what kind of report can he deliver? He doesn't know the first thing about agriculture. He doesn't even know agricultural terminology." Stalin said this in Malenkov's presence. He was absolutely correct, but it was all the more astounding that Stalin had assigned Malenkov to handle agriculture if he knew that Malenkov was totally incompetent in this area. The paradox was interesting to me, and I have no ready explanation for it. But then, anything was possible with Stalin.

Suddenly Stalin said to me, "You make the General Report."

I was simply terrified by this instruction and said, "Comrade Stalin, please don't assign this to me."

"Why not?"

"I could deliver a report on the Ukraine. I've been concerned with the Ukraine for some years now, and I know more or less what the situation is there. But I don't know anything about agriculture in the Russian Federation, and I haven't the slightest idea about Siberia. I've never even been in Central Asia. I've never seen cotton, and I don't know how it grows. Actually, before going to the Ukraine, I had almost nothing to do with agriculture at all. I'm an industrialist. I've been concerned with industry and with the city administration."

But he was insistent: "That doesn't matter. You'll make the General Report anyway."

I said, "No, Comrade Stalin, I ask you please to release me from this. I don't want to mislead the Central Committee, nor do I want to put myself in a stupid position by trying to make a report on subjects which I really don't understand."

He thought about it for a few moments and then said, "Well, all right. We'll assign the report to Andreyev." [5] Andreyev had earned

5. A. A. Andreyev, one of Stalin's senior lieutenants in his rise to power and thereafter, had been a Bolshevik since 1914 and a Politbureau member since 1932. A dour and featureless organization man, he turned his hand to every job, which he pursued ruthlessly in Stalin's interest. In 1943 he was put in charge of agriculture. He came to grief in 1950, incurring Stalin's displeasure, ostensibly over a technical matter of agricultural policy, but survived to make an abortive comeback under the protection of Malenkov. It was in 1950 that Khrushchev emerged as the spokesman for Soviet agriculture.

himself a reputation as the Party's expert on agriculture. Compared with the other members of the Politbureau, he knew quite a bit about agriculture, although personally I wasn't very impressed by his knowledge. He was a rather dry and formal person. I knew he would throw together his General Report by drawing on papers written by other agricultural experts. In any event, I couldn't suggest anyone better, and I was relieved that this cup had passed from me.

Andrei Andreyevich Andreyev was confirmed as speaker for the Central Committee Plenum. The Plenum took place in Sverdlov Hall [of the Kremlin]. Andrei Andreyevich's report turned out to be fairly coherent and logically constructed as Andrei Andreyevich's reports usually were. I sat next to Stalin and saw that he was listening attentively. During the recess, we went into a lounge where members of the Politbureau got together for refreshments. We sat down at a table, tea was served, and Stalin asked me, "What did you think of Andreyev's report?"

I said, "It certainly cast light on all the main problems."

"But you were sitting there absolutely indifferent to what he was saying. I was watching you."

"If you want me to be frank, I'll tell you I think these problems should have been posed somewhat differently. All the necessary matters were touched on, but in a very stereotyped fashion."

Stalin was furious. "First you refuse to deliver the report yourself and now you're criticizing it." I hadn't wanted to criticize the report, especially since I had declined to give it myself. However, I still told Stalin honestly that I thought Andreyev had done a pretty second-rate job. Now I could see Stalin was very displeased with me indeed.

After the recess, we started discussing the report. Many people spoke, including myself. I talked about the problems of reconstructing the economy of the Ukraine. I said I considered mechanization and the questions of seed stocks to be the key subjects. Before this Plenum there had been a decree laying down the first commandment for a collective farm worker: his first obligation was to meet his output quota and make his required deliveries to the State; only then could he supply seed and other products to his fellow laborers on his collective farm. I believed that this first commandment, which had been Stalin's idea, should be revoked and seed should be set aside for sowing on the farm before grain was turned over to the State. In the old days a peasant would starve to death before eating grain he had set aside for seed.

His seed was his future, the very life of his farm. How could we take his seed away from him? It made little difference that the State was supposed to compensate him with new seed for sowing, the farmer had no way of knowing what strain of seed it was or where it had come from. The State was making farmers sow their fields with unknown seed which may not have been acclimatized to their own region. It was no way to manage agriculture.

My remarks during the discussion of Andreyev's report aggravated Stalin even more. A still darker cloud hung over me after Maltsev's speech. He was an experienced farmer who managed the agriculture of the Urals excellently.[6] In his speech he said that everything was going very well in the Urals and that they were bringing in a good harvest of spring wheat. As soon as Maltsev mentioned spring wheat, I knew that I was in even deeper trouble than before. I knew that Stalin wouldn't stop to examine details but that he would grab the question of spring wheat and throw it in my face. I had already declared myself against the sowing of spring wheat according to rigid, compulsory rules. Spring wheat was less high-yielding in the Ukraine, especially in the south, but it yielded a decent harvest on certain collective farms. Therefore I thought Ukrainian collective farms should be able to sow it if they wanted to, but there should be no blanket order from Moscow compelling every collective farm to sow a specified percentage of spring wheat. In some cases a harvest of spring wheat didn't even yield enough of a harvest to pay for the cost of the seed. Stalin didn't understand this, and he didn't want to hear anything about it. I had told him about our problem with spring wheat before the war. At that time he had agreed with me and approved a decision to release Ukrainian collective farms from compulsory cultivation of spring wheat.

There was another recess. When we went into the lounge, Stalin snapped menacingly at me, "Did you hear what Maltsev said about spring wheat?"

"Yes, but Comrade Stalin, he was speaking about the Urals. In the Ukraine our highest-yielding crop is winter wheat. In the Urals they don't sow winter wheat at all. They sow only spring wheat. They have studied it. They know how to cultivate it and how to harvest it profitably."

6. T. S. Maltsev, a gifted and energetic agronomist with powerful Party connections, was for a long time in the forefront of experimental attempts to increase productivity; some of the attempts were good, some bad.

"That doesn't matter. If they're able to get such a good harvest of spring wheat in the Urals and if we" — he slapped himself on the stomach — "have such good rich, dark soil, then we should get an even better harvest. There should be a resolution taken to that effect."

I said, "If you want to put it in a resolution, then go ahead. You can also record that I'm opposed. Everyone knows I'm against spring wheat. But if it's what you want to do, then issue a resolution to the northern Caucasus and to the Rostov Region."

"No, this resolution will apply directly to you." By that he meant that I would have to take the initiative so that the other grain-growing areas would follow my lead.[7]

A commission was created with Andrei Andreyevich as chairman. I was appointed to this commission, too. When the Central Committee Plenum ended, I had to get back to the Ukraine. The commission hadn't yet finished its work, and Malenkov and Andrei Andreyevich were left to work out the resolution Stalin wanted. Just before I left, I proposed that the commission recommend revoking the first commandment for collective farm workers. I proposed that the stocking of seed for the collective farms should proceed in parallel with the delivery of grain to the State in a certain proportion. This was a concession on my part, but I believed it would be better than no change at all. As it was, the State wasn't leaving anything at all for the farmers. According to my proposal, the farmers would deliver a certain percentage of their grain to the State while retaining a certain percentage for their own seed stores.

Then I left for Kiev. Malenkov phoned me a few days later and said, "The resolution is ready. We have not included your proposal regarding seed stores for collective and state farms. We are now going to report to Stalin. Do you want us to report your proposal separately? Or perhaps we shouldn't mention it at all?"

This was clearly a provocation. Everyone knew, and Stalin knew, that I had fought hard for my proposal at the commission meetings. If I were to tell Malenkov not to mention my proposal to Stalin, I would look like a coward, so I answered, "No, Comrade Malenkov, please go ahead and report my point of view to Comrade Stalin."

7. The drama of spring versus winter wheat was characteristic of Stalin's interference in technical matters about which he knew nothing. He was incapable of realizing that what might be suitable in the Urals could be unsuitable in the Ukraine. Curiously, Khrushchev showed much the same failing in years to come when he insisted on the wholesale growing of maize, regardless of local conditions.

"Very well," he said. So they reported it. Not long afterwards Malenkov phoned me again and said that my proposal had angered Stalin and he had rejected it out of hand.

The next thing that happened was that Stalin suddenly raised the question of what sort of help I should be given in the Ukraine.[8] This meant he had his eye on me. "Apparently we'd better bolster up Khrushchev's leadership in Kiev," he said. "The Ukraine is being ruined, which could be a disaster for our whole country." He was obviously up to something, but I wasn't sure what he was driving at. Then he said, "I think we had better send Kaganovich to help you. What do you think about that?"

"Well," I said, "Kaganovich was once Secretary of the Central Committee in the Ukraine, and he knows the Ukraine very well. Naturally, since the Ukraine is such a huge Republic, there's enough for tens or hundreds of people to do, not to mention just two."

Stalin then said, "We'll send Patolichev to help you, too."

I answered, "By all means. That will be fine." The decision was recorded and published. Stalin suggested that the post of Chairman of the Council of Ministers in the Ukraine be separated from that of First Secretary of the Central Committee. A few years before, when these two offices had been merged at Stalin's suggestion, I had tried to persuade him that it was a bad idea. Now Stalin said, "Khrushchev will be Chairman of the Council of People's Commissars of the Ukraine, Kaganovich will be First Secretary of the Central Committee, and Patolichev will be the Central Committee Secretary in charge of agriculture."[9]

"Very well," I said. We convened a Central Committee plenum in the Ukraine and ratified Stalin's decision. Everyone went to his post and proceeded with his duties. I told Kaganovich and Patolichev, "We have to get ready for the sowing campaign. People are starving. Cannibalism has broken out. If we don't organize famine relief, there's no point in talking about a sowing campaign."

8. When Stalin suggested that one of his subordinates needed "help," it could be taken to mean that he was about to be replaced.

9. This was the most ominous setback for Khrushchev. It meant only one thing: he was on the way out. N. S. Patolichev, though Khrushchev does not mention it, was a Malenkov protégé, which made his appointment all the more sinister from Khrushchev's point of view. Incidentally, it was this Patolichev who was head of the Yaroslavl tire factory referred to in Chapter 4. After his Ukrainian appointment he fell into disgrace for a time, but survived to become in 1950 First Secretary of the Communist Party of Belorussia. He also survived the eclipse of Malenkov in 1957 and became Minister of Foreign Trade in 1958.

We feared it might already be too late to secure a good harvest in 1947 and to lay in grain for 1948. We asked Stalin for aid and received a certain amount of seed and food rations from Moscow. It was February. The sowing had already started in some places in the south. By March many collective farms all over the Ukraine would be sowing. We would have to be finished with a massive sowing campaign in the Kiev Region by April.

I said to Kaganovich, "Let's make up our minds about what to do."

"We should make a tour of the Ukraine," he replied.

"Yes, but right now that's not the most important thing. You haven't been in the Ukraine for a long time, so you make a tour around the Republic. I'll stay in Kiev. Right now it won't do much good for me to make an appearance at a handful of collective farms. The main thing is to rush the seed consignments out by rail and get them to the farms where they're needed. The success of the sowing campaign depends on this." So Kaganovich left and I stayed in Kiev like a telephone dispatcher, trying to push through the seed, fuel, and other supplies vital to the sowing campaign. There was no thought of supplying mineral fertilizers because we simply didn't have any.

Kaganovich made a trip to the Poltava Region. What he saw there convinced him that, however honored his position as First Secretary may have been, it was also a grievously responsible position. He saw that collective farmers were virtually blowing over in the wind. They couldn't work, and many of them were dying of starvation. After he returned to Kiev he shared his impressions with me about one collective farm in particular. He told me about its chairman, a man named Mogilchenko. "I've never met anyone like him," said Kaganovich, "He's so grim and stubborn. I'm afraid he may really get a good harvest after all."

"And what's the matter with that?" I asked.

"Well, when I got to Mogilchenko's collective farm, I saw they were using a shallow-tillage method." You'd have to know Kaganovich to imagine how he would have barked at this collective farm chairman — "Why the hell are you plowing so shallow?"

Mogilchenko, who knew his business well, said, "I'm plowing the way I should be plowing."

Kaganovich snapped back at him, "If you plow this shallow, you'll end up having to beg for bread from the State."

"Not me, Comrade Kaganovich, never," answered Mogilchenko

proudly. "I've never asked for bread from the State. I myself give bread to the State. And what's more, I don't care if you are First Secretary of the Party; I'm going to keep plowing like this no matter what you say. We'll sow these fields my way, and we'll get a good harvest, you'll see." A year later I made a special trip to meet this Mogilchenko. His collective farm was one of the most prosperous in the country. It would deliver its quota to the State six months or more in advance. All this disturbed Kaganovich very much. That's why he had said to me, "I'm afraid this Mogilchenko really will have a good harvest using shallow tillage."

I should mention that Kaganovich had a personal stake in discrediting Mogilchenko; he had had a hand in the struggle against the proponents of the shallow-tillage method. People who used this method were actually put on trial and in some cases even condemned to death. The practice of shallow tillage had been declared "against the law." The theory behind it had been developed in Saratov by some professor who was later punished. I think they put him in jail or maybe worse.[10]

From the very beginning of his activities in the Ukraine, Kaganovich looked for every opportunity to show off and to throw his weight around. He took it into his mind to distinguish himself by making the Ukraine exceed its industrial output plan, especially for local industry.

I remember one year, as Chairman of the Council of Ministers for the Ukraine, I had to introduce to the Ukrainian Politbureau the target figures which had been proposed by the State Planning Commission. Kaganovich very reluctantly agreed to accept this plan. He thought the figures were too high and doomed us to failure, and he didn't want to accept an output plan which we would fall short of. He wanted one which could be exceeded. It's much easier to put lower figures into a plan and then shout later about how the plan has been fulfilled and even exceeded. Unfortunately, this is a very common device. I think it's still used fairly widely today.

About this time I ran into some bad luck. I caught a cold, and it developed into pneumonia. I had to lie for a long time in an oxygen tent. I barely survived. While I was sick, Kaganovich had a chance to do whatever he pleased without me around, looking over his shoulder. He bullied Patolichev so much that Patolichev came to me while I was still sick in bed, just after I had passed my crisis, and complained. "I

10. Another small example of the fatality attached to disagreements about agricultural practice.

can't take being pushed around by Kaganovich any more," he said. "I don't know what to do." I could see he had been driven to his wits' end. Later he wrote a letter to Comrade Stalin requesting that he be relieved of his job because he couldn't work with Kaganovich. Patolichev was released from his post in Kiev and transfered to Rostov.

My health soon started to get better, but I stayed in bed for another two months before returning to work. After my recovery and resumption of my duties, my own relations with Kaganovich went from bad to worse. He became simply unbearable. He developed his intensive activities in two directions: against the so-called Ukrainian nationalists and against the Jews. A Jew himself, Kaganovich was against the Jews! His anti-Semitism was directed mainly against the Jews who happened to be on friendly terms with me. For instance, there was a newspaper editor in Kiev named Traskunov. Kaganovich had him fired. He treated him very badly. He mocked and taunted him. Traskunov was an honest man. During the war he had been the editor of one of the very best Front newspapers. I knew him from the Yuzovka Workers' Faculty, where he had edited the newspaper. I had also endorsed his candidacy when he applied for Party membership. Kaganovich punished Traskunov simply for his association with me.

All the while Kaganovich was grinding out a steady stream of political complaints against everybody in sight. As Chairman of the Ukrainian Council of Ministers, I left the Party Secretariat to take care of them. Many of Kaganovich's political complaints against Party members found their way to Stalin in the form of interoffice personnel reports. One day Stalin called me and said, "Why isn't your signature on these memoranda of Kaganovich's?"

"Comrade Stalin, these memoranda aren't government business, they're Party business: therefore my signature isn't required."

"Not so. I've told Kaganovich that I won't accept any more of his memoranda unless they're co-signed by you."

Almost as soon as I hung up, the phone rang again. It was Kaganovich.

"Has Stalin called you yet?" he asked.

"Yes."

"Did he tell you?" He didn't even have to say what about; we understood each other completely.

"Yes. He told me that now we're both supposed to sign all memoranda."

The stream of official complaints from Kaganovich soon dried up because he knew that he could never get me to sign them. That was certainly a welcome development in itself, but the most important thing about this story is that it shows that Stalin's trust in me had been restored. I took his telephone call as a signal that I had been returned to good standing as a member of the Politbureau. My morale improved immeasurably.[11]

In the end we fulfilled our bread quota and delivered something like 400 million pood of grain — not an overly impressive amount compared to the prewar level; but compared to what we'd started with after the war, it wasn't a bad harvest at all.

In the fall Stalin transferred Kaganovich back to Moscow.

My last year in the Ukraine was 1949. It was also our best year. In inter-Republic competitions, we outstripped Belorussia and all the other regions of the Union which, like ourselves, were recovering from the ravages of German occupation. Our agricultural successes elevated the stature of the Ukraine and the prestige of the Ukrainian leadership in the eyes of the whole country. I look back on that period with warm memories. Stalin more than once instructed me to deliver reports on agricultural topics such as livestock raising in the Ukraine, and on his instructions my reports were reprinted in *Pravda* as examples for others to follow. But far be it from me to take all the credit. I myself am a Russian and wouldn't want to slight the Russian people, but I must attribute our success in the restoration of Ukrainian agriculture and the reconstruction of Ukrainian industry to the Ukrainian people themselves.

11. In March, 1947, Khrushchev relinquished the First Secretaryship of the Ukraine to Kaganovich. A week later he publicly blamed the shortcomings of Ukrainian agriculture on his own Ukrainian Minister of Agriculture. Ten days later he lost the secretaryship of the Kiev Regional Party Committee. In June he failed to appear at the Ukrainian Central Committee Plenum. It appeared that he had been sunk without a trace. The fact that he was still nominally Prime Minister of the Ukraine and a member of the Moscow Politbureau proved nothing: on several occasions Stalin kept senior lieutenants nominally "on the strength" for some time after they had in fact been discarded. Khrushchev now tells us that this period of total eclipse was in fact due to illness, which may well have been so. It is only recently that the illnesses of members of the Soviet Government have been declassified from top secret. It was in December, 1947, that Kaganovich went back to Moscow and Khrushchev, quite suddenly, reemerged in all the panoply of power.

8

Stalin's Last Years

The Leningrad Affair

Until Khrushchev's Secret Speech to the Twentieth Party Congress, the so-called Leningrad Affair was never publicly mentioned in the Soviet Union. All that the outer world knew was that soon after the sudden death in 1948 of Andrei Zhdanov, the Leningrad Party chieftain and at one time the most likely successor to Stalin, there was a vicious and large-scale purge of the Leningrad apparatus and of Zhdanov's supporters in Moscow and elsewhere. A. A. Kuznetzov, a Secretary of the Central Committee, long Zhdanov's number two in Leningrad and a hero of the wartime siege, was executed; so were all the Leningrad City and Regional Party secretaries, together with M. I. Rodionov, Prime Minister of the Russian Federal Republic, and many more besides. N. A. Voznesensky, the brilliant young Chairman of State Planning, who seemed to have the world at his feet, was also shot at this time. A. N. Kosygin, another Leningrader, now Prime Minister of the Soviet Union, escaped with a temporary demotion. The chief and immediate beneficiary of this bloody operation was Malenkov, for whom the death of his rival, Zhdanov, had been providential. Malenkov men at once moved to the front in Leningrad and in some Moscow appointments too. Khrushchev is almost certainly right in suggesting that Stalin brought him back to Moscow from Kiev at the end of 1949 to act as a counterweight to Malenkov, who was becoming too strong. It may be doubted, however, whether Stalin was immediately planning to replace Malenkov with Kuznetzov. It is far more likely that with Zhdanov dead, Malenkov, assisted by Beria, decided to move in on the Zhdanov empire and succeeded in poisoning Stalin's mind against the Lenin-

graders, who were at least potential rivals. Be that as it may, Malenkov's position was temporarily strengthened and his chief rival from now on was to be Khrushchev.

M Y transfer from the Ukraine back to Moscow at the end of 1949 was partly a consequence of the sickness which began to envelop Stalin's mind in the last years of his life.

One day when I was in Lvov, conducting a meeting among the students at the forestry institute, where the writer Galan had been murdered by Ukrainian nationalists, I suddenly got a call from Malenkov. He said that Stalin wanted me to come to Moscow.

"How urgent is it?" I asked.

"Very. Get a plane first thing tomorrow morning."

I left ready for anything, trying to anticipate all sorts of unpleasant surprises. I didn't know what my status would be when I returned to the Ukraine — or even if I would return at all. But my fears turned out to be unfounded. Stalin greeted me warmly when I arrived in Moscow.

"Tell me," he said, "don't you think you've been in the Ukraine long enough? You're turning into a regular Ukrainian agronomist! It's time you came back to Moscow to work. Our opinion is that you should take up your old post as First Secretary of the Moscow City and Regional Party committees."

I thanked him for his confidence in me and told him I agreed that twelve years was a respectable term of service in the Ukraine: "I've been treated well, and I'm thankful to everyone who has helped me with the supervision of the Ukraine. But I will nonetheless be glad to get back to Moscow."

"Good. We need you here. Things aren't going very well. Plots have been uncovered. You are to take charge of the Moscow organization so that the Central Committee can be sure to count on the local Party structure for support in the struggle against the conspirators. So far, we've exposed a conspiracy in Leningrad, and Moscow, too, is teeming with anti-Party elements. We want to make the city a bastion for the Central Committee."

"I'll do everything in my power."

"Good. Here's an important letter which has fallen into our hands. Familiarize yourself with its contents, and we'll talk about it after you've moved up here." He handed me a lengthy document. There was

Conversing with Voroshilov

a list of signatures at the end, but it read like an anonymously written statement. It said that there existed in Moscow a group of people who were conspiring against the Central Committee, and it named Popov,[1] Secretary of the Moscow and Central committees as the leader of the group, which consisted of district committee secretaries, factory directors, and engineers. My immediate reaction was that either a madman or a scoundrel must be behind these charges. Whoever he was, his intentions were obviously malicious. I put the document in my safe and decided not to mention it again unless Stalin brought the subject up himself. I felt the longer I let the matter rest, the better.

I went back to Kiev to arrange for my transfer. When I got home Wanda Lvovna and Korneichuk came by to see me at my apartment.[2] I told them about my new assignment, and Wanda Lvovna literally broke down and burst into tears.

"How can you go? How can you leave the Ukraine?" she wailed. Here was a Polish woman bewailing the departure of a Russian from the Ukraine!

I convened a plenum in Kiev at which we elected a new leadership for the Ukraine. I was in a rush to get back to Moscow because Stalin had asked me to be sure to return in time for his seventieth birthday celebration, which was on the twenty-first of December, 1949.

Shortly after I was officially installed as First Secretary of the Moscow Committee,[3] Stalin raised the subject of the letter which he had given me to look over.

"Did you familiarize yourself with that document I gave you?" He was watching me intently.

"Yes. I familiarized myself with it."

"Well?" As he said this, his eyes narrowed and bored into mine; then he tossed his nose into the air and snorted — it was one of his favorite mannerisms.

"The letter must have been put together by scoundrels or madmen," I said.

"What!" He never liked it when someone seemed to have less than

1. G. M. Popov. It was into his shoes as Moscow Party chief that Khrushchev now stepped on his return from the Ukraine.

2. A. Korneichuk was a prominent Ukrainian writer-politician much favored by the Party establishment (see page 145).

3. When he returned to Moscow at the end of 1949, Khrushchev was, of course, much more than First Secretary of the Moscow Party Committee. He was still a member of the Politbureau, and he was now put on the Central Committee Secretariat, too.

absolute faith in statements that exposed and denounced conspiracies.

"Comrade Stalin, I'm one hundred percent certain that the charges made in the letter have nothing whatsoever to do with reality. I am personally acquainted with many of the people who are named as conspirators in it. They are all honest, loyal men. I'm sure that Popov is no conspirator. No doubt he's handled himself stupidly and his work hasn't been up to snuff, but he couldn't be involved in any sort of plot. He's an honest man. I've never had any doubts about him, and this letter doesn't change my opinion of him in the slightest."

My air of certainty must have had some effect on Stalin. He looked at me closely and said, "You mean you don't think this document should be taken seriously?"

"Absolutely not, Comrade Stalin. Of course, I don't know for sure, but my guess is that it's the work of a provocateur."

He cursed angrily, but he let the matter drop. Clearly, it would have been easy enough for me to have improved my own position and to have won Stalin's confidence simply by supporting the fabricated charges in the letter. All I would have had to do was say: "Yes, Comrade Stalin, this looks serious. We'd better investigate." That's all the encouragement Stalin would have needed to order Popov and all the others arrested. They would have confessed, of course, and we would have had a conspiracy trial in Moscow every bit as disgraceful as the one in Leningrad. And I would have gotten credit as the man whose vigilance made it possible to stamp out the plot at its roots.

Even though Popov was saved for the moment, I knew Stalin would be looking for a chance to do him in. He wouldn't rest until Popov was out of the way. I suggested we transfer Popov out of Moscow. We found him a job as director of a large factory in Kuibyshev.

Stalin would occasionally remember the charges made in the letter, and he'd ask menacingly, "Where's that Popov, anyway?"

"He's in Kuibyshev," we would answer.

Stalin would then calm down, but he must have wondered to himself from time to time: "Maybe Khrushchev was wrong. Maybe Popov is plotting against me." I later found out that Popov had denounced me bitterly after we got him out of Moscow. He must not have known that if it hadn't been for me, he would have been dead. I'd saved him at considerable risk to myself, by the way. I was running the chance that if Stalin didn't trust me, he might take it into his head that I was involved in the conspiracy with Popov. Popov was too blind to know who his real friends were, and he turned against someone who had gone out on a limb for him.

After taking up my job in Moscow I could see that my arrival on the scene got in the way of Beria and Malenkov's plans. I even began to suspect that one of the reasons Stalin had called me back to Moscow was to influence the balance of power in the collective and to put a check on Beria and Malenkov. It seemed sometimes that Stalin was afraid of Beria and would have been glad to get rid of him but didn't know how to do it. Naturally, Stalin never told me this, but I could sense it.[4] Stalin certainly treated me well. He seemed to trust and value me. Even though he frequently criticized me, he gave me support when I needed it, and I appreciated that very much. I was constantly running up against Beria and Malenkov. Malenkov had become a member of the Politbureau after the war. Essentially, he was a typical office clerk and paper-pusher. Such men can be the most dangerous of all if given any power. They'll freeze and kill anything that's alive if it oversteps its prescribed boundaries.

Meanwhile the hunt was on in Leningrad. I don't know how Stalin himself really felt about the Leningrad affair. He never spoke to me about it, except when he touched on the matter of the "Moscow conspirators" in connection with my transfer from the Ukraine. The people arrested in Moscow were mostly Party workers who had been promoted by Zhdanov from the Gorky organization to the Moscow organization.[5]

By the time I started working as the Central Committee Secretary responsible for the Moscow organization, A. A. Kuznetsov — the Leningrad Kuznetsov, as we always called him — had already been arrested, and the Leningrad Party organization was being torn to shreds. The campaign was concentrated against a troika [threesome] of promising young men: Kuznetsov, Voznesensky, and Kosygin. I more or less knew Kuznetsov, and I knew Voznesensky very well. He still hadn't been arrested when I arrived in Moscow, but he had been removed from all his posts. He was out of work and was expecting them to come for him any day.

4. There is a good deal of evidence to suggest that Stalin was in fact turning against Beria at this time.

5. Andrei Zhdanov had been the Gorky (Nizhny Novgorod) Party Secretary until he was sent to Leningrad to take over from the murdered Kirov. He had brought some of his protégés to Leningrad with him and managed to get others well placed in Moscow.

For a period after Voznesensky was put on ice, he still used to come to dinner at Stalin's. He was a changed man. He wasn't the same bright, self-assured, tough-minded Voznesensky I'd known earlier. In fact, it was precisely these virtues which had been his undoing. While Chairman of State Planning, he had been brave enough to tangle with Beria. He had sought to redistribute the country's economic resources more evenly, and this meant taking money away from certain commissariats which enjoyed Beria's patronage. Beria had many commissariats under him, and he always demanded that they receive much more than their share of funds. Beria was extremely powerful because of his closeness to Stalin. You'd have to have seen Beria's Jesuitical shrewdness in action to imagine how he was able to pick the exact moment when he could turn Stalin's goodwill or ill will for someone to his own advantage. Voznesensky dared to cross Beria's path, and before Beria finished with him, Voznesensky was just a shadow of his former self.[6]

I remember that more than once during this period Stalin asked Malenkov and Beria, "Isn't it a waste not letting Voznesensky work while we're deciding what to do with him?"

"Yes," they would answer, "let's think it over."

Some time would pass and Stalin would bring up the subject again: "Maybe we should put Voznesensky in charge of the State Bank. He's an economist, a real financial wizard."

No one objected, but nothing happened. Voznesensky was still left hanging.

Stalin obviously felt a certain residual respect for Voznesensky. Before the whole Leningrad affair started he had nourished high hopes for that troika of bright young men and in fact had been systematically promoting them before the "plot" was "exposed." Kuznetsov once seemed destined to replace Malenkov. Voznesensky had been made a first deputy of Stalin's and was often entrusted with the job of presiding over the Council of Ministers. Kosygin had been given a responsible post in charge of trade and finance. It's my opinion that the downfall of these men was determined by precisely this fact: Stalin had been preparing them as successors to the Kremlin Old Guard — which meant that Beria first and foremost, then Malenkov, Molotov, and Mikoyan, no longer enjoyed Stalin's confidence.[7] It's difficult for me to say ex-

6. The shooting of N. A. Voznesensky, the most up-and-coming of the younger generation, has always been associated with the Leningrad affair, but Khrushchev gives here, for the first time, a plausible account of what happened.
7. This is going too far. It seems probable that Khrushchev is anticipating Sta-

actly how the Old Guard managed to undermine Stalin's confidence in these young men and how he was, to put it crudely, sicced on them. I can only offer the conclusions which I reached on the basis of my own observations and on the basis of remarks which I overheard in conversations between Malenkov and Beria.

I could plainly see how Beria and Malenkov behaved with Stalin when the names of these three young men were mentioned. I quickly formed the impression that Beria and Malenkov were doing everything they could to wreck this troika of Kuznetsov, Voznesensky, and Kosygin. As I've already mentioned, Beria was the most accomplished at undermining Stalin's confidence in others, and he had Malenkov to use as a battering ram. Malenkov sat on the Central Committee Secretariat and had access to all the information which was given to Stalin. He could manipulate it in such a way as to provoke Stalin's anger and distrust.

Beria and Malenkov's scheming against the Leningrad troika involved another, earlier case, that of A. I. Shakhurin, who was already in jail when the imprisonment of the Leningraders began in earnest. He had been People's Commissar of the Aviation Industry during the war. I'd known him very well when he was a Party organizer for the Central Committee in charge of the Thirtieth Aviation Factory. While I was in the Ukraine, Shakhurin was arrested for having allegedly allowed the production of defective airplanes during the war. Malenkov later told me that Vasya [Vasily] Stalin, who was a pilot, had denounced Shakhurin to his father, and Stalin had ordered an investigation.[8] Malenkov was indirectly implicated in the Shakhurin case him-

---

lin's plans. It is much more likely that Malenkov and Beria resented the rise of A. A. Kuznetsov, G. M. Popov, and N. A. Voznesensky and successfully intrigued for their destruction. With the top men safely eliminated, it followed as night follows day (according to time-honored Soviet custom) that all their assistants and protégés would be destroyed.

8. Stalin's son was notorious for his arrogant and vindictive nature. He was also an alcoholic. He presumed excessively on his heredity, and his elevation to be a lieutenant general in the air force was flagrant nepotism. Stalin himself was compelled to remove him from the command of the Moscow Military District air arm shortly before his death. Svetlana Alliluyeva in *Twenty Letters to a Friend* confirms that Vasily was responsible for the disgrace and imprisonment of Marshal A. A. Novikov, commander in chief of the Soviet air force. After Stalin's death Vasily was sentenced to eight years' imprisonment by a military tribunal because of this and other offenses. He was released before serving his term largely because Khrushchev took pity on him and "treated him like a father." He was given back his air force rank, his Party membership, and his pension, but had another spell in prison, then was released again to drink himself to death in 1962.

self. Part of his job during the war had been to supervise the aviation industry, which made him responsible for the bad job being done by the People's Commissar. There was some justice here because the drive for quantity during the war certainly had been conducted at the expense of quality. Anyway, Shakhurin was thrown in prison, and Malenkov was discharged from the Central Committee Secretariat and sent somewhere in Central Asia — to Tashkent, I think. Beria used his influence to get Stalin to let Malenkov come back to Moscow, and the two of them, Beria and Malenkov, had been inseparable ever since.

Aviation Marshal A. A. Novikov was also in jail at the beginning of the Leningrad affair.[9] He'd been arrested after the war for having accepted defective airplanes. He, too, was reportedly denounced by Vasya Stalin. I knew Novikov well. He commanded the Red Army air force through most of the war and had visited our command post during the battle of Stalingrad. He had his faults. He drank more than was probably good for him, but he was a devoted, honest, and honorable man.

Apparently even after these arrests, Stalin felt a certain amount of goodwill toward Shakhurin and Novikov. He used to turn to Beria and Malenkov during dinner and ask, "Say, are Shakhurin and Novikov still in jail?"

"Yes."

"Don't you think it might be all right to release them?" But Stalin was asking the question to himself. He was just thinking out loud. No one would say anything, and the matter would be left up in the air until some time later when he'd bring it up again. Once he even went so far as to say, "You should give serious thought to releasing Shakhurin and Novikov. What good are they doing us in jail? They can still work." He always directed these remarks to Malenkov and Beria because they were in charge of the case against Shakhurin and Novikov.

After dinner at Stalin's we used to collect in the bathroom to wash our hands. It was a big, roomy bathroom, and we sometimes stood around in there before and after sessions — we always called dinners with Stalin "sessions" — discussing what needed to be done and what the consequences of a session were likely to be. Once I overheard Beria say to Malenkov in the bathroom, "Stalin's brought up the sub-

9. Novikov was a first-class commander who was also a brilliant pilot and an attractive man. The fact that he and Shakhurin could be broken and imprisoned by this sort of intrigue is a fair commentary on life in Stalin's Russia.

With his wife, Nina Petrovna, in Kiev, 1944

With his youngest daughter, Helen, looking at German trophies in Gorky
Park, Moscow, 1945

With their granddaughter Julia in Kiev, 1947

The Khrushchev family in 1947. Standing in back: Julia (left), Khruschev's daughter by his first wife, Galina; and Rada. Middle row: Julia, the daughter of Khrushchev's son Leonid, who was killed in the war; Sergei; and the Khrushchevs. Seated on the grass: Helen and an unidentified child.

ject of those two aviators again. You know, if they're released, it could spread to others."

What did Beria mean, "It could spread to others"? Who were "the others"? Beria must have been afraid that if Shakhurin and Novikov were released, Stalin might return to the matter of Kuznetsov and Voznesensky. He might start thinking about having them released before they were brought to trial. Malenkov and Beria were afraid that if Kuznetsov and Voznesensky, who were considered the ringleaders of the Leningrad plot, were released, the campaign against the whole Leningrad organization might collapse. Therefore Malenkov and Beria did everything they could to keep Shakhurin and Novikov in jail. They succeeded, and consequently the Leningraders weren't released either.

I never saw the indictments in the Leningrad case, but I assume — also on the basis of conversations I overheard between Malenkov and Beria — that the charges against Kuznetsov's group were Russian nationalism and opposition to the Central Committee. The investigation began. And who directed the investigation? Stalin himself did. But if Stalin was the conductor, then Beria was the first violinist. Why do I say that? Because [V. S.] Abakumov, who actually supervised the prosecution, was Beria's man; he never reported to anyone, not even to Stalin, without checking first with Beria.

I was never really in on the case myself, but I admit that I may have signed the sentencing order. In those days when a case was closed — and if Stalin thought it necessary — he would sign the sentencing order at a Politbureau session and then pass it around for the rest of us to sign. We would put our signatures on it without even looking at it. That's what was meant by "collective sentencing."

In comparison with Stalin's usual method for dealing with enemies of the people, the Leningrad case was a model of justice. It gave the appearance of being handled in accordance with all the proper judicial procedures. Investigators conducted the investigation, a prosecutor handled the prosecution, and a court trial was held. The active members of the Leningrad organization were invited to observe when the accused were interrogated in the courtroom. Then the accused were given a chance to say something in their defense before the sentence was read.

I was with Stalin when he was told about what Voznesensky said just before it was announced that he had been sentenced to be shot. Voznesensky stood up and spewed hatred against Leningrad. He cursed the day he had set foot in the city when he came there to study from the Donbass. He said that Leningrad had already had its share of conspiracies; it had been subjected to all varieties of reactionary influence, from Biron [10] to Zinoviev. Obviously he had lost his sanity. It's nonsense to talk about Biron and Zinoviev in one breath, as though they were the same thing. Zinoviev represented a political view, conflicting with Stalin's, on how to build Socialism in our country. You could be either for him or against him. For my part, I always stood for the Stalinist position and therefore fought against Zinoviev and his followers. But Biron! — he was something else altogether.

I don't know what Kuznetsov and the others said in their last words, but whatever they said, it didn't have any bearing on their fate. They had already been sentenced a considerable time before the sentence was officially passed and even before the trial began. In fact, they had been sentenced by Stalin himself at the time of their arrest.

Many people perished in Leningrad. So did many people who had been transferred from Leningrad to work in other regions.

As for Kosygin, his life was hanging by a thread. Men who had been arrested and condemned in Leningrad made ridiculous accusations against him in their testimonies. They wrote all kinds of rot about him. Kosygin was on shaky ground from the beginning because he was related by marriage to Kuznetsov. Even though he'd been very close to Stalin, Kosygin was suddenly released from all his posts and assigned to work in some ministry. The accusations against him cast such a dark shadow over him that I simply can't explain how he was saved from being eliminated along with the others. Kosygin, as they say, must have drawn a lucky lottery ticket, and this cup passed from him [a favorite Khrushchevism].[11]

In those days anything could have happened to any one of us. Everything depended on what Stalin happened to be thinking when he

10. Biron was the notorious Count von Bühren, later Duke of Courland, a German of fairly obscure origin who started as the lover and secretary of the Empress Anna Ivanovna before she came to the throne, and rose to become one of the most hated tyrants in Russian history. He presumed too much and finished up by being sent off to Siberia for twenty years.

11. Khrushchev is not alone in wondering how Kosygin managed to escape with his life. It may well have been because, although a prominent figure in the Leningrad organization, Kosygin managed to keep out of Party intrigues and concentrate on administration and the industrial economy. Stalin brought him back to be a candidate member of the enlarged Presidium after the Nineteenth Party Congress in 1952.

glanced in your direction. Sometimes he would glare at you and say, "Why don't you look me in the eye today? Why are you averting your eyes from mine?" or some other such stupidity. Without warning he would turn on you with real viciousness. A reasonable interrogator wouldn't behave with a hardened criminal the way Stalin behaved with friends whom he'd invited to eat with him at his table.

Bulganin once described very well the experience we all had to live with in those days. We were leaving Stalin's after dinner one night and he said, "You come to Stalin's table as a friend, but you never know if you'll go home by yourself or if you'll be given a ride — to prison!" Bulganin was fairly drunk at the time, but what he said accurately depicted how precarious our position was from one day to the next.

Stalin's Anti-Semitism

One of the most interesting aspects of this narrative is the way in which Khrushchev goes out of his way to condemn anti-Semitism. Guilt feelings must play their part here. There is no evidence to indicate that Khrushchev himself was ever committed actively to anti-Semitic policies, but time and time again he is on record as making disparaging remarks about Jews and insisting that they should be kept in their place. He may have been horrified by the pogroms of his childhood, but he did not like Jews, and as master of the Ukraine, he kept silent about the mass-murdering carried out by the Nazis (including the massacre at Babi Yar on the outskirts of Kiev). In accordance with Stalin's policy, which he later made his own, he refused to admit that Jews had suffered more than non-Jews on Soviet territory; he must also have connived at Stalin's own postwar deportation of Jews from the Ukraine into deep Siberia. Everything he has to say about the fate of individual Jews in this period is true; he might have said much more. It is interesting to get the story of Mikhoels' murder officially confirmed and to have an illuminating sidelight on the fate of poor Lozovsky. None of this, incidentally, was mentioned in the Secret Speech. Nor was the arrest and imprisonment of Molotov's wife. On the other hand, the Secret Speech contained more information than occurs in this chapter on Stalin's destruction of whole peoples in the Crimea and the Caucasus (tartars, Chechens, Ingushes, and so on), as a punishment for "col-

laboration" with the Germans. Khrushchev's own slapdash attitude toward violence and arbitrary rule comes out in this chapter, as in the earlier chapters on the great purges. "I'm all for arresting people" he says, but with the implication that it should be done in the proper form.

WHILE we were still pushing the Germans out of the Ukraine, an organization had been formed called the Jewish Anti-Fascist Committee of the Sovinformbureau [Soviet Bureau of Information]. It was set up for gathering materials — positive materials, naturally — about our country, about the activities of our Soviet Army against the common enemy, Hitlerite Germany, and for the distribution of these materials to the Western press, principally in America where there is a large, influential circle of Jews. The committee was composed of Jews who occupied high positions in the Soviet Union and was headed by Lozovsky, a member of the Central Committee and former chairman of Profintern [the Trade Union International]. Another member was Mikhoels, the most prominent actor of the Yiddish theater. Yet another was Molotov's wife, Comrade Zhemchuzhina. I think this organization was first created at the suggestion of Molotov, although it may have been Stalin's own idea. The Sovinformbureau and its Jewish Anti-Fascist Committee were considered indispensable to the interests of our State, our policies, and our Communist Party.[12]

Lozovsky used to get in touch with me whenever I came to Moscow, and sometimes he would call me on the telephone asking for material to use as propaganda about the Hitlerite fascists. I gave orders for the preparation of such material over the signatures of various authors, and it was sent to America, where it was widely used to publi-

12. Lozovsky was well known to Western correspondents and respected by them as the Soviet official spokesman. He simply vanished in 1948 and was sadly missed. Soon it was known that he had been shot, along with a number of Jewish writers, after the sudden disbandment of the Jewish Anti-Fascist Committee. Khrushchev's first reference to the "Crimean Affair" was in an interview with a delegation of Canadian Communists in 1956. The famous Jewish actor Mikhoels also vanished at this time. It was soon known, though not admitted, that he had been shot. He was the brother of one of the Kremlin doctors falsely accused of poisoning activities and was himself built into the so-called plot by the NKVD. Madame Molotova (Zhemchuzhina) had been an important figure in her own right, at one time head of the State Cosmetic Trust (which introduced perfumes and lipstick to the Soviet young). Molotov had to stand by and suffer her arrest and exile without murmuring at the very time when he was turning his iron front to the West in the early days of the Cold War.

cize the successes of the Red Army and to expose the atrocities committed by the Germans in the Ukraine. On the whole, Lozovsky's activities were very worthwhile. He was an energetic person and sometimes almost annoyingly persistent. He used virtually to extort material from me, saying, "Give me more material! More! More!" We were busy with the reconstruction of the economy and didn't have much time for such matters. He wouldn't let up on me: "You must understand how important it is for us to show the face of our common enemy to the world, to expose his atrocities, and to show the process of reconstruction which is taking place in our cities and villages."

Once the Ukraine had been liberated, a paper was drafted by members of the Lozovsky committee. It was addressed to Stalin and contained a proposal that the Crimea be made a Jewish Soviet Republic within the Soviet Union after the deportation from the Crimea of the Crimean Tartars. Stalin saw behind this proposal the hand of American Zionists operating through the Sovinformbureau. The committee members, he declared, were agents of American Zionism. They were trying to set up a Jewish state in the Crimea in order to wrest the Crimea away from the Soviet Union and to establish an outpost of American imperialism on our shores which would be a direct threat to the security of the Soviet Union. Stalin let his imagination run wild in this direction. He was struck with maniacal vengeance. Lozovsky and Mikhoels were arrested. Soon Zhemchuzhina herself was arrested. The investigation of the group took a long time, but in the end almost all of them came to a tragic end. Lozovsky was shot. Zhemchuzhina was exiled. I thought at first she had been shot, too, because nothing of what had happened was reported to anyone except Stalin, and Stalin himself decided whom to execute and whom to spare.

I remember Molotov calling to ask my advice about this whole affair. Apparently Zhemchuzhina had pulled him into it. Molotov never did agree with Stalin about the necessity for arresting Zhemchuzhina. When the question of removing her from the staff of the Central Committee came up at a Central Committee plenum and everyone else voted aye, Molotov abstained. He didn't vote nay, but he still abstained. Stalin blew up at this, and the incident left its imprint on Stalin's attitude toward Molotov. He started kicking Molotov around viciously. Kaganovich's maliciousness was a particularly good barometer of Molotov's precarious position. Incited by Stalin, Kaganovich played the part of a vicious cur who was unleashed to tear limb from limb any member of the Politbureau toward whom he sensed Stalin's coolness, and Kaganovich was turned loose on Molotov.

I didn't find out that Zhemchuzhina was still alive until after Stalin's death, when Molotov told me that she was living in exile. We all agreed she should be freed. Beria released her and solemnly handed her over to Molotov. Beria used to describe how Molotov came to his office at the Ministry of Internal Affairs to be reunited with Zhemchuzhina. Molotov was overjoyed that she was still alive and threw himself into her arms. Beria expressed his sympathy to Molotov and Zhemchuzhina at the time, but he made a point of reminding them that she had been freed on his initiative and he told this story with a touch of irony in his voice.

A question of substance: was it necessary to create a Jewish Union or autonomous Republic within the Russian Federation or within the Ukraine? I don't think it was. A Jewish autonomous Region had already been created which still nominally exists, so it was hardly necessary to set one up in the Crimea.[13] But this question was never discussed in substance. We had been conditioned to accept Stalin's reasoning, and we gave in to his absolute authority. He contended that if a Jewish Republic were created in the Crimea, then Zionism, which is rampant in America, would gain a foothold in our country. That was all there was to it. He had made up his mind, and he had people arrested, arbitrarily and without any regard for legal norms, regardless of the important and positive role which the accused had played during the war in helping to bring to light the atrocities committed by the Germans. Theirs had been constructive work, but now it counted for nothing. They were deprived of their liberty and in many cases their lives. I consider the whole affair to have been a disgrace. Stalin could have simply rejected their suggestion and rebuked them. But no, he had to destroy all those who actively supported the proposal. It was only by some miracle that Zhemchuzhina stayed alive and got off with a long term of exile. More typical was the cruel punishment of Mikhoels, the greatest actor of the Yiddish theater, a man of culture. They killed him like beasts. They killed him secretly. Then his murderers were rewarded and their victim was buried with honors. The mind reels at the thought! It was announced that Mikhoels had fallen in

13. This refers to the Autonomous Republic of Birobidzhan in Siberia, designated as a national home for Soviet Jews. It never came to much. Understandably, the Jews took to it only in small numbers.

front of a truck. Actually he was thrown in front of a truck. This was done very cleverly and efficiently. And who did it? Stalin did it, or at least it was done on his instructions. After Stalin's death, when we opened the archives of the Ministry of State Security and interrogated Beria's men, we found out that they had planned to murder Litvinov [Molotov's predecessor as foreign minister] by a similar method. Litvinov was to have been ambushed and killed on the road while he was traveling from Moscow to his dacha.[14]

Later, a group of Jews at the Stalin Automobile Factory were put on trial. In this case, too, Stalin was looking for schemes of American imperialism operating through Zionists. It was all pure nonsense, of course. But this was the sort of thing that happened as a result of Stalin's arbitrary rule and the absolute absence of any restraints on his authority.

It still seems inconceivable to me that this kind of thing happened in our time. I'm all for arresting people, but the accused should be given a fair trial and exiled or imprisoned only if an honest approach to their cases proves that they really are criminal or political offenders. A prosecution and a trial should proceed according to the norms of the law. Trials should be conducted in the open so there will be no doubt in anyone's mind that the accused actually are guilty. That way no one will come to the defense of people who have been punished, and public opinion will genuinely support the punitive agencies. In our day we had people lifting up their voices in court, vouching for the truth of accusations, beating their breasts, and swearing that the accused were enemies of the people — all without any real knowledge about what had happened. A witness would endorse the verdict and raise his hand, voting for the elimination of the accused without really knowing about the facts of the alleged crime, much less the role of the alleged criminal. These were not real trials anyway. They were closed courts in the hands of troikas. And who made up the troikas? Three men who arrested, prosecuted, and judged the accused all by themselves. Most of the people who lost their heads in Stalin's time were tried by this kind of court.

I've tried to give Stalin his due and to acknowledge his merits, but there was no excuse for what, to my mind, was a major defect in his

14. M. M. Litvinov, Soviet foreign minister, was replaced by Molotov after the failure of his "collective security" drive in 1939. The story of his planned assassination is new. In the end he died a natural death.

character — his hostile attitude toward the Jewish people. As a leader and a theoretician he took care never to hint at his anti-Semitism in his written works or in his speeches. And God forbid that anyone should quote publicly from any private conversations in which he made remarks that smelled sharply of anti-Semitism. When he happened to talk about a Jew, Stalin often imitated in a well-known, exaggerated accent the way Jews talk. This is the same way that thick-headed, backward people who despise Jews talk when they mock the negative Jewish traits. Stalin also liked to put on this accent, and he was pretty good at it.

I remember when I was working in Moscow, some kind of trouble at the Thirtieth Aviation Factory was reported to Stalin through Party channels and by State Security. During a meeting with Stalin, while we were sitting around exchanging opinions, Stalin turned to me and said, "The good workers at the factory should be given clubs so they can beat the hell out of those Jews at the end of the working day." When he said this, I wasn't alone. Molotov, Beria, and Malenkov were there. (However, Kaganovich was not there. Stalin never permitted anti-Semitic remarks in Kaganovich's presence.) I thought to myself, "What is he saying? How can he say that?"

As we left the room, Beria asked me ironically, "Well, have you received your orders?"

"Yes," I said, "I've received them. My father was illiterate, but he never took part in a pogrom. It was considered a disgrace. And now this directive is given to me as a Secretary of the Central Committee of the Communist Party of the USSR."

Even though Stalin had given me a direct order, I knew that if something like what he suggested were done and if it were to become public knowledge, a commission would no doubt be appointed and the culprits would be severely punished. Stalin would have stopped at nothing to punish anti-Semitism publicly. Orders or no orders, he would have strangled anyone whose actions would have discredited his name, especially with something as indefensible and shameful as anti-Semitism. There were many conversations like the one about the Thirtieth Aviation Factory, and we became accustomed to them. We listened to what Stalin told us and then put it out of our heads right away.

After I was transferred from the Ukraine to Moscow, my successor as First Secretary in the Ukraine, Melnikov, and Korotchenko were

with me in Moscow.[15] Stalin invited us to the Nearby Dacha for dinner. He pressed them to drink and achieved his goal. Melnikov and
Korotchenko were at Stalin's for the first time. They drank eagerly;
they considered it an honor that Stalin was entertaining them. I knew
Stalin better than they did. I knew that he liked to get people drunk
and that hospitality wasn't the main thing he had in mind. He was interested in getting his guests into a state where their tongues would be
loosened. He wanted them to start blabbing out things which they
would have thought twice about if they'd been sober. I sat there nervously while this was going on. I had to answer for Melnikov since I
had summoned him to Moscow. There's nothing much to say about Korotchenko. I knew him to be an honest but a very limited man. At that
time Stalin couldn't seem to keep his anti-Semitism hidden, and he
started to make anti-Semitic remarks. Melnikov's own attitudes made
him most receptive. He was ripe for just the sort of thing Stalin started
saying. He and Korotchenko let their jaws drop and listened to Stalin
without saying a word. The dinner ended and we left. Melnikov and
Korotchenko went back to the Ukraine.

After my transfer to Moscow, the Politbureau of the Central Committee passed a resolution instructing me to keep an eye on the activities of the Ukrainian Communist Party. In this capacity I received all
the Ukrainian newspapers. I checked the central papers, and my assistants handled the others, reporting to me anything that deserved attention. Shortly after that dinner at Stalin's dacha my assistant Shuisky
brought me a Ukrainian newspaper and showed me an editorial criticizing some defects and deficiencies. Sixteen names were singled out
for criticism in this editorial, and they were all Jewish. I read it and
became indignant. How could this kind of thing be permitted? I immediately understood which way the wind was blowing. Melnikov and
Korotchenko, who were typical Ukrainians, had taken it into their
heads that Stalin was launching a criticism campaign against the Jewish people. Thinking they were following Stalin's lead, they had started
to act on their own. I telephoned Melnikov and said, "I've read your
editorial. You should be ashamed. How dare you let this sort of thing
get into the newspaper! Why, this is an invocation of anti-Semitism!
Why are you doing this? I know what you're thinking, but you misun-

15. Korotchenko was a high-powered figure who stood at Khrushchev's right
hand in the Ukraine, became Prime Minister of the Ukraine in 1947, President of
the Ukraine in 1954, and was for a time a candidate member of the Central Committee Presidium. Melnikov succeeded Khrushchev as Ukrainian First Secretary.

derstood Stalin. Keep it in mind that if Stalin should read this editorial — well, I don't know what will happen to you as Secretary of the Central Committee of the Ukraine. Here is the central organ of the Ukrainian Party preaching anti-Semitism! How can you fail to see that this is ammunition for our enemies to use against us? Our enemies will exploit this disgrace and say that the Ukraine is raising the banner of the struggle against the Jews, the banner of anti-Semitism!" [16]

Melnikov started to justify himself. Then he began sobbing. I didn't let up on him: "If this scandal continues any further, I will report it to Stalin myself." Of course, I was taking a risk because I had no guarantee that our telephone conversations weren't being monitored. And I wasn't certain that Melnikov wouldn't write to Stalin himself, saying that Khrushchev was giving him directives contradictory to those which he had received from Stalin when he was at Stalin's dacha. Stalin would never have stood for that from me.

A little later Nina Petrovna [Madame Khrushcheva] received a letter from Kiev and told me another story which relates to Melnikov and anti-Semitism. In Kiev there is a clinic for children with tuberculosis of the bone. The head of this clinic was Professor Frumina. In the days when we lived in Kiev, before I was transferred to Moscow, Professor Frumina was often at our apartment. She treated my son Seryozha [affectionate form of Sergei] when he had tuberculosis, and she cured him. Now Sergei has no signs of the disease. He is completely recovered. We attribute this mainly to Frumina. Another specialist in tuberculosis of the bone, an academician in Leningrad, had told Nina Petrovna that there was no better specialist for dealing with this disease than Frumina. Then, after we moved to Moscow, Frumina wrote Nina Petrovna a letter telling us that she had been fired from her job at the clinic. The reason given was that she lacked the necessary qualifications. I was indignant and telephoned Melnikov again. I said, "How could you allow this? How is this possible — to discharge so deserving a person, and with such an excuse? How can you say she's not qualified when this academician in Leningrad says that no one knows more than she does about tuberculosis of the bone? Who could have evaluated her differently and said she isn't qualified?" Melnikov started to justify himself. In cases like this there are always people

16. In referring to Melnikov's anti-Semitic activity, Khrushchev ignores that fact that there was a mass deportation of Jews from the Ukraine soon after the war, when Khrushchev was in charge.

available who will assure you that everything has been handled correctly. I said, "You're simply disgracing the name of Communism!" As I recall, Frumina was restored in her position, but the outrage of anti-Semitism has persisted.

Why does this shameful phenomenon keep cropping up? Partly it's because anti-Semitism was very much with us in the old days and it's hard to get rid of. The older generation remembers countless pogroms, and it remembers Vladimir Purishkevich, who was the leading representative of the Black Hundreds in the Duma [Tsarist Parliament].[17]

In my childhood in the Donbass, I once witnessed a pogrom with my own eyes. I went to school four versts [two and two-thirds miles] from the mine where my father worked. One day I was coming home from school. It was a lovely, sunny, autumn day, with spiderwebs flying about in the air like snow. We were barefoot that day, like every day from spring until late autumn. Every villager dreamed of owning a pair of boots. We children were lucky if we had a decent pair of shoes. We wiped our noses on our sleeves and kept our trousers up with a piece of string. It was a beautiful day, and we were in a carefree mood. My schoolmates and I met a man driving a wagon. When he saw us he stopped and started to weep. "Children," he said, "If only you knew what they're doing in Yuzovka!" We started to walk faster. As soon as I arrived home, I threw down my book bag and ran all the way to Yuzovka. When I approached the town, I saw a huge crowd lined up on top of the heaps of iron ore that were being stored next to the railway tracks. The ore had been brought there from Krivoi Rog for use in the blast furnaces during the winter. The sides of these red mounds of iron ore were crisscrossed by footpaths which the miners used coming to and from the market in Yuzovka. I saw that the Cossacks had already arrived. A bugle started to blow. I had never seen soldiers before. We had no soldiers in Yuzovka, so it was all an exciting novelty for me. When the bugle started to blow, the old soldiers among the workers around me explained it was the signal to get ready to open fire and any minute we would hear the first fusillade. The mob surged to the south side of the slope, but the soldiers didn't let the workers into the city. A volley of rifle fire rang out. Someone shouted that they were

17. The so-called Black Hundreds were extreme reactionary organizations, supplied with Tsarist secret police funds, whose mission was to terrorize supporters of reformist and revolutionary movements as well as Jews. The most successful and vicious of these organizations, responsible for the worst pogroms, was the Union of Russian People.

shooting into the air. Someone else shouted that they were shooting with blanks and that only one or two soldiers were shooting with live bullets, just to scare the Jews a little. Everyone was inventing his own version of what was happening. The crowd dispersed late in the evening. The workers from our mine were bragging the next day about how many boots and other trophies they'd picked up during the looting. One man said he had made off with ten pairs of boots. Some of the miners were telling about how the "yids" marched around calling the Russians abusive names, carrying banners, and bearing their "yid tsar" on their shoulders. When the Russians attacked them with clubs, he hid in a leather factory. The Russians set this factory on fire, and the "yid tsar" was burned alive inside.

The day after the pogrom started I ran straight from school to Yuzovka to see what was going on here. There was still a lot of looting. I saw clock repair shops which had been broken into, and feathers were flying along the streets where the looters were ripping open mattresses and shaking the feathers out the windows of Jewish homes.

Then a rumor started that there had been a decree that for three days you could do whatever you wanted to the Jews. For three days there was no check on the looting. After the three days were up, the police, who along with the Black Hundreds had taken advantage of the workers' primitive mentality to incite the pogrom in the first place, started to restore order. But nothing was done about all the looting and rampage. The powers who had decreed the pogrom kept their word: three days had been put at the disposal of the Black Hundreds, and all the pillage and murder went unpunished. I heard that many of the Jews who had been beaten were in the factory infirmary. I decided to go there and have a look with one of my friends, another little boy. We found a horrible scene. The corpses of Jews who had been beaten to death were lying in rows on the floor.

Later the workers came to their senses. They realized that the pogroms were a provocation staged against the people by the tsarist police. The workers realized that the Jews were not their enemies when they saw that many leaders of the factory strikes were Jews, and the main speakers whom the workers eagerly listened to at political meetings were Jews.

In the late fall my father's brother Martin took me with him from the mines to the village. My mother and father sent me with him because they wanted me to be close to the soil. Before taking a job in the

At unveiling of Lenin monument, near Moscow, 1950

mines, my father had been a farmhand. We had been poor then, and we were poor now. My mother earned extra money by taking in washing. I used to make a few kopeks cleaning boilers after school and on Saturdays. Both my father and mother, but particularly my mother, dreamed of the day when they could return to the village, to a little house, a horse, and a piece of land of their own. That's why I lived sometimes with my father at the pit and sometimes with my grandfather in a village in Kursk Province. I left for the village when the strikes started in the Donbass. Red flags were flying, and huge meetings were taking place. When I returned to town from the village, I was told about all that had happened. I was told about the organizers and leaders of the strikes. I noticed that the large majority of them had Jewish names. People were saying good things about these orators. The workers all spoke warmly of them. Thus, the workers realized they had been duped into taking part in the pogroms, and they were ashamed of themselves for not resisting the Black Hundreds and disguised policemen who organized the persecution of the Jews.

Years later, after Stalin came to power, instead of setting an example of how to liquidate anti-Semitism at its roots, he helped spread it. Anti-Semitism grew like a growth inside Stalin's own brain. Then, after Stalin's death, we arrested the spread a bit, but only arrested it. Unfortunately, the germs of anti-Semitism remained in our system, and apparently there still isn't the necessary discouragement of it and resistance to it. My guards aren't bad fellows, but anti-Semitism crops up even in my conversations with them.

Stalin's Theoretical Writings

Here Khrushchev touches on an aspect of Stalin which was incomprehensible to his entourage. Stalin wished to leave his mark on Communist theory (he was, after all, highly literate and had been trained as a seminarian), and he felt the need to establish theoretical justification for certain of his actions. Stalin's operations in the field of linguistics, Greek to Khrushchev, important for an understanding of Stalin's mentality, were scarcely noticed in the West. The Georgian scholar referred to must have been a disciple of the linguist Professor N. Y. Marr.

In the summer of 1950, Stalin, who had made no public utterance for years (with the exception of occasional answers to questions of privileged journalists) suddenly burst into print in Pravda *with a long and abstruse article about the falseness of the theories of Marr (of whom not one* Pravda *reader in a million had ever heard) — and then followed it up with "answers to correspondents," in which he elaborated his own ideas.* Pravda *readers were bewildered, but the essence was this: Marr, with official approval, had argued in Marxist terms that language was an aspect of the superstructure of society and would change as society changed; that is, in due course, with the global advance of Communism, language differences would wither away and there would be one universal language. Stalin decided it was time to put a stop to woolly internationalism of this kind. The language of the future would be Russian. It was necessary, therefore, to prove in Marxist terms that language was an aspect of the unchanging base of society, not of its superstructure. Far from getting nothing out of this foray into linguistics, as Khrushchev suggests, Stalin must have derived extreme satisfaction from a theoretical exercise in the grand manner.*

The second example of Stalin's theorizing, to which Khrushchev here refers, was delivered to the world on the eve of the Nineteenth Party Congress as a pamphlet entitled The Economics of Socialism. *The speakers at the Congress, the delegates too, must have been given this to digest before it was finally published. None of them seems to have made much of it. It was a long and dreary polemic, but it contained one line of thought of great importance for the future. Until October, 1952, Stalin had to all appearances accepted Lenin's thesis that the way to world revolution must lead through wars — wars seen as stresses in the disintegration of capitalist society. He clung to this article of faith long after the advent of the atom bomb had made nonsense of it. But in his* Economics of Socialism *Stalin at last announced, in effect, that things had changed, that the Soviet Union was now so strong that with good luck and good judgment she could keep out of future wars, leaving the capitalist powers to destroy themselves in the struggle for dwindling world markets.*

By the time of the Nineteenth Party Congress [1952], Stalin had already taken on the role of great thinker and was the author of a number of theoretical works. It all started a few years before the Congress, when he became involved in a polemic about linguistics. It was a very strange debate, and it was of absolutely no use to him whatsoever. He invited a Georgian scholar friend of his to dinner and for some reason started talking about linguistics with the man. Subsequently Stalin wrote his articles on linguistics in which he attacked this same Georgian friend of his. That's how Stalin's theoretical works started to appear during the last stage of his life.

He struck out at economic problems, too. He organized a public debate and published his own theories. When Stalin began to dictate and publish installments of his work on the economic problems of Socialism just before his death, he made everyone read and study them. The whole Party was supposed to sit down and pore over his pamphlet. Stalin went so far as to propose that the speakers at the Nineteenth Party Congress address themselves to the theoretical questions he had raised. Malenkov doted at great length over Stalin's theories in his General Report to the Congress. All the other speakers, with the exception of myself, did the same, but it wasn't because I was daring or clever or because I was critical of Stalin's writings that I omitted any mention of them in my speech. No, it was because at the Nineteenth Party Congress I wasn't a regular speaker. I was supposed to make a report on the Party Statutes, and there was nothing in the Party Statutes that compelled me to mention Stalin's writings on linguistics and economics. Besides, Malenkov had given them more than enough attention in his General Report.

One fine summer day we were all gathered at Stalin's dacha. We sat down to a typical Stalin-style dinner, long and painful. Suddenly Voroshilov launched into the strangest tirade. I couldn't image what had gotten into him. "Koba!" he said — he often called Stalin by his nickname—"you haven't read the paper this scholar so-and-so has sent around, have you?" And then Voroshilov started calling this scholar all sorts of names, saying, "Look what a piece of scum, what a scoundrel he is! He writes such-and-such . . . You don't remember? You haven't read it?"

Stalin said, "No, I haven't read it."

Voroshilov looked at the rest of us. We all said we hadn't read whatever he was talking about. Malenkov said he knew that some specialist in economics had written a book and requested that the Academy of Sciences organize a symposium based on his theories. I don't remember the scholar's name, but it sounded Ukrainian. He had gone on a rampage, writing letters to the Central Committee, demanding that we intervene and see that his work be given the attention he felt it deserved. Malenkov went on to explain that this scholar had also sent copies of his book around to the Central Committee. Voroshilov renewed his stream of abuse against the author: "This chiseler should be arrested, he should be arrested!"

Stalin supported Voroshilov: "What a swine! Arrest him."

A short time later Stalin gave us a fierce dressing down for carelessness in selecting people for our office staffs. He complained that secret documents were leaking out through our secretariats. He said there would have to be an investigation to find out who the culprit was. We all looked at him in bewilderment, wondering what he was driving at. Suddenly Stalin was coming straight for me: "It's you, Khrushchev! The leak is through your secretariat."

I said, "Comrade Stalin, I'm certain that's not true. My assistants are all trustworthy. I have great confidence in them. They're honest Party people. It's simply impossible that one of them would divulge secret information."

"That doesn't matter. Information has still been leaking out through someone in your secretariat." And Stalin started telling us that some position he had formulated in his work on economics coincided almost word for word with the formulation of the scholar whom Voroshilov had denounced. "How did this man get hold of my work?" he asked. "How did he find out what I've written? He couldn't have overheard. This means he received the materials which I dictated and distributed to you. And now he's published this formulation as his own."

As Stalin talked, he got angrier and angrier. Then I understood what had happened, or at least why he was blaming me. The scholar in question had a Ukrainian name. Stalin knew that I had a number of Ukrainians in my secretariat, notably my assistant Shuisky, an irreproachably honest man. So Shuisky and the other Ukrainians on my staff had fallen under suspicion! Stalin thought they were the leak. I realized he was trying to stun an admission out of me. He often did this. He would look you in the eye, make an accusation, and watch to see if you would blink.

The next morning, I went to the Moscow Committee office and summoned Shuisky. "Do you know this scholar so-and-so?" I asked him calmly.

"No," he said, "I don't know him."

"And you've never heard of him?"

"Yes, I've heard of him."

"Is he an acquaintance of yours?"

"No, I've never met him."

"All right. Get me his file."

Shuisky brought me the scholar's file. I familiarized myself with it and noted that even though he had a Ukrainian name, he was actually a Siberian. His grandfather had left Poltava Province in the Ukraine and moved out to Siberia. The scholar himself had been a Party member since 1918 or 1919, and had been through an important part of the struggle for Socialism as a partisan fighter against the White-Guardist Cossacks in Siberia during the Civil War.

The next day I told Stalin, "Comrade Stalin, you were asking me about this scholar. I got out his file. You know, he's not from the Ukraine at all. He wasn't even born in the Ukraine. His grandfather left the Ukraine, and he's a Siberian." I was trying to prove that my secretariat wasn't involved in the leak of information.

Stalin looked at me fiercely and growled, "Hell!" That was his way of apologizing for having accused me. Then he softened and said, "So he's from Siberia, is he?"

"Yes, he's a Siberian. And where won't you find people with Ukrainian names? They're spread out over the whole earth. There are many of them in the Far East, in Canada, and in other countries beyond the limits of our borders."

So I had succeeded in deflecting the blow from myself, but Stalin didn't let the matter rest. He was still stung because his formulation coincided word for word with the formulation of this "half-baked scholar," as he called him. No one was allowed to come up with the same ideas that Stalin came up with. Only Stalin was a genius. Everything new had to be said by him, and everyone else was supposed to repeat after him and to spread the new laws for the building of Socialism which he had discovered and proclaimed. And now some Siberian nincompoop, unknown to anyone, had come along and written the same thing as Stalin.

If Stalin had been objective, if he hadn't been so egotistical, if he'd been capable of analyzing his own theories self-critically, then it wouldn't have taken too much effort to see that the book of this "half-baked Party theoretician" had been written considerably before Stalin started writing and publishing his own work. It was actually the Siberian scholar who could have said to Stalin, "You stole my formulation because you already had my paper." After all, it often happens that a relatively unknown man makes an important discovery. Every great man is a plain, average man before he takes the step which makes him great. But Stalin would never allow for this possibility. As long as he was alive, as long as he was the Great Leader, he had to have the first and last word in deciding theoretical questions.

This episode ended with the Siberian scholar's being hounded and eventually thrown out of the Party, attacked in the press, disgraced, arrested, and put in jail. How could such a thing happen? The man had simply written a paper. Maybe it was bad, maybe even destructive. But he had sent it directly to the Central Committee! It was his own point of view. He was a Party member of long standing and a veteran of the Civil War. Now people were branding him as a criminal. What for? They didn't know themselves. All they knew was that he had written a treatise on economics which displeased Stalin. If Voroshilov hadn't brought the matter up, this scholar would probably have persisted in calling everyone bureaucrats, and that would have been the end of it. As it was, he ended up in prison.

After Stalin's death we released him. He complained to the Moscow Committee about the way he had been treated and took out his indignation on me personally. Of course, he didn't know anything about my role in the case. He criticized me for not intervening on his behalf and for not appreciating his work. Perhaps his work did deserve recognition. In any case, it never came to anything. The so-called scholars who had followed Stalin's lead in the affair, who had praised Stalin's writings and attacked the Siberian scholar, had no interest in changing their minds now that Stalin was dead. Possibly this man never received the recognition he deserved, but it's not for me to judge. Economics is a highly specialized subject. Let expert economists go back to his treatise, appraise it, analyze it, and put it on the bookshelf where it belongs.

The incident about the "leak" of Stalin's economics writings did not end with the arrest of the Siberian scholar. After I'd convinced Stalin that the leak wasn't through my secretariat, he came to the conclusion that the leak must have been through Poskrebyshev. This was shocking because Poskrebyshev had worked for Stalin for many years. He was Stalin's faithful dog. How could anyone believe that Poskrebyshev had divulged official secrets? He couldn't have had sinister connections with anyone because everyone knew exactly who Poskrebyshev was and feared and avoided him. He wasn't a stupid man, but he had accumulated so much power that he had started putting on airs. He behaved haughtily with everyone and downright despicably with any member of the Presidium who had fallen out of Stalin's favor. He used to snarl viciously at Molotov and Mikoyan, for instance, when they fell from grace. Poskrebyshev could be unbearably offensive. He kept close to Stalin and found out before the rest of us who had fallen under the shadow of Stalin's suspicion or displeasure. Therefore anyone whom Poskrebyshev turned against was likely to be the next sacrificial victim.

And now Poskrebyshev suddenly fell under Stalin's suspicion himself. Naturally Poskrebyshev had access to all the documents in question. He himself had written them down at Stalin's dictation. Stalin used to pace up and down while dictating. He couldn't stay seated when he was thinking. He dictated while walking around. He never used stenographers. He always dictated to Poskrebyshev, and then Poskrebyshev would read it back to him. If Poskrebyshev had written down some formulation incorrectly or if a more concise wording occurred to Stalin, then Poskrebyshev would amend the manuscript. I want to give Stalin his due here. Right up to his very death, Stalin could express himself clearly and concisely. His formulations were short, comprehensible, and to the point. It was one of Stalin's great gifts. In this regard Stalin was possessed of a tremendous power which can neither be denied nor debased. Everyone who knew Stalin admired this talent of his, and because of it we were proud to work with him.

Stalin removed Poskrebyshev from his post and promoted someone else. Poskrebyshev was put on ice. I'm convinced that if Stalin had lived much longer, Poskrebyshev would undoubtedly have been arrested and eliminated as a traitor. Stalin's last word on the subject was, "I caught Poskrebyshev passing secret material. Nobody else could have done it. The leak of secret documents was through Poskrebyshev. It was he who broke secrecy." Some secrecy! What kind of secrecy is it when everything that Stalin said had been "leaked" had actually been published already?

The Nineteenth Party Congress

When he presided over the Nineteenth Party Congress in October, 1952, Stalin was an old, sick man with less than five months to live. Something of his mood in those days is conveyed by Khrushchev in this and the following sections of the chapter. Khrushchev also suggests, as he did in his Secret Speech, that Stalin was embarking on a new purge, which would have involved the liquidation of some of his closest colleagues, senior members of the old Politbureau. But Khrushchev is content to suggest. Indeed, he ignores the real significance of a number of Stalin's actions. And he gives no indication at all of the personal struggle for influence and power between himself and Malenkov (allied with Beria) which was becoming more deadly every day. Stalin, of course, dominated the Congress, even though he spoke for only seven minutes. The two chief performers were Malenkov, who delivered the Central Committee General Report, and Khrushchev himself, who made a speech of equal importance on the reform of the Party Statutes. The two rivals were thus elevated above the heads of their seniors, and it seems likely that at this time Stalin was putting these two forward as joint successors — and at the same time playing them off against each other. For what Khrushchev does not mention is that each in his speech sniped viciously at the other — Malenkov attacking Khrushchev, though not by name, for his abortive agricultural reforms; Khrushchev similarly attacking Malenkov for corruption and demoralization within the Party.

IN 1952 Stalin called us together and suggested that we should convene a Party Congress. He didn't need to persuade us. We all considered it incredible that there hadn't been a Party Congress for thirteen years. Nor had there even been a Central Committee plenum for some time. The Central Committee hadn't met in either its policy-making or its consultative capacity for years.[18] In short, the Party at large and the

18. The Party Statutes called for a Party Congress every three years. It was part of the Congress's function to elect a new Central Committee from which the members of the Politbureau, Secretariat, and other leading organs were chosen. Stalin had ruled without a Congress since 1939, paying no attention to the Central Committee and making his own appointments to the Politbureau, etc. (see Appendix 2).

Central Committee in particular had been taking no part whatever in the collective leadership. Stalin did everything himself, bypassing the Central Committee and using the Politbureau as little more than a rubber stamp. Stalin rarely bothered to ask the opinion of Politbureau members about a given measure. He would just make a decision and issue a decree.

At any rate, it was decided we would convene a Party Congress in October, 1952. For some time Stalin said nothing about the agenda or whom he wanted to speak. We were all trying to guess whether Stalin would take on the General Report himself or whether he would assign it to someone else. And if he assigned it to someone else, who would it be? We figured that if he didn't make the report himself, it would mean he didn't feel up to it physically and was unable to stand for that long on the podium. Of course, he could always distribute copies of the address to the delegates and not bother to read it aloud at all.

Finally, Stalin decided on the agenda for the Congress and announced that we would assign the General Report to Malenkov. Stalin went on to say, "Let's give the report on the Party Statutes to Khrushchev and the report on the Five-Year Plan to Saburov." Saburov was Chairman of the State Planning Commission.[19] As Stalin told us our assignments, they were recorded forthwith. We listened and received our instructions in silence. That's how the agenda for the Nineteenth Party Congress came to be determined and accepted.

I admit that when I was instructed to prepare the report on the Party Statutes, I became very nervous. Of course, the assignment was a great honor for me, but at the same time I knew that it was difficult to prepare a report on this particular subject that would be approved by the collective. I knew that when I submitted a draft of the report, I could expect the others to attack it — especially Beria, who would pull Malenkov along with him. And that's exactly what happened. Stalin never saw my report. He instructed Malenkov, Beria, myself, and someone else to look over all the reports. Beria insisted that mine was too long and that it be abbreviated. A great deal of material was cut out so that in the end my report took only about an hour to read. I don't think the substance suffered. It was shortened by taking out examples, and these were just literary frills for the sake of illustrating

19. M. Z. Saburov, an engineer, had spent most of his career in the State Planning Commission. A Deputy Prime Minister in 1947, he did not enter the Central Committee until 1952. His rise was then swift. He ran into serious trouble in 1957 by supporting the "Anti-Party Group" against Khrushchev.

some statements. By padding my report with supporting examples, I had been imitating Zhdanov to some degree. Zhdanov had given a report on the Party Statutes at the Eighteenth Party Congress [in 1939], and he had used many examples in it. I don't know how necessary they were, but I figured that because that particular style of report had already been approved, I would follow it.[20]

You might ask why Stalin didn't assign the General Report to Molotov or Mikoyan, both of whom held higher posts in the Party than Malenkov, and who were well-known Party figures. Some of us in the prewar leadership had even considered Molotov as our future leader and Stalin's most likely successor, but after the war we put any such notions out of our heads. In the days before and after the Nineteenth Party Congress, Stalin attacked Molotov and Mikoyan at every meeting. These two men were out of favor, and their lives were in danger.

The Congress was convened, the reports were delivered, and the discussion started. The discussion periods were brief. The atmosphere in the Party at that time was hardly conducive to debating the proposals made in the reports delivered by the leadership. As the Congress was drawing to a close, we discussed Saburov's report on the Five-Year Plan. It was the worst Five-Year Plan ever accepted by a Party Congress. It was poorly conceived and poorly presented. Later, after Stalin's death, we were compelled to assume the responsibility for fulfilling it. Since the plan was an impossible one, we had no choice but to introduce some amendments. As a rule it would be unthinkable to amend a document once it has been ratified by a Party Congress, but this was a special case: it was obvious to us that this particular Five-Year Plan wasn't going anywhere. As I recall, in our search for some democratic way of amending the Five-Year Plan so that its goals would correspond with some semblance of reality, we even distributed the suggested amendments among the delegates. In short, we took the only rational course left open to us.

At the end of the Congress, Stalin delivered his own speech. It lasted no more than six or seven minutes. Everyone burst into joyous applause, shouting that he was a genius and so on and so forth. After Stalin left the podium and the Congress was adjourned, we all gathered in the Presidium lounge. Stalin said, "There, look at that! I can still do it." He could still do it, my foot! He could stand on the podium for six

20. Khrushchev's account of his method of tackling this speech, the supreme moment of his career up to then, is engaging. Certainly it read like that.

or seven minutes, and he considered it a great triumph! It was incredibly difficult for him to give a six- or seven-minute speech, and he thought he was still strong enough to go on working!

Stalin himself opened the first Central Committee Plenum after the Congress and proposed the creation of a Presidium of twenty-five members. He took some papers out of his pocket and read a list of names to us — the new membership. The proposal and the nominations were accepted without discussion. We were all too accustomed to such undemocratic procedures. When Stalin proposed something, there were no questions, no comments. A "proposal" from Stalin was a God-given command, and you don't haggle about what God tells you to do — you just offer thanks and obey. While Stalin was reading out the list of members, we all lowered our eyes and squirmed in our seats. Twenty-five people! It would certainly be difficult to work in such a large collective. It would be difficult to decide operational questions.

When the plenum session was over, we all exchanged glances. What had happened? Who had put this list together? Stalin himself couldn't possibly have known most of the people whom he had just appointed. He couldn't have put the list together himself. I confess that at first I thought Malenkov was behind the new Presidium and wasn't telling the rest of us. Later I quizzed him about it in a friendly way. "Listen," I said, "I think that you had a hand in this. But I detect other minds at work here, too. There must have been some adjustments on Stalin's part, weren't there?"

Malenkov answered, "I swear I had absolutely nothing to do with the list. Stalin didn't even ask for my help nor did I make any suggestions at all about the composition of the Presidium." Malenkov's denial made it even more mysterious. I couldn't imagine that Beria was involved because there were people on the list whom Beria would never have recommended to Stalin. But I asked him about it nevertheless. "Lavrenty, did you put Stalin up to this?"

"No, at first I was sure it was Malenkov. But he swears he didn't have anything to do with it."

Molotov and Mikoyan were out of the question. Bulganin didn't know anything about it either. We kept turning these thoughts over in our minds, trying to figure out who the man behind the scenes was. Naturally the author was Stalin himself, but who had helped him? Poskrebyshev was in charge of Stalin's personal secretariat, but he couldn't have put together the list without drawing from Malenkov's apparatus, and Malenkov would have found out. There were people in Malenkov's apparatus who had worked for him for many years, and they would have told him even if they had received secret instructions from Stalin. So we were stumped. The list remained a puzzle. I now guess on the basis of certain indications that Stalin bypassed Malenkov altogether and made use of Kaganovich's assistance. Some of the names were little known in the Party, and Stalin certainly had no idea who the people were. But Kaganovich knew them. He probably told Stalin about them and that's how their names ended up on the list.

You see what sort of leadership we had? Stalin was supposedly running the Congress, putting together a new Central Committee, and creating a new Presidium, but in fact he had very little idea of what he was doing. I remember exchanging knowing glances with Beria and Malenkov. The new Presidium was too large to be workable, and the membership was too heterogeneous. The twenty-five people selected were of all different sorts, of different degrees of merit. They all enjoyed the confidence of the Party and no doubt were all worthy men. But many of them weren't prepared for a job of this importance.[21]

When Stalin read off the list of the new Presidium members, I listened anxiously and wondered, would Molotov, Mikoyan, and Voroshilov be included? I doubted it. They were men whom Stalin had cast aside. The danger of being considered spies and accordingly declared enemies of the people hung over their heads. But no, they were included. I took this as a good sign.

After Stalin proposed the twenty-five names, he said that because a group of that size would be cumbersome, we had to select a Bureau from the Presidium membership.[22] Now, this was a nonstatutory proposal. We had just adopted new Party Statutes at the Nineteenth Party Congress, and we had made no provision for a Presidium Bureau. We

21. The appointment of a twenty-five-man Presidium to replace the much smaller Politbureau was a surprise to all those not in the know. But were Khrushchev and Malenkov as unknowing as the rest of us? The interesting thing about the newcomers, both full members and candidate members, was that there was a fairly even division between Malenkov men (above all the technocrats) and Khrushchev men. This, to use Stalin's favorite phrase, was clearly no accident. It is worth noting that the candidate members included A. N. Kosygin, brought back from the limbo into which he was cast after the Leningrad affair, and L. I. Brezhnev, then very much a Khrushchev protégé, making his first appearance on the national stage. Stalin was obviously enlarging the supreme Party organ in order to cover in advance the proposed liquidation of some of its most senior members.

22. It was assumed at the time that there must be a small inner cabinet, or bureau, of Stalin's favored subordinates. Its precise composition has been hitherto unknown.

were violating the Statutes already! Stalin said the Bureau would meet more often than the full Presidium and would make decisions on all operational questions that might come up. He proposed a Bureau of nine men and straightway appointed the staff: himself, Malenkov, Beria, Khrushchev, Voroshilov, Kaganovich, Saburov, Pervukhin,[23] and Bulganin. Molotov and Mikoyan were left out, but Voroshilov was included. Voroshilov's inclusion was strange because Stalin had started having doubts about him long before Molotov and Mikoyan fell out of favor. I very much regretted that Molotov and Mikoyan weren't put on the Bureau. I thought they should have been. Stalin made a speech at the Plenum giving some very surprising and confused explanations of why Molotov and Mikoyan didn't deserve the confidence of the Party. He said they appeared to be agents of certain Western governments. There was no logic in this, of course. If they were foreign agents and didn't deserve our confidence, then why were they being kept on the Central Committee and the Presidium? Be that as it may, Molotov and Mikoyan were in fact excluded from the ruling circle of the Government. But I was glad to see that Voroshilov had been put on the Bureau. I thought Stalin had finally realized that it was a mistake to consider Voroshilov an English spy and God knows what else. It all depended on Stalin's fertile imagination, who was an agent of what imperialistic country from one day to the next.

After the Nineteenth Party Congress and the creation of the large Presidium and the new Presidium Bureau at the Plenum, our work continued according to the same pattern we had followed before all the supposed changes and improvements. Out of the nine members in the Bureau Stalin selected an inner circle of five, according to his will and benevolence. It was considered a great honor to be invited to meet with Stalin. On the other hand it was considered a bad omen if you were invited once but weren't invited back. The usual five were Stalin himself, Malenkov, Beria, Bulganin, and Khrushchev. He rarely invited Kaganovich and Voroshilov and absolutely never invited Molotov or Mikoyan. In actual fact, the Presidium was never convened. The Bureau decided all questions, and the Bureau usually meant the inner circle of five. All decisions were made by the same methods which Stalin had put into practice after 1939. Before the Eighteenth Party Congress

23. M. G. Pervukhin was one of the technocrat ministers (like Saburov) who made their name in industry and in Stalin's last years rose rapidly to the top. He, too, found himself in trouble after the defeat of the Anti-Party Group.

the Politbureau had preserved more or less democratic methods. But gradually democracy had been giving way to autocracy. Stalin had been barking orders and stifling discussion ever since the annihilation of the basic staff of the Central Committee which had been elected at the Seventeenth Party Congress [1934], the "old men," as we called them, who had been through the struggle for the creation of our Party since before the Revolution.

So much for collective leadership.

The Doctors' Plot

The arrest of the Kremlin doctors in January, 1953, on charges of poisoning Andrei Zhdanov and other Soviet luminaries was a preliminary move in what was to have been Stalin's last purge, one designed to get rid of some of his closest colleagues: Beria above all, but probably Molotov and Mikoyan, too. Khrushchev tells us one thing new about what came to be known as the Doctors' Plot: the case had already been prefabricated at some time before the Nineteenth Party Congress in October, 1952; otherwise Khrushchev would not have known that the doctor who was treating his own illness during the Congress was about to be charged. Unless he is muddled in his chronology, this leaves a particularly nasty taste. Indeed, Khrushchev's role in this whole sinister affair is suspect. S. D. Ignatiev, a man very close to Khrushchev, had replaced Beria's supporter, Abakumov, as Minister of State Security. In 1952 he was actively engaged in a savage purge of Beria's men in the security services, and heart condition or no heart condition, it was his task to fabricate the evidence against the doctors (the alleged letter from Lydia Timashuk was obviously a put-up job, as Khrushchev himself suggested in his Secret Speech) and beat confessions out of them. When the affair was "reexamined" after Stalin's death, it was none other than Beria who publicly denounced the frame-up, alleging Ignatiev's responsibility. Soon after that, Beria himself was arrested and shot, along with his chief associates, Abakumov included. Ignatiev, who according to Khrushchev had been on the brink of death in 1932, recovered sufficiently to emerge as a member of Khrushchev's own Party Secretariat. Khrushchev's sketchy version of this story diverts attention away from the larger implications of the affair — and from the

truth, which is still obscure in detail. He treats it as an example of Sta-
lin's nastiness in attacking such innocents as doctors. The unfortunate
doctors, most of whom were Jews, were no more than pawns in a major
operation directed against some of Khrushchev's colleagues, an opera-
tion which was also intended to involve Soviet Jewry in a wholesale
pogrom.

ONE day Stalin called us to the Kremlin and read us a letter from a woman doctor named Timashuk. She claimed that Zhdanov died because the doctors on the case purposely administered improper treatment to him, treatment intended to lead to his death. Naturally if this had been true, it would have been the most outrageous villainy. For doctors to destroy life rather than save it is the worst sort of crime against nature.

If Stalin had been a normal person, he wouldn't have given Timashuk's letter a second thought. A few such letters always turn up from people who are psychologically unbalanced or who are scheming to get rid of their enemies. But Stalin was more than receptive to this sort of literature. In fact, I believe this woman Timashuk was herself a product of Stalinist policies. Stalin had instilled in the consciousness of us all the suspicion that we were surrounded by enemies and that we should try to find an unexposed traitor or saboteur in everyone. Stalin called this "vigilance" and used to say that if a report was ten percent true, we should regard the entire report as fact. But how could you find even ten percent truth in a letter like Timashuk's?

Stalin's version of vigilance turned our world into an insane asylum in which everyone was encouraged to search for nonexistent facts about everyone else. Son was turned against father, father against son, and comrade against comrade. This was called "the class approach." I realize that the class struggle cannot help but divide families and divide them unmercifully. The class struggle defines the position of every member of a family. I welcome the unrelenting combat of the class struggle. It's necessary for the building of Socialism and the attainment of a better future. The class war isn't a festive parade, but a bloody, tortuous battle. I know this. I myself have been a participant in the class struggle. I came to understand the class approach during the Civil War, when I joined the bloody struggle waged by the Red Army against the shattered bands of Makhnovites, Grigorievites, Antonovites, and remnants of other White units that were still at large. The northern Caucasus was literally swarming with bandits; I myself took part in the assembly to organize the struggle against them. Once, a group of us was photographed with Furmanov, the Chief of the Political Directorate. My comrade-in-arms in the army political affairs department, Vera Shutskina, sent me a copy of this picture. She's now a pensioner. I'm glad she's alive and well. I don't know how the cup passed from her when the Stalinist butchery was going on. Anyway, even back when the struggle was under way against the White Cossack bands in the northern Caucasus, Lenin, in his foresight, showed great restraint and humanity. He did everything he could not to harm those who were innocent; and when he saw that someone was guilty, he did everything he could to rehabilitate him rather than punish him. Even if a man had slipped up, Lenin would strive to support him and to reestablish him on positive positions: first, by neutralizing the man's negative traits and then by gradually reenlisting him into the active struggle for the building of a new Socialist life. But we left the Leninist stage behind. We moved into the Stalinist stage, and the irrational policies, policies of a sick man, terrorized us all.

Getting back to Timashuk's letter, I should mention that Zhdanov had been treated by Kremlin physicians. These doctors could only have been the best and most trusted of their profession. Only men well known and much respected in the Soviet medical world had been enlisted to work in the Kremlin hospital. But they were arrested and thrown in jail like common criminals.

Before his death, Zhdanov had been in poor health for some time. I don't know what he was suffering from, but one of his ailments was that he had lost his will power and wasn't able to control himself when it came to drinking. He was pitiful to watch. I even remember that in the last days of Zhdanov's life, Stalin used to shout at him to stop drinking. This was an astounding thing because Stalin usually encouraged people to get drunk. But he compelled Zhdanov to drink fruit water and suffer while the rest of us were drinking wine or something stronger. And it's easy to imagine that if Stalin held him back like this, Zhdanov would go completely out of control at home. This same vice killed Shcherbakov, and it certainly hastened Zhdanov's death to a considerable degree.

By no means am I putting Shcherbakov and Zhdanov on the same level. Since Stalin's death I've realized that our intelligentsia harbors a deep-seated resentment against Zhdanov for his role in closing the Leningrad journals. But it should be remembered that Zhdanov was only discharging Stalin's orders. I think Stalin's cultural policies, especially the cultural policies imposed on Leningrad through Zhdanov, were cruel and senseless.[24] You can't regulate the development of literature, art, and culture with a stick or by barking orders. You can't lay down a furrow and then harness all your artists to make sure they don't deviate from the straight and narrow. If you try to control your artists too tightly, there will be no clashing of opinions, consequently no criticism, and consequently no truth. There will be just a gloomy stereotype, boring and useless. Not only will this stereotype fail to encourage the people to benefit from their art; it will poison and kill their relationship to art.

Anyway, the doctors connected with Zhdanov's case were arrested. Among them was V. N. Vinogradov. He had once treated Stalin, which was a rare distinction because Stalin almost never let doctors treat him. But Stalin didn't spare Vinogradov. He had him arrested and beaten. I got to know Vinogradov after he was released. He was brought in more than once to consult on my own health. They also arrested V. K. Vasilenko, a reputable physician and professor. I didn't know him very well personally, but I had heard many good things about him from Strazhesky, whom I respected very much. I knew Strazhesky from Kiev. He was a leading light not only in the Soviet medical world but abroad as well. When the war ended, Strazhesky asked me to take Vasilenko out of the army so that he could work in the clinic which Strazhesky directed. "Vasilenko is my pupil," Strazhesky had said, "and I would like him to take over from me so that the clinic will be sure to pass into reliable hands." Strazhesky had founded his clinic before the Revolution, and it had an excellent reputation. Vasilenko was in China when the arrests started. He was called home, and the minute he stepped across the Soviet border he was thrown in chains.

I remember after I made my report on the Party statutes to the Nineteenth Party Congress, I fell ill. I couldn't leave home when my report was being discussed at the Congress. I had to stay in bed for a

24. The reference here is to Zhdanov's sweeping purge of the arts, known as the Zhdanovshchina, which was a major scandal in 1947–48. Magazines were closed down, celebrated writers were proscribed, distinguished composers had to confess to past errors and promise to compose for the masses. It was, in effect, a cultural Terror.

few days. An elderly doctor came to examine me. While he was listening to my heart, he put his ear against my chest. I was touched by his thoughtfulness and his care. I felt terrible at that moment, but not because I was sick. I was tormented because I had already read the testimony against this old doctor, whose concern for my health I found so touching, and I knew that no matter what I said Stalin wouldn't spare him.

After Vinogradov, Vasilenko, and the others had been arrested, Stalin circulated and published copies of Timashuk's letter with his own postscript, in which he invoked the anger of the masses against the doctors who had "committed such villainy" by doing away with Zhdanov. More letters started pouring in branding the doctors as traitors. These letters reflected the opinion of people who believed that if Stalin had released such a document, the crime must have already been proved, and they were revolted that such a thing could have happened.

Konev,[25] himself a sick man at the time, sent a long letter to Stalin in which he claimed that he, too, was being poisoned with the same medicines which had allegedly been used to do in Zhdanov. Konev's letter compounded the travesty. Apparently all the members of the Presidium sensed the lack of substance in Konev's accusation, but we never discussed it openly because, once Stalin had made up his mind and started to deal with a problem, there wasn't anything to do. When we got together and exchanged opinions in private, we admitted we were indignant about Konev's letter: since the people accused of Zhdanov's murder were behind bars, the letter widened the circle of suspects and fanned Stalin's distrust of doctors in general.

The interrogations began. I heard myself how Stalin talked to S. D. Ignatiev, who was then Minister of State Security. I knew Ignatiev personally, and I knew he was a very sick man. He had had a near-fatal heart attack. He was mild, considerate, and well liked. We all knew what sort of physical condition he was in. Stalin used to berate him viciously over the phone in our presence. Stalin was crazy with rage, yelling at Ignatiev and threatening him, demanding that he throw the

---

25. Marshal I. S. Konev, an outstanding general in World War II, later showed an inclination to dabble in political intrigue. He was at various times commander in chief of Soviet land forces (in succession to Zhukov, after the latter's rustication in 1946), First Deputy Minister of Defense, and Supreme Commander of the Warsaw Pact forces. Two other marshals, one general and one admiral, were also said to have been poisoned (not fatally) by the unfortunate doctors.

doctors in chains, beat them to a pulp, and grind them into powder. It was no surprise when almost all the doctors confessed to their crimes. I can't blame them for slandering themselves. Too many people have passed before me, different sorts of people, honest men and traitors, men of the Revolution and saboteurs, all of whom confessed. For example, take Meretskov. He's now nearing the end of his life. He walks about crippled, almost bent in two. He admitted he was an English spy. The Kremlin doctors landed in this same situation, and they, too, confessed.[26]

That's how the so-called Doctors' Plot arose. It was a shameful business. After the crushing of the enemy in World War II, after our own Soviet intelligentsia had come into its own and achieved world stature, suddenly our intelligentsia — or at least the doctors in its midst — fell subject to Stalin's suspicion. The doctors' case was a cruel and contemptible thing.

Back in 1902 there were cholera riots in Makeyevka [a city in the Donbass], during which the doctors in the area were beaten unmercifully. Then I remember early in my youth, around 1910, there was a cholera epidemic throughout the Donbass. Many miners were dying at the mines where my father and I worked. When the miners got sick they were taken off to the cholera barracks from which no one returned. A rumor started to circulate among the miners that the doctors were poisoning the patients. Witnesses were found who claimed they had seen someone throw powder into the well. I heard all kinds of absurdities like that. And now, in our own time, these same dark powers were rearing their heads again, and the persecution of intellectuals and doctors came back out into the open.

Svetlanka

Khrushchev's impressions of Stalin's daughter, her relationship with her father, and their homelife may be compared with the record in Svetlana Alliluyeva's own two books, Twenty Letters to a Friend *and* Only One Year. *There are small discrepancies, but in general, Svetlana herself confirms Khrushchev's account, which shows him at his best and Stalin at his very remarkable worst. The chronology, as always, is a little vague; but Svetlana's story bears out Khrushchev's account of*

26. The doctors were cleared of the charges against them by a commission of inquiry set up by Beria immediately after Stalin's death. But two had already died under interrogation.

Stalin and Svetlana

Mikoyan's intervention on her behalf and Khrushchev's own benevolent attitude. Unfortunately, Khrushchev was deposed at what, for Svetlana and Brajesh Singh, was the critical moment. It was left for Kosygin and Suslov, in person, to forbid her to marry and then to forbid her to take Brajesh Singh back to India to die. When he did die and she was at last allowed to take his ashes back to India, the authorities tried to rush her home. Benediktov, then the Soviet ambassador to India, whom Khrushchev calls "straitlaced," was merely frightened. He had been Minister of Agriculture at one time, and then was demoted by Khrushchev himself. Khrushchev's comments on what Soviet citizens may naturally expect when they are summoned back to Moscow are sufficiently revealing.

STALIN's character was brutish, and his temper was harsh; but his brutishness didn't always imply malice toward people to whom he acted so rudely. His was a sort of inborn brutishness. He was coarse and abusive with everyone. I often experienced his rudeness myself. Stalin liked me. If he hadn't liked me or if he had felt the slightest suspicion toward me, he could have gotten rid of me anytime he pleased in the same way he got rid of so many people who were undesirable to him. More than once, after being rude or spiteful to me, he would express his goodwill. But God forbid that there should have been any kind of apology! No. Apologies were alien to his very nature. There is a story that gives a clearer idea of how Stalin allowed himself to insult and abuse those closest to him.

It happened in the last year of his life. Stalin had invited us all to the Nearby Dacha to celebrate the New Year with him. We were all in a state of great elation. A new year! We could count to our credit one more year of victories and successes! There were tables spread with hors d'oeuvres. We had a huge dinner and a great deal to drink. Stalin was in high spirits and was therefore drinking a lot himself and urging everyone else to do the same. A considerable quantity of wine was consumed.

Stalin went over to the record player and put on some records of Russian and Georgian folk music. We all listened and started singing along with the records. Then he put on some dance music, and we started to dance. There was one acknowledged dancer among us — Anastas Ivanovich Mikoyan. All the steps he did were based on the

"Lezghinka" [a Caucasian folk dance]. Then Voroshilov started dancing, and we all joined in. When I dance, I don't move my feet. I dance like a cow on the ice. But I joined in nonetheless. So did Kaganovich. He was a dancer of not much higher class than myself. Bulganin apparently had done some dancing in his youth. He was trying to stomp out something vaguely Russian in rhythm. Stalin danced, too. He shuffled around with his arms spread out. It was evident that he had never danced before. (It was too bad that Molotov wasn't with us on that occasion. He was the city dancer among us. He had grown up in an intellectual family, and as a university student, he had been at many student parties and knew how to dance the way students did. He loved music and could even play the violin. In general he was a very musical person. I'm not an expert in this, in fact I'm a pretty bad judge, but in my eyes Molotov was a first-class dancer.)

I would say that the general mood of the party was good. Then Svetlanka [affectionate form of Svetlana] appeared. I don't know if she'd been summoned or if she came on her own. She found herself in the middle of a flock of people older than she, to put it mildly. As soon as this sober young woman arrived, Stalin made her dance. I could see she was tired. She hardly moved while dancing. She danced for a short time and tried to stop, but her father still insisted. She went over and stood next to the record player, leaning her shoulder against the wall. Stalin came over to her, and I joined them. We stood there together. Stalin was lurching about. He said, "Well, go on, Svetlanka, dance! You're the hostess, so dance!"

She said, "I've already danced, Papa, I'm tired." With that, Stalin grabbed her by the forelock of her hair with his fist and pulled. I could see her face turning red and tears welling up in her eyes. I felt so sorry for Svetlanka. He pulled harder and dragged her back onto the dance floor.

Here you have a father's expression of tenderness for his daughter. No doubt Stalin loved Svetlanka very much. He loved Vasya, too, but he was critical of Vasya's drinking and general lack of discipline. Svetlanka, on the other hand, was a good student. Her behavior as a little girl was always excellent. I never heard anything bad about her. Stalin was very proud and fond of her. Yet look how he showed his fatherly feelings toward his daughter! He behaved so brutishly not because he wanted to cause Svetlanka pain. No, his behavior toward her was really an expression of affection, but in a perverse, brutish form which was peculiar to him.

As I've said, I had held Svetlanka's mother, Nadezhda Alliluyeva, in high esteem. She was very different from Stalin. I had always liked her for her modesty. Vasya [Vasily] was a good boy, clever but headstrong. In his early youth he started to drink heavily. He was an undisciplined student and brought Stalin much grief. I think Stalin used to whip him regularly and assigned Chekists to keep Vasya under surveillance.

Svetlanka was different. As a little girl she would be running around the house whenever we were there. Stalin always called her "the hostess," and we started calling her "the hostess," too. She was always dressed smartly in a little Ukrainian skirt and an embroidered blouse. She looked just like a dressed-up doll, but at the same time very much like her mother with her auburn hair and tiny freckles. "The hostess" grew up before our eyes. I remember that whenever we came by, Stalin would say, "Well, hostess, entertain the guests," and she would run out into the kitchen. Stalin explained, "Whenever she gets angry with me, she always says, 'I'm going out to the kitchen and complain about you to the cook.' I always plead with her, 'Spare me! If you complain to the cook, it will be all over with me!'" Then Svetlanka would say firmly that she would tell on her papa if he ever did anything wrong again.

Stalin had an older son Yasha [Yakov] by his first wife, a Georgian woman. Yasha was an engineer. I never knew him. When I started to see Stalin at home, Yasha was there only rarely. He lived in a separate house with his wife and baby daughter. The few times he did come to Stalin's family dinners, he always came alone. He never brought his wife and daughter along.

Then Nadya committed suicide. She died under mysterious circumstances. However she died, it was because of something Stalin did, and Svetlanka must have known that. There was even a rumor that Stalin shot Nadya. According to another version, which is more plausible to me, Nadya shot herself because of an insult hurled at her honor as a woman. Certainly Svetlanka knew something about the way her mother died, and she suffered very much.

After Nadya's death, Vasya and Svetlanka were always around whenever we came by to see Stalin at his apartment. I grew accustomed to seeing Svetlanka. I was very attached to her. I felt like a parent toward her. I felt a certain human pity for her, as I would feel for an orphan. Stalin himself was brutish and unattentive. He never showed any parental tenderness. When he wasn't being downright abusive toward her, he was cold and unfeeling. Everywhere he went he left a trace of disagreeableness in his relations with others. He had a bully's personality. Svetlanka's relations with her father were complicated. He loved her, but he used to express these feelings of love in a beastly way. His was the tenderness of a cat for a mouse. He broke the heart first of a child, then of a young girl, then of a woman and mother. It all resulted in Svetlanka's gradual psychic breakdown. Stalin always went on holidays alone. He never took his children with him. Even animals like their mothers to coddle them in the sunshine. All creatures need affection, and a human being who is deprived of affection becomes psychologically stratified. This is what happened to Svetlanka.

I don't know what sort of people brought Svetlanka up. I remember seeing a young, beautiful Georgian woman around. Somebody said she was Svetlanka's tutor. I don't know what kind of tutor she was or where she came from. There was a rumor that she was planted by Beria, and that she was there for Beria's benefit, not Svetlanka's. One day she just disappeared.

Svetlanka married a man named Morozov. His name was Russian, but he was a Jew. They lived some time together. Stalin barely tolerated him. I never saw Morozov invited anywhere by Stalin. After Svetlanka's first son was born, I don't think Stalin ever saw him. This, too, distressed Svetlanka very much. Then suddenly, after the war, Stalin was seized by a fit of anti-Semitism. Svetlanka and Morozov were divorced. He is a bright man. I'm told that he's now a good economist and that he has a doctorate and a teaching degree in economics. In short, he's a fine, upstanding Soviet citizen.

When Stalin told Svetlanka to divorce her husband, he apparently said something about it to Malenkov. Malenkov's daughter, a very good girl named Volya, had married the son of Malenkov's friend Shamberg, who had worked for years in Malenkov's apparatus. Then one day Malenkov's wife, Valeriya Alekseyevna Malenkova, a bright woman for whom I had great respect, told me that Volya had divorced young Shamberg and married someone else, an architect. I won't try to compare the two men. That's Volya's business. I think her second husband is a good fellow, too. But I couldn't understand why she would throw out the son of her father's friend Shamberg. It was very upsetting to me at the time. Malenkov wasn't an anti-Semite, and he never told me for sure that Stalin had spoken to him disapprovingly about his daughter being married to a Jew. But I'm sure that even if Stalin didn't say anything to Malenkov directly, Malenkov heard from others that Stalin had ordered Svetlanka to divorce her husband because he was a Jew, and no doubt Malenkov figured that he had better do the same with his daughter. The episode was another manifestation of that same debasing, disgraceful anti-Semitism I've already talked about. I'm not ascribing this sentiment to Malenkov. On his part, it was just a lackey's servility to his master. Stalin had made his daughter divorce a Jew, so Malenkov had to do it, too. Generally speaking, I considered Malenkov a normal, healthy human being, uncontaminated by this vile disease.

Then Svetlanka married a second time. It was Stalin who wanted her to marry Zhdanov's son Yury. He's now the rector of Rostov University. I've always liked him, and I still do. He's a bright, well-educated, sensible fellow. Stalin liked him, too, but Svetlanka did not. After Stalin's death they were divorced. I was very sorry about the whole thing. I've never liked to listen to people gossip about Svetlanka's bad behavior and her infidelity to her husbands. She lived for a long time in loneliness, without a husband. This was unnatural. She had two children, a boy by her first husband and a little girl by young Zhdanov. The revelations about her father's abuses of power were another severe shock for her.

Later, Mikoyan told me that Svetlanka had come to ask his advice. She wanted to marry an Indian journalist [Brajesh Singh]. She told Mikoyan she loved this man. He was older than she, but she had known him for a long time and he was a decent man, a Communist. Mikoyan said, "She asked me to find out what your attitude is." I was surprised that she would ask my opinion. As far as I was concerned, it was her own business. I told Mikoyan, "If she considers him a worthy person, then let her marry him. It's her choice. Whatever she decides, we won't interfere. The fact that he's not a citizen of the Soviet Union shouldn't be an obstacle if she really is fond of him. Let her decide for herself." So she married him. I was satisfied. I wanted her simply to be able to lead her own life.

Then came the last straw — the death and funeral of her third husband.

I talk of Svetlanka at such length partly because she's now very unfortunate. When I found out that she had gone to bury her husband in his homeland and that she wouldn't return, I wanted to believe it was just the latest slanderous hoax concocted by bourgeois journalists. I refused to believe it for a few days, but then I received indisputable confirmation. I can't understand how she decided to take this step. She abandoned her Homeland and her children. She gave the enemies of the Soviet way of life something to gossip about, and she allowed her name, the name of Stalin's daughter, to be exploited by the enemies of Socialism to the disservice of our country. It was an unforgivable thing for a Soviet citizen to do. Nonetheless, I still feel very sorry for her. When I think of her and her misfortune, I recall those lines by Nekrasov: [27]

> *The sight of the clearing brings tears to her eyes;*
> *She remembers the birches that flourished there.*

The very thought of Svetlanka brings tears to my eyes. It saddens me that she has come to this end. From the very beginning of her life her fate was very complex, and things were never easy for her. None of this excuses what she's done, but still, it makes me more sad than angry when I think about her.

I haven't read her book, but I've heard excerpts from it over the radio. The West is broadcasting those passages which serve its purposes. Perhaps the parts I heard weren't characteristic of the book as a whole, but what was broadcast sounded, at the very least, strange. It sounded as though it were written as a result of a mental or emotional breakdown of some kind. For instance, she writes in her book that she used to cross herself and that she was very religious. I don't think that she was ever really religious. There's something odd and even sick about her book. I can't reconcile myself to it. How could a Soviet citizen who grew up in our society write this kind of stuff?

For her to run away to the West was terribly wrong. It can't be justified. But there's another side to the whole case. She did something stupid, but Svetlanka was dealt with stupidly, too — stupidly and rudely. Apparently, after her husband's funeral she went to our embassy in New Delhi. Benediktov was our ambassador there. I knew him. He's a very straitlaced person. Svetlanka said she wanted to stay in India for a few months, but Benediktov advised her to return immediately to the Soviet Union. This was stupid on his part. When a Soviet

27. N. A. Nekrasov was a nineteenth-century poet; the lines are from his poem "Sasha."

ambassador recommends that a citizen of the Soviet Union return home immediately, it makes the person suspicious. Svetlanka was particularly familiar with our habits in this regard. She knew it meant she wasn't trusted. It didn't mean they were concerned for her welfare. It meant distrust — political distrust — and it could have meant a bad end for her. This was an offensive, humiliating tactic, which would throw even a stable person off balance, and Svetlanka wasn't a stable person. Her instability is evident from the contents of her book. She broke down and turned to foreign powers for help. Her defection was partly the fault of people who used police measures instead of showing tact and respect to a citizen of our Soviet Homeland.

What do I think should have been done? I'm convinced that if she had been treated differently, the regrettable episode would never have happened: When Svetlanka came to the embassy and said that she had to stay in India for two or three months, they should have told her, "Svetlana Iosifovna, why only three months? Get a visa for a year or two or even three years. You can get a visa and live here. Then, whenever you're ready, you can go back to the Soviet Union." If she had been given freedom of choice, her morale would have been boosted. They should have showed her that she was trusted. I'm convinced that if they had dealt with her in that way and even if she had already written her book, either she would have not published it at all or else she would have rewritten it. But they treated her in such a way as to show her she was under suspicion. She's a clever woman and understood this, so she went to the American ambassador. That's how she got to Switzerland and from there to America. She severed her ties with her Homeland forever. She parted with her children — her son and her daughter — and her friends. She lost everything she had known. And thus ended her life as a Soviet citizen. It is very, very sad. I feel so sorry for Svetlanka. I still call her that automatically, even though she's been Svetlana Iosifovna, and not Svetlanka, for many years.

And what if we had acted the way I think we should have and Svetlanka still hadn't returned home from India? Well, that would have been too bad but no worse than what happened. As it was, even under the existing system of issuing visas, she didn't come back. What has happened to Svetlanka grieves me very much, but I still think that everything has not yet been lost. She can still return. Her thoughts about returning to her children might grow stronger. She should be given another chance. She should know that if she wants to come back she's welcome and that the weakness she showed when she left and went to America won't be held against her. I don't excuse Svetlanka for what she did, but neither do I excuse those people who — instead of giving her a helping hand to find the proper course — pushed her into taking this improper, unjustifiable, and irrational step when she threw herself into the mire of émigré life.

Feasts and Holidays with Stalin

Of this chapter there is little that need be said. It offers a vivid and horrifying picture of the dictator in decline — and of the sycophancy, the self-seeking duplicity of his entourage, Khrushchev included. For it should be remembered that Khrushchev was now engaged in a deadly struggle with Malenkov and was contriving to ingratiate himself with Stalin to very considerable effect. Anyone who doubts the essential truth of this picture should read Conversations with Stalin *by the Yugoslav rebel Milovan Djilas. Here Stalin is shown by Djilas among his marshals and "closest colleagues" as early as 1947:*

"An ungainly dwarf of a man passed through gilded and marbled imperial halls, and a path opened before him; radiant, admiring glances followed him, while the ears of the courtiers strained to catch every word. And he, sure of himself and his works, obviously paid no attention to all this. His country was in ruins, hungry and exhausted. But his armies and his marshals, heavy with fat and drunk with vodka and victory, had already trampled half of Europe underfoot, and he was convinced that they would trample over the other half in the next round. He knew that he was the most cruel and despotic figure in history. But this did not worry him a bit, for he was convinced that he was carrying out the will of history."

The descriptions by Djilas of Stalin's way of doing business tally closely with Khrushchev's. In 1947 Stalin was still strong and overwhelmingly confident. Khrushchev shows him also in his last phase — the degeneration of this Attila figure into a broken and paranoid old man, scheming to destroy his closest colleagues before they destroyed him, afraid of the food from his own kitchens, but still striking terror into the hearts of all around him. The colleagues, Khrushchev among them, thought it was the most natural thing in the world to lie low and never to speak up in the face of the iniquity of the moment.

THOSE last years with Stalin were hard times. The government virtually ceased to function. Stalin selected a small group which he kept close to him at all times, and then there was always another group of people whom he didn't invite for an indefinite period in order to punish them. Any one of us could find himself in one group one day and in the other group the next. After the Nineteenth Party Congress, Stalin created among the new Presidium members some wide-ranging commissions to look into various matters. In practice these commissions turned out to be completely ineffectual because everyone was left to his own devices. There was no guidance. There was nothing assigned for the commissions to look into, so they made up their own assignments. Everyone in the orchestra was playing on his own instrument anytime he felt like it, and there was no direction from the conductor.

We usually got together for Bureau meetings in the following way: There were no official sessions as such. When Stalin was coming into town from the Nearby Dacha, where he was living then, he would call us together through the Central Committee Secretariat. We would meet either in his study at the Kremlin or, more often, in the Kremlin movie theater. We would watch movies and talk about various matters between reels. Stalin would get up from an afternoon nap around seven or eight o'clock in the evening and drive to the Kremlin. We would meet him there. He used to select the movies himself. The films were usually what you might call captured trophies; we got them from the West. Many of them were American pictures. He liked cowboy movies especially. He used to curse them and give them the proper ideological evaluation but then immediately order new ones. The films didn't have subtitles, so the Minister of Cinematography, I. I. Bolshakov, would translate them out loud. He would translate from all languages. Actually, he didn't know any of these languages. He had been told the plot in advance. He would take pains to memorize it and then would "translate" the movie. We often joked about his translations, Beria especially. In many of the scenes, Bolshakov would simply get the plot wrong, or else he would just explain what anyone could see was happening on the screen: "Now he's leaving the room . . . Now he's walking across the street." Beria would then chime in and give Bolshakov some help: "Look! He's started running! Now he's running!"

Stalin never went to the movies anywhere but in the Kremlin theater, which was equipped with a projector outdated even at that time. The hall is no longer used for a movie theater. We used to watch all kinds of movies there — German, English, French, American, and from other countries, too. The film archive was huge. On the whole we didn't like these films very much. I remember once we saw a gloomy, unpleasant, historical movie. It was set in England. Some treasure had to be transported from India to London, and there were Spanish pirates all along the way who were raiding English ships and murdering their crews. When it came time to transport the treasure, the English remembered a pirate captain who was in one of their jails. He was a very crafty pirate, a ruffian and a daredevil. The English decided to ask him if he would do the job for them. The pirate captain said he would, but only if he were allowed to choose his own crew from the other pirates who were in jail with him. The English agreed. They gave him a ship and he headed for India, where he picked up the treasure. On the way back he started to get rid of his pirate crewmen one by one. This was his system: in his cabin he would put up a picture of the next friend he intended to eliminate, just to remind himself. After he had eliminated that person and thrown him overboard, he would put up a picture of his next victim. I think in the end the pirate captain was eliminated himself. They say it was a true story. As we watched the movie and saw the treachery of this captain, we were reminded of how people working around Stalin often disappeared. We were haunted by the thought, "Weren't the enemies of the people being killed off in just this way?"

As a rule, when a movie ended, Stalin would suggest, "Well, let's go get something to eat, why don't we?" The rest of us weren't hungry. By now it was usually one or two o'clock in the morning. It was time to go to bed, and the next day we had to go to work. But Stalin didn't have to work in the morning, and he didn't think about us. Everyone would say, yes, he was hungry, too. This lie about being hungry was like a reflex. We would all get into our cars and drive out to the Nearby Dacha. Beria and Malenkov would usually get in Stalin's car, and the rest of us were distributed according to choice. I usually rode in a car with Bulganin. Our caravan used to make detours into side streets from the Kremlin to the Moscow River. I often asked those who rode with Stalin, "Why did you make detours off the main road?"

They answered, "Don't ask us. We didn't decide the route. Stalin himself chose the streets we would take." Apparently Stalin had a street plan of Moscow and marked out a different route every time. He didn't even tell his bodyguard in advance what route he would take.

You don't have to be too clever to guess that he was taking measures to deceive any enemies who might have had designs on his life. As for the Kremlin itself, no one was allowed into it in those days. The building where the theater was located was closed off to everyone except those who came with Stalin.

Every time we got to the Nearby Dacha, we used to whisper among ourselves about how there were more locks than the time before. All sorts of bolts were attached to the gate, and a barricade had been set up. In addition there were two walls around the dacha, and between the walls there were watchdogs. An electric alarm system and all sorts of other security devices were installed. In a way this was all quite proper. Holding the position he did, Stalin was a very tempting target for any enemy of the Soviet regime. This was nothing to joke about, and the precautions he took seemed to make sense — although it would have been dangerous for any of us to have tried to imitate him.

When we got to the dacha, "the session" continued, if you can call it a session. This system of work, if you can call it work, continued from after the war until Stalin's death. Neither the Central Committee, nor the Politbureau, nor the Presidium Bureau worked regularly. But Stalin's regular sessions with his inner circle went along like clockwork. If he didn't summon us for two or three days, we would think something had happened to him, that he'd gotten sick.

He suffered terribly from loneliness. He needed people around him all the time. When he woke up in the morning, he would immediately summon us, either inviting us to the movies or starting some conversation which could have been finished in two minutes but was stretched out so that we would stay with him longer. This was an empty pastime for us. It's true that sometimes State and Party questions were decided, but we spent only a fraction of our time on those. The main thing was to occupy Stalin's time so he wouldn't suffer from loneliness. He was depressed by loneliness and he feared it.

He had a deep fear of more than just loneliness and being ambushed by his enemies on the road to the dacha. Whenever we had dinner with him, Stalin wouldn't touch a single dish or hors d'oeuvre or bottle until someone else had tested it. This shows that he had gone off the deep end. He didn't even trust the people serving him, people who had served him for years and who were undoubtedly loyal to him. He didn't trust anyone at all. When we went for dinner at Stalin's we always had his favorite dishes, and the cooks prepared them very well.

They were delicious. But we had to eat according to the following routine:

Let's say Stalin wanted something to eat; everyone was assigned a dish which he was supposed to try before Stalin would taste it.

"Look, here are the giblets, Nikita. Have you tried them yet?"

"Oh, I forgot." I could see he would like to take some himself but was afraid. I would try them and only then would he start to eat them himself.

Then he would say, "Look! Here's some herring!" He liked it very much. He was always served his herring unsalted and everyone else salted theirs to taste. I would taste Stalin's, and then he would have some. And so it was with every dish. Every dish had its own appointed taster who would find out if it was poisoned or not.

Beria was the only one of us who didn't have to be a taster at Stalin's table. He was exempt because he never ate the same dishes the rest of us were served. Even when having dinner with Stalin, Beria always had his own meal brought over from his dacha. Stalin's old retainer Matryona Petrovna used to serve Beria and say in her thick nasal voice, "Well, Comrade Beria, here's your grass." We all used to get a big laugh out of that. Beria really did eat greens, just as they do in Central Asia, and sometimes he stuffed them into his mouth with his fingers. Every now and then he used a fork, but usually he ate with his fingers.

These dinners were frightful. We would get home from them early in the morning, just in time for breakfast, and then we'd have to go to work. During the day I usually tried to take a nap in my lunch hour because there was always a risk that if you didn't take a nap and Stalin invited you for dinner, you might get sleepy at the table; and those who got sleepy at Stalin's table could come to a bad end. There were often serious drinking bouts, too. I remember Beria, Malenkov, and Mikoyan had to ask the waitresses to pour them colored water instead of wine because they couldn't keep up with Stalin's drinking.

There had been excessive drinking at Stalin's table ever since before the war. Prior to their deaths, Shcherbakov and Zhdanov had been two of the worst offenders in this vile activity — and two of its first casualties as well. Once, Shcherbakov even went so far as to expose Beria, Malenkov, and Mikoyan's arrangement with the waitresses to be served colored water instead of wine. When Stalin realized he had been deceived he fumed with anger and raised a terrible uproar. We were all disgusted with Shcherbakov, but of course we couldn't say anything about it. Shcherbakov ended up drinking himself to death — and he drank not so much because he had a craving for alcohol, but simply because it pleased Stalin when the people around him drank themselves under the table. To put it more generally, I'd say that Stalin found it entertaining to watch the people around him get themselves into embarrassing and even disgraceful situations. For some reason he found the humiliation of others very amusing. I remember once Stalin made me dance the "Gopak" [a Ukrainian folk dance] before some top Party officials. I had to squat down on my haunches and kick out my heels, which frankly wasn't very easy for me. But I did it and I tried to keep a pleasant expression on my face. As I later told Anastas Ivanovich Mikoyan, "When Stalin says dance, a wise man dances."

At these interminable, agonizing dinners, Stalin used to regale us with stories. I've never forgotten how he described his first exile. The tale helped explain why he drank so much. He was sent somewhere in Vologda Province. Many political and criminal convicts were sent there. Stalin used to say, "There were some nice fellows among the criminal convicts during my first exile. I hung around mostly with the criminals. I remember we used to stop at the saloons in town. We'd see who among us had a ruble or two, then we'd hold our money up to the window, order something, and drink up every kopek we had. One day I would pay; the next, someone else would pay and so on, in turn. These criminals were nice, salt-of-the-earth fellows. But there were lots of rats among the political convicts. They once organized a comrades' court and put me on trial for drinking with the criminal convicts, which they charged was an offense."

I don't know what sort of sentence this comrades' court passed on Stalin. No one ever dared ask him. We just exchanged glances. Only afterward would we exchange remarks, such as, "You see, even in his youth, he was inclined to drink too much. It's probably inherited." Stalin had also told us stories about his father. He said his father was a simple shoemaker and that he drank a lot. He used to say that his father drank so much he had to sell his belt for drinking money, and a Georgian has to be in desperate straits before he will sell his belt. "My father sold his belt a number of times," said Stalin, "and when I was still in the cradle, he used to dip his finger in a glass of wine and let me suck on it. He was teaching me to drink even when I was still in the cradle!"

I don't know what's been written in Stalin's biography about his father, but in the early days of my career there was a rumor going around that his father wasn't a worker and simple shoemaker at all, but that he had a workshop with at least ten employees under him. For those days that was a big enterprise. If this fact had been revealed during the purges in connection with anybody but Stalin, that person would have undergone an interrogation that would have made his bones rattle. People were very particular about your background after the Revolution. If it was discovered that you came from a nonworker's background, you were considered a second-class citizen. This attitude was understandable. The working class is the most revolutionary and the most stable class in society. It has carried the weight of all the other classes on its shoulders throughout history. Therefore the people's attitude toward any class other than the proletariat has always been guarded and critical.

Here's another sample of the kind of story Stalin used to tell:

"One winter I went on a hunt. I took my gun and crossed the Yenisei River on skis. I went about twelve versts [eight miles]. I saw some partridges sitting in a tree. To tell the truth, I didn't know they were partridges at first. I'd hunted partridges before, but I'd always thought they were field game and that they kept to the grass. Anyway, live and learn. I came nearer and started to shoot. I had twelve rounds and there were twenty-four partridges. I killed twelve, and the rest just sat there. So I decided to go back for more shells. I went back, got some more shells, and returned." We were ready for him to say anything at this point. "I arrived and they were still sitting there."

I interrupted and asked, "What do you mean, they were still sitting there?"

"That's right," he said, "they were still sitting there." Beria urged him to go on with the story. "I killed the remaining twelve partridges, took a piece of string, attached them to it, tied the end of the string to my belt, and dragged them home with me."

After dinner, while we were washing up before leaving, we were literally spitting with scorn in the bathroom. So he had made twelve versts on a winter day, killed twelve partridges, gone back and forth another twelve versts, shot twelve more partridges, and returned home another twelve versts — that's forty-eight versts on skis! Beria said, "Listen, how could a man from the Caucasus, who never had much chance to ski, travel a distance like that? He's lying!"

Of course he was lying. None of us had any doubt about that. It's hard to say why Stalin felt he had to lie. I don't know what motivated him. He must have had some sort of inner urge. This particular story was an entertaining lie and it didn't do the cause any harm, but he often lied in more serious conversations, too. As far as his boasts about his skill with a gun were concerned — I had even seen with my own eyes that Stalin couldn't shoot at all, much less kill twenty-four partridges with twenty-four shots. He once picked up a gun when we were having dinner at the Nearby Dacha and went outside to drive away some sparrows. All he succeeded in doing was wounding one of the Chekists in his bodyguard. Another time he was fiddling with a gun, and it went off and just barely missed killing Mikoyan. Stalin was sitting next to Mikoyan. The shot ripped into the ground and spewed gravel all over the table and all over Mikoyan. No one said a word, but we were all horrified.

If there was anything worse than having dinner with Stalin, it was having to go on a vacation with him. To have dinner with him or to go on vacation with him was, of course, a great honor. But it was also a terrible physical strain. If only people realized what an ordeal it was, how much unpleasantness had to be swallowed in order to preserve relations! The friendliest relations always had to be demonstrated outwardly. You had to make this sacrifice. But putting up with the ordeal had its rewards and advantages, too. Conversations were always going on which you could use profitably and from which you could draw useful conclusions for your own purposes.

After I started working in Moscow, Stalin frequently invited me to come along with him when he went to the Caucasus for a vacation. These frequent invitations were all part of his fear of being alone. Stalin must have liked me particularly, because before he left for vacation he would often call me up and say, "Let's go south. You need a vacation, too."

"Good," I'd answer, "I'd be glad to come along." I clearly would have preferred not to go, but to have said so would have been absolutely unthinkable. I always went along and suffered. I once spent a whole month on vacation with him. He put me right next door to him. It was sheer torture. I had to spend all my time with him, sitting over endless meals. Whenever I was offered up in sacrifice, Beria used to cheer me up by saying, "Look at it this way: someone has to suffer; it might as well be you."

Stalin usually vacationed in Sochi, and he used to let Voroshilov come down to Sochi for old times' sake. Back when Voroshilov had been People's Commissar of Defense and still in Stalin's good graces, he had built himself a huge, ostentatious dacha modeled on the Livadia Palace [in Yalta].

Once I was vacationing by myself in Sochi, and Mikoyan was somewhere else — in Sukhumi, I think. Stalin phoned us from his resort in Borzhomi. I think this was the only time he spent his vacation there. He summoned everyone who was vacationing in the Caucasus plus Beria, who was working in Moscow at the time. We all gathered in Borzhomi. The house was big but poorly equipped. It had previously been a museum so there were no bedrooms, and we used to sleep all crowded together. It was awful. We depended on Stalin for everything. We were on an entirely different schedule from his. In the morning we would be up and have taken a walk, and Stalin would still be sleeping. Then he would get up, and the day would officially begin.

One day Stalin called us to him and said, "Rakosi [the Hungarian dictator] has come for a vacation in the Caucasus. He called and asked my permission." So what? This wasn't the first time Rakosi had come to the Caucasus for a vacation. But we were silent. "Somebody better call Rakosi and tell him to come over here." Someone phoned Rakosi. Then Stalin said, "How does Rakosi know whenever I'm in the Caucasus? Apparently some sort of intelligence network is informing him. He should be discouraged from this." So Rakosi had fallen onto the list of suspects! So he was some sort of agent! Actually it was no mystery how Rakosi found out when Stalin was going to the Caucasus. He simply called up the Central Committee Secretariat and was told that Stalin was vacationing in the Caucasus. That's all he had to do, and that's probably exactly what he did.

When Rakosi arrived at Stalin's, he joined us for dinner and took part in our drinking parties. Once, after he'd had a bit to drink himself, Rakosi said, "Listen, what's going on here? Look at all this drunkenness!" Rakosi was calling a spade a spade. We knew he was right, but we had all found some sort of justification for our behavior. None of us wanted to live like this. We were all victims of Stalin's will. But nonetheless we took offense at Rakosi's remark.

Beria told Stalin that Rakosi had called us a bunch of drunkards. Stalin answered, "All right, we'll see about that." That very night when we sat down to dinner, Stalin started pumping drinks into Rakosi. He pumped two or three bottles of champagne into him and I don't know how much wine. I was afraid Rakosi wouldn't be able to stand it and would drink himself to death. But no, somehow he pulled through. The next morning he left. Stalin was in a good mood all day and joked, "You see what sort of a state I got him into?"

Stalin stayed there for some time, and Mikoyan and I were detained for a while longer to keep him company. Finally we escaped and went back to our own vacation homes.

Stalin used to have Georgian house guests when he was in the Caucasus, mostly old men whom he'd known in his childhood. I remember there was one old railway man whom Stalin was particularly fond of. Apparently he was a good, honest fellow. He was a Communist. He told Stalin about the bad situation among the young people in Georgia. When young men finished their education, they were unable to find suitable jobs in Georgia, and they didn't want to leave. They would just loaf around or start profiteering. Everyone who had anything to do with Georgia knew all about this, but it was all news to Stalin — bad news. He told me later, "Do you know what's going on in Georgia? The young men are either loafing or profiteering! It's disgusting!"

Beria was the boss of Georgia. He had been Secretary of the Central Committee of Georgia for many years, and he was Stalin's only informant about the Republic where Stalin himself had been born. Beria had effectively sealed off Stalin from news about the real situation in Georgia, but now a draft had come through and fanned Stalin's anger. There's no question that there really were many defects and deficiencies which had to be combated in Georgia, but by no means do I ascribe them to national faults in the Georgians themselves. No, the problems were the result of conditions of life in Georgia. Georgia is the Soviet Union's corner of paradise. It has a warm climate, ideal for citrus crops and vineyards. There are also many human charms. Naturally it's hard for a Georgian of limited background to leave, and there are many temptations for profiteers. The vices so infectious among the unstable elements of Georgia would be present in any nationality group living in the same conditions. I even hear my guards complaining: "Georgians are all over the place, profiteering everywhere you go." I always tell them that if Russians lived in Georgia, they would do exactly the same.

I remember that after I had been in the leadership for a few years, the Georgians started profiteering in bay leaves. I told V. P. Mzhavanadze [Khrushchev's own Georgian Party chieftain] and the Crimean leaders to make sure that bay trees were grown only on state plantations. They tell me that now there's no profiteering in bay leaves at all.

Naturally, there's always a temptation to try to make a little extra money. That's the basic reason for profiteering. It isn't a matter of nationality but a fact of life. If Georgians are speculating in vegetables, then the State should start growing those vegetables in hotbeds and hothouses so that it will no longer be profitable for speculators to transport these products from Georgia and resell them in Moscow. They will be cheaper if they're produced by state enterprises. And once illegal trade has been discouraged, the whole Georgian nation will be ennobled, and Georgians in Moscow will lose their notoriety as profiteers. But Stalin never considered such a sensible, constructive solution. He thought the way to deal with the problem of profiteering in Georgia was by administrative measures, and that meant arresting and exiling people.

Fear and Intrigue in the Inner Circle

Here Khrushchev gives further examples of Stalin's paranoia and vindictiveness, some dating back to the war years when, to all appearances, he was the stern-faced, imperturbable generalissimo. What is missing here, and throughout this narrative (except in brief flashes), is an insight into the qualities which enabled Stalin to hold his own and argue closely and knowledgeably with Churchill and Roosevelt. Perhaps only Molotov could speak with authority on these. Here also are revealing glimpses, directed above all at Beria, of the sort of undercover intriguing that went on all the time among Stalin's "closest colleagues." The anecdote about the Georgian cook is comic relief of a high order.

I REMEMBER a striking incident that occurred when Stalin spent his holiday in Afon. It must have been in 1951 because in 1952 he didn't go anywhere for vacation. And when Stalin didn't go on vacation, nobody went. When he was in Afon, Stalin summoned me from Sochi and Anastas Ivanovich Mikoyan from Sukhumi. One day Mikoyan and I were taking a walk around the grounds and Stalin came out on the porch of the house. He seemed not to notice Mikoyan and me. "I'm finished," he said to no one in particular. "I trust no one, not even myself."

This was a shocking admission. We had seen this mistrust of people for a long time, but now he was acknowledging it himself, and so categorically. Can you imagine such a statement coming from a man who decided the fate of his country and influenced the fate of the world? It's one thing not to trust people. That was his right, even if his extreme mistrust did indicate that he had a serious psychological problem. But it's another thing when a man is compulsively driven to eliminate anyone he doesn't trust.

All of us around Stalin were temporary people. As long as he trusted us to a certain degree, we were allowed to go on living and working. But the moment he stopped trusting you, Stalin would start to scrutinize you until the cup of his distrust overflowed. Then it would be your turn to follow those who were no longer among the living. That's what it was like for all the people who worked with him and struggled beside him in the ranks of the Party for the Party's sake. Many of these people, Stalin's most dedicated comrades-in-arms, were eliminated. Kamenev and Zinoviev are good examples of what I mean. I don't know what sort of relations existed between Stalin and Trotsky in the early period after the Revolution. In his written Testament just before his death, Lenin says that Trotsky had never been a Marxist, while Stalin possessed the necessary qualities of a real Marxist.[28] But Lenin also said that Stalin was intolerant and vengeful. Stalin's own admission of this in Afon in 1951 gave us a glimpse behind the curtain which had hidden some of the reasons for the tragedy which was played out during the years when he led the Party and the country. And his reign lasted a long time, a very long time. Many completely honest, innocent people lost their heads while Stalin ruled.

In the last days before his death, we usually met with Stalin in a group — Beria, Malenkov, Bulganin, and myself. Bulganin wasn't always present at these dinner sessions of the inner circle. Every year it became more and more obvious that Stalin was weakening mentally as

---

28. Trotsky, of course, was a Menshevik for years before he joined the Bolsheviks. As a former Menshevik he did not qualify as a true Marxist in Lenin's eyes. But he made up for it afterward. And in his Testament, to which Khrushchev here refers, Lenin did not say that Trotsky had never been a Marxist.

well as physically. This was particularly evident from his eclipses of mind and losses of memory. When he was well and sober, he was still a formidable leader, but he was declining fast. I recall once he turned to Bulganin and started to say something but couldn't remember his name. Stalin looked at him intently and said, "You there, what's your name?"

"Bulganin."

"Of course, Bulganin! That's what I was going to say." Stalin became very unnerved when this kind of thing happened. He didn't want others to notice. But these slips of memory occurred more and more frequently, and they used to drive him crazy.

Kaganovich attended our meetings of the inner circle even more rarely than Bulganin, and Voroshilov was almost never invited. Very occasionally, Voroshilov broke into these sessions without being invited, and sometimes he would even call ahead to say he was coming. But he was hardly ever around. For ten years Stalin had suspected Voroshilov of being an English spy, which was the greatest stupidity.[29] I don't know how far one has to go in one's distrust of people to reach such an extreme. Stalin had worked and fought side by side with Voroshilov for many, many years. Voroshilov's honesty in the Party's eyes and in the eyes of the working class couldn't possibly have been subjected to any doubt. It's one thing to appraise the job he did as People's Commissar of Defense, when he showed himself to be ill prepared, careless and lazy. But he certainly was loyal and honest. I remember once Stalin suddenly got indignant in the middle of one of our sessions and asked, "How did Voroshilov worm his way into the Bureau?"

We answered, "He didn't worm his way in. You appointed him yourself." Later, Beria, Malenkov, and I talked this over and shook our heads, wondering how Stalin could have said such a thing.

Kaganovich was a less engaging man than Voroshilov, but in terms of industriousness, Kaganovich was a whirlwind. He worked as hard as he possibly could. He drove himself mercilessly and never kept track of time. All his time he devoted to the Party. He was a careerist, but that's another matter. I'm talking now about his style of work.

I remember once in my presence Stalin started voicing his suspicions

29. It seems improbable that Stalin thought of his very old crony, Voroshilov, as an English spy as early as 1943, whatever he may have come to believe in his failing years.

of Molotov. We were in the south — in Afon, I think — when it suddenly came into Stalin's head that Molotov was an agent of American
imperialism. And what was the evidence for this charge? It seemed
that when Molotov was in the United States he traveled from Washington to New York by train. Stalin reasoned that if Molotov traveled
by train, then he must have had his own private railway car. And if he
had his own private railway car, then where did he get the money?
Hence, Molotov must have sold himself to the Americans. We explained to Stalin that Molotov couldn't possibly have owned a railway
car while he was abroad. In the United States, all cars belong to private railway companies. Nevertheless, Stalin sent a telegram to Vyshinsky [chief prosecutor of the open trials in the thirties], who was then
working in the UN, and asked him to find out as much as possible
about Molotov's activities there. Did Molotov have a personal railway
car in the USA? Of course Vyshinsky answered immediately that Molotov did not have, and could not have had, a railway car. I bring this
incident up so that it will be clear what sort of eclipses came over Stalin's mind during his last years and what the atmosphere in the leadership was.

As I've already described, as a consequence of Stalin's suspicion Molotov and Mikoyan were put on ice after the Nineteenth Party
Congress. We were all very much alarmed about their fate. We knew
that Stalin had thought up some scheme against them when he didn't
include them in the Bureau. After the Congress, Stalin began a policy
of isolation against Mikoyan and Molotov. I personally took their removal from the inner circle very much to heart. I respected them both.
I considered Molotov to be very experienced, especially in matters of
foreign policy. He often talked about foreign policy matters in my
presence, and he always expressed himself knowledgeably, logically,
and forcefully. That's why I worried that his removal would affect the
quality of the leadership's work. I also liked Anastas Ivanovich Mikoyan. I valued his judgment on international matters, too, especially
ones relating to foreign trade.

After the Nineteenth Congress, Mikoyan and Molotov, continuing an
old practice, used to come along when we got together with Stalin. They
wouldn't bother to call Stalin and ask permission. They would find out
whether Stalin was at the Kremlin or at his dacha and then simply appear. They were always allowed in, but it was obvious Stalin wasn't
very glad to see them. They were trying to stay close to Stalin because

they wanted to save themselves — and not just save their positions in the Party and the leadership. They wanted to stay alive. They were trying to regain Stalin's confidence. I realized the danger they were in, and was completely on their side.

Then one day Stalin said, "I don't want these two coming around any more." He gave orders to his staff not to tell Molotov and Mikoyan where he was. Afterward, Molotov and Mikoyan had a talk with Beria, Malenkov, and me. We agreed to try to soften Stalin's attitude toward them. We also agreed to notify them when Stalin was going out to the Nearby Dacha or coming in to the Kremlin movie theater so that they could meet us there. For a while, whenever we went to the movies with Stalin, Molotov and Mikoyan showed up too. Stalin checked with his staff and was told that whenever Molotov and Mikoyan called, they were never told where he was, just as Stalin had ordered. Then Stalin noticed our maneuverings and figured out that we were acting as Molotov and Mikoyan's agents. One day he raised an uproar. He didn't accuse any of us by name, but he was looking mostly at Malenkov as he stormed: "You think I don't see how you let Molotov and Mikoyan know when we're going to the movies so that they can come along? Stop this! Stop telling them where I am! I won't tolerate it!"

We saw it was useless to persist. It wouldn't do Molotov and Mikoyan any good, and it might jeopardize our own positions in Stalin's eyes. No one wanted that. Stalin was irritated, and when that happened you could expect your relationship with him to take a sudden turn for the worse. So without bringing the subject up again among ourselves, we decided to wait for the natural outcome of this situation. I'm convinced that if Stalin had lived much longer, Molotov and Mikoyan would have met a disastrous end.

I would also like to say something about Beria's relationship with Stalin toward the end of Stalin's life. During the war Beria had become more brazen than ever. As Stalin lost control, and even lost his will during the period of our retreat from the Germans, Beria became the terror of the Party. His growing influence was obvious to me from the composition of Stalin's entourage. When I returned to Moscow from the Front during the war, I noticed that Stalin was surrounded by Georgians. There was a Caucasian chef who made shashlik for Stalin. He had been made a major general. Every time I came to Moscow, I saw that this chef had more and more ribbons and medals, apparently in recognition of his skill at cooking shashlik. Once Stalin caught me staring at the chef's ribbons and medals and scowled at me. He knew what I was thinking, and I knew what he was thinking, but neither of us said anything. Everyone felt that having this chef around in his uniform all covered with medals was downright offensive, but we never mentioned it because it wouldn't have done any good. In addition to the major-general chef, there was a Georgian in charge of supplying wine, lamb for shashlik, and various other provisions for Stalin's kitchen. He was made a lieutenant general during the war. Whenever I came back from the Front, I noticed that he, too, had been awarded one or two more decorations in my absence. I think everyone else was as revolted by this practice as I was. I remember that once Stalin gave me a dressing down in front of this lieutenant general in charge of provisions. He had gotten drunk with Stalin and the rest of us. This fellow wasn't suitable company for us in any way. It was one thing to let him deliver all kinds of food and drink for our table, but it was another thing to let him sit down and eat and drink at the same table with us. Nobody knew him, yet we were supposed to talk intimately and freely in his company. In my opinion it was during the war that Stalin started to be not quite right in the head.

After the war Beria became a member of the Politbureau, and Stalin started to worry about Beria's increasing influence. More than that, Stalin started to fear Beria. I didn't know at the time what the roots of this fear were, but later, when Beria's entire machinery for eliminating people was uncovered, it all became clear. The practical means for achieving Stalin's goals were all in Beria's hands. Stalin realized that if Beria could eliminate anyone at whom Stalin pointed his finger, then Beria could also eliminate someone of his own choosing, on his own initiative. Stalin feared that he would be the first person Beria might choose. Naturally Stalin never told anyone about this, but I could sense it nonetheless. I first began to realize the intensity of Stalin's fear one day after the war when I was at Stalin's for dinner. All of a sudden Stalin looked around him at the people waiting on him and asked angrily, "Why am I surrounded by Georgians?"

Beria was immediately on his guard and said, "Comrade Stalin, these people are your faithful servants; they're all devoted to you."

Stalin became indignant: "Does that mean Russians are unfaithful? Does that mean Russians aren't devoted to me?"

"No," answered Beria, "I didn't say that. But the people who have been selected here are all loyal servants."

Stalin shouted, "I don't need their loyalty! Clear these people out of here!" The Georgians — including the shashlik cook and the provisions officer — were immediately whisked away, and Beria shuffled out of the room like a man who had been beaten up.

Once he had thrown out all the Georgian help and replaced them with Russians, Stalin probably believed he had closed off Beria's access to his kitchen through his entourage. However, Stalin was getting old and didn't realize how powerful Beria still was. For instance, the Minister of State Security, Abakumov, would report to Stalin only after Beria had reported to Stalin himself and received Stalin's instructions. But, as I say, Stalin was getting old, and he didn't understand what was happening. He thought he had found in Abakumov a bright young man who was dutifully carrying out his orders, but actually Abakumov was reporting to Stalin what Beria had told him Stalin wanted to hear. Furthermore, Beria still did in fact control Stalin's entourage, even after the Georgian service personnel had been thrown out. Beria had worked in the Cheka for a long time, and all the Chekists were known to him. They were all trying to get in Beria's good graces, and it was easy for him to use these people for his own aims. Therefore Stalin couldn't even trust his Russian entourage, including his Chekist bodyguard.

My feeling that Stalin was afraid of Beria was confirmed when Stalin concocted the Mingrelian affair. I am absolutely certain that the "conspiracy" charge was fabricated as a way of doing away with Beria, who was a Mingrel himself. Stalin published a decree saying that the Mingrels had connections with the Turks, and that some of them were politically oriented toward Turkey. Of course the allegation was utter nonsense. Because Stalin was old and sick, he wasn't consistent in following through on his scheme. Beria turned the whole thing around in his favor and shrewdly insinuated himself as Stalin's henchman. None of the rest of us would have dared interfere in a matter relating to the Georgian Republic. Beria assigned himself to go to Georgia and administer the punishment of the Mingrels, the imaginary enemies. Those poor fellows were led to the slaughter like sheep.[30] All this left an awful taste in our mouths. It convinced me personally that only if a

30. In the Secret Speech Khrushchev implied that the Mingrelian affair — the smashing of an alleged nationalist conspiracy in Georgia — was engineered by Beria. In fact, as he now suggests, it was part of a plot to discredit Beria. It was trumped up on behalf of Stalin by Khrushchev's own ally, S. D. Ignatiev, who also masterminded the Doctors' Plot.

leadership is under public control will it be protected from actions which are incompatible with our Socialist doctrine and harmful to our Socialist way of life.

Beria's arrogance grew and grew. He was able — and I was astonished that Stalin stood for it — to make some point over dinner and then, if Stalin rejected it, Beria would slap down someone else who tried to make the same point later on in the meal. "I've already told you," Beria would say. "This question needn't be raised." Stalin wouldn't say anything even though he'd heard with his own ears that it had been Beria himself who had raised the question in the first place.

Beria was arrogant about everything. Nothing could be decided without him. You couldn't even report to Stalin without getting Beria's support in advance; if you made a report to Stalin in Beria's presence and if you hadn't cleared it with him beforehand, he would be sure to tear your report down in Stalin's eyes with all sorts of questions and contradictions. All the while Beria was consolidating his forces.

During the period after the war Malenkov began consolidating his forces, too, even though his situation periodically took a turn for the worse. One time Stalin even removed Malenkov from the Central Committee Secretariat and sent him to Central Asia. Beria gave Malenkov a helping hand and arranged for his transfer back to Moscow. From then on Beria and Malenkov appeared to be inseparable friends. Stalin used to joke over dinner about them as "those two rogues." I watched with great interest as this "friendship" between the two rogues developed. I could see Beria neither liked nor respected Malenkov but was simply using him for his own political ends. Beria once said to me something like the following:

"Listen, about this spineless fellow Malenkov. He's nothing but a billy goat. He'll bolt if you don't hold him on a leash. But he's a Russian and very proper. He may come in handy." This business about "coming in handy" was the key to Beria's friendship with Malenkov.[31]

I had been friends with Malenkov since the days when I worked in the Moscow organization before the war. We often spent our days off together. We had dachas near each other in the country. Therefore,

---

31. Throughout this narrative Khrushchev so successfully writes off Malenkov as a characterless intriguer that it requires an effort to remember that this same "billy goat" came within a hairsbreadth of deposing Khrushchev in 1957. He was certainly an intriguer; he was also extremely able, ruthless, and tough. In addition, he was well educated and cultivated, perhaps inclined to look down on Khrushchev. (See Appendix 3.)

even though Malenkov showed a certain amount of condescension toward me during the war, especially when Stalin displayed his dissatisfaction with me, Malenkov and I never had a falling out.

Once Malenkov and I were together at Stalin's vacation home in Sochi. I had come from Kiev and Malenkov had come from Moscow. We went for a walk together, and I said to him, "I'm surprised you don't realize what Beria's attitude is toward you. Don't you see what it is?" He was silent. "You think he respects you? I think he mocks you."

Finally Malenkov answered, "Yes, of course, I see. But what can I do?"

"What can you do? I would just like you to understand. It's true, right now you can't do anything. But the time will come."

My own anxiety was growing. Stalin was at an age which put the rest of us in a difficult position. Far from looking forward to Stalin's death, I actually feared it. I was afraid of the consequences. What would happen to the country? Even though I already had my doubts about the campaign against the enemies of the people, I still had confidence in Stalin. I figured that perhaps there had been some excesses, but basically everything had been handled properly. Not only did I not condemn Stalin, I exalted him for being unafraid to purge the Party and thereby to unify it. In the late forties I was already convinced that when Stalin died, we would have to do everything possible to prevent Beria from occupying a leading position in the Party. Otherwise it would be the end of the Party. I even thought that Beria's success might mean the failure of the Revolution. It might mean losing the gains of the Revolution. It was already my opinion that Beria might divert the progress of the country from a Socialist to a capitalist course.

In the last years of Stalin's life Beria used to express his disrespect for Stalin more and more baldly. He used to talk more candidly with Malenkov than with me, but he often spoke disrespectfully and even insultingly about Stalin in my presence. This always offended me and put me on my guard. It particularly put me on my guard. The way I looked at it, Beria's apparent disrespect toward Stalin was probably a provocation designed to pull me into making similar remarks or even just agreeing with him so that he could then go and denounce me to Stalin as an anti-Stalinist and an enemy of the people. However, I was familiar with Beria's treachery, so I listened but never said anything. I never closed my ears, but I never opened my mouth either. Nevertheless Beria continued in the same spirit, even though I was careful not to encourage him. He was confident that nothing threatened him. He knew that I wasn't able to play the informer. Also I knew he was considerably closer to Stalin than I was and could afford to be less cautious. When Beria and Stalin fought, Beria could always pretend it was just a lovers' quarrel. When two Georgians fight, they're just amusing themselves. They'll always make up in the end.

So much for Beria's method of provocation. He was a master of it. He was very skillful at anything that was filthy and treacherous. Therefore I was always on my guard with him. I knew he was looking for a chance to denounce me and get rid of me. He used this trick on Bulganin, too, but Bulganin knew what Beria was up to as well as I did. I'm sure, however, that Beria never allowed himself to say anything against Stalin in Kaganovich's presence. Beria not only didn't trust Kaganovich — he hated him with a passion.

That was the general situation on the eve of Stalin's death.

Stalin's Death

Radio Moscow announced to the world on the morning of March 4, 1953, that Stalin had been stricken with a cerebral hemorrhage "while in his Moscow apartment." In fact, as Khrushchev confirms here, Stalin was at his dacha. The communiqué was accompanied by an appeal from the Central Committee and the Council of Ministers for the Soviet people to redouble their "unity, solidarity, fortitude of spirit and vigilance in these troubled days." The Russian Orthodox Patriarch and the Chief Rabbi ordered that special services be held. Two days later about four o'clock in the morning came the announcement, preceded by a roll of drums, that "the heart of Lenin's comrade-in-arms, the standard-bearer of his genius and his cause, the wise leader and teacher of the Communist Party and the Soviet Union, has ceased to beat."

Khrushchev's account of the macabre circumstances surrounding Stalin's death is broadly correct and is essentially confirmed by Svetlana Alliluyeva's account in Twenty Letters to a Friend. *Each has details omitted by the other, but it is interesting to see that both versions agree on Beria's almost unbelievable behavior at the deathbed.*

Khrushchev makes much of his fear that Beria would take the Ministry of State Security. The reason for this is that although for years Beria had been in control of the secret police, since 1946 he had had no formal position as such. As a member of the Politbureau he retained general control over the Ministry of Internal Affairs and the Ministry of State Security (MVD and MGB). Both these ministries (successors to the old commissariats) were headed by his protégés until 1951, when Khrushchev's friend, S. D. Ignatiev, was made head of the MGB. Khrushchev's worry was that with his great following in the security services Beria would be able to get rid of Ignatiev and regain control of the MGB. This in fact happened, but it did not last long.

STALIN fell ill in February, 1953. Malenkov, Beria, Bulganin, and I had been at the Nearby Dacha with him on a Saturday night after watching a movie at the Kremlin. As usual, dinner lasted until around five or six o'clock in the morning. Stalin was pretty drunk after dinner and in very high spirits. He didn't show the slightest sign that anything was wrong with him physically. When it was finally time for us to leave, he came into the vestibule to show us out. He was joking boisterously, jabbing me playfully in the stomach with his finger and calling me "Nikita" with a Ukrainian accent, as he always did when he was in a good mood. So after this particular session we all went home happy because nothing had gone wrong at dinner. Dinners at Stalin's didn't always end on such a pleasant note.

The next day, Sunday, was supposed to be a day off, and I was sure Stalin would call us all in for a meeting of some kind. On Sunday evening, expecting his call at any moment, I delayed dinner at home. Finally I gave up waiting and had something to eat. After dinner there was still no call. I couldn't believe that a whole day off would go by without Stalin summoning us. But no, he didn't call. It was already very late when I undressed and got into bed.

Suddenly the telephone rang. It was Malenkov, who said, "Listen, the Cheka boys have just called from Stalin's dacha. They think something has happened to him. We'd better get over there. I've already notified Beria and Bulganin. You'd better leave at once."

I sent for my car right away. I had it with me at my dacha. I dressed quickly and drove to Stalin's. It took fifteen minutes to get there. When we'd all convened, we stopped by to see the duty officers before going to Stalin's room. They explained why they were worried: "Comrade Stalin almost always calls someone and asks for tea or something to eat at eleven o'clock. Tonight he didn't." The Chekists said they had sent Matryona Petrovna to check up on him. Matryona Petrovna was an aging maid who had worked for Stalin for many years. She wasn't very bright, but she was honest and devoted to Stalin. After Matryona Petrovna had looked around, she came back and told the Chekists that Comrade Stalin was lying asleep on the floor of the large room where he usually slept. Apparently Stalin had gotten out of bed and fallen. The Chekists lifted him up off the floor and laid him on a sofa in the small, adjoining dining room.

When we were told about all this, we decided that it wouldn't be suitable for us to make our presence known while Stalin was in such an unpresentable state. We separated and all went home. Later that night there was another call from Malenkov. "The boys have called again from Comrade Stalin's," he said. "They say that something is definitely wrong with him. Matryona Petrovna said he was sleeping soundly when we sent her to look in on him again, but it's an unusual sort of sleep. We'd better go back."

We arranged for Malenkov to call the other members of the Bureau, Voroshilov and Kaganovich, who hadn't been at dinner the night before and who hadn't come to the Nearby Dacha the first time when Malenkov, Beria, Bulganin and I went to check on the situation. We arranged for doctors to come, too. Among them I remember Professor Lukomsky. After meeting at the duty officers' station, we went into the room where Stalin was sleeping on the sofa. We told the doctors to do what was necessary and to find out what condition Stalin was in. Professor Lukomsky approached Stalin very cautiously. I knew what he was thinking. Shaking nervously, he touched Stalin's hand as though it were a hot iron. Beria said gruffly, "You're a doctor, aren't you? Go ahead and take hold of his hand properly."

Professor Lukomsky said Stalin's right arm wouldn't move. His left leg was also paralyzed. He couldn't even speak. His condition was grave. They undressed him and moved him back into the large room onto the sofa where he usually slept and where there was more air.

The doctors arranged a rotating watch over him. We arranged our own round-the-clock vigil among the Presidium Bureau members, di-

viding it up as follows: Beria and Malenkov were on together, Kaganovich and Voroshilov, and Bulganin and I. It was obvious that Malenkov and Beria determined how the vigil would be divided up. They
took the day shift for themselves and gave the night shift to Bulganin
and me. I admit I was very upset. I was very sorry we were losing Stalin.

Stalin was in a bad way. The doctors told us that after such an illness it was extremely unlikely he would be able to return to work. He
might live, but he wouldn't be able to work again. They told us that
usually illnesses like this didn't last long and ended fatally.

We did everything we could to raise Stalin to his feet. We saw he
was unconscious and therefore completely oblivious of his condition.
But then, while the doctors were taking a urine sample, I noticed he
tried to cover himself. He must have felt the discomfort. Once, during
the day, he actually returned to consciousness. Even though he still
couldn't speak, his face started to move. They had been spoon-feeding
him soup and sweet tea. He raised his left hand and started to point to
something on the wall. His lips formed something like a smile. I realized what he was trying to say and called for attention. I explained
why he was pointing with his hand. There was a picture hanging on
the wall, a clipping from the magazine *Ogonyok*. It was a reproduction
of a painting by some artist of a little girl feeding a lamb from a horn.
At that moment Stalin was being spoon-fed and was trying to say, "I'm
in the same position as that lamb which the girl is feeding from the
horn. You're doing the same for me with a spoon."

Then he began to shake hands with us one by one. I gave him my
hand, and he shook it with his left hand because his right wouldn't
move. By these handshakes he conveyed his feelings.

No sooner had Stalin fallen ill than Beria started going around spewing hatred against him and mocking him. It was simply unbearable to
listen to Beria. But, interestingly enough, as soon as Stalin showed
these signs of consciousness on his face and made us think he might recover, Beria threw himself on his knees, seized Stalin's hand, and
started kissing it. When Stalin lost consciousness again and closed his
eyes, Beria stood up and spat. This was the real Beria — treacherous
even toward Stalin, whom he supposedly admired and even worshiped
yet whom he was now spitting on.

Bulganin and I arrived one evening for the night watch. We had
been there during most of the day as well. We had to keep an eye on

the doctors while they were there, and we had to stand watch at night, too. I was more candid with Bulganin than with the others and even confided to him my innermost thoughts. I told him, "Nikolai Aleksandrovich, Stalin's not going to pull through. The doctors have already said he won't live. You know what kind of situation we're going to find ourselves in when Stalin passes away? You know what post Beria will take for himself?"

"Which one?"

"He'll try to make himself Minister of State Security. No matter what happens, we can't let him do this. If he becomes Minister of State Security it will be the beginning of the end for us. He'll take that post for the purpose of destroying us, and he will do it, too, if we let him. Therefore no matter what happens, we can't let him do it, absolutely no matter what!"

Bulganin said he agreed with me, and we began to discuss what we should do from there. I said, "I'll talk to Malenkov. I think he will see it our way. He must also understand that something must be done. If we don't do something and do it right away, it will mean disaster for the Party. This issue involves more than just us personally, although of course we don't want to let Beria stab us in the back. If Beria has his way, he could turn back the clock to 1937–38 — and he could do worse, too."

As I've mentioned, I had already started having my doubts whether Beria was even a true Communist. I'd begun to think of him as someone who had wormed his way into the Party. I recalled the words of Grisha Kaminsky when he said Beria had been an agent of the English counterintelligence service in Baku in the first years of the Revolution [see page 100]. Beria was a wolf in sheep's clothing who had sneaked into Stalin's confidence and been able to secure a high position by deceit and treachery.

Bulganin agreed with everything I said. Our watch ended and I went home. I wanted to get some sleep because I hadn't slept for a long time, so I took a sleeping pill and went to bed. No sooner had I lain down than the telephone rang. It was Malenkov, who said, "Come quickly. Stalin has had a setback. Come over here right away." I called for my car immediately and was on my way. When I arrived at the Nearby Dacha I found that Stalin was indeed in a very bad way. The others arrived. We could all see that Stalin was near death. The doctors told us that he was dying and that we were watching his death throes. Suddenly he stopped breathing. A huge man came from some-where and started giving him artificial respiration, massaging him to get him breathing again. I must admit I felt very sorry for Stalin, this man was racking him so. It was painful for me to watch him working Stalin over. I said, "Listen! Stop it, please! Can't you see the man is dead? What do you want? You won't bring him back to life. He's al-ready dead." They gave up trying to resuscitate him. It was true — Stalin was dead.

The moment Stalin died, Beria got in his car and drove off.

9

Succession

Plotting Beria's Downfall

As far as Khrushchev was concerned, the plotting evidently started while he, his colleagues, and Svetlana Alliluyeva stood by Stalin's deathbed. Once again, Svetlana and Khrushchev agree about Beria's extraordinary attitude. Both were struck by his triumphant smile as he called for his car the moment Stalin was dead; and it was plain that he was in a hurry to be away from Kuntsevo to take control of the security forces and put himself in the strongest possible position. (It may be mentioned that Svetlana Alliluyeva goes out of her way to pay tribute to Khrushchev's sympathetic attitude toward her, then and thereafter. There can be no doubt at all that Beria was determined to make a bid for supreme power. So was Malenkov, who emerged for the time being as Stalin's successor — as Prime Minister and First Secretary of the Communist Party — with Beria second in the hierarchy. The two men were temporary allies, each no doubt believing that he could use the other. But Khrushchev also had set his sights very high. For the moment he bowed to the coalition of Malenkov and Beria, but within ten days Malenkov, while still remaining Prime Minister, was compelled to relinquish the First Secretaryship of the Party, which was formally assumed by Khrushchev six months later. Khrushchev's implicit claim to have been the leading spirit in the plot against Beria is no doubt broadly true; but it is permissible to doubt whether it happened quite like that. Others besides Khrushchev were aware of Beria's pretensions and the danger arising from the concentration of power in his hands. Apart from individual members of the Presidium, these in-

cluded, most importantly, virtually the whole of the army high com-
mand, which also detested Malenkov for the way he had acted as Sta-
lin's spy during the war. It is likely that some of the marshals, many of
whom had worked closely with Khrushchev and got on well with him,
were far more active in the preliminary plotting than is suggested here.
There were also far more serious issues than the proposed dacha-build-
ing operation at Sukhumi, fantastic and bizarre as that episode was.
And the plotting itself must have been a grimmer undertaking than a
simple matter of lobbying the faint-hearted for support. Khrushchev's
actual description of the arrest and detention of Beria differs a good
deal from some of the more lurid accounts with which he regaled for-
eign Communist visitors from time to time, but it is probably authentic.
The official communiqués about the trial and sentencing of Beria and
a number of his subordinates are included in Robert Conquest's Power
and Policy in the USSR. *Conquest also offers the fullest and most co-*
herent account of the infighting in the Kremlin between 1945 and 1960,
about which Khrushchev has all too little to say in this narrative.

S TALIN was dead, and at the time, his death seemed like a terrible
tragedy; but I feared that the worst was still to come. Each of
us took Stalin's death in his own way. I took his death very hard.
To be honest, I took it hard not so much because I was attached to
Stalin — although I *was* attached to him. He was an old man, and
death had been one step behind him for a long time. After all, death is
inevitable. Everyone is born and everyone dies. It's a fact of life. More
than by his death itself, I was disturbed by the composition of the Presidium which Stalin left behind and particularly by the place Beria
was fixing for himself. It all portended serious complications and some
unpleasant surprises — I would even say catastrophic consequences.

As soon as Stalin died, Beria was radiant. He was regenerated and
rejuvenated. To put it crudely, he had a housewarming over Stalin's
corpse before it was even put in its coffin. Beria was sure that the moment he had long been waiting for had finally arrived. There was no
power on earth that could hold him back now. Nothing could get in
his way. Now he could do whatever he saw fit. You could see these
triumphant thoughts in his face as he called for his car and drove off to
the city, leaving us at the Nearby Dacha.

I knew that Malenkov had never really had a position or a role of his own and that he was just an errand boy. Stalin used to say very accurately during conversations with his inner circle, "This Malenkov is a good clerk. He can write out a resolution quickly. He's a good person for allocating responsibilities to, but he has no capacity at all for independent thought or initiative." [1] Malenkov had always thought it was profitable to play up to Beria, even though he knew Beria pushed him around and mocked him. And Malenkov was quite right — it was profitable to play up to Beria. It was mainly because he was so close to Beria that Malenkov stayed in favor with Stalin despite Stalin's low opinion of him as a leader. Now that Stalin was dead, Malenkov was sure to "come in handy" for Beria's plans, as Beria himself had once told me he would.

These were the thoughts going through my mind while I stood over Stalin's dead body at the Nearby Dacha.

When Beria had gone, the rest of us decided to call together all the members of the Bureau and the Presidium. While waiting for them to arrive, Malenkov paced up and down nervously. I decided to have a talk with him then and there. I went over and said, "Yegor [Georgi], I want to talk to you."

"What about?" he asked coldly.

"Now that Stalin is dead, we have something to discuss. What do we do now?"

"What's there to talk about? We'll all get together and then we'll talk. That's why we're having a meeting." This seemed like a democratic enough answer, but I took it differently. I took it to mean that Malenkov had already talked things over with Beria and everything had been decided for some time.

"Well, all right," I said, "then we'll talk later."

Everyone gathered at the Nearby Dacha and saw that Stalin was dead. Then Svetlanka arrived. I went over to meet her. She was very upset and started to cry. I couldn't control myself. I started to weep, too, and I wept sincerely over Stalin's death.

I wasn't just weeping for Stalin. I was terribly worried about the future of the Party and the future of the country. I already sensed that Beria would start bossing everyone around and that this could be the beginning of the end. I'd known for a long time that he was no Com-

1. Only five months before, in October, 1952, Stalin had showed his far from low opinion of Malenkov by putting him up to make the General Report to the Nineteenth Party Congress.

munist. I considered him a treacherous opportunist who would stop at nothing to get what he wanted. Ideologically, I didn't recognize his position as a Communist one. He was a butcher and an assassin.

When the meeting was convened, the distribution of our new portfolios began. Beria immediately proposed Malenkov for Chairman of the Council of Ministers. On the spot Malenkov proposed that Beria be appointed his first deputy. He also proposed the merger of the ministries of State Security and of Internal Affairs into a single Ministry of Internal Affairs with Beria as Minister — a seemingly modest post for Beria to settle for.[2] I was silent. I was afraid that Bulganin might object to this improper procedure, but Bulganin was silent, too. I could see what the attitude of the others was. If Bulganin and I had objected to the way Beria and Malenkov were running the meeting, we would have been accused of being quarrelsome and disorderly and of starting a fight in the Party before the corpse was cold. I could see that things were moving in the direction I had feared.

Molotov and Kaganovich were each nominated First Deputy Prime Minister along with Beria. Voroshilov was nominated Chairman of the Presidium of the Supreme Soviet [President of the USSR], replacing Shvernik.[3] Beria was most disrespectful in his remarks about Shvernik, saying he was unknown to the nation at large and therefore unsuited to an important position in the leadership. I could see that all these rearrangements of positions fitted squarely into Beria's master plan. For instance, by promoting Voroshilov to the Chairmanship of the Presidium of the Supreme Soviet, Beria was trying to make Voroshilov into someone whom he could rely on when he started his next round of butchery. Then Beria proposed that I be released from my duties as Secretary of the Moscow Committee so that I could concentrate on my work in the Central Committee Secretariat. More nominations and proposals were made. Then we decided on the funeral arrangements and how best to announce Stalin's death to the people.[4]

2. Not so modest. Earlier Khrushchev said that this was just what he feared. Beria was also chosen to be a First Deputy Chairman of the Council of Ministers (First Deputy Prime Minister).

3. N. M. Shvernik, one of Stalin's senior old faithfuls, spent most of his career at the head of the Soviet Trades Unions. The Chairmanship of the Presidium of the Supreme Soviet, or Presidency of the USSR, was a largely ceremonial function. Bulganin was also appointed a First Deputy Chairman of the Council of Ministers, along with Beria, Kaganovich, and Molotov. Khrushchev held no ministerial appointment. His strength reposed in his position as a member of the Presidium and of the Party Secretariat.

4. The announcement, when it came, included the celebrated plea to the people of the Soviet Union to avoid "panic and disarray."

Thus we lost Stalin and started to run the government by ourselves.

During the funeral and right after it, Beria was attentive and respectful to me, which surprised me. He didn't sever his demonstratively friendly connections with Malenkov, but he did begin to establish equally friendly relations with me. Beria and Malenkov started including me in their strolls around the Kremlin grounds. Naturally I didn't resist or object, but my opinion of Beria didn't change. On the contrary, it was confirmed. I understood that his friendly behavior toward me was a trick. It was, as we often put it, Beria's Asiatic cunning coming into play. By this term we meant the quality of a man who thinks one thing but says something else. I knew that Beria was pursuing a hypocritical policy toward me; he was toying with me and trying to put me off my guard, all the while waiting for the opportunity to dispose of me before anyone else.

It was decided that Malenkov and I would work out the agenda for Presidium sessions. Malenkov would preside over the sessions, and I would work with him in setting the agenda.

Beria consolidated his forces with each passing day, and his arrogance grew proportionally. All his shrewdness as a provocateur was called into play.

Then came the first clash between Beria and Malenkov on the one hand and the rest of the Presidium on the other. The Presidium had already changed quite a bit. We had liquidated the large Presidium and small Bureau which Stalin had set up at the first Central Committee Plenum after the Nineteenth Party Congress. We had reverted to a narrow circle of about eleven people. At one Presidium session Beria made the following proposal:

"Since many prison and exile terms are coming to an end and all these former convicts and exiles will be returning to their homes, I propose that we pass a resolution not allowing any of them to return without special permission from the Ministry of Internal Affairs. And I propose that we require them to live in regions dictated by the Ministry of Internal Affairs." That meant dictated by Beria himself. This proposal was an alarming sign of what Beria was up to.

I got angry and spoke against him, saying, "I categorically object to the sort of arbitrary rule you're proposing. We've already had this sort of thing in the past. Now that we've started thinking more critically and more correctly about how to evaluate the past, we know we can't impose this sort of illegality disguised as law on the people any more. These convicts and exiles you're talking about were arrested, interrogated, tried, and sentenced by State Security troikas.[5] They were never given the benefit of witnesses, prosecutors, or judge — they were just hauled in and imprisoned, or killed. Now you're saying that these people, whose terms of punishment were set by the troikas, should again be deprived of all their rights, treated as criminals, and not allowed to choose where they will live. This is totally unacceptable."

The others supported me. Beria shrewdly withdrew his proposal, and since Malenkov was taking the minutes, the motion was never recorded. Later Beria introduced what seemed to be a liberal motion. He proposed we alter an old ruling which set prison and exile terms at a maximum of twenty years for people arrested and charged by the troikas; he suggested lowering the maximum term from twenty to ten years. This seemed like a liberal enough proposal, but I knew what Beria had in mind.

I said, "I'm categorically opposed to this proposal, too. I'm against it because we should be reviewing the whole system of arrests and investigations, not just modifying the details. Once again, you're trying to promote arbitrary rule. Whether the maximum term is twenty or ten years doesn't really matter because you can always sentence someone to ten years and then another ten years. If necessary you could keep sentencing someone you don't like to one ten-year term after another, right up until he dies. What's required is a radical revision of the inadmissible practice of arresting and sentencing people which prevailed during Stalin's time. What you want to do is legalize arbitrary rule — you want to legalize the status quo. Documents are being put together to show how the methods you're proposing have been applied in the past arbitrarily and illegally, and how the Party has been damaged as a result."

Once again Beria withdrew his motion. I had vigorously spoken out against him twice already. I had no doubt that he knew exactly where I stood and that he was planning his next move. Beria could never reconcile himself to the fact that someone was standing in his way.

And what was this scoundrel Beria's next move? Here's what happened. One day we were walking somewhere together — Beria, Malenkov, and I — just taking a stroll, and Beria began to develop the following idea: "All of us are in God's hands, as they used to say. We're not getting any younger. Anything could happen to any one of us, and

5. Ad hoc groups of three, who combined the duty of prosecutor and judge and operated with extreme and arbitrary dispatch.

we would leave our families behind. We should give some thought to our old age and to our families. Therefore I'd like to propose that the Government build dachas which it would then turn over to the leaders of the country for their personal use." The suggestion was typical of Beria. I had come to expect this sort of un-Communist thinking from him. It was completely in keeping with his way of doing things. I was sure that the dacha idea was part of some kind of provocation. But I didn't say anything; I just listened. Then he said, "I propose building these dachas in Sukhumi [on the Black Sea coast] rather than on the outskirts of Moscow — and not on the outskirts of Sukhumi, but right in the center. We could clear the center of the city and turn it into a park with peach trees." He started raving about what a marvelous city Sukhumi was and about the peaches and grapes that grew there. He had it all worked out — which personnel would be used and what resources would be needed. He was thinking on a grand and lordly scale. He continued: "The Ministry of Internal Affairs will supervise this project. First of all we'll have to build a dacha for you, Yegor [Malenkov] — then for you, Nikita, and then for Molotov, Voroshilov, and the others."

I heard him out and didn't try to argue with him. All the while he was talking, I just said, "Yes, yes, we'll have to give it some thought" — as though I were agreeing with him.

When we finished talking and returned to our cars, Beria, Malenkov, and I went off to our own dachas in the country. The three of us rode in one car as far as the turnoff on the Rublev road, where Malenkov and I were supposed to turn left and Beria was supposed to keep going straight. Malenkov and I got out of his car and into another one. Once we were alone I said to Malenkov, "Listen, what do you think about this idea of Beria's? It's the most blatant provocation."

"Why do you think so?"

"I can see Beria's a provocateur. He wants to build these dachas as a provocation and nothing else. Let's not object for a while. We'll let him do what he wants, and he'll think no one knows what he's up to."

So Beria began to put his idea into effect. He ordered plans for the dachas to be drawn up. When these were finished, he invited us to come over and showed them to us. He proposed that the construction start at once. A well-known builder gave a report on the project. This comrade is now in charge of building atomic energy plants. Beria considered him a trusty ally. He worked for Beria and did whatever Beria told him. At the meeting Beria said that the site for Malenkov's dacha had been carefully chosen so that Malenkov would be able to view the Black Sea from his window and keep an eye on the Turks. Beria joked, "Yegor, you'll be able to see Turkey. It's beautiful. You see what a nice house this will be?"

When everyone else had gone, I stayed behind with Malenkov. I said to him, "It's crucial to Beria's plans that your dacha be built in the very center of Sukhumi. The plans call for a great many people to be displaced. The Minister of Housing has said that the dacha project will mean the eviction of a huge number of people. The whole thing will be a calamity for them. They have lived on their property for generations, and now suddenly they're all to be evicted. This is no joke. You still don't see the point of his provocation? Beria wants to start a sort of pogrom, to throw people out of their homes and tear down their houses in order to build you some kind of palace. The dacha and grounds will be walled in. The city will be seething with resentment and indignation. People will ask, "Who are they doing all this building for?" And when it's all finished, you'll arrive and people will see you, the Chairman of the Council of Ministers, get out of your car and disappear into your palace. They'll see that the pogrom and the eviction of people from their homes was all done for you. The hatred against you will spread not only through the whole city of Sukhumi, but everywhere, throughout the land. And this is exactly what Beria wants to happen. He's trying to maneuver you into such a hopeless scandal that you'll be forced to resign. Don't you see? Beria says he's going to have plans drawn up for a dacha of his own, but you'll see, he won't have it built. He'll build one for you and then use it to discredit you."

"How can you say that? Beria talked it all over with me!"

But this conversation started Malenkov thinking.

One day when Beria was showing me the plans for the dachas, he said again, in his thick Georgian accent, "Won't these be lovely houses?"

"Yes, very," I said. "It's a great idea."

"Why don't you take the plans home with you?"

So I took them home, but I didn't know what to do with them. Nina Petrovna [Madame Khrushcheva] came across them and asked, "What's this here?" I told her what they were, and she was furious. "That's a disgraceful idea!"

I couldn't explain, so I said, "Let's just put them aside and we'll talk about it later." [6]

Beria tried to push through the construction of the dachas in Sukhumi, but nothing had been done by the time of his arrest. After he was arrested we canceled the whole project. I kept the plans for the dachas at home for a long time afterward.

But in the meantime, things started spinning. Beria was trying to interfere in the workings of the Party, particularly the Cheka. He fabricated some sort of document about the state of affairs in the Ukrainian Party leadership. So he had decided to strike his first blow against the Ukrainian organization! I was ready for this because I figured he would try to implicate me. I was still largely responsible for the Ukraine. Beria started collecting evidence through the regional departments of the Ministry of Internal Affairs in the Ukraine. Strokach was Chief of the MVD [Ministry of Internal Affairs] office in Lvov.[7] He's dead now. He was an honest Communist and a good soldier. Before the war he had been a colonel in command of border troops in the Ukraine. Then, during the war, he had been in charge of the Ukrainian partisan troops' headquarters, so he used to report to me on the situation in occupied territory behind enemy lines. I could see he was an honest, decent person. After the war he was made a representative for the Ministry of Internal Affairs in the Lvov Region. We found out later that when the Minister of Internal Affairs for the Ukraine, who was Beria's henchman, got in touch with Strokach and demanded material from him about local Party workers. Strokach said that he wasn't responsible for personnel and that they should get in touch with the local Regional Party Committee. Then Beria himself phoned Strokach and said that if he was going to split hairs, he would be pounded into camp dust. We found out about this incident later, after we detained Beria, but at the time we had no idea that the Party was being undermined and subordinated to the Ministry of Internal Affairs in the Ukraine.

The Presidium began to discuss a memorandum by Beria about the ethnic composition of governing bodies in the Ukraine. Beria's idea was that local [that is, non-Russian] officials should be kept in posi-

6. A fascinating sidelight on the domestic life of Khrushchev and his very remarkable wife.

7. T. A. Strokach, lieutenant general in the security police. Later (1955–56) he was Chief of the Ukrainian MVD.

tions of leadership in their own Republics and shouldn't be promoted to the central organization in Moscow. As a result of his memorandum, it was decided to release Melnikov from his duties as First Secretary of the Ukrainian Central Committee and to put Kirichenko [a Ukrainian] in his place. Beria also proposed putting Korneichuk on the Presidium of the Central Committee of the Ukrainian Party. This was done, and a Ukrainian Central Committee Plenum was held. Korneichuk didn't realize he had been promoted in order to further Beria's anti-Party aims, so he said all sorts of favorable things about Beria and Beria's memorandum during the course of the Plenum. Then a memorandum appeared concerning the Baltic states, followed by another concerning Belorussia. Both stressed the principle of drawing the Republic leadership from the local population. We passed a decision that the post of First Secretary in every Republic had to be held by a local person and not by a Russian sent from Moscow.[8]

It so happened that Beria's position on this question was correct and that it coincided with the position of the All-Union Central Committee, but he was taking this position in order to further his own anti-Party goals. He was preaching that the predominance of Russians in the leadership of the non-Russian Republics had to be reversed. Everyone knew that this was right and that it was consistent with the Party Line, but at first people didn't realize that Beria was pushing this idea in order to aggravate nationalist tensions between Russians and non-Russians, as well as tensions between the central leadership in Moscow and the local leadership in the Republics.

At this point I took Malenkov aside and said, "Listen, Comrade Malenkov, don't you see where this is leading? We're heading for disaster. Beria is sharpening his knives."

Malenkov asked, "Well, what can we do? I see what's happening, but what can we do about it?"

"The time has come to resist. Surely you must see that Beria's position has an anti-Party character. We must not accept what he is doing. We must reject it."

"You mean you want me to oppose him all by myself? I don't want to do that."

8. This refers to the still obscure operation conducted by Beria to encourage local leadership in the component Republics. He was arrested and shot before his long-range purpose was clearly manifest, though Khrushchev's explanation is probably correct. A. I. Kirichenko was, in fact, a protégé of Khrushchev, who was to rise to great heights in his master's shadow until his sudden and unexplained downfall in 1960.

"What makes you think you'll be alone if you oppose him? There's you and me — that's already two of us. I'm sure Bulganin will agree. I've exchanged opinions with him more than once. I'm sure the others will join us if we put forward our argument from a firm Party position. The trouble is that you never give anyone a chance to speak at our Presidium sessions. As soon as Beria introduces a motion, you always jump immediately to support him, saying, 'That's fine, Comrade Beria, a good motion. I'm for it. Anyone opposed?' And you put it right to a vote. Give the rest of us a chance to express ourselves for once and you'll see what happens. Control yourself. Don't be so jumpy. You'll see you're not the only one who thinks the way you do. I'm convinced that many people are on our side against Beria. You and I put the agenda together, so let's include for discussion some matters on which we believe Beria is mistaken. Then we'll oppose him. I'm convinced we can mobilize the other Presidium members behind us and our resolutions will carry. Let's just try it."

Malenkov finally agreed. I was surprised and delighted. We wrote up the agenda for the next Presidium session and included some issues on which the others supported us, and Beria was defeated. This pattern was repeated at a number of sessions, and only then did Malenkov become confident that we could use Party methods against Beria in order to defeat proposals which, in our view, were harmful to the Party and to the country. When Beria realized that the other Presidium members were overriding him, he tried to speed things up. He put on a tremendous show of self-importance, trying to demonstrate his superiority in every way he could. We were going through a very dangerous period. I felt it was time to force the situation to a confrontation. It was time to act.

I told Malenkov that we had to talk with the other members of the Presidium and get them behind us. Obviously it was no good trying to do this during a session with Beria present. We'd have to talk face to face with each individual in order to discover his real attitude toward Beria. At last Malenkov agreed and said, "Yes, we must act."

I already knew Bulganin stood for the Party position and fully understood the danger to the Party which Beria represented. Malenkov and I arranged that to begin with, I would talk to Comrade Voroshilov. Voroshilov and I served together on some commission or other. I decided this would be my pretext for going to see him. I telephoned him and said I wanted to meet with him about the commission. Comrade Voroshilov said he would rather come see me at the Central Committee building. "No," I said, "please let me come to your office." He insisted that he should come to me, but in the end I had my way. Malenkov and I arranged that I would stop in at his place on my way home so that we could have dinner together and talk over how my meeting with Voroshilov had gone. Malenkov and I lived in the same house and on the same staircase. My apartment was immediately above his.

I went to Comrade Voroshilov's office at the Supreme Soviet, but I didn't accomplish what I'd come for. I was barely inside his office when Voroshilov started singing Beria's praises: "What a remarkable man we have in Lavrenty Pavlovich, Comrade Khrushchev! What a remarkable man!"

I answered, "Maybe not. Maybe you overestimate him." But after Voroshilov had greeted me in this way, I couldn't possibly talk to him frankly about Beria. I thought perhaps Voroshilov had spoken as he did because he thought he was being overheard and that he'd said it for "Beria's ears" [slang for bugging devices]. On the other hand, maybe it was because he considered me Beria's ally. This was conceivable since Beria, Malenkov, and I were often seen together. In any case, my opinion of Beria was completely opposite to Voroshilov's. But if I'd said outright what I wanted to say, I would have put Voroshilov in a very awkward position. He would have been unable to agree with me simply out of pride. He couldn't have come straight over to my position after having just praised Beria as soon as I came through the door. After all, my own position was committed to the need for eliminating Beria.

So Voroshilov and I exchanged a few words on the matter about which I had officially made an appointment with him. It was some trivial question, and I quickly left to have dinner as I'd arranged with Malenkov. I told Malenkov that nothing had come of my visit to Voroshilov and that I hadn't been able to talk openly with him.

Comrade Malenkov and I then agreed that I should talk to Comrade Molotov, who was Minister of Foreign Affairs and who had called me earlier asking if we could meet at the Central Committee office to discuss some matter concerning Foreign Ministry personnel. I used his call as a pretext to set up a meeting and phoned him back, saying, "You wanted to get together with me. I'm ready to see you anytime. If you can, come over here right away. We'll talk about personnel." He arrived shortly and I said, "Let's talk about personnel, but not Foreign Ministry personnel." I gave him my views about Beria's role. I told Molotov what sort of person Beria was and what kind of danger threatened the Party if we didn't thwart his scheming against the Party leadership. I had earlier told him how Beria had already set his plan in motion for aggravating nationalist tensions in the Republics.

Apparently Molotov had been thinking a lot about this himself. Of course, he couldn't help but think about it, since he knew about everything that had happened during Stalin's rule. Back when Molotov still enjoyed Stalin's full confidence, I had often heard him speak out strongly against Beria, although never in Stalin's presence. Molotov had personally been a victim of Beria's hypocrisy and treacherous provocations during sessions with Stalin, and more than once I heard him call Beria's activities by their proper names to Beria's face. Therefore, as soon as I got down to the serious matter at hand with Molotov, I could see he was in full agreement with me.

"Yes," he said, "I agree with you fully. But I want to ask you one thing. What is Malenkov's position?"

"I'm discussing this with you on Malenkov's and Bulganin's behalf. We've already exchanged views on the subject."

Then Molotov said, "It's quite right that you should raise this question. I agree with you fully and you'll have my complete support. But tell me something else. What do you want to do exactly? Where is all this leading?"

"First, we have to relieve Beria of his duties as a Presidium member, Deputy Chairman of the Council of Ministers, and Minister of Internal Affairs."

Molotov said that wasn't enough: "Beria's very dangerous. Therefore I think we must, so to say, resort to more extreme measures."

"You think maybe we should detain him for investigation?" I said "detain" rather than "arrest" because there were still no criminal charges against Beria. I could easily believe that he had been an agent of the Mussavatists, as Kaminsky had said, but Kaminsky's charge had never been verified. There had never been an investigation of Beria's role in Baku. As far as Beria's provocational behavior was concerned, we had only our intuition to go on, and you can't arrest a man on intuition. That's why I said we would have to "detain" him for an investigation. Molotov and I agreed and parted. Later I told Comrade Malenkov and Comrade Bulganin what had happened.

We decided that we'd better speed things up because we might be overheard by "Beria's ears" or someone might let the cat out of the bag. In short, information about the steps we were taking might reach Beria, and Beria could easily have us all arrested.

We agreed that I should talk to Saburov, who was then a member of the Presidium. When I talked to Saburov, he answered very quickly: "I'm fully in agreement with you." Then he asked, "But what about Malenkov?" Everyone I talked to asked this same question.

At that time Kaganovich wasn't in Moscow. He was making an inspection tour of the lumber industry. When he returned, I asked him to stop in at the Central Committee office. He arrived in the evening, and we sat and talked for a long time. He told me in great detail about Siberia and about the sawmills. I didn't try to interrupt him, although I had other things than sawmills on my mind. I showed proper courtesy and tact and waited for him to get tired of talking. When he finished his report, I said, "What you've told me is all very well. Now I want to tell you about what's going on here." I told him what the circumstances were and what conclusions we had reached.

Kaganovich immediately pricked up his ears and asked, "Who is 'we'?" He put the question like that in order to assess the distribution of power. I said that Malenkov, Bulganin, Molotov, Saburov, and I were of one mind, and I told him that without him we had a majority. Kaganovich declared right away, "I'm with you, too. Of course I'm with you. I was only asking." But I knew what he was thinking, and he knew what I was thinking. Then he asked me, "And what about Voroshilov?" I told him about my awkward meeting with Voroshilov and how Voroshilov had praised Beria. "He really said that?" Kaganovich exclaimed. He was incredulous.

"Yes," I said. "He started to sing Beria's praises the moment I came into his office."

Kaganovich cursed Voroshilov, but not maliciously: "That sly old bastard! He was lying to you. He's told me himself that he can't stand Beria, that Beria's dangerous, and that Beria's likely to be the ruin of us all."

"I thought Voroshilov wasn't being straightforward with me, but that's what he said, all the same."

"What he said doesn't mean a thing."

"Then it seems we'll have to try talking to him one last time. Perhaps Malenkov will talk to him. Since I've already spoken to him, it might be better if I didn't bring up the subject of Beria with him again. I wouldn't want to put him in an awkward position." We agreed on this.

Then Kaganovich said, "And what about Mikoyan?"

"I haven't talked to Mikoyan yet. His case is a bit more complicated." Everyone knew that Mikoyan was on the very best of terms with Beria. They were always together and always following each other around. We'd have to talk to Mikoyan at some point, but it would have to be done later on.

I told Malenkov about my conversation with Kaganovich, and he agreed that it would be better if he talked to Voroshilov himself. That left Pervukhin. Malenkov suddenly said, "I want to talk to Pervukhin myself."

"By all means, if you want to, but Pervukhin is a complex man. I know him."

"I know him, too."

"Very well then, you talk to him."

Malenkov invited Pervukhin to come see him and then got in touch with me later, "You know, I sent for Pervukhin and told him everything. Pervukhin said he'd think it over. That's very dangerous. I think you should get hold of him yourself, and you'd better do it immediately. Who knows what might happen? 'I'll think it over' — that's very dangerous."

I phoned Comrade Pervukhin. He came to see me. I told him everything, very frankly. He said, "If Malenkov had put it to me as clearly as you have done, there wouldn't have been any question in my mind. I agree with you entirely. There's no alternative." I don't know what Malenkov had told Pervukhin, but now it was settled.

In this way we made the rounds of all the Presidium members except Voroshilov and Mikoyan. We arranged for me to speak to Mikoyan and for Malenkov to speak to Voroshilov. Later, I went by to see Malenkov and asked him about his conversation with Voroshilov. "Well, what happened?" I asked. "Was he still singing Beria's praises?"

"As soon as I told him about our plan," said Malenkov, "Voroshilov embraced me and started crying." I don't know if this really happened, but Comrade Malenkov had no need to lie about it.

Still another question arose. Once we had formally resolved to strip Beria of his posts, who would actually detain him? The Presidium bodyguard was obedient to him. His Chekists would be sitting in the next room during the session, and Beria could easily order them to arrest us all and hold us in isolation. We would have been quite helpless because there was a sizable armed guard in the Kremlin. Therefore we decided to enlist the help of the military. First, we entrusted the detention of Beria to Comrade Moskalenko, the air defense commander, and five generals.[9] This was my idea. Then, on the eve of the session, Malenkov widened our circle to include Marshal Zhukov and some others. That meant eleven marshals and generals in all. In those days all military personnel were required to check their weapons when coming into the Kremlin, so Comrade Bulganin was instructed to see that the marshals and generals were allowed to bring their guns with them. We arranged for Moskalenko's group to wait for a summons in a separate room while the session was taking place. When Malenkov gave a signal, they were to come into the room where we were meeting and take Beria into custody.

We arranged to convene a session of the Presidium of the Council of Ministers but invited all the members of the Presidium of the Central Committee as well. Malenkov opened the meeting as a Central Committee Presidium session rather than a Council of Ministers Presidium session so that we could discuss the situation in the Party. Comrade Voroshilov had to be specially invited, since he was Chairman of the Presidium of the Supreme Soviet and therefore didn't regularly attend sessions of either the Council of Ministers or the Party Presidium.

As soon as Malenkov opened the session he said, "Let us discuss Party questions. There are some matters which we must deal with right away." Everyone agreed. As had been arranged in advance, I requested the floor from Chairman Malenkov and proposed that we discuss the matter of Beria. Beria was sitting on my right. He gave a start, grabbed me by the hand, looked at me with a startled expression on his face, and said, "What's going on, Nikita? What's this you're mumbling about?"

I said, "Just pay attention. You'll find out soon enough." And here is what I said. I recalled the Central Committee Plenum of February, 1939, at which Comrade Grisha Kaminsky had accused Beria of having worked for the Mussavatist counterintelligence service, and therefore for the English intelligence service, when he was Secretary of the Baku Party organization. I then recalled how immediately after that meeting Grisha Kaminsky had dropped out of sight like a stone in the water:

9. General K. S. Moskalenko, later marshal. At the time of Beria's arrest he was commander of the air defense of Moscow.

"I've always wondered about Kaminsky's statement and why no one made any attempt to explain what he said." Then I reviewed the moves Beria had made since Stalin's death, his interference in the Party organizations of the Ukraine, Belorussia, and the Baltic states. I described how Beria, like all enemies of the Communist Party, was relying on nationalist antagonisms to undermine Soviet unity. I mentioned his latest proposal concerning policy toward people in exile and in prison camps, stressing that Beria was trying to legalize arbitrary rule. I concluded by saying, "As a result of my observations of Beria's activities, I have formed the impression that he is no Communist. He is a careerist who has wormed his way into the Party for self-seeking reasons. His arrogance is intolerable. No honest Communist would ever behave the way he does in the Party."

After I had spoken, Bulganin asked for the floor and said something very much along the same lines. Then the others spoke in turn. Molotov expressed the proper Party position on the matter. The other comrades stressed the same principles, with the exception of Mikoyan, who spoke last. He repeated what he had told me before the session when we had our talk: namely, that Beria would take our criticisms to heart and reform himself, that he wasn't a hopeless case, and that he could still be useful in the collective leadership.

When everyone had spoken, Malenkov, as Chairman, was supposed to sum things up and to formulate a consensus, but at the last moment he lost his nerve. After the final speech, the session was left hanging. There was a long pause. I saw we were in trouble, so I asked Comrade Malenkov for the floor in order to propose a motion. As we had arranged in advance, I proposed that the Central Committee Presidium should release Beria from his duties as Deputy Chairman of the Council of Ministers and Minister of Internal Affairs and from all the other government positions he held. Malenkov was still in a state of panic. As I recall, he didn't even put my motion to a vote. He pressed a secret button which gave the signal to the generals who were waiting in the next room. Zhukov was the first to appear. Then Moskalenko and the others came in. Malenkov said in a faint voice to Comrade Zhukov, "As Chairman of the Council of Ministers of the USSR, I request that you take Beria into custody pending investigation of charges made against him."

"Hands up!" Zhukov commanded Beria.

Moskalenko and the others unbuckled their holsters in case Beria tried anything. Beria seemed to reach for his briefcase which was lying behind him on the windowsill. I seized his arm to prevent him from grabbing a weapon from the briefcase. We checked later and found that he had no gun, either in his briefcase or in his pockets. His quick movement had simply been a reflex action.

Beria was immediately put under armed guard in the Council of Ministers building next to Malenkov's office. At this point a new question arose. Now that we had detained Beria, where could we put him? We couldn't hand him over to the Ministry of Internal Affairs because those were all his own men. Beria's deputies were Kruglov [10] and Serov. I hardly knew Kruglov, but I knew Serov well, and I trusted him. I thought, and still think, Serov is an honest man. If there are a few dubious things about him, as there are about all Chekists, then let's just say he was a victim of Stalin's general policy. At first I proposed that Serov should take Beria into custody, but the others were against this. Finally we agreed to entrust him to the air defense commander, Comrade Moskalenko, who had his men transfer Beria to a bunker at his headquarters. I could see that Comrade Moskalenko would do what was necessary for the Party cause.

After it was all over, Malenkov took me aside and said, "Listen to what my chief bodyguard has to say." The man came over to me and said, "I have only just heard that Beria has been arrested. I want to inform you that he raped my stepdaughter, a seventh-grader. A year or so ago her grandmother died and my wife had to go to the hospital, leaving the girl at home alone. One evening she went out to buy some bread near the building where Beria lives. There she came across an old man who watched her intently. She was frightened. Someone came and took her to Beria's home. Beria had her sit down with him for supper. She drank something, fell asleep, and he raped her."

I told this man, "I want you to tell the prosecutor during the investigation everything you've told me." Later, we were given a list of more than a hundred girls and women who had been raped by Beria. He had used the same routine on all of them. He gave them some dinner and offered them wine with a sleeping potion in it.

10. S. N. Kruglov, colonel general of the security police, was at one time Deputy Director of Smersh (acronym for "Death to Spies and Diversionists") and responsible for the security of Stalin, Roosevelt, and Churchill at Yalta and Teheran. Even in that gallery he had a reputation for outstanding vengefulness and cruelty. Unlike some of his colleagues, however, he was personally brave. He succeeded Beria as Minister of the Interior, with reduced powers, until his fall in 1957. The head of the MGB at this time was not Serov, but Khrushchev's ally, S. D. Ignatiev.

When Beria was put in solitary confinement, he asked for pencil and paper. We consulted among ourselves. Some of us were doubtful, but we decided to give him what he wanted in case an urge had come over him to tell us candidly what he knew about the things we had charged him with. He started writing notes. The first was to Malenkov: "Yegor, don't you know me? Aren't we friends? Why did you trust Khrushchev? He's the one who put you up to this, isn't he?" and so on. He also sent me two or three notes swearing he was an honest man and so on and so forth.

We had no confidence in the ability of the State Prosecutor to investigate Beria's case objectively, so we sacked him and replaced him with Comrade Rudenko.[11] When Rudenko started to interrogate Beria, we found ourselves faced with a really awful man, a beast, to whom nothing was sacred. When we opened the archives and brought him to trial, we found out what methods Beria had used to achieve his goals. Not only was there nothing Communist about him — he was without the slightest trace of human decency.

After Beria's arrest the question arose of what to do about Merkulov, who was Minister of State Control.[12] I admit that I held him in high regard and considered him a good Party member. He was unquestionably a cultured person, and in general I liked him. Therefore I said to the comrades, "Just because Merkulov was Beria's assistant in Georgia doesn't mean he was an accomplice to Beria's crimes. Perhaps he wasn't. We can't treat everyone who worked for Beria as his accomplice. Let's call Merkulov in and have a talk with him. He might even help us to clear up some of the remaining questions about Beria." By arrangement with the others, I summoned Merkulov to the Central Committee office and told him what had happened, that we had detained Beria, and that an investigation was under way. "You worked for Beria for many years, Comrade Merkulov," I said, "and therefore we thought you might be able to help the Central Committee with our investigation."

"I will do whatever I can, with pleasure."

"Then write us a report."

11. R. A. Rudenko, a Ukrainian who was chief USSR prosecutor at the Nuremberg Trials of the Nazi leaders and became General Public Prosecutor in 1953.
12. V. N. Merkulov, an extremely presentable but no less unpleasant secret policeman and a very close associate of Beria's. He was replaced by Abakumov as head of the MGB in 1946, but soon became Minister of State Control. He was tried with Beria and shot.

A few days passed and Merkulov turned in a lengthy memorandum. It was absolutely worthless. It was more like a piece of fiction. This man Merkulov was something of a writer. He'd written plays and was good at fiction writing. After I sent this material to the prosecutor's office, Rudenko called me and asked for an appointment. When he came to my office he told me that without Merkulov's arrest our investigation into Beria's case would be incomplete. The Central Committee approved Merkulov's arrest. To my regret, since I had trusted him, Merkulov turned out to have been deeply implicated in some of Beria's crimes, so he too was convicted and had to bear the same responsibility. In his last words, after his sentence had been announced by the court, Merkulov cursed the day and the hour when he first met Beria. He said Beria had led him to this end. Thus, in the final analysis, Merkulov recognized the criminality of his actions and pronounced his own judgment against the man who had incited him to crime.

One of the people we were able to return to a useful, active life after Beria's downfall was Aleksandr Petrovich Dovzhenko, the brilliant film director who was so unjustly disgraced during the war [see page 172]. Shortly after Beria was arrested, Dovzhenko asked me for an appointment. He came by my office and told me the following story:

One day the director Chiaureli, who made *The Fall of Berlin,* asked Dovzhenko to come and see him. Chiaureli was totally dependent on Stalin's patronage, and it was no accident that his film on the fall of Berlin showed Stalin pondering military strategy in a huge hall surrounded by empty chairs — in solitary grandeur except for General Poskrebyshev, Chief of the Special Section of the Central Committee. In short, Chiaureli was a wretched little toady. After Stalin's death and Beria's arrest we sent him off to the Urals. I don't know what place he holds in the world of film arts today or whether he learned any lessons from the criticism that came his way after his protector Stalin died. Anyway, Chiaureli summoned Dovzhenko and told him, "Comrade Dovzhenko, I'd advise you to go and see Comrade Beria. He's very interested in you and has a proposition to make. It will be to your advantage to go hear what he has to say." Dovzhenko was perplexed: Why was Chiaureli telling him to go and see Beria? What business did he have with the Ministry of Internal Affairs? In the end he decided not to go.

I explained to Dovzhenko: "You see, Aleksandr Petrovich, Chiaureli was trying to recruit you as an agent for Beria. He understood, quite correctly, that you were an influential person and would have been useful to Beria in his plans for the Ukraine. Beria wanted to make you his henchman so that he could count on you when his blood bath began. His plans could only have been bloody because Beria knew no other methods."

I considered Dovzhenko an honest, loyal, upright citizen. He may have sometimes said things which were unpleasant for the leaders to hear, but it's always better to hear such things from an honest man than from an enemy. You can always talk sense to an honest man if he's wrong, and you can learn from him if he's right. After Aleksandr Petrovich's death I urged the Ukrainians to rename the Kiev Film Studio after him, and they did so.

Dovzhenko's story about Beria's attempt to compromise him was only one of the first — and by no means one of the most shocking — in a spate of revelations into Beria's past activities which came to light after his arrest.

The Twentieth Party Congress

The arrest of Beria took place in June, 1953. As far as domestic politics are concerned, we now jump forward to the climacteric Twentieth Party Congress of February, 1956 — and thereafter all is silence. The period from June, 1953, to February, 1956, was make-or-break for Khrushchev. In September, 1953, he assumed the First Secretaryship of the Party, a post which had been left vacant since Malenkov had been forced to relinquish it (while retaining the Premiership) within ten days of Stalin's death. Thenceforth, the fiction of collective leadership, so sedulously maintained, began rapidly to disintegrate. In February, 1955, Malenkov was forced to resign as Prime Minister. He was replaced by Bulganin, whose role was subsidiary and indeterminate. But Malenkov was still a power in the Politbureau, and it was clear that Molotov, Mikoyan, and others were keeping a very close eye on the man they had chosen to lead their Party. Nevertheless, signs multiplied that Khrushchev was engaged in a more or less open bid for supremacy. He was turning industry and agriculture upside down, above all in his Virgin Lands campaign. He was making himself known both at home and abroad as the real boss, even when some of his colleagues were actively opposing some of his policies. Mikoyan, for example (others too), objected to the Virgin Lands campaign; Molotov objected and was publicly humiliated in consequence. Khrushchev was actively building up his own personality cult. He was also (and this continued until Malenkov's fall) adopting the Stalinist attitude about Russia's invulnerability in the case of an atomic war and about the primacy of heavy industry over consumer goods (Malenkov had declared that the Soviet Union would be annihilated along with the rest of the world in any nuclear war, and he had embarked on a program of diverting money and resources from heavy industry to the manufacture of consumer goods).

By the time of the Twentieth Party Congress, Khrushchev had reached a very commanding position indeed, but he had another sixteen months to go before he emerged supreme (in June, 1957, with the destruction of the so-called Anti-Party Group — Malenkov, Molotov, Kaganovich, and others). Even so, he was, unlike Stalin, vulnerable if ever his closest colleagues should decide to act unanimously against him, as they were to do in October, 1964. In February, 1956, however, he was still maneuvering on the last stages of his ascent. Few students of Soviet affairs will be satisfied with Khrushchev's account of the background to the famous Secret Speech attacking Stalin. Khrushchev was obviously forced into a highly exposed position by his colleagues (Malenkov prominent among them), who were divided in their aims. Some were concerned above all with reminding the Party that Stalin was dead and his successors firmly in control. Others, reluctantly perceiving the necessity for this, thought that by forcing Khrushchev to make the speech, he would be the first victim of an inevitable storm. Khrushchev, who had opened the Congress with his formal General Report, clearly had no intention of denouncing his late master before the Congress was over. He then determined to turn the tables and by sheer boldness gain the credit for the new course which he had been resisting. It was a touch-and-go affair, but his gamble paid off.

An ambiguous situation had arisen. Stalin was dead and buried, but until Beria's arrest, Stalinist policies were still in force. Business went on as usual. No one thought to rehabilitate the people who had gone to their graves branded as enemies of the people or to release the prisoners from the camps, and most of them stayed there until the Twentieth Party Congress, three years after Stalin's death! For three years we were unable to break with the past, unable to muster the courage and the determination to lift the curtain and see what had been hidden from us about the arrests, the trials, the arbitrary rule, the executions, and everything else that had happened during Stalin's reign. It was as though we were enchained by our own activities under Stalin's leadership and couldn't free ourselves from his control even after he was dead. Not until 1956 could we rid ourselves of the psychological aftereffects of the hysteria which had gripped us during the hunt for enemies of the people. We persisted in believing the delusion perpetrated by Stalin that we were surrounded by enemies, that we had to do battle against them, and that by following the methods justified in theory and established in practice by Stalin, we were intensifying the class struggle and consolidating the gains of the Revolution. We couldn't imagine that all those executions during the purges were, from a legal standpoint, crimes themselves. But it was true! Criminal acts had been committed by Stalin, acts which would be punishable in any state in the world except in fascist states like Hitler's and Mussolini's.[13]

Then came Beria's arrest and the investigation into his case. There were shocking revelations about the secret machinery which had been hidden from us and which had caused the deaths of so many people. I remember I was particularly shocked at the revelation that Kedrov had been executed as an enemy of the people. Kedrov had been the first commander in the North to organize the defense of our country against the English. But even when our eyes were opened during Beria's trial, we refused to believe that Stalin himself could have been behind the terror which Beria oversaw. For a while we gave the Party and the people incorrect explanations about what had happened; we blamed everything on Beria. He was a convenient figure. We did everything we could to shield Stalin, not yet fully realizing that we were harboring a criminal, an assassin, a mass murderer! I repeat: Not until 1956 did we set ourselves free from our subservience to Stalin.

I first sensed the falsity of our position when we went to Yugoslavia and talked with Comrade Tito in 1955. When we touched on the whole subject of the terror and mentioned Beria as the culprit behind the crimes of the Stalin period, the Yugoslav comrades smiled scornfully and made sarcastic remarks. We were irritated, and we launched into

13. This is the first time that Khrushchev, or any other Soviet politician, has gone to the lengths of equating Stalin's actions with Hitler's.

a long argument in defense of Stalin. Later I spoke out publicly in defense of Stalin when the Yugoslavs criticized him. It's now clear to me that my position was wrong. I didn't fully realize the necessity not only of exposing the crimes but of putting the blame where it belonged so that Stalinist methods would never again be used in our Party.

I still mourned Stalin as an extraordinarily powerful leader. I knew that his power had been exerted arbitrarily and not always in the proper direction, but in the main Stalin's strength, I believed, had still been applied to the reinforcement of Socialism and to the consolidation of the gains of the October Revolution. Stalin may have used methods which were, from my standpoint, improper or even barbaric, but I hadn't yet begun to challenge the very basis of Stalin's claim to a place of special honor in history. However, questions were beginning to arise for which I had no ready answer. Like others, I was beginning to wonder why of all those arrested no one had ever been acquitted and why of all those imprisoned no one had ever been released. I was beginning to doubt whether all the arrests and convictions had been justified from the standpoint of judicial norms. But then Stalin had been Stalin. Even in death he commanded almost unassailable authority, and it still hadn't occurred to me that he had been capable of abusing his power.

Nonetheless, partly because of the revelations made during the investigation into Beria's case, I felt an urge to lift the curtain a bit further — to find out who exactly had been arrested, what methods had been used in their interrogation, and what evidence there had been for arresting them in the first place. I brought the matter up at a Presidium session and proposed that we conduct an investigation in order to get a clearer picture of what had happened under Stalin.[14] I was especially anxious to do this in view of the approaching Twentieth Party Congress.

Not surprisingly, Voroshilov, Molotov, and Kaganovich weren't very enthusiastic about my suggestion. As I recall, Mikoyan didn't support me actively, but he didn't do anything to block my proposal either. I explained to those who were against the idea that since the Twentieth was to be the first Party Congress after Stalin's death, we would have to prove that we were able to assume full responsibility for governing

14. An investigatory committee was in fact set up by the Party Presidium in 1954, soon after Beria's execution. In the Secret Speech Khrushchev announced that 7,379 individuals had been rehabilitated as a result of the findings of this commission.

the Party and the country; that meant we had to know exactly what had happened under Stalin and what had motivated Stalin's decisions on various issues, particularly concerning all the people who had been arrested. One question was sure to come up at the Congress: Why were so many people still in prison and what was to be done about them now? In short, we would have to answer both for what happened while Stalin was alive and for problems stemming from his policies, which were still with us after his death.

We set up a commission and put Pospelov in charge of it.[15] The evidence gathered by Pospelov's commission came as a complete surprise to some of us. I'm speaking about myself, Bulganin, Pervukhin, Saburov, and some others. I think Molotov and Voroshilov were the best informed about the true dimensions and causes of the Stalinist repressions, and therefore they had the least reason to be surprised by the commission's findings. Mikoyan was also more prepared than most of us to believe the facts that were brought to light. I can't be certain that he knew everything, but nevertheless he had been very close to Stalin. Many people who worked with Mikoyan and whom he trusted had been eliminated. Knowing Anastas Ivanovich, his perceptiveness and his ability to generalize about what is happening on the basis of scant indications, I'd say that he must have known what had been going on. If he didn't know, then he at least guessed how little justification there had been for all the arrests and executions.

As for Kaganovich, I don't think he knew all the details of what happened. Stalin hardly needed to confide in him. Kaganovich was such a yes-man that he would have cut his own father's throat if Stalin had winked and said it was in the interests of the cause — the Stalinist cause, that is. Stalin never needed to keep Kaganovich reined in. Kaganovich had always been a detestable sycophant, exposing enemies and having people arrested right and left.

A word about Malenkov. He had been in charge of personnel for the Central Committee during the purges and had played a pretty active role in the whole business. He had actually helped promote people from the ranks only to have them eliminated later on. I'm not saying he took the initiative in the repressions and executions, but the fact

15. P. N. Pospelov (real name, Feigelson) was one of the chief Party ideologists. He was editor of *Pravda* from 1940–49 and director of the Marx-Engels-Lenin-Stalin Institute from 1949–52. A bleak and thoroughgoing dogmatist, he worked closely with Suslov. It was not previously known that he was responsible for the commission which produced the evidence for the Secret Speech.

speaks for itself that hundreds of people were repressed and eliminated in those regions where Stalin sent Malenkov to establish order.[16]

We were on the eve of the Twentieth Party Congress. I didn't want to give the General Report at the Congress. It was my opinion that if we were going to announce collective leadership, it was unwise for the General Report to be delivered by the First Secretary of the Central Committee. At a Presidium session just before the Congress I proposed that we discuss who should make the General Report. As the senior member among us, Molotov had the best credentials for being the speaker, but he and everyone else were unanimously agreed that I should give the report. I felt they were saying this sincerely and not just for the sake of appearances. One of their considerations was that it would cause no friction if I, as First Secretary of the Central Committee, gave the report, whereas if we chose another speaker — and there were plenty of candidates available — it would pose complications. After Stalin's death no single man was acknowledged as our leader. There were aspirants, but no clear-cut, recognized leader.[17] That's why I, as First Secretary, was instructed to make the General Report.

I prepared a draft and submitted it at a Central Committee plenum for discussion and approval. The report was the fruit of collective authorship. The Central Committee drew from research institutes and other groups who were, as a rule, called upon to help in preparing general reports.

The Congress opened. I delivered the report and discussion started. We were facing a real test. Everyone was asking, what kind of a Congress would this be after Stalin's death? I would say the Congress was going well. One speaker after another approved the Central Committee Line. No one sensed any opposition.[18]

16. Molotov and Malenkov were active in seconding and encouraging Stalin's crimes. So, at least in the Ukraine, was Khrushchev himself. The others all knew about them and connived at them.

17. Indeed there were "candidates" for the "recognized" leadership: Khrushchev and Malenkov. For over a year inside the Soviet Union, and abroad — in Belgrade, in Delhi, and in Geneva — Khrushchev had been presenting himself on every possible occasion as the Master. In those Republics where his own supporters were strongly in the ascendant (especially the Ukraine and Kazakhstan) a new Khrushchev "personality cult" was in full bloom. But Malenkov was still fighting back. Khrushchev would never, without admitting defeat, have allowed anybody else to make the General Report to the Twentieth Party Congress.

18. Should we be surprised? The new leadership had had three years to sort out any potential opposition.

Despite the fact that the Congress was going smoothly and my report had been favorably received, I wasn't satisfied. I was tormented by the following thought: "The Congress will end, and resolutions will be passed, all as a matter of form. But then what? The hundreds of thousands of people who were shot will stay on our consciences, including two-thirds of those elected to the Central Committee at the Seventeenth Party Congress [in 1934]. Almost all the active Party members of that time were either shot or repressed." In short, the findings of Pospelov's commission weighed heavily on my mind. Finally I gathered myself together and during a recess, when only the members of the Presidium were in the room, I brought the whole matter up:

"Comrades, what are we going to do about Comrade Pospelov's findings? What are we going to do about all those who were arrested and eliminated? The Congress is coming to a close, and we'll all disperse without having said a single word about the abuses committed under Stalin. We now know that the people who suffered during the repressions were innocent. We have indisputable proof that, far from being enemies of the people, they were honest men and women, devoted to the Party, devoted to the Revolution, devoted to the Leninist cause and to the building of Socialism and Communism in the Soviet Union. We can't keep people in exile or in the camps any longer. We must figure out how to bring them back." [19]

As soon as I finished speaking, everyone started attacking me, especially Voroshilov: "What's the matter with you? How can you talk like that?" he exclaimed. "You think you can bring all this out at the Congress and get away with it? How do you think it will reflect on tne prestige of our Party and our country? You won't be able to keep what you say secret. Word will get out about what happened under Stalin, and then the finger will be pointed straight at us. What will we be able to say about our own roles under Stalin?"

Kaganovich chimed in, fiercely opposing me along the same lines. His position wasn't one of profound philosophical analysis of the Party issues involved. No, he was arguing against me out of a selfish fear for his own hide. He was motivated entirely by his eagerness to escape

19. Khrushchev does not mention that Mikoyan had exploded a bomb at the Congress by making observations highly critical of Stalin (and, by implication, of Khrushchev himself). Others had made derogatory remarks about the "personality cult," as yet undefined. Khrushchev alone had gone out of his way to praise Stalin for his determined smashing of the "enemies of the people" — although eleven days later he was, in his Secret Speech, to denounce the use of this term.

any responsibility for what had happened. If crimes had been committed, Kaganovich wanted to make sure his own tracks were covered.

I answered these attacks as calmly and convincingly as I could: "Even looking at it from your position," I said, "I still think it's impossible to cover everything up. Sooner or later people will be coming out of the prisons and the camps, and they'll return to the cities. They'll tell their relatives, friends, comrades, and everyone back home what happened. The whole country and the whole Party will find out that people have spent ten to fifteen years in prison — and all for what? For nothing! The accusations against them were trumped up! If they were brought to trial, the prosecution's cases against them were conjured out of thin air! I ask you to think about something else, comrades: we are conducting the first Congress after Stalin's death, and therefore we're obliged to make a clean breast to the delegates about the conduct of the Party leadership during the years in question. We're supposed to be giving an account of ourselves for the period after Stalin's death, but as members of the Central Committee while Stalin was still alive, we must tell about that period as well. How can we pretend not to know what happened?

"Therefore, comrades, I ask you to support me. The Congress is coming to an end, and the delegates will soon be dispersing. Shortly after we adjourn, newly released prisoners will start coming home and begin informing people in their own way about what happened. Then the delegates to Congress will rightly ask, 'How can this be? Why didn't you tell us about these terrible things at the Twentieth Party Congress? You must have known.' And they will be quite right. We won't have an answer. To say that we didn't know anything would be a lie. We have Comrade Pospelov's findings in hand, and now we know everything. We know there was a reign of repression and arbitrary rule in the Party, and we must tell the Congress what we know."

Once again the reaction was stormy. Voroshilov and Kaganovich repeated as though in one voice, "We'll be taken to task! The Party has the right to hold us responsible for what happened under Stalin! We were in the leadership and even if we didn't know what was happening, that's just too bad — we'll still be made to pay!"

"If you consider our Party to be founded on the principle of democratic centralism," I replied, "then we, as the Party's leaders, had no right *not* to know what was happening. Some of us didn't know many things because we were part of a regime in which you were told what you were supposed to know and you kept your nose out of everything else. So we kept our noses out. But not everyone was in that position. Some knew what was happening, and some even got their own noses dirty in the events we're speaking about. But while the degree of responsibility for what happened varies among us, I'm prepared, as a member of the Central Committee since the Seventeenth Congress, to bear my share of the responsibility before the Party — even if the Party should see fit to bring to task all those who were in the leadership under Stalin when arbitrary rule was imposed on the Party."

This time Molotov objected, "Don't you see what will happen?"

Voroshilov protested vehemently that what I was proposing needn't be done and couldn't be done without calling down the wrath of the Party on our own heads. He kept saying over and over, "Who's asking us to do this? Who says we have to tell the Congress these things?"

"No one," I replied. "But the crimes have still been committed, haven't they? We have at least to admit that much to ourselves. It's inevitable that people will find out what happened; if they start asking us about it after we've kept silent, they'll already be sitting in judgment over us. I don't want that to happen. I don't want to accept responsibility in that way. I'd rather we raised the matter ourselves."

But we were still a long way from an agreement. I saw that it would be impossible to get the Presidium to reach a decision at this rate, and I knew we couldn't bring the question to the Congress floor until we had reached a consensus among ourselves. I decided to try the following device: "The Party Congress is under way and going very smoothly, but the internal discipline required for unified leadership by the Central Committee has broken down. Now that the General Report has been given, may I remind you that every Presidium member has the right to speak at the Congress and to express his own point of view, even if it doesn't coincide with the line set by the General Report." I didn't need to tell them that I was prepared if necessary to make such a speech myself, presenting my views on the arrests and executions. I added: "In the life of anyone who has committed a crime, there comes a moment when a confession will assure him leniency if not exculpation. If we are going to make a clean breast of the abuses committed by Stalin, then we must do so now, at the Twentieth Party Congress. The Twenty-first Congress will already be too late, even if we get that far without being brought to task."

We had reached the point where someone took the initiative and said, "All right, then, if that's where we stand, someone had better make a speech about Stalin's abuses." Everybody finally agreed reluctantly that a speech should be given. I think Bulganin, Pervukhin, Saburov, and possibly Malenkov gave me their personal support. That left the question of who should actually get up and deliver the speech. I suggested it be Pospelov since he had been the chairman of the commission whose findings we would be using. The others objected. They said I should make the speech. I refused. I had already delivered the General Report without saying a word about Pospelov's findings, so how could I now make a new speech based on them? But the others insisted, saying, "If Pospelov, another Central Committee Secretary, delivers the speech, it will make people wonder, 'Why didn't Khrushchev say anything about this business in his General Report? Why is Pospelov bringing up such an important matter now? How could Khrushchev not have known — or if he knew, how could he not have placed any importance on it?' If you don't give the speech, it could contribute to the impression of dissension in the leadership."

This argument deserved consideration, and finally I gave in. It was decided that I would give the speech based on the commission's findings. Pospelov was instructed to turn his report into a speech.[20] We arranged for a special closed session of the Congress, and I delivered my speech. The delegates listened in absolute silence. It was so quiet in the huge hall you could hear a fly buzzing. You must try to imagine how shocked people were by the revelations of the atrocities to which Party members — Old Bolsheviks and up-and-coming young men alike — had been subjected. This was the first that most of them had heard of the tragedy which our Party had undergone — a tragedy stemming from the sickness in Stalin's character which Lenin had warned us against in his Testament and which Stalin himself had confirmed in his confession to Mikoyan and me — "I trust no one, not even myself" [see page 307].

20. The genesis of the Secret Speech must have been more complicated than Khrushchev suggests here. The speech, twenty thousand words long, packed with detail, a composite effort if ever there was one (with short passages obviously interpolated at the last minute by Khrushchev himself), must have been in existence before the Congress opened. If Khrushchev had intended to denounce Stalin he would have prepared the way in his General Report (as Mikoyan did in his own speech). It can only have been that Khrushchev was under pressure to speak, pressure such as would make it impossible for him to develop his own personality cult further. Then, boldly acting to make the best of a bad situation, he contrived to turn the occasion to his own advantage by presenting himself as the one man who dared to speak out.

And so the Twentieth Party Congress speech on Stalin's abuses was born. It was supposed to have been secret, but in fact it was far from being secret. We took measures to make sure that copies of it circulated to the fraternal Communist Parties so that they could familiarize themselves with it. That's how the Polish Party received a copy. At the time of the Twentieth Party Congress the Secretary of the Polish Central Committee, Comrade Bierut, died. There was great turmoil after his death, and our document fell into the hands of some Polish comrades who were hostile toward the Soviet Union. They used my speech for their own purposes and made copies of it. I was told that it was being sold for very little. So Khrushchev's speech delivered in closed session to the Twentieth Party Congress wasn't appraised as being worth much! Intelligence agents from every country in the world could buy it cheap on the open market.

That's how the document came to be published. But we didn't confirm it. I remember that when journalists would ask me, "What can you tell us about this speech which has been attributed to you?" I used to say I knew nothing about it and they'd have to direct their questions to Mr. [Allen] Dulles — that is, American intelligence.[21]

In retrospect I think the matter of what to do with Pospelov's findings was handled absolutely correctly and at the right time. I'm satisfied that I seized the proper moment when I insisted that the speech be made at the Twentieth Congress.

It could have turned out differently. We were just coming out of a state of shock. People were still in prison and in the camps, and we didn't know how to explain what had happened to them or what to do with them once they were free. We could have fallen back on what might crudely be called "the Beria version" — and have claimed that Beria was completely responsible for the abuses committed by Stalin. After Beria's trial we had found ourselves trapped by the version which we'd created in the interests of protecting Stalin's reputation. It would have been easier, perhaps, to continue blaming Beria and to have left the illusion unchallenged that Stalin was "the People's Father and Friend." Even today, long after the Twentieth Party Congress, there are still people who have clung to the Beria version and who refuse to accept the truth about Stalin. Some people want to believe that it wasn't God who was guilty but one of his angels; one of his angels

21. It is worth recording that Khrushchev has never before admitted publicly that the Secret Speech in fact existed.

gave God false reports, and that's why God sent hail and thunder and other disasters down on mankind; the people suffered not because God wanted them to, but because that evil angel Beria sat at God's right hand.

Not too long ago I was listening to the radio and heard a reading of a chapter from Sholokhov's novel, *They Fought for Their Homeland.* Mikhail Aleksandrovich tries to explain, in a conversation between two fishermen, what happened during the period of Stalin's abuses. One fisherman asks the other, "What do you make of Comrade Stalin? They say he overlooked all these terrible things that were going on. All sorts of honest, loyal people were brought to trial and put to death. How could Comrade Stalin have let it happen?"

The other fisherman says, "Yes, it's hard to believe."

Then the first asks, "Wasn't Beria the main culprit? Wasn't it he who reported to Stalin?"

"Yes, it was all that awful Beria's doing."

Now, Mikhail Aleksandrovich is an intelligent man and a fine writer, but it's no credit to him that he's perpetuating this explanation of the tragedy which Stalin inflicted on our Party. One thing is absolutely elementary: Beria didn't create Stalin, Stalin created Beria. And before him Stalin created Yezhov. "The Blackberry" and "the Mailed Fist" — those were Stalin's nicknames for Yezhov. And before Yezhov there was Yagoda. Stalin invented Yagoda, too. One by one they made their entrances and exits. The rapid turnover among the main characters created by Stalin was very much part of Stalin's logic. He used henchmen to destroy honest men who he knew perfectly well were guiltless in the eyes of the Party and the people. Then Stalin stood above it all while the terror consumed its own executors. When one band of thugs got too embroiled in the terror, he simply replaced it with another. That's how the three echelons came about: first Yagoda, then Yezhov, then Beria. The chain was broken with Stalin's death, and Beria faced the people's court as a criminal.

Just before the Twentieth Party Congress I summoned the State Prosecutor, Comrade Rudenko, who had been involved in many of the cases during the purges of the thirties. I asked him, "Comrade Rudenko, I'm interested in the open trials. Tell me, how much basis in actual fact was there for the accusations made against Bukharin, Rykov, Syrtsov, Lominadze, Krestinsky, and many, many other people well known to the Central Committee, to the Orgbureau, and to the Polit-bureau?"

Comrade Rudenko answered that from the standpoint of judicial norms, there was no evidence whatsoever for condemning or even trying those men. The case for prosecuting them had been based on personal confessions beaten out of them under physical and psycholog-ical torture, and confessions extracted by such means are unacceptable as a legitimate basis for bringing someone to trial.

Nevertheless, we decided not to say anything about the open trials in my speech to the Twentieth Party Congress. There was a certain ambiguity in our conduct here. The reason for our decision was that there had been representatives of the fraternal Communist parties pres-ent when Rykov, Bukharin, and other leaders of the people were tried and sentenced. These representatives had then gone home and testified in their own countries to the justice of the sentences. We didn't want to discredit the fraternal Party representatives who had attended the open trials, so we indefinitely postponed the rehabilitation of Bukharin, Zinoviev, Rykov, and the rest. I can see now that our decision was a mistake. It would have been better to tell everything. Murder will al-ways out. You can't keep things like that a secret for long.

But despite that one mistake, the Twentieth Party Congress still ac-complished a great deal. Its main achievement was that it touched off the process of purifying the Party of Stalinism and reestablishing in the Party those Leninist norms of life for which the best sons of our coun-try had struggled.

TWO

The World Outside

The Fraternal Countries

Khrushchev's expedition to Warsaw in 1945 was more important than he suggests. He was chairman of the committee that planned the reconstruction of an appallingly devastated city, whose center then appeared to be nothing more than an immense heap of fire-blackened rubble. Indeed, it says something for Khrushchev that he makes so little of the immense difficulties that faced him in Warsaw and, more intimately, in the ruined towns and cities of his own Ukraine, where sometimes nothing at all was left to show that a town had once existed — apart from irregular rows of brick chimney breasts sticking up out of the snow to give the effect of monstrous cemeteries. On the other hand, Khrushchev's account of Soviet relations with the satellites is so remote from reality that, apart from a handful of anecdotes, its chief interest is in the light it throws on the mentality of a man who can blandly say about Moscow's attitude toward Poland, Czechoslovakia, Rumania, Bulgaria, and Hungary with their puppet governments: ". . . we deliberately avoided applying pressure on other Socialist countries." He is referring to a part of the world where Communist rule had been established by Stalin's agents backed by the might of the Soviet Army, and where the Russians later inspired and supervised the notorious series of trials and judicial murders (Rajk in Hungary, Kostov in Bulgaria, Slansky in Czechoslovakia, and others too numerous to mention) which were to transform the Communist Parties of Central and Eastern Europe into faithful replicas of the Soviet Communist Party as it had been shaped by the great purges of the 1930's.

IN January, 1945, Stalin phoned me in the Ukraine and asked, "Can you come to Moscow immediately? We need you here urgently." I flew to Moscow from Kiev. Stalin met me in high spirits. He said, "The

Khrushchev and Gomulka of Poland in the 1960's

Hunting near Kiev with Gomulka and Podgorny, December 22, 1962

Polish comrades have asked us to help them restore their municipal services, especially their water supply and sewage system. We have liberated Warsaw, but they're in a helpless situation. They say Warsaw is in ruins, and they don't know what to do or where to begin. You've already had considerable experience with the rapid restoration of essential city services, so we want to send you to Warsaw to oversee the work there."

"Very well," I answered. "I will go with pleasure. But I would like to take with me some municipal administrators and electrical engineers. The first thing is to get the Poles' power station working, then their water and sewage works." I asked Comrade Stramentov to come along. I knew he was a good organizer and an expert manager of electrical facilities. I also included some engineers who specialized in power stations, water supply, and sewage. We all flew to Warsaw.

The Polish government, or "Committee," as it was called at that time, was situated in Praga, a suburb of Warsaw on the right bank of the Vistula. Osobka-Morawski was Prime Minister, and Comrade Bierut was Secretary of the Central Committee of the Polish Communist Party.[1] General Spychalski was mayor of Warsaw. I had met Bierut earlier, but this was the first time I met Spychalski. I liked them both. Spychalski was young, energetic, and hard-working. He was an architect by training. As for Bierut, I considered him an honest Communist, devoted to the cause of Marxism-Leninism. He had one weakness: he was too mild, good-natured, and trusting. This led to some complications in Poland later when his colleagues took advantage of him.

Our engineers divided up into three groups with the Polish engineers. One group was detailed to restore electric power as quickly as possible. The second group was to take care of the water supply, and the third was to repair the sewage system. The Poles were to look after cleaning up the city by themselves. Our services weren't required for that job. I put Comrade Stramentov in charge of the whole operation, so he had both Polish and Russian specialists under him. He was to handle all the specific problems which arose and then report to me and the other Polish comrades on the general situation.

1. These were all members of the notorious "Lublin Committee," formed by the Russians to act as the first puppet government of Communist Poland. Osobka-Morawski was the first Prime Minister, 1944–47. He was then demoted and finally disgraced in the purge of 1949. Bierut was very quickly to become the first President. The office of Secretary General of the Party was in fact assumed by W. Gomulka in 1945.

Our men soon had some good news to report. It turned out that only the outside of the power station had been ruined and the equipment inside was still in working order. The Poles had thought that the station was completely destroyed. The machinery to pump water through the city was also still usable. The sewage system apparently wasn't badly damaged either. I was very glad to hear all this. After a few days of exhaustive investigation into the condition of the machinery and turbines, I jokingly said to Comrade Bierut, "Why don't you pay for our trip and our consultations by giving us half the electric power which we will restore in Warsaw? We could certainly use it in Kiev." I was referring to the disastrous situation in Kiev at that time. The power station there had been completely demolished by the Germans.

Warsaw got its electricity and water supply back. Bierut was radiant. He thanked us profusely and asked us to pass on his thanks to Comrade Stalin. He was obviously speaking very sincerely. Before we left, Comrade Bierut made a suggestion to me: "We have a very important figure in the Polish Communist Party here, a comrade named Wladyslaw Gomulka. I would like to ask that you pay a call on him at his apartment. He's quite sick and can't come out."

"All right," I said. "I will be pleased to." I was given someone to accompany me and went to see Comrade Gomulka. I remember being taken to a gloomy, sooty, one-room apartment. Gomulka's wife was washing clothes when we arrived. Gomulka himself was sitting in a chair with some sort of black kerchief drawn up high around his neck.

Comrade Gomulka didn't speak Russian very well, but with the help of the interpreter we could understand each other. Gomulka gave me his appraisal of the general state of affairs in Poland and told me how Party work was being organized. He impressed me. He seemed to know where to start in organizing the activities of the Party and government. In short, he impressed me as being an able political leader and statesman. "I'm sick for the time being," he said, "but I will be up and around before long."

When I reported to Comrade Stalin about my trip, I told him about Gomulka. I don't know if Stalin had heard of him earlier. None of the rest of us had, and I doubt Stalin had either. I recommended Gomulka very highly to Stalin.[2]

2. Gomulka had survived Stalin's deliberate destruction of the Polish Communist Party only because he was lucky enough to be in prison in Poland when his colleagues were being murdered in Moscow. Almost immediately after this first encounter with

Stalin was very satisfied with my report about Poland. He was pleased that we had been able to help the Poles, and he knew this assistance would make good marks for us with the Polish people, especially the citizens of Warsaw. The treaty of 1939 [the Ribbentrop-Molotov Pact] had deeply wounded the Poles, and the wound was still fresh. Stalin wanted to do everything he could to heal it as soon as possible. Naturally, he didn't say this to me outright, but I could sense what he was thinking.

At the end of the war we had troops stationed in Poland and Hungary. Stalin took an active personal interest in the affairs of these countries,[3] as well as of Czechoslovakia, Bulgaria, and Rumania. The rest of us in the leadership were careful not to poke our noses into Eastern Europe unless Stalin himself pushed our noses in that direction. He jealously guarded foreign policy in general and our policy toward other Socialist countries in particular as his own special province. Stalin had never gone out of his way to take other people's advice into account, but this was especially true after the war. The rest of us were just errand boys, and Stalin would snarl threateningly at anyone who overstepped the mark.

One reason for Stalin's obsession with Eastern Europe was that the Cold War had already set in. Churchill had given his famous speech in Fulton urging the imperialistic forces of the world to mobilize against the Soviet Union. Our relations with England, France, the USA, and the other countries who had cooperated with us in crushing Hitlerite Germany were, for all intents and purposes, ruined.

America was conducting its foreign policy from a position of strength. The Americans had the atomic bomb, and they knew we didn't. For the atomic bomb to be in our enemy's hands was bad enough. To make matters worse, the President at that time was Truman, who had neither an ounce of statesmanship nor a flexible mind and who was hostile and spiteful toward the Soviet Union. I can't imagine how anyone ever considered Truman worthy of the Vice-Presi-

---

Khrushchev he became Secretary General of the Polish Party, reborn, until he was imprisoned again (this time by Stalin) in 1949 — accused of Titoism. He was lucky not to be shot. Khrushchev was to meet him again in very different circumstances, when he put himself at the head of the Polish revolt in the autumn of 1956 and, in a head-on collision, rejected the demands made by a high-powered Soviet delegation (Khrushchev, Kaganovich, Mikoyan, and Molotov) which had flown to Warsaw to intimidate the Poles.

3. This, conceivably, is the biggest understatement in this book.

dency, much less the Presidency. The whole world knows from the newspapers how he slapped a journalist who criticized his daughter for being a poor singer.[4] That incident alone told us something about Truman's statesmanship, to say nothing of his suitability for so important a post as the Presidency of the United States. America's air force at that time was the best in the world both in the quality and quantity of its planes. The American "flying fortresses" and "super-fortresses" had played a big part in winning the war against Germany and Japan, and they were still unmatched by any other planes in the world. I would even say that America was invincible, and the Americans flaunted this fact by sending their planes all over Europe, violating borders and even flying over the territory of the Soviet Union itself, not to mention a country like Czechoslovakia. Not a single day went by when American planes didn't violate Czechoslovak airspace. In the Soviet Union there was considerable alarm that the US might send its troops into Czechoslovakia and try to restore the capitalist government which had been overthrown in 1948 by the working classes under the leadership of the Communist Party.

This danger was another reason for Stalin to take such a direct, and jealous, interest in the affairs of the fraternal Socialist countries and Czechoslovakia in particular. The Czechoslovak Communist Party was outstanding among European Parties. It had good proletarian leadership and enjoyed high prestige. Gottwald was President.[5] I had heard many good things about Gottwald over the years, and I knew Stalin thought very highly of him. I had met Gottwald myself in 1948, after the victory of the Communist Party in Czechoslovakia over the bourgeoisie and the proletariat's assumption of the leadership. One day I got a telephone call from Stalin. He was in a good mood and invited me to come to the Crimea, where he was spending his vacation. He told me that Gottwald and his wife had also come to the Crimea on vacation. "Come on down here," he said. "Gottwald says he can't live another day without you." I flew to the Crimea the very next day.

Stalin was then staying in a tsarist palace in Yalta which had been

4. In fact, Truman did not hit the man at all. He did write a scurrilous letter to a Washington music critic who had written an unfavorable review of his daughter Margaret's singing.

5. Klement Gottwald was Czechoslovak Prime Minister in 1946–48 and President from the Communist take-over in 1948 until his death in 1953. The Party Secretary from 1945 until his arrest in November 1951 was Rudolf Slansky. After Slansky's arrest, Gottwald assumed his duties as Party Secretary without taking the title.

the site of his meeting with Roosevelt and Churchill during the war. Gottwald was staying in the same palace. We had many long talks, usually at the dinner table. These were just casual conversations; there was nothing formal or official about them, but we talked about serious subjects — namely, agriculture and the economy.

For some time Stalin kept asking me incredulously, "Is this true what Gottwald says — that the Czechs get sugar beet harvests of 250 to 300 centners [563 to 675 pounds], and that before the war we were getting only 160 or so centners [366 or so pounds] in the Ukraine?"

"Comrade Stalin, that is true," I answered. Gottwald's claim was completely new to him. He asked how it was possible. I had our agronomists look into it. They reported that, in the first place, Czechoslovakia wasn't plagued by the species of weevil that devours the sugar beet crop in the Ukraine and that, furthermore, Czechoslovakia gets more precipitation in the summer months than the regions of the Ukraine where we grow sugar beets.[6]

Stalin was obviously displeased. He wanted to lord the superiority of our agriculture and our collective farm system over Gottwald. He wanted us to be the best in every way, in agriculture and in industry. Since our best agriculture was then in the Ukraine, he had summoned me to the Crimea so that I could back up his claims in his dispute with Gottwald over whose agriculture was the more advanced. But I set the record straight at the outset of our discussion. There was nothing to argue about: the Czechs had clearly reached a higher level in this regard than we had in the Ukraine.

A few years later I saw Gottwald again, when he led a Czechoslovak delegation to Stalin's funeral. Gottwald fell seriously ill himself in Moscow and had to be taken back to Prague. He died not long afterwards.

Bulganin, who was then our Minister of Defense, was instructed to represent the Soviet Union at Gottwald's funeral. When he returned to Moscow he reported that the situation in Prague was very fluid and that it was difficult to predict what Gottwald's successors would be like. Even though our relations with Czechoslovakia were excellent, Gottwald's death caused us some apprehension because our close relationship with him had been the main thread binding our Parties and our states together.

---

6. Czechoslovak agriculture was, of course, as advanced as any in Europe and more advanced than most. This had more to do with skill and fertilizers than with the absence of weevils.

Zapotocky, who had been Prime Minister under Gottwald, was made President of the Czechoslovak Republic. After the death, or rather the arrest [and execution], of General Secretary Slansky, Novotny became head of the Party.[7] I don't know very much about the events leading up to Novotny's ascendancy. I can tell only about the period when I visited Czechoslovakia, after Novotny had already become Secretary of the Central Committee.

I had very little idea who Novotny was when word of his promotion reached us. This was his first entrance into the international arena. We were told, however, that he had been Secretary of the Prague City Committee, which was the most powerful Party organization in Czechoslovakia, and that he enjoyed wide prestige throughout the Czechoslovak Party. But this was little more than rumor.

When I first met Novotny I liked him very much. I still think that he is a good, honest Communist, dedicated to Marxism-Leninism and the cause of the working class. I've never had any doubt about it. When I saw him in action, I realized that here was a man whose whole life was devoted to the Communist Party of Czechoslovakia. In short, my relations with him were good.

I also met Novotny's Minister of Internal Affairs.[8] He was a loyal and active friend of the Soviet Union. But then he was arrested and brought to trial and so on. I admit I felt very bad about this, but there was nothing I could say in his defense because indisputable, damning evidence had been brought against him.

7. Gottwald died soon after Stalin in 1953 and was succeeded as President by Zapotocky, who had been Prime Minister since 1948. A. Novotny then became Party Secretary. Zapotocky died in 1957 and was succeeded as President by Novotny, who also retained the Party Secretaryship, so that he was, in effect, dictator of Czechoslovakia. Novotny had gained a bad reputation for himself during the four years he spent in a Nazi concentration camp (Mauthausen): he had quickly established himself as a *Kapo*, or trusty, winning privileges for himself and his friends at the expense of less fortunate prisoners and using his special position to break his enemies. Novotny's swift rise after the war was largely due to the part he played in helping to unmask the alleged conspiracy of his colleague Slansky and others, which led to charges of treason and to trials and executions in the manner of the Soviet treason trials of the 1930's. Once Novotny had established himself, he ruled Czechoslovakia in the Stalinist manner, resisting change, until in the spring of 1968 he was overwhelmed by a tidal wave of popular indignation, expressing itself in the great reform movement, presided over by Alexander Dubcek, which was to end so tragically with the Soviet invasion.
8. Rudolf Barak. Novotny had him arrested and sentenced to fifteen years' imprisonment in 1962, by this means getting rid of his only dangerous rival and at the same time making him a scapegoat for his, Novotny's, own failure to satisfy Khrushchev's rather sharp demands for a little more progress toward de-Stalinization in Czechoslovakia.

Furthermore, in those days we deliberately avoided applying pressure on other Socialist countries. We assumed that every Communist Party should, and would, handle its own internal problems by itself. Therefore when we received information about developments which we didn't approve of, we sometimes expressed our opinions and our doubts, but we usually let the fraternal Party make its own decisions. This practice held true in the case of the Czechoslovak Party.

However, I do remember one episode when there was a certain amount of tension between the Czechoslovak leaders and myself. I was to be part of a Soviet delegation which was preparing to leave for Czechoslovakia. I told my comrades during a meeting before we left that I wanted very much to pay a special visit to General Svoboda and to take him some typical Russian souvenirs as a token of both my own personal esteem for him and the gratitude of the Soviet people for his role in the war.

In 1943, Vatutin and I had a Czechoslovak battalion under the command of Colonel Svoboda that was attached to our army. This battalion distinguished itself outside Kharkov. Later I got to know Svoboda better after his men formed a crack brigade. I remember the Czechoslovak Communists telling me during the war that he was an active political leader as well as an outstanding military commander. According to the constitution of Czechoslovakia at that time, it was forbidden to set up political cells in the ranks of military units, and therefore the Communist organization in the Czechoslovak brigade was technically illegal. But that didn't stop Svoboda from summoning the leader of the Party organization and telling him what sort of political work needed to be done. The Czechoslovaks fought side by side with us on the First Ukrainian Front. I was a member of the Military Council, and Svoboda was one of my subordinates. I had another chance to meet Svoboda and the other Czechoslovak leaders after their country was liberated by our troops. The newly formed Czech government traveled back to Prague through Kiev where I received them. Svoboda was decorated by the Soviet Union with the Order of Lenin. Thus, his record and my own association with him meant it would have been simply indecent for me to go to Czechoslovakia without paying a personal visit to him.

However, by the time I finally had a chance to go to Czechoslovakia with our delegation, Svoboda was in disgrace. According to information we received, he was working as a bookkeeper on a collective farm.

It hardly made sense. He had done nothing to deserve this humiliation. I told my comrades I thought Svoboda should be put to constructive use and given a position worthy of his important contribution as the only military leader of the Czechoslovak army who had fought by our side against Germany. We had to do something to boost his prestige and to return him to active political life. My comrades in the leadership of the Soviet Communist Party and the Soviet Government agreed with me.

When I spoke to our Czechoslovak friends about my desire to see General Svoboda, I tried to impress on them that I considered him a good warrior and an honest comrade and therefore I couldn't just forget about him, as though he'd never existed. I asked them if they had anything against my meeting with Svoboda. I could tell that they weren't very happy about my request, but they knew I wouldn't take no for an answer. I wouldn't say they gave me their blessing, but they didn't do anything to stop me. They said that if I wanted to meet with Svoboda it was my own business. So I made a point of seeing him during our trip to Czechoslovakia.[9]

There are strong brotherly feelings for the Soviet Union among all the peoples of the Socialist countries, but I've always found the Bulgarians' friendship for us to be particularly ardent. Their feelings are understandable. Not all that many years have passed since the battlefields of Bulgaria were littered with the bones of Russian warriors who died winning Bulgaria's independence from the Turks.

9. L. Svoboda became President of Czechoslovakia after Novotny's fall in 1968 and put up a gallant resistance to Soviet bullying. Much earlier he had been the pro-Communist Minister of Defense under Benes and, as such, had played an active part in the overthrow of parliamentary democracy in Czechoslovakia. He did not actually join the Communist Party until 1948 and was regarded with extreme suspicion by Stalin, who had him demoted in 1950. In 1951 he vanished from the scene, spent some time in prison, was released, and made a living as an accountant on a beekeeping cooperative. It is perfectly true that his return from obscurity was due entirely to Khrushchev. He had sunk so deep into anonymity that it took Novotny's minions quite a long time to discover where he was.

The Korean War

Here again the predominant impression is of the almost casual ama-teurishness with which Stalin approached problems not immediately af-fecting the security of the Soviet Union as he understood it. Presum-ably he received detailed advice about the Korean situation from his Foreign Ministry; but he seems to have encouraged the North Koreans without giving the matter serious thought. The important point emerg-ing from this chapter is that Khrushchev makes no bones about North Korean responsibility for the war: he does not pretend that South Korea was guilty of aggression or even provocation. The whole affair, as presented by Khrushchev, was a North Korean invasion com-pounded by a gross miscalculation on Stalin's part. But it is also clear that Stalin saw his own error a great deal sooner than Khrushchev did. Khrushchev could not understand why his master withdrew all Soviet advisors and stood aloof — except for a propaganda barrage — when what should have been a walkover for the North Koreans developed into a major war. No wonder Stalin showed contempt for Khrushchev's suggestions. They were the suggestions of a man still wholly ignorant of the actual working of world forces — unaware, even, of the leading role played in the whole affair by the United Nations, as distinct from the USA.

ABOUT the time I was transferred from the Ukraine to Moscow at the end of 1949, Kim Il-sung arrived with his delegation to hold con-sultations with Stalin. The North Koreans wanted to prod South Korea with the point of a bayonet. Kim Il-sung said that the first poke would

touch off an internal explosion in South Korea and that the power of
the people would prevail — that is, the power which ruled in North
Korea. Naturally Stalin couldn't oppose this idea. It appealed to his
convictions as a Communist all the more because the struggle would
be an internal matter which the Koreans would be settling among
themselves. The North Koreans wanted to give a helping hand to their
brethren who were under the heel of Syngman Rhee. Stalin persuaded
Kim Il-sung that he should think it over, make some calculations, and
then come back with a concrete plan. Kim went home and then returned to Moscow when he had worked everything out. He told Stalin
he was absolutely certain of success. I remember Stalin had his doubts.
He was worried that the Americans would jump in, but we were inclined to think that if the war were fought swiftly — and Kim Il-sung
was sure that it could be won swiftly — then intervention by the USA
could be avoided.

Nevertheless, Stalin decided to ask Mao Tse-tung's opinion about
Kim Il-sung's suggestion. I must stress that the war wasn't Stalin's idea,
but Kim Il-sung's. Kim was the initiator. Stalin, of course, didn't try to
dissuade him. In my opinion, no real Communist would have tried to
dissuade Kim Il-sung from his compelling desire to liberate South
Korea from Syngman Rhee and from reactionary American influence.
To have done so would have contradicted the Communist view of the
world. I don't condemn Stalin for encouraging Kim. On the contrary, I
would have made the same decision myself if I had been in his place.

Mao Tse-tung also answered affirmatively. He approved Kim Il-
sung's suggestion and put forward the opinion that the USA would not
intervene since the war would be an internal matter which the Korean
people would decide for themselves.

I remember a high-spirited dinner at Stalin's dacha. Kim Il-sung told
us about the conditions of life in Korea, and he stressed the many attractive things about South Korea — the good soil and excellent climate for growing rice, the prosperous fishing industry, and so on. He
said that after the reunification of South and North Korea, Korea
as a whole would benefit. Korea would be able to ensure the supply
of raw materials for her industry from the north and to meet the food
requirements to feed her people from the fish, rice, and other agricultural products which flourished in the south. We wished every success to Kim Il-sung and toasted the whole North Korean leadership,
looking forward to the day when their struggle would be won.

We had already been giving arms to North Korea for some time. It was obvious that they would receive the requisite quantity of tanks, artillery, rifles, machine guns, engineering equipment, and antiaircraft weapons. Our air force planes were being used to shield Pyongyang and were therefore stationed in North Korea.

The designated hour arrived and the war began. The attack was launched successfully. The North Koreans swept south swiftly. But what Kim Il-sung had predicted — an internal uprising after the first shots were fired and Syngman Rhee was overthrown — unfortunately failed to materialize. The elimination of Syngman Rhee and his clique was supposed to be accomplished with the advance of the North Korean troops. At first it looked as though Kim Il-sung had been right. The South Korean regime was unstable and wasn't able to defend itself. The resistance was weak. Syngman Rhee indeed didn't have much support within South Korea, but there still weren't enough internal forces for a Communist insurrection in South Korea. Apparently the Party's preparatory organizational work had been inadequate. Kim had believed that South Korea was blanketed with Party organizations and that the people would rise up in revolt when the Party gave the signal. But this never happened.

The North Koreans occupied Seoul. We were all delighted and again wished Kim Il-sung every success because this was a war of national liberation. It was not a war of one people against another, but a class war. Workers, peasants, and intelligentsia under the leadership of the Labor Party of North Korea, which then stood and today still stands on Socialist principles, were united in battle against the capitalists. This in itself was a progressive development.

However, just as Kim Il-sung's army got as far as Pusan, its strength gave out. This was the last port city in the south. It would have to be seized before the war could end. If it had been seized, Korea would have been united. It would no longer have been divided. It would have been a single powerful Socialist country, rich in raw materials, industry, and agriculture.

But that didn't happen. The enemy took advantage of the resistance organized by Syngman Rhee in Pusan. He had prepared his troops for a landing at Chemulpo. The landing assault was staged, and the situation became very serious for the North Koreans. Actually, the entire North Korean army in the south was cut off by this landing, and all its weapons fell into the hands of Syngman Rhee. It was a moment of crisis, and the threat of catastrophe was hanging over North Korea itself.

Stalin was partly to blame for the precarious situation which the North Koreans were in. It's absolutely incomprehensible to me why he did it, but when Kim Il-sung was preparing for his march, Stalin called back all our advisors who were with the North Korean divisions and regiments, as well as all the advisors who were serving as consultants and helping to build up the army. I asked Stalin about this, and he snapped back at me, "It's too dangerous to keep our advisors there. They might be taken prisoner. We don't want there to be evidence for accusing us of taking part in this business. It's Kim Il-sung's affair." So our advisors were recalled. As a result, the North Korean army was in trouble from the very start. When the pitched battles began after Che-mulpo, I took very much to heart the reports we received about the tragic situation Kim Il-sung had gotten himself into. I felt sorry for Kim Il-sung and once even suggested to Stalin:

"Comrade Stalin, wouldn't it be a good idea to lend more qualified help to Kim Il-sung? He wants to fight for his people to make all Korea free and independent. But he's not a military man himself, and now he's facing crack American units. Our ambassador to North Korea is a former Second Secretary of the Leningrad Regional Committee. Even though he's been given a wartime rank of lieutenant general, he's not a professional soldier. He hasn't ever had even basic military training, and his advice couldn't possibly substitute for the advice of a qualified man trained in the conduct of military operations. Now take Malinov-sky, for instance [Khrushchev's future defense minister]. He's in com-mand of the Far Eastern Military District. Why shouldn't we send Ma-linovsky to North Korea so that, incognito, he could help Kim Il-sung to wage the war more effectively?"

Stalin reacted to my remarks with extreme hostility. I was aston-ished. Hadn't Stalin given his blessing to Kim Il-sung? Hadn't we given arms to Kim Il-sung? Weren't we on Kim's side? Without our help he wouldn't have stood a chance, but this aid had been in arms only. If we hadn't refused him aid in qualified personnel to assess the distribution of forces and to direct operations, there's no doubt that North Korea would have been victorious. I think if Kim had received just one tank corps, or two at the most, he could have accelerated his advance south and occupied Pusan on the march. The war would have ended then and there. Later, the American press said that if Pusan had been captured, the USA would not have intervened with its armed forces.[1]

As it was, after a long delay, the Americans staged a landing strike of their own. Their troops retook Seoul and moved north, past the 38th parallel — the demarcation line established by the peace treaty after the fall of Japan. The situation had turned catastrophic for North Korea and for Kim Il-sung.

The North Korean air force was armed mostly with MIG-15's, our newest, best, and most maneuverable jet fighters. In the course of the war, the Americans rearmed their air force and introduced a new fighter which was faster and more powerful than ours. Our MIG-15's were simply outclassed and began to suffer defeat. We lost our dominance in the air. The Americans could cut through our air defenses and bomb North Korea with impunity. We weren't able to provide air cover for cities and power stations any more.

While this tragic situation in North Korea was developing and while we were feeling most sorry for Kim Il-sung and the people of the North Korean Republic, Chou En-lai suddenly appeared. I wasn't present during his meeting with Stalin. Stalin was then in the South [in Sochi], and Chou En-lai flew directly there to see him. Afterward, when Stalin returned to Moscow, he said that Chou En-lai had flown to see him on the instructions of Mao Tse-tung. By this time the North Korean army was nearly decimated. Chou asked Stalin whether Chinese troops ought to be moved into North Korean territory in order to block the path of the Americans and South Koreans. At first, Stalin and Chou seemed to conclude that it was fruitless for China to intervene. However, just before Chou En-lai was to return home, one of them — either Chou En-lai on Mao Tse-tung's instructions or else Stalin himself — reopened the whole matter. They then agreed that China should give active support to North Korea. Chinese troops were already stationed along the border. Stalin and Chou believed these

1. Khrushchev's memory fails him here. Immediately following the North Korean attack, the Americans "intervened" with air power, then with such ground forces as General Douglas MacArthur could assemble from his under-strength garrisons in Japan. The Americans took heavy casualties in the early days of the war and lost one divisional major general taken prisoner. But there were enough men left to hang onto the Pusan beachhead at the southern tip of Korea by their fingernails. Without the Americans, Pusan certainly would have been overrun. Meanwhile, MacArthur was preparing the shattering amphibious blow at Inchon which for the time being destroyed the North Korean army. The Chinese intervention in the autumn of 1950 then turned the war around again.

troops could manage the situation completely. They would beat back the American and South Korean troops and save the situation from disaster.

Chou En-lai flew back to Peking. He was Mao Tse-tung's most influential and most brilliant advisor, and Stalin regarded him with respect. We all considered him a bright, flexible, and up-to-date man with whom we could talk sensibly.

China didn't declare war but simply sent volunteers into Korea. These troops were commanded by P'eng Te-huai, whom Mao Tse-tung held in the highest esteem. Mao used to say that P'eng was the brightest star on the Chinese military horizon.

The fighting started anew. The Chinese succeeded in stopping the advance of the Americans and South Koreans. Pitched battles were fought. In the archives you can find documents in which P'eng Te-huai gave his situation reports to Mao Tse-tung. P'eng composed lengthy telegrams expounding elaborate battle plans against the Americans. He declared categorically that the enemy would be surrounded and finished off by decisive flanking strikes. The American troops were crushed and the war ended many times in these battle reports which P'eng sent to Mao, who then sent them along to Stalin.

Unfortunately, the war wasn't ended quickly at all. The Chinese suffered many huge defeats. We received the news that Mao Tse-tung's son, a general, was killed in an air raid on a command post. So Mao Tse-tung's own son was killed in South Korea! China bore terrible losses because her technology and armaments were considerably inferior to those of the Americans. On both the offensive and the defensive, Chinese tactics depended mostly on sheer manpower.

The war began to draw out. As the two sides dug in, the fighting became bloodier and bloodier. The fronts seemed to be stabilizing. When the North Koreans started to put pressure on the South Koreans, the American troops occupied Pyongyang and pushed the North Koreans back to the border which had been set by the Japanese surrender treaty.

My memories of the Korean War are unavoidably sketchy. I didn't see any of the documents in which the question of military-technical aid to the North Koreans was discussed. But I basically understood our policies. I read all the documents we received from our ambassador. By the time the war started, I had been given my citizenship rights and was put on the government mailing list. While working in the Ukraine I hadn't received any Politbureau mail except on those subjects which related directly to the Ukraine or to me personally. Then, when I was transferred to Moscow, Stalin said that confidential documents could be distributed to me because I hadn't been getting any interoffice mail before. That's how I started to see the battle reports which Mao Tse-tung received from P'eng Te-huai and transmitted to Stalin, and that's how I was able to familiarize myself with the situation which was developing in South Korea.

12

Burying the Hatchet with Tito

Khrushchev's journey to Yugoslavia in the summer of 1955 to repair the damage done by Stalin when he excommunicated Tito in 1948 was his first appearance in the international arena. He was accompanied by Bulganin, then Prime Minister of the Soviet Union, and also by Mikoyan and the new foreign minister, Shepilov. Bulganin acted throughout as an amiable and boozy stooge, doing what Khrushchev told him to do. Mikoyan kept in the background, making occasional warning noises when Khrushchev talked too much and too wildly — for at this time Khrushchev was still drinking very heavily and was at times spectacularly drunk. In these wholly unfamiliar surroundings Khrushchev made mistake after mistake, beginning with his speech at the airport in which he angered Tito by pretending that Soviet treatment of Yugoslavia had been Beria's fault, not Stalin's. But he never made the same mistake twice and showed himself to be a quick learner and to possess unsuspected reserves of personal authority. It should be recalled that in 1949 Stalin had used every method short of war — frontier troop movements, economic blockade, active subversion, and violent and vicious propaganda — to bring about Tito's downfall.

At the time of Stalin's death I was a Secretary of the Central Committee of the CPSU, and First Secretary of both the Moscow City and Regional committees. After Stalin's death I was released from my duties on the Moscow Party Committee but remained on the Secretariat of the Central Committee. For a while we had no First Secretary of the Party at all. Then Bulganin proposed at a Central Committee plenum that we reinstate the position of First Secretary and nominated me for the job. That's how, with the sanction of the Presidium, I became First Secretary of the Central Committee of the CPSU. In that capacity I led a delegation to Yugoslavia in 1955 to restore good relations with Comrade Tito.

Tito had been well known, and well liked, in the Comintern before World War II. During the great struggle of the Yugoslav people against the Hitlerite invaders, Tito achieved widespread fame as a partisan leader. I don't think anybody would take offense if I were to say that the most impressive resistance against the Nazi occupation in any country early in the war was waged by the national partisan movement organized by the Communist Party of Yugoslavia. There were great movements in France, Italy, and other European countries, too, but Yugoslavia's was the first and the most massive.

I first met Tito after the war when he came to Moscow with Kardelj and Djilas to see Stalin. The Yugoslav comrades returned to their homeland by train and came by way of Kiev. They wanted to see some of the country, even if only from a railway car window. Stalin phoned me and said, "Organize a good reception and look after them well while they're in Kiev. Make Tito feel that our country harbors a deep sense of friendship toward Yugoslavia, and see that the Ukraine goes all out for them."

"Very well," I said. "Everything will be done as you say. We will be happy to meet Comrade Tito."

When they arrived, we gave them the appropriate reception, laying on everything that Russian and Ukrainian hospitality could offer. We were still poor, but we were able to treat our guests well. At Tito's request, I organized a visit to a collective farm. He said he was impressed by what he saw, even though our economy was still devastated and our agriculture wasn't much to brag about.

I liked Tito. He had a lively personality, and he was a simple man. I liked Kardelj, too. When I first met Djilas, he impressed me with his quick and subtle wit. He struck me as a good man. I won't deny that I now have quite a different opinion of him, but that's beside the point. I remember that one evening between acts at the opera [in Kiev], Djilas told us a number of fables which he'd thought up himself. One in particular sticks in my mind, and I'd like to tell it here:

Once upon a time a dog, a cow, and an ass lived in a village somewhere in Yugoslavia. Things went from bad to worse there, and finally the dog, the cow, and the ass decided to run away into the mountains. They wandered around in the mountains for some time until they started to get hungry and homesick. They decided to send the dog back to town to see if the situation there had improved. Soon the dog came running back as fast as his legs would carry him. "It's still too hard to live in the village," he reported. "They don't allow barking. How can a dog live if he's forbidden to bark?" So the three of them continued to wander through the mountains for a little while longer. Then they decided to send the cow to reconnoiter. "Since you don't bark," said the dog and the ass to the cow, "it won't bother you that they don't allow barking." So off the cow went. Some time passed, and the cow returned, obviously in great distress. "It's impossible," she said, "simply impossible, I tell you! As soon as I arrived in town people started attacking me. They grabbed me by my nipples and started sucking and tugging! I kept bolting away, and they almost tore my nipples off! I just barely escaped!" So they continued to live in the mountains. Finally they decided to try one last time, and the ass agreed to go down to the village. A short time passed, and the ass came running back as fast as his legs would carry him. "It's impossible, absolutely impossible to live in town!" he cried. "Why?" the others asked. "What happened?" "Well," said the ass, "as soon as I arrived in town they tried to put me up for office. They were having their elections, and they wanted to elect me to parliament. I barely got away!"

Tito looked at Djilas sternly and said, "Are you trying to tell us by your fable that we elect asses to parliament?" But Tito was just joking. He laughed, Djilas laughed, and we all laughed.

Later I told Stalin about the friendly, casual atmosphere which had prevailed during the Yugoslavs' visit. Stalin was very pleased that we had been able to play host to Tito and that the Yugoslavs had enjoyed their stopover in the Ukraine. At that time Stalin wanted us to have, and was sure we *would* have, the best, most fraternal relations with Yugoslavia.

Some time later, our ambassador in Belgrade, an academician and philosopher named Yudin [P. F. Yudin, later Ambassador to Peking], informed Stalin that at some Party meeting the Yugoslavs had started making all sorts of sarcastic, disrespectful, and even insulting remarks about the Soviet Union and particularly about our military and technical advisors who had been sent there at Tito's request to help with the reconstruction of the country. Yudin described this meeting in detail, and Stalin sent copies of his report to members of the Politbureau. I received it in Kiev.

Then the official Yugoslav leadership started finding fault and trying to pick a fight with us. Many Yugoslavs who were our friends and who didn't agree with this new anti-Soviet line taken by their government were put in prison. Some of them even paid with their lives. They were punished not because they were our friends, but because they were against the leadership of the Yugoslav Communist Party and the Yugoslav government. This situation came to a head when the Soviet Union recalled all of its advisors who had been helping Yugoslavia reorganize its industry, science, economy, and army.[1]

After Stalin died, we began to exchange opinions in our leadership about the possibility of reestablishing contact with the Yugoslavs and liquidating the hostility which had been created by Stalin between the Soviet Union and Yugoslavia. This idea ran into sharp opposition from the outset. How could we restore relations with the Yugoslavs, "people argued," when they had already slipped back into capitalism? Their economy had been swallowed up by American monopolistic capital; private property had been reinstated; private banks had been set up. Mikhail Suslov was particularly adamant in resisting the idea of trying to relieve the tension between us and the Yugoslavs. He insisted that Yugoslavia was no longer a Socialist country.

I think the reason for all these ridiculous claims was that we had been so estranged from the Yugoslavs and we had thought up so many accusations against them that we'd started to believe what we'd been telling ourselves. It's like in that old story about the mullah [a Muhammadan religious teacher] who is walking through the village square telling people that back where he's just come from they're giving away free lamb and rice. Word quickly spreads through the town, and everyone starts running in the direction where he pointed. When

1. It is not clear why at this stage Khrushchev suggests that the Yugoslavs were to blame for the quarrel. In his Secret Speech he categorically blamed Stalin, who is reported as saying: "I will shake my little finger — and there will be no more Tito. He will fall." Khrushchev commented: "It was a shameful role that Stalin played here." Edvard Kardelj and Milovan Djilas were both close colleagues of Marshal Tito's. Kardelj, who was his Prime Minister, is still an elder statesman. Djilas, a passionate and intelligent Montenegrin, was to fall from grace and be twice imprisoned by his old master for turning against the Communist bureaucracy and in his *The New Class* attacking the very foundations of the Communist system. His *Conversations with Stalin* caused, if possible, even more offense. It is evident that the seeds of his disillusionment with Stalin in particular and Communism in general were sown on this visit.

the mullah sees everyone running, he stops somebody and asks, "What's happening?" "They're giving away free lamb and rice over there!" So the mullah hikes up his skirts and runs along with the crowd to get free food, even though he made the whole story up himself. It was just the same with Yugoslavia. We'd made up a story about all the terrible things the Yugoslavs were doing, and we'd heard the story so often that we started to believe it ourselves.

In trying to deal with the stubbornness of some people who refused to budge from their old position, which had been formed during Stalin's time, we obviously had to counter their arguments with arguments of our own. We weren't going to get anywhere simply by denying that Yugoslavia was a capitalist state. We had to prove it. So I suggested, "Why don't we study the problem objectively? We can set up a commission of economists and other specialists who will analyze all the pertinent factors and decide what sort of economy and social-political structure Yugoslavia really has. We'll study all the evidence very carefully, point by point."

Shepilov and some other comrades were appointed to this commission, and after a thorough investigation they presented us with a report, which can be found in the Central Committee archives. Their conclusion was that there was no reason for considering Yugoslavia a capitalist state. Granted, the peasantry lived in conditions of private ownership and had personal use of their land, but there were still collective and state farms. Banks, commerce, and the means of production were all in the hands of the state, and the power of the state was in the hands of the people; the state relied on the dictatorship of the working class. Therefore Yugoslavia qualified as a Socialist state. I had never had any doubts about this myself, but it took an authoritative commission to prove it to others.

Once Yugoslavia's good standing in the Socialist community had been established, the basis for the conflict which had been created by Stalin was no longer valid, and the arguments against reconciliation collapsed like a house of cards. We decided to reestablish contacts and restore good relations between our Parties. But since other Parties, particularly those of the Socialist countries, had been implicated in our own conflict with Yugoslavia, we had to get their agreement before we could approach Tito directly. We sent a letter to the Communist Parties of the Socialist states as well as to the English, French, Italian, and other Western Parties. They all gave us their approval.

When the question arose of how best to approach Tito, there were voices raised which said we should ask the Yugoslavs to come to us for negotiations. I said that this was out of the question. First, I doubted they would accept. It would have looked as though they had come begging, with their hats in their hands. Second, we had taken the initiative in breaking off relations with them; we had attacked them publicly before they attacked us. Therefore we should take the initiative in closing the rupture. Third, we were a big country, a big Party, with great authority and prestige in the world Communist arena. The Yugoslav leaders would have been running a big risk if they had met us on our territory and we hadn't been able to reach an agreement.

So we decided to send a delegation to Belgrade. I would lead the delegation, and it was to include Bulganin, Mikoyan, and Shepilov. At that time, our embassy in Yugoslavia was operating with only a skeleton staff. We addressed ourselves to the Yugoslav comrades with our proposal, and they agreed to receive our delegation and to exchange views. When we landed in Yugoslavia, we were met with all the courtesy due a visiting foreign delegation. However, there were no displays of brotherly feeling. Both the leadership and the people seemed restrained and cautious. I was offered the microphone to make a speech. My remarks had been drafted by the collective leadership. Therefore they weren't as much my own personal opinion as the opinion of the leadership of the Central Committee of the CPSU. After I finished speaking, Tito said, "Well, we don't need to have your speech translated because everyone here understands Russian," I think he was deliberately demonstrating the restraint which we sensed in the atmosphere. After all, I know Ukrainian, but I can't catch everything when an orator speaks Ukrainian rapidly, and Ukrainian is much closer to Russian than Russian is to Serbo-Croatian.

I must confess that I was somewhat disappointed by the cool reception we got at the airport because I knew it might encourage those in our own leadership who opposed the restoration of good relations.[2]

When discussions started, we took the initiative in suggesting that we bury our differences. I said I was absolutely sure we would be able to reach some sort of mutual understanding. I admit there were still

---

2. Khrushchev was more than disappointed by Tito's snub at the airport. He was visibly furious. It is worth noting that earlier Khrushchev accepts responsibility for his unfortunate speech. He put the blame on Beria because, he says, neither he nor his colleagues had yet quite taken in the wickedness of Stalin.

some flaws in our position. The Yugoslavs quite correctly blamed Stalin for the split between our Parties. They didn't hold it against us personally, but against Stalin. We, too, were proceeding from the assumption that Stalin had started the conflict, but we tried to avoid bringing up the subject of who was to blame when we actually set about normalizing our relations with Yugoslavia. We were only beginning to realize the extent of Stalin's abuses of power and the carnage he had caused when he cut down the flower of our Party. As I've said before [see pages 343–344], psychologically we were not prepared for our meeting with the Yugoslavs. We still hadn't freed ourselves from our slavish dependence on Stalin. However, the Yugoslavs agreed that we could come to some sort of understanding. They seemed receptive to our intentions.

The Yugoslav leaders organized a tour of the country for us. Once again, our reception in cities and towns was restrained. It was evident that the people lined up in the streets hadn't come out spontaneously to meet us. They were organized Party people. Not that they were hostile, but I wouldn't say they were very friendly, either. Mostly they chanted, "Long live Tito, Tito, Tito!" [3]

We were, however, glad to see during our trip around the country that the Yugoslav people treated with all due respect the memory of our soldiers who had given their lives in the liberation of Yugoslavia from Hitler.[4] The graves of our fallen warriors were in good condition, and marked with plaques giving their names.

The country, of course, was very poor. It had been a poor peasant country before the war, and the Hitlerite occupation had been long and hard. We saw that the farmers had only very primitive agricultural implements and were still largely without tractors. Their backwardness was very understandable. Yugoslavia was an isolated and ravaged country, even though the capitalists were pretending to help.[5]

I remember talking to Vukmanovic-Tempo. He impressed me very

3. Khrushchev is quite correct about the attitude of the Yugoslav people. They were politely hostile.
4. The Yugoslavs liberated themselves from the Germans, although their fate depended absolutely on Allied victory in other theaters. This was one reason for Tito's refusal to take orders from Stalin.
5. The capitalist West was for some time extremely reluctant to give aid to Tito, being skeptical about the seriousness of his quarrel with Stalin. In due course it helped a good deal, not to swallow up Yugoslavia, as Khrushchev says, but certainly to enable her to maintain her independent nationalist existence outside the Soviet bloc.

much with his sincerity, his genuineness, his human naturalness. I liked him even though he spoke out very strongly against us. I don't think he should have let himself get so carried away. He told us how he had gone to America to negotiate a credit loan. "We were facing the most severe hardships," he explained. "Our harvest had failed and we were threatened with famine. The tension between our country and the Soviet Union was at its height. The Americans knew how desperate we were and tried to take advantage of it. They tried to impose on us the most one-sided, shackling sort of conditions in exchange for their credit loan. They thought we had no choice but to accept. Their conditions were clearly of a political character, designed to throw Yugoslavia off its Socialist course and force us toward capitalism. I told them we'd rather die than face conditions like that. I walked out and slammed the door. I stayed around for a few days and gave the Americans a chance to reopen negotiations. They were compelled to give in a little because they were afraid of pushing us too far. They knew that if we went home angry they would have lost all hope of prying Yugoslavia away from the Socialist camp. Their prime goal was to prevent our reconciliation with the Soviet Union — or, as they said it, to protect us from having to capitulate to Stalin. They wanted to encourage a schism in the Socialist world and to fortify their own imperialistic camp."

I liked to see a man with such a flair for expressing class hatred, but I did resent it when Vukmanovic-Tempo had sharp words for me. I said at one meeting, "If ever again you want to aggravate tensions in your relations with some country, the man for the job is Comrade Tempo." Tito glanced at me, then burst out laughing. Later Vukmanovic-Tempo and I got along fine. I respected him very much. His fierce temper stemmed from his hatred for the enemies of the working class. That's why he permitted himself some intemperate language with us. After all, we had shown, to put it mildly, a certain lack of sympathy for Yugoslavia when it was facing the most arduous hardships.[6]

6. The negotiations were extremely tense and often on the point of being broken off. Khrushchev was determined to reestablish intimate relations between the Soviet and Yugoslav Communist Parties — in a word, to reincorporate Yugoslavia into the monolithic Communist bloc. Tito would have nothing to do with this. He wished to reestablish relations with the Soviet Union on a government level as between independent states. This is what happened. Vukmanovic-Tempo, for long head of the Yugoslav trade union organization, and an old partisan, was, and is, an exceptionally honest and forthright man. On the occasion of Khrushchev's visit he expressed in undiplomatic terms what others were thinking.

At the end of our first visit to Yugoslavia, we released a joint communiqué. This declaration was only a point of departure. Tito insisted on our commitment to the principles of complete noninterference in the internal affairs of other countries and other Parties and the right of every country to assert its own will without pressure from the outside. We agreed to this, believing sincerely as we did that relations must be built on mutual trust. The joint communiqué raised some questions that might better have been avoided, but most of the rough spots were smoothed over. This accord, of course, was only the beginning. After such a long period of hostility, there was more to restoring relations than just sitting down at a table and drinking a glass of wine together.

Once we arrived back in Moscow we reported on how our meetings with the Yugoslavs had gone. We said that Yugoslavia appeared to be a country firmly set on the course of Socialism; both the people and the Party seemed to be solidly committed to Marxism-Leninism. We decided in Moscow that in order to meet the Yugoslavs halfway and in order to lay the foundation for further economic cooperation with them, we would write off their large debt to us. Then the Yugoslavs asked us for credit. I forget how much, but it was a considerable sum. They wanted it in order to build a steel mill. We gave them the credit loan they asked for, on the condition that we could make the loan in the form of machinery to use in building and equipping the mill.

Tito has always been a good Communist and a man of principle, but before our relations with him began to improve, Yugoslavia had been trading mostly with American, British, and other Western companies in exchange for credit loans. The rumor had even been spread that Yugoslavia was forbidden by treaty to trade with the Soviet Union. In fact, this was a fabrication circulated by Yugoslavia's many ill-wishers in the USSR. Yugoslavia had no such treaty with the West. But at the same time, there's no question that the imperialists weren't giving the Yugoslavs gifts just because they liked their looks. It was very profitable for the capitalist countries then, and it's still profitable for them today, to use tempting trade agreements to try and coax the fraternal countries away from the Socialist camp one by one. In this connection I remember a conversation of a private but friendly nature that I once had with Comrade Gomulka. He had requested that we sell grain to Poland. I saw through to the real motive for his request and said to him very frankly, "Comrade Gomulka, I have a feeling that you'd like to buy grain from us for some reason other than to meet your own internal needs. Of all the Socialist countries, with the exception of the

Soviet Union of course, Poland has the best-developed agriculture. Surely you have enough grain to satisfy your own needs. Consequently, I think you must have something else in mind."

He looked at me intently for a moment; then, seeing that I understood him, he smiled: "Yes, Comrade Khrushchev, you're quite right. Of course we don't need grain as a food product. We need it as fodder. We want to buy grain from you so that we can feed the hogs on which our bacon industry depends." The Poles make excellent bacon, and it brings a very good price on the American market. When the Americans were blockading imports from the Soviet Union and other Socialist countries, they made sure there was a loophole for Polish bacon.

Similarly, the West was always making special deals with Yugoslavia. There was naturally a lot of resentment in the Soviet Union against Yugoslavia because of the amount of trade it did with the West. This resentment was based more on jealousy than ideology. It would have been profitable for us to have bought machine equipment from the United States, but the Americans wouldn't sell to us. All right, so the Americans did sell to the Yugoslavs, but I don't see why we should have taken out our anger at the Americans on the Yugoslavs, who were simply taking advantage of an opportunity we would have loved to have had ourselves. Therefore I didn't see any reason for irritation with Yugoslavia.

Yugoslavia always took a special, independent position in its foreign policy, especially when it came to coping with the antagonistic forces of the imperialist countries. Yugoslavia always took care not to affiliate itself with one bloc or the other. This policy of theirs was not always compatible with our own foreign policy, and there was sometimes friction between us. The Yugoslavs refused to join the Warsaw Pact because they had a special commercial relationship with the West. That refusal left an unextinguished spark between us even after our relations began to improve in 1955. Of course, another reason the Yugoslavs refused to sign the Warsaw treaty was that they had a border dispute with Bulgaria.

Our relations became strained again after the events of 1956 in Hungary, and we abandoned some of the measures which we had taken to improve relations with Yugoslavia. For example, we suspended our agreement on credit loans. But we had no reason to let another rupture develop with the Yugoslavs, so Tito and I smoothed this conflict over at a special meeting in Bucharest.

In this connection, consider Yugoslavia's position at the two impor-

tant Party Conferences which were held in 1957 and 1960. The Yugoslav delegation attended the conferences in little more than an observer's capacity. They may have taken some part in the discussions, but
they didn't sign the conference resolutions. I won't deny that their position irritated me very much at the time.[7] I couldn't understand why
they were behaving like that, but there was nothing we could do about
it. Apparently the Yugoslav comrades didn't want to take on any of the
mutual obligations which signing the resolutions would have meant. I
think their refusal to commit themselves was a mistake, but now at
least I can understand their reasons. As Tito said during a conversation with me, "Surely you'll agree that if we want to remain unaligned
to any one bloc, we can't sign the conference resolution." The Yugoslavs wanted to be able to speak for the newly emerging countries, the
countries which were just liberating themselves from colonialism, and
which found themselves somewhere in between the Socialist and capitalist worlds. The Yugoslavs were, and still are, perfectly entitled to
take this position and we should be able to preserve our own relations
with them despite their refusal to join forces with us more closely.
Nonetheless, the Yugoslav Communist Party's policy of aloofness has
been something of a stumbling block over the years.

After our trip to Yugoslavia in 1955, we invited a Yugoslav delegation led by Comrade Tito to visit the Soviet Union. He made more
than one such trip and became well acquainted with our country.
Once we invited him to the Crimea for a few days of rest and for a
hunting trip. The hunt, of course, has been used for centuries as an opportunity for leaders of two or three different countries to get together
and discuss issues of mutual interest and importance. The atmosphere
of my discussions with Tito during our hunt together was warm and
friendly.

The Yugoslavs invited us to make a return visit to their country. I
went a number of times. These trips gave me a chance to see at first
hand many of the new and rather unusual things Yugoslavia was doing
with its economy.

As the whole world knows, Yugoslavia claims to have discovered
new administrative methods and economic procedures to facilitate the
transition from capitalism to Socialism. Their claim is that these new

7. Irritation is a mild word for Khrushchev's feelings toward Tito for his refusal
to participate actively in the two big Moscow conferences of all the Communist
parties in 1957 and 1960. He raged. And heavy pressure was put on the Yugoslavs
in consequence.

organizational forms are more democratic because they permit more participation by workers, office personnel, and scientists in the management of the people's economy. At first, we came out against these supposed reforms. However, I was interested to see them in operation when I visisted factories in Yugoslavia. I wanted to ascertain to what extent these new procedures might be applicable to our own conditions in the Soviet Union.

I remember once the Yugoslav comrades took me to see a tractor factory on the outskirts of Belgrade. Engineers, directors, supervisors, trade-union representatives, and Party organizers all tried to explain to me how their output plan was determined by democratic methods. I never could really make sense out of what they were trying to tell me about their new conception of property and ownership. All their talk about participation in ownership seemed like so much window dressing to me. No matter what they said, it still looked to me as though the government prescribed their output plan and tightly controlled how it was put into effect. I expressed my doubts to the Yugoslav comrades very candidly, and they seemed to be half in agreement with me. But they still tried to convince me that their system was somehow different from what we had in the Soviet Union, and that theirs was more democratic and more conducive to the participation of the people in the establishment of production goals.[8]

Despite my doubts, their reasoning unquestionably deserved a certain amount of attention. During the period that I have lived, worked, and been in the leadership of the government, our economy has always had centralized management. I think that for my time, centralization was the best and most efficient system. But recently I have begun to feel that while centralized management is still necessary, it's no less important for the workers in a given enterprise to have more say than they did before in determining their quotas and conditions. While output plans will always have to be worked out at the top and supervised from above, I think in the future there will certainly have to be more active participation by the workers themselves in the establishment of plans and quotas and the determination of how these plans shall be carried out. In other words, I think there was at least a grain of sense, at least the beginnings of a useful contribution to the management of

8. Here Khrushchev is referring specifically to the workers' councils set up in Yugoslavia in an attempt to achieve a new sort of socialism, free of centralized planning, by making factories, banks, enterprises, and institutions of all kinds self-governing. On his first visit to Yugoslavia Khrushchev poured scorn on this idea.

our economy in the new organizational forms introduced by the Yugo-slavs, and there's no point in denying this.

The Yugoslavs claimed that they were creating better economic con-ditions for meeting consumer demands, but they had their share of problems, too. During one of my visits Tito confessed to me, "We're trying to cope with some unfortunate developments here. I think some of our people who administer the state enterprises have foreign cur-rency accounts in capitalist banks abroad. In other words they're em-bezzling from us." Well, in my opinion, this sort of abuse was a natural and inevitable result of Tito's economic policies. Perhaps by now the Yugoslavs have either liquidated the problem or devised some sort of control for it.

Abuses and blunders will always occur when a society experiments with a new system, and it's hardly surprising that not all aspects of the Yugoslav experiment have proved successful. But by the same token, not all aspects of the Yugoslav experiment can be rejected out of hand, either. We should examine the situation dispassionately and decide what features of the Yugoslav system might profitably be adapted to the economic organization of other Socialist countries. I admit that our own examination of these issues wasn't always calm and objective. Sometimes there were mutual recriminations and reproaches, with both sides claiming to have found the one and only truth. I never felt that either side was completely right. It's always a mistake to pretend to have an exclusive claim on truth. To insist stubbornly that yours is the only way of doing something is wrong, and it's stupid.

One area in which the Yugoslavs seemed to be on the right track was agriculture. I once had a very interesting conversation with Tito on this subject. "When our relations with the Soviet Union were sev-ered," he said, "we wanted to make very sure that we weren't consid-ered renegades from Socialism, so we took administrative measures to see collectivization through to the end. In strictly quantitative terms, we may have done all right with collectivization, but we had great dif-ficulty producing sufficient harvests to meet the demands of the urban population and the working class. Nevertheless, only after we had fol-lowed through on collectivization did we begin to make the transition from collective farms to state farms." He cited a large figure represent-ing the percentage of land on which state agricultural enterprises had been set up for wheat growing, truck farming, dairying, and poultry and cattle raising. The state was buying up farms from the peasants and turning this land into state farms very much along the lines of our own Soviet state farms.

Far from contradicting our conception about how to build Socialism, Comrade Tito's policy of cooperative state agriculture deserved our careful attention. Lenin himself used to say that peasant cooperatives and state farms represented the most advanced stage in the development of agriculture. I think the Yugoslavs took the right step when they began to replace collective farms with state farms.[9]

We ourselves tried to make sweeping improvements in our agricultural system when we tried to resettle collective farmers on the Virgin Lands. You can imagine the difficulties that the Virgin Lands campaign posed for a family which had to be picked up and moved from the home where it had lived for generations. It was a great hardship for them, but we had to resettle many such families — Ukrainians, Belorussians, and Russians—thousands of kilometers from the graves of their ancestors. Enormous material expenditures went into the resettlement campaign. Among other things, we had to give credit loans and financial aid to the youths who went out to build settlements in the Virgin Lands. We became convinced that we shouldn't set up collective farms out there; a collective farm is an artificial organization; that is, it's not a real community, and it would have been too expensive to resettle people on collective farms. Therefore we decided on the alternative of state farms. While I was in the leadership, our cheapest bread was grown by state farms on the Virgin Lands.[10]

I was glad to see that Tito, while he saw the benefits of cooperative farming over collectivization, also came to understand the importance

9. Before the quarrel with the Soviet Union in 1948, and for some time afterward, the Yugoslav economy, industry, and agriculture were run most rigidly on Soviet lines. In industry, central control gave way to "self-management"; in agriculture, the collective farms were abolished in the teeth of peasant hostility, in favor of peasant cooperatives which small-holding peasants were urged to join. Most did. State farms, always dear to Khrushchev (very large farms owned by the state, managed by paid officials, and worked by wage-earning workers) are not in fact widespread in Yugoslavia and were chiefly set up for special purposes, for example, stockbreeding. Collective farms are theoretically owned by the peasants of a village, or group of small villages, and worked by them for communal profit.

10. The Virgin Lands campaign to which Khrushchev here refers was a gargantuan operation designed to open up a vast tract of steppe land, mainly in Kazakhstan, for grain. The area initially plowed up in 1954 was no less than ninety million acres — more than the whole cultivated area of England, France, and Spain combined. Half a million "volunteers" were moved from European Russia into the empty steppe, where they lived in primitive conditions, organized into huge state farms. After an initial (but costly) success, the experiment had to be heavily curtailed: as many had predicted, the land was rapidly being turned into a dust bowl.

of central planning. Central planning, the function which the State Planning Commission fulfills in the Soviet Union, is essential to the management of a Socialist economy. Without central planning, the rule of the marketplace—supply and demand, which are the elements of a capitalist state — will undermine and soon replace true Socialist relationships between individuals and enterprises. It was gratifying to me when the Yugoslav state, under the leadership of Comrade Tito, realized that central planning is crucial to maintaining a true Socialist economy.

During my visits to Yugoslavia and my conversations with Tito, I developed great respect and trust for his abilities as an imaginative and enterprising leader. Once, when I went out into the country with him, I saw that conditions were much improved from what they had been when our delegation first traveled there in 1955. The people were much better off. Factories were going up all over the place. I remember visiting the construction site of a plastic fiber plant which was equipped with machinery purchased from the United States. It was very interesting equipment, and the plant promised to be a great boon for the people of Yugoslavia when it was finished.

Comrade Tito once told me that in the year 1963 Yugoslavia received a revenue of something like $70 million from tourists. This amount would have been negligible for countries like Italy, Switzerland, Sweden, and other Western countries; but for any Socialist country, including the Soviet Union, it was an impressive sum. Tito told me the Yugoslavs were building hotels and new roads in order to attract more tourists. Tourism yields foreign currency, which is necessary for foreign trade. I would even say that we, the Soviet Union, were somewhat envious at Yugoslavia's success in attracting tourism.

I started asking around to find out how the Yugoslavs managed to build up such a flourishing tourist trade. They said that good roads were the most important thing, followed by decent hotels and restaurants. They explained that in order to guarantee good service for tourists in Yugoslav hotels, they sent their people to capitalist countries to study how to receive visitors, how to prepare food, and how to manage a hotel properly. I visited some of their tourist hotels; they were sparkling clean and modern; the service was excellent.

Of course Yugoslavia has a big natural advantage. It's one of the most beautiful of all the European Socialist countries. Before visiting Yugoslavia, I thought that our own Crimea and our Caucasian coast

Mme. Khrushcheva and Janos Kadar of Hungary

Mmes. Khrushcheva and Tito in Yugoslavia (1963?)

were the scenic masterpieces of the world, and they certainly are breathtaking. But when I saw Dubrovnik and other spots in Yugoslavia, I was humbled. I realized that we weren't the only Socialist country who could claim such natural charms. Perhaps Yugoslavia's climate, coastal landscape, and wealth of historical monuments even surpass the beauties of our own country.

Tourists, of course, sometimes cause problems, and I once asked Comrade Tito, "Tell me, how do you check all the Western tourists who enter Yugoslavia by car?" In the USSR we have a huge bureaucratic apparatus that puts many roadblocks in a tourist's way.

He laughed and said, "You know, we've solved the problem very simply. There are all kinds of ways that undesirable tourists, spies, and so forth, can get into our country. Border checks are no guarantee against them, and there are other ways of waging the struggle against infiltration. Therefore border guards in our country subject tourists to a minimum of formal checks. The whole routine takes a matter of minutes, both on entering and leaving the country. There's usually no identity check at all. A man simply says where he's going, the barrier is raised, and he drives through. This goes for people coming into Yugoslavia from other countries, and it's just as free for citizens of Yugoslavia going abroad. For instance, we have many miners who leave Yugslavia to work for a while in West Germany. They simply tell the border guard, 'I'm leaving to earn enough money to buy a car,' and they're let right through."

I was intrigued by this whole approach to the problem of border control. When I returned to our Homeland, I reported this practice to our comrades who were in charge of tourism and told them to think about it. We also began a large program to build hotels and to take advantage of our own tourist attractions.

During another conversation with Comrade Tito, I asked him, "Would you permit us to send our people here so that they could learn from your great experience how to handle a large tourist trade?"

"By all means," said Tito. "We'll be happy to show you and tell you anything that's of interest to you. Of course, the average tourist who comes here isn't rich; he's not a big capitalist. He's probably a working man, from West Germany or Italy. He has a middle-range income and drives his own car. Our tourists don't bring huge amounts of capital with them to spend right and left, but they patronize our services and pay with foreign currency."

I also asked Comrade Tito if they had much of a problem with fashion-conscious young men and women chasing after tourists, trying to buy all sorts of trinkets off them, especially around the hotels. "In our country," I said, "we are ashamed to see our own people buying and bartering and begging from foreigners. How do you deal with this problem?"

"We don't really have that problem here," said Tito, "and I'll tell you why. When some item becomes fashionable among our young people, we buy the necessary equipment for a factory and start manufacturing the item ourselves. Of course consumer tastes are always changing, but all you have to do is use your head and make sure your industries keep up with fashions and adapt to changing consumer demands."

I proposed to my comrades that we follow Tito's example and thereby put an end to the disgrace of our young people running around after tourists.

I don't know how many of my suggestions were ever actually put in practice, but I think we did send some of our people to study the tourist trade in Yugoslavia. I see from the press that there are a great many hotels going up around the Soviet Union.

My experience with Comrade Tito showed me that there are different ways of going about the building of Socialism. There's no single model or mold which fits all the countries of the world. To think that there is is just plain stupid. Every Party knows how best to assure unity in its own ranks. More patience should be shown to Parties that are experimenting with slightly different approaches to the basic problems of the people. Every working class should be able to choose its own course of development on the basis of local historical and economic circumstances — on the one vital condition, of course, that the means of production and the banks belong to the people, and that the state is run by the dictatorship of the proletariat.

In the interaction and interrelationship of different Parties and states, we should be tolerant of others and avoid faultfinding, especially in public. Unfortunately, however, there are times when it's impossible to restrain ourselves, but I won't cite examples. All right-thinking people know very well whom I'm talking about.

13

The Geneva Summit

At Belgrade, Khrushchev found himself for the first time meeting a foreign head of state and subjected to the scrutiny of foreign diplomats and foreign journalists away from his own base. At Geneva a month or two later he had his first meeting with the leaders of the imperialist powers — President Eisenhower and Messrs. Eden and Faure, to say nothing of Mr. John Foster Dulles. It was clearly an ordeal. It was also a climacteric. The peasant from Kalinovka, the Party chieftain who had worked his way up in Stalin's shadow, was meeting as an equal the elected heads of the Western world with their backgrounds of West Point, Eton and Oxford, the Lycée and the Sorbonne. Khrushchev and Bulganin were still dressed as they had dressed for Yugoslavia — in their baggy pale-mauve summer suits with flapping trousers; and Bulganin wore his light-beige summer overcoat coming down to the ground, which made him look like a pre-1914 motorist (it was after Geneva that the Soviet leadership took an interest in good tailoring). Khrushchev gives a fairly vivid idea of the strain, the strangeness, and the deep inferiority complex from which he, not unnaturally, suffered. His feelings of embarrassment about the two-engined Ilyushin in which they arrived from Moscow are very revealing.

RIGHT up until his death Stalin used to tell us, "You'll see, when I'm gone the imperialistic powers will wring your necks like chickens." We never tried to reassure him that we would be able to manage. We knew it wouldn't do any good. Besides, we had doubts of our own about Stalin's foreign policy. He overemphasized the importance of military might, for one thing, and consequently put too much faith in our armed forces. He lived in terror of an enemy attack. For him foreign policy meant keeping the antiaircraft units around Moscow on a twenty-four-hour alert.

After Stalin died it was an interesting challenge for us to try to deal with the foreign powers by ourselves. In 1955 we went abroad a number of times to meet with the representatives of the bourgeois states and to feel them out on various issues. Our trip to Geneva that year gave the bourgeois heads of state a chance to look us over. The Geneva meeting was a crucial test for us: Would we be able to represent our country competently? Would we approach the meeting soberly, without unrealistic hopes, and would we be able to keep the other side from intimidating us? All things considered, I would say we passed the test.

A word about the background of the Geneva meetings:

Ever since Churchill gave his speech in Fulton calling for the capitalist countries of the world to encircle the Soviet Union, our relations with the West had been strained.[1] I think it was actually Churchill's idea for the Western powers to open lines of communication with the new Soviet Government after Stalin's death and to do so quickly. Churchill believed that the West could take advantage of the fact that the new Soviet Government wasn't yet fully formed and would therefore be more vulnerable to pressure. The Western press was suddenly filled with articles urging a meeting of the four great powers. We, too, were in favor of such a meeting. It was our feeling in the Soviet leadership that after such a bloody war, we and the West could come to terms and agree among ourselves on rational principles of peaceful coexistence and noninterference in the internal affairs of other states.

Through diplomatic channels a place for the meeting, Geneva, and a date in the summer of 1955 were set. By that time Bulganin was already Chairman of the Council of Ministers. I think that one reason we were able to agree to the Geneva meeting at all was that Malenkov had by then been released from his duties as Chairman. As anyone who knew Malenkov will tell you, after Stalin's death he was completely without initiative and completely unpredictable. He was unstable to the point of being dangerous because he was so susceptible to the pressure and influence of others. It was no accident that he had

1. It is interesting to find Khrushchev using the term "encirclement" here. What he is referring to is the American policy of containment inaugurated after the sovietization of a great part of Central and Eastern Europe. From the Soviet side of the hill, defensive containment no doubt looked like potentially offensive encirclement.

fallen into Beria's clutches. Beria may have been no smarter than Malenkov, but he was much more shrewd and strong-willed.

As Prime Minister, Bulganin was to head our delegation to Geneva
even though he wasn't very well versed in foreign policy nor very
adept at diplomatic negotiations. Since the foreign ministers of the
other three governments — the United States, England, and France —
would be accompanying their premiers, the Presidium of the Central
Committee decided to send our Minister of Foreign Affairs, Molotov. It
was then suggested that I should be included in the delegation. I
warned that my presence might be difficult for the other delegations to
understand since I didn't hold any ministerial post; I only represented
the Party [as First Secretary]. Molotov replied, "It's our own business
whom we decide to include. And besides, you're also a member of the
Presidium of the Supreme Soviet, which is the highest governing body
of the Soviet Union. I think you should come."

I'm still not sure whether or not it was proper for me to attend the
Geneva meeting; but it's too late to worry about that now, and I won't
deny that I was very anxious to have a chance to meet the representatives of the USA, England, and France and to join in the solution of international problems.

The basis of Soviet foreign policy at that time was peaceful coexistence. The Western leaders, however, had other things on their minds.
They wanted to reach an agreement with us about the political situation in the Near East, but they wanted to do so on their own terms.
They had no desire to consider the interests or wishes of the Soviet
Union and the other Socialist countries. It was also their goal, of
course, to restore capitalism in the countries which had been liberated
by the Soviet Army after World War II, and they particularly wanted
to tear Poland away from the Socialist bloc. But we knew that the number one goal which the English, American, and French would be
pursuing in Geneva would be what they called "the reunification of
Germany," which really meant the expulsion of Socialist forces from
the German Democratic Republic: in other words, the liquidation of
Socialism in the German Democratic Republic and the creation of a
single capitalist Germany which would, no doubt, be a member of
NATO. As for our own position on this issue, we wanted simply to sign
a peace treaty that would recognize the existence of two German
states and would guarantee that each state be allowed to develop as its
own people saw fit.

I felt at the time of the Geneva meeting that the main thing was to preserve peace, but the Western powers were still reluctant to take even the basic measures necessary for laying the foundations of a secure peace. Therefore the Geneva meeting was probably doomed to failure before it even began. But it was still useful in a number of important respects. For one thing, it gave the leaders of the four great powers an opportunity to see each other at close quarters and to exchange views informally among themselves, usually over dinner after the official sessions.

Unfortunately, our own delegation found itself at a disadvantage from the very moment we landed at the Geneva airport. The leaders of the other three delegations arrived in four-engine planes, and we arrived in a modest two-engine Ilyushin [Il-14]. Their planes were certainly more impressive than ours, and the comparison was somewhat embarrassing.

There was a ceremony in honor of the four delegations at the airport, a military parade followed by an invitation for the head of each delegation to review the troops. An unpleasant incident occurred during this ceremony. Bulganin, as the head of our delegation, was supposed to step forward after the parade and inspect the honor guard.[2] Just before he did so, a Swiss protocol officer suddenly stepped right in front of me and stood with his back up against my nose. My first impulse was to shove him out of the way. Later I realized he had done this on the instructions of the Swiss government. He had been told to make sure that I couldn't step forward with Bulganin to review the troops. I wasn't permitted to join in that part of the ceremony, so the Swiss government very rudely had that man stand in front of me!

As we drove off to our residences, I noticed that Eisenhower's bodyguards had to run along behind his car. This struck us as being extremely odd. For a man to keep up with a moving car is no mean trick, nor is it easy for a car to pace itself to a man on foot. Four years later I saw the same thing again when Eisenhower met me at the airport in Washington at the beginning of my visit to America. Once again, there were those hearty fellows from his personal bodyguard running along behind the car in which he drove me back into the city.

The Geneva meeting was not the first time I met Eisenhower. I'd

2. Khrushchev still likes to pretend that he was not in charge of the Soviet delegation. Indeed, he went through the motions of deferring to Bulganin. But his commanding position was clear for all to see.

At the Geneva summit meeting, 1955. Left to right: Molotov, Bulganin, Khrushchev, Zhukov, Faure, Macmillan, Eden, and Dulles

Khrushchev and Bulganin in India with Nehru and other Indian leaders, 1955

met him at the end of the war when he came to Moscow and was on the reviewing stand of the Lenin Mausoleum to view the Victory Parade on June 24, 1945. But that had been earlier in our careers, when Eisenhower was a general and I was head of the Ukrainian Party and State. Now, in Geneva ten years later, we met again as representatives of our respective countries. Before we had stood side by side on a reviewing stand together; now we were to sit on opposite sides of the negotiating table from each other.

If I had to compare the two American presidents with whom I dealt — Eisenhower and Kennedy — the comparison would not be in favor of Eisenhower. Our people whose job it was to study Eisenhower closely have told me that they considered him a mediocre military leader and a weak President. He was a good man, but he wasn't very tough. There was something soft about his character. As I discovered in Geneva, he was much too dependent on his advisors. It was always obvious to me that being President of the United States was a great burden for him.

Our conversations with the American delegation were generally constructive and useful for both parties, although neither side changed its position substantially on any of the issues facing us. The United States in those days refused to make even the most reasonable concessions because John Foster Dulles was still alive. It was he who determined the foreign policy of the United States, not President Eisenhower. To illustrate that statement, I can describe something I observed at a plenary session in Geneva. The heads of all four delegations took turns chairing the plenary sessions, and when Eisenhower's turn came, there was Dulles at his right. I was on Bulganin's left, which put me right next to Dulles, or maybe there was an interpreter between us. In any case I watched Dulles making notes with a pencil, tearing them out of a pad, folding them up, and sliding them under President Eisenhower's hand. Eisenhower would then pick up these sheets of paper, unfold them, and read them before making a decision on any matter that came up. He followed this routine conscientiously, like a dutiful schoolboy taking his lead from his teacher. It was difficult for us to imagine how a chief of state could allow himself to lose face like that in front of delegations from other countries. It certainly appeared that Eisenhower was letting Dulles do his thinking for him.

A word about Dulles. A few years later, when I led the Soviet delegation to the United Nations General Assembly in New York, Mr. Nehru asked me about Dulles. Nehru, by the way, was a most attractive person. He was always smiling and had such a gentle expression on his face. "Tell me, Mr. Khrushchev," he said, "how did you get along with Mr. Dulles in your negotiations in Geneva?" His question didn't surprise me; Nehru knew that Dulles's policies and our own were unalterably opposed. I answered that I had had a chance to talk with Dulles informally over dinner in Geneva and had found him to be a very dry character; we hadn't talked about anything much except what dishes we liked most.

Dulles often said that the goal of the United States was to push Socialism in Europe back to the borders of the Soviet Union, and he seemed to be obsessed with the idea of encirclement. He extended America's economic embargo of the Soviet Union to include a boycott on cultural exchange. Not even Soviet tourists and chess players were permitted to visit the United States. I remember, too, that when the US sponsored some sort of international convention of chefs, our own delegation wasn't allowed to attend.

However, I'll say this for him: Dulles knew how far he could push us, and he never pushed us too far. For instance, when the forces of our two countries confronted each other in the Near East during the events in Syria and Lebanon in 1958, Dulles stepped back from the brink of war. The reactionary forces of the United States and England pulled back their troops, partly under the pressure of world opinion but also partly as a result of Dulles's prudence. The prestige of the Soviet Union was enhanced in all the progressive countries of the world.

When Dulles died, I told my friends that although he had been a man who lived and breathed hatred of Communism and who despised progress, he had never stepped over that brink which he was always talking about in his speeches; and for that reason alone we should lament his passing.

Because Eisenhower brought his Secretary of Defense [Charles E. Wilson] with him to Geneva in 1955, we made a point of including our own Minister of Defense, Marshal Zhukov, in our delegation. Zhukov had been a friend of Eisenhower's during the war, and we thought their acquaintance might serve as the basis for conversations that would lead to an easing of the tension between our countries. We hoped that Eisenhower and Zhukov might have a chance to talk alone together and that they would exchange views about the need for peaceful coexistence. But that vicious cur Dulles was always prowling around Eisenhower, snapping at him if he got out of line. Dulles could not tolerate the idea of peaceful coexistence with the Soviet Union. Eisenhower, however, did give Zhukov a spinning reel and sent personal greetings to Zhukov's wife and daughter; but other than such pleasantries, nothing came of Zhukov's conversations with Eisenhower.

After the Geneva meetings got under way, Eisenhower suggested that after each plenary session we meet for refreshments so that we might end the day on a pleasant note. His idea was that if there had been any hard feelings or tensions aroused during the day's session, we could wash them away with martinis. I remember at one of these informal gatherings Eisenhower introduced me to [Nelson] Rockefeller, who was accompanying the American delegation as an advisor of some sort. There was nothing special about him as far as I could tell. He was dressed fairly democratically and was the sort of man who didn't make much of an impression one way or the other.[3] When I met him, I said, "So this is Mr. Rockefeller himself!" and I playfully poked him in the ribs with my fists. He took this as a joke and did the same thing to me.

We were interested in talking to Rockefeller about the possibility of getting credit from the United States, something on the order of six billion dollars. But the Americans were already pressing us to repay them the money we owed them from the Lend-Lease. We told them we were willing to pay them a certain amount, but not all, of what we owed from the Lend-Lease if they would give us six billion dollars' credit. We had some discussions about this, but nothing ever came of it.

Our best relations in Geneva were with the French. Edgar Faure, whom we nicknamed "Edgar Fyodorovich," was a very prepossessing man who went out of his way to be friendly and hospitable toward us. However, in those days there was a rapid turnover in the French government, and therefore there was no point in paying serious attention to the French delegation to the Geneva meetings.[4]

Our relations with the British delegation weren't quite as friendly as with the French, but the atmosphere of our conversations with Eden was certainly warm. Naturally he was following the same general line as the Americans, but he seemed to be more flexible and receptive to reasonable arguments. During dinner one evening Eden asked us, "What would you say if you were invited to make an official visit to Great Britain? Don't you think such a trip would be useful for both of

3. The remark about Nelson Rockefeller being dressed "fairly democratically" is a gem and throws a great deal of light on the Soviet image of the West.

4. Khrushchev's dismissal of the need to take M. Faure seriously, although he liked him, because French ministries kept on changing, is an interesting commentary on the limitations of Soviet governmental thinking.

our governments?" We said that it would indeed be useful and we would accept such an invitation with pleasure. We almost agreed then and there. The British were to issue us a formal invitation, and we would accept.

At the end of the Geneva meeting we prepared a joint statement setting forth the position of the four delegations. This statement was formulated in such a way as to leave each delegation with the possibility of interpreting it in its own way. The wording was the result of various compromises which allowed all of us to sign. We didn't want to disperse without having anything to show for the meeting. On the other hand none of us wanted any point in the statement to be interpreted as a concession in principle or policy to the other side.

We stopped off in West Berlin on the way back to our Homeland, and there we joined the leaders of the German Democratic Republic and issued another joint statement. We were greeted with full honors in Berlin. Huge crowds of people came out to cheer us. I had been to Germany before, but this was the first time I had been there in an official capacity. I expected there to be some displays of hostility toward us, but there were none. There were a few sour faces, but not many. On the main we were welcomed enthusiastically. Our warm reception in Berlin reinforced our conviction that the Germans were fed up with making war, and that now they wanted to build strong, friendly relations with us.

We returned to Moscow from Geneva knowing that we hadn't achieved any concrete results. But we were encouraged, realizing now that our enemies probably feared us as much as we feared them. They rattled their sabers and tried to pressure us into agreements which were more profitable for them than for us because they were frightened of us. As a result of our own showing in Geneva, our enemies now realized that we were able to resist their pressure and see through their tricks. They now knew that they had to deal with us honestly and fairly, that they had to respect our borders and our rights, and that they couldn't get what they wanted by force or by blackmail. They realized that they would have to build their relations with us on new assumptions and new expectations if they really wanted peace. The Geneva meeting was an important breakthrough for us on the diplomatic front. We had established ourselves as able to hold our own in the international arena. Our success was confirmed by Eden's invitation for us to pay a state visit to Great Britain.

14

Visit to London

By the time he made his London visit with Bulganin in the spring of 1956, Khrushchev had already been to Peking in 1954, and in 1955 he had made his notorious tour of India as well as his pilgrimage to Belgrade and his journey to Geneva. He was becoming a seasoned traveler. He had the Twentieth Party Congress and the Secret Speech behind him, and even though Bulganin was Prime Minister, there was no question at all of who was in command — though it was not until the summer of 1957 that Khrushchev shattered the opposition, finally breaking Malenkov, Molotov, Kaganovich, and others. Khrushchev does not mention the fact that Malenkov, no longer Prime Minister but still a member of the Party Presidium, had made an earlier and very successful visit to England to prepare the way and take the country's temperature. The arrival of Khrushchev and Bulganin was somewhat marred by the fact that they had sent the notorious police chief General Serov to supervise the security aspects of the great visit. The British press was loud in protest, and Serov had to go back to the Soviet Union. Khrushchev was never able to understand why the British disapproved of Serov.

THE Labour government in England after the war had been fairly unfriendly toward the Soviet Union, and our efforts to develop good trade ties didn't get very far. Our relations with Great Britain were only slightly improved after Stalin's death, when the Labourites came to see us and opened discussion on various matters. Then the Conservatives replaced the Labourites, and Eden became Prime Minister.[1] We considered Eden relatively progressive for a Conservative, and we still remembered with appreciation that when he had been in the Foreign Office before the war he had favored a treaty uniting the forces of Great Britain and the Soviet Union against Hitlerite Germany. Eden had resigned when Chamberlain started his harshly anti-Soviet policies designed to incite Hitler against us.[2] Therefore Eden's return to power gave us hope that we would be able to improve relations with Great Britain.

After agreeing with Eden in Geneva on the desirability of a state visit to England, we arranged everything by an exchange of diplomatic notes, and our delegation was to leave for London in April, 1956. It must have been in the second half of April because I remember very well celebrating my birthday on the way to England, and my birthday is April 17.

Bulganin was still Chairman of the Council of Ministers and therefore formally head of our delegation.[3] I was included because I had developed the best working relationship with Eden in Geneva. He had talked more to me than to anybody else, and I had spoken for our delegation in answering his questions. We also took Academician Kurchatov with us to London because we wanted to establish contacts with the British scientific community.[4] Kurchatov is an attractive and witty man as well as a brilliant scientist.

We traveled to England on a battle cruiser. We wanted to come by ship so that we could then take the train to London. That way we would be able to see much more of the countryside. Before we left, the British Embassy in Moscow asked us if we could let one of their naval attachés accompany us on the trip. We consented. Of course there were some people who worried that the British attaché would be on the lookout for military secrets and technical specifications on board our cruiser. Such stupidity was a holdover from the Stalinist period. The English naval attaché turned out to be well-mannered and pleas-

1. Churchill was Prime Minister when the Conservatives returned to power. Eden succeeded him later.

2. Anthony Eden resigned as Foreign Secretary primarily because of Neville Chamberlain's attempted appeasement of Mussolini in an attempt to detach him from Germany. Chamberlain did nothing to "incite Hitler" against Russia: Hitler needed no inciting. Chamberlain's policy was to appease Hitler by allowing him to take part of Czechoslovakia. When that did not work, he did in fact make a half-hearted attempt to achieve an alliance of sorts with Russia.

3. As already observed, Khrushchev was in fact in command.

4. I. V. Kurchatov, the famous atomic physicist, who was father of the Russian A-bomb.

ant. On April 17, my birthday, we decided to invite him to dine with our delegation. Naturally there was some drinking, and the Englishman showed that he had a well-developed taste for spirits. In fact, he drank so much that he was barely able to get back to his cabin, much less go snooping around the ship looking for military secrets. Later I joked with Eden about this. He asked, "Well, Mr. Khrushchev, did our military attaché behave himself on board your ship?"

"He behaved himself very well indeed. He represented Great Britain very conscientiously."

"You mean he didn't spy on you? He didn't crawl around the whole ship, examining everything?"

"Oh, yes, he was simply impossible! He kept squeezing himself into corners that a bug couldn't have fitted into. He saw everything there was to see." Eden laughed. I don't know if he'd already been told how drunk this attaché had been. In any case, he was willing to joke with Bulganin and me about him.

When our ship came to port in England, we were met with full military honors and a regulation salute. We took the train up to London. We could see much more of the country than we'd been able to see of Switzerland. Not counting Geneva, I'd never been to the West before. My first and most lasting impression of England is the long stretches of the little red-brick houses. They stuck in my memory because they reminded me so much of houses I had seen during my boyhood in the Donbass. My father worked in a mine near the Yuzovka Metal Factory which once belonged to the Welshman John Hughes.[5] Hughes had built for his technicians and administrators little red-brick houses just like the ones I saw on my trip to England. I remember that during the summertime in the Donbass you could only see the windows of these houses because ivy covered all the rest.

Our hotel in England was excellent. The service was superb. All this was very new to us. We had never had much contact with foreigners before. I think we made quite an impression on the local population. I remember one day we were walking to our hotel from our cars, and Londoners immediately started crowding around us. They were particularly fascinated by Academician Kurchatov, who had a beard. Little boys pointed at him, laughed, and jumped up and down in excitement, as little boys do the world over.

After we were settled, we began discussions with the British govern-

5. Yuzovka — or Hughes-ovka — was named after John Hughes.

ment leaders. Their side was led by Eden and Lloyd. I think Macmillan also took part in these negotiations. Substantively our talks didn't add much to what had come out of our Geneva meeting. The main issues were still Germany, disarmament, and peaceful coexistence. We had already seen that the West wasn't yet ready to deal seriously with these very important issues. The Western powers were still trying to coax us into an accommodation on their terms.

I remember one incident that captures the atmosphere of our talks in London. Bulganin, Lloyd, and I were riding in the same car on our way to visit some educational institution. Lloyd was very proper and friendly. At one point he turned to me and said, "You know, a little birdie perched on my shoulder the other day and chirped into my ear that you are selling arms to Yemen."

I said, "Well, apparently there are all sorts of little birds flying about these days, chirping all kinds of different things, because one perched on my shoulder, too, and told me that you're selling arms to Egypt and Iraq. This little birdie told me that you'll try to sell arms to anyone who will buy them from you and sometimes even to people who don't want to buy them from you."

"I guess it's true: there are all sorts of birdies. Some of them are chirping in your ear, and some in ours."

"Yes," I said, "but wouldn't it be nice if all the little birdies started chirping the same thing in both of our ears — that we should assume a mutually binding obligation not to sell arms to anyone? Then wouldn't all the birdies be making a contribution to the common cause of peace?" [6]

This kind of conversation was just banter, of course. It shouldn't be taken to mean we didn't have a very serious interest in our meetings with the English. Above all, these meetings gave us a chance to clarify our position. The West was interested in our talks for the same reason. Moreover, I think Britain had a special interest in preventing a military conflict, particularly in the Near East. They wanted us to agree not to sell arms to Egypt. We were willing in principle, but we told them we could sign an agreement only on the condition that the pact would be binding on them not to sell arms to countries in the Near East.

One Sunday, Eden invited Bulganin and me out to his "dacha," as

6. Only Mr. Selwyn Lloyd can say whether this inane conversation is accurately reported.

we called his country house. He explained to us that some wealthy capitalist had given this country house to the government for the personal use of whoever happened to be Prime Minister, regardless of party. Before dinner, Bulganin and I went for a walk along a road near the house. The landscape reminded us of the countryside in our own Orel and Kursk provinces.

Eden's country house, which was called Chequers, had flowers planted all around it. It was heated by iron stoves which burned anthracite coal. As I knew from my own experience in the Donbass, anthracite coal contains large amounts of sulphur, which explains why there was an unpleasant odor and a sticky film all over everything inside the house.

Macmillan, Lloyd, and some influential Conservative politician joined us for dinner. Eden's wife was the hostess. Our embassy had informed us that she was Churchill's niece and that apparently she had inherited some of Churchill's traits in the matter of drinking. Well, she certainly didn't refuse us her company when drinks were served, but as far as we could tell, I wouldn't say she abused this particular Churchill tradition.

During dinner Mrs. Eden asked us, "Tell me, what sort of missiles do you have? Will they fly a long way?"

"Yes," I said, "they have a very long range. They could easily reach your island and quite a bit farther." She bit her tongue. It was a little rude of me to have answered her as I had. Perhaps she took it as some sort of a threat. We certainly didn't mean to threaten anyone. We were simply trying to remind other countries that we were powerful and deserved respect, and that we wouldn't tolerate being talked to in the language of ultimatums.

Eden invited Bulganin and me to spend the night at Chequers. We were shown to separate rooms upstairs. In the morning I woke up early and went out into the hall, looking for Bulganin's room so I could wake him up. I knocked on a door, thinking it was Bulganin's. A woman's voice rang out; she was obviously surprised and frightened. I realized that I had almost walked in on Eden's wife. I turned around and hurried back to my room without apologizing or identifying myself. Bulganin and I had a good laugh over this incident, but we decided not to mention it to our hosts.

The next day we had an appointment to visit with Queen Elizabeth. We didn't have to wear any special sort of clothes. We had told Eden

in advance that if the Queen didn't mind receiving us in our everyday
business suits, it was fine. If she did object, then it was just too bad.
We had some preconceived notions about this kind of ceremony, and
we weren't going to go out of our way to get all dressed up in tails and
top hats or anything else that they might have insisted on for an audience with the Queen. I remember once in Moscow we were watching a
documentary film which showed Anastas Ivanovich Mikoyan all
decked out as our official emissary in Pakistan. We all roared with
laughter at the sight of him. He really did look like an old-fashioned
European gentleman. I might mention that the fancy airs required of
ambassadors by foreign diplomats were not alien to Anastas Ivanovich.

Anyway, we arrived at the Queen's palace on a warm, pleasant day.
According to Eden, April is the best time of year, with the least rain.
There were throngs of tourists sight-seeing on the palace grounds.
Eden told us that we would find the Queen to be a simple, but very
bright and very pleasant woman. She met us as we came into the palace. She had her husband and two of her children with her. We were
introduced. She was dressed in a plain, white dress. She looked like the
sort of young woman you'd be likely to meet walking along Gorky
Street on a balmy summer afternoon.

She gave us a guided tour around the palace and then invited us to
have a glass of tea with her.[7] We sat around over tea and talked about
one thing and another. Her husband showed a great interest in Leningrad. He said he'd never been there and dreamed of going someday.
We assured him it was a very interesting city and said we were very
proud of it. We also told him that it would be easy for us to make his
dream come true. We offered to invite him to Leningrad anytime he
cared to come and said he could visit us in any capacity he wished —
as a government representative or as a commander of the army. He
thanked us and said he'd take us up on our kindness when he had the
opportunity to do so.

The Queen was particularly interested in our plane, the Tu-104,
which flew our mail to us while we were in England. Actually, part of
the reason we had the Tu-104 fly to London while we were there was
to show the English that we had a good jet passenger plane. This was
one of the first jet passenger planes in the world, and we wanted our
hosts to know about it. The Queen had seen the plane in the air as it
flew over her palace on its way to land. We thanked her and agreed

7. Russians drink tea by the glass, not by the cup.

that, yes, it was an excellent plane — very modern, undoubtedly the best in the world.

I was very impressed by the Queen. She had such a gentle, calm voice. She was completely unpretentious, completely without the haughtiness that you'd expect of royalty. She may be the Queen of England, but in our eyes she was first and foremost the wife of her husband and the mother of her children. I remember sometime later during our trip around England I met an English woman who said, "So you met the Queen. What did you think of her?" I answered that we'd liked the Queen very much. The woman shook her head sadly and said, "I feel so sorry for her. She doesn't have an easy life."

"Why do you say that?" I asked.

"Well, she's a young woman. She'd probably like to live the normal life of a woman her age, but she can't because she's the Queen. She lives in a fishbowl. She's always on display, and she has to make sure she bears herself in a manner suitable to her royal position at all times. It's a very weighty responsibility, and it makes her life hard. That's why I feel great sympathy and even sorrow for her." I liked this woman. What she said about the Queen was a very human and feminine reaction. Maybe Nekrasov [N. A. Nekrasov, the nineteenth-century poet] was right when he said in "Who in Russia Lives a Carefree Life?" that not even the tsar had it easy. The same thing applies to Queen Elizabeth II.

Technically Bulganin was our chief of state and the head of our delegation, and I was simply a member of the delegation. But as it turned out, I had to handle our end of the negotiations with the English. I certainly didn't intend it to be this way, but Bulganin kept asking me to take over for him. There were times when a statement of some kind would be required by our side, and I would wait for Bulganin to say something; there would be an awkward pause, and he would turn to me and say, "You go ahead and answer." Of course, I had no choice but to say something myself if we were going to avoid embarrassment.

For example, the First Lord of the Admiralty held an informal reception for us. There were all sorts of people there, mostly naval officers. When we had to decide how we would reply to the First Lord's speech, Bulganin said, "You do the talking." I decided to make a fairly hard-hitting, straightforward speech and to take the offensive against the English. I said, "Gentlemen, here you are, the representatives of Great Britain, and the whole world knows there was a time when Britannia ruled the waves. But all that era is now past, and we must look at things realistically. Everything has changed. Your specialists have told me how much they admire the battle cruiser which brought us here. Well, I'll tell you something. We will be happy to sell you this cruiser if you really want it because it's already obsolete. Its weapons have been outdated by new weapons. Besides, cruisers like ours no longer play a decisive role. Nor do bombers. Now it's submarines that rule the sea, and missiles that rule the air — missiles that can strike their targets from great distances." [8] During the question-and-answer period following my speech, we had a frank exchange of views in which neither side had to commit itself to any particular position. Nobody was being threatening or warlike. There was an undercurrent of irony in the questions the English asked, and there were even a few chuckles. It was not a formal negotiation, but just a casual chat over a bottle of whiskey.

When we met with Eden the next day, he asked with a smile, "Well, how did you get along with our sailors?"

"You have good sailors. They're known the world over. But I see from your smile that you must already know about our discussion."

"Yes," he said, "I know about it. It was reported to me. So were your remarks."

"And what did you think of my remarks?"

"Well, you know, I rather agree with you. But I'm the Prime Minister and I can't talk to our naval officers the way you can; I can't very well tell them that their ships and weapons are obsolete. After all, except for some bombers, our surface fleet is all we have. I can't undermine their faith in the only weapons they've got, now can I?"

My remarks to the Admiralty were eventually published amid great hue and cry in the American press. The Americans hurled all kinds of arguments against my claim that surface ships and bombers were out of date. But life has borne me out, and now the Americans admit that bombers have outlived their usefulness and should be replaced by missiles.

Eden had planned an exhausting itinerary for our tour of the country. From early morning until late at night we rushed about in cars and planes. The pace was grueling, and I began to let my dissatisfac-

---

8. This was in fact Khrushchev's view at the time. But, as everybody knows, the Russians have since changed their minds and constructed a powerful surface fleet. This construction was started while Khrushchev was still in power.

tion be known. I finally put my foot down just before we were supposed to dash off for some city in England and then fly on to Scotland. I took Eden aside and said, "Mr. Eden, my legs won't carry me another step. Tomorrow I'm going out on strike, and I'm not going to set foot outside the hotel."

He laughed. "Mr. Khrushchev, please, I implore you. We'll skip the city we were supposed to visit today, but please go ahead with the trip to Scotland. We'll fly there directly. Haven't you heard about the Scots? They're fierce nationalists. They don't give me a moment's peace. If you don't go to Scotland, they'll stage a rebellion and secede from the British Commonwealth. I beg you, please!"

Bulganin and I exchanged glances, and we agreed to go even though neither of us thought the trip would be worth it. As it turned out, Scotland was very interesting, but we only saw it in passing — at a gallop, so to say. We were prevented from having any contact with the local citizenry other than the officials whom we were scheduled to meet. This was true generally of our stay in Great Britain.

When we arrived in Scotland there was an honor guard which marched and played music for us. We watched the parade under a tent which protected us from the light, freezing rain. We had been warned that it always rains in Scotland. I had heard about the Scottish military uniforms before, and I had seen them a few times in Berlin and Vienna at the end of the war. Their uniforms are very unusual — steel-gray skirts — and their music is odd, too; it's played on special Scottish musical instruments.[9]

We were told that a dinner had been prepared in our honor, with the compliments of the Queen. So she was the Queen of Scotland, too! The house where the dinner was served had been, we were told, the palace of Mary Stuart. Our hosts all spoke very reverently about this queen and about their country's past. My son Seryozha [Sergei] was with me on this trip. He was seated at a table with two elderly women. One of them was an interpreter. She kept trying to impress Seryozha with the fact that the other woman at their table was some sort of princess. When she saw that this made no particular impression on him, she said very emphatically that this was no commoner dining with them but a real princess. Seryozha later told me what had happened and we had a good laugh about it. I don't think that his interpreter was pretending; I think she really was thrilled at the idea of sitting at

9. Scots will be interested to see themselves through Russian eyes.

the same table with a princess, and she was a bit irritated that this young man from Russia didn't appreciate the full significance of the honor.

When we returned from Scotland to London, Eden gave a dinner for us somewhere in the government complex. Before dinner we went by Eden's office. There I saw what I first took to be a portrait of Tsar Nicholas II on the wall. I mentioned that the man in the portrait bore a striking resemblance to our former tsar. Eden explained that it was Nicholas's cousin [King George V]. I let the subject drop because it would have been unpleasant for them if I had reminded them that the cousin of the man in the portrait was killed in Sverdlovsk in 1918.[10]

Before we went in to dinner Eden warned us that Churchill would be there, too. I was seated right next to Churchill. He was very old and fat and doddering. We sat there exchanging occasional phrases, not really saying much of anything to each other. Then we were served oysters. Churchill asked me, "Have you ever eaten oysters?"

"No, Mr. Churchill."

"Then watch how I eat them. I love oysters."

"All right, I'll watch you and learn how it's done." He started eating while I sipped my soup and watched. He downed his oysters, and I finished my portion, too.

"Well," he asked, "did you like them?"

"Frankly, not very much."

"Well, that's because you're not used to them." That may have been true, but I still didn't like them.

That was the extent of my conversation with Churchill. He once brought up the subject of Stalin: "You know, I had the greatest respect for Mr. Stalin during the war." Churchill was obviously making an effort to avoid business talk. He wasn't head of the government any more, and he left serious matters for Eden to discuss.

I saw Churchill a second time when we were invited to watch a session of Parliament from the visitors' gallery. A young Conservative who spoke excellent Russian was attached to our delegation as a guide and interpreter. He had complete mastery of Russian and could even express himself in the language of truck drivers. He was trying very hard both to impress us with his command of Russian and at the same time

10. King George V of England had a close resemblance to the last Tsar, who was in fact murdered with his wife and children in a cellar at Sverdlovsk, then Ekaterinburg.

to appear to be a man of the common people, but we pretended to be indifferent to him and not to notice the act he was putting on for us. While the debate was going on down on the floor of the Parliament, this young fellow suddenly whispered to us, "Look, here comes Churchill!" Churchill entered the chamber and went to his seat. "He can't sit for more than five or ten minutes without going to sleep," said our guide. We watched, and sure enough, after a short time Churchill leaned his head against the side of his seat and went fast asleep.

We were once taken on a sight-seeing tour of London. We saw the Tower, the place where the kings and queens used to have people executed, and we watched the changing of the guard. Such a colorful ceremony! I could see why it was such a great tourist attraction. In general I enjoyed seeing how the English paid tribute to their past and how they reenacted their history in pageants such as the changing of the guard. However, there was one tradition I saw that struck me as ludicrous. When we visited the House of Lords, the chairman [Lord Chancellor] came out to meet us wearing an absolutely comic outfit. He had on a red gown and a red robe and a huge wig. He showed us the seat from which he chaired sessions of the House of Lords. It was nothing but a sack of wool! I was astonished that serious men could conduct serious meetings in such silly clothes surrounded by so much humbug. I couldn't help smiling as I watched this bizarre theatrical spectacle.

Unfortunately, there were two unpleasant incidents toward the end of our stay in England.

One occurred in the harbor where our battle cruiser was docked. We had told the captain to take the necessary security precautions. Suddenly we got a report that our sailors had noticed someone swimming underwater around our cruiser, but apparently he evaded our men before they could do anything; that was the last that was seen of him. We reported what had happened to our hosts. I forget what sort of explanation they had. We let the subject drop, although we didn't overlook the possibility that someone might have been trying to attach a magnetic mine to the hull of our cruiser. Some of our military people proposed that as one theory to explain what had happened. Later, after the corpse of an intelligence officer named Commander Crabbe was discovered in England, our own intelligence service suggested that the English might have been trying to gather information on the propellers and hull construction of our ship. In any case, we didn't make too much out of this episode. But it was worth noting that the English weren't satisfied that we had let their naval attaché travel on board our ship from the Soviet Union, and that they weren't above trying to spy on their guests. Partly because of this incident, but not completely because of it, we decided not to waste any more time in England and to return to our Homeland.[11]

During our stay in London a meeting was arranged for us with the Labour Party opposition. The Labourites suggested that we have dinner with them. We consented, even though we didn't expect that this meeting would serve any useful purpose. We had found that the Labourites were consistently more hostile toward us than the Conservatives. I think I can explain this seeming paradox. We were completely at opposite poles from the Conservatives. They represented big capital and big business; we represented the working class and the Communist Party. We knew where they stood, and they knew where we stood. They made no pretenses to being anything except what they were, and we, of course, didn't have any illusions about them or high expectations of them. Therefore we could deal with each other on a down-to-earth, statesmanly basis. The Labourites were another matter altogether. They considered themselves the representatives of the working people, and they believed that theirs were the policies of the working class. In short, they made all sorts of claims which we neither accepted nor recognized. Hence there was considerable tension between us.

The Labour Party's dinner for us was held in some sort of restaurant in the Parliament building. One of the leaders of the Labour Party at that time was Wilson, who was considered our friend. Even though he was fairly conservative, he claimed that if he were in power his policy toward us would be friendlier than that of the Eden government. But look how many years he's been in power now, and he's had exactly the same policy toward us as the Conservatives before him!

When we took our seats for dinner, out came the inevitable English [sic] whiskey. The first toast was, as always at a public dinner, to the Queen. We, too, raised our glasses and drank to the Queen. Then our two delegations toasted each other.

Gaitskell at least showed a certain amount of tact in his after-dinner

11. The affair of Commander Crabbe created a great scandal at the time, and as far as the public is concerned, it remains a mystery. Did the Russians kill him or was he drowned? And why was he swimming under the Soviet battle cruiser at all?

remarks, but suddenly [George] Brown butted in and took the floor. At that time Brown had ambitions for the leadership of the Labour Party, and he was extremely hostile toward us. He delivered a speech that was absolutely scandalous and completely unacceptable. Here we were, his guests, and he launched into a harangue against our policies! I didn't mince words in responding to his attack. I said, "Mr. Brown, I'm going to tell you exactly what I think of your speech. We are your guests and expect to be treated accordingly. If you insist on insulting us, then I'm afraid we have no choice but to thank you for your invitation and to leave." With that, we made a demonstrative exit, and the dinner ended.[12]

A day or so later, there was a reception for us at the House of Lords. Brown was there. He came up and offered me his hand. I looked him in the eye and said, "Mr. Brown, after the other evening's incident, I simply cannot shake hands with you."

"You mean you won't shake my hand?" He thrust out his hand and pulled it back twice.

I didn't move and said: "No, I won't."

He let his hand drop to his side, and we walked away from each other. The other Labourites who watched as I gave this rebuff to Brown were very cautious as they came up to say hello to me; they offered me their hands very tentatively, as if to determine whether I would accept their hand or not. I shook hands with all of them. We exchanged pleasantries even though I was still upset about Brown and told them so. Later, a delegation of three Labourites apologized for Brown's rudeness and assured us that he had been speaking only for himself. Brown was considered very anti-Soviet. He had decided to take advantage of our visit as an opportunity to poison our relations and he had succeeded.[13]

12. The affair of the Labour Party dinner, which took place at the House of Commons, was headline news at the time. Gaitskell was then leader of the British Labour Party. And Gaitskell himself annoyed Khrushchev by handing him a list of East European Socialist politicians who had vanished, asking him to find out what had happened to them (they had all, of course, been shot). Mr. George Brown lost his temper and shouted at Khrushchev, who took extreme offense. For the reasons indicated by Khrushchev, the Soviet Communists have always detested European socialists far more wholeheartedly than they detest conservatives.

13. The remark about poisoning relations is revealing. Neither Khrushchev nor any other Soviet leader is capable of understanding that a man may speak out against Communist oppression out of honest depth of feeling and without an ulterior purpose.

When I saw Eden after the incident with Brown, he was, so to say, smiling in his moustache. "Well, how did your party with the Labour-ites go?" Naturally he knew very well what had happened.

I smiled back at him and said, "Well, you know, it wasn't everything it might have been."

"I told you that you'd be better off dealing with the Conservatives. Those Labourites are just impossible." Eden wasn't about to miss his chance to take full political advantage of the conflict we had had with the Labour Party. The Conservatives were delighted that our first contact with the Labour leaders had turned out badly.

We jokingly told Eden that we were trying to make up our minds about which Party to join. He laughed and said, "I'd strongly urge that you choose the Conservatives."

"We'll think it over. Perhaps we'll do as you suggest."

In the course of our negotiations in London we invited Eden to let us return his hospitality by visiting the Soviet Union. He thanked us for our invitation and accepted. However, it never worked out for him to make the trip. After our return from London, there occurred the events in Poland, the events in Hungary, and — most important — the attack by Great Britain, France, and Israel against Egypt. We were on Egypt's side and took firm diplomatic steps to put pressure on the aggressors to halt the war. The war ended only twenty-two hours after we stepped in. But the polemics in the press had reached fever pitch, and therefore it was out of the question for Eden to visit the Soviet Union.

15

Restoring Order in Hungary

Khrushchev's highly defensive account of the Hungarian uprising of 1956 diverges so widely from the generally accepted facts that it would require a small book to counter his version point by point and set out the true sequence of events. But a few major points should be made. Imre Nagy was not responsible for the uprising. He was swept into temporary power by a popular revolt, which he was never able to control. The Stalinist Party Secretary, Matyas Rakosi, was deposed in July, 1956, at a Hungarian Central Committee meeting presided over by Mikoyan. (Mikoyan had flown out from Moscow because the Soviet ambassador to Budapest had reported that there would be a revolution unless Rakosi was removed.) Rakosi was replaced as First Secretary by Gero, who continued with oppressive measures. Nagy at that time was under arrest. Students and intellectuals were soon joined by Communists in demanding greater freedom. The explosion took place on October 23, when more than two hundred thousand demonstrators marched through Budapest demanding freedom and Imre Nagy. There was bloodshed. When Gero called out the army and the ordinary police, they handed over their arms to the students and sometimes joined them. Imre Nagy did not come forward himself. In response to popular demand he was belatedly put forward by Mikoyan and Suslov in the hope that he would be able to rally the Party and control the revolt. Even now, Nagy was held back at Party headquarters by the rump of the Stalinists, who appealed to the Soviet Army. The result was that the greater part of the Hungarian army turned against the Russians. The Hungarian Communist Party virtually ceased to exist. All were behind Nagy, who requested the Russians to pull out their troops. The Russians did so only after much indecision, but they returned in strength.

It was after the violent smashing of all resistance that Janos Kadar, who had sought sanctuary with the Russians, came forward to establish, under Soviet protection, the regime which continues today.

IN 1956 a bloody struggle broke out in Budapest. Imre Nagy used deceit and intimidation to draw people into mutiny and a fratricidal war. He shoved prominent citizens in front of microphones and forced them to endorse his leadership and to denounce the Rakosi regime. Some people gave in to Nagy's demands out of fear, some out of incomprehension of what was happening. Active Party members and especially Chekists were being hunted down in the streets. Party committees and Chekist organizations were crushed. People were being murdered, strung up from lampposts, and hanged by their feet — there were all kinds of outrages. At first, the counterrevolution was waged mostly by boys. They were well armed because they had pillaged military depots and munitions warehouses. Then armed detachments joined in, and skirmishes started in the streets of Budapest. Some of these armed detachments captured artillery, mostly antiaircraft guns, which they turned against the city. Hungarian émigrés started returning to Budapest, mostly from Vienna. These were reactionary elements who had been forced to flee after Hitler was crushed and a Socialist government was established. The NATO countries were already insinuating themselves into the affair. They were adding fuel to the flames of the civil war in hopes that the revolutionary government would be overthrown, the gains of the revolution would be liquidated, and capitalism would be restored in Hungary.

Imre Nagy issued a demand that we pull all Soviet troops out of Hungary. According to our obligations under the Warsaw treaty, we could pull out our troops only if asked to do so by a legally constituted government. We certainly had no intention of doing what the leader of a putsch told us to do. From our viewpoint, a small clique, taking advantage of the blunders committed by the Rakosi regime, had overthrown the legitimate government of Hungary. From a strictly legal viewpoint, Nagy's demands had no parliamentary backing and therefore did not have the force of law.

Although he was a Communist, Nagy no longer spoke for the Hungarian Communist Party. He spoke only for himself and a small circle of émigrés who had returned to help the counterrevolution.

We quickly determined that the uprising and the Nagy government were without a mandate from the workers, the peasants, and the intelligentsia of the country as a whole. The working class refused to support the counterrevolution, and despite Nagy's appeals for the collective farmers to join him, the peasantry stayed on the sidelines and didn't let itself be duped by Nagy. Many collective farms went right on working and ignored the anti-collective farm slogans that were broadcast from Budapest.[1]

Completely independently of Imre Nagy's demands, we decided to pull our troops out of Budapest and to station them at the airfield outside the city. But even though our troops were no longer in Budapest, we kept ourselves advised of the situation through our embassy staff, which remained in the city.

We discussed the mutiny in the Presidium of the Central Committee and came to the conclusion that it would be inexcusable for us to stay neutral and not to help the working class of Hungary in its struggle against the counterrevolution. We passed a unanimous resolution to this effect. Anastas Ivanovich Mikoyan and Suslov were not present at this meeting. They were in Budapest. They went into the city during the day and returned at night to the airport where our troops were stationed.

This was a historic moment. We were faced with a crucial choice: Should we move our troops back into the city and crush the uprising, or should we wait and see whether internal forces would liberate themselves and thwart the counterrevolution? If we decided on the latter course, there was always the risk that the counterrevolution might prevail temporarily, which would mean that much proletarian blood would be shed. Furthermore, if the counterrevolution did succeed and NATO took root in the midst of the Socialist countries, it would pose a serious threat to Czechoslovakia, Yugoslavia, and Rumania, not to mention the Soviet Union itself.

Whichever course we chose, we would not be pursuing nationalist goals, but the internationalist goal of fraternal proletarian solidarity. To make sure that all countries understood us correctly on this point, we decided to consult with the other Socialist countries — first and foremost with the fraternal Communist Party of China.

1. The only grain of truth here is that many of the peasants did keep out of the fighting. They went on working in the fields, leaving the battle to be fought by the workers and the students in the cities — and by parts of the Hungarian army.

We asked Mao Tse-tung to send a representative to consult with us about the events in Hungary. The Chinese responded quickly. A delegation led by Liu Shao-chi flew in. Liu was a man of great experience and prestige, much respected by us.

The Central Committee Secretariat delegated me to represent our side. Ponomarev was also a member of our delegation.

Our consultations with the Chinese were held at Lipky, which had formerly been one of Stalin's dachas and is now a rest home. We sat up the whole night, weighing the pros and cons of whether or not we should apply armed force to Hungary. First Liu Shao-chi said it wasn't necessary; we should get out of Hungary, he said, and let the working class build itself up and deal with the counterrevolution on its own. We agreed.

But then, after reaching this agreement, we started discussing the situation again, and someone warned of the danger that the working class might take a fancy to the counterrevolution. The youth in Hungary was especially susceptible.

I don't know how many times we changed our minds back and forth. Every time we thought we'd made up our minds about what to do, Liu Shao-chi would consult with Mao Tse-tung. It was no problem for Liu to get in touch with him on the telephone because Mao is like an owl; he works all night long. Mao always approved whatever Liu recommended. We finally finished this all-night session with a decision not to apply military force in Hungary. Once we had agreed on that, I went home. Liu and his delegation stayed on at the dacha.

When I climbed into bed that morning, I found I was still too preoccupied with the whole problem to rest. It was like a nail in my head and it kept me from being able to sleep.

Later in the morning the Presidium of the Central Committee met to hear my report on how our discussion with the Chinese delegation had gone. I told them how we had changed our position a number of times and how we had finally reached a decision not to apply military force in Hungary. However, I then told the Presidium what the consequences might be if we didn't lend a helping hand to the Hungarian working class before the counterrevolutionary elements closed ranks.

After long deliberation, the Presidium decided that it would be unforgivable, simply unforgivable, if we stood by and refused to assist our Hungarian comrades. We asked Marshal Konev, who was the commander of the Warsaw Pact troops, "How much time would it take if

we instructed you to restore order in Hungary and to crush the counterrevolutionary forces?"

He thought for a moment and replied, "Three days, no longer."

"Then start getting ready. You'll hear from us when it's time to
begin."

So it was decided. But Liu Shao-chi was supposed to fly to Peking
that same evening, and he still thought we had agreed not to apply
military force in Hungary. We thought we should inform him that we
had reconsidered our position, so we arranged to consult with him at
Vnukovo airport. We asked him to leave earlier than he had planned
so we might meet him at the airport; that way he would be able to
take off without delay.

The entire Presidium went out to the airport. Liu and his comrades
arrived, and we had our meeting. There were no arguments at all. The
conversation proceeded in a particularly fraternal atmosphere, and the
Chinese side showed that it obviously shared the concerns of the Soviet people. We were all thinking about the well-being of the Hungarian working class and about the future of the Hungarian people. Liu
agreed that our revised decision to go ahead and send in the troops
was right.

"I can't get Comrade Mao Tse-tung's consent at this moment," he
said, "but I think he will support you. As soon as I arrive in Peking I'll
inform the Politbureau of the Chinese Communist Party, and we will
relay back to you our formal decision. But you may assume that you
have our backing."

Once that was settled, we saw the Chinese delegation off.[2]

The next thing we had to do was to consult with Poland. The trouble we had had there was far less serious than the trouble in Hungary.
There hadn't been an armed uprising in Poland, and an acceptable
Polish leadership had already been formed by Comrades Gomulka and
Cyrankiewicz and by other comrades we trusted. We had reason to believe that the situation in Poland was stabilizing.[3] We had all the more
reason to consult with Poland in view of the Polish people's concern

2. The Chinese had earlier advised against military action in Poland. After much
hesitation they pressed for it in Hungary. Later they took much credit for this.

3. Khrushchev appears to have nothing to say about the attempted Soviet intervention in Poland. The army was poised to strike there, but Marshal Rokossovsky,
then Polish Minister of Defense, though a Soviet army commander, warned the
Kremlin leadership that the Polish army was hostile and would put itself behind
Gomulka and fight as a body. J. Cyrankiewicz was Prime Minister of Poland at the
time of the 1956 upheaval.

about the fate of their own country; they had a large stake in the outcome of the events in Hungary. We not only wanted to know the opinion of the Polish comrades before taking such a decisive step as sending troops into Budapest — we also wanted the Polish comrades' response to be positive. We wanted their support. So we arranged for Comrade Gomulka along with Cyrankiewicz and the other comrades to meet us at a spot just inside Soviet territory on the Soviet-Polish border. The Presidium appointed a troika of Khrushchev, Molotov, and Malenkov to represent our side.

After consulting with the Poles, Malenkov and I flew to Bucharest. In addition to the Rumanian comrades, the representatives of the Czechoslovak Party led by Novotny were there and the Bulgarian comrades led by Zhivkov. All we had to do was explain the state of affairs. We didn't have to convince anyone of the need to take decisive action because these comrades had already been thoroughly informed by their ambassadors in Budapest about the situation which was developing there. Furthermore, some of the border regions in Hungary were already starting to seek arms from Czechoslovakia and Rumania in order to defend themselves against the counterrevolutionary government of Imre Nagy. The leaders of the fraternal Socialist countries were unanimous: we had to act, and we had to act swiftly.

The Rumanians and the Bulgarians said that they wanted to join us in contributing military aid to the revolutionary workers of Hungary in their struggle against the counterrevolution. We replied that there was no need to involve any troops in this operation other than the Soviet troops who were already stationed in Hungary in accordance with the Potsdam agreement. We joked with the Rumanian comrades about how Rumania was now so eager to throw itself into battle against counterrevolution, while in 1919 Rumania had been on the side of the counterrevolution which crushed the Hungarian revolution of Bela Kun. The Rumanian comrades laughed. Then they wished us success and told us to hurry.

Late that evening Malenkov and I took off for Yugoslavia to consult with Comrade Tito. The weather couldn't have been worse. We had to fly through the mountains at night in a fierce thunderstorm. Lightning was flashing all around us. I didn't sleep a wink. I had flown a great deal, especially during the war, but I'd never flown in conditions this bad. We had a very experienced pilot named General Tsybin. During the storm we lost contact with our escort reconnaissance plane which was flying ahead of us. We were heading toward Brioni Island off the coast of Yugoslavia. The local airfield was poorly equipped. It was one of those primitive airstrips built during the war. But thanks to the skill of Comrade Tsybin, we made it. When we landed, we asked if our other plane had arrived. The Yugoslavs told us they didn't know anything about it. We were very distressed about the fate of the crew.

There was a car waiting for us which took us to a pier. We climbed into a motor launch and headed toward Comrade Tito's place on Brioni Island. Malenkov was pale as a corpse. He gets carsick on a good road. We had just landed after the roughest flight imaginable, and now we were heading out into a choppy sea in a small launch. Malenkov lay down in the boat and shut his eyes. I was worried about what kind of shape he'd be in when we docked, but we didn't have any choice. As the old Russian saying goes, we couldn't sit on the beach and wait for good weather.

Tito was waiting for us when we arrived at the island. He welcomed us cordially. We embraced and kissed each other, although until recently our relations had been strained, and they were becoming more and more strained as the events in Hungary developed. We differed over the most advisable course of action.

We reported to Tito on why we had come and confronted him with our decision to send troops into Budapest. We asked for his reaction. I expected even more strenuous objections from Tito than the ones we had encountered during our discussions with the Polish comrades. But we were pleasantly surprised. Tito said we were absolutely right and that we should send our soldiers into action as quickly as possible. He said we had an obligation to help Hungary crush the counterrevolution. He assured us that he completely understood the necessity of taking these measures. We had been ready for resistance, but instead we received his wholehearted support. I would even say he went further than we did in urging a speedy and decisive resolution of the problem.

Once that was decided we said, "Well, we'd better get some rest now because we have to return to Moscow early in the morning."

"No," said Tito, "don't go. Why don't you stay here for a day or two?" We thanked Comrade Tito but explained that we didn't have time because we had to get back to Moscow right away. "Tell me," he asked, "when are you planning to begin restoring order in Budapest?"

I said that we still hadn't decided on the exact day but that it would have to be soon. Tito must have realized that this wasn't entirely true and that we had already designated the day to strike, but I didn't want to tell anyone when our troops were going to move into Budapest. The Yugoslavs were taking no direct part in this business, and therefore they didn't need to know. The fewer people who knew, including our friends, the better. It would have cost us dearly if word had leaked out about when we were going to begin.

I said, "I think we'll try to get some sleep now."

"Listen," he said, "why go to bed now? What's your hurry? Why don't we spend the night talking? There are still a few hours until dawn, and I'd like to spend with you what little time we have together."

"Well, all right," I said. "We'll take a nap in the plane on the way back to Moscow."

We managed to stay up until dawn. In the morning Tito said he'd see us off. He took the wheel of the car himself and drove us to the pier. We said farewell like old friends and kissed each other on both cheeks. He wished us a good journey and success in what we had to do.[4]

We arrived in Moscow toward evening. The members of the Presidium came to meet us at the airport, and we went straight to the Kremlin.

We told Konev to move in his troops, and order was restored almost immediately everywhere in Hungary except in Budapest, where the people put up rather stubborn resistance. Officers of the Hungarian army had joined the uprising, and our troops found themselves faced with well-organized defenses. Cannons were even pulled to the upper floors of buildings and used to cover the streets. But, as Marshal Konev had predicted, the resistance in Budapest lasted less than three days. The mutiny could have been crushed more quickly but we would have had to take more destructive measures and it would have required more sacrifices. That wouldn't have been in our interest.

Imre Nagy hid in the Yugoslav Embassy along with a great many other leaders of his movement. This development put a definite strain on our relations with Yugoslavia. The Hungarian comrades demanded that Nagy and his men be handed over so that they could be brought

4. Tito's attitude toward the Hungarian affair was uncertain. He had urged on the Russians the imperative need to get rid of Rakosi, but he seems to have been alarmed at the violence of the uprising, though highly sympathetic toward Nagy.

to justice for their crimes. The Yugoslavs resisted stubbornly. The Temporary Revolutionary Government of Hungary led by Kadar and Munnich simply waited until the Yugoslav comrades couldn't keep Nagy and all his men any longer.[5] When the Yugoslavs released Nagy, they insisted on assurances concerning his safety. The Hungarian comrades refused, and as soon as Nagy was delivered to his apartment, he was put under arrest — as well he should have been! [6] Then Comrade Kadar proposed that Nagy be flown to Bucharest until order was completely restored and the new government had a chance to normalize the situation in Hungary.

The Temporary Revolutionary Government of Hungary, which had moved into Hungary from Uzhgorod [in the Soviet Ukraine] when order was first restored, changed its name to the Socialist Workers' Party. The new leaders began to gather their forces, and the situation began to stabilize very satisfactorily.

When everything had settled down, the Rumanian comrades returned Imre Nagy to Hungary. Some tension had arisen between the Soviet Union and Yugoslavia because of the position Yugoslavia took during the events in Hungary, so Comrade Tito proposed that we meet and talk in order to restore our good relations. At first he suggested

5. The Temporary Revolutionary Government of Hungary, so called, was set up by the Russians on their own soil when it looked as though the Nagy government in Budapest had come to stay. It was a puppet organization made up of remnants of the old Hungarian Communist Party, which had completely disintegrated. Janos Kadar, the present ruler of Hungary, had actually joined the Nagy government and appeared publicly in support of it, together with Ferenc Munnich, who for a few days was Nagy's Minister of the Interior. But these two men suddenly disappeared without warning on November 2, deserted Nagy at the moment of crisis, and turned up in the Soviet camp at Uzhgorod. Two days later Kadar made his famous broadcast, allegedly from eastern Hungary, claiming that he had formed a new government and appealed to the Russians to send in troops to crush the revolt. Together with Munnich he returned to Budapest in the wake of the Russian troops, and backed by Russian tanks, he established the new regime, which he has headed ever since. Munnich, as Minister of Defense and Minister of the Interior, was responsible for the harshly repressive measures which brought Hungary back into line. He became Prime Minister in 1958, while Kadar remained Party Secretary. Since Munnich's death (natural), Kadar has contrived, after many false starts, to introduce a degree of reform in Hungary and thus in a measure to live down his treacherous and quisling past. Khrushchev's evaluation of Munnich illuminates his own character as well as his attitude, that of a no-nonsense Soviet leader, to the satellites.

6. This is untrue. The Hungarians did in fact promise Tito that no harm would come to Nagy if he left the sanctuary of the Yugoslav Embassy in Budapest. Tito was furious when he was arrested. Khrushchev does not mention the little fact that Nagy was later taken from prison and shot. Nor does he refer to the arrest and shooting of General Pal Maleter when he met the Russians under safe-conduct to negotiate.

meeting secretly on a boat in the Danube River, on the border between Rumania and Yugoslavia. Then, just before I left, he changed his mind and suggested that we meet openly in Bucharest instead. We had already liquidated one conflict with Yugoslavia after Stalin's death, and we had no reason to want to start another. We talked about how to improve our trade relations. I said that we made no claims to hegemony as far as Yugoslavia was concerned, and I reiterated our commitment to the principle of noninterference in the internal affairs of Yugoslavia.

Some time passed, and we saw that things weren't going very well in Hungary. We discussed the situation in the Presidium and decided that we couldn't let it go on any longer. The Presidium instructed me to fly to Budapest for talks with the Hungarian leaders.

My own hopes rested with Munnich. I thought I could deal with him better than with Kadar. Munnich was a cunning and battered old wolf who had been through the Hungarian revolution with Bela Kun. He'd lived in the Soviet Union for a long time, and I thought he was better prepared than anyone else to handle the problems which were still facing Hungary.

I was met at the airport and driven into the city. I'd been in Budapest in 1946, and it was still as beautiful as I remembered it, although there were some traces of the street fighting such as bullet-scarred walls and even some ruins.

A banquet was given for me in a dark hall. I don't know why the lighting was so bad. In the West I had attended candlelight banquets, but those were always held on triumphal occasions. Here in Budapest it wasn't a triumphal occasion, and it was dimly lit simply because the lighting was poor. The entire leadership was there. The Hungarians served their delicious goulash and excellent wine.

The conversation soon came around to politics. In answer to my criticisms, Munnich said, "You know, I was our country's amabassador to Moscow during the Rakosi period, so I can't be held responsible for what happened then." I asked about the Hungarian press, which was obviously still out of line, and he said, "Look here, Comrade Khrushchev, I'm not in charge of overseeing the newspapers. That's the job of other comrades."

In short, there were still problems. It's always like that when a country and a Party undergo such a severe upheaval. One unhealthy after-effect of the mutiny was that the Hungarian army was demoralized. The army as a whole had not taken part in the counterrevolution, but individual officers in small numbers had participated actively.[7] After the counterrevolution was crushed and Imre Nagy's gang was toppled, there remained a certain amount of vacillation among the army officers. Therefore, the new government of Comrades Kadar and Munnich required that all army officers define their political attitude toward the events which had transpired by signing an oath swearing that they would honorably serve the Hungarian people and carry out the orders of the Hungarian government. A few officers were reluctant to take this oath. Their vacillation led to a purge of those elements who refused to accept the necessary conditions for the building of Socialism in Hungary. As a result, the army was diminished in quantity but improved in quality.

The life of the country was already beginning to return to normal, despite the accusatory howls of the bourgeois press and slanderous propaganda from abroad to the effect that the Soviet Union had suppressed a popular revolution in Hungary.

Comrade Kadar and the Central Committee of the Hungarian Communist Party appealed to the Central Committee of the Communist Party of the Soviet Union to send consultants to help them reorganize their coal industry which was in a shambles. At the behest of the Hungarian government and the Hungarian Central Committee I made a number of trips to Hungary in 1957.

Once, when I was there in the summer, Kadar said that they were holding a rally on the square in front of the United States Embassy. It was to be a particularly important meeting because [Cardinal] Mindszenty and the staff of the American Embassy were sure to be watching from the balcony. Mindszenty was head of the Catholic Church in Hungary. He represented the most reactionary wing of the counterrevolutionary forces which had struck against the Hungarian government and the building of Socialism in Hungary in 1956. After the counterrevolution was crushed, he hid in the American Embassy, and he was there for years afterward.

Even if Mindszenty and the Americans were unable to hear the speeches on the square, they were sure to have agents circulating through the crowd, taking notes on everything that happened.

7. The greater part of the Hungarian army did in fact join the revolt.

We had another reason to be interested in the meeting. When it became known that I had come to Hungary, American journalists started tooting their horn that Khrushchev wouldn't dare show his face in public because Khrushchev knew he'd be in trouble if he followed his usual custom and went walking in the streets; the Hungarians would never forgive him for having used military force to crush the counterrevolution. We knew what sort of bunk to expect from the American press!

Kadar opened the meeting. The Hungarian comrades urged me to speak, and I couldn't very well refuse. In my speech, I reproached the workers and intelligentsia of Hungary for permitting a counterrevolutionary mutiny to take place in their country.

During the meeting Kadar said, "Look over there to the left and you'll see the American ambassador standing with his men. I can see Mindszenty, too."

When the meeting was over, I said, "Comrade Kadar, let's go down from the speaker's platform and walk straight into the crowd."

He smiled and said, "There're a lot of people down there, you know."

"All the better. This way we'll show the American journalists and the American ambassador and Mindszenty that Khrushchev isn't afraid to stick his neck out, and that he still mixes with the people. We'll give them a good brainwashing, as the American journalists would say — those ill-wishers of the Soviet Union and Hungary!"

I gave a similar speech at the biggest machine tool factory in Hungary. From there Comrade Kadar and I went to the coal-mining region where he had been an underground Party leader during the war. Because I was a former miner myself, I felt I could take a tough line with the coal miners. I said I was ashamed of my brother miners who hadn't raised either their voices or their fists against the counterrevolution. They hadn't taken an active part in the mutiny, but they hadn't put up any resistance either. They had let themselves become demoralized and apathetic. When I finished speaking, the miners said they were sorry. They repented for having committed a serious political blunder, and they promised that they would do everything they could not to let such a thing happen ever again.

Next we went to a rally at a steel factory on the Danube which had been equipped on a credit loan from us. It was in a town which used to be called Stalinovarash, but its name had been changed. At one point Comrade Kadar asked me, "Would it be all right if we met with representatives of our intelligentsia? We'll call a meeting of the workers from the Academy of Sciences and other institutions of intellectual labor." I consented and was pleased to find at the meeting that the intelligentsia, too, understood the necessity for the measures which had been taken.

At all of these meetings we gave speeches exposing the schemes of world counterrevolution and world imperialism to reestablish capitalism in Hungary. For their part, the Hungarian comrades demonstrated to the bourgeois press that, far from harboring any ill-will toward the Soviet Union, the Hungarian people were grateful to us and our army for having fulfilled our internationalist duty in helping to liquidate the counterrevolutionary mutiny. And it wasn't because only people who sided with us were allowed to speak at these meetings, either. Everyone who spoke expressed his true feelings, and anyone present was perfectly free to say what was on his mind. The atmosphere at the meetings was charged with great elation and enthusiasm. The Hungarian people put their stamp of approval on the measures which were being taken by the new leadership of the Hungarian Party and government.

We agreed with the new leadership that the mutiny had been engendered by Stalin's abuse of power and that the seeds of discontent had been sown in Hungary by Stalin's advisor, Rakosi. In other words, the counterrevolution was another consequence of Stalin's sick character, which Lenin had warned us about in his Testament.[8]

I remember when we proposed a plan to reduce the size of the Soviet Army garrisoned throughout Eastern Europe, I asked the Hungarians for their reaction: "Comrade Kadar, what do you think about the prospect of us pulling our troops out of Hungary? Is this advisable? We rely on your judgment here. We'll do whatever you decide."

"Comrade Khrushchev, I think you had best decide this for yourself. I can only tell you two things. First, there is absolutely no resentment whatsoever in our country against the presence of your troops on our territory. I say this very frankly. Second, I think there's only one thing which worries the Hungarian people — workers, peasantry, and intelligentsia alike: that is, that Rakosi not return to Hungary." At the time Rakosi was living in the Soviet Union. Apparently there were still

8. Having once declared that the whole affair was due to Nagy, Khrushchev now turns around and says it was due to Stalin and Rakosi.

forces in Hungary which sympathized with him and regretted his fall from power, just as there were forces in the Soviet Union who would have given their vote to Stalin even after we established his guilt in the eyes of the Party.

Now, I realize there are some people who might claim that the Kadar government was pro-Moscow, that it had been created under our sponsorship and influence. Well, we can kick this ball back to the other end of the field simply by asking, under whose sponsorship was the government of Imre Nagy created? In whose planes were waves of bourgeois agents and counterrevolutionary émigrés flown back into Hungary? The answer is, under the sponsorship and in the planes of the imperialistic forces of the world, especially the United States.[9] Besides, the members of the Kadar government had been elected to their original positions of leadership at a Hungarian Party Congress presided over by none other than Rakosi himself.

Thus I refute the reasoning of those people who claim that Kadar and his government were, to put it crudely, our stooges.

I want to make myself quite clear on this point: we, the Soviet Union, support the revolutionary forces of the world. We do so out of our internationalist obligations. We wholeheartedly join in the struggle being waged by the working classes under the red banner emblazoned with the slogan, "Proletarians of the World Unite!" We are against the export of revolution, but we are also against the export of counterrevolution. That is why it would be unthinkable and unforgivable for us to refuse help to the working class of any country in its struggle against the forces of capitalism.

Our goal in Hungary was to support progressivism and to assist the people's transition from capitalism to Socialism. The enemies of Socialism had the opposite goal: wherever a Socialist way of life had been achieved, they wanted to liquidate it, to suppress the working class, and to restore capitalism.

By helping the Hungarian people to crush the counterrevolutionary mutiny we have prevented the enemy from impairing the unity of the entire Socialist camp, rigorously tested during the Hungarian events. We were aware that by helping Hungary to suppress the uprising and

9. It is impossible to tell whether Khrushchev really believes that the West played an effective part in the Hungarian revolt. Certainly a number of Hungarian émigrés found their way back to Hungary in the first flush of the revolt. But the Western powers, with Suez on their hands, held aloof and passed by on the other side.

eliminate its aftermath as quickly as possible we were also helping all the other countries of the Socialist camp. The help we gave the Hungarian people in crushing the counterrevolution was approved unanimously by the working people in the Socialist countries, by all progressives throughout the world.

So I say, yes! We did help Hungary in 1956. As I once said at a Party rally, we repaid a debt to Hungary which had been hanging over our heads since 1848. In that year there was a successful revolution in Budapest, but Nicholas I threw in his legions, crushed the revolution, and helped restore the rule of the Austrian monarchy in Hungary. That was a disgrace. Of course that black deed was committed by Nicholas I and those around him; the disgrace did not rub off onto the working class and peasantry of the former Russian Empire. But our country still owed a historical debt to the people of Hungary. In 1956 we finally paid it off. Now we're even.[10]

10. The Hungarians saw it differently. In 1848 their national revolt against Austria was crushed by the Russians; in 1956 the Russians were back again.

16

Nasser, Suez, and the Aswan Dam

In his account of the Kremlin's relations with President Nasser, Khrushchev is fuller, more detailed, more straightforward, and less inhibited than he is about Eastern Europe. Soviet penetration of the Middle East, facilitated by the American withdrawal from the Aswan Dam project and the subsequent Suez crisis, has been very much a success story; and although Khrushchev twists certain facts to make the Soviet role appear more decisive and creditable than it was, he has little to hide about the actions, as distinct from the motives, of the Kremlin. The most interesting general point that emerges is Soviet ignorance of the real state of affairs in Egypt before the nationalization of the Suez Canal in 1956 — and later, in Iraq.

I won't deny that it created certain difficulties for us when anti-Soviet elements stirred up a critical situation in Poland and Hungary. While we were dealing with those problems, second-echelon English and French diplomats in London and Paris met with our embassy people over a cup of coffee or a glass of wine and said, "You seem to have some trouble on your hands in Poland and Hungary. We understand how it is sometimes. We're having some troubles of our own in Egypt. Let's have a tacit understanding between us that you'll liquidate your difficulties by whatever means you see fit, and you won't interfere while we do the same." In other words, the imperialists tried to take advantage of the troubles we were having in Poland and Hungary so that they could send their troops into Egypt to reestablish colonial rule.[1]

1. Khrushchev's remarks about Western diplomats offering the Russians a free hand in Poland and Hungary are in direct contradiction to his earlier insistence that the Hungarian revolt, at least, was supported and sustained by the "imperialist" powers.

Well, we disposed of the troubles in Poland quickly, and as soon as we had liquidated the mutiny in Hungary, we faced head-on the task of how to end the war which the colonialists were waging against President Nasser of Egypt.[2]

Our use of our international influence to halt England, France, and Israel's aggression against Egypt in 1956 was a historic turning point. Before that time, the Soviet Union — and Imperial Russia before it — had always treated the Near East as belonging to England and France. King Farouk had once asked Stalin to give him arms so that he could force Great Britain to evacuate its troops from Egypt, but Stalin refused. Stalin said in my presence that the Near East was part of Britain's sphere of influence and that therefore we couldn't go sticking our nose into Egypt's affairs. Not that Stalin wouldn't have liked to move into the Near East — he would have liked to very much — but he realistically recognized that the balance of power wasn't in our favor and that Britain wouldn't have stood for our interference.

Things changed during the intervening years. Our economy, our armed forces, and the weight of our influence in international affairs all increased mightily, and by 1956 we were able to step in and assist President Nasser and the Arab peoples. It wasn't that we wanted to replace England as an exploiter of Egypt and other Arab countries. We weren't motivated by self-centered, mercantile interests. Quite the contrary, we wanted only to help these peoples to cast off the yoke of their servile dependence on their colonialist masters. Ours has been a noble mission in the Near East. We have incorporated into our diplomacy the tenets of Lenin's own foreign policy, and we have already begun to reap the fruits of our investment in the future of the Arab nations.

When we first began to take an active interest in the affairs of Egypt, our attitude was cautious and our optimism was guarded. When Nasser came to power after the revolution in Egypt,[3] we were not convinced by his policies that he was going to do what was necessary to reform the social-political structure of his country. For a certain period after the coup and Colonel Nasser's emergence as chief of state, we couldn't be sure what direction this new government of army officers would take, either in foreign or in domestic policies. The new Egyptian

2. The use of the word "mutiny" is revealing. The Hungarian revolt was finally crushed on November 9; the Suez war was opened on October 29.

3. Events are somewhat telescoped in these paragraphs. General Naguib launched the Egyptian nationalist and republican movement; he was then replaced by Nasser.

leadership came mostly from the upper ranks of the Egyptian army, in other words from the bourgeoisie and not from the working class. On the whole these were men of privileged background and propertied status, although the new regime was far from being socially homogeneous.

We were inclined to think that Nasser's coup was just another one of those military take-overs which we had become so accustomed to in South America. We didn't expect much new to come of it. However, we had no choice but to wait and see what would happen.

We liked what we saw. The Egyptians began to pursue a policy that had considerable merit. They started actively to put pressure on the English to pull their troops out. The English were left with no alternative, and they complied with the Egyptians' demand.

Now we respected Nasser and realized that his wasn't just another in a series of new governments that seize power and then follow old policies. No, the new Egyptian government had the national interest of its people at heart and therefore deserved our respect and support. We wanted to help Nasser continue his struggle against the colonialists.

But it remained very difficult to define the social-political goals of the new government in Egypt. There was still a great deal of foreign capital in the country, and the government had left the private banks alone. Nasser's government was obviously nationalistic, but it looked as if it were turning out to be a bourgeois government. Nevertheless, it was in our interest to support Nasser's bourgeois leadership because it promised to weaken the influence of English colonialism in the Near East — and that was in the interest of the Soviet Union.[4]

Nasser's relations with Comrade Tito were even better than his relations with us. When Tito traveled to India, he went by ship through the Suez Canal. The Yugoslav press lavished praise on the Egyptian government. At that time we still hadn't improved our own relations with Yugoslavia; but shortly afterward, when Comrade Tito and I first met to exchange views on international matters, Tito spoke very flatteringly about Nasser and his policies.

We were impressed but pointed out that it was hard to be sure from Nasser's speeches whether or not he intended to create a progressive

4. Khrushchev seems unable to make up his mind whether Russia helped Egypt "in the interest of the Soviet Union" as part of the campaign against Western imperialism, or for purely altruistic motives of the most noble kind.

regime in Egypt. He still hadn't laid a finger on the bourgeoisie and the banks.

Comrade Tito replied that Nasser was a young man without much political experience; he had good intentions, but he hadn't yet found his fulcrum of power. Tito pointed out that if we gave Nasser the benefit of the doubt, we might later be able to exert a beneficial influence on him, both for the sake of the Communist movement and for the sake of the Egyptian people. In Egypt, the interests of the people and the interests of Socialism were interwoven. After all, Socialism can bear its fruits to all the peoples of the world. Therefore, our desire to affect the course of the Egyptian government was not a conspiracy by one country against another; it was the natural outgrowth of our desire to share our experience with another nation.[5]

Soon after the coup, when the Egyptians decided to try to oust the English, Nasser's representatives came to us with a request for military aid. They said they needed to have their own army in order to put pressure on the English. We agreed. We gave them weapons ranging from rifles to regular artillery, but as I recall, we didn't give them any planes at first. We did, however, give them tanks and naval equipment. Nasser said he particularly needed torpedo boats. I think we gave them military aid on a commercial basis, but at a reduced price.

After buying arms from us, Nasser — who was by now very close to Tito — started to talk about building Socialism in his country. However, he talked about Socialism in such a way as to make us uncertain whether he really understood what he was saying. It also seemed possible that he might have some ulterior motive for espousing the Socialist cause. In modern times the word Socialism has become very fashionable, and it has also been used very loosely. Even Hitler used to babble about Socialism, and he worked the word into the name of his Nazi [National Socialist] party. The whole world knows what sort of Socialism Hitler had in mind. Therefore we were cautious toward people who adopted the word Socialism but who seemed mostly interested in getting military aid from us.

The fondest dream of the Egyptian people was to harness the mighty Nile River to their economy. Since ancient times the Egyptians had

5. Here we see the Soviet Union assuming what used to be called the White Man's Burden. Compare his earlier remarks about Stalin's attitude to Soviet penetration of the Middle East.

used the waters of the Nile to irrigate their farmlands along its banks. In addition to being the lifeblood of their agriculture, the waters of the Nile were also an untapped source of hydroelectric power. When Nasser came to power, he began vigorously promoting the idea of building a dam which would use the Nile to drive generator turbines. He entered into negotiations on this subject with the United States and eventually reached an agreement with some American bank, a so-called "international" bank, which promised to give Egypt credit loans for the construction of the dam. The Egyptians let themselves be deluded into thinking that the dream which they had cherished for centuries was about to come true.

But their delusion didn't last long. Egypt refused to follow the path set for it by the United States, England, and France, and as a result the imperialists were irritated. Suddenly it was announced that the credit loans which had been promised for the dam were canceled.

President Nasser exploded with rage and announced that Egypt was going to nationalize the Suez Canal. This action sent the temperature of the international political situation soaring dangerously.

When the imperialists attacked Egypt, I consulted with Molotov. Even though he was no longer very active, he had been Minister of Foreign Affairs for a long time and was our most experienced statesman. I called him on the phone to get his reaction to an idea I had: "Vyacheslav Mikhailovich, I think that we should address ourselves to the President of the United States with a proposal to take joint action against the aggressors who have attacked Egypt."

Molotov pointed out, quite correctly, "Eisenhower will never agree to join forces with us against England, France, and Israel."

"Of course he won't, but by putting him in the position of having to refuse, we'll expose the hypocrisy of his public statement condemning the attack against Egypt. We'll make him put his money where his mouth is. If he were really against the aggression, then he'd accept the Soviet Union's proposal for us jointly to safeguard Egypt's independence."

I told Molotov we should put this matter to the Presidium right away. I summoned the members of the Presidium to the Kremlin for an urgent meeting. We discussed my suggestion and drafted a proposal which Shepilov, our new Minister of Foreign Affairs, sent to President Eisenhower. Our note to Eisenhower stressed that we should join forces under the flag of the United Nations. We also sent notes to the prime ministers of Britain, France, and Israel demanding the immediate halt of their aggressive attack on Egypt.

Shortly after delivering our message to Eisenhower, we published it in the press. We were informed that when the President received our note, he told journalists, "This is incredible! Can the Russians be serious? To think that we would join them against Britain, France and Israel! It's inconceivable!" So our note had done exactly what it was supposed to do; it had put the lie to the Americans' claim of being fighters for peace and justice and nonaggression. They may have been fighters in words, but not in deeds, and we had unmasked them.[6]

In the spring of 1956, when we were in London and had talks with Messrs. Eden, Lloyd, Macmillan, Butler, and other British statesmen, we told them frankly that we had rockets of various ranges. Later, when Israel, Britain, and France attacked Egypt, the Soviet Government stated in a message to the British Prime Minister: What would be the position of Britain herself if she were attacked by stronger states possessing modern destructive weapons of all kinds? And such countries, the message said, could even do this without sending a navy or an air fleet to British shores, but could use other means, for instance rocketry. This statement by the Soviet Government evidently influenced them. Previously they had apparently thought that we were simply bluffing when we openly said that the Soviet Union possessed powerful rockets. But then they saw that we really had rockets. And this had its effect.

It was about this time that I flew to Brioni Island off the coast of Yugoslavia for consultations with Tito on the events in Hungary [see pages 420–422]. Tito was on the island because he was ill and his physicians had prescribed saltwater baths for him. I remember asking him, "Don't you think it's dangerous to be here while there's a war raging in Egypt? A plane could easily drop a bomb on this island and there'd be nothing left of you or your dacha. No one could prove it wasn't an accident. Remember, the English and the French know all about your relations with Nasser, and anything could happen."

Rankovic [the Yugoslav Minister of Internal Affairs] said, "Yes, I keep telling Comrade Tito to go back to Belgrade for the duration of the conflict in the Near East, but he doesn't want to. He says he needs

6. Khrushchev seems to be unaware of the fact that the Suez operation was called off because of extreme American pressure. It is impossible to tell whether he really believed, and believes, that the operation was launched without reference to Washington and in the teeth of American disapproval.

these saltwater baths for his health." But even though he didn't admit that he was in personal danger, I could see that Comrade Tito was very alarmed about the situation in the Near East. He was worried for Yugoslavia as well as for Egypt and Nasser.

In our notes to the three governments who led the aggression against Egypt, we said, "You have attacked Egypt, knowing that it is considerably weaker than you are, that it does not have much of an army, and that it does not have many weapons. But there are other countries which are entirely capable of coming to Egypt's defense." We were clearly hinting that the Soviet Union was such a country, and that we were ready to intervene if necessary. We warned that we couldn't remain neutral because, if the conflict in the Near East spread, it would threaten our own national interests. The governments of England and France knew perfectly well that Eisenhower's speech condemning their aggression was just a gesture for the sake of public appearances. But when we delivered our own stern warning to the three aggressors, they knew that we weren't playing games with public opinion. They took us very seriously. I've been told that when Guy Mollet received our note, he ran to the telephone in his pajamas and called Eden. I don't know if this story is true, but whether or not he had his trousers on doesn't change the fact that twenty-two hours after the delivery of our note the aggression was halted. We only had to issue our warning once — unlike the Chinese variety, which has to be repeated about a thousand times before it has any impact.[7]

I think I can explain why Israel retreated from the territory it had captured with the help of France and England. In addition to getting the United Nations to censure the aggression, we announced in the press that we were recruiting volunteers to serve with the Egyptian army as tank operators, pilots, artillery specialists, and so on. In other words we decided to give Egypt concrete assistance in the form of men who were able to handle sophisticated weaponry. We put our conditions to Israel in very unambiguous terms: either the Israelis pull back their troops and obey the United Nations resolution, or else they would clash with the armed forces of Egypt — and in so doing, they might find themselves faced with our volunteers.

Our policy was very much appreciated by the Egyptian people and by President Nasser. It was a great victory for us when we ended the

7. See note 6 above. The Soviet warnings were not issued until the danger was past, although most people did not realize this at the time.

crisis. It was also a great victory for the progressive forces of the world. It enhanced the prestige of the Soviet Union not only among the Egyptian people, but among all peoples who had recently freed themselves from colonial slavery or who were still waging their struggles for independence.

Nasser said many flattering but nonetheless accurate things about our policies after we intervened on Egypt's behalf in 1956. There had been no strings attached to our defense of Egypt. Our actions were based on purely humanitarian, not mercenary, concerns. Mercantile interests had nothing to do with it. In fact, we didn't really need anything that we might have been able to get from Egypt. We have almost everything they produce and many things they don't produce. We have rice and oil of our own. We're a much richer country, and we can rely on our own natural wealth. And if there is something we do need, we always try to acquire it from other countries by fair trade arrangements. Unlike the colonialists, we don't need to resort to war or political machinations to get what we want.

Even after the threat of colonialist aggression had been removed, the Egyptians were in serious difficulty. Prior to July, 1956, the service personnel managing the facilities of the Suez Canal and the pilots who took ships through the canal had mostly been Frenchmen. When Nasser nationalized the canal, all these people were called home, and there was no one to operate the canal. The West believed, and hoped, that Egypt would prove itself unable to run the canal by itself, that it would founder in financial and political troubles, and that the Nasser regime would discredit itself. The Egyptian government turned to us for assistance, and we immediately sent them pilots and engineers. As a result, Egypt managed the take-over smoothly, and the canal was soon reopened under Egyptian management.

This whole situation had generated white-hot friction between the Great Powers in the Near East. The crisis was another result of Dulles's high-handed pressure politics. But in the final analysis, Dulles's policies backfired and helped bring us and Egypt closer together. In a way Dulles did Egypt a service by showing Nasser who his real friends and his real enemies were. Nasser appreciated this fact, and [in 1958] he asked us if he might visit the Soviet Union. After discussing his request in the collective leadership, we said we were ready to receive him any time. We exchanged views in the leadership about all the issues which Egypt might care to discuss. We made sure that there was a consensus on our own position, and then I was instructed to meet with Nasser on a one-to-one basis. It was to be my first acquaintance with him.

Nasser came to see us after vacationing in Yugoslavia. He impressed me from the moment I met him. He was still a young man, self-contained and intelligent, and there was always a smile twinkling at the corners of his mouth. If you want to know my personal impression, I liked him very much. Our meeting was held just outside the city of Novoye Ogarevo. Nasser had his ambassador Ghaleb with him. Ghaleb was a bright and very interesting man, completely deserving of our respect. He spoke Russian well and served as Nasser's interpreter.

Suddenly word came to us that there had been a military coup in Baghdad. Naturally we welcomed the news because it meant the long-overdue end of one of the most reactionary, terroristic regimes in the world. The dictator, a sly old agent of English imperialism, was killed.[8] The coup could justly be called a revolutionary overthrow, and we could see that the new leader Kassem represented the progressive forces of Iraq. We already had some information on Kassem. He had had sporadic contacts with Communists and even called himself a Communist. We could tell from Nasser's reaction when he was told about the coup that the news came as a complete surprise to him. He was obviously very excited and said he must return to the Near East immediately. Shortly before the coup in Iraq, Egypt and Syria had formed the United Arab Republic, and Nasser nourished the hope that the new Iraqi government would fall into line with the policies of Egypt. This was a completely understandable desire, but as it turned out, neither Nasser's hopes nor our own information about Kassem were borne out. Kassem turned out to be highly unstable politically.

But I'm getting ahead of myself. When word of the coup in Iraq first reached us, Nasser was determined to return to Yugoslavia and travel from there with his family to Alexandria by boat.

I thought about this for a moment and then offered my own thoughts on the matter for his consideration. "Mr. President," I said, "I wouldn't advise you to return by boat across the Mediterranean. The coup in Iraq has touched off a very volatile situation throughout that whole area. The USA, England, and other countries are moving their military units into place and preparing for action. Tension is mounting. You

8. The reference here is to the assassination of Nuri Pasha. The Russians appear to have been wholly ignorant of the situation in Iraq. They knew as little about Kassem as anybody else.

don't exactly enjoy the sympathy of the Western countries. It would be easy for them to sink your ship at sea and impossible for anyone to prove what happened. There you would be, the President of the United Arab Republic, aboard an unarmed yacht — a sitting duck for any airplane or submarine that happened to be snooping around in the area. I would strongly advise you to fly from Baku [in Soviet Azerbaidzhan] to Iran, then on to Iraq, and from there to Syria. You won't have any trouble getting back to Cairo from Damascus."

Nasser thought it over and agreed. At that time our relations with Iran weren't bad, but they weren't very good either. Therefore we never used Iran's territorial airspace without requesting special permission to do so. However, I was sure that the Shah wouldn't refuse because during his visit to the Soviet Union we had sensed on his part considerable interest in improving our relations. Naturally, when we requested permission to fly over Iran, we didn't say that our passenger was going to be the President of the UAR. We thought up some story and received permission almost immediately. Not long after Nasser left we got word that he had arrived safely in Syria.

The Egyptian military delegations which visited us regularly were usually led by Amer, the commander in chief of the Egyptian army.[9] I should mention that this man Amer later came to a tragic end. He committed suicide as a result of the disastrous defeat suffered by the Egyptian army. He took responsibility for the defeat. Perhaps he was partially to blame; it's hard for me to judge. However, when I knew him he always impressed me as an honest, decent man, devoted to the cause of the Egyptian people.

After preliminary approaches to our embassy people in Cairo, Amer came to Moscow with a proposal that we should build the Aswan Dam. At first we refused.

I thought at the time that Tito had put this idea in the Egyptians' heads, urging them to bring to bear on us all the friendly pressure they could muster in order to persuade us to build the dam for them. The reason I believed that, and still do, is that whenever Tito and I met, he always defended Nasser vigorously and praised him to the skies. He always said that we must help Egypt, and he was absolutely right. Life has borne him out [a favorite Khrushchevism]. And, in the long run, we've followed Tito's advice. Of course we've had our differences. Our

9. Deputy Supreme Commander of the Egyptian forces, arrested after the six-day war in August, 1967; he committed suicide in September, 1967.

press has sometimes had critical things to say about Egypt, but the Egyptians have always been able to count on us to take their side at crucial moments.

The Egyptians wouldn't take no for an answer about the Aswan Dam. Amer knew how to be persistent without being annoying. Whenever he came to Moscow he always asked for a personal appointment with me. He kept trying to convince me that Egypt's request that we build the dam was based on a consideration of our mutual interests, and that it would be profitable for us as well as for Egypt. He stressed that the dam would allow the Egyptians to increase their arable land by one third, and that this would mean great wealth for his country and for anyone willing to invest in its future.

I told him we agreed, but that we couldn't afford the huge capital investments required to build the dam. After one of these meetings we talked over the Egyptian request in the leadership and instructed our economists at the State Planning Commission to study the Egyptian proposal carefully. They did so and some time later gave us a projection of what the dam would yield in the way of an economic as well as political return on our investment. We were interested in determining whether it would be a profitable business transaction. Naturally we would be glad to have an opportunity to bolster the economy of our friends and in so doing to strengthen our relations with them. But that was a political consideration, and we had also to make sure that we wouldn't simply be giving our money away. We had to make sure that the Egyptians could repay us in regular deliveries of their best long-fiber cotton, rice, and other goods.[10]

However, I don't want to give the impression that we were helping them out of mercenary motives. Not at all. We were more interested in politics than economics. By building the dam we would be winning the priceless prize of the Egyptian people's trust and gratitude. And not just the trust of the Egyptian people, but the trust of all Arabs. And not just the trust of all Arabs, but of all other underdeveloped countries, especially in Africa. Our assistance to the Egyptians would demonstrate that the Soviet Union could be counted on to aid needy peoples the world over who were liberating themselves from colonial rule. Furthermore, we knew that strengthening the Arab countries meant weakening the camp of our enemies.

10. Compare with Khrushchev's earlier remark: "We didn't really need anything we might have been able to get from Egypt."

So we signed an agreement with the Egyptians on the building of the Aswan Dam.

During the negotiations the Egyptians suggested that we should take the role of contractor in the project. We had rejected this arrangement in the past with other countries, and we rejected it now with Egypt. We refused to put ourselves in the position of contractor because it would have meant hiring Egyptian manpower. It would have led to an employer-employee relationship between us and the Egyptian people, and they would have begun to resent us as exploiters. In order to avoid conflict with local populations we had made it a matter of policy never to be a contractor in countries to whom we gave credit loans.

Therefore we told the Egyptians, "We'll supply you with all the equipment, plans, maintenance facilities, and technical supervision you need; but our specialists will report to you for approval on all matters, and you will take care of hiring the work crews yourselves."

The signing of the Aswan Dam treaty was another turning point in our relations with Egypt. It gave them an accurate and promising picture of our intentions with regard to all countries who were emerging from under the yoke of colonialism.

Our engineers and scientists started by studying the blueprints for the dam which had been drawn up and submitted by Western engineers. Our men believed they could find a more advanced, more ingenious, and more efficient way of harnessing the resources of the river to a hydrostation. I think it's a realistic assessment of the facts, and not just boasting, when I say that our specialists are the most experienced in the world when it comes to building hydroelectric plants.

When work was ready to start, the Egyptian leaders suggested that a Soviet delegation come to Aswan to acquaint itself on the spot with Soviet-Egyptian cooperation in action. The Egyptians made a point of inviting me to lead the Soviet delegation, and I understood why: they wanted to foster better relations, and they thought they had best go straight to the top and talk to me personally.

I don't deny that I had a great desire to visit Egypt and to see that fabled land and its ancient culture with my own eyes. I would have loved to attend the foundation-stone ceremony at the site of the Aswan Dam project, but I was unable to accept the invitation.

Some time passed. The work went on apace, in the construction of the Aswan Dam and of other projects as well. We built, or rather financed, a steel mill, a pharmaceutical factory, and a number of other plants, too. The construction of the Aswan Dam brought us together with the Egyptian people as well as with the Egyptian government. Our specialists worked side by side on the same machines with their engineers and peasants, and a great reservoir of mutual trust and respect was built up.

As the construction of the Aswan power plant neared its final stage — the closing of the river channel and the mounting of the hydroturbines — the Egyptians insisted that I be present for the triumphant occasion when the prayers of the Egyptian people would finally be answered. Nasser asked me not to come just for the ceremony but to stay for a while, to take a vacation in Egypt. He said it would give us a chance to conduct talks in a relaxed atmosphere, and that it would be very useful for both of us. As an added incentive for me to come, the Egyptians reminded us that there were still a few Communists left in jail in Egypt, and the Premier promised that these prisoners would be released in honor of my visit.

We agreed to make the trip. We went in May, 1964. I was accompanied by our Minister of Foreign Affairs, Andrei Andreyevich Gromyko, and Deputy Minister of Defense Grechko. We included Grechko in our delegation because we wanted him to handle negotiations with the military comrades from the Arab Republic. As for Gromyko, his wide knowledge of foreign affairs was indispensable to us.

The moment we arrived in Aswan we felt as though we had stepped into an oven. I had been warned that it was scorching hot in Egypt and that it rained only once every few years. Of course, for some illnesses this is the most therapeutic sort of climate, but for us it was almost unbearable. There was no escape from the burning sun. Fortunately, our quarters were air-conditioned, but there was no way of taking a cold shower. The cold water was "cold" only in the sense that it wasn't heated artificially.

We were given a welcome appropriate to my high position and to our good relations with Egypt. When the triumphant hour came for the damming of the river, President Nasser turned to me during the ceremony and said, "This is our dam, but in fact you have built it, you have financed it, your people designed it, and without you we would never have been able to begin. Therefore I ask you please to join me in throwing the switch which will divert the waters of the Nile from their ancient course." Well, this was certainly a great honor, and there was no sense in my refusing, so I thanked him and agreed with pleasure.

The President and I threw the switch together. An explosion shook the air, and the water rushed into its new course. There were huge crowds of people attending the ceremony, and I can't express how marvelous it was to see all the faces light up and the eyes sparkle with triumph as the mighty waters of the Nile began to turn the turbines which would give Egypt a new way of life. Later I was told that two men were caught in the tunnels and washed away. This accident was certainly careless and shortsighted on somebody's part.

That afternoon there was a reception for me at a club which belonged to our own specialists. They invited me to appear before them and to give a speech. I accepted with pleasure. Their spirits were high. I brought them good news about the state of affairs back home.

That evening, about sunset, a large meeting was scheduled. President Nasser was going to give a speech, and we were invited. The meeting was held in the evening because it would have been impossible for people to sit outside in the heat listening to speeches during the day.

I believe that evening in his speech was the first time Nasser said Egypt was going to build Socialism. Actually, he said the Egyptians were going to build their society on the basis of "scientific socialism," which we took to mean Marxism. He did not cite Marx or Lenin by name for a number of reasons. First, he was still having trouble coming to terms with Marxism in his own mind. Second, he had to take into account the attitude of some of his enemies. But most important, some of his allies still failed fully to understand what Marxism had to offer them. Therefore his choice of the phrase "scientific socialism" was a concession to all these different elements and considerations, but it also represented a big step forward. In short, I was pleased by his speech.

I had a brief speech of my own prepared, and it was well received by the audience. The next person to speak was Ben Bella [of Algeria]. He was one of the most impressive men I met in Egypt. He struck me as a man of culture, an educated man who understood the issues involved in the building of Socialism. He gave an excellent speech.

Then Aref [of Iraq] spoke. His speech was full of talk about the Arab people this, the Arab people that, the interests of the Arab people, and so on. While Aref was speaking, Ben Bella kept glancing over in my direction. He was smiling. He knew I shared his disagreement with Aref's speech. After Aref finished, Ben Bella came over to me and

tried to persuade me that I should reply to what Aref had said. I said
that I'd already spoken once and that I didn't have another speech prepared. Furthermore, it would be inappropriate for me as a guest to
turn the meeting into a debate. I said it would be very unpleasant for
Nasser if I started an argument. But at this point Nasser himself intervened and said to me, "I'd like to ask you to go ahead and answer
Aref. You won't be starting a polemic. You don't even have to mention
Aref by name. Go ahead and express your viewpoint on this subject. It
will be useful for Aref as well as for the rest of us to hear."

So I agreed. I took the floor and here is what I said:

Aref seemed to be suggesting that all Arabs have the same interests,
that Arab peoples are not divided into classes, and that Arab leaders
have a commitment to the Arab people as a whole. Well, I had had a
dispute with Nasser on this same subject a few years earlier, but now
Nasser had left that stage behind in the development of his own thinking. Apparently Aref had yet to overcome a very common misunder-
standing about the nature of Arab society. I said it was certainly a mistake to regard the Arab people as a single, unified entity. Arab society,
I explained, has a complicated social structure like every other society.
The Arab world is not a monolith. There are Arab slaves and Arab
capitalists; there are Arab peasants and Arab landowners; there is an
Arab working class and an Arab bourgeoisie. I said I felt it was reasonable to ask an Arab leader exactly whom he was speaking for
when he talked about "the Arab people" and "Arab interests." An Arab
peasant wants to work his own land, while an Arab landowner doesn't
want to give up his land; he wants to exploit the peasant. Arab workers want shorter hours and higher wages, while Arab capitalist employ-
ers want them to work longer hours for lower wages. "So what Arabs
are you speaking for?" I asked, "For Arab workers or Arab capitalists?"

It was perfectly clear to everyone that I was taking issue with Aref,
but no one seemed to mind. When I finished, I was pleased with what
I had said. I felt I had sown the seeds of a correct understanding of the
class structure of society.

I could, however, sympathize with the reasons for Aref's emphasis on
"Arab socialism." For years the Arab people had been under the yoke
of the English colonialists, and then they had to wage war against the
Israelis, who had seized their lands. To them, "Arab socialism" meant
Arab unity against a common external enemy. I knew that when Aref
espoused the cause of "Arab socialism" rather than "scientific social-

ism," it wasn't because he opposed Nasser. Not at all. In Aref's eyes, Nasser represented absolute authority. I think Aref simply hadn't gone far enough in his own thinking. The fruit of class consciousness still hadn't ripened in him, and he hadn't yet come to grips with the question of the class struggle.

Ben Bella and Nasser were both very pleased with my speech. Ben Bella was obviously delighted because he had been the first to encourage me to speak. He came up to me afterwards and said — now calling me comrade, I noticed — "Comrade Khrushchev, I'm sure you understand that even though you're quite right in your criticism of Aref's position, we still have to deal with him. More than that, we will support him to the end. Aref is with us all the way and he will never stray. For the time being he stands for Arab unity as he understands it, but the day will come when he will understand what you're saying."

Later, our people who understood Arabic informed me that my speech had been exceptionally well received among the Arabs in the audience. One of our specialists told me that his Arab chauffeur had told him that my speech had opened his eyes to a whole new conception of Arab unity. "I'd never realized it before," this chauffeur told our specialist, "but of course we Arabs have different class interests among ourselves!" For us, of course, this realization is as elementary as A-B-C, but for the Arabs it was something new. No one had told them before. Part of the reason was that the Communist Party had to remain underground in the Arab world, and as a result its message never reached the common people.

My stay in Egypt was very pleasant. We visited the Nile Delta, took a train ride along the Suez Canal, and spent two or three days on board a ship in the Red Sea. Some of our comrades went swimming, but I passed that up. I did do some fishing, however. The fishing was excellent. The coastal landscape of the Red Sea reminded us very much of the shoreline along our own Caspian Sea. We had many informal but useful conversations during this boat trip. For one thing, it was much easier to breathe here than in the desert around Aswan.

We visited Luxor, the ancient capital of the Egyptian kingdom, with rich historical monuments which we would have to save from being submerged in the flood caused by the Aswan Dam.[11]

11. The saving of the ancient Egyptian monuments and sculptures from being submerged forever by the waters of the dam was, of course, an international operation on a tremendous scale.

We also visited factories, some of them already in operation, which had been built with our assistance and cooperation. I remember being shown around a pharmaceutical plant which we had financed. In the old days, the Egyptians, who are a poor people, had been paying huge sums of money for medicines from England, and now they would be able to produce drugs much cheaper by themselves.

I knew enough geography to realize that the land on either side of the Nile Valley was desert, but I was still startled when I flew over the area and could see from the air how the rim of green, which was life, met the waterless expanse of the desert, which was death. I can't compete with people who have a gift for fancy description, but I'd still like to offer my own impressions of Egypt. Despite the climate, which is so hard to get used to, with its sweltering, enervating atmosphere, it's nonetheless a rich and beautiful country. When, as a boy, I studied the scriptures in the parish school, the priest used to show us pictures and tell us stories about paradise. The Nile Valley reminded me very much of what I had imagined heaven would be like in my childhood. It's a country rich in all the fabled beauties of nature, lush green foliage, and exotic birds.

One interesting thing about my Egyptian hosts was that they abstained from drinking any liquor. I had known before, of course, that Muslims are forbidden by their religion to drink, but not all Muslims abide by the counsel of their prophet. However, at banquets in Egypt I found that my hosts served nothing but fruit juice. These juices were delicious and thirst-quenching. They were made from many different kinds of fruit. My experience was that Egyptian fruit juices provided the best possible relief from the awful heat, and I'd like to express my own gratitude for the wisdom their prophet showed when he told the Muslims not to drink alcohol.

I was very much impressed by Nasser's tremendous prestige as a leader among the Egyptian people. Everywhere we went, he was hailed enthusiastically with chants of "Nasser! Nasser! Nasser!" I was, however, somewhat alarmed about Nasser's health. During one excursion with him — I think it was outside of Alexandria — he suddenly felt faint. He had the car stop. His eyeballs rolled back in his head, and he lay down on the back seat. He excused himself and was driven back to Alexandria, but he insisted that we continue our tour. Amer was almost always with us. He and Nasser were the closest of friends. They had neighboring apartments, and their two families lived together like one. Their children played with each other and so on. I was pleased to see two such good friends, both men of intelligence and sound judgment, working together to elevate Egypt from its primitiveness and poverty into a progressive society and a prosperous economy.

When Nasser and Amer took me out into the countryside, I could see that the farmers were trying their best to put their plots of land to good use and that the government was trying to create more humane conditions for the population of rural villages. But my general impression was that the agricultural reforms then under way were not based on any very advanced principles of revolutionary organization. Naturally I kept my observations to myself. As a guest I should look and listen, not offer unsolicited advice. Yet I couldn't help but compare all the trouble the Egyptians were having with the remarkable success we were having in our own agricultural campaigns in such Central Asian Republics as Uzbekistan, Turkmenistan, and Tadzhikistan. As an old pro at opening up new lands, I felt a strong urge to tell Nasser what I thought.

A few days later Nasser and I were having dinner together alone at his villa in Alexandria. I raised the subject very cautiously. I forget whether I called him Comrade Nasser or Mr. President, but I remember the gist of what I said: "I have a few thoughts I'd like to share with you, although I'm hesitant to comment on what is completely your own business."

"Go ahead. Tell me what's on your mind."

"I've been thinking about the lands which you're going to open up when you start using the dam for irrigation."

"Well, what about them? We're going to develop the land by dividing it up and distributing it among the people. Right now there's a terrible shortage of land for our peasants."

This was nothing new to me. I decided to push a little further. "Of course, you're undertaking a huge project, and I know it will yield enormous rewards for you. But please permit me to make a few observations. I'll ask you in advance not to be offended. I realize that it is inappropriate for me, as your guest, to impose on your indulgence like this. These are my own thoughts, and they're in no way binding on you. You can just hear me out, and it will be up to you whether or not to take my advice."

"Please go ahead," he said. "I'm listening."

"If I were in your place, I would not divide up the land and portion

it out to individual peasants. I would instead set up state farms —
what we call Soviet State Agricultural Enterprises. We've had a lot of
experience with this system in the Central Asian Republics where climate and soil conditions are very comparable to yours. We are proceeding with huge land-development projects on the barren steppes.
We have decided not to set up collective farms there but rather to
found city-like communities with everything from schools to barbershops, everything that's necessary to service the farmers' daily needs.
Naturally this requires enormous funds and capital investments, but
our experience has shown us that three or four good harvests are
enough to recoup our investment in a state farm. I guarantee, a state
farm system will make a mint of money for you.

"And I hope you won't be offended if I tell you something else.
When I was in school in the old pre-Revolutionary days, we used to
see pictures of the irrigation system that was used in Egypt back in the
time of Rameses I. From what I've seen, I'd say Egypt uses exactly the
same system today, under Nasser I, yet thousands of years have gone
by. Why is this? It's because a man working a tiny plot of land can't
possibly afford to install a pump in his well, just as he can't afford a
seed-sowing machine or a cotton baler. Big pieces of modern equipment like that wouldn't even have room to turn around on a tiny patch
of land.

"I realize that if you share out the land the peasants will accept it
and they will deify you for your progressivism and your generosity.
But you still won't be able to introduce technology as part of your agricultural reforms because modern farm machinery is neither necessary
nor even feasible on a tiny plot. Believe me, if you share out small
pieces of land to individual farmers, the Egyptian peasant will remain
just as much a slave to his own land as he has been for centuries."

Nasser listened to me attentively and said, "I'm afraid what you're
suggesting simply isn't possible for us. We don't have the necessary
specialists and supervisors to institute a state farm system. There's also
the problem of corruption. We simply wouldn't be able to establish sufficient controls to prevent embezzlement and black-marketeering, and
as a result our state farms would run at a heavy loss."

"Well," I said, "that's up to you to decide. I've told you my recommendation. You know your people better than I do, and you know the
problems and potential of your economy better than I. But on the matter of controlling corruption, I can tell you that we've had to put up

with a certain amount of pilfering, too, but we've managed to keep it under control. Now, as far as specialists are concerned, you can simply take them from among your army officers. Send them to us in the Soviet Union. We'll let them work for a year on our own state farms so that they can learn the system there while we're finishing the Aswan Dam here. That way, you'll be ready to develop the land to its full potential without losing time when the dam is finished and the new lands are opened up."

On the subject of irrigation I told him about a French farm I once visited at de Gaulle's invitation near the border of Spain. I was amazed at how fertile it was. I was entranced at how the irrigation system worked. The water was channeled through reinforced concrete races so that there would be no leakage. The hillslopes were carefully angled to control the level of water, and the whole system was mechanized. I had been very impressed and subsequently sent our own engineers to France to study their system.[12] I told Nasser I thought the French irrigation method might be very effective in Egypt and easy to introduce. I could see that he was starting to listen even more closely and began to ask some questions.

A few days later we were driving from the palace where I was staying to Nasser's villa. He turned to me and smiled, "You know, Comrade Khrushchev, I've been thinking about our conversation of the other day. I told Amer about it. That was a very alluring offer you made, and I now see that it would be much to our advantage for us to take you up on it. It might be profitable for you, too."

I replied, "If you think that what I suggested might be a progressive course for you to follow, then it will have been more than worth my while to have made this trip." I told him that in order to consummate the revolution, the Egyptian leadership should take all the peasants who were trying to cultivate their own tiny farms with primitive equipment and techniques and consolidate them into large administrative units — in other words, collectivize them. I told Nasser I fully appreciated how difficult a task this was. We had experienced troubles of our own when agriculture in the Soviet Union was collectivized — and when I say "troubles," that's an understatement. But once the Egyptians brought all the land under state control, they could organize the

12. In his genuine admiration of and enthusiasm for the French irrigation system below the Pyrenees Khrushchev shows his liveliest and most sympathetic side, which does not appear in this narrative as often as it might.

peasants into cooperatives and set up state farms. From then on they would develop smoothly and profitably. Later I found out from the newspapers that Nasser followed through on the idea he and I had discussed. An Egyptian delegation did come to the Soviet Union to study the state farm system. I was very pleased to read that my counsel had remained in force even after I retired from the post which I held during the time I was in Egypt. It proved that Nasser wasn't simply deferring to my position when he expressed interest in my offer; he must have really been convinced of the wisdom of my advice.

In summary, I think our policy toward Egypt was unquestionably sound, and it has already repaid us in full. I'm still convinced my own judgments were correct — despite the grumbling of those skunks, those narrow-minded skunks who raised such a stink and tried to poison the waters of our relations with Egypt.[13]

Egypt is in grave straits today. I remember my last conversation with President Nasser during my visit there in 1964. He told me that he had a troublesome situation on his hands within his own country and within the Arab world. He said that the wounds inflicted on the Arab people by the creation of the state of Israel would never heal because Arabs had been driven off their lands, and these Arabs now found themselves in severe trouble, both economically and politically. Before I retired, I made speeches from time to time against Israel's aggressive policy. I certainly sumpathized with Nasser's position.

There's no question in my mind that Israel started the war against Egypt [in 1967], and I think it's only a propaganda trick when Israel says it's ready to enter into direct negotiations with Egypt to work out a negotiated settlement of the conflict. In fact, since the war Israel has taken a more aggressive stance than ever and is looking for a chance to use military means to destroy the Egyptian armed forces and to compel Egypt to sign a peace treaty on Israel's own terms.

But there are a couple of things I can't understand that happened before Israel's attack on Egypt. It's not at all clear to me why Egypt demanded that U Thant remove the UN troops from the border between Egypt and Israel. These forces were a restraining influence on the Israeli aggressors. They were helping to neutralize the threat of a clash along the border. I remember we voted in favor of sending a UN

13. This sudden and surprisingly bitter outburst evidently refers to some conflict inside the Kremlin about which we know nothing.

peace-keeping force to the Near East in order to prevent war from breaking out between the two hostile states, Egypt and Israel. It's simply incomprehensible to me why Egypt demanded that these forces be removed.

Nor can I understand what goal Egypt thought it was pursuing when it closed the Suez Canal, which was the main waterway used by Israel from the Mediterranean Ocean to the Red Sea.

Israel took advantage of these actions on Egypt's part. The Israeli aggressors seized Egyptian territories, and Israel is still exploiting them today, thereby making things very hard on Egypt.

And another thing: If Egypt was prepared for war against Israel, then why was Israel able to crush the Egyptian army in six days?

All these questions puzzle me, and I don't have any idea what the answer to them is because I was already in retirement when these events developed. All I know is that during the period when we were actively concerned with the Near East, we conducted a policy which was Leninist in spirit. Our policy has already borne fruit for our own Soviet people and for the peoples of all countries of the world who believe in peaceful coexistence and self-determination.

17

The Berlin Crises

Here we are offered a view from Moscow of all-too-familiar ground: the conflict over Germany as seen through Khrushchev's eyes. Of particular interest is the account of the armed confrontation between Soviet and American forces at the time of the building of the Berlin Wall, which Khrushchev refers to as the establishment of border control. Khrushchev telescopes the chronology of the two Berlin crises: the first was in November, 1958, when Moscow gave the Western powers six months to evacuate Berlin; the second was in 1961, after the meeting in Vienna between Khrushchev and President Kennedy, from which Khrushchev gained the erroneous idea that he could bully the new President.

A FTER Hitler was crushed, East and West Germany each chose a different political system. East Germany decided in favor of building Socialism, and West Germany went the route of capitalism.[1]

When we began to face up to the problem of West Berlin after Stalin's death, we realized that the agreement which had liquidated the blockade of West Berlin [1948–49] was unfair.[2] The West had managed to exploit the tension generated by the blockade and to impose conditions on East Germany which were even more constraining and

1. East Germany had no choice. It was sealed off from the West by Soviet troops and ruled by Moscow-trained Communists (Otto Grotewohl, Wilhelm Pick, and Walter Ulbricht). Three months after Stalin's death in 1953, a popular uprising was put down expeditiously by Soviet tanks.
2. The blockade, defeated by the Allied airlift, was imposed by the Russians to strangle West Berlin by preventing access to it. The tensions referred to here were thus set up by Stalin.

one-sided than the ones set by the Potsdam agreement. The international situation throughout Europe was highly unstable, and therefore internal stabilization was impossible for the German Democratic Republic [East Germany]. Germany was a sort of barometer. The slightest fluctuation in the pressure of the world political atmosphere naturally registered at that point where the forces of the two sides were squared off against each other.

We wanted very much to relieve the tension which was building up dangerously over West Berlin, and we knew that the only way we could do it would be to conclude a peace treaty with the West. This posed a problem: on what basis would it be possible to reach an agreement with the Western powers? It was already too late to talk about a treaty that would reunify Germany because neither East Germany nor West Germany wanted to accept the social-political system of the other side. That much we understood and accepted. But we still sincerely wanted to find some workable and mutually beneficial terms for a treaty that would stabilize the situation, further the cause of peace, and uphold the rights of everyone involved. It was clear that the existing situation was dangerous, and also that both sides wanted to avoid military confrontation.

Therefore we came to the conclusion that we should work out a peace treaty which would consolidate the status of Germany as fixed by the Potsdam agreement. The Potsdam agreement was considered a temporary solution pending the Allies' conclusion of a peace treaty with Germany. Our proposal would have legitimized the provisional de facto situation and made it permanent. We were simply asking the other side to acknowledge that two irreconcilable social-political structures existed in Germany, Socialism in East Germany and capitalism in West Germany. We were asking only for formal recognition of two German Republics, each of which would sign the treaty. According to our proposal West Berlin would have special status as a free city.[3]

Clearly, some of the terms of the Potsdam agreement were already out of date. At the very least, adjustments in the treaty were required as regarded the use of East German territory for access to West Berlin. Strictly for the sake of adhering to international law, the West should have come to terms with us on this account. As it was, the West was

3. This refers to the 1958 crisis. The Russians were asking for much more than a formal recognition of the divisions of Germany. They demanded the evacuation of West Berlin by Allied forces.

putting its own, very one-sided interpretation on the question of the GDR's right to control its borders. The problem had not been foreseen by the Potsdam agreement — an omission in the treaty which the West was turning to its own purposes.[4] This was another reason why a permanent peace treaty was required. The legal rights of the GDR were at stake. The issue still exists today.

The Western powers rejected our proposal for the recognition of two German Republics. In response, we warned that we might have no choice but to initiate a peace treaty unilaterally, and we proposed a date for a meeting of all countries who wanted to sign the treaty. We warned that even if certain countries refused to sign, the rest of us would go ahead and conclude a treaty with the GDR. We would then be obliged to act according to the terms of the new treaty on various matters, including the matter of access to West Berlin.

Meanwhile, Walter Ulbricht and our other comrades in the GDR were facing serious troubles directly stemming from the ambiguous status of West Berlin. Berlin was an open city, which posed two problems: First, there was the problem of people crossing from East Berlin into West Berlin. The GDR had to cope with an enemy who was economically very powerful and therefore very appealing to the GDR's own citizens. West Germany was all the more enticing to East Germans because they all spoke the same language. An East German with adequate professional qualifications had no difficulty finding a job if he moved to West Germany. The resulting drain of workers was creating a simply disastrous situation in the GDR, which was already suffering from a shortage of manual labor, not to mention specialized labor. If things had continued like this much longer, I don't know what would have happened. I spent a great deal of time trying to think of a way out. How could we introduce incentives in the GDR to counteract the force behind the exodus of East German youths to West Germany? Here was an important question — the question of incentives. How could we create conditions in the GDR which would enable the state to regulate the steady attrition of its working force?[5]

4. The Potsdam Agreement had not foreseen the forcible and permanent division of Germany.

5. Khrushchev has now moved on to the makings of the 1961 crisis. By July the flood of refugees pouring out of East Germany into West Germany had assumed monstrous proportions (ten thousand a week) and the East German economy was becoming impossibly strained in consequence.

The second problem was the problem of the West Berliners' easy access to East Berlin. Residents of West Berlin could cross freely into East Berlin, where they took advantage of all sorts of communal services like barbershops and so on. Because prices were much lower in East Berlin, West Berliners were also buying up all sorts of products which were in wide demand — products like meat, animal oil, and other food items, and the GDR was losing millions of marks.

Of course, even if we had a peace treaty, it wouldn't have solved these problems because Berlin's status as a free city would have been stipulated in the treaty and the gates would have remained open.

I discussed this situation with Comrade Ulbricht and the other leaders of the member Parties of the Warsaw Pact. I stressed that Ulbricht had an especially heavy burden on his shoulders. Every other country had its own laws, its own border rights, and was free to decide domestic and foreign policy for itself, in the interests of its own people. But the GDR had neither these rights nor this freedom.

The GDR's economic problems were considerably relieved by the establishment of border control between East and West Berlin.[6] Comrade Ulbricht himself told me that the economy of the GDR immediately began to improve after the establishment of border control. The demand for food products in East Berlin went down because West Berliners were no longer able to shop there. This meant that the limited supply of consumer products was available exclusively to the citizens of East Berlin.

Furthermore, the establishment of border control in Berlin had a very positive effect on the consciousness of the people. It strengthened them and reminded them that the task of building Socialism was a challenge of solid and lasting importance, dwarfing the temporary phenomenon of West German propaganda which had been used to tempt East Germans over to the side of capitalism. The establishment of border control restored order and discipline in the East Germans' lives (and Germans have always appreciated discipline). Seeing that their government had reasserted control over its own frontiers, the East Germans were heartened by the solidification and fortification of their state.

Of course there were some difficulties. The East Berliners who had jobs in West Berlin were suddenly out of work. But there was never

6. The phrase "establishment of border control" refers to the Berlin Wall, started on August 13, 1961.

any problem of unemployment. On the contrary, most of the people affected were construction workers, who were very much needed in East
Germany. They were all given jobs suitable to their qualifications.

There were illegal attempts to cross over to the West, resulting in
some incidents along the border, some of them with unpleasant outcome. Such unpleasantness had to be expected. Border guards were
forced to use the means which had been put at their disposal to prevent violation of the border.[7] The incidents were exploited by the West
and blown completely out of proportion.

I know there are critics, especially in bourgeois societies, who say
we ignored the will of the East German citizens when we reinforced
the sovereignty of the GDR by closing the borders. I know there are
people who claim that the East Germans are imprisoned in paradise
and that the gates of the Socialist paradise are guarded by armed
troops. I'm aware that a defect exists, but I believe it's a necessary and
only temporary defect. We have always wanted to create the conditions in the GDR which the citizens want. If the GDR had fully tapped
the moral and material potential which will someday be harnessed by
the dictatorship of the working class, there could be unrestricted passage back and forth between East and West Berlin. Unfortunately, the
GDR — and not only the GDR — has yet to reach a level of moral and
material development where competition with the West is possible.
The reason is simply that West Germany possesses more material potential and therefore has more material goods than the GDR. Of
course, there are some of our more clever Communists who will protest, "No, you are underestimating our achievement!" and so on. Well,
let's just look at the whole thing soberly. If we had at our disposal
more material potential and had more ability to supply our material
needs, there's no question but that our people would be content with
what they would have and they would no longer try to cross over to
the West in such numbers that the drain has become a major threat to
a state like the GDR.[8]

It was my dream to create such conditions in Germany that the
GDR would become a showcase of moral, political, and material
achievement — all attractively displayed for the Western world to see
and admire. Part of the reason for struggling to convince our former al-

7. Border guards in most countries are employed to keep undesirable strangers
out, not to keep their fellow citizens in.
8. The frankness of these admissions does Khrushchev credit. It strikes a new
note in the utterances of Soviet politicians.

lies to sign a peace treaty and thereby to normalize relations between our states, was to permit the development of trade, cultural exchange, and tourism.

Even if we were able to create the conditions in the GDR which its citizens want, we would still have to guard the borders. We would introduce as much freedom as the material conditions would permit, but naturally under the dictatorship of the working class there can be no such thing as absolute freedom. As for other countries which brag about all their freedoms, if we analyze their societies carefully, we'll find that they have no such thing as absolute freedom either. In order to feel moral constraint, moral oppression, or moral bondage, a man must have a highly developed and highly refined conception of what human freedom is all about. Most people still measure their own freedom or lack of freedom in terms of how much meat, how many potatoes, or what kind of boots they can get for one ruble.[9]

When we established control on the borders of the GDR, we relied heavily on our own armed forces which were stationed in Germany after the war. But even as we took measures to protect the interests of our German comrades, we didn't withdraw our proposal, which would have legitimized the existing borders and guaranteed the neutrality and self-determination of West Berlin as a free city. But the West again rejected our proposal and now demanded that the border which we had established be removed. The Western powers threatened to resort to force. They said they would use bulldozers to knock out the roadblocks and to level the barriers which we had erected. They said if necessary they would back up these measures with military force, and that they were going to take it upon themselves to restore conditions which would allow unobstructed passage back and forth between East and West Berlin.

We had erected what we thought were solid structures along the border, but some trucks smashed through them at full speed and hurtled into West Berlin. Even more solid structures were then built in those spots so that the same thing wouldn't happen again.

If the Western powers had so desired, they could have gone ahead and staged a provocation. But such an action on their part would have had fairly serious consequences. Fortunately, articles written with at least a grain of sense were beginning to appear in the American press

9. These philosophical observations on the nature of freedom strike an equally unusual note.

about the risks involved in trying to use military means to liquidate the situation which had developed.

We assumed that the West didn't want to start a war and our assumption turned out to be correct. Starting a war over Berlin would have been stupid. There was no reason to do so. Our establishment of border control in the GDR didn't give the West either the right or the pretext to resolve our dispute by war.

By this time President Kennedy was in the White House. Not long before the events in Berlin came to a head, I had met Kennedy in Vienna. He impressed me as a better statesman than Eisenhower. Unlike Eisenhower, Kennedy had a precisely formulated opinion on every subject [see page 397]. I joked with him that we had cast the deciding ballot in his election to the Presidency over that son-of-a-bitch Richard Nixon. When he asked me what I meant, I explained that by waiting to release the U-2 pilot Gary Powers until after the American election, we kept Nixon from being able to claim that he could deal with the Russians; our ploy made a difference of at least half a million votes, which gave Kennedy the edge he needed.

Actually, I had met Kennedy two years before, during my visit to America, when Lyndon Johnson introduced me to the young Senator at a Senate Foreign Relations Committee reception in my honor. I was impressed with Kennedy. I remember liking his face, which was sometimes stern but which often broke into a good-natured smile. As for Nixon, I had been all too familiar with him in the past. He had been a puppet of [Joseph] McCarthy until McCarthy's star began to fade, at which point Nixon turned his back on him. So he was an unprincipled puppet, which is the most dangerous kind. I was very glad Kennedy won the election, and I was generally pleased with our meeting in Vienna. Even though we came to no concrete agreement, I could tell that he was interested in finding a peaceful solution to world problems and in avoiding conflict with the Soviet Union. He was a reasonable man, and I think he knew that he wouldn't be justified in starting a war over Berlin.

Nevertheless, Kennedy decided to demonstrate his strength. He reinforced the American garrison and appointed a general named Clay to take command of the Western forces in Berlin. Kennedy seemed to be turning back the clock to the period just after World War II.[10]

10. General Lucius Clay, who had been commandant of the American sector of Berlin during the blockade. The clock had certainly been turned back. But by whom?

The bourgeois press started to grind out propaganda against us. At this point we were heading toward the Twenty-second Party Congress. We decided to accept the challenge which Kennedy had issued. We knew from our intelligence what steps the West was taking to intensify its concentration of troops in Berlin, and we built up our own garrison accordingly. We appointed Marshal Konev commander of our troops in Berlin. We had picked up the gauntlet and were ready for the duel.

I should make it clear that our appointment of Marshal Konev as commander was actually just an "administrative" appointment to demonstrate to the West that we regarded the situation as seriously as they did.[11] Our regular commander in Berlin, who was junior in rank to Konev, remained in charge while Konev reported to us in Moscow. The fact that Konev spent most of his time in Moscow proves that we weren't expecting the confrontation to escalate into a full-scale military conflict.

Konev reported that he had learned through intelligence channels on what day and at what hour the Western powers were going to begin their actions against us. They were preparing bulldozers to break down our border installations. The bulldozers would be followed by tanks and wave after wave of jeeps with infantrymen. This action was timed to coincide with the opening of the Twenty-second Party Congress.

We went into consultation and worked out in advance what our response would be. We concentrated our own infantry units in side streets near the checkpoints along the border. We also brought in our tanks at night and stationed them nearby. Then there was nothing for us to do but wait and see what the West would do next.

Then Konev reported that the American bulldozers, tanks, and jeeps had moved out and were heading in the direction of our checkpoints. Our men were waiting calmly and did not move, even when the bulldozers came right up to the border. Then all at once our tanks rolled out of the side streets and moved forward to meet the American tanks.

The American bulldozers and tanks came to a halt. The jeeps drove past them and crossed over the border into East Berlin. We didn't try to stop them because, according to special terms in the Potsdam agreement, Allied military vehicles were allowed to cross from one zone to another in Berlin. Therefore we opened the gates and let the American

11. Marshal I. S. Konev had recently relinquished command of the Warsaw Pact forces. His bogus, or "administrative," appointment was an interesting example of Soviet bluff.

jeeps through. After they'd gone a short distance beyond the check-point, the Americans saw our troops stationed in the side streets and our tanks coming toward them. The Americans immediately turned their jeeps around and sped back into West Berlin.

The tanks and troops of both sides spent the night lined up facing each other across the border. It was late October and chilly. It certainly must have been invigorating for our tank operators to sit up all night in cold metal boxes. The next morning Marshal Konev reported to us that both the American tank crews and our own had climbed out of their tanks in turn to warm themselves, but that the barrels of their cannons remained trained on each other across the border.

After Marshal Konev's report I proposed that we turn our tanks around, pull them back from the border, and have them take their places in the side streets. Then we would wait and see what happened next. I assured my comrades that as soon as we pulled back our tanks, the Americans would pull back theirs. They had taken the initiative in moving up to the border in the first place, and therefore they would, so to say, have been in a difficult moral position if we forced them to turn their backs on the barrels of our cannons. Therefore we decided that at this point we should take the initiative ourselves and give the Americans an opportunity to pull back from the border once the threat of our tanks had been removed. My comrades agreed with me. I said I thought that the Americans would pull back their tanks within twenty minutes after we had removed ours. This was about how long it would take their tank commander to report our move and to get orders from higher up of what to do.

Konev ordered our tanks to pull back from the border. He reported that just as I had expected, it did take only twenty minutes for the Americans to respond.

Thus the West had tested our nerve by prodding us with the barrels of their cannons and found us ready to accept their challenge. They learned that they couldn't frighten us. I think it was a great victory for us, and it was won without firing a single shot.[12] By refusing to back down in the face of intimidation by the West, we guaranteed the GDR's right to control its own territory and its own borders. We had good reason to celebrate this moral and material victory, for we had forced the West to recognize the GDR's unwritten rights.

12. By all means the Western Allies gave way over the Wall. But their troops remained in West Berlin.

18

Mao Tse-tung and the Schism

In this highly personal and anecdotal account of Khrushchev's and Stalin's relations with Mao Tse-tung there is nothing to contradict the accepted Western reconstruction of the genesis and development of the Sino-Soviet split and there is a good deal to confirm it. Khrushchev does not add to the story (indeed, he leaves out much that we know) so much as embroider it. He concentrates on the personal aspects of the great schism (whether seen primarily as an ideological conflict, or as a conflict of interest between two great powers) and its seismic effects on the world Communist movement. He does give us, nevertheless, new and valuable insights into the bitterness of the conflict, and above all, his own emotional approach to the whole affair. It is clear that, like most Russians, he found, and still finds, the Chinese character incomprehensible and distasteful in the extreme. It is with a visible effort that he pulls himself together and forces himself to differentiate Mao and his supporters from the Chinese people, who, he declares with striking lack of conviction, "are human beings just as we are." Here we have an echo of the old, loud-mouthed Khrushchev with his contempt for Chinese ways made strident by an undercurrent of fear.

P<small>OLITICS</small> is a game, and Mao Tse-tung has played politics with Asiatic cunning, following his own rules of cajolery, treachery, savage vengeance, and deceit. He deceived us for a number of years before we saw through his tricks. Talleyrand once said that a diplomat is given a tongue in order to conceal his thoughts. The same goes for a politician, and Mao Tse-tung has always been a master at concealing his true thoughts and intentions. Why, I remember after the Twentieth Party Congress, Mao said, "Comrade Khrushchev has opened our eyes and given us light that we might see. He has told us the truth at last. We will reform." But I was always on my guard with him. I could tell when he was wheedling us.

A few years after I retired, the story started circulating that I was the one who started the quarrel between the USSR and China. I won't even bother to refute this slander. History has already made nonsense out of that allegation.

Ever since I first met Mao, I've known — and I've told my comrades — that Mao would never be able to reconcile himself to any other Communist Party being in any way superior to his own within the world Communist movement. He would never be able to tolerate it. If Stalin had lived a little longer, our conflict with China would have come out into the open earlier, and it probably would have taken the form of a complete severance of relations.[1]

Stalin was always fairly critical of Mao Tse-tung. He had a name for Mao, and it describes him accurately from a purely Marxist point of view. Stalin used to say that Mao was a "margarine Marxist" [*peschany marksist*].

When Mao's victorious revolutionary army was approaching Shanghai, he halted their march and refused to capture the city. Stalin asked Mao, "Why didn't you take Shanghai?"

"There's a population of six million there," answered Mao. "If we take the city, then we'll have to feed all those people. And where do we find food to do it?"

Now, I ask you, is that a Marxist talking?

Mao Tse-tung has always relied on the peasants and not on the working class. That's why he didn't take Shanghai. He didn't want to take responsibility for the welfare of the workers. Stalin properly criticized Mao for this deviation from true Marxism. But the fact remains that Mao, relying on the peasants and ignoring the working class, achieved victory. Not that his victory was some sort of miracle, but it

1. This is a dubious thesis. There was indeed no love lost between Stalin and Mao. Stalin had supported Chiang Kai-shek and insulted Mao in doing so. He had also told Mao, shortly before he achieved his victorious drive in 1948, that any idea of revolution in China was premature. But Mao respected him as he never dreamed of respecting Khrushchev. And Stalin would never have allowed himself to be carried away on a highly emotional tide of indignation as Khrushchev did. Had Stalin lived longer, sooner or later Mao would have collided with him, but later rather than sooner.

was certainly a new twist to Marxist philosophy since it was achieved without the proletariat. In short, Mao Tse-tung is a petty-bourgeois whose interests are alien, and have been alien all along, to those of the working class.

After Mao came to power, his relations with Stalin soon became strained at the level of trade and industrial cooperation as well as at the level of ideology. At one point Stalin concluded a treaty with China for the joint exploitation of mineral resources in Sinkiang. The treaty was a mistake on Stalin's part. I would even say it was an insult to the Chinese people. For centuries the French, English, and Americans had been exploiting China, and now the Soviet Union was moving in. This exploitation was a bad thing, but not unprecedented: Stalin had set up similar "joint" companies in Poland, Germany, Bulgaria, Czechoslovakia, and Rumania. Later we liquidated all these companies.

There was another such incident. One day Stalin called around to all of us and asked if anyone knew where China's gold and diamond mines were. Of course, none of us knew. We had no way of knowing. We used to joke about it in whispers among ourselves. Beria said, "You know who knows? Kozlovsky does.[2] He's always singing that song, 'You can't count the diamonds . . .' [from Bizet's opera *The Pearl Fishers*]." Beria liked to egg Stalin on, saying that there were enormous riches in China, that Mao Tse-tung was hiding them from us, and that if we gave Mao a credit loan he would have to give us something in return.

Then one day we were sitting around at Stalin's, trying to figure out some way to meet the demands of our rubber industry without having to buy crude rubber from the capitalists. I suggested getting Mao to let us set up a rubber plantation in China in exchange for credit loans and technical assistance. We sent Mao a cable proposing this plan. The Chinese replied that if we would give them credit, they would let us use the island of Hainan for our plantation. We drew up an agreement between us, but it turned out that the area we were given on Hainan was too small for a decent rubber plantation, and the idea was dropped.

Then all of a sudden Stalin took a liking to canned pineapple. He immediately dictated a message to Malenkov, who was always a handy

2. I. S. Kozlovsky, the great Russian tenor of the Bolshoi Opera; in his prime, though unknown in the West, he was perhaps the greatest tenor since Caruso.

clerk: "Get off a message to the Chinese that I'd like them to give us an area where we can build a pineapple cannery."

I spoke up and said, "Comrade Stalin, the Communists have just recently come to power in China. There are already too many foreign factories there, and now the Soviet Union, a fellow Socialist country, is going to put up a factory of its own in China! This is sure to offend Mao Tse-tung."

Stalin snapped at me angrily, and I said nothing more. The cable was sent. A day or two later we received the Chinese reply. Mao Tse-tung said, "We accept your proposal. If you are interested in canned pineapples, then give us a credit loan and we will build the cannery ourselves. We will then pay back your loan with the produce from this cannery." I was silent while Stalin cursed and fumed. Just as I had suspected, Stalin had offended Mao.

No such cables proposing to exploit China were ever sent to Mao over my signature or the signature of our government in my time. We took great care never to offend China until the Chinese actually started to crucify us. And when they did start to crucify us — well, I'm no Jesus Christ, and I didn't have to turn the other cheek.

When the malicious rumor started circulating that I was responsible for the Soviet Union's quarrel with China, I was particularly astounded, distressed, and angered that Yudin was among those spreading the story that I goaded Mao into becoming the sort of person he is now. Well, if Yudin were here and said this to me in person, I would be able to give him documentary proof that it was actually he who first brought our conflict with Mao Tse-tung to a head. He was our ambassador to China at the beginning of the quarrel. And if Yudin were to force me to embark on such an unsavory exchange of accusations with him, then I might remark with some justification that we were sure to have discord with any country where Yudin was sent as ambassador. Yudin was sent to Yugoslavia, and we had a falling-out with Tito [see pages 376–377]. Yudin went to China, and we had a falling-out with Mao. This was no coincidence.

At one point I had respect for Yudin. Why was he sent to China in the first place? It happened like this: Mao Tse-tung wrote a letter to Stalin asking him to recommend a Soviet Marxist philosopher who might come to China to edit Mao's works. Mao wanted an educated man to help put his works into proper shape and to catch any mistakes in Marxist philosophy before Mao's writings were published. Yudin was chosen and sent to Peking.[3]

For a while Yudin worked hand in glove with Mao. Mao went to see Yudin more often than the other way around. Stalin was even a bit worried that Yudin wasn't treating Mao with proper respect because he permitted Mao to come to him instead of going to Mao. Everything was going along fine.

Then, out of the blue, we received from Yudin a long coded dispatch in which he described all sorts of incredible things which he had heard from Mao Tse-tung about the Soviet Union, our Communist Party, and about Yudin himself. There was no longer any need to worry that Mao was fawning over Yudin. Now it was obvious that Mao had no respect for Yudin at all. We decided we'd better get Yudin out of China. As an ambassador, Yudin had been a weak administrator and poor diplomat, but he had been useful as long as his personal relations with Mao remained friendly. To hell with his strictly ambassadorial work; we could always let our embassy officials in Peking take care of that. But when he clashed with Mao on philosophical grounds, he was no good to us either as an ambassador or as a contact with Mao. So we recalled him.

And now this philosopher is trying to pin the blame on others.

As far as my own relations with Mao are concerned, I always bent over backwards to be fair and friendly. Unlike Stalin, I never tried to take advantage of Mao. In fact, just the opposite happened: the Chinese tried to take advantage of us. For instance, in 1954, when our country was still hungry and poverty-ridden from the war, we were in Peking and Chou En-lai asked, "Perhaps you could make us a gift of a university?"

"We're poor ourselves, you know," I said. "We may be richer than

3. P. F. Yudin was the onetime editor of the Cominform newspaper with the stirring title *For Lasting Peace, for People's Democracy!*, which was published in Belgrade until the Stalin-Tito quarrel. He was a byword for his combination of servility toward those set above him and pompous arrogance toward those below him. He appeared to nourish the illusion that the latter included all foreigners, which did not go down well with the Yugoslavs and the Chinese with whom he was required to work. In Moscow he was known as the best philosopher in the Cheka and the best Chekist among the philosophers. His philosophy consisted in dressing up the turns and twists of the Kremlin line in quasi-Marxist jargon. Khrushchev was quite right to hold him in contempt; but it was largely Khrushchev's fault that he was retained as Soviet ambassador to China from 1953 until the great quarrel.

you, but the war has just ended and we are still not back on our feet."
Even though we had troubles of our own, we had given Port Arthur
and Dalny to the Chinese free, and we had invested huge amounts of
money in China.[4]

We had also built the road from Ulan Bator to Peking. When Mao
mentioned this in 1957, he said, "The road from Ulan Bator isn't much
use to us. What we really need is a road from Peking through the
mountains to Kazakhstan."

I said, "You know your own territory better than we do. We thought
the road from Ulan Bator would be a more direct route for you, but
we'd be willing to open a road to China through Kazakhstan, too. Why
don't you build the road on your territory, and we'll build our section
of the road so that it connects at the border?"

Later Chou En-lai brought up the subject of this road again: "Maybe
you could build the section of the road on our territory, too?" We
looked at the map and saw that this would have meant cutting through
mountains and building bridges over rivers.

We answered, "No, let's each build our own sections of the road as
we originally agreed."

We started our share of the work. During the process of the construction, the Chinese came to us again asking us to build their part of
the road, and when we finally reached the border, the Chinese were
nowhere to be seen.

I remember that when I came back from China in 1954 I told my
comrades, "Conflict with China is inevitable." I came to this conclusion
on the basis of various remarks Mao had made. During my visit to Peking, the atmosphere was typically Oriental. Everyone was unbelievably courteous and ingratiating, but I saw through their hypocrisy.
After I had arrived, Mao and I embraced each other warmly and
kissed each other on both cheeks. We used to lie around a swimming
pool in Peking, chatting like the best of friends about all kinds of
things. But it was all too sickeningly sweet. The atmosphere was nauseating. In addition, some of the things Mao said put me on my guard.
I was never exactly sure that I understood what he meant. I thought at
the time that it must have been because of some special traits in the
Chinese character and the Chinese way of thinking. Some of Mao's

4. The reference is to the handing over to the Chinese of Port Arthur and Dalny
(Dairen) in May, 1955, after a long, unsettled history involving China, Japan, and
Russia. Soviet credits were in fact no more than a drop in the ocean of Chinese
need.

pronouncements struck me as being much too simplistic, and others struck me as being much too complex.

I remember, for example, that Mao once asked me, "Comrade Khrushchev, what do you think of our slogan, 'Let a Hundred Flowers Bloom'?" [5]

I answered, "Comrade Mao Tse-tung, we simply can't figure out what this slogan of yours means. There are all kinds of flowers — beautiful flowers, nauseating flowers, and even lethal flowers." Mao agreed that maybe it wasn't a good slogan for Russians. We had made a point of not publishing anything in our own press about the "Hundred Flowers" slogan. Mao was no fool; he realized that our silence meant we didn't agree with him. In fact, of course, I realize perfectly well what "Let a Hundred Flowers Bloom" means. It means let different tendencies develop in art and culture. But now it's clear to everyone that the slogan was intended as a provocation. It was proclaimed in order to encourage people to express themselves more openly so that any flowers whose blossom had the wrong color or scent could be cut down and trampled into the dirt.

Then there was Mao's other famous slogan: "Imperialism Is a Paper Tiger." I found it perfectly incredible that Mao could dismiss American imperialism as a paper tiger when in fact it is a dangerous predator. The "Paper Tiger" slogan was first proclaimed when our relations with China were still good, and it caused us a certain amount of embarrassment, coming as it did from our friend Mao Tse-tung, the leader of the Chinese people. Now it seems the Chinese have quieted down for the time being about the "Paper Tiger." They're not chanting it all the time the way they used to.

I remember once in Peking, Mao and I were lying next to the swimming pool in our bathing trunks, discussing the problems of war and peace. Mao Tse-tung said to me, "Comrade Khrushchev, what do you think? If we compare the military might of the capitalist world with that of the Socialist world, you'll see that we obviously have the advantage over our enemies. Think of how many divisions China, the USSR, and the other Socialist countries could raise."

I said, "Comrade Mao Tse-tung, nowadays that sort of thinking is out of date. You can no longer calculate the alignment of forces on the

5. "Let a hundred flowers bloom, let a hundred schools contend": Mao introduced this short-lived policy of apparent toleration early in 1957. Khrushchev then and thereafter was obsessively irritated by the phrase.

In China, 1954. Above: Khrushchev and Bulganin at the Canton airport

Khrushchev, Bulganin (in uniform), and security chief Serov (center)

Mao Tse-tung, Khrushchev, and Mikoyan

basis of who has the most men. Back in the days when a dispute was settled with fists or bayonets, it made a difference who had the most men and the most bayonets on each side. Then when the machine gun appeared, the side with more troops no longer necessarily had the advantage. And now with the atomic bomb, the number of troops on each side makes practically no difference to the alignment of real power and the outcome of a war. The more troops on a side, the more bomb fodder."

Mao replied by trying to assure me that the atomic bomb itself was a paper tiger! "Listen, Comrade Khrushchev," he said. "All you have to do is provoke the Americans into military action, and I'll give you as many divisions as you need to crush them — a hundred, two hundred, one thousand divisions." I tried to explain to him that one or two missiles could turn all the divisions in China to dust. But he wouldn't even listen to my arguments and obviously regarded me as a coward.[6]

Mao certainly changed his tune in 1957, when he came to the Moscow Conference of Communist and Workers' Parties and said, during an amiable and candid conversation, "Comrade Khrushchev, I see in the newspaper that your defense minister, Zhukov, says that if any Socialist country is attacked by any imperialist power, you will strike back swiftly. That would be a mistake."

I said, "Comrade Mao Tse-tung, Zhukov wasn't just speaking for himself. He was speaking for the Central Committee and voicing our collective decision. I've said the same thing myself." We weren't quarreling; we were just having a friendly discussion.

Mao replied, "I think if the imperialists were to attack China, you shouldn't intervene. We would fight them by ourselves. Your job would be to survive. Let us watch out for ourselves. What's more, if you were attacked, I don't think you should retaliate."

"And what should we do?"

"Retreat."

"Where to?"

"You've retreated before. You retreated all the way to Stalingrad during World War II, and if you're attacked again you could retreat

6. In this precious vignette of the two leaders of the Communist world, relaxing in the shallow end of a Peking swimming pool as they discuss war, peace, and the atom bomb in kindergarten terms, we see the beginning of Khrushchev's personal exasperation with the man who was later to say that even after an atomic war there would still be three hundred million Chinese left.

all the way to the Urals and hold out for two or three years. You'd have China at your back."

"Comrade Mao Tse-tung, if a war started now, how long do you think it would last? It wouldn't be like the last war. That was a war of air forces and tanks. Now there are missiles and atomic bombs. What makes you think we'd have three years in which to retreat to the Urals? We'd probably have only a few days, and after that there would be nothing left of us but a few tattered remnants scratching along. If we told the enemy that we won't retaliate, we'd be inviting him to attack. That's why we must let him know that our warning serves to deter him."

Clearly, there was a fairly basic disagreement between us. But our split with China went even deeper. The Chinese knew that they were in a dangerous position in the world Communist movement after the Twentieth Party Congress. They understood the implications for themselves of the Congress's repudiation of personality cults, autocratic rule, and all other antidemocratic, anti-Party forms of life. Stalin was exposed and condemned at the Congress for having had hundreds of thousands of people shot and for his abuse of power. Mao Tse-tung was following in Stalin's footsteps.

Mao's own personality cult is a complicated phenomenon. A personality cult is a little like a religion. For centuries people have been droning, "Lord, have mercy upon us; Lord, help us and protect us." And have all the prayers helped? Of course not. But people are set in their ways and continue to believe in God despite all the evidence to the contrary.

There have even been echoes of the Maoist personality cult here in our country. In about 1962, I discovered that our military men had been printing Mao Tse-tung's works on warfare. I immediately sent for the Minister of Defense and said, "Comrade Malinovsky, I understand your department is publishing the works of Mao. This is absurd! The Soviet Army crushed the crack forces of the German army, while Mao Tse-tung's men have spent between twenty and twenty-five years poking each other in the backsides with knives and bayonets. Now you're publishing Mao's works on warfare! What for? To learn how to make war in the future? What were you using for your head when you made this decision?" Malinovsky and the other military comrades were intelligent men, but publishing Mao Tse-tung on warfare was a stupid waste of time. I don't know whatever happened to the copies they printed. They're probably lying in some storeroom somewhere, or maybe they've been burned.

I remember well how Mao Tse-tung rebuffed our efforts to cooperate on military matters in 1958. According to a treaty, our planes were supposed to be able to use airfields in China for layovers and refueling. Then, when we put our long-range submarines into service, we needed a radio station in China to keep in contact with our fleet. The Chinese, by the way, had already asked that we turn over our submarine designs to them and teach them how to build submarines. So we felt justified in asking them for permission to build a radio station on their territory. Their answer was no. It wasn't long afterward that we got Yudin's coded dispatch about the anti-Soviet attitudes of the Chinese leadership.

I said to my comrades, "According to protocol, it's Mao's turn to make a state visit here before we go there again. But given the present situation, maybe we'd better go talk to him. It had better be a private meeting so that we can find out where we stand with the Chinese comrades."

This was our last trip to China. It was in 1959.[7] Our discussions were friendly but without concrete results. Among the things discussed was the subject of the radio station. I said, "Comrade Mao Tse-tung, we will give you the money to build the station. It doesn't matter to us to whom the station belongs, as long as we can use it to keep in radio contact with our submarines. We would even be willing to give the station to you, but we'd like to have it built as soon as possible. Our fleet is now operating in the Pacific Ocean, and our main base is in Vladivostok. Comrade Mao Tse-tung, couldn't we come to some sort of agreement so that our submarines might have a base in your country for refueling, repairs, shore leaves, and so on?"

"For the last time, *no*, and I don't want to hear anything more about it."

"Comrade Mao Tse-tung, the countries of the Atlantic Pact have no

7. This meeting took place immediately after Khrushchev's first visit to America, when he was full of what was called "the spirit of Camp David" and infuriated Mao by his warm praise of the statesmanlike qualities of President Eisenhower. The ill-feeling arising from this unfortunate meeting resulted in the precipitate withdrawal of Soviet technicians engaged in supervising the construction of a number of factories: they took their blueprints back to Moscow with them, leaving the factories unfinished.

trouble cooperating and supplying each other, and here we are —
unable to reach an agreement on so simple a matter as this!"

"No!"

I couldn't understand why he got so angry. I made one last attempt
to be reasonable: "If you want, you can use Murmansk as a port for
your submarines."

"No! We don't want anything to do with Murmansk, and we don't
want you here. We've had the British and other foreigners on our territory for years now, and we're not ever going to let anyone use our land
for their own purposes again." We never did get his permission for the
submarine base.[8]

When Mao started pushing the idea that China could catch up with
America in five years, he took the offensive against us, and he did so
out in the open. It was about this same time that he started to organize
communes and to build his samovar blast furnaces.[9] At Mao's instiga-
tion, the Chinese started to claim that the Soviet belief in the distribution of material goods according to the quantity and quality of labor
expended was a bourgeois concept. Statements started appearing in
China to the effect that we, the Soviet Union, were hanging on the
coattails of the bourgeoisie. So some basic questions of principle had
arisen about the future direction of our movement and we had reached
a parting of the ways with China.

Mao Tse-tung also declared that peaceful coexistence was a bourgeois pacifist notion. Since then China has recklessly slandered the
Communist Party of the Soviet Union for its policy of peaceful coexistence. But, as I say, it's always difficult to know what the Chinese are
really thinking. It's difficult to figure out whether China is really for or
against peaceful coexistence. I remember that after I retired I heard on
the radio that Mao had given an interview to some American writer
who put the question to him directly: "Do you really want to unleash
war upon the world?" Mao answered, "No, the Chinese don't want
war. We'll go to war only if there is a direct attack against our territory." Under the pressure of questioning by bourgeois journalists, Mao

8. The Chinese, on their part, asked for atomic know-how, which the Russians
refused to give them.

9. The reference is to the celebrated Great Leap Forward of 1958, which involved
an attempt to turn peasants into proletarians by building "backyard" blast furnaces
and "rural steelworks" and organizing the farmworkers into regimented communes.
The whole conception was anathema to the Russians.

Tse-tung has repeated several times that China stands behind peaceful coexistence. It's my own feeling that the so-called Mao Tse-tung Declaration was actually authored by Chou En-lai. I've never known for sure Mao's own position. It's impossible to pin these Chinese down.

There is, however, one thing I know for sure about Mao. He's a nationalist, and at least when I knew him, he was bursting with an impatient desire to rule the world. His plan was to rule first China, then Asia, then . . . what? There are seven hundred million people in China, and in other countries like Malaysia, about half the population is Chinese. The following innocent conversation which Mao and I once had over tea is very interesting for the light it throws on Mao's own version of Chinese nationalism.

He asked me, "How many conquerors have invaded China?" He answered the question himself: "China has been conquered many times, but the Chinese have assimilated all of their conquerors."

He was setting his sights on the future. "Think about it," he said. "You have two hundred million people, and we have seven hundred million."

Then he started to discourse on the distinctiveness of China. As an example he mentioned that there are no foreign words in the Chinese language. "All the rest of the world uses the word 'electricity,'" he boasted. "They've borrowed the word from English. But we Chinese have our own word for it!" His chauvinism and arrogance sent a shiver up my spine.

Later the Chinese press took Mao's lead and started to claim that Vladivostok was on Chinese territory. They wrote that the Russians had stolen it from China. It's true; at one point in history the Chinese ruled in that part of Siberia before our tsars expanded into the area. We consented to negotiate with the Chinese about our borders. They sent us their version of how the map should read. We took one look at it, and it was so outrageous that we threw it away in disgust.[10]

Mao Tse-tung may be a nationalist, but he's no fool. When China began its supposedly egalitarian reforms, literature on the subject came

---

10. This refers to the border conflict which has persisted until this day, now smoldering, now flaring up. In the nineteenth century a weak China had been compelled to cede considerable territories, which included Vladivostok and what is now the Soviet Maritime Province, to Imperial Russia. At the height of the Sino-Soviet quarrel, Mao was to insist that the "unequal treaties" which had formalized these cessions could no longer be considered valid: the whole border question was thrown open.

across the border and started circulating widely in Soviet Siberia. When I found out what was happening, I told my comrades, "This must stop immediately. The slogans of the Chinese reforms are very alluring. You're mistaken if you don't think the seeds of these ideas will find fertile soil in our country."

We had to respond in substance to Mao's assumptions and propositions. To put it mildly, we didn't agree with his position. Actually, I had already run out of patience with him. If you read my report to the Twenty-second Party Congress, you'll see that I dedicated many of my remarks to the problems of China, although I didn't mention China by name. But it was there at the Twenty-second Party Congress that we rejected the main tenets of Mao's position.[11]

However, I do subscribe to one of Mao's "egalitarian" reforms. He was right to remove epaulets from Chinese army uniforms. I think this was a sensible thing to do, and by the same token, I think it was a mistake on our part when we put epaulets and stripes back onto our own military uniforms. Who the hell needs them? We won the Civil War, and I didn't have any epaulets or stripes even though I held the rank of commissar. The soldiers didn't need to see fancy stripes to know who their commissar and their commander were. Back in those days we were able to crush our enemies without epaulets. Nowadays our military men are all dressed up like canaries.

During the Conference of Communist and Workers' Parties at the Kremlin in 1960, the Chinese delegation — which was led by Liu Shao-chi — opposed us right down the line, and the Albanians spoke out against us in support of China.[12] Especially shameless was the behavior of that agent of Mao Tse-tung, Enver Hoxha. He bared his

11. At the Twenty-second Party Congress in October, 1961, Khrushchev first brought the quarrel out into the open with a sharp attack on Albania (China's improbable ally) and without mentioning China by name.

12. Khrushchev's first major onslaught on China occurred at the Third Congress of the Rumanian Communist Party at Bucharest in June, 1960, immediately after the abortive Paris Summit meeting (wrecked, ostensibly, by the U-2 affair). It shocked all the foreign Party leaders present, but was kept very secret. The second stage of his attack was mounted at the Moscow Conference of the world Communist Parties in November of the same year. On both occasions Khrushchev attacked Mao bluntly, not to say coarsely, in highly emotional terms which are reflected, though more diffusely, in this chapter. The Chinese gave as good as they got. The Albanian leader, Enver Hoxha, made the most vicious speech of all, arraigning Khrushchev for blackmailing Albania and trying to starve her into submission and for betraying Stalin. But the quarrel was still hidden from the outer world. For an account of these climacteric meetings, and the development of the quarrel generally, see *The New Cold War: Moscow Versus Peking* by Edward Crankshaw.

fangs at us even more menacingly than the Chinese themselves. After his speech, Comrade Dolores Ibarruri, an old revolutionary and a devoted worker in the Communist movement, got up indignantly and said, very much to the point, that Hoxha was like a dog who bites the hand that feeds it.

We wanted to do everything we could to prevent a schism between the Albanians and ourselves, but all our efforts were to no avail. Our conflict with the Albanians developed in stages, as we gradually became aware that the Albanians were conspiring with the Chinese against us. We got wind of their treachery when an Albanian delegation was passing through Moscow on its way back from China. One of the Albanians, an honest woman, came to us and told us what was going on. I think she was strangled a short time later, poor woman. And it wasn't the Gestapo who strangled her. No, it was her own "brothers." I say this because she was a Communist and they were Communists, too. They strangled her because she, a Communist, had come to us at the Central Committee of the Communist Party of the Soviet Union and told us about the Albanians' secret meetings with the Chinese.

How naïve we were! At the same time Mehmet Sheku was in a hospital in the USSR, taking some sort of medical treatment. When we confronted him with the fact that we knew talks were going on between his country and China, he jumped up from his hospital bed and flew straight back to Albania.

Enver Hoxha, Mehmet Sheku, and Ballutu had come to power in Albania by staging an uprising and overthrowing the original First Secretary of the Albanian Party, a very good comrade whom Tito had always spoken well of and whom the Yugoslavs had generally supported. He had been from solid workers' stock, and he was the founder of the Communist Party of Albania. Tito told me that Mehmet Sheku personally strangled this man. These three — Hoxha, Sheku, and Ballutu — used to bring someone to trial and sentence him themselves, without ever putting anything in writing; then they would look for an opportunity to have their victim murdered secretly. It was all very similar to the system used by Stalin and Beria.[13]

13. Enver Hoxha, First Secretary of the Albanian Communist Party, rose to power as a member of the Albanian wartime resistance by using arms supplied to him by the Allies and the Yugoslavs against his nationalist rivals as well as against the Germans. Khrushchev is evidently referring to Hoxha's liquidation of Koci Xoxce, Vice-Premier and Minister of the Interior, in 1949. This was after Stalin's

The rift which developed between the Soviet Union and Albania stemmed mainly from the Albanians' fear of democratization. Even though there was a time when I thought all was not lost, I now believe that the rift was inevitable. The final break with the Albanians occurred at the Rumanian Communist Party Congress in Bucharest in July, 1960, where we met to exchange views on international matters and in particular matters pertaining to relations between fraternal Communist Parties on the one hand and the Chinese Communist Party on the other. Now that our break with the Albanians is complete, I stand all the more firmly for those principles of democratic leadership which the Albanians could never accept.

Democracy is certainly desirable, but in a democracy it is difficult for a leader to stay in power if he doesn't make a point of consulting with his followers. A democratic leader must have a good mind and be able to take advice. He must realize that his position of leadership depends on the people's will to have him as their leader, not on his own will to lead the people. And the people will accept a leader only if he shows himself to be of the same flesh and blood as the Party. A leader must be motivated by the interests of the people, and not by greed or vanity. A leader must have mastered knowledge, humility, and the ability to live as part of the collective. I repeat, he holds his position of leadership by the will of the Party. In other words, he is not above the Party, but the servant of the Party, and he can keep his position only as long as he enjoys the Party's satisfaction and support.[14]

In their own Party careers, Enver Hoxha, Mehmet Sheku, and Ballutu haven't lived up to these principles. Neither has Mao Tse-tung.

However, while Mao Tse-tung may have abused his power and misled his Party, he's not — as some claim — a madman. People are starting to say that Mao Tse-tung is a lunatic, that he has taken leave of his senses. This isn't true. Mao is very intelligent and very cunning. I remember how only a few years ago people were predicting that Mao

---

excommunication of Tito. Xoxce had been a friend of Yugoslavia. Khrushchev has forgotten (but he may never have known) that it was Stalin who egged Hoxha on to get rid of Xoxce. Mehmet Sheku, the most ruthless of the Albanian Communists, was Minister of the Interior in succession to Xoxce and a merciless purger; he later became Prime Minister. Bequir Ballatu, Albanian Minister of Defense and a member of the Politbureau, attended a course at the Moscow Military Academy in 1952–53. Khrushchev's account of the *modus operandi* of this triumvirate is close enough to the truth.

14. In the light of these observations it would be interesting to see what would happen if Khrushchev could live his life over again.

Tse-tung would never win the power struggle which was going on in China. At that time I said, "Nonsense, of course Mao will win." And I was right. Mao certainly seems to be getting the upper hand in China now. But by what means? The Chinese don't recognize any law except the law of power and force. If you don't obey, they tear your head off. And they do this very artfully: they strangle you in the middle of a square in front of thousands of people. What sort of "politics" is that? You can't even call it barbarism. It's something more than that. After all, we're living in the twentieth century!

Even though Mao is winning in China, Liu Shao-chi hasn't given up. He's against Mao's policies, and he's putting up a fight. Liu Shao-chi is a very intelligent man, and he has a great many people on his side, but they don't have any real power. The reason Liu Shao-chi is still alive is his popularity. Mao could have Liu strangled without much effort. But Liu's murder would incur the wrath of the masses. Mao Tse-tung knows this, and he doesn't fight against Liu Shao-chi as an individual, but as a standard-bearer of a particular political system. In other words, Mao wants to defeat Liu by isolating him politically.[15]

Of course, it's one thing for us to talk about Mao Tse-tung and another thing to talk about China as a whole. If we started reviling the Chinese people, we would be stepping over the line that separates objective analysis from nationalistic prejudice. We are being nationalistic when we let ourselves believe that one nation has special rights and superiorities over other nations. That's how Nazism got started.

Therefore we must realize that the Chinese are our brothers. They are human beings just like us. And if Chinese youths attack our embassy in Peking, it doesn't mean we should hate the Chinese people as a whole. A country's youth is not the entire nation. Besides, there are all different kinds of youths. Not everyone in China was on that square stoning our embassy, and not everyone who was on that square was shouting in support of Mao Tse-tung's policies, either. Think how many Chinese there must be who are bemoaning what has happened to their country. There's a great struggle going on in China, and people are killing each other.

I believe that all our efforts should be devoted to resolving the conflict which now exists between the Communist Party of the Soviet

15. Liu Shao-chi, a moderate, was for a long time Mao's heir apparent. He led the Chinese delegation to the Moscow Conference in 1960, but took a back seat to the fierce hard-liner P'eng Chen. In his recent conflict with Mao, Liu was lucky to escape with his life.

Union and the other Communist Parties on the one hand and the Communist Party of China on the other. We should do everything we can to see that the Communist movement will once again be united and monolithic. This goal must be achieved! It is in the interests of the peoples of the Soviet Union. It is in the interests of the Chinese people, and it is in the interests of all peace-loving peoples of the world. Long live the struggle for peace — and peaceful coexistence!

19

Ho Chi Minh and the War in Vietnam

Khrushchev, the elder statesman, reflects on the Vietnam tragedy without dwelling on the barbarity of the war. In so doing he offers a glimpse of the conflict as seen from "the other side of the hill." His view, at least in part, is shared by many on this side.

WHEN the American aggressors were forced to stop their bombing attacks against the territory of North Vietnam, they suffered an important defeat. It's now obvious from the press that the United States is not strictly abiding by the commitment it made when it ceased the bombing, but the very fact that the bombing was halted attests to the courageous resistance of the Vietnamese people. Their resistance was organized under the leadership of their late president, that remarkable man, Comrade Ho Chi Minh. I've met many people in the course of my political career, but Ho Chi Minh impressed me in a very special way. Religious people used to talk about the holy apostles. Well, by the way he lived and by the way he impressed other people, Ho Chi Minh was like one of those "holy apostles." He was an apostle of the Revolution.

I'll never forget the look in his eye, the way his gaze shone with a special kind of sincerity and purity. It was the sincerity of an incorruptible Communist and the purity of a man devoted in principle and in practice to the cause. He could win anyone over with his honesty and his unshakable conviction that the Communist cause was the right one for his people and for all people. His every word seemed to underscore his belief that all Communists are class brethren and consequently that all Communists must be sincere and honest in their dealings with each other. Ho Chi Minh really was one of Communism's "saints."

I first met him while Stalin was still alive. Ho Chi Minh had flown to Moscow directly from the jungles of Vietnam. He told us how he had made his way through the jungles for days on foot until he came to the Chinese border and how from there he had traveled to the Soviet Union.

During our conversation, Ho Chi Minh kept watching Stalin intently with his unusual eyes. I would say that there was in his gaze an almost childlike naïveté. I remember once he reached into his briefcase and took out a copy of a Soviet magazine — I think it was *The USSR Under Construction* — and asked Stalin to autograph it. In France everyone chases after autographs, and apparently Ho Chi Minh had picked up this bug. He liked the idea of being able to show people Stalin's autograph back in Vietnam. Stalin gave Ho his autograph but shortly afterward had the magazine stolen back from him because he was worried about how Ho might use it.

Ho Chi Minh told us about the struggle his people were waging against the French occupation forces and asked us to give him material aid, particularly arms and ammunition. After he left Moscow, Ho Chi Minh asked us in writing to send him quinine because his people were suffering from a malaria epidemic. Our pharmaceutical industry produced quinine on a large scale, so Stalin went overboard with generosity and said, "Send him half a ton."

Subsequently I met with Ho Chi Minh many times. I remember our work together during the Geneva Conference [of 1954].[1] At that time we still had very good relations with the Communist Party of China. Before the Geneva Conference there was a preparatory meeting in Moscow. China was represented by Chou En-lai and Vietnam by President Ho Chi Minh and Prime Minister Pham Van Dong. We worked

1. This was the historic conference of the spring and early summer of 1954 that brought to an end the fighting between the French and the Vietnamese Communists, partitioning Vietnam along the 17th parallel, on July 20. Dienbienphu fell while the conference was sitting on May 7, and there seemed nothing to prevent the whole of Vietnam from being overrun by the Communists. The Americans debated intervention with carrier-based air power but Eisenhower decided against it. Khrushchev himself was not in Geneva on this occasion. The main negotiators were Mr. Anthony Eden (later Lord Avon) for Britain, M. Mendès-France for France, Chou En-lai for China, and Ho Chi Minh himself.

out the position we would take in Geneva, basing it on the situation in Vietnam. The situation was very grave. The resistance movement in Vietnam was on the brink of collapse. The partisans were counting on the Geneva Conference to produce a cease-fire agreement which would enable them to hold on to the conquests which they had won in the struggle of the Vietnamese people against the French occupation. Hanoi was securely in the hands of the French. If you looked at a map on which our own demands for a settlement were marked out, you'd see that North Vietnam was pockmarked with enclaves which had been captured and occupied by the French.

After one of these sessions in Catherine Hall of the Kremlin, Chou En-lai buttonholed me and took me into a corner. He said, "Comrade Ho Chi Minh has told me that the situation in Vietnam is hopeless and that if we don't attain a cease-fire soon, the Vietnamese won't be able to hold out against the French. Therefore they've decided to retreat to the Chinese border if necessary, and they want China to be ready to move troops into Vietnam as we did in North Korea. In other words, the Vietnamese want us to help them drive out the French. We simply can't grant Comrade Ho Chi Minh's request. We've already lost too many men in Korea — that war cost us dearly. We're in no condition to get involved in another war at this time." [2]

I made a request of my own to Comrade Chou En-lai. "An important struggle is going on," I said, "and the Vietnamese are putting up a good fight. The French are taking heavy losses. There's no reason why you should tell Ho Chi Minh that you will refuse to help him if his troops retreat to your border under the blows of the French. Why don't you just tell him a white lie? Let the Vietnamese believe that you'll help them if necessary, and this will be a source of inspiration for the Vietnamese partisans to resist the French." Chou En-lai agreed not to tell Comrade Ho Chi Minh that China wouldn't come into the war against the French on Vietnamese territory.

Then a miracle happened. When the delegations arrived in Geneva for the conference, the Vietnamese partisans won a great victory and captured the fortress of Dienbienphu. At the first session of the conference, the French head of state, Mendès-France, proposed to restrict the northern reach of the French forces to the 17th parallel. I'll confess that when we were informed of this news from Geneva, we gasped

2. Nobody in the West knew that the situation of the Vietnamese was so desperate.

with surprise and pleasure. We hadn't expected anything like this. The 17th parallel was the absolute maximum we would have claimed ourselves. We instructed our representatives in Geneva to demand that the demarcation line be moved farther south, to the 15th parallel, but this was only for the sake of appearing to drive a hard bargain. After haggling for a short time, we accepted Mendès-France's offer, and the treaty was signed. We had succeeded in consolidating the conquests of the Vietnamese Communists.[3]

I should take this opportunity to give Mendès-France his due. He soberly and accurately evaluated the situation facing him. Granted, the partisans were having trouble in Vietnam, but they weren't having any more trouble than the French army. Mendès-France took the only sensible step when he ended the war which the French were waging in Vietnam. France pulled out of the war and evacuated its troops.

All would have been well if everyone had adhered to the commitments of the Geneva Accords. After two years, general elections should have been held, and we had no doubt that Ho Chi Minh — that is, the Communists and the progressive forces of Vietnam — would have emerged victorious. But then that sinister man Dulles and the United States stepped in and imposed a long, bloody war on the Vietnamese people, a war which is still going on today.

I won't go into the war itself because the whole thing has been thoroughly covered in the press. However, I would like to say something about the difficulties which face the Vietnamese because of the Soviet Union's conflict with China.

During the concluding stage of the Conference of Communist and Workers' Parties in 1960,[4] everyone agreed to sign the Conference Declaration except for the Chinese, who stubbornly refused to accept one point in the document. This was an important point, and its inclusion in the declaration was a matter of principle for us. Therefore we couldn't meet the Chinese halfway.

Ho Chi Minh came up to me and said, "Comrade Khrushchev, you'll have to concede to the Chinese on this point."

3. The British and the French were extremely pleased with the 17th parallel agreement. It is nice to know that Ho Chi Minh and Khrushchev were too. Mr. Dulles was not.

4. This was the Conference of Communist and Workers' Parties (eighty-one of them were represented) referred to in the previous chapter. The fact that the Chinese did in the end sign a face-saving, compromise resolution induced the world to believe in the monolithic character of the world Communist movement for some time to come.

"How can we concede?" I replied. "This is a matter of principle."

"Comrade Khrushchev, China is a very big country with a very big Party. You can't permit a schism in the movement. You must make sure that the Chinese sign this declaration along with the rest of us. Only if it is unanimously endorsed will this document have great international importance."

"Comrade Ho Chi Minh, our delegation is devoting all its efforts to maintaining unity in the Communist movement. Don't think we under-estimate the stature and power of the Communist Party of China. We're doing everything we can to keep China inside the fold of frater-nal Communist Parties. But surely you will understand that we cannot compromise our principles. That's what we would be doing if we yielded to the Chinese on this point. Their position contradicts our whole Communist world outlook. You say that China is a big country and the Chinese Party is a big party. Surely you'd agree that ours is not a small country nor a small party. But that's beside the point. All Communist Parties are equal and must enjoy equal rights and equal opportunities. And as long as that is the case, all our aspirations must be subordinated to one goal, and that goal is the victory of the Com-munist movement."

Ho Chi Minh agreed with me, but he said, "For us it is doubly diffi-cult. Don't forget, China is our neighbor." After speaking to me, he ap-parently went to talk to the Chinese. Eventually, after prolonged efforts on the part of our representatives to negotiate with the Chinese, we found a mutually acceptable formula, and China agreed to sign the declaration.

I was very grieved when China finally did in fact break off all work-ing political relations with us. When the rupture between the Commu-nist Party of the Soviet Union and the Communist Party of China came out into the open, China began to lead the Vietnamese Laborers' Party around by a halter. A large segment of the population in Vietnam — and therefore of the Party — is Chinese. China began to use its considerable influence to start quarrels between Vietnam and the So-viet Union and to turn the Vietnamese Party against us. Some of the key positions in the leadership of the Vietnamese Party are now held by pro-Chinese comrades. At a time when we have been doing every-thing we could to help Vietnam, the pro-Chinese elements in Vietnam have been doing everything they could to please China. In other words, they have been working not only against us, but against Viet-nam's own best interests. It's a great pity.

We have been sincere and unsparing in our efforts to assist Vietnam, and the hostility toward us of the pro-Chinese elements in Vietnam has been a bitter pill to swallow. Why am I bringing this up now? I'm bringing it up because it relates to the subject of what we can expect now that Ho Chi Minh is dead.

According to what I read in the press, it appears that all is going smoothly in Soviet-Vietnamese relations. Vietnamese delegations are visiting the Soviet Union, and delegations of our reporters go to Vietnam to report on the struggle of the Vietnamese people. Their reports are regularly in the press as well as on television and on the newsreels.

But certain information that has reached me indicates that, as a matter of fact, everything is not going as smoothly as the newspaper articles and the television reports proclaim. According to my information, the Vietnamese are showing a certain unwarranted restraint toward the Soviet Government and Party. This must mean that there still exist some pro-Chinese forces in the Vietnamese government and in the leadership of the Vietnamese Laborers' Party. From the outside, it would seem that friendly relations and mutual understanding are developing between Vietnam and the Soviet Union. But it's possible that this appearance is just a façade thrown up by the Vietnamese leadership — perhaps even with China's blessing — in order not to lose the help of the Soviet Union and the other fraternal Communist Parties. I certainly hope this is not the case, although I would still allow for the possibility that it is. I would like to believe that Vietnam really does desire good relations with the Soviet Union, but I don't think China will release Vietnam from its paws, and pro-Chinese forces will remain powerful in Vietnam. They will do all they can to make Vietnam eat out of China's hand.

Now, with the death of Comrade Ho Chi Minh, the infectious growth of pro-Chinese influence will be able to spread more virulently than ever before. If that happens, it will be a great pity, and it will be a poor memorial to Comrade Ho Chi Minh, who invested so much of his thought and energy in the strengthening of his country's friendship with the Soviet Union.

Since Comrade Ho Chi Minh's death there have been many speeches and articles, by people of various political inclinations, all trying to answer the questions which are troubling everyone: How will Vietnam's relations develop with the Soviet Union? With capitalist countries? With Communist Parties whose views differ from those of Mao Tse-tung? How will Vietnam's relations develop with the leadership of the

Chinese Party? What changes will there be in the policies of Vietnam? I would like now to share my own impressions about the things I've read and heard and try to express a few of my own thoughts about the prospects for the development of Soviet-Vietnamese relations.

No one can predict what will happen, of course. There are some signs of what to expect next, but we should be cautious about making predictions because nothing is constant. Everything is in a state of flux. Things can change anytime. For instance, there were once flawless relations between the Soviet Union and the Chinese People's Republic. There were even good relations between the Soviet leadership and Mao Tse-tung. But now all that has changed. The same thing could happen with Vietnam. Our relations were originally very good; and if they later deteriorated, it wasn't the fault of the Communist Party of the Soviet Union. Rather, I believe, it was entirely the result of Mao Tse-tung himself and his influence on Vietnam.

The documents which give me a basis for predicting, or at least guessing, the future course of Vietnam are the so-called "Testament" of Ho Chi Minh and the famous speech by Le Duan.[5] I've read both documents twice, and I made myself read them attentively in order to interpret them correctly.

In the Testament of Ho Chi Minh there is nothing said about the enormous, unselfish help which the Soviet Union is giving Vietnam. Our assistance has been decisive because, without material aid from the Soviet Union, it would have been impossible for Vietnam to survive under the conditions of modern warfare and to resist as rich and powerful an aggressor as the United States. In order to receive adequate arms and equipment, Vietnam has had no choice but to rely on the Soviet Union. In order to achieve victory, they must have the appropriate arms, and these arms they can obtain only from the Soviet Union. China can't give Vietnam what it needs today. The world press, including the enemies of Communism, acknowledge that Vietnam wouldn't be able to conduct its policies of military resistance against American aggression if it weren't for the economic and material aid provided by the Soviet Union. For example, take an announcement that the North Vietnamese army of liberation has launched a rocket attack on a US air base. Naturally these rockets weren't manufactured in the jungles of Vietnam. They came from factories in the Soviet Union. The Soviet Union, untainted by any mercenary motives, is dedicated to

5. Le Duan, senior member of North Vietnamese leadership after Ho's death.

assisting all those forces and all those peoples who are fighting for their independence, who are fighting for economic and political freedom, and who are fighting against imperialist aggression.

More recently, even the pro-Chinese elements in Vietnam have begun to understand the necessity of friendship with the Soviet Union and Ho Chi Minh's tradition has been partly restored. The Vietnamese acted wisely when they reoriented their policies. I say "reoriented" because they didn't change their policy fundamentally, they just reoriented it — taking into account the necessity of continuing the war into the future and realizing that only the Soviet Union, and not China, can give them the help they need.

Today the brutal struggle rages on and victory is still far from won. But the light of Vietnam's victory over American imperialism can already be seen, glimmering in the distance. Therefore our efforts must not flag. Everything must be mobilized in order to bring the struggle of the Vietnamese people to a successful conclusion. There is more at stake in this war than just the future of the Vietnamese people. The Vietnamese are shedding their blood and laying down their lives for the sake of the world Communist movement. Will Ho Chi Minh's successors show sufficient wisdom for the struggle to be won? Only time will tell.

20

Fidel Castro and the Caribbean Crisis

Khrushchev's account of the Cuban crisis is perhaps the most open, coherent, and circumstantial passage in his entire narrative. The omission of certain details from so familiar a story hardly matters. It was clear at a very early date to most sensible observers that Khrushchev's motives were more or less precisely as he now describes them. In the West too much was made (though not by President Kennedy) of his humiliation in being forced to withdraw his missiles. The Chinese exploited this up to the hilt, and so did Khrushchev's adversaries at home. The fact remains that he achieved what he set out to do, though not quite in the manner he intended: he secured Castro's Cuba from the standing threat of invasion. And he achieved an understanding with President Kennedy, whose assassination was for him a profound and very personal misfortune.

I WILL explain what the Caribbean crisis of October, 1962, was all about. It came to a head this way:

At the time that Fidel Castro led his revolution to victory and entered Havana with his troops, we had no idea what political course his regime would follow. We knew there were individual Communists participating in the movement which Castro led, but the Communist Party of Cuba had no contact with him. The Secretary of the Central Committee of the Cuban Party had even resigned from the Party in order to join Castro in the hills. When Castro's men captured Havana, we had to rely completely on newspaper and radio reports, from Cuba itself and from other countries, about what was happening. The whole situation was very unclear. The man Fidel appointed to be president was someone we'd never heard of. Furthermore, Cuba hadn't recognized our Government, so for a long time we had no diplomatic relations with the new regime.

However, our people who handled Latin American affairs and who had traveled in the area did know some of the Cuban leaders. They knew Raúl Castro in particular. Apparently by chance, one of our comrades had been on a ship to Mexico with Raúl Castro. This comrade told me that he and Raúl had met and talked together, and that later in Mexico Raúl Castro was arrested before our comrade's very eyes. Based on information gathered through various channels, we knew that Raúl Castro was a good Communist, but it appeared that he kept his true convictions hidden from his brother Fidel. Ché Guevara was a Communist, too, and so were some of the others — or so we thought. We had no official contacts with any of the new Cuban leaders and therefore nothing to go on but rumors.

Events started to develop quickly.

We decided to send Anastas Ivanovich Mikoyan to America as a guest of our ambassador, Anatoly Dobrynin. Mikoyan's mission was to establish unofficial contacts with the leaders of the American business world. We wanted to find out what the prospects were for developing trade with America. Anastas Ivanovich was the logical person to lead such a mission. He had been in the US before the war and still had some of his old contacts. We believed that when he appeared in Washington he would be approached by people from the business world who would want to look into opportunities for trade with us. In any event, Anastas Ivanovich would be able to get a sense of which way the wind was blowing.

While Mikoyan was in the US, Fidel invited him to visit Cuba. Mikoyan accepted. He traveled around Cuba, looked things over, and talked with people. We still had no diplomatic relations with Cuba, and Castro was pursuing a very cautious policy toward us. There is a story that characterizes the situation in Cuba and Fidel Castro's role at that time: The leaders of the Cuban revolution go up to heaven; Saint Peter comes out to meet them as God's official representative and orders them all to line up. Then he says, "All Communists, three steps forward!" Guevara steps forward; Raúl steps forward; so does someone else. But all the rest, including Fidel, stay in line. Peter glares at Fidel and shouts, "Hey! you, the tall one with the beard! What's wrong, didn't you hear what I said? All Communists three steps forward!"

The point of this story is that while Saint Peter and everyone else considered Fidel a Communist, Fidel himself did not. He thought Peter's command didn't pertain to him.

Shortly after Mikoyan's visit we established diplomatic relations with Cuba, and we sent a delegation there. The Americans had cut off the Cubans' supply of oil, their main source of power, and the Cubans were obliged to turn to us for help. Life on the island was in danger of coming to a standstill. It was urgent that we organize an oil delivery to Cuba on a massive scale. But that was easier said than done. We didn't have enough oceangoing vessels in our own tanker fleet. Our efforts to provide Cuba with the petroleum products it needed put a heavy burden on our own shipping system and forced us to order extra tankers from Italy. When Italy agreed to sell us the necessary tankers, it caused a sharp conflict between Italy and America. The Americans accused the Italians of violating the spirit of solidarity with their fellow capitalists. The lesson of the whole incident was that if a capitalist country sees a chance to make some extra money from trade with a Communist country, it couldn't care less about economic solidarity.

Once we set up diplomatic relations with Cuba, we sent a veteran diplomat to be our ambassador in Havana. We also had Alekseyev there, a journalist who was friendly with Fidel and even more so with Raúl. When the Cuban leaders needed something from us, they would more often address themselves to Alekseyev than to our ambassador. Alekseyev would immediately get in touch with Moscow and inform us of the Cubans' request. It was a lucky thing we had Alekseyev there because our ambassador turned out to be unsuited for service in a country just emerging from a revolution. One of his problems was that he got bogged down in bureaucracy. Another problem was that when the situation heated up and shooting started, he demanded that the Cubans give him a special bodyguard. The Cuban leaders, who were all guerrilla fighters fresh from the hills, were astonished and irritated by this request. Here they were, offering the enemies of the revolution far more enticing targets and going around without any bodyguards at all, and now this Communist aristocrat of ours starts demanding some sort of special protection from any possible unpleasantness! We could see that our ambassador was doing more to harm our relations with

Cuba than to help them, so we recalled him and made Alekseyev ambassador in his place. The Cubans already knew and trusted Alekseyev, and he turned out to be an excellent choice; he was their kind of diplomat.

Meanwhile the plot was thickening. Castro was no longer sitting on the fence; he was beginning to behave like a full-fledged Communist, even though he still didn't call himself one. He was enlisting Communists into his government.

Castro's policies, however, were earning him many enemies. The President whom he'd appointed when he first came to power fled to America, and many of the men who had fought at his side during the struggle for independence were turning away from him. The reason for this was that many of them didn't want Socialist reforms. They had been fed up with Batista and eager to overthrow the corrupt old regime, but they were against Castro's nationalization of all businesses, his restrictive policies against the landowners, and his confiscation of property belonging to wealthy Americans.

All the while the Americans had been watching Castro closely. At first they thought that the capitalist underpinnings of the Cuban economy would remain intact. So by the time Castro announced that he was going to put Cuba on the road toward Socialism, the Americans had already missed their chance to do anything about it by simply exerting their influence: there were no longer any forces left which could be organized to fight on America's behalf in Cuba. That left only one alternative — invasion!

The Cubans asked us for arms. We gave them tanks and artillery and sent them instructors. In addition we sent them antiaircraft guns and some fighter planes. As a result of our assistance Cuba was solidly armed. The Cuban army lacked mainly in experience. They had never used tanks before; they had always fought with light arms only — automatic rifles, grenades, and pistols. But with the help of our instructors they learned quickly how to use the modern weapons that we supplied them with.

We first heard on the radio that a counterrevolutionary invasion had been launched against Cuba.[1] We didn't even know who the invaders were: were they Cuban conspirators or Americans? However, we knew that no matter under whose banner the invasion was launched, it had to have the backing of the Americans.

1. This was the Bay of Pigs fiasco in April, 1961.

Fidel's forces swung into action and made short work of the invaders. The Americans had put too much faith in the conspirators. They had assumed that with American support behind the invasion, the Cubans would rally to the conspirators and topple Castro by themselves.

After Castro's crushing victory over the counterrevolutionaries, we intensified our military aid to Cuba. We gave them as many arms as the Cuban army could absorb. But the real problem remained a matter not of the quantity or quality of the weapons, but of the availability of personnel who knew how to handle modern equipment.

Before the forces of invasion had been entirely crushed, Castro came out with a declaration that Cuba would follow a Socialist course. We had trouble understanding the timing of this statement. Castro's declaration had the immediate effect of widening the gap between himself and the people who were against Socialism, and it narrowed the circle of those he could count on for support against the invasion. As far as Castro's personal courage was concerned, his position was admirable and correct. But from a tactical standpoint, it didn't make much sense.[2]

However, Castro was victorious anyway. He defeated the counterrevolutionaries and took many of them prisoner. We welcomed Castro's victory, of course, but at the same time we were quite certain that the [Bay of Pigs] invasion was only the beginning and that the Americans would not let Cuba alone. The United States had put its faith in the Cuban emigrés once and it would do so again. The emigré conspirators had learned some lessons from their defeat, and they wouldn't refuse a chance to repeat their aggression.

Cuba's geographical position has always made it very vulnerable to its enemies. The Cuban coast is only a few miles from the American shore, and it is stretched out like a sausage, a shape that makes it easy for attackers and incredibly difficult for the island's defenders. There are infinite opportunities for invasion, especially if the invader has naval artillery and air support.

We were sure that the Americans would never reconcile themselves to the existence of Castro's Cuba. They feared, as much as we hoped, that a Socialist Cuba might become a magnet that would attract other Latin American countries to Socialism. Given the continual threat of American interference in the Caribbean, what should our own policy

---

2. Castro's open declaration of Socialist principles at this stage of the game flew in the face of Lenin's teaching on revolutionary tactics, which places a high value on deception.

be? This question was constantly on my mind, and I frequently discussed it with the other members of the Presidium. Everyone agreed that America would not leave Cuba alone unless we did something. We had an obligation to do everything in our power to protect Cuba's existence as a Socialist country and as a working example to the other countries of Latin America. It was clear to me that we might very well lose Cuba if we didn't take some decisive steps in her defense.

The fate of Cuba and the maintenance of Soviet prestige in that part of the world preoccupied me even when I was busy conducting the affairs of state in Moscow and traveling to the other fraternal countries. While I was on an official visit to Bulgaria, for instance, one thought kept hammering away at my brain: what will happen if we lose Cuba? I knew it would have been a terrible blow to Marxism-Leninism. It would gravely diminish our stature throughout the world, but especially in Latin America. If Cuba fell, other Latin American countries would reject us, claiming that for all our might the Soviet Union hadn't been able to do anything for Cuba except to make empty protests to the United Nations. We had to think up some way of confronting America with more than words. We had to establish a tangible and effective deterrent to American interference in the Caribbean. But what exactly? The logical answer was missiles. The United States had already surrounded the Soviet Union with its own bomber bases and missiles. We knew that American missiles were aimed against us in Turkey and Italy, to say nothing of West Germany. Our vital industrial centers were directly threatened by planes armed with atomic bombs and guided missiles tipped with nuclear warheads. As Chairman of the Council of Ministers, I found myself in the difficult position of having to decide on a course of action which would answer the American threat but which would also avoid war. Any fool can start a war, and once he's done so, even the wisest of men are helpless to stop it — especially if it's a nuclear war.

It was during my visit to Bulgaria that I had the idea of installing missiles with nuclear warheads in Cuba without letting the United States find out they were there until it was too late to do anything about them. I knew that first we'd have to talk to Castro and explain our strategy to him in order to get the agreement of the Cuban government. My thinking went like this: if we installed the missiles secretly and then if the United States discovered the missiles were there after they were already poised and ready to strike, the Americans would think twice before trying to liquidate our installations by military means. I knew that the United States could knock out some of our installations, but not all of them. If a quarter or even a tenth of our missiles survived — even if only one or two big ones were left — we could still hit New York, and there wouldn't be much of New York left. I don't mean to say that everyone in New York would be killed — not everyone, of course, but an awful lot of people would be wiped out. I don't know how many: that's a matter for our scientists and military personnel to work out. They specialize in nuclear warfare and know how to calculate the consequences of a missile strike against a city the size of New York. But that's all beside the point. The main thing was that the installation of our missiles in Cuba would, I thought, restrain the United States from precipitous military action against Castro's government. In addition to protecting Cuba, our missiles would have equalized what the West likes to call "the balance of power." The Americans had surrounded our country with military bases and threatened us with nuclear weapons, and now they would learn just what it feels like to have enemy missiles pointing at you; we'd be doing nothing more than giving them a little of their own medicine. And it was high time America learned what it feels like to have her own land and her own people threatened. We Russians have suffered three wars over the last half century: World War I, the Civil War, and World War II. America has never had to fight a war on her own soil, at least not in the past fifty years. She's sent troops abroad to fight in the two World Wars — and made a fortune as a result. America has shed a few drops of her own blood while making billions by bleeding the rest of the world dry.

All these thoughts kept churning in my head the whole time I was in Bulgaria. I paced back and forth, brooding over what to do. I didn't tell anyone what I was thinking. I kept my mental agony to myself. But all the while the idea of putting missiles in Cuba was ripening inside my mind. After I returned to Moscow from Bulgaria I continued to think about the possibility. Finally we convened a meeting and I said I had some thoughts to air on the subject of Cuba. I laid out all the considerations which I've just outlined. I presented my idea in the context of the counterrevolutionary invasion which Castro had just resisted. I said that it would be foolish to expect the inevitable second invasion to be as badly planned and as badly executed as the first. I warned that Fidel would be crushed if another invasion were launched against Cuba and said that we were the only ones who could prevent such a disaster from occurring.

In the course of discussions inside the Government, we decided to install intermediate-range missiles, launching equipment, and Il-28 bombers in Cuba. Even though these bombers were obsolete, they would be useful against an enemy landing force. The Il-28 was too slow to fly over enemy territory because it could easily be shot down, but was well suited for coastal defense. The Il-28 was our first jet bomber. In its time it had been god of the air, but by the time we gave military assistance to Cuba, the Il-28 had already been taken out of production.

Soon after we began shipping our missiles to Cuba, the Americans became suspicious. Their intelligence told them that the number of our ships going to Cuba had suddenly and substantially increased and that our own people were unloading the ships once they reached Cuban ports. We didn't allow the Cubans to do any of the unloading or installation of the missiles themselves. While the Americans had no direct information about what we were delivering, they knew that whatever we were doing, we were doing with our own hands. It was not long before they concluded on the basis of reconnaissance photographs that we were installing missiles. They also knew about our Il-28 bombers which had been flown to Cuba.

The Americans became frightened, and we stepped up our shipments. We had delivered almost everything by the time the crisis reached the boiling point.

There are people who argue with the benefit of hindsight that antiaircraft missiles should have been installed before the ballistic missiles so as to close the airspace over Cuba. This doesn't make sense. How many surface-to-air missiles can you fit on a tiny sausage-shaped island? There's a limit to the number of missile installations you can put on an island as small as Cuba. Then, after you've launched all your missiles, you're completely unprotected. Moreover, antiaircraft missiles have a very short range. Antiaircraft batteries can easily be knocked out from the sea and air.

I want to make one thing absolutely clear: when we put our ballistic missiles in Cuba, we had no desire to start a war. On the contrary, our principal aim was only to deter America from starting a war. We were well aware that a war which started over Cuba would quickly expand into a world war. Any idiot could have started a war between America and Cuba. Cuba was eleven thousand kilometers away from us. Only a fool would think that we wanted to invade the American continent from Cuba. Our goal was precisely the opposite: we wanted to keep the Americans from invading Cuba, and, to that end, we wanted to make them think twice by confronting them with our missiles. This goal we achieved — but not without undergoing a perod of perilous tension.

When the Americans figured out what we were up to in Cuba, they mounted a huge press campaign against us, claiming that we were threatening the security of the United States and so on and so forth. In short, hostility began to build up, and the American press fanned the flames. Then one day in October President Kennedy came out with a statement warning that the United States would take whatever measures were necessary to remove what he called the "threat" of Russian missiles on Cuba. The Americans began to make a belligerent show of their strength. They concentrated their forces against Cuba, completely surrounding the island with their navy. Things started churning. In our estimation the Americans were trying to frighten us, but they were no less scared than we were of atomic war. We hadn't had time to deliver all our shipments to Cuba, but we had installed enough missiles already to destroy New York, Chicago, and the other huge industrial cities, not to mention a little village like Washington. I don't think America had ever faced such a real threat of destruction as at that moment.

Meanwhile we went about our own business. We didn't let ourselves be intimidated. Our ships, with the remainder of our deliveries to Cuba, headed straight through an armada of the American navy, but the Americans didn't try to stop our ships or even check them. We kept in mind that as long as the United States limited itself to threatening gestures and didn't actually touch us, we could afford to pretend to ignore the harassment. After all, the United States had no moral or legal quarrel with us. We hadn't given the Cubans anything more than the Americans were giving to their allies. We had the same rights and opportunities as the Americans. Our conduct in the international arena was governed by the same rules and limits as the Americans'.

We had almost completed our shipments. As the crisis approached the boiling point, the Western press began to seeth with anger and alarm. We replied accordingly, although not so hysterically. Our people were fully informed of the dangerous situation that had developed, although we took care not to cause panic by the way we presented the facts.

I remember a period of six or seven days when the danger was particularly acute. Seeking to take the heat off the situation somehow, I suggested to the other members of the government: "Comrades, let's go to the Bolshoi Theater this evening. Our own people as well as foreign eyes will notice, and perhaps it will calm them down. They'll say to themselves, 'If Khrushchev and our other leaders are able to go to the opera at a time like this, then at least tonight we can sleep peacefully.'" We were trying to disguise our own anxiety, which was intense.[3]

Then the exchange of notes began. I dictated the messages and conducted the exchange from our side. I spent one of the most dangerous nights at the Council of Ministers office in the Kremlin. I slept on a couch in my office — and I kept my clothes on. I didn't want to be like that Western minister who was caught literally with his pants down by the Suez events of 1956 and who had to run around in his shorts until the emergency was over [see page 436]. I was ready for alarming news to come any moment, and I wanted to be ready to react immediately.

President Kennedy issued an ultimatum, demanding that we remove our missiles and bombers from Cuba. I remember those days vividly. I remember the exchange with President Kennedy especially well because I initiated it and was at the center of the action on our end of the correspondence. I take complete responsibility for the fact that the President and I entered into direct contact at the most crucial and dangerous stage of the crisis.

The climax came after five or six days, when our ambassador to Washington, Anatoly Dobrynin, reported that the President's brother, Robert Kennedy, had come to see him on an unofficial visit. Dobrynin's report went something like this:

"Robert Kennedy looked exhausted. One could see from his eyes that he had not slept for days. He himself said that he had not been home for six days and nights. 'The President is in a grave situation,' Robert Kennedy said, 'and he does not know how to get out of it. We are under very severe stress. In fact we are under pressure from our military to use force against Cuba. Probably at this very moment the President is sitting down to write a message to Chairman Khrushchev. We want to ask you, Mr. Dobrynin, to pass President Kennedy's message to Chairman Khrushchev through unofficial channels. President Kennedy

3. When the top men in the Kremlin turn up at the Bolshoi Theater in a body, all smiles, it frequently (though not infallibly) means that a crisis of some kind is brewing. One of the best remembered of such occasions was the evening before Beria's arrest. Beria himself, of course, was included in the party.

implores Chairman Khrushchev to accept his offer and to take into consideration the peculiarities of the American system. Even though the President himself is very much against starting a war over Cuba, an irreversible chain of events could occur against his will. That is why the President is appealing directly to Chairman Khrushchev for his help in liquidating this conflict. If the situation continues much longer, the President is not sure that the military will not overthrow him and seize power. The American army could get out of control.' " [4]

I hadn't overlooked this possibility. We knew that Kennedy was a young President and that the security of the United States was indeed threatened. For some time we had felt there was a danger that the President would lose control of his military, and now he was admitting this to us himself. Kennedy's message urgently repeated the Americans' demand that we remove the missiles and bombers from Cuba. We could sense from the tone of the message that tension in the United States was indeed reaching a critical point.

We wrote a reply to Kennedy in which we said that we had installed the missiles with the goal of defending Cuba and that we were not pursuing any other aims except to deter an invasion of Cuba and to guarantee that Cuba could follow a course determined by its own people rather than one dictated by some third party.

While we conducted some of this exchange through official diplomatic channels, the more confidential letters were relayed to us through the President's brother. He gave Dobrynin his telephone number and asked him to call at any time. Once, when Robert Kennedy talked with Dobrynin, he was almost crying. "I haven't seen my children for days now," Robert Kennedy said, "and the President hasn't seen his either. We're spending all day and night at the White House; I don't know how much longer we can hold out against our generals."

We could see that we had to reorient our position swiftly. "Comrades," I said, "we have to look for a dignified way out of this conflict. At the same time, of course, we must make sure that we do not compromise Cuba." We sent the Americans a note saying that we agreed to remove our missiles and bombers on the condition that the President give us his assurance that there would be no invasion of Cuba by the forces of the United States or anybody else. Finally Kennedy gave in and agreed to make a statement giving us such an assurance.

I should mention that our side's policy was, from the outset, worked

4. Obviously, this is Khrushchev's own version of what was reported to him. There is no evidence that the President was acting out of fear of a military take-over.

out in the collective leadership. It wasn't until after two or three lengthy discussions of the matter that we had decided it was worth the risk to install missiles on Cuba in the first place. It had been my feeling that the initial, as well as the subsequent, decisions should not be forced down anyone's throat. I had made sure to give the collective leadership time for the problem to crystallize in everyone's mind. I had wanted my comrades to accept and support the decision with a clear conscience and a full understanding of what the consequences of putting the missiles on Cuba might be — namely, war with the United States. Every step we had taken had been carefully considered by the collective.

As soon as we announced publicly that we were ready to remove our missiles from Cuba, the Americans became arrogant and insisted on sending an inspection team to the island. We answered that they'd have to get the Cuban government's permission to do that. Then the Chinese and American press started hooting and shouting about how Khrushchev had turned coward and backed down. I won't deny that we were obliged to make some big concessions in the interests of peace. We even consented to the inspection of our ships — but only from the air. We never let the Americans actually set foot on our decks, though we did let them satisfy themselves that we were really removing our missiles.

Once the evacuation was begun, there was some question in our minds whether the Americans would pull back their naval forces which surrounded the island. We were worried that as soon as we retreated the Americans might move in on the offensive. But no, good sense prevailed. Their ships started to leave Cuba's territorial waters, but their planes continued to circle the island. Castro gave an order to open fire, and the Cubans shot down an American U-2 reconnaissance plane. Thus another American spy, just like Gary Powers, was downed by one of our missiles.[5] The incident caused an uproar. At first we were concerned that President Kennedy wouldn't be able to stomach the humiliation. Fortunately, however, nothing happened except that the Americans became more brazen than ever in their propaganda. They did everything they could to wound our pride and to make Kennedy look good. But that didn't matter as long as they pulled back their troops and called off their air force.

The situation was stabilizing. Almost immediately after the President

5. Major Rudolf Anderson, Jr., the pilot of the U-2, was in fact killed when his plane was shot down on October 27, 1962.

and I had exchanged notes at the peak of the crisis, our relations with the United States started to return to normal. Our relations with Cuba, on the other hand, took a sudden turn for the worse. Castro even stopped receiving our ambassador. It seemed that by removing our missiles we had suffered a moral defeat in the eyes of the Cubans. Our shares in Cuba instead of going up, went down.

We decided to send Mikoyan to Cuba. "We have no better diplomat than Mikoyan for a mission like this," I said. "He will discuss the situation with the Cubans calmly." Not everyone understands what Mikoyan is saying when he talks, but he's a reasonable man. He had, over the years, played an important role in the development of our foreign trade and had proved himself a skillful negotiator.

Then Castro came out with his four or five conditions for normalizing relations with the United States. We wholeheartedly supported him in his demand that the Americans should give up their naval base at Guantánamo Bay. To this very day we support him in this demand, but the Americans are still there and no one knows when they will leave.

In our negotiations with the Americans during the crisis, they had, on the whole, been open and candid with us, especially Robert Kennedy. The Americans knew that if Russian blood were shed in Cuba, American blood would surely be shed in Germany. The American government was anxious to avoid such a development. It had been, to say the least, an interesting and challenging situation. The two most powerful nations of the world had been squared off against each other, each with its finger on the button. You'd have thought that war was inevitable. But both sides showed that if the desire to avoid war is strong enough, even the most pressing dispute can be solved by compromise. And a compromise over Cuba was indeed found. The episode ended in a triumph of common sense. I'll always remember the late President with deep respect because, in the final analysis, he showed himself to be sober-minded and determined to avoid war. He didn't let himself become frightened, nor did he become reckless. He didn't overestimate America's might, and he left himself a way out of the crisis. He showed real wisdom and statesmanship when he turned his back on right-wing forces in the United States who were trying to goad him into taking military action against Cuba. It was a great victory for us, though, that we had been able to extract from Kennedy a promise that neither America nor any of her allies would invade Cuba.

With Castro at Lake Ritsa in the Caucasus, 1962, after the Cuban missile crisis

Castro and Khrushchev's grandson Nikita

Castro photographing the Khrushchev family

Drinking wine from traditional Georgian horns, May, 1962

But Castro didn't see it that way. He was angry that we had removed the missiles. All the while, the Chinese were making a lot of noise publicly as well as buzzing in Castro's ear, "Just remember, you can't trust the imperialists to keep any promises they make!" In other words the Chinese exploited the episode to discredit us in the eyes of the Cubans.

After consulting with Mikoyan on his return from Havana, I decided to write a letter to Castro, candidly expressing my thoughts about what had happened. "The main point about the Caribbean crisis," I wrote, "is that it has guaranteed the existence of a Socialist Cuba. If Cuba had not undergone this ordeal, it's very likely the Americans would have organized an invasion to liquidate Cuba's Socialist way of life. Now that the climax of the tension has passed and we have exchanged commitments with the American government, it will be very difficult for the Americans to interfere. If the United States should invade now, the Soviet Union will have the right to attack. Thus we have secured the existence of a Socialist Cuba for at least another two years while Kennedy is in the White House. And we have reason to believe that Kennedy will be elected for a second term. Consequently, he may be in office for another six years altogether. To make it through six years in this day and age is no small thing. And six years from now the balance of power in the world will have probably shifted — and shifted in our favor, in favor of Socialism!"

My letter to Castro concluded an episode of world history in which, bringing the world to the brink of atomic war, we won a Socialist Cuba. It's very consoling for me personally to know that our side acted correctly and that we did a great revolutionary deed by not letting American imperialism intimidate us. The Caribbean crisis was a triumph of Soviet foreign policy and a personal triumph in my own career as a statesman and as a member of the collective leadership. We achieved, I would say, a spectacular success without having to fire a single shot!

A number of years have passed, and we can be gratified that the revolutionary government of Fidel Castro still lives and grows. So far, the United States has abided by its promise not to interfere in Cuba nor to let anyone else interfere.

I remember my very last conversation with Comrade Fidel Castro. We were at Pitsunda [a resort in the Caucasus, the site of a government dacha] and were discussing Cuba's sugar crop. Castro's eyes burned with the desire to get started as soon as possible with the task of revolutionizing Cuban agriculture. He knew that the only realistic way to elevate the Cuban economy was to increase the sugar output, and in order to do that he needed tractors, harvesting combines, and modern sugar refineries. During our conversation Castro said his goal was to dominate the international sugar market. I pointed out to him that world sugar prices, which were sharply inflated after the blockade against Cuban sugar, would undoubtedly return to normal when other countries expanded their own sugar production to meet the world demand. It turned out that I was right: the inflated sugar prices, which would have been so lucrative for Cuba if the transitory market situation which caused them had lasted longer, quickly fell back to normal.

But the fact remains that Cuba has done extremely well. I've read in the newspapers that Cuba assigned itself the task of producing a sugar crop of ten million tons for 1970, a year which is significant for all progressive humanity because it is the one hundredth anniversary of the Great Lenin's birth. I'm very happy for the Cuban people that they have come this far.

Today Cuba exists as an independent Socialist country, right in front of the open jaws of predatory American imperialism. Cuba's very existence is good propaganda for other Latin American countries, encouraging them to follow its example and to choose the course of Socialism. Other Latin American peoples are already beginning to realize what steps they can take to liberate themselves from American imperialists and monopolists. Hopefully Cuba's example will continue to shine.

As for Kennedy, his death was a great loss. He was gifted with the ability to resolve international conflicts by negotiation, as the whole world learned during the so-called Cuban crisis. Regardless of his youth he was a real statesman. I believe that if Kennedy had lived, relations between the Soviet Union and the United States would be much better than they are. Why do I say that? Because Kennedy would have never let his country get bogged down in Vietnam.

After President Kennedy's death, his successor, Lyndon Johnson, assured us that he would keep Kennedy's promise not to invade Cuba. So far the Americans have not broken their word. If they ever do, we still have the means necessary to make good on our own commitment to Castro and to defend Cuba.

21

Defending the Socialist Paradise

This chapter offers a remarkably clear picture of the limitations and the no less striking virtues of Khrushchev as statesman. It opens with a view of the international scene which, apart from individual obliquities of outlook, is blinkered by Communist preconceptions; but it moves on to show a breadth of understanding and a depth of vision unusual in politicians of any stamp. With all his faults, which he carried with him to the end of his career, the extraordinary thing about Khrushchev is that he went on growing and developing. The peasant from Kalinovka, rough, domineering, violent, sometimes vindictive, boastful, filled with peasant cunning, quite uneducated in the conventional sense, and with a mind that was never fully trained, nevertheless embodied certain qualities of character, imagination, perhaps even humility, which set him apart from his colleagues and above all of them. He could never escape entirely from the prison of his own past and the defects of his temperament; but in these pages he emerges, as he showed himself increasingly in his last years of activity, as a courageous statesman with flashes of deep wisdom, who in other circumstances might have become an outstanding world figure held in wide respect.

Iᴛ's no small thing that we have lived to see the day when the Soviet Union is considered, in terms of its economic might, the second most powerful country in the world. Macmillan once said to me, "What is England today? England isn't the power she was when she ruled the waves and had the deciding voice in world politics. Nowadays it's the United States and you, the Soviet Union, who decide everything." Mr. de Gaulle, the President of France, told me the same thing, almost in the same words, and he's a sober-minded man: "Well, Mr. Khrushchev, today the United States and the Soviet Union are the two great powers. France doesn't have the stature and influence she once had." So you see, both Macmillan and de Gaulle readily acknowledged our importance in the world arena.

Over the years the Soviet Union has gained great prestige in the eyes of all people who fight for peace, progress, and liberation from colonialism. The goal of our foreign policy hasn't been to enrich our own state at the expense of other states; we have never believed in the exploitation of man by man, of state by state. On the contrary, both by our stated policies and by our deeds we have encouraged countries to enjoy the fruits of their own labor. We have aided these countries not only with our counsel and by the example we have set, but we have also given them gratuitous material aid or sold them goods and equipment at reduced prices. Our foreign policy is rooted in our conviction that the way pointed out to us by Lenin is the way of the future not only for the Soviet Union, but for all countries and all peoples of the world.

Take for example our policy toward Afghanistan. I went there with Bulganin, who was then head of our delegation, on our way back from India [in 1955]. We were invited by the king of Afghanistan to stop over in Kabul. As a result of our discussions with the king and his ministers, we had a fairly clear idea of what an economically backward country Afghanistan was. We could sense that the Afghans were looking for a way out of all their problems.

It was also clear that America was courting Afghanistan. In its desire to encircle us with military bases, America will throw itself all over a country like Afghanistan, appearing to give that country economic aid but actually being much more interested in currying political favors. The Americans were undertaking all kinds of projects at their own expense — building roads, giving credit loans, and so on. But they weren't offering their help out of some compassionate or charitable desire on the part of the rich to assist the poor. No, America's so-called foreign aid program is actually part of a campaign to take advantage of the severe economic difficulties of a country like Afghanistan. And the Americans don't even go to much trouble to conceal their real aims; they hardly bother to put a fig leaf over their self-centered, militaristic motives. We have already seen what has happened when the American capitalists, imperialists, monopolists, and militarists — the whole gang of them — have gone poking their noses into other countries' business in Asia. They would go in offering all kinds of economic aid and come out with another signature to the SEATO treaty. Pakistan joined SEATO, and the Americans tried to get India to join, too. But India, thanks to Nehru's progressive leadership, refused, and India stood firm as a country independent of all military blocs.

At the time of our visit there, it was clear to us that the Americans were penetrating Afghanistan with the obvious purpose of setting up a military base.

For our part, we have built a bakery, a railroad, and educational institutions, and we have undertaken the construction of several hundred kilometers of road. The road is now of great political and economic importance because it passes near the Afghan-Iranian border.

It's my strong feeling that the capital which we've invested in Afghanistan hasn't been wasted. We have earned the Afghans' trust and friendship, and it hasn't fallen into the Americans' trap; it hasn't been caught on the hook baited with American money.

There's no doubt that if the Afghans hadn't become our friends, the Americans would have managed to ingratiate themselves with their "humanitarian aid," as they call it. The amount of money we spent in gratuitous assistance to Afghanistan is a drop in the ocean compared to the price we would have had to pay in order to counter the threat of an American military base on Afghan territory. Think of the capital we would have had to lay out to finance the deployment of our own military might along our side of the Afghan border, and it would have been an expense that would have sucked the blood of our people without augmenting our means of production one whit.

I think our foreign policy should be based in part on an old folk custom which I remember from my own childhood. If a housewife went to another village to visit friends or relatives, she would never go without taking a bundle of pastries — or, in our Kursk Province, a dozen eggs — as a house present for her hosts. I think this tradition should be adopted by one state in its dealings with another. This custom should be practiced reasonably and moderately, mind you. It doesn't take much brains or skill to earn the reputation of the kindly uncle who squanders money on gifts for other families without leaving enough to buy the groceries for his own family. That's obviously an extreme to be

Meeting cosmonaut Titov, August, 1961, at Vnukovo airport. In the background, left: Kozlov, Suslov, Brezhnev, and Gagarin. Beyond Titov: a group of cosmonauts' wives

On a cruise along the Dnieper River in the Ukraine, 1962

With his grandson Nikita, 1963

Khrushchev and his wife at a house in Usovo, in the Ukraine, with their children Helen, Sergei, Julia, and Rada, and their son-in-law, A. I. Adzhubei, Rada's husband

Vacationing at a former palace of Tsar Alexander III, in the Crimea, 1961.
Far left: Ulbricht of East Germany and Gomulka of Poland. Far right:
Suslov and Brezhnev

At Zavidova, near Moscow, 1963

avoided. The policy of giving "house presents" to other countries must be pursued intelligently and in moderation so that our generosity will always repay us both economically and politically.[1]

We must never forget that our enemies are always working against us, always looking for a chance to exploit some oversight on our part. There is a battle going on in the world to decide who will prevail over whom: will the working class prevail, or the bourgeoisie? The working class is convinced that the bourgeoisie has exhausted itself, while the bourgeoisie believes it can rule forever. Every right-thinking person can see clearly that the basic questions of ideology can be resolved only by struggle and only by the victory of one doctrine over the other.

We Communists, we Marxists-Leninists, believe that progress is on our side and victory will inevitably be ours. Yet the capitalists won't give an inch and still swear to fight to the bitter end. Therefore how can we talk of peaceful coexistence with capitalist ideology? Peaceful coexistence among different systems of government is possible, but peaceful coexistence among different ideologies is not. It would be a betrayal of our Party's first principles to believe that there can be peaceful coexistence between Marxist-Leninist ideology on the one hand and bourgeois ideology on the other.

We have always said this. When I spoke out on this subject at press conferences, during the years when the direction of our policies depended largely on me, I always said that there can be no such thing as ideological peaceful coexistence. I always stressed that we would fight to the end, and that we were sure we would prevail.

Therefore I allowed myself at one point to use the expression, "We will bury the enemies of the Revolution." I was referring, of course, to America. Enemy propaganda picked up this slogan and blew it all out of proportion — "Khrushchev says the Soviet people want to bury the people of the United States of America!" I had said no such thing. Our enemies were distorting and exploiting a phrase which I'd simply let drop. Later at press conferences I elaborated and clarified what I had meant: We, the Soviet Union, weren't going to bury anyone; the working class of the United States would bury its enemy the bourgeois class of the United States. My slogan had referred to an internal question which every country will decide for itself: namely, by what course and

1. Even on Khrushchev's showing there does not seem much difference between Soviet motives and the motives he attributes to the USA for giving aid to underdeveloped countries.

by what methods will the working class of a given country achieve its victory over the bourgeoisie?

The main thing that I noticed about the capitalist West when I was in New York, which Gorky once called the City of the Yellow Devil, is that it's not the man that counts but the dollar. Everyone thinks of how to make money, how to get more dollars. Profits, the quest for capital, and not people are the center of attention there.

The ruling quarters of the United States describe the so-called American way of life as a model for the "free world." But what kind of freedom is that? It is the freedom to exploit, the freedom to rob, the freedom to die of starvation when there are surpluses, the freedom to be unemployed when production capacities stand idle. Freedom in the United States is a freedom for monopoly capital to oppress the working people, to bamboozle people with the bi-partisan system, to impose its will on their partners in military blocs. Such a society provides the basis for wars between countries because the tendency toward reaction inside the country and toward expansion and aggression outside is characteristic of monopoly capitalism and imperialism.

The liquidation of the capitalist system is the crucial question in the development of society. After the victory of the working class, working peasantry, and working intelligentsia, there will be neither social, national, nor any other causes for the outbreak of war in any country. But this will be only under the complete domination of the Socialist, communist system throughout the world. Mankind will then be united in a true commonwealth of equal nations. This was said long ago and scientifically proved by the founders of Marxism-Leninism.

The crucial struggle, then, is the struggle going on within each country between its own bourgeoisie and its own proletariat. This fact has some bearing on the question of how large a standing army the Soviet Union should try to maintain on its own territory and on the territories of the fraternal Socialist countries. My own thinking on this subject has evolved considerably over the years.

Not long after Stalin's death I was in Rumania and had a talk with the Rumanian Minister of War, Comrade Bodnaras.[2] He was a good friend of the Soviet Union, an Old Bolshevik who had spent some time

2. E. Bodnaras started life as an artillery subaltern in the Rumanian army; he became a Communist and deserted to the Soviet Union in 1932. After various vicissitudes he took out Soviet citizenship and underwent training in the Moscow secret police school. Back in Rumania after the war he was active and effective in assisting the Communists, backed by Soviet bayonets, in destroying all non-Com-

in prison in Rumania and who enjoyed our absolute confidence and respect. Without warning he brought up the question, "What would you
think about pulling your troops out of Rumania?"

I must confess that my initial reaction to his suggestion wasn't very
sensible. I would even go so far as to say I lost my temper. "What are
you saying? How can you ask such a question?"

"Well," he explained, "Rumania shares borders only with other Socialist countries and there's nobody across the Black Sea from us except the Turks."

"And what about the Turks?" I asked.

"Well, we have you right next door. If it were necessary, you could
always come to our assistance."

"It's not just the Turks I'm thinking about. They control the Bospo-
rus and the Dardanelles. Hence the enemy could always invade Rumania by bringing landing forces into the Black Sea."

The Rumanians exchanged glances. Obviously they had already
talked this matter over among themselves. "Well, all right," they said,
"if that's how you feel, we'll withdraw the question. We just didn't
want you to think that we were standing firm on Socialist positions because your troops are stationed on our territory. We're standing firm
because we believe in building Socialism and in following Marxist-
Leninist policies, and because our people recognize us as their leaders
and support us completely." I was more than satisfied with this eluci-
dation of their reason for proposing the removal of Soviet troops from
their territory. I believed that the Rumanian comrades were sincere in
reaffirming their dedication to the building of Socialism.

A few years later we did start reducing the size of the Soviet Army,
cutting it to almost half of what it had been under Stalin. We exchanged opinions in the leadership of the Central Committee and
came to the conclusion that we would be able to pull troops out of Poland, Hungary, and Rumania. We didn't have any troops in Czechoslovakia or in Bulgaria.[3] We left troops only in Germany. It was perfectly
clear to everyone that until our former allies — who had organized

---

munist parties. He became Minister of National Defense in the fellow-traveling
Groza government in December, 1947, thus bringing the army under Communist
control at the moment when Rumania became a People's Republic. He went on
from strength to strength.

3. Under Khrushchev the Soviet Army was indeed very sharply reduced. Stalin
had not considered it necessary to keep troops in Czechoslovakia: it was left to
Brezhnev to remedy this omission. But there were still Soviet troops in Hungary,
Poland, and Rumania.

NATO — agreed to a peace treaty, our troops would have to stay in East Germany.

We had a number of reasons for deciding to pull our troops out of the fraternal countries. One reason was political. We didn't want anyone to think that we didn't trust the Polish, Hungarian, and Rumanian people. These were our allies. They were building Socialism in their countries because it was in their own interest to do so, not because there were Soviet troops stationed in their midst. Marxist-Leninist internationalism has been the main attraction and unifying force for the people of the other Socialist countries. You can't herd people into paradise with threats and then post soldiers at the gates. People have to choose a better life on their own, and given the opportunity, they will. Therefore we wanted to remove a trump card from the hand of enemy propaganda. We wanted to give the lie to the enemy's insinuation that the Hungarian, Polish, and Rumanian people were being prodded along the path of Socialism at bayonet point by Soviet troops.

There was, of course, an economic reason as well as a political one for pulling our troops out of the fraternal countries. The maintenance of a division abroad, on the territory of another Socialist country, costs twice as much as the maintenance of a division on our own territory. We had to economize on our standing army at home as well as abroad. So we cut back substantially on military spending, particularly in the area of personnel. After I retired from my posts as First Secretary of the Party and Chairman of the Council of Ministers, I heard repercussions of dissatisfaction from people who ascribed to me the decision to cut salaries in the Soviet Army. I don't deny that military salaries were cut under me, but it was actually Marshal Zhukov's idea. I certainly supported him because there were obviously many excesses which had to be curtailed. These matters were worked out when Zhukov was Minister of Defense and then later after Malinovsky became Minister. I have to give Zhukov his due here. He realized the necessity of reducing expenses in the army, and he took the initiative in trimming expendable personnel from the command staff and ordered salary cuts for some categories of officers.

Now, I know you can find people — especially in the military — who will tell you that our reduction of the Soviet Union's armed forces was a mistake. They'll tell you that the imperialist camp has been dreaming for years of a chance to annihilate the Soviet Union, and that the only thing holding back the aggressors has been our armed might. Well, people who say this are wrong. Once it was important how many troops, how many rifles, how many bayonets a country had. But we live in a new and different age. The number of troops and rifles and bayonets is no longer decisive. Now the important thing is the quality and quantity of our nuclear missile arsenal. The defense of our country and our ability to deter imperialist aggression depends on our nuclear and thermonuclear fire power.[4]

Even honest people who want to avoid the use of atomic and hydrogen weapons can't ignore the question of how many such arms are available to us in case a global war should break out. That's why we must decide realistically on priorities for the allocation of funds.

When I was the leader of the Party and the Government, I decided that we had to economize drastically in the building of homes, the construction of communal services, and even in the development of agriculture in order to build up our defenses. I even suspended the construction of subways in Kiev, Baku, and Tblisi so that we could redirect those funds into strengthening our defense and attack forces. We also built fewer athletic stadiums, swimming pools, and cultural facilities. I think I was right to concentrate on military spending, even at the expense of all but the most essential investments in other areas. If I hadn't put such a high priority on our military needs, we couldn't have survived. I devoted all my strength to the rearmament of the Soviet Union. It was a challenging and important stage of our lives. Now that I'm living with my memories and little else, I think back often to that period when in a creative surge forward we rearmed our Soviet Army. I'm proud that the honor of supervising the transition to the most up-to-date weaponry fell on me as the Chairman of the Council of Ministers and the First Secretary of the Central Committee.

Our potential enemy — our principal, our most powerful, our most dangerous enemy — was so far away from us that we couldn't have reached him with our air force. Only by building up a nuclear missile force could we keep the enemy from unleashing war against us. As life has already confirmed, if we had given the West a chance, war would have been declared while Dulles was alive. But we were the first to launch rockets into space; we exploded the most powerful nuclear devices; we accomplished those feats first, ahead of the United States,

4. Khrushchev came under very heavy fire indeed for running down conventional forces in favor of reliance on the nuclear deterrent. It was one of the contributory factors behind his downfall in October, 1964.

England, and France. Our accomplishments and our obvious might had a sobering effect on the aggressive forces in the United States, England, France, and, of course, inside the Bonn government. They knew that they had lost their chance to strike at us with impunity.

Now that it's the size of our nuclear missile arsenal and not the size of our army that counts, I think the army should be reduced to an absolute minimum. There's no question in my mind that we have indeed reached the stage where that's possible. When I led the Government and had final authority over our military allocations, our theoreticians calculated that we had the nuclear capacity to grind our enemies into dust, and since that time our nuclear capacity has been greatly intensified. During my leadership we accumulated enough weapons to destroy the principal cities of the United States, not to mention our potential enemies in Europe.

I remember that President Kennedy once stated in a speech or at a press conference that the United States had the nuclear missile capacity to wipe out the Soviet Union two times over, while the Soviet Union had enough atomic missiles to wipe out the United States only once. When journalists asked me to reply to Kennedy's statement, I said jokingly, "Yes, I know what Kennedy claims, and he's quite right. But I'm not complaining as long as the President understands that even though he may be able to destroy us two times over, we're still capable of wiping out the United States, even if it's only once. I'm grateful to the President for recognizing that much. We're not a bloodthirsty people. We're satisfied to be able to wipe out the United States the first time around. Once is quite enough. What good does it do to annihilate a country two times over?" These remarks of mine always drew some smiles.

In this regard I must give our departed enemy Adenauer credit for his sober-mindedness. Whenever journalists attacked him and accused West Germany of being a potential aggressor bent upon unleashing another world war, Adenauer always pretended to be a perfect little Christ. "I don't know what you're talking about," he would say. "If a third world war is unleashed, West Germany will be the first country to perish." I was pleased to hear this, and Adenauer was absolutely right in what he said. For him to be making public statements like that was a great achievement on our part. Not only were we keeping our number one enemy in line, but Adenauer was helping us to keep our other enemies in line, too.

I have always been against war, but at the same time I've always realized full well that the fear of nuclear war in a country's leader can paralyze that country's defenses. And if a country's defenses are paralyzed, then war really is inevitable: the enemy is sure to sense your fright and try to take advantage of it. I always operated on the principle that I should be clearly against war but never frightened of it. Sometimes retreat is necessary, but retreat can also be the beginning of the end of your resistance. When the enemy is watching your every move, even death is a thing to be faced bravely. And if the enemy starts a war against you, then it is your duty to do everything possible to survive the war and to achieve victory in the end.

We must not lower our guard. Under no circumstances should we let our nuclear missile force fall below the necessary level. There are other weapons, too, which are necessary to have in any eventuality, namely, chemical and bacteriological weapons. Fortunately, the Second World War passed without these arms being used, but they were used in the First World War. Our army would be in a miserable situation if our enemy were to use chemical and bacteriological weapons against us and we didn't have any of our own. As long as two opposing systems exist, we will be obliged to keep all possible means of warfare stockpiled. I'm emphasizing this because I want my belief in the importance of vigilance and effective deterrence against imperialist aggression to be clearly understood.

However, we must also keep in mind the true character of all imperialists, capitalists, monopolists, and militarists who are interested in making money out of the political tension between nations. We must make sure that we don't allow ourselves to get involved in a lot of senseless competition with the West over military spending. If we try to compete with America in any but the most essential areas of military preparedness, we will be doing two harmful things. First, we will be further enriching wealthy aggressive capitalistic circles in the United States who use our own military buildups as a pretext for overloading their own country's arms budget. Second, we will be exhausting our material resources without raising the living standard of our people. We must remember that the fewer people we have in the army, the more people we will have available for other, more productive kinds of work, This realization would be a good common point of departure for the progressive forces of the world in their struggle for peaceful coexistence. If one side were to curtail its accumulation of military means, it would be easier for the other side to do the same. We must be prepared to strike back against our enemy, but we must also ask, "Where is the end to this spiraling competition?"

I know from experience that the leaders of the armed forces can be very persistent in claiming their share when it comes time to allocate funds. Every commander has all sorts of very convincing arguments why he should get more than anyone else. Unfortunately there's a tendency for people who run the armed forces to be greedy and self-seeking. They're always ready to throw in your face the slogan "If you try to economize on the country's defenses today, you'll pay in blood when war breaks out tomorrow." I'm not denying that these men have a huge responsibility, and I'm not impugning their moral qualities. But the fact remains that the living standard of the country suffers when the budget is overloaded with allocations to unproductive branches of consumption. And today as yesterday, the most unproductive expenditures of all are those made on the armed forces. That's why I think that military leaders can't be reminded too often that it is the government which must allocate funds, and it is the government which must decide how much the armed forces can spend.

Apparently the control of military spending is a universal problem. I remember a conversation I once had with President Eisenhower when I was a guest at his dacha at Camp David. We went for walks together and had some useful informal talks. During one of these talks, he asked, "Tell me, Mr. Khrushchev, how do you decide the question of funds for military expenses?" Then, before I had a chance to say anything, he said, "Perhaps first I should tell you how it is with us."

"Well, how is it with you?"

He smiled, and I smiled back at him. I had a feeling what he was going to say. "It's like this. My military leaders come to me and say, 'Mr. President, we need such and such a sum for such and such a program.' I say, 'Sorry, we don't have the funds.' They say, 'We have reliable information that the Soviet Union has already allocated funds for their own such program. Therefore if we don't get the funds we need, we'll fall behind the Soviet Union.' So I give in. That's how they wring money out of me. They keep grabbing for more and I keep giving it to them. Now tell me, how is it with you?"

"It's just the same. Some people from our military department come and say, 'Comrade Khrushchev, look at this! The Americans are developing such and such a system. We could develop the same system, but it would cost such and such.' I tell them there's no money; it's all been allotted already. So they say, 'If we don't get the money we need and if there's a war, then the enemy will have superiority over us.' So we discuss it some more, and I end up by giving them the money they ask for."

"Yes," he said, "that's what I thought. You know, we really should come to some sort of an agreement in order to stop this fruitless, really wasteful rivalry."

"I'd like to do that. Part of my reason for coming here was to see if some sort of an agreement would come out of these meetings and conversations."

But we couldn't agree then, and we can't agree now. I don't know. Maybe it's impossible for us to agree. On the basis of my own experience, I can certainly say it's very difficult. But even if a Soviet-American agreement on bilateral reduction in military spending is impossible, I keep coming back to my own feeling that we should go ahead and sharply reduce our own expenditures, unilaterally. If our enemy wants to go ahead inflating his military budget, spending his own money right and left on all kinds of senseless things, then he's sure to lower the living standards of his own people. By so doing he will be strengthening the position of the Communist and progressive forces in his own midst, enabling them to cry out in a still louder voice against the reactionary forces of monopolistic capital.

There you have it. That's the substance of my viewpoint, and I think it has some merit. My time has already come and gone. There's nothing I can do now but share my experience with anyone who cares to listen and hope that somebody pays attention. It's too late for me to do anything active. I make all these observations as a man who no longer works. But from my position as a pensioner, I can't help noticing that the economizing trend we started seems to have been reversed, that now money is being wasted on unnecessary items and categories, and that this new trend of military overspending is putting a pinch on some of the more important, but still underfinanced, areas of our country's life.

When I was the head of the government, the young pianist Ashkenazy married an Englishwoman who had studied in one of our conservatories. They had a baby and went to England to visit the wife's parents. Shortly afterwards Gromyko reported to me that our ambassador in London had cabled the following story: Ashkenazy came to our embassy in London and said that his wife refused to go back to the Soviet Union. He loved her very much and asked our embassy what to do. Now, I should mention that I had heard Ashkenazy play and had personally congratulated him when he won first prize at the Tchaikovsky Competition. He's an excellent pianist, and I often hear him on the radio. I consulted with my comrades and proposed, "Let's give Ashkenazy permission to live in England however long he wants. That way he'll always be able to return to the Soviet Union. We really have no alternative. If we insist that he leave his wife and return home, he'll refuse. He's not an anti-Soviet, but we could turn him into one if we put him in the position of having to choose between staying with his wife and obeying his government. He would immediately fall into the clutches of emigrés and other types who would start working on him, beating all sorts of anti-Soviet ideas into his head. We don't want that to happen. What's wrong with him living in London while keeping his Soviet citizenship? He can come back to Moscow anytime to give concerts. After all, he's a musician, and that's a free profession."

Everyone agreed, and my suggestion was accepted.

These days I often listen to the radio. My radio is my constant companion when I go out for walks. I get both information and pleasure from it. I love folk music and folk songs. I also like some contemporary music, but I'll confess that a man of my age is more inclined to the things which were part of his youth. Most radio programs are pretty good, but there's a certain amount of trash polluting the air. It always gives me special pleasure when I turn on the radio and hear it announced that Ashkenazy has come to Moscow to give a concert. I'm glad we protected his good name as a great Soviet pianist and saved his family life in the process. Perhaps the time will come when Ashkenazy and his wife will want to come back and settle in Moscow for good. Or perhaps they will settle in London. I'm not excluding that possibility. So what. Let them live where they want. I think the time has come to give every Soviet citizen that choice. If he wants to leave our country and live somewhere else for a while, all right; we should give him that opportunity. It's incredible to me that after fifty years of Soviet power, paradise should be kept under lock and key.[5]

We Communists believe that capitalism is a hell in which laboring

5. In August, 1969, Soviet diplomats pointed to Ashkenazy as an example of a Soviet artist who could travel freely in and out of the USSR. Ashkenazy branded the statement as untrue. He said, "When an official Soviet spokesman says I move freely between Russia and the West, as I only wish I could, it is a gross and unfair distortion of the truth."

people are condemned to slavery. We are building Socialism. We have already been successful in many respects, and we will be even more successful in the future. Our way of life is undoubtedly the most progressive in the world at the present stage of humanity's development. To use the language of the Bible again, our way of life is paradise for mankind. It's not paradise in the sense that the horn of plenty is overflowing and that all you have to do is open your mouth and you will be fed. No, we don't have that kind of paradise — at least not yet. I don't know if we ever will. But, as they say, everything is relative. And relative to the capitalist world, our way of life is a great accomplishment. We have accomplished many things, and we have created the conditions for still greater successes.

So why should we contradict ourselves? Why should we build a good life for a people and then keep our border bolted with seven locks? Sometimes our own Soviet citizens scoff, "So you're driving us into paradise with a club, eh?" People used to make that sort of complaint when compulsory collectivization and other campaigns were under way. I think it's time to show the world that our people are free; they work willingly; and they are building Socialism because of their convictions, not because they have no choice.

I have no doubt that it's practically as well as theoretically feasible for us to open our borders. If it were not feasible, then what kind of freedom would we have? All right, I know some people argue, "Look, we have a class structure of society, and we can't let the class enemies of the proletariat come and go at will." For thinking people, that's a different period of our existence. We liquidated the hostile classes fifty years ago, and any argument that raises the specter of class enemies inside the Soviet Union is for fools.

I can think of another incident from my own leadership which illustrates how we can rid ourselves of this disgraceful heritage of the closed border which lies like a chain on the consciousness of the Soviet State. Our number one ballerina, Maya Plisetskaya — who was not only the best ballerina in the Soviet Union, but the best in the whole world — used to be excluded from the company whenever the Bolshoi Theater went abroad. It was reported to me that she couldn't be trusted, that she might not come back. Well, I didn't know her personally; I'd never even spoken to her; I had no idea what her attitudes were. There's no question that it would have been very unpleasant if someone of Plisetskaya's reputation were suddenly to abandon the So-

Official portrait, 1963

viet Union. Her defection would have been useful for the West as anti-Soviet propaganda, and we would have been painfully stung.

Then one day, when a ballet troupe was getting ready to go abroad, I received a letter from Maya Plisetskaya. It was addressed to me in my capacity as Secretary of the Central Committee. It was a long and forthright letter. She wrote that she was a patriot and that she was hurt and insulted by the distrust which was being shown toward her. I made copies of her letter and passed it around among the other members of the Presidium. I raised the question of what we should do. It was my recommendation that she be allowed to go on the tour. There were some doubts expressed that she might not come back. "Maybe," I replied. "That's something that could happen. But I trust her, even though I don't know her. It's impossible to live without trusting people. If she wrote this letter dishonestly, if she's just trying to trick us into letting her break out . . . well, it will certainly be a big loss for us, and very embarrassing. But we'll survive."

Maya Plisetskaya went on the tour, and I was rewarded many times over by her brilliant performances abroad. She enhanced the fame of Soviet ballet and Soviet culture. And she came back. This was our reward for the labor invested in building a Socialist society of which Plisetskaya was proud to be a citizen.

And what if we had continued our "no exit permit" policy? What if we had continued to keep Maya Plisetskaya securely locked in? We probably would have turned her into a crippled human being and an anti-Soviet as well. The human psyche is a terribly fragile thing. It has to be treated with the utmost respect. One careless move can throw it fatally out of balance. I'm proud of my decision to let Maya Plisetskaya travel abroad, and I'm glad she properly appreciated our gesture of confidence in her.

If we were to open our borders, is it possible that our confidence and trust in individuals will ever be betrayed? Of course it is. Among 240 million people you're bound to find some impure elements. And the impure will come bobbing to the surface as the light, less substantial matter in a solution always does. So let the garbage, the dregs, the scum of our society float to the surface, and let the waves carry it far away from our shores. What I'm saying here is perfectly consistent with Lenin's policy in the first years of the Revolution, when we used to send the enemies of the Soviet Union into exile abroad. All those desiring to leave found no obstacles in their way. "You want to leave?" we told them. "Fine, pack your bag and get out!" And they left.

Now, fifty years later, we've got to stop looking for a defector in everyone. We've got to stop designing our border policy for the sake of keeping the dregs and scum inside our country. We must start thinking about the people who don't deserve to be called scum — people who might undergo a temporary vacillation in their own convictions, or who might want to try out the capitalist hell, some aspects of which may still appear attractive to our less stable elements. We can't keep fencing these people in. We've got to give them a chance to find out for themselves what the world is like.

If we don't change our position in this regard, I'm afraid we will discredit the Marxist-Leninist ideals on which our Soviet way of life is based.

Appendixes

Appendix 1

Chronology of Khrushchev's Career

1894   April 17. Born in Kalinovka,   *Accession of Tsar Nicholas II.*
Kursk Province, near Ukrainian
border.

1903   *Lenin splits Russian Social Democratic
Labor Party into Bolshevik and Menshevik
wings at Second Party Congress in London.*

1904–5   *Russo-Japanese War.*
1905   *The 1905 Revolution.*
1906   *First Duma (Parliament).*

1909   Moves to Yuzovka (later Stalino,
now Donetsk) in Donbass region
of Ukraine, where father works
in mine.

1909–12   Learns metal fitter's trade at
Bosse factory in Yuzovka.

1912–18   Works as metal fitter in generator plants of French-owned
Ruchenkov and Pastukhov mines.

1914   *Outbreak of World War I.*

1915   Becomes "avid reader of
Pravda."

1917   Represents miners at political   *February Revolution; abdication of Tsar;
meetings and rallies, meets Lazar   formation of Provisional Government.*
Kaganovich.

*October Revolution; Lenin overthrows
Provisional Government and establishes
Soviet Rule.*

1918   Becomes Bolshevik.

1919   Joins Red Army.

1919–21   Soldier and Party worker in   *Civil War and Allied Intervention.*
ranks of Ninth Rifle Division,
then attached to Budyonny's
First Mounted Army for offensive to Black Sea.

1921   Death of first wife in famine.   *Famine; introduction of New Economic Policy (NEP).*

1922   Back to Yuzovka from Front.

       Assigned by Yuzovka Party organization to be deputy director of Ruchenkov mines.

       Offered directorship of Pastukhov mines but asks permission to study at Yuzovka Workers' Faculty.

1923   Student and political leader at Yuzovka Workers' Faculty.

1924   Holds various posts in Yuzovka Party organization.   *Death of Lenin.*

       Marries Nina Petrovna.

1925   Appointed Party Secretary of Petrovsko-Marinsk District of Stalino (formerly Yuzovka) Region.

       Attends Ninth Ukrainian Party Congress with Kaganovich in chair.

       Consulting (i.e., nonvoting) delegate to Fourteenth All-Union Party Congress in Moscow; first exposure to Stalin.   *Stalin moves against Zinoviev and Kamenev.*

1926   First recorded public speech at Ukrainian Party Conference in Kharkov.

1927   Delegate to Fifteenth All-Union Party Congress in Moscow.   *Defeat of Zinoviev and Kamenev.*

       Promoted from Stalino District to Regional Party apparatus.

1928   Promoted by Kaganovich to be Deputy Chief of Organizational Section of Ukrainian Central Committee in Kharkov.   *First Five-Year Plan; start of collectivization.*

       Promoted by Kaganovich to be Chief of Organizational Section of Kiev Party apparatus.

1929   Thirty-five years old; requests permission to study metallurgy at Stalin Industrial Academy in Moscow.   *Kaganovich transferred to Moscow.*

1929–30 Political worker and student *Trotsky banished.*
at Industrial Academy.

Voted down as academy delegate to Sixteenth Party Congress; candidacy to bureau of Party cell blocked.

"Leads struggle for Party Line against rightists, parasites, and Old Guard in academy."

Associated with Nadezhda Alliluyeva, Stalin's wife and group organizer at academy.

Sent to inspect Stalin Collective Farm in Samara Region; first glimpse of conditions caused by collectivization.

Recruited by Mekhlis to lead pro-Stalin forces at academy; chairs meeting to recall "rightist" delegates to Bauman District Party Conference; leads new delegation to Conference.

1931 Elected First Secretary of Bauman District; six months later promoted to First Secretary of Red Presnya District.

1932 Leaves academy without grad- *Death of Nadezhda Alliluyeva, Stalin's*
uating; promoted to Second Sec- *wife.*
retary under Kaganovich of Moscow City Party Committee.

Associated with Nadezhda Krupskaya, Lenin's widow, in Moscow City administration.

1933 Becomes Second Secretary of Moscow Regional Committee.

Active in reconstruction of Moscow and building of Metro under Kaganovich.

1934 Elected to Central Committee at *Kirov murdered.*
Seventeenth Party Congress ("Congress of Victors").

1935 Takes Kaganovich's place as *Years of blood purges, great terror, and*
First Secretary of Moscow City *show trials begin.*
and Regional committees.

1936		*Zinoviev and Kamenev tried and executed (August).*
		Yezhov replaces Yagoda as secret police chief (September).
1937		*Death of Ordzhonikidze (February).*
		Execution of Tukhachevsky and generals (June).
1938	Appointed First Secretary of Ukrainian Central Committee.	*Bukharin and Rykov tried (March).*
1939	Attends February Central Committee Plenum at which Kaminsky denounces Beria; Kaminsky then disappears.	*Beria replaces Yezhov (December).*
	Made full member of Politbureau (March).	*Ribbentrop-Molotov Pact (August).*
	As Ukrainian First Secretary and civilian member of Kiev Military Council, moves into Western Ukraine (occupied Poland).	
1939–40		*Winter War with Finland (November-March).*
1940	Supervises sovietization of Western Ukraine.	
1941–43	As member of Military Council and Politbureau representative, serves on various fronts as commissar with wartime rank of lieutenant general.	*Germany invades Russia (June '41); Operation Barbarossa begins.*
		Fall of Kiev (September '41).
		Battle of Moscow (winter '41–42).
		Kharkov disaster (May '42).
		Battle of Stalingrad (July '42–winter '43).
		Battle of Kursk (summer '43).
	Begins reconstruction of Ukrainian economy and Party.	*Liberation of Kiev (November '43).*
		Teheran Conference (November '43).
1944	Appointed Chairman of Ukrainian Council of Ministers while retaining position as First Secretary of Ukrainian Party.	*Soviet offensive toward Berlin (spring).*
		Allied invasion of France (June).
1945		*Soviet troops capture Berlin (May).*
	Meets Eisenhower in Moscow.	*Victory Parade in Moscow (June).*
	Leads commission of experts to help Poles with reconstruction of Warsaw.	

1946–47   Temporary eclipse and demotion; replaced by Kaganovich as First Secretary of Ukraine; near-fatal bout with pneumonia.

Famine in Ukraine.

1948   Restored to full power in Ukraine.

Stalin breaks with Tito.

1949   Recalled by Stalin to Moscow, made head of Moscow Party organization (December).

The Leningrad Affair.

1950   Made overlord of agriculture; amalgamates collective farms and pushes agro-town scheme.

Stalin publishes letter on linguistics in Pravda.

Outbreak of Korean War.

1952   Delivers report on amendments to Party Statutes at Nineteenth Party Congress (October).

Stalin lets Malenkov deliver General Report on his behalf at Nineteenth Party Congress.

1953

Doctors' Plot (January-February).

Ranked behind Malenkov, Molotov, Beria, and Kaganovich.

Stalin's death; Malenkov becomes Prime Minister and First Secretary (March).

Replaces Malenkov as First Secretary (September).

1954   Visits Peking with Bulganin.

Begins Virgin Lands campaign.

1955   Visits Yugoslavia (buries hatchet with Tito); Geneva for summit meeting; Afghanistan; and India ("We shall bury you!").

Bulganin replaces Malenkov as Prime Minister.

1956   Delivers Secret Speech on crimes of Stalin at Twentieth Party Congress (February).

Visits London (April).

Defiance of Poland (June).

Suez Crisis (October-November).

Hungarian Revolt (October).

1957   Begins decentralization of industry (May).

Smashes opposition of "Anti-Party Group" — Malenkov, Molotov, Kaganovich, Shepilov, and others (July).

Dismisses Marshal Zhukov from post of Minister of Defense (October).

Sputnik I launched (October).

1957

Moscow meeting of world Communist Parties, attended by Mao Tse-tung (November).

1958 Takes over Premiership from Bulganin (March).

Middle East Crisis (July-August).

First Berlin Crisis (autumn).

1959 Refuses to give China atomic weapons information (summer).

First visit to USA, consultations with Eisenhower at Camp David (September).

1960 Announces downing of U-2 reconnaissance plane and capture of Gary Powers (May).

Wrecks Paris summit meeting (May).

Attacks China behind closed doors at Rumanian Party Congress in Bucharest (June) and at Moscow Conference of World Communist Parties (November).

1961

Major Y. Gagarin, first man in space (April).

Meets with Kennedy in Vienna.

Second Berlin Crisis (June).

Makes public attack on China, thinly disguised as Albania, at Twenty-second Party Congress (October).

Has Stalin's body removed from Mausoleum.

1962 Goes to brink of war over missiles in Cuba — and steps back (October).

1963 Cracks down on writers and artists.

Nuclear test-ban treaty (August).

Disastrous harvest.

1964 Prepares for showdown with China at world Party Conference scheduled for December.

Resigns all offices; succeeded by Brezhnev as First Secretary and Kosygin as Prime Minister (October).

Appendix 2

Soviet Institutions and Terminology

THE Soviet Union consists of fifteen constituent Republics (the Russian Federation and the Ukraine are two), each formally a sovereign state with the constitutional right of secession.

The institutions of Party and State, which have their counterparts at both Republic and All-Union levels, are theoretically separate but equal. In fact, however, real power resides in the Party.

THE PARTY

The Party, which includes about five percent of the Soviet population in its membership, is administered by a pyramidal hierarchy of committees. The lowest organizational unit is formed around an enterprise, such as a factory, a mine, a collective farm, a military outfit, or an educational establishment. The primary Party organization was for many years called a *cell*; for example, the Party cell of the Industrial Academy. The Party pyramid is built of territorial boxes-within-boxes, each with its own steering committee called a *bureau* and its executive adjunct called a *secretariat*. The Party committees in ascending order of purview and power are: *district, city, region, Republic Central Committee*, and at the apex, the *All-Union Central Committee*.

Party procedure is constitutionally governed by a set of rules called the *Party Statutes*, which were codified before the Revolution and are regularly amended.

According to the Party Statutes, the "supreme organ" of the Communist Party of the Soviet Union is the *Party Congress*, a meeting of delegates from all the Republics who elect the All-Union Central Committee. The Party Statutes stipulate that a Congress shall be convened at least every three years. How much authority the Party Congress and, for that matter, the Party Statutes themselves really have is indicated by the fact that Stalin let thirteen years elapse between the Eighteenth and Nineteenth Party Congresses.

Business at the district, city, regional, and Republic levels is conducted at *Party Conferences.*

The All-Union Central Committee meets semiannually in *plenums,* or plenary sessions. Between plenums, the work of the Central Committee is carried out by its administrative organ, the *Central Committee Secretariat,* which does the bidding of the innermost circle of the Party leadership, the *Politbureau* (renamed the *Presidium* just before Stalin's death and changed back to Politbureau after Khrushchev's downfall). Although technically elective and accountable to the Central Committee, the Politbureau is virtually self-perpetuating and is the real power center of the Partocracy. The First Secretary of the Party Central Committee is always the head of the Politbureau or Presidium, and he is able to pack the whole Party apparatus with his supporters.

THE STATE

The State is divided into executive and legislative branches, the former supposedly responsible to the latter, but both in fact subservient to the Party.

The executive function is fulfilled at the Republic and All-Union levels by *ministries* (which until shortly after World War II were called *commissariats*) and at the district, city, and regional levels by *executive committees.* At both the Republic and All-Union levels the various areas of management (transport, electricity, mining, agriculture, industry, and the like) are overseen by a *Council of Ministers* (formerly, *Council of People's Commissars*). The Chairman of the Council of Ministers of the USSR is commonly referred to as the Prime Minister of the Soviet Union. He is always a member of the Politbureau or Presidium.

The structure of the legislative system corresponds closely to the territorial breakdown of the Party organization.

The basic representative unit is the *soviet* or council, ranging from a rural or district soviet at the primary level to the *Supreme Soviet* at both the Republic and All-Union levels.

The chairman of a city soviet is, in effect, the mayor of the city, and the Chairman of the Presidium of the Supreme Soviet of the USSR is titularly the President and chief of state.

Stalin's 1936 Constitution declares the Supreme Soviet to be "the highest organ of State power in the USSR" and invests it with the law-making powers of a democratic parliament. In fact, however, the Supreme Soviet is the rubber stamp of the State just as the Central Committee is the rubber stamp of the Party. The Politbureau controls both with a firm hand.

THE SECRET POLICE

The Soviet police establishment has undergone a complex evolution and has been known by ten different names, depending on period and realm of activity (that is, State, Party, or military). It figures in this book primarily as the NKVD, or *People's Commissariat of Internal Affairs*, during the purge years. During World War II it was the *Political Directorate* of the armed forces. After the war the police establishment was split for a time into the *Ministry of Internal Affairs* and the *Ministry of State Security*, often referred to here simply as "State Security." As Khrushchev's own occasional confusion attests, it is almost impossible to keep the profusion of initials straight, so the original acronym *Cheka* (for Lenin's "Extraordinary Commission for Combating Counterrevolution, Profiteering, and Sabotage") is still common parlance for the secret police, as is the term *Chekist* for a functionary of the security apparatus.

Until Stalin's death the Cheka was a leviathan of surveillance and repression which infiltrated every level and organ of State and Party life and did its best to penetrate the private life of the individual citizen as well. It had at its command a vast administrative bureaucracy, its own armed forces, and unchecked powers of extralegal, summary procedure as well as facilities for arresting, interrogating (often under torture), trying, and executing its victims. The secret police organization reached its apotheosis as a kind of para-government under Lavrenty Beria, when prisons and concentration camps provided the state with an enormous work force of slave labor.

Stalin himself was never so secure in his autocracy that he did not fear the NKVD's immense accretions of power. When he decided that the Yezhov purges were gathering dangerous momentum, he had Yezhov himself, the "bloodthirsty dwarf," thrown under its wheels in order to halt the Juggernaut. Khrushchev says that Stalin toward the end of his life began to fear Beria *but did not know how to get rid of him*. The urgency of getting rid of Beria was apparently the one thing on which Khrushchev and the other contenders for Stalin's throne could agree. Shortly after Beria's elimination, the State Security apparatus was relegated from its status as a ministry and empire to that of a committee (the KGB) firmly subordinated to the Council of Ministers.

Appendix 3

Khrushchev's Kremlin Colleagues

Lavrenty P. Beria. Promoted by Stalin as a reliable countryman and courtier to be overlord of the NKVD's state-within-the-state, he was then liquidated by Stalin's heirs as an evil genius and traitor. Beria fully deserved his reputation as Stalin's bloody right hand, but his role in the history of Stalinist terror was nonetheless paradoxical. It was under his supervision, and partially on his initiative, that the brakes were applied to the Yezhov purges in the late thirties (see Appendix 2). Furthermore, Beria may have been an intended victim, rather than an instigator, of three notorious postwar purges: the Crimean affair (he was responsible for organizing the Jewish Anti-Fascist Committee, which Stalin accused of harboring a Zionist-imperialist conspiracy), the Mingrelian affair, and the Doctors' Plot.

Beria's origins are obscure. He is thought to have come from a middle-class background. Until Stalin brought him to Moscow to replace Yezhov, Beria's career was confined to Georgia, first in the Cheka, then in the Party apparatus. Through effective scheming against other Georgians (like Ordzhonikidze and Yenukidze), he made himself indispensable to Stalin as the Kremlin's number one informer and inquisitor in Transcaucasia. In 1935 he delivered to the Ninth Congress of the Georgian Party a two-day address, "On Stalin's Early Writings and Activities," thus establishing himself as one of Stalin's official biographers.

Compared to his colleagues Malenkov, Voroshilov, Molotov, Kaganovich, Bulganin, Mikoyan, and Khrushchev, Beria was a late-comer to Stalin's inner circle. But once he was transferred to Moscow in July, 1938, he made up for lost time. He was able to ingratiate himself with Stalin and at the same time to manipulate Stalin's suspicions of others in his own interest. Before the war he became Deputy Chairman of the Council of People's Commissars and national coordinator of security operations. He was almost certainly the main culprit behind the massacre of some four thousand Polish officers at Katyn Forest near Smolensk. When the Germans invaded, Stalin appointed Beria to the State Defense Committee (along with Molotov, Voroshilov, and Malenkov) and put him in charge of domestic policy. He played an important part in the evacuation and resettlement of industry during the German advance, and during the German retreat two years later, he was made a member of Malenkov's Committee on the Rehabilitation of Liberated Areas; both jobs brought him into frequent and, by all evidence, not very harmonious contact with Khrushchev. The day after the Americans dropped an atomic bomb on Hiroshima, Stalin designated Beria to supervise a Soviet version of the Manhattan Project, an assignment which culminated in the nuclear explosion on the Ust-Urt Desert between the Caspian and Aral seas in July, 1949.

Beria often opposed Khrushchev, particularly on issues of agricultural policy. He and Malenkov led the attack against Khrushchev's agro-town scheme in 1951. Beria may have been a master of intrigue, but he arrogantly flaunted his power and his ambition in the faces of his comrades, and this was his undoing. In his last years Stalin himself began to fear and distrust Beria, but it remained for Stalin's successors to close their otherwise divided ranks against Beria and have him shot within months after the dictator's death in 1953.

Nikolai A. Bulganin. The son of an office worker and a consummate *apparatchik*, Bulganin spent his early Party career in the ranks of the Cheka, combating "counterrevolution" in the Russian Federation and in Turkestan. He was elected Chairman of the City Soviet — in effect, mayor — of Moscow in 1931, a position which brought him into close contact with Khrushchev. A beneficiary of the purges, Bulganin was appointed Chairman of the Council of People's Commissars for the Russian Federation in 1937 and a full member of the All-Union Central Committee in 1939. During the war he was Khrushchev's counterpart as commissar on the Moscow, Western, Baltic, and Belorussian fronts with the rank of lieutenant general. He was promoted to full general and made a member of Stalin's war cabinet in 1944. At the end of the war he succeeded Stalin himself as Minister of the Armed Forces and became a Marshal of the Soviet Union. In 1948 he became a full member of the Politbureau.

Bulganin's greatest asset seems to have been that he was relatively tolerable to the men around him, who were at each other's throats. A compromise candidate acceptable to everyone, as well as a trusty stalking horse for Khrushchev, he became Minister of Defense shortly after Stalin's death and replaced Malenkov as Prime Minister in 1955. The low-keyed, goateed Bulganin made a good straight man to the livelier and shrewder Khrushchev during the celebrated "B & K road shows" to Peking, Delhi, Belgrade, Geneva, and London.

When Khrushchev had maneuvered himself into a position from which he could seize the Premiership, he toppled Bulganin with the back of his hand, adding his name almost as an afterthought to the black list of the Anti-Party Group. Bulganin obediently bowed out of active life at a Central Committee plenum in 1958 at which he confessed his own guilt and roundly denounced his alleged co-conspirators, Molotov, Malenkov, and Kaganovich. He was given a comfortable pension and retired to a dacha on the outskirts of Moscow.

Lazar M. Kaganovich. In these reminiscences Kaganovich figures as the number three villain, ranking behind only Stalin and Beria in general despicableness. The reader might be forgiven for not realizing that Khrushchev owed his career to Kaganovich. Ever since he first met the Bolshevik organizer known as "Zhirovich" during the February, 1917, Revolution, Khrushchev was Kaganovich's protégé and right-hand man. It was largely on Kaganovich's coattails that Khrushchev was pulled up the Party ladder in the Ukrainian organization during the twenties; and notwithstanding Khrushchev's implausible claim that his real benefactor in Moscow was Stalin's wife, it was Kaganovich who promoted him quickly through the Moscow apparatus all the way to the Central Committee and the Politbureau. The hard-driving, untir-

ing, and thoroughly ruthless Kaganovich had a reputation for being the
best administrator in the USSR. His heyday was during the reconstruction of Moscow in the thirties, and his crowning glory was the Moscow
Metro, which he superintended and which for years bore his name. As
head of the Party Control Commission, he was one of Stalin's most reliable henchmen during the collectivization, when he was dispatched to
accelerate "the liquidation of the kulaks as a class" in the Ukraine and
Siberia, and during the purges, when he was turned loose against "oppositionist elements" in the trade unions.

Khrushchev's enmity toward Kaganovich probably stems from 1947,
when his former mentor replaced him as Ukrainian First Secretary during Khrushchev's brief fall from grace. Kaganovich was First Deputy
Chairman of the Council of Ministers after Stalin's death. A "Malenkov
man" during the rivalry among Stalin's would-be successors, Kaganovich was lumped into the Anti-Party Group and expelled from the Presidium in 1957, twenty-seven years after being elected to a full membership in that august body. Khrushchev has accused Kaganovich, a
Ukrainian Jew, of being anti-Ukrainian and anti-Semitic as well as
"having exaggerated his contribution to the development of transport
and construction" and being Stalin's "chained cur and toady." There is
basis for the charges, but Khrushchev is hardly the one to be casting
these particular stones. In disgrace, Kaganovich was appointed manager of a cement works in Sverdlovsk. More recently he has been seen
browsing in libraries, taking in the theater, and giving advice to students on park benches in Moscow.

Georgi M. Malenkov. Far from being what Khrushchev makes him out to be — Stalin's half-wit clerk and Beria's obsequious "billy goat" —"Yegor" Malenkov was a man of formidable intelligence, ability, toughness, and ambition. He was much more sophisticated in background and manner than Khrushchev, whom he probably considered a loud-mouthed, ham-handed bumpkin. With the death in 1948 of Andrei Zhdanov (whom Khrushchev damns here by ignoring altogether), Malenkov became the second most important and powerful figure in the Soviet leadership. He was widely regarded as Stalin's heir apparent, an impression which seemed to be confirmed when Stalin designated him to deliver the General Report on his behalf at the Nineteenth Party Congress in 1952.

For a short time after Stalin's death, Malenkov was both Party First Secretary and Prime Minister. During the interregnum, while Khrushchev was consolidating his forces, Malenkov led the way in reshaping Soviet foreign and domestic policies to fit the realities of the postwar world. It was Malenkov who first publicly suggested that the Leninist dogma about the inevitability of all-out war between Communism and capitalism might be obsolete in the age of thermonuclear weapons — a suggestion which Khrushchev initially attacked as revisionist heresy but later canonized as his own "peaceful coexistence" doctrine. It was Malenkov who first called for a higher standard of living for the people and a higher priority on the production of consumer goods — long before Khrushchev began to rail against the "steel-eaters" of the military-industrial complex who were devouring state resources at the expense of the people's material interests. And it was under Malenkov that the Doctors' Plot was repudiated as a fabrication and the defendants rehabilitated — an action which might be taken as precursory to the Twentieth Party Congress's repudiation of Stalin's methods and its rehabilitation of his victims.

As the rivalry between Malenkov and Khrushchev developed, Malenkov tried unsuccessfully to turn the ministries, the State apparatus, and the technocracy into a power base from which he could hold Khrushchev and the Partocracy in check. Outmaneuvered and outvoted, Malenkov was forced to relinquish the Premiership on grounds of "inexperience" to Khrushchev's alter ego, Bulganin, in 1955. After forming a loose, ad hoc coalition of old Stalinists in an abortive effort to oust Khrushchev from the top spot in the Party, Malenkov was eclipsed once and for all in 1957. Khrushchev threw the book at Malenkov a year later, charging him with everything from incompetence during the war and responsibility for the 1949 Leningrad purge to un-Leninist economic and agricultural policies and participation in an "anti-Party plot." Malenkov was packed off to be the director of a power station in a remote part of Kazakhstan. For a long time he seemed to have dropped out of sight altogether, but recently he has been seen alive and well in Moscow.

Rodion Y. Malinovsky. The rugged, burly, outspoken commander was a favorite with rank-and-file troops and commissars alike. As these reminiscences make clear, he had an admirer of long standing in Nikita Khrushchev. Born of peasant stock in Odessa, Malinovsky joined the Tsarist army at the age of sixteen and served as a machine gunner with the Russian Expeditionary Force in France until the Revolution. He commanded a Red Army battalion against the White forces of Admiral Kolchak in Siberia during the Civil War and joined the Party in 1926. Except for a temporary demotion after the Soviet defeat at Rostov, Malinovsky distinguished himself during World War II. Throughout the war he was in close, and apparently friendly, contact with Khrushchev: first as the architect of a masterful Soviet delaying action against the

Germans in Bessarabia and the Ukraine; then as one of the commanders under Zhukov, who turned the tide of the German advance at Stalingrad; then as the director of an operation to drive the Germans out
of Khrushchev's native Donbass region and the southern Ukraine, including Malinovsky's own birthplace, Odessa. In 1944 he accepted the
German surrender in Rumania and spearheaded the Soviet thrust from
Budapest to Vienna. The end of the war found him fighting the Japanese (and wreaking havoc on the Chinese as well) in Manchuria. He
remained in the Far East until he was recalled to Moscow to become
First Deputy Minister of Defense in 1956, when he also became a full
member of the Central Committee. A year later he replaced as Defense
Minister his old superior from Stalingrad days, Marshal Zhukov.

Malinovsky was at Khrushchev's right hand during the abortive
Paris Summit Conference in 1960. He did some tough talking of his
own on his return to Moscow from Paris, when he warned that from
then on immediate action would be taken against the bases from which
any aircraft violating USSR airspace operated. Malinovsky was succeeded by his own deputy, Marshal Grechko, with whom Khrushchev
was on friendly terms during the war. Malinovsky died in 1967.

Anastas I. Mikoyan. The dour and wily Armenian, known to the West as the Soviet Union's number one traveling salesman, is a classic — but at the same time an almost unique — study in survival. His biography and political ascendancy were, one would have thought, much too close to Stalin's for his own good. Like Stalin a Caucasian and like Stalin a onetime seminarian, Mikoyan joined the Bolsheviks in 1915, the same year he received his theological degree. He was prominent in the Baku and Tiflis Party organizations, and narrowly escaped execution at the hands of the Menshevik, White, German, Turkish, and British forces, who vied with the Reds for control of the Caucasus after the Revolution. He was an early ally of Stalin's against Trotsky and —

along with the less fortunate, perhaps less flexible Sergo Ord-zhonikidze — a member of the Kremlin's Caucasian threesome. Miko-yan became a candidate member of the Politbureau in 1926, when he was appointed People's Commissar of Internal Trade and later, of Foreign Trade. Foreign trade has been his specialty ever since. He toured the United States in 1936 to study food production methods and again in 1959, drumming up commerce between what he billed "the two greatest powers." According to Khrushchev, Mikoyan along with Molotov fell out of favor with Stalin during the dictator's last years; Stalin ostracized them from the ruling circle and was gunning for them until the day he died. Khrushchev doubts that either of the foreign policy overlords would have survived if Stalin had lived much longer.

Mikoyan's role in the scenario of Khrushchev's own career is ambiguous: he apparently defended Lavrenty Beria against the kangaroo court of his peers which Khrushchev claims to have organized in 1953; then, in 1956, "Anastas Ivanovich" primed the Twentieth Party Congress for Khrushchev's Secret Speech by openly criticizing Stalin at a regular session. Mikoyan exuded charm and a good-natured sense of humor when traveling on his own. But when attached to Khrushchev on trips abroad, he had the thankless task of trying to head off his boss's most outrageous indiscretions and to neutralize the embarrassment of Khrushchev's frequent drunkenness with his own doleful sobriety. Mikoyan was the only member of the Old Guard (Malenkov, Molotov, Kaganovich, et al.) to survive Khrushchev's assault on the Anti-Party Group. After a short term as titular President of the USSR, he passed from the active scene a little over a year after Khrushchev's downfall. He retired at the Twenty-third Party Congress and now lives quietly on a state pension in downtown Moscow.

Vyacheslav M. Molotov. Born Scriabin, he was the nephew of the Russian composer of that name, the son of a shop assistant, and one of the few Bolsheviks with a bourgeois background to attach himself to Stalin from the very early days. As a young man in his twenties he held the tiny Petrograd Party together while Lenin, Trotsky, Zinoviev, and others were in exile abroad and Stalin and Kamenev were in Siberia. Lenin once called him "the best filing clerk in Russia," and Trotsky, less generously, dismissed him as "mediocrity incarnate." When the Tsarist regime was overthrown in the February Revolution, he was a twenty-seven-year-old with a bad stammer, a pince-nez, and a stuffed-shirt manner which were to stay with him throughout his career; he was also the senior Bolshevik in Petrograd. Molotov took the name "hammer" just as Stalin had taken the name "steel," and Stalin did indeed use Molotov to smash his opposition into submission and to pound his own power base into shape. On Stalin's behalf Molotov led the liquidation of the Mensheviks and then, with Voroshilov, went to Leningrad in 1926 to crush the Zinoviev opposition. He preceded Kaganovich and Khrushchev as head of the Moscow Party organization, and in 1931 he was promoted to take the place of the deposed "rightist" Rykov as nominal Prime Minister (Chairman of the Council of People's Commissars). In 1939 he surrendered the Premiership to Stalin and became foreign minister when Maxim Litvinov's policy of collective security was abandoned in favor of Stalin's preparations to make a deal with Hitler. Molotov's first major act as foreign minister was to sign a nonaggression and friendship pact with his Nazi opposite number, Joachim von Ribbentrop. According to Khrushchev, Molotov fell into perilous disfavor during Stalin's last years; the decrepit and paranoid old dictator took it into his head that Molotov, perhaps his most loyal lieutenant, was in the employ of the American government. An inveterate Stalinist nonetheless and a poker-faced master of "stonewalling," Molotov acquired an international reputation as the principal exponent of hard-line foreign policy in the first, grim days of the Cold War.

After Stalin's death Molotov opposed Khrushchev at every major turn: he was against de-Stalinization, against reconciliation with Tito, and against a restrained response to the Polish defiance of 1956. Khrushchev branded him an enemy of the Party along with Malenkov and Kaganovich in 1957. Molotov was accused of having been the "chief theoretician" for the opposition. He was dispatched to the most obscure foreign service outpost of all, Ulan Bator, as ambassador. His successor as foreign minister was Shepilov, who soon became another casualty of Khrushchev's vengeance against the Anti-Party Group. Shepilov was in turn replaced by his own deputy, the current foreign minister, Andrei Gromyko. Molotov reemerged from Outer Mongolian limbo in 1960 to become the Soviet representative at the International Atomic Energy Agency in Vienna. However, any thought of his return to good standing was dispelled at the Twenty-second Party Congress in 1961, when he was accused of having been an accomplice in Stalin's crimes and specifically of having drawn up death lists during the purges. Molotov was most recently seen by foreigners in Moscow at the funeral of his wife Zhemchuzhina in 1970.

Kliment E. Voroshilov. A "political general" rather than a professional soldier, he had a long career, marked by vainglory, folly, and durable good luck. After breaking the White Army's siege of Tsaritsyn (later Stalingrad) during the Civil War and suppressing the Kronstadt insurrection in 1921, Voroshilov rose swiftly to be People's Commissar of Defense, a marshal of the Soviet Union, and Stalin's "top marksman." He relished the limelight, spending, as Khrushchev says, most of his time being seen at the opera and posing in his medals for photographers. And all the while, Hitler was preparing for war and Voroshilov's charge, the Red Army, was in a shambles. With some justification Stalin blamed Voroshilov for the humiliation the USSR suffered at the hands of the Finns in the Winter War of 1939–40. Voroshilov was sacked and "kept around only as a whipping boy," according to Khrushchev. Having risen so high and suddenly sunk so low, he managed to secure a place for himself as the battered but venerable old pro of Stalin's war cabinet. Stalin was apparently reluctant to put the old warhorse out to pasture — or to send him to the glue factory along with a number of Voroshilov's former subordinates (they were punished for "treason" during the first year of the war, when Hitler's blitzkrieg rolled right over the Red Army's defenses). In the years between the end of the war and Stalin's death, Voroshilov managed to avoid both Stalin's serious suspicion and the enmity of Stalin's heirs. Khrushchev tells us that Stalin in his dotage used to mumble sometimes about Voroshilov's being an English spy, but that did not keep him from letting Voroshilov vacation next door to him in Sochi.

On Stalin's death in 1953, Voroshilov was elected Chairman of the Presidium of the USSR Supreme Soviet. He remained titular President of the Soviet Union until 1960, when he retired on grounds of ill-health. A year and a half later, at the Twenty-second Party Congress, he was suddenly denounced for having participated in the Anti-Party Group's activities of the mid-1950's. Voroshilov confessed his sins, and Khrushchev asked clemency for him. Surprisingly, Voroshilov was re-elected to the Presidium of the Supreme Soviet in April, 1962. He died at the age of eighty-nine in 1969.

Georgi K. Zhukov. Marshal Zhukov was Stalin's most outstanding commander in the USSR's painful triumph over Germany and Khrushchev's most important ally in his narrow victory over the Anti-Party Group. He began his military career as an ensign in a Cossack cavalry unit of the Tsarist army during World War I. He joined the Red Army in 1918 and the Party the following year. In 1936 Zhukov was the principal Soviet observer in the Spanish Civil War. He escaped the fate of many other "Spaniards," who were liquidated in Stalin's purge of the Red Army high command. Three years later he commanded a brilliant counteroffensive against the Japanese in Outer Mongolia near the Halkin-Gol River. As recently as the summer of 1969 Soviet propaganda has been reminding the world — and China in particular — of the Halkin-Gol battle as historic proof that the USSR is ready and able to protect its Far Eastern frontier. During World War II, Zhukov directed the first major Soviet success in the defense of Moscow, turned the German tide at the Battle of Stalingrad, lifted the siege of Leningrad, and led the Russian advance from Warsaw to Berlin. Zhukov's immense professional prestige and grass-roots popularity provoked Stalin's resentment, and after the war he was relegated to a series of secondary commands.

It was Khrushchev who brought Zhukov out of the obscurity into which Stalin had cast him. He became First Deputy Minister of Defense in 1953 and replaced Bulganin as Minister two years later — the first time in Soviet history that a professional soldier, as opposed to a commissar or "political general," had been put in charge of the armed forces. He continued to rise and became a full member of the Presidium in return for his help in mustering Central Committee support for Khrushchev against the Anti-Party Group in June, 1957. Four months later Zhukov was sent to Belgrade on a state visit and returned to find himself dismissed as defense minister, divested of his Central Committee and Presidium memberships, and disgraced for "adventurism" and "Bonapartism." The most cynical charge made against him by Khrushchev was complicity in Stalin's negligence at the beginning of World War II. Zhukov retired and wrote his own war memoirs, which have been published in the West. As an example of a Soviet military leader who briefly wielded spectacular political power, Zhukov has proved to be an exception rather than a precedent. Neither of his successors as defense minister, Malinovsky or Grechko, has been admitted to the Party Presidium or Politbureau.

Appendix 4

Khrushchev's Secret Speech

(*as released by the U.S. Department of State on June 4, 1956*)

COMRADES! In the report of the Central Committee of the Party at the XXth Congress, in a number of speeches by delegates to the Congress, as also formerly during the plenary CC/CPSU sessions, quite a lot has been said about the cult of the individual and about its harmful consequences.

After Stalin's death the Central Committee of the Party began to implement a policy of explaining concisely and consistently that it is impermissible and foreign to the spirit of Marxism-Leninism to elevate one person, to transform him into a superman possessing supernatural characteristics akin to those of a god. Such a man supposedly knows everything, sees everything, thinks for everyone, can do anything, is infallible in his behavior.

Such a belief about a man, and specifically about Stalin, was cultivated among us for many years.

The objective of the present report is not a thorough evaluation of Stalin's life and activity. Concerning Stalin's merits, an entirely sufficient number of books, pamphlets and studies had already been written in his lifetime. The role of Stalin in the preparation and execution of the Socialist Revolution, in the Civil War, and in the fight for the construction of Socialism in our country is universally known. Everyone knows this well. At the present we are concerned with a question which has immense importance for the Party now and for the future — [we are concerned] with how the cult of the person of Stalin has been gradually growing, the cult which became at a certain specific stage the source of a whole series of exceedingly serious and grave perversions of Party principles, of Party democracy, of revolutionary legality.

Because of the fact that not all as yet realize fully the practical consequences resulting from the cult of the individual, the great harm caused by the violation of the principle of collective direction of the Party and because of the accumulation of immense and limitless power in the hands of one person — the Central Committee of the Party considers it absolutely necessary to make the material pertaining to this matter available to the XXth Congress of the Communist Party of the Soviet Union.

Allow me first of all to remind you how severely the classics of Marxism-Leninism denounced every manifestation of the cult of the individual. In a letter to the German political worker, Wilhelm Bloss, Marx stated: "From my antipathy to any cult of the individual, I never made public during the existence of the International the numerous addresses from various countries which recognized my merits and which annoyed me. I did not even reply to them, except sometimes to rebuke their authors. Engels and I first joined the secret society of Communists on the condition that everything making for superstitious worship of authority would be deleted from its statute. Lassalle subsequently did quite the opposite."

Sometime later Engels wrote: "Both Marx and I have always been against any public manifestation with regard to individuals, with the exception of cases when it had an important purpose; and we most strongly opposed such manifestations which during our lifetime concerned us personally."

The great modesty of the genius of the revolution, Vladimir Ilyich Lenin, is known. Lenin had always stressed the role of the people as the creator of history, the directing and organizational role of the Party as a living and creative organism, and also the role of the Central Committee.

Marxism does not negate the role of the leaders of the workers' class in directing the revolutionary liberation movement.

While ascribing great importance to the role of the leaders and organizers of the masses, Lenin at the same time mercilessly stigmatized every manifestation of the cult of the individual, inexorably combated the foreign-to-Marxism views about a "hero" and a "crowd" and countered all efforts to oppose a "hero" to the masses and to the people.

Lenin taught that the Party's strength depends on its indissoluble unity with the masses, on the fact that behind the Party follow the people — workers, peasants and intelligentsia. "Only he will win and retain the power," said Lenin, "who believes in the people, who submerges himself in the fountain of the living creativeness of the people."

Lenin spoke with pride about the Bolshevik Communist Party as the leader and teacher of the people; he called for the presentation of all the most important questions before the opinion of knowledgeable workers, before the opinion of their Party; he said: "We believe in it, we see in it the wisdom, the honor, and the conscience of our epoch."

Lenin resolutely stood against every attempt aimed at belittling or weakening the directing role of the Party in the structure of the Soviet State. He worked out Bolshevik principles of Party direction and norms of Party life, stressing that the guiding principle of Party leadership is its collegiality. Already during the pre-revolutionary years Lenin called the Central Committee of the Party a collective of leaders and the guardian and interpreter of Party principles. "During the period between congresses," pointed out Lenin, "the Central Committee guards and interprets the principles of the Party."

Underlining the role of the Central Committee of the Party and its authority, Vladimir Ilyich pointed out: "Our Central Committee constituted itself as a closely centralized and highly authoritative group. . . ."

During Lenin's life the Central Committee of the Party was a real expression of collective leadership of the Party and of the nation. Being a militant Marxist-revolutionist, always unyielding in matters of principle, Lenin never imposed by force his views upon his co-workers. He tried to convince; he patiently explained his opinions to others. Lenin always diligently observed that the norms of Party life were realized, that the Party statute was enforced, that the Party congresses and the plenary sessions of the Central Committee took place at the proper intervals.

In addition to the great accomplishments of V. I. Lenin for the victory of the working class and of the working peasants, for the victory of our Party and for the application of the ideas of scientific Communism to life, his acute mind expressed itself also in this, that he detected in Stalin in time those negative characteristics which resulted later in grave consequences. Fearing for the future fate of the Party and of the Soviet nation, V. I. Lenin made a completely correct characterization of Stalin, pointing out that it was necessary to consider the question of transferring Stalin from the position of the Secretary General because of the fact that Stalin is excessively rude, that he does not have a proper attitude toward his comrades, that he is capricious and abuses his power.

In December 1922 in a letter to the Party Congress Vladimir Ilyich wrote: "After taking over the position of Secretary General Comrade Stalin accumulated in his hands immeasurable power and I am not certain whether he will be always able to use this power with the required care."

This letter — a political document of tremendous importance, known in the Party history as Lenin's "testament" — was distributed among the delegates to the XXth Party Congress. You have read it, and will undoubtedly read it again more than once. You might reflect on Lenin's plain words, in which expression is given to Vladimir Ilyich's anxiety concerning the Party, the people, the State, and the future direction of Party policy.

Vladimir Ilyich said: "Stalin is excessively rude, and this defect, which can be freely tolerated in our midst and in contacts among us Communists, becomes a defect which cannot be tolerated in one holding the position of the Secretary General. Because of this, I propose that the comrades consider the method by which Stalin would be removed from this position and by which another man would be selected for it, a man, who above all, would differ from Stalin in only one quality, namely, greater tolerance, greater loyalty, greater kindness and more considerate attitude toward the comrades, a less capricious temper, etc."

This document of Lenin's was made known to the delegates at the XIIIth Party Congress, who discussed the question of transferring Stalin from the position of Secretary General. The delegates declared themselves in favor of retaining Stalin in this post, hoping that he would heed the critical remarks of Vladimir Ilyich and would be able to overcome the defects which caused Lenin serious anxiety.

Comrades! The Party Congress should become acquainted with two new documents, which confirm Stalin's character as already outlined by Vladimir Ilyich Lenin in his "testament." These documents are a letter from Nadezhda Konstantinovna Krupskaya to Kamenev, who was at that time head of the Political Bureau, and a personal letter from Vladimir Ilyich Lenin to Stalin.

I will now read these documents:

Lev Borisovich!

Because of a short letter which I had written in words dictated to me by Vladimir Ilyich by permission of the doctors, Stalin allowed himself yesterday an unusually rude outburst directed at me. This is not my first day in the Party. During all these thirty years I have never heard from any comrade one word of rudeness. The business of the Party and of Ilyich are not less dear to me than to Stalin. I need at present the maximum of self-control. What one can and what one cannot discuss with Ilyich — I know better than any doctor, because I know what makes him nervous and what does not, in any case I know better than Stalin. I am turning to you and to Grigory as to much closer comrades of V. I. and I beg you to protect me from rude interference with my private life and from vile invectives and threats. I have no doubt as to what will be the unanimous decision of the Control Commission, with which Stalin sees fit to threaten me; however, I have neither the strength nor the time to waste on this foolish quarrel. And I am a living person and my nerves are strained to the utmost.

N. KRUPSKAYA

Nadezhda Konstantinovna wrote this letter on December 23, 1922. After two and a half months, in March 1923, Vladimir Ilyich Lenin sent Stalin the following letter:

The Letter of V. I. Lenin

To Comrade Stalin.

Copies for: Kamenev and Zinoviev.

Dear Comrade Stalin!

You permitted yourself a rude summons of my wife to the telephone and a rude reprimand of her. Despite the fact that she told you that she agreed to forget what was said, nevertheless Zinoviev and Kamenev heard about it from her. I have no intention to forget so easily that which is being done against me, and I need not stress here that I consider as directed against me that which is being done against my wife. I ask you, therefore, that you weigh carefully whether you are agreeable to retracting your words and apologizing or whether you prefer the severance of relations between us.

[*Commotion in the hall*]

Sincerely,

LENIN

March 5, 1923

Comrades! I will not comment on these documents. They speak eloquently for themselves. Since Stalin could behave in this manner during Lenin's life, could thus behave toward Nadezhda Konstantinovna Krupskaya, whom the Party knows well and values highly as a loyal friend of Lenin and as an active fighter for the cause of the Party since its creation — we can easily imagine how Stalin treated other people. These negative characteristics of his developed steadily and during the last years acquired an absolutely insufferable character.

As later events have proven, Lenin's anxiety was justified: in the first period after Lenin's death Stalin still paid attention to his [i.e., Lenin's] advice, but later he began to disregard the serious admonitions of Vladimir Ilyich.

When we analyze the practice of Stalin in regard to the direction of the Party and of the country, when we pause to consider everything which Stalin perpetrated, we must be convinced that Lenin's fears were justified. The negative characteristics of Stalin, which, in Lenin's time, were only incipient, transformed themselves during the last years into a grave abuse of power by Stalin, which caused untold harm to our Party.

We have to consider seriously and analyze correctly this matter in order that we may preclude any possibility of a repetition in any form whatever of what took place during the life of Stalin, who absolutely did not tolerate collegiality in leadership and in work, and who practiced brutal violence, not only toward everything which opposed him, but also toward that which seemed to his capricious and despotic character, contrary to his concepts.

Stalin acted not through persuasion, explanation, and patient co-operation with people, but by imposing his concepts and demanding absolute submission to his opinion. Whoever opposed this concept or tried to prove his viewpoint, and the correctness of his position, was doomed to removal from the leading collective and to subsequent moral and physical annihilation. This was especially true during the period following the XVIIth Party Congress, when many prominent Party leaders and rank-and-file Party workers, honest and dedicated to the cause of Communism, fell victim to Stalin's despotism.

We must affirm that the Party had fought a serious fight against the Trotskyites, rightists and bourgeois nationalists, and that it disarmed ideologically all the enemies of Leninism. This ideological fight was carried on successfully, as a result of which the Party became strengthened and tempered. Here Stalin played a positive role.

The Party led a great political ideological struggle against those in its own ranks who proposed anti-Leninist theses, who represented a political line hostile to the Party and to the cause of socialism. This was a stubborn and a difficult fight but a necessary one, because the political line of both the Trotskyite-Zinovievite bloc and of the Bukharinites led actually toward the restoration of capitalism and capitulation to the world bourgeoisie. Let us consider for a moment what would have happened if in 1928–1929 the political line of right deviation had prevailed among us, or orientation toward "cotton-dress industrialization," or toward the kulak, etc. We would not now have a powerful heavy industry, we would not have the kolkhozes, we would find ourselves disarmed and weak in a capitalist encirclement.

It was for this reason that the Party led an inexorable ideological fight and explained to all Party members and to the non-Party masses the harm and the danger of the anti-Leninist proposals of the Trotskyite opposition and the rightist opportunists. And this great work of explaining the Party line bore fruit; both the Trotskyites and the rightist opportunists were politically isolated; the overwhelming Party majority supported the Leninist line and the Party was able to awaken and organize the working masses to apply the Leninist Party line and to build socialism.

Worth noting is the fact that even during the progress of the furious ideological fight against the Trotskyites, the Zinovievites, the Bukharinites and others, extreme repressive measures were not used against them. The fight was on ideological grounds. But some years later when socialism in our country was fundamentally constructed, when the exploiting classes were generally liquidated, when the Soviet social structure had radically changed, when the social basis for political movements and groups hostile to the Party had violently contracted, when the ideological opponents of the Party were long since defeated politically — then the repression directed against them began.

It was precisely during this period (1935–1937–1938) that the practice of mass repression through the government apparatus was born, first against the enemies of Leninism — Trotskyites, Zinovievites, Bukharinites, long since politically defeated by the Party, and subsequently also against many honest Communists, against those Party cadres who had borne the heavy load of the Civil War and the first and most difficult years of industrialization and collectivization, who actively fought against the Trotskyites and the rightists for the Leninist Party line.

Stalin originated the concept "enemy of the people." This term automatically rendered it unnecessary that the ideological errors of a man or men engaged in a controversy be proven; this term made possible the usage of the most cruel repression, violating all norms of revolutionary legality, against anyone who in any way disagreed with Stalin, against those who were only suspected of hostile intent, against those who had bad reputations. This concept, "enemy of the people," actually eliminated the possibility of any kind of ideological fight or the making of one's views known on this or that issue, even those of a practical character. In the main, and in actuality, the only proof of guilt used, against all norms of current legal science, was the "confession" of the accused himself; and, as subsequent probing proved, "confessions" were acquired through physical pressures against the accused.

This led to glaring violations of revolutionary legality, and to the fact that many entirely innocent persons, who in the past had defended the Party line, became victims.

We must assert that in regard to those persons who in their time had opposed the Party line, there were often no sufficiently serious reasons for their physical annihilation. The formula, "enemy of the people," was specifically introduced for the purpose of physically annihilating such individuals.

It is a fact that many persons, who were later annihilated as enemies of the Party and people, had worked with Lenin during his life. Some of these persons had made errors during Lenin's life, but, despite this, Lenin benefited by their work, he corrected them and he did everything possible to retain them in the ranks of the Party; he induced them to follow him.

In this connection the delegates to the Party Congress should familiarize themselves with an unpublished note by V. I. Lenin directed to the Central Committee's Political Bureau in October 1920. Outlining the duties of the Control Commission, Lenin wrote that the Commission should be transformed into a real "organ of Party and proletarian conscience."

As a special duty of the Control Commission there is recommended a deep, individualized relationship with, and sometimes even a type of therapy for, the representatives of the so-called opposition —those who have experienced a psychological crisis because of failure in their Soviet or Party career. An effort should be made to quiet them, to explain the matter to them in a way used among comrades, to find for them (avoiding the method of issuing orders) a task for which they are psychologically fitted. Advice and rules relating to this matter are to be formulated by the Central Committee's Organizational Bureau, etc.

Everyone knows how irreconcilable Lenin was with the ideological enemies of Marxism, with those who deviated from the correct Party line. At the same time, however, Lenin, as is evident from the given document, in his practice of directing the Party demanded the most intimate Party contact with people who had shown indecision or temporary nonconformity with the Party line, but whom it was possible to return to the Party path. Lenin advised that such people should be patiently educated without the application of extreme methods.

Lenin's wisdom in dealing with people was evident in his work with cadres.

An entirely different relationship with people characterized Stalin. Lenin's traits — patient work with people; stubborn and painstaking education of them; the ability to induce people to follow him without using compulsion, but rather through the ideological influence on them of the whole collective — were entirely foreign to Stalin. He [Stalin] discarded the Leninist method of convincing and educating; he abandoned the method of ideological struggle for that of administrative violence, mass repressions, and terror. He acted on an increasingly larger scale and more stubbornly through punitive organs, at the same time often violating all existing norms of morality and of Soviet laws.

Arbitrary behavior by one person encouraged and permitted arbitrariness in others. Mass arrests and deportations of many thousands of people, execution without trial and without normal investigation created conditions of insecurity, fear and even desperation.

This, of course, did not contribute toward unity of the Party ranks and of all strata of working people, but on the contrary brought about annihilation and the expulsion from the Party of workers who were loyal but inconvenient to Stalin.

Our Party fought for the implementation of Lenin's plans for the construction of socialism. This was an ideological fight. Had Leninist principles been observed during the course of this fight, had the Party's devotion to principles been skillfully combined with a keen and solicitous concern for people, had they not been repelled and wasted but rather drawn to our side — we certainly would not have had such a brutal violation of revolutionary legality and many thousands of people would not have fallen victim of the method of terror. Extraordinary methods would then have been resorted to only against those people who had in fact committed criminal acts against the Soviet system.

Let us recall some historical facts.

In the days before the October Revolution two members of the Central Committee of the Bolshevik Party — Kamenev and Zinoviev — declared themselves against Lenin's plan for an armed uprising. In addition, on October 18 they published in the Menshevik newspaper, *Novaya Zhizn,* a statement declaring that the Bolsheviks were making preparations for an uprising and that they considered it adventuristic. Kamenev and Zinoviev thus disclosed to the enemy the decision of the Central Committee to stage the uprising, and that the uprising had been organized to take place within the very near future.

This was treason against the Party and against the revolution. In this connection, V. I. Lenin wrote: "Kamenev and Zinoviev revealed the decision of the Central Committee of their Party on the armed uprising to Rodzyanko and Kerensky. . . ." He put before the Central Committee the question of Zinoviev's and Kamenev's expulsion from the Party.

However, after the Great Socialist October Revolution, as is known, Zinoviev and Kamenev were given leading positions. Lenin put them in positions in which they carried out most responsible Party tasks and participated actively in the work of the leading Party and Soviet organs. It is known that Zinoviev and Kamenev committed a number of other serious errors during Lenin's life. In his "testament" Lenin warned that "Zinoviev's and Kamenev's October episode was of course not an accident." But Lenin did not pose the question of their arrest and certainly not their shooting.

Or let us take the example of the Trotskyites. At present, after a sufficiently long historical period, we can speak about the fight with the Trotskyites with complete calm and can analyze this matter with sufficient objectivity. After all, around Trotsky were people whose origin cannot by any means be traced to bourgeois society. Part of them belonged to the Party intelligentsia and a certain part were recruited from among the workers. We can name many individuals who in their time joined the Trotskyites; however, these same individuals took an active part in the workers' movement before the revolution, during the Socialist October Revolution itself, and also in the consolidation of the victory of this greatest of revolutions. Many of them broke with Trotskyism and returned to Leninist positions. Was it necessary to annihilate such people? We are deeply convinced that had Lenin lived such an extreme method would not have been used against many of them.

Such are only a few historical facts. But can it be said that Lenin did not decide to use even the most severe means against enemies of the revolution when this was actually necessary? No, no one can say this. Vladimir Ilyich demanded uncompromising dealings with the enemies of the revolution and of the working class and when necessary resorted ruthlessly to such methods. You will recall only V. I. Lenin's fight with the Socialist Revolutionary organizers of the anti-Soviet uprising, with the counter-revolutionary kulaks in 1918 and with others, when Lenin without hesitation used the most extreme methods against the enemies. Lenin used such methods, however, only against actual class enemies and not against those who blunder, who err, and whom it was possible to lead through ideological influence, and even retain in the leadership.

Lenin used severe methods only in the most necessary cases, when the exploiting classes were still in existence and were vigorously opposing the revolution, when the struggle for survival was decidedly assuming the sharpest forms, even including a civil war.

Stalin, on the other hand, used extreme methods and mass repressions at a time when the revolution was already victorious, when the Soviet state was strengthened, when the exploiting classes were already liquidated and Socialist relations were rooted solidly in all phases of national economy, when our Party was politically consolidated and had strengthened itself both numerically and ideologically. It is clear that here Stalin showed in a whole series of cases his intolerance, his brutality and his abuse of power. Instead of proving his political correctness and mobilizing the masses, he often chose the path of repression and physical annihilation, not only against actual enemies, but also against individuals who had not committed any crimes against the Party and the Soviet government. Here we see no wisdom but only a demonstration of the brutal force which had once so alarmed V. I. Lenin.

Lately, especially after the unmasking of the Beria gang, the Central Committee has looked into a series of matters fabricated by this gang.

This revealed a very ugly picture of brutal willfulness connected with the incorrect behavior of Stalin. As facts prove, Stalin, using his unlimited power, allowed himself many abuses, acting in the name of the Central Committee, not asking for the opinion of the Committee members nor even of the members of the Central Committee's Political Bureau; often he did not inform them about his personal decisions concerning very important Party and government matters.

Considering the question of the cult of an individual we must first of all show everyone what harm this caused to the interests of our Party.

Vladimir Ilyich Lenin had always stressed the Party's role and significance in the direction of the socialist government of workers and peasants; he saw in this the chief precondition for a successful building of socialism in our country. Pointing to the great responsibility of the Bolshevik Party, as a ruling party in the Soviet state, Lenin called for the most meticulous observance of all norms of Party life; he called for the realization of the principles of collegiality in the direction of the Party and the state.

Collegiality of leadership flows from the very nature of our Party, a party built on the principles of democratic centralism. "This means," said Lenin, "that all Party matters are accomplished by all Party members — directly or through representatives — who without any exceptions are subject to the same rules; in addition, all administrative members, all directing collegia, all holders of Party positions are elective, they must account for their activities and are recallable."

It is known that Lenin himself offered an example of the most careful observance of these principles. There was no matter so important that Lenin himself decided it without asking for advice and approval of the majority of the Central Committee members or of the members of the Central Committee's Political Bureau.

In the most difficult period for our Party and our country, Lenin considered it necessary regularly to convoke congresses, Party conferences, and plenary sessions of the Central Committee at which all the most important questions were discussed and where resolutions, carefully worked out by the collective of leaders, were approved.

We can recall, for an example, the year 1918 when the country was threatened by the attack of the imperialistic interventionists. In this situation the VIIth Party Congress was convened in order to discuss a vitally important matter which could not be postponed — the matter of peace. In 1919, while the Civil War was raging, the VIIIth Party Congress convened which adopted a new Party program, decided such important matters as the relationship with the peasant masses, the organization of the Red Army, the leading role of the Party in the work of the Soviets, the correction of the social composition of the Party, and other matters. In 1920 the IXth Party Congress was convened which laid down guiding principles pertaining to the Party's work in the sphere of economic construction. In 1921, the Xth Party Congress accepted Lenin's New Economic Policy and the historical resolution called "About Party Unity."

During Lenin's life Party Congresses were convened regularly; always, when a radical turn in the development of the Party and the country took place, Lenin considered it absolutely necessary that the Party discuss at length all the basic matters pertaining to internal and foreign policy and to questions bearing on the development of Party and government.

It is very characteristic that Lenin addressed to the Party Congress as the highest Party organ his last articles, letters and remarks. During the period between congresses the Central Committee of the Party, acting as the most authoritative leading collective, meticulously observed the principles of the Party and carried out its policy.

So it was during Lenin's life.

Were our Party's holy Leninist principles observed after the death of Vladimir Ilyich?

Whereas during the first few years after Lenin's death Party Congresses and Central Committee plenums took place more or less regularly, later, when Stalin began increasingly to abuse his power, these principles were brutally violated. This was especially evident during the last 15 years of his life. Was it a normal situation when over 13 years elapsed between the XVIIIth and XIXth Party Congresses, years during which our Party and our country had experienced so many important events? These events demanded categorically that the Party should have passed resolutions pertaining to the country's defense during the Patriotic War and to peacetime construction after the war. Even after the end of the war a Congress was not convened for over 7 years.

Central Committee plenums were hardly ever called. It should be sufficient to mention that during all the years of the Patriotic War not a single Central Committee plenum took place. It is true that there was an attempt to call a Central Committee plenum in October 1941, when Central Committee members from the whole country were called to Moscow. They waited two days for the opening of the plenum, but in vain. Stalin did not even want to meet and to talk to the Central Committee members. This fact shows how demoralized Stalin was in the first months of the war and how haughtily and disdainfully he treated the Central Committee members.

In practice Stalin ignored the norms of Party life and trampled on the Leninist principle of collective Party leadership.

Stalin's willfulness *vis-à-vis* the Party and its Central Committee became fully evident after the XVIIth Party Congress which took place in 1934.

Having at its disposal numerous data showing brutal willfulness toward Party cadres, the Central Committee has created a Party Commission under the control of the Central Committee Presidium; it was charged with investigating what made possible the mass repressions against the majority of the Central Committee members and candidates elected at the XVIIth Congress of the All-Union Communist Party (Bolsheviks).

The Commission has become acquainted with a large quantity of materials in the NKVD archives and with other documents and has established many facts pertaining to the fabrication of cases against Communists, to false accusations, to glaring abuses of socialist legality — which resulted in the death of innocent people. It became apparent that many Party, Soviet and economic activists who were branded in 1937–1938 as "enemies" were actually never enemies, spies, wreckers, etc., but were always honest Communists; they were only so stigmatized, and often, no longer able to bear barbaric tortures, they charged themselves (at the order of the investigative judges — falsifiers) with all kinds of grave and unlikely crimes. The Commission has presented to the Central Committee Presidium lengthy and documented materials pertaining to mass repressions against the delegates to the XVIIth Party Congress and against members of the Central Committee elected at that Congress. These materials have been studied by the Presidium of the Central Committee.

It was determined that of the 139 members and candidates of the Party's Central Committee who were elected at the XVIIth Congress, 98 persons, i.e., 70 percent, were arrested and shot (mostly in 1937–1938). (*Indignation in the hall.*)

What was the composition of the delegates to the XVIIth Congress? It is known that 80 percent of the voting participants of the XVIIth Congress joined the Party during the years of conspiracy before the Revolution and during the Civil War; this means before 1921. By social origin the basic mass of the delegates to the Congress were workers (60 percent of the voting members).

For this reason, it was inconceivable that a Congress so composed would have elected a Central Committee, a majority of which would prove to be enemies of the Party. The only reason why 70 percent of the Central Committee members and candidates elected at the XVIIth Congress were branded as enemies of the Party and of the people was that honest Communists were slandered, accusations against them were fabricated, and revolutionary legality was gravely undermined.

The same fate met not only the Central Committee members but also the majority of the delegates to the XVIIth Party Congress. Of 1,966 delegates with either voting or advisory rights, 1,108 persons were arrested on charges of anti-revolutionary crimes, i.e., decidedly more than a majority. This very fact shows how absurd, wild and contrary to common sense were the charges of counter-revolutionary crimes made out, as we now see, against a majority of participants at the XVIIth Party Congress. (*Indignation in the hall.*)

We should recall that the XVIIth Party Congress is historically known as the Congress of Victors. Delegates to the Congress were active participants in the building of our socialist state; many of them suffered and fought for Party interests during the pre-revolutionary years in the conspiracy and at the Civil War fronts; they fought their enemies valiantly and often nervelessly looked into the face of death. How then can we believe that such people could prove to be "two-faced" and had joined the camps of the enemies of socialism during the era after the political liquidation of Zinovievites, Trotskyites and rightists and after the great accomplishments of socialist construction?

This was the result of the abuse of power by Stalin, who began to use mass terror against the Party cadres.

What is the reason that mass repressions against activists increased more and more after the XVIIth Party Congress? It was because at that time Stalin had so elevated himself above the Party and above the nation that he ceased to consider either the Central Committee or the Party. While he still reckoned with the opinion of the collective before the XVIIth Congress, after the complete political liquidation of the

Trotskyites, Zinovievites and Bukharinites, when as a result of that fight and socialist victories the Party achieved unity, Stalin ceased to an ever greater degree to consider the members of the Party's Central Committee and even the members of the Political Bureau. Stalin thought that now he could decide all things alone and all he needed were statisticians; he treated all others in such a way that they could only listen to and praise him.

After the criminal murder of S. M. Kirov, mass repressions and brutal acts of violation of socialist legality began. On the evening of December 1, 1934, on Stalin's initiative (without the approval of the Political Bureau — which was passed two days later, casually) the secretary of the Presidium of the Central Executive Committee, Yenukidze, signed the following directive.

I. Investigative agencies are directed to speed up the cases of those accused of the preparation or execution of acts of terror.

II. Judicial organs are directed not to hold up the execution of death sentences pertaining to crimes of this category in order to consider the possibility of pardon, because the Presidium of the Central Executive Committee [of the] USSR does not consider as possible the receiving of petitions of this sort.

III. The organs of the Commissariat of Internal Affairs [NKVD] are directed to execute death sentences against criminals of the above-mentioned category immediately after the passage of sentences.

This directive became the basis for mass acts of abuse against socialist legality. During many of the fabricated court cases the accused were charged with "the preparation" of terroristic acts; this deprived them of any possibility that their cases might be re-examined, even when they stated before the court that their "confessions" were secured by force, and when, in a convincing manner, they disproved the accusations against them.

It must be asserted that to this day the circumstances surrounding Kirov's murder hide many things which are inexplicable and mysterious and demand a most careful examination. There are reasons for the suspicion that the killer of Kirov, Nikolayev, was assisted by someone from among the people whose duty it was to protect the person of Kirov. A month and a half before the killing, Nikolayev was arrested on the grounds of suspicious behavior, but he was released and not even searched. It is an unusually suspicious circumstance that when the Chekist assigned to protect Kirov was being brought for an interrogation, on December 2, 1934, he was killed in a car "accident" in which no other occupants of the car were harmed. After the murder of Kirov, top functionaries of the Leningrad NKVD were given very light sentences, but in 1937 they were shot. We can assume that they were shot in order to cover the traces of the organizers of Kirov's killing. (*Movement in the hall.*)

Mass repressions grew tremendously from the end of 1936 after a telegram from Stalin and Zhdanov, dated from Sochi on September 25, 1936, was addressed to Kaganovich, Molotov and other members of the Political Bureau. The content of the telegram was as follows:

"We deem it absolutely necessary and urgent that Comrade Yezhov be nominated to the post of People's Commissar for Internal Affairs. Yagoda has definitely proved himself to be incapable of unmasking the Trotskyite-Zinovievite bloc. The OGPU is 4 years behind in this matter. This is noted by all Party workers and by the majority of the representatives of the NKVD." Strictly speaking we should stress that Stalin did not meet with and therefore could not know the opinion of Party workers.

This Stalinist formulation that the "NKVD is 4 years behind" in applying mass repression and that there is a necessity for "catching up" with the neglected work directly pushed the NKVD workers on the path of mass arrests and executions.

We should state that this formulation was also forced on the February-March plenary session of the Central Committee of the All-Union Communist Party (Bolsheviks) in 1937. The plenary resolution approved it on the basis of Yezhov's report, "Lessons flowing from the harmful activity, diversion and espionage of the Japanese-German-Trotskyite agents," stating:

> The Plenum of the Central Committee of the All-Union Communist Party (Bolsheviks) considers that all facts revealed during the investigation into the matter of an anti-Soviet Trotskyite center and of its followers in the provinces show that the People's Commissariat of Internal Affairs has fallen behind at least 4 years in the attempt to unmask these most inexorable enemies of the people.

The mass repressions at this time were made under the slogan of a fight against the Trotskyites. Did the Trotskyites at this time actually constitute such a danger to our Party and to the Soviet state? We should recall that in 1927 on the eve of the XVth Party Congress only some 4,000 votes were cast for the Trotskyite-Zinovievite opposition, while there were 724,000 for the Party line. During the 10 years which passed between the XVth Party Congress and the February-March Central Committee Plenum Trotskyism was completely disarmed; many former Trotskyites had changed their former views and worked in the various sectors building socialism. It is clear that in the situation of socialist victory there was no basis for mass terror in the country.

Stalin's report at the February-March Central Committee Plenum in 1937, "Deficiencies of Party work and methods for the liquidation of the Trotskyites and of other two-facers," contained an attempt at theoretical justification of the mass terror policy under the pretext that as we march forward toward socialism, class war must allegedly sharpen. Stalin asserted that both history and Lenin taught him this.

Actually Lenin taught that the application of revolutionary violence is necessitated by the resistance of the exploiting classes, and this referred to the era when the exploiting classes existed and were powerful. As soon as the nation's political situation had improved, when in January 1920 the Red Army took Rostov and thus won a most important victory over Denikin, Lenin instructed Dzerzhinsky to stop mass terror and to abolish the death penalty. Lenin justified this important political move of the Soviet state in the following manner in his report at the session of the All-Union Central Executive Committee on February 2, 1920:

> We were forced to use terror because of the terror practiced by the Entente, when strong world powers threw their hordes against us, not avoiding any type of combat. We would not have lasted two days had we not answered these attempts of officers and White Guardists in a merciless fashion; this meant the use of terror, but this was forced upon us by the terrorist methods of the Entente.
>
> But as soon as we attained a decisive victory, even before the end of the war, immediately after taking Rostov, we gave up the use of the death penalty and thus proved that we intend to execute our own program in the manner that we promised. We say that the application of violence flows out of the decision to smother the exploiters, the big landowners and the capitalists; as soon as this was accomplished we gave up the use of all extraordinary methods. We have proved this in practice.

Stalin deviated from these clear and plain precepts of Lenin. Stalin put the Party and the NKVD up to the use of mass terror when the exploiting classes had been liquidated in our country and when there were no serious reasons for the use of extraordinary mass terror.

This terror was actually directed not at the remnants of the defeated exploiting classes but against the honest workers of the Party and of the Soviet state; against them were made lying, slanderous and absurd accusations concerning "two-facedness," "espionage," "sabotage," preparation of fictitious "plots," etc.

At the February-March Central Committee Plenum in 1937 many members actually questioned the rightness of the established course regarding mass repressions under the pretext of combating "two-facedness."

Comrade Postyshev most ably expressed these doubts. He said:

> I have philosophized that the severe years of fighting have passed; Party members who have lost their backbones have broken down or have joined the camp of the enemy; healthy elements have fought for the Party. These were the years of industrialization and collectivization. I never thought it possible that after this severe era had passed Karpov and people like him would find themselves in the camp of the enemy. (Karpov was a worker in the Ukrainian Central Committee whom Postyshev knew well.) And now, according to the testimony, it appears that Karpov was recruited in 1934 by the Trotskyites. I personally do not believe that in 1934 an honest Party member who had trod the long road of unrelenting fight against enemies, for the Party and for Socialism, would now be in the camp of the enemies. I do not believe it . . . I cannot imagine how it would be possible to travel with the Party during the difficult years and then, in 1934, join the Trotskyites. It is an odd thing. . . .

(Movement in the hall.)

Using Stalin's formulation, namely that the closer we are to socialism, the more enemies we will have, and using the resolution of the February-March Central Committee Plenum passed on the basis of Yezhov's report — the provocateurs who had infiltrated the state security organs together with conscienceless careerists began to protect with the Party name the mass terror against Party cadres, cadres of the Soviet state and the ordinary Soviet citizens. It should suffice to say that the number of arrests based on charges of counter-revolutionary crimes had grown ten times between 1936 and 1937.

It is known that brutal willfulness was practiced against leading Party workers. The Party Statute, approved at the XVIIth Party Congress, was based on Leninist principles expressed at the Xth Party Congress. It stated that in order to apply an extreme method such as exclusion from the Party against a Central Committee member, against a Central Committee candidate, and against a member of the Party Control Commission, "it is necessary to call a Central Committee Plenum and to invite to the Plenum all Central Committee candidate members and all members of the Party Control Commission"; only if two thirds of the members of such a general assembly of responsible Party leaders find it necessary, only then can a Central Committee member or candidate be expelled.

The majority of the Central Committee members and candidates elected at the XVIIth Congress and arrested in 1937–1938 were expelled from the Party illegally through the brutal abuse of the Party Statute, because the question of their expulsion was never studied at the Central Committee Plenum.

Now when the cases of some of these so-called "spies" and "saboteurs" were examined it was found that all their cases were fabricated. Confessions of guilt of many arrested and charged with enemy activity were gained with the help of cruel and inhuman tortures.

At the same time Stalin, as we have been informed by members of the Political Bureau of that time, did not show them the statements of many accused political activists when they retracted their confessions before the military tribunal and asked for an objective examination of their cases. There were many such declarations, and Stalin doubtless knew of them.

The Central Committee considers it absolutely necessary to inform the Congress of many such fabricated "cases" against the members of the Party's Central Committee elected at the XVIIth Party Congress.

An example of vile provocation, of odious falsification and of criminal violation of revolutionary legality is the case of the former candidate for the Central Committee Political Bureau, one of the most eminent workers of the Party and of the Soviet government, Comrade Eikhe, who was a Party member since 1905. (*Commotion in the hall.*)

Comrade Eikhe was arrested on April 29, 1938, on the basis of slanderous materials, without the sanction of the Prosecutor of the USSR, which was finally received 15 months after the arrest.

Investigation of Eikhe's case was made in a manner which most brutally violated Soviet legality and was accompanied by willfulness and falsification.

Eikhe was forced under torture to sign ahead of time a protocol of his confession prepared by the investigative judges, in which he and several other eminent Party workers were accused of anti-Soviet activity.

On October 1, 1939, Eikhe sent his declaration to Stalin in which he categorically denied his guilt and asked for an examination of his case. In the declaration he wrote:

> There is no more bitter misery than to sit in the jail of a government for which I have always fought.

A second declaration of Eikhe has been preserved which he sent to Stalin on October 27, 1939; in it he cited facts very convincingly and countered the slanderous accusations made against him, arguing that this provocatory accusation was on the one hand the work of real Trotskyites whose arrests he had sanctioned as First Secretary of the West Siberian Krai Party Committee and who conspired in order to take revenge on him, and, on the other hand, the result of the base falsification of materials by the investigative judges.

Eikhe wrote in his declaration:

> . . . . On October 25 of this year I was informed that the investigation in my case has been concluded and I was given access to the materials of this investigation. Had I been guilty of only one hundredth of the crimes with which I am charged, I would not have dared to send you this pre-execution declaration; however, I have not been guilty of even one of the things with which I am charged and my heart is clean of even the shadow of baseness. I have never in my life told you a word of falsehood and now, finding my two feet in the grave, I am also not lying. My whole case is a typical example of provocation, slander and violation of the elementary basis of revolutionary legality. . . .
>
> . . . . The confessions which were made part of my file are not only absurd but contain some slander toward the Central Committee of the All-Union Communist Party (Bolsheviks) and toward

the Council of People's Commissars because correct resolutions of the Central Committee of the All-Union Communist Party (Bolsheviks) and of the Council of People's Commissars which were not made on my initiative and without my participation are presented as hostile acts of counter-revolutionary organizations made at my suggestion. . . .

I am now alluding to the most disgraceful part of my life and to my really grave guilt against the Party and against you. This is my confession of counter-revolutionary activity. . . . The case is as follows: not being able to suffer the tortures to which I was submitted by Ushakov and Nikolayev—and especially by the first one —who utilized the knowledge that my broken ribs have not properly mended and have caused me great pain — I have been forced to accuse myself and others.

The majority of my confession has been suggested or dictated by Usakov, and the remainder is my reconstruction of NKVD materials from western Siberia for which I assumed all responsibility. If some part of the story which Ushakov fabricated and which I signed did not properly hang together, I was forced to sign another variation. The same thing was done to Rukhimovich, who was at first designated as a member of the reserve net and whose name later was removed without telling me anything about it; the same was also done with the leader of the reserve net, supposedly created by Bukharin in 1935. At first I wrote my name in, and then I was instructed to insert Mezhlauk. There were other similar incidents.

. . . . I am asking and begging you that you again examine my case and this not for the purpose of sparing me but in order to unmask the vile provocation which like a snake wound itself around many persons in a great degree due to my meanness and criminal slander. I have never betrayed you or the Party. I know that I perish because of vile and mean work of the enemies of the Party and of the people, who fabricated the provocation against me.

It would appear that such an important declaration was worth an examination by the Central Committee. This, however, was not done and the declaration was transmitted to Beria while the terrible maltreatment of the Political Bureau candidate, Comrade Eikhe, continued.

On February 2, 1940 Eikhe was brought before the court. Here he did not confess any guilt and said as follows:

In all the so-called confessions of mine there is not one letter written by me with the exception of my signatures under the protocols which were forced from me. I have made my confession under pressure from the investigative judge who from the time of my arrest tormented me. After that I began to write all this nonsense. . . . The most important thing for me is to tell the court, the Party and Stalin that I am not guilty. I have never been guilty of any conspiracy. I will die believing in the truth of Party policy as I have believed in it during my whole life.

On February 4 Eikhe was shot. (*Indignation in the hall.*) It has been definitely established now that Eikhe's case was fabricated; he has been posthumously rehabilitated.

Comrade Rudzutak, candidate member of the Political Bureau, member of the Party since 1905, who spent 10 years in a Tsarist hard labor camp, completely retracted in court the confession which was forced from him. The protocol of the session of the Collegium of the Supreme Military Court contains the following statement by Rudzutak:

. . . . The only plea which he places before the court is that the Central Committee of the All-Union Communist Party (Bolsheviks) be informed that there is in the NKVD an as yet not liquidated center which is craftily manufacturing cases, which forces innocent persons to confess; there is no opportunity to prove one's nonparticipation in crimes to which the confessions of various persons testify. The investigative methods are such that they force people to lie and to slander entirely innocent persons in addition to those who already stand accused. He asks the Court that he be allowed to inform the Central Committee of the All-Union Communist Party (Bolsheviks) about all this in writing. He assures the Court that he personally had never any evil designs in regard to the policy of our Party because he has always agreed with the Party policy pertaining to all spheres of economic and cultural activity.

This declaration of Rudzutak was ignored, despite the fact that Rudzutak was in his time the chief of the Central Control Commission which was called into being in accordance with Lenin's concept for the purpose of fighting for Party unity. . . . In this manner fell the chief of this highly authoritative Party organ, a victim of brutal willfulness: he was not even called before the Central Committee's Political Bureau because Stalin did not want to talk to him. Sentence was pronounced on him in 20 minutes and he was shot. (*Indignation in the hall.*)

After careful examination of the case in 1955 it was established that the accusation against Rudzutak was false and that it was based on slanderous materials. Rudzutak has been rehabilitated posthumously.

The way in which the former NKVD workers manufactured various fictitious "anti-Soviet centers" and "blocs" with the help of provocatory methods is seen from the confession of Comrade Rozenblum, Party member since 1906, who was arrested in 1937 by the Leningrad NKVD.

During the examination in 1955 of the Komarov case Rozenblum revealed the following fact: when Rozenblum was arrested in 1937 he was subjected to terrible torture during which he was ordered to confess false information concerning himself and other persons. He was then brought to the office of Zakovsky, who offered him freedom on condition that he make before the court a false confession fabricated in 1937 by the NKVD concerning "sabotage, espionage and diversion in a terroristic center in Leningrad." (*Movement in the hall.*) With unbelievable cynicism Zakovsky told about the vile "mechanism" for the crafty creation of fabricated "anti-Soviet plots."

"In order to illustrate it to me," stated Rozenblum,

> Zakovsky gave me several possible variants of the organization of this center and of its branches. After he detailed the organization to me, Zakovsky told me that the NKVD would prepare the case of this center, remarking that the trial would be public.
>
> Before the court were to be brought 4 or 5 members of this center: Chudov, Ugarov, Smorodin, Pozern, Shaposhnikova (Chudov's wife) and others together with 2 or 3 members from the branches of this center. . . .
>
> . . . . The case of the Leningrad center has to be built solidly and for this reason witnesses are needed. Social origin (of course, in the past) and the Party standing of the witness will play more than a small role.

"You, yourself," said Zakovsky,

will not need to invent anything. The NKVD will prepare for you a ready outline for every branch of the center; you will have to study it carefully and to remember well all questions and answers which the Court might ask. This case will be ready in 4–5 months, or perhaps a half year. During all this time you will be preparing yourself so that you will not compromise the investigation and yourself. Your future will depend on how the trial goes and on its results. If you begin to lie and to testify falsely, blame yourself. If you manage to endure it, you will save your head and we will feed and clothe you at the government's cost until your death.

This is the kind of vile things which were then practiced. (*Movement in the hall.*)

Even more widely was the falsification of cases practiced in the provinces. The NKVD headquarters of the Sverdlov oblast "discovered" the so-called "Ural uprising staff" — an organ of the bloc of rightists, Trotskyites, Socialist Revolutionaries, church leaders — whose chief supposedly was the Secretary of the Sverdlov Oblast Party Committee and member of the Central Committee, All-Union Communist Party (Bolsheviks), Kabakov, who had been a Party member since 1914. The investigative materials of that time show that in almost all krais, oblasts and republics there supposedly existed "rightist Trotskyite, espionage-terror and diversionary-sabotage organizations and centers" and that the heads of such organizations as a rule — for no known reason — were first secretaries of oblast or republic Communist Party committees or Central Committees. (*Movement in the hall.*)

Many thousands of honest and innocent Communists have died as a result of this monstrous falsification of such "cases," as a result of the fact that all kinds of slanderous "confessions" were accepted, and as a result of the practice of forcing accusations against oneself and others. In the same manner were fabricated the "cases" against eminent Party and state workers — Kossior, Chubar, Postyshev, Kosarev, and others.

In those years repressions on a mass scale were applied which were based on nothing tangible and which resulted in heavy cadre losses to the Party.

The vicious practice was condoned of having the NKVD prepare lists of persons whose cases were under the jurisdiction of the Military Collegium and whose sentences were prepared in advance. Yezhov would send these lists to Stalin personally for his approval of the proposed punishment. In 1937–1938, 383 such lists containing the names of many thousands of Party, Soviet, Komsomol, Army and economic workers were sent to Stalin. He approved these lists.

A large part of these cases are being reviewed now and a great part of them are being voided because they were baseless and falsified. Suffice it to say that from 1954 to the present time the Military Collegium of the Supreme Court has rehabilitated 7,679 persons, many of whom were rehabilitated posthumously.

Mass arrests of Party, Soviet, economic and military workers caused tremendous harm to our country and to the cause of socialist advancement.

Mass repressions had a negative influence on the moral-political condition of the Party, created a situation of uncertainty, contributed to the spreading of unhealthy suspicion, and sowed distrust among Communists. All sorts of slanderers and careerists were active.

Resolutions of the January Plenum of the Central Committee, All-Union Communist Party (Bolsheviks), in 1938 had brought some measure of improvement to the Party organizations. However, widespread repression also existed in 1938.

Only because our Party has at its disposal such great moral-political strength was it possible for it to survive the difficult events in 1937–1938 and to educate new cadres. There is, however, no doubt that our march forward toward socialism and toward the preparation of the country's defense would have been much more successful were it not for the tremendous loss in the cadres suffered as a result of the baseless and false mass repressions in 1937–1938.

We are justly accusing Yezhov for the degenerate practices of 1937. But we have to answer these questions: Could Yezhov have arrested Kossior, for instance, without the knowledge of Stalin? Was there an exchange of opinions or a Political Bureau decision concerning this? No, there was not, as there was none regarding other cases of this type. Could Yezhov have decided such important matters as the fate of such eminent Party figures? No, it would be a display of naivete to consider this the work of Yezhov alone. It is clear that these matters were decided by Stalin, and that without his orders and his sanction Yezhov could not have done this.

We have examined the cases and have rehabilitated Kossior, Rudzutak, Postyshev, Kosarev and others. For what causes were they arrested and sentenced? The review of evidence shows that there was no reason for this. They, like many others, were arrested without the Prosecutor's knowledge. In such a situation there is no need for any sanction, for what sort of a sanction could there be when Stalin decided everything. He was the chief prosecutor in these cases. Stalin not only agreed to, but on his own initiative issued, arrest orders. We must say this so that the delegates to the Congress can clearly undertake and themselves assess this and draw the proper conclusions.

Facts prove that many abuses were made on Stalin's orders without reckoning with any norms of Party and Soviet legality. Stalin was a very distrustful man, sickly suspicious; we knew this from our work with him. He could look at a man and say: "Why are your eyes so shifty today," or "Why are you turning so much today and avoiding to look me directly in the eyes?" The sickly suspicion created in him a general distrust even toward eminent Party workers whom he had known for years. Everywhere and in everything he saw "enemies," "two-facers" and "spies."

Possessing unlimited power he indulged in great willfulness and choked a person morally and physically. A situation was created where one could not express one's own will.

When Stalin said that one or another should be arrested, it was necessary to accept on faith that he was an "enemy of the people." Meanwhile, Beria's gang, which ran the organs of state security, outdid itself in proving the guilt of the arrested and the truth of materials which it falsified. And what proofs were offered? The confessions of the arrested, and the investigative judges accepted these "confessions." And how is it possible that a person confesses to crimes which he has not committed? Only in one way — because of application of physical methods of pressuring him, tortures, bringing him to a state of unconsciousness, deprivation of his judgment, taking away of his human dignity. In this manner were "confessions" acquired.

When the wave of mass arrests began to recede in 1939, and the leaders of territorial Party organizations began to accuse the NKVD workers of using methods of physical pressure on the arrested, Stalin dispatched a coded telegram on January 20, 1939, to the committee secretaries of oblasts and krais, to the Central Committees of republic Communist Parties, to the People's Commissars of Internal Affairs and to the heads of NKVD organizations. This telegram stated:

The Central Committee of the All-Union Communist Party (Bolsheviks) explains that the application of methods of physical pressure in NKVD practice is permissible from 1937 on in accordance with permission of the Central Committee of the All-Union Communist Party (Bolsheviks). . . . It is known that all bourgeois intelligence services use methods of physical influence against the representatives of the socialist proletariat and that they use them in their most scandalous form. The question arises as to why the socialist intelligence service should be more humanitarian against the mad agents of the bourgeoisie, against the deadly enemies of the working class and the kolkhoz workers. The Central Committee of the All-Union Communist Party (Bolsheviks) considers that physical pressure should still be used obligatorily, as an exception applicable to known and obstinate enemies of the people, as a method both justifiable and appropriate.

Thus Stalin had sanctioned in the name of the Central Committee of the All-Union Communist Party (Bolsheviks) the most brutal violation of socialist legality, torture and oppression, which led as we have seen to the slandering and self-accusation of innocent people.

Not long ago — only several days before the present Congress — we called to the Central Committee Presidium session and interrogated the investigative judge Rodos, who in his time investigated and interrogated Kossior, Chubar and Kosarev. He is a vile person, with the brain of a bird, and morally completely degenerate. And it was this man who was deciding the fate of prominent Party workers; he was making judgments also concerning the politics in these matters, because having established their "crime," he provided therewith materials from which important political implications could be drawn.

The question rises whether a man with such an intellect could alone make the investigation in a manner to prove the guilt of people such as Kossior and others. No, he could not have done it without proper directives. At the Central Committee Presidium session he told us: "I was told that Kossior and Chubar were people's enemies and for this reason, I, as an investigative judge, had to make them confess that they are enemies." (*Indignation in the hall.*)

He could do this only through long tortures, which he did, receiving detailed instructions from Beria. We must say that at the Central Committee Presidium session he cynically declared: "I thought that I was executing the orders of the Party." In this manner Stalin's orders concerning the use of methods of physical pressure against the arrested were in practice executed.

These and many other facts show that all norms of correct Party solution of problems were invalidated and everything was dependent upon the willfulness of one man.

The power accumulated in the hands of one person, Stalin, led to serious consequences during the Great Patriotic War.

When we look at many of our novels, films and historical "scientific studies," the role of Stalin in the Patriotic War appears to be entirely improbable. Stalin had foreseen everything. The Soviet Army, on the basis of a strategic plan prepared by Stalin long before, used the tactics of so-called "active defense," i.e., tactics which, as we know, allowed the Germans to come up to Moscow and Stalingrad. Using such tactics the Soviet Army, supposedly, thanks only to Stalin's genius, turned to the offensive and subdued the enemy. The epic victory gained through the armed might of the Land of the Soviets, through our heroic people, is ascribed in this type of novel, film and "scientific study" as being completely due to the strategic genius of Stalin.

We have to analyze this matter carefully because it has a tremendous significance not only from the historical, but especially from the political, educational and practical point of view.

What are the facts of this matter?

Before the war our press and all our political-educational work was characterized by its bragging tone: when an enemy violates the holy Soviet soil, then for every blow of the enemy we will answer with three blows and we will battle the enemy on his soil and we will win without much harm to ourselves. But these positive statements were not based in all areas on concrete facts, which would actually guarantee the immunity of our borders.

During the war and after the war Stalin put forward the thesis that the tragedy which our nation experienced in the first part of the war was the result of the "unexpected" attack of the Germans against the Soviet Union. But, Comrades, this is completely untrue. As soon as Hitler came to power in Germany he assigned to himself the task of liquidating Communism. The Fascists were saying this openly; they did not hide their plans. In order to attain this aggressive end all sorts of pacts and blocs were created, such as the famous Berlin-Rome-Tokyo axis. Many facts from the pre-war period clearly showed that Hitler was going all out to begin a war against the Soviet state and that he had concentrated large armed units, together with armored units, near the Soviet borders.

Documents which have now been published show that by April 3, 1941, Churchill, through his ambassador to the USSR, Cripps, personally warned Stalin that the Germans had begun regrouping their armed units with the intent of attacking the Soviet Union. It is self-evident that Churchill did not do this at all because of his friendly feeling toward the Soviet nation. He had in this his own imperialistic goals — to bring Germany and the USSR into a bloody war and thereby to strengthen the position of the British Empire. Just the same, Churchill affirmed in his writings that he sought to "warn Stalin and call his attention to the danger which threatened him." Churchill stressed this repeatedly in his dispatches of April 18 and in the following days. However, Stalin took no heed of these warnings. What is more, Stalin ordered that no credence be given to information of this sort, in order not to provoke the initiation of military operations.

We must assert that information of this sort concerning the threat of German armed invasion of Soviet territory was coming in also from our own military and diplomatic sources; however, because the leadership was conditioned against such information, such data was dispatched with fear and assessed with reservation.

Thus, for instance, information sent from Berlin on May 6, 1941, by the Soviet military attaché, Capt. Vorontsov, stated: "Soviet citizen Bozer . . . communicated to the deputy naval attaché that according to a statement of a certain German officer from Hitler's Headquarters, Germany is preparing to invade the USSR on May 14 through Finland, the Baltic countries and Latvia. At the same time Moscow and Leningrad will be heavily raided and paratroopers landed in border cities. . . ."

In his report of May 22, 1941, the deputy military attaché in Berlin, Khlopov, communicated that ". . . the attack of the German army is reportedly scheduled for June 15, but it is possible that it may begin in the first days of June. . . ."

A cable from our London Embassy dated June 18, 1941, stated: "As of now Cripps is deeply convinced of the inevitability of armed conflict between Germany and the USSR which will begin not later than the middle of June. According to Cripps, the Germans have presently concentrated 147 divisions (including air force and service units) along the Soviet borders. . . ."

Despite these particularly grave warnings, the necessary steps were not taken to prepare the country properly for defense and to prevent it from being caught unawares.

Did we have time and the capabilities for such preparations? Yes, we had the time and capabilities. Our industry was already so developed that it was capable of supplying fully the Soviet army with everything that it needed. This is proven by the fact that although during the war we lost almost half of our industry and important industrial and food production areas as the result of enemy occupation of the Ukraine, northern Caucasus and other western parts of the country, the Soviet people was still able to organize the production of military equipment in the eastern parts of the country, install there equipment taken from the western industrial areas, and to supply our armed forces with everything which was necessary to destroy the enemy.

Had our industry been mobilized properly and in time to supply the army with the necessary materiel, our wartime losses would have been decidedly smaller. Such mobilization had not been, however, started in time. And already in the first days of the war it became evident that our army was badly armed, that we did not have enough artillery, tanks and planes to throw the enemy back.

Soviet science and technology produced excellent models of tanks and artillery pieces before the war. But mass production of all this was not organized and as a matter of fact we started to modernize our military equipment only on the eve of the war. As a result, at the time of the enemy's invasion of the Soviet land we did not have sufficient quantities either of old machinery which was no longer used for armament production or of new machinery which we had planned to introduce into armament production. The situation with antiaircraft artillery was especially bad; we did not organize the production of antitank ammunition. Many fortified regions had proven to be indefensible as soon as they were attacked, because the old arms had been withdrawn and new ones were not yet available there.

This pertained, alas, not only to tanks, artillery and planes. At the outbreak of the war we did not even have sufficient numbers of rifles to arm the mobilized manpower. I recall that in those days I telephoned to Comrade Malenkov from Kiev and told him, "People have volunteered for the new army and demand arms. You must send us arms."

Malenkov answered me, "We cannot send you arms. We are sending all our rifles to Leningrad and you have to arm yourselves." (*Movement in the hall.*)

Such was the armament situation.

In this connection we cannot forget, for instance, the following fact. Shortly before the invasion of the Soviet Union by the Hitlerite army, Kirponos, who was Chief of the Kiev Special Military District (he was later killed at the front), wrote to Stalin that the German armies were at the Bug River, were preparing for an attack and in the very near future would probably start their offensive. In this connection Kirponos proposed that a strong defense be organized, that 300,000 people be evacuated from the border areas and that several strong points be organized there: antitank ditches, trenches for the soldiers, etc.

Moscow answered this proposition with the assertion that this would be a provocation, that no preparatory defensive work should be undertaken at the borders, that the Germans were not to be given any pretext for the initiation of military action against us. Thus, our borders were insufficiently prepared to repel the enemy.

When the Fascist armies had actually invaded Soviet territory and military operations began, Moscow issued the order that the German fire was not to be returned. Why? It was because Stalin, despite evident facts, thought that the war had not yet started, that this was only a provocative action on the part of several undisciplined sections of the German army, and that our reaction might serve as a reason for the Germans to begin the war.

The following fact is also known. On the eve of the invasion of the territory of the Soviet Union by the Hitlerite army a certain German citizen crossed our border and stated that the German armies had received orders to start the offensive against the Soviet Union on the night of June 22, at 3 o'clock. Stalin was informed about this immediately, but even this warning was ignored.

As you see, everything was ignored: warnings of certain army commanders, declarations of deserters from the enemy army, and even the open hostility of the enemy. Is this an example of the alertness of the Chief of the Party and of the state at this particularly significant historical moment?

And what were the results of this carefree attitude, this disregard of clear facts? The result was that already in the first hours and days the enemy had destroyed in our border regions a large part of our air force, artillery and other military equipment; he annihilated large numbers of our military cadres and disorganized our military leadership; consequently we could not prevent the enemy from marching deep into the country.

Very grievous consequences, especially in reference to the beginning of the war, followed Stalin's annihilation of many military commanders and political workers during 1937–1941 because of his suspiciousness and through slanderous accusations. During these years repressions were instituted against certain parts of military cadres beginning literally at the company and battalion commander level and extending to the higher military centers; during this time the cadre of leaders who had gained military experience in Spain and in the Far East was almost completely liquidated.

The policy of large-scale repression against the military cadres led also to undermined military discipline, because for several years officers of all ranks and even soldiers in the Party and Komsomol cells were taught to "unmask" their superiors as hidden enemies. (*Movement in the hall.*) It is natural that this caused a negative influence on the state of military discipline in the first war period.

And, as you know, we had before the war excellent military cadres which were unquestionably loyal to the Party and to the Fatherland. Suffice it to say that those of them who managed to survive despite severe tortures to which they were subjected in the prisons, have from the first war days shown themselves real patriots and heroically fought for the glory of the Fatherland; I have here in mind such comrades as Rokossovsky (who, as you know, had been jailed), Gorbatov, Meretskov (who is a delegate at the present Congress), Podlas (he was an excellent commander who perished at the front), and many, many others. However, many such commanders perished in camps and jails and the army saw them no more.

All this brought about the situation which existed at the beginning of the war and which was the great threat to our Fatherland.

It would be incorrect to forget that after the first severe disaster and defeats at the front, Stalin thought that this was the end. In one of his speeches in those days he said: "All that which Lenin created we have lost forever."

After this Stalin for a long time actually did not direct the military operations and ceased to do anything whatever. He returned to active leadership only when some members of the Political Bureau visited him and told him that it was necessary to take certain steps immediately in order to improve the situation at the front.

Therefore, the threatening danger which hung over our Fatherland in the first period of the war was largely due to the faulty methods of directing the nation and the Party by Stalin himself.

However, we speak not only about the moment when the war began, which led to serious disorganization of our army and brought us severe losses. Even after the war began, the nervousness and hysteria which Stalin demonstrated, interfering with actual military operations, caused our army serious damage.

Stalin was very far from an understanding of the real situation which was developing at the front. This was natural because during the whole Patriotic War he never visited any section of the front or any liberated city except for one short ride on the Mozhaisk Highway during a stabilized situation at the front. To this incident were dedicated many literary works full of fantasies of all sorts and so many paintings. Simultaneously, Stalin was interfering with operations and issuing orders which did not take into consideration the real situation at a given section of the front and which could not help but result in huge personnel losses.

I will allow myself in this connection to bring out one characteristic fact which illustrates how Stalin directed operations at the fronts. There is present at this Congress Marshal Bagramyan who was once the Chief of Operations in the Headquarters of the Southwestern front and who can corroborate what I will tell you.

When there developed an exceptionally serious situation for our army in 1942 in the Kharkov region, we had correctly decided to drop an operation whose objective was to encircle Kharkov, because the real situation at that time would have threatened our army with fatal consequences if this operation were continued.

We communicated this to Stalin, stating that the situation demanded changes in operational plans so that the enemy would be prevented from liquidating a sizable concentration of our army.

Contrary to common sense, Stalin rejected our suggestion and issued the order to continue the operation aimed at the encirclement of Kharkov, despite the fact that at this time many army concentrations were themselves actually threatened with encirclement and liquidation.

I telephoned to Vasilevsky and begged him, "Alexander Mikhailovich, take a map (Vasilevsky is present here) and show Comrade Stalin the situation which has developed." We should note that Stalin planned operations on a globe. (*Animation in the hall.*) Yes, comrades, he used to take the globe and trace the frontline on it. I said to Comrade Vasilevsky: "Show him the situation on a map; in the present situation we cannot continue the operation which was planned. The old decision must be changed for the good of the cause."

Vasilevsky replied saying that Stalin had already studied this problem and that he, Vasilevsky, would not see Stalin further concerning this matter, because the latter didn't want to hear any arguments on the subject of this operation.

After my talk with Vasilevsky I telephoned to Stalin at his villa. But Stalin did not answer the telephone and Malenkov was at the receiver. I told Comrade Malenkov that I was calling from the front and that I wanted to speak personally to Stalin. Stalin informed me through Malenkov that I should speak with Malenkov. I stated for the second time that I wished to inform Stalin personally about the grave situation which had arisen for us at the front. But Stalin did not consider it convenient to raise the phone and again stated that I should speak to him through Malenkov, although he was only a few steps from the telephone.

After "listening" in this manner to our plea Stalin said, "Let everything remain as it is!"

And what was the result of this? The worst that we had expected. The Germans surrounded our army concentrations and consequently we lost hundreds of thousands of our soldiers. This is Stalin's military "genius"; this is what it cost us. (*Movement in the hall.*)

On one occasion after the war, during a meeting of Stalin with members of the Political Bureau, Anastas Ivanovich Mikoyan mentioned that Khrushchev must have been right when he telephoned concerning the Kharkov operation and that it was unfortunate that his suggestion had not been accepted.

You should have seen Stalin's fury! How could it be admitted that he, Stalin, had not been right! He is after all a "genius," and a genius cannot help but be right! Everyone can err, but Stalin considered that he never erred, that he was always right. He never acknowledged to anyone that he made any mistake, large or small, despite the fact that he made not a few mistakes in the matter of theory and in his practical activity. After the Party Congress we shall probably have to re-evaluate many wartime military operations and to present them in their true light.

The tactics on which Stalin insisted without knowing the essence of the conduct of battle operations cost us much blood until we succeeded in stopping the opponent and going over to the offensive.

The military know that already by the end of 1941 instead of great operational maneuvers flanking the opponent and penetrating behind his back, Stalin demanded incessant frontal attacks and the capture of one village after another. Because of this we paid with great losses until our generals, on whose shoulders rested the whole weight of conducting the war, succeeded in changing the situation and shifting to flexible maneuver operations, which immediately brought serious changes at the front favorable to us.

All the more shameful was the fact that after our great victory over the enemy which cost us so much, Stalin began to downgrade many of the commanders who contributed so much to the victory over the enemy, because Stalin excluded every possibility that services rendered at the front should be credited to anyone but himself.

Stalin was very much interested in the assessment of Comrade Zhukov as a military leader. He asked me often for my opinion of Zhukov. I told him then, "I have known Zhukov for a long time; he is a good general and a good military leader."

After the war Stalin began to tell all kinds of nonsense about Zhukov, among others the following, "You praised Zhukov, but he does not deserve it. It is said that before each operation at the front Zhukov used to behave as follows: he used to take a handful of earth, smell it and say, 'We can begin the attack,' or the opposite, 'The planned operation cannot be carried out.'" I stated at that time, "Comrade Stalin, I do not know who invented this, but it is not true."

It is possible that Stalin himself invented these things for the purpose of minimizing the role and military talents of Marshal Zhukov.

In this connection Stalin very energetically popularized himself as a great leader; in various ways he tried to inculcate in the people the version that all victories gained by the Soviet nation during the Great Patriotic War were due to the courage, daring and genius of Stalin and to no one else. Exactly like Kuzma Kryuchkov [a famous Cossack who performed heroic feats against the Germans] he put one dress on 7 people at the same time. (*Animation in the hall.*)

In the same vein, let us take, for instance, our historical and military films and some literary creations; they make us feel sick. Their true objective is the propagation of the theme of praising Stalin as a military genius. Let us recall the film, "The Fall of Berlin." Here only Stalin acts; he issues orders in the hall in which there are many empty chairs and only one man approaches him and reports something to him — that is Poskrebyshev, his loyal shield-bearer. (*Laughter in the hall.*)

And where is the military command? Where is the Political Bureau? Where is the Government? What are they doing and with what are they engaged? There is nothing about them in the film. Stalin acts for everybody; he does not reckon with anyone; he asks no one for advice. Everything is shown to the nation in this false light. Why? In order to surround Stalin with glory, contrary to the facts and contrary to historical truth.

The question arises: And where are the military on whose shoulders rested the burden of the war? They are not in the film; with Stalin in, no room was left for them.

Not Stalin, but the Party as a whole, the Soviet Government, our heroic army, its talented leaders and brave soldiers, the whole Soviet nation — these are the ones who assured the victory in the Great Patriotic War. (*Tempestuous and prolonged applause.*)

The Central Committee members, ministers, our economic leaders, leaders of Soviet culture, directors of territorial Party and Soviet organizations, engineers, and technicians — every one of them in his own place of work generously gave of his strength and knowledge toward ensuring victory over the enemy.

Exceptional heroism was shown by our hard core — surrounded by glory is our whole working class, our kolkhoz peasantry, the Soviet intelligentsia, who under the leadership of Party organizations overcame untold hardships and, bearing the hardships of war, devoted all their strength to the cause of the defense of the Fatherland.

Great and brave deeds during the war were accomplished by our Soviet women who bore on their backs the heavy load of production work in the factories, on the kolkhozes, and in various economic and cultural sectors; many women participated directly in the Great Patriotic War at the fronts; our brave youth contributed immeasurably at the front and at home to the defense of the Soviet Fatherland and to the annihilation of the enemy.

Immortal are the services of the Soviet soldiers, of our commanders and political workers of all ranks; after the loss of a considerable part of the army in the first war months they did not lose their heads and were able to reorganize during the progress of combat; they created and toughened during the progress of the war a strong and heroic army and not only stood off pressure of the strong and cunning enemy but also smashed him.

The magnificent and heroic deeds of hundreds of millions of people of the East and of the West during the fight against the threat of Fascist subjugation which loomed before us will live centuries and millenia in the memory of thankful humanity. (*Thunderous applause.*)

The main role and the main credit for the victorious ending of the war belongs to our Communist Party, to the armed forces of the Soviet Union, and to the tens of millions of Soviet people raised by the Party. (*Thunderous and prolonged applause.*)

Comrades, let us reach for some other facts. The Soviet Union is justly considered as a model of a multinational state because we have in practice assured the equality and friendship of all nations which live in our great Fatherland.

All the more monstrous are the acts whose initiator was Stalin and which are rude violations of the basic Leninist principles of the nationality policy of the Soviet state. We refer to the mass deportations from their native places of whole nations, together with all Communists and Komsomols without any exception; this deportation action was not dictated by any military considerations.

Thus, already at the end of 1943, when there occurred a permanent breakthrough at the fronts of the Great Patriotic War benefiting the Soviet Union, a decision was taken and executed concerning the deportation of all the Karachai from the lands on which they lived. In the same period, at the end of December 1943, the same lot befell the whole population of the Autonomous Kalmyk Republic. In March 1944 all the Chechen and Ingush peoples were deported and the Chechen-Ingush Autonomous Republic was liquidated. In April 1944, all Balkars were deported to faraway places from the territory of the Kabardino-Balkar Autonomous Republic and the Republic itself was renamed the Autonomous Kabardin Republic. The Ukrainians avoided meeting this fate only because there were too many of them and there was no place to which to deport them. Otherwise, he would have deported them also. (*Laughter and animation in the hall.*)

Not only a Marxist-Leninist but also no man of common sense can grasp how it is possible to make whole nations responsible for inimical activity, including women, children, old people, Communists and Komsomols, to use mass repression against them, and to expose them to misery and suffering for the hostile acts of individual persons or groups of persons.

After the conclusion of the Patriotic War the Soviet nation stressed with pride the magnificent victories gained through great sacrifices and tremendous efforts. The country experienced a period of political enthusiasm. The Party came out of the war even more united; in the fire of the war Party cadres were tempered and hardened. Under such conditions nobody could have even thought of the possibility of some plot in the Party.

And it was precisely at this time that the so-called "Leningrad Affair" was born. As we have now proven, this case was fabricated. Those who innocently lost their lives included Comrades Voznesensky, Kuznetsov, Rodionov, Popkov, and others.

As is known, Voznesensky and Kuznetsov were talented and eminent leaders. Once they stood very close to Stalin. It is sufficient to mention that Stalin made Voznesensky first deputy to the Chairman of the Council of Ministers and Kuznetsov was elected Secretary of the Central Committee. The very fact that Stalin entrusted Kuznetsov with the supervision of the state security organs shows the trust which he enjoyed.

How did it happen that these persons were branded as enemies of the people and liquidated?

Facts prove that the "Leningrad Affair" is also the result of willfulness which Stalin exercised against Party cadres.

Had a normal situation existed in the Party's Central Committee and in the Central Committee Political Bureau, affairs of this nature would have been examined there in accordance with Party practice, and all pertinent facts assessed; as a result such an affair as well as others would not have happened.

We must state that after the war the situation became even more complicated. Stalin became even more capricious, irritable and brutal; in particular his suspicion grew. His persecution mania reached unbelievable dimensions. Many workers were becoming enemies before his very eyes. After the war Stalin separated himself from the collective even more. Everything was decided by him alone without any consideration for anyone or anything.

This unbelievable suspicion was cleverly taken advantage of by the abject provocateur and vile enemy, Beria, who had murdered thousands of Communists and loyal Soviet people. The elevation of Voznesensky and Kuznetsov alarmed Beria. As we have now proven, it had been precisely Beria who had "suggested" to Stalin the fabrication by him and by his confidants of materials in the form of declarations and anonymous letters, and in the form of various rumors and talks.

The Party's Central Committee has examined this so-called "Leningrad Affair"; persons who innocently suffered are now rehabilitated and honor has been restored to the glorious Leningrad Party organization. Abakumov and others who had fabricated this affair were brought before a court; their trial took place in Leningrad and they received what they deserved.

The question arises: Why is it that we see the truth of this affair only now, and why did we not do something earlier, during Stalin's life, in order to prevent the loss of innocent lives? It was because Stalin personally supervised the "Leningrad Affair," and the majority of the Political Bureau members did not, at that time, know all of the circumstances in these matters, and could not therefore intervene.

When Stalin received certain materials from Beria and Abakumov, without examining these slanderous materials, he ordered an investigation of the "Affair" of Voznesensky and Kuznetsov. With this their fate was sealed. Instructive in the same way is the case of the Mingrelian nationalist organization which supposedly existed in Georgia. As is known, resolutions by the Central Committee [of the] Communist Party of the Soviet Union, were made concerning this case in November 1951 and in March 1952. These resolutions were made without prior discussion with the Political Bureau. Stalin had personally dictated them. They made serious accusations against many loyal Communists. On the basis of falsified documents it was proven that there existed in Georgia a supposedly nationalistic organization whose objective was the liquidation of the Soviet power in that Republic with the help of imperialist powers.

In this connection, a number of responsible Party and Soviet workers were arrested in Georgia. As was later proven, this was a slander directed against the Georgian Party Organization.

We know that there have been at times manifestations of local bourgeois nationalism in Georgia as in several other republics. The question arises: Could it be possible that in the period during which the resolutions referred to above were made, nationalist tendencies grew so much that there was a danger of Georgia's leaving the Soviet Union and joining Turkey? (*Animation in the hall, laughter.*)

This is, of course, nonsense. It is impossible to imagine how such assumptions could enter anyone's mind. Everyone knows how Georgia has developed economically and culturally under Soviet rule.

Industrial production of the Georgian Republic is 27 times greater than it was before the revolution. Many new industries have arisen in Georgia which did not exist there before the revolution: iron smelting, an oil industry, a machine construction industry, etc. Illiteracy has long since been liquidated, which, in pre-revolutionary Georgia, included 78 percent of the population.

Could the Georgians, comparing the situation in their Republic with the hard situation of the working masses in Turkey, be aspiring to join Turkey? In 1955 Georgia produced 18 times as much steel per person as Turkey. Georgia produces 9 times as much electrical energy per person as Turkey. According to the available 1950 census, 65 percent of Turkey's total population are illiterate, and of the women, 80 percent are illiterate. Georgia has 19 institutions of higher learning which have about 39,000 students; this is 8 times more than in Turkey (for each 1,000 inhabitants). The prosperity of the working people has grown tremendously in Georgia under Soviet rule.

It is clear that as the economy and culture develop, and as the socialist consciousness of the working masses in Georgia grows, the source from which bourgeois nationalism draws its strength evaporates.

As it developed, there was no nationalistic organization in Georgia. Thousands of innocent people fell victim of willfulness and lawlessness. All of this happened under the "genial" leadership of Stalin, "the great son of the Georgian nation," as Georgians liked to refer to Stalin. (*Animation in the hall.*)

The willfulness of Stalin showed itself not only in decisions concerning the internal life of the country but also in the international relations of the Soviet Union.

The July Plenum of the Central Committee studied in detail the reasons for the development of conflict with Yugoslavia. It was a shameful role which Stalin played here. The "Yugoslav Affair" contained no problems which could not have been solved through Party discussions among comrades. There was no significant basis for the development of this "affair"; it was completely possible to have prevented the rupture of relations with that country. This does not mean, however, that the Yugoslav leaders did not make mistakes or did not have shortcomings. But these mistakes and shortcomings were magnified in a monstrous manner by Stalin, which resulted in a break of relations with a friendly country.

I recall the first days when the conflict between the Soviet Union and Yugoslavia began artificially to be blown up. Once, when I came from Kiev to Moscow, I was invited to visit Stalin who, pointing to the copy of a letter lately sent to Tito, asked me, "Have you read this?" Not waiting for my reply he answered, "I will shake my little finger — and there will be no more Tito. He will fall."

We have dearly paid for this "shaking of the little finger." This statement reflected Stalin's mania for greatness, but he acted just that way: "I will shake my little finger — and there will be no Kossior"; "I will shake my little finger once more and Postyshev and Chubar will be no more"; "I will shake my little finger again — and Voznesensky, Kuznetsov and many others will disappear."

But this did not happen to Tito. No matter how much or how little Stalin shook, not only his little finger but everything else that he could shake, Tito did not fall. Why? The reason was that, in this case of disagreement with the Yugoslav comrades, Tito had behind him a state and a people who had gone through a severe school of fighting for liberty and independence, a people which gave support to its leaders.

You see to what Stalin's mania for greatness led. He had completely lost consciousness of reality; he demonstrated his suspicion and haughtiness not only in relation to individuals in the USSR, but in relation to whole parties and nations.

We have carefully examined the case of Yugoslavia and have found a proper solution which is approved by the peoples of the Soviet Union and of Yugoslavia as well as by the working masses of all the People's Democracies and by all progressive humanity. The liquidation of the abnormal relationship with Yugoslavia was done in the interest of the whole camp of socialism, in the interest of strengthening peace in the whole world.

Let us also recall the "Affair of the Doctor-Plotters." (*Animation in the hall.*) Actually there was no "Affair" outside of the declaration of the woman doctor Timashuk, who was probably influenced or ordered by someone (after all, she was an unofficial collaborator of the organs of state security) to write Stalin a letter in which she declared that doctors were applying supposedly improper methods of medical treatment.

Such a letter was sufficient for Stalin to reach an immediate conclusion that there were doctor-plotters in the Soviet Union. He issued orders to arrest a group of eminent Soviet medical specialists. He personally issued advice on the conduct of the investigation and the method of interrogation of the arrested persons. He said that the academician Vinogradov should be put in chains, another one should be beaten. Present at this Congress as a delegate is the former Minister of State Security, Comrade Ignatiev. Stalin told him curtly, "If you do not obtain confessions from the doctors we will shorten you by a head." (*Tumult in the hall.*)

Stalin personally called the investigative judge, gave him instructions, advised him on which investigative methods should be used; these methods were simple — beat, beat and, once again, beat.

Shortly after the doctors were arrested we members of the Political Bureau received protocols with the doctors' confessions of guilt. After distributing these protocols Stalin told us, "You are blind like young kittens; what will happen without me? The country will perish because you do not know how to recognize enemies."

The case was so presented that no one could verify the facts on which the investigation was based. There was no possibility of trying to verify facts by contacting those who had made the confessions of guilt.

We felt, however, that the case of the arrested doctors was questionable. We knew some of these people personally because they had once treated us. When we examined this "case" after Stalin's death, we found it to be fabricated from beginning to end.

This ignominious "case" was set up by Stalin; he did not, however, have the time in which to bring it to an end (as he conceived that end), and for this reason the doctors are still alive. Now all have been rehabilitated; they are working in the same places they were working before; they treat top individuals, not excluding members of the government; they have our full confidence; and they execute their duties honestly, as they did before.

In organizing the various dirty and shameful cases, a very base role was played by the rabid enemy of our Party, an agent of a foreign intelligence service — Beria, who had stolen into Stalin's confidence. In what way could this provocateur gain such a position in the Party and in the state, so as to become the First Deputy Chairman of the Council of Ministers of the Soviet Union and a member of the Central Committee Political Bureau? It has now been established that this villain had climbed up the government ladder over an untold number of corpses.

Were there any signs that Beria was an enemy of the Party? Yes, there were. Already in 1937, at a Central Committee Plenum, former People's Commissar of Health Protection, Kaminsky, said that Beria worked for the Mussavat intelligence service. But the Central Committee Plenum had barely concluded when Kaminsky was arrested and then shot. Had Stalin examined Kaminsky's statement? No, because Stalin believed in Beria, and that was enough for him. And when Stalin believed in anyone or anything, then no one could say anything which was contrary to his opinion; anyone who would dare to express opposition would have met the same fate as Kaminsky.

There were other signs also. The declaration which Comrade Snegov made at the Party's Central Committee is interesting. (Parenthetically speaking, he was also rehabilitated not long ago, after 17 years in prison camps.) In this declaration Snegov writes:

> In connection with the proposed rehabilitation of the former Central Committee member, Kartvelishvili-Lavrentiev, I have entrusted to the hands of the representative of the Committee of State Security a detailed deposition concerning Beria's role in the disposition of the Kartvelishvili case and concerning the criminal motives by which Beria was guided.
>
> In my opinion it is indispensable to recall an important fact pertaining to this case and to communicate it to the Central Committee, because I did not consider it as proper to include it in the investigation documents.
>
> On October 30, 1931, at the session of the Organizational Bureau of the Central Committee, All-Union Communist Party (Bolsheviks), Kartvelishvili, Secretary of the Trans-Caucasian Krai Committee made a report. All members of the Executive of the Krai Committee were present; of them I alone am alive. During this session J. V. Stalin made a motion at the end of his speech concerning the organization of the Secretariat of the Trans-Caucasian Krai Committee composed of the following: First Secretary, Kartvelishvili; Second Secretary, Beria (it was then for the first

time in the Party's history that Beria's name was mentioned as a candidate for a Party position). Kartvelishvili answered that he knew Beria well and for that reason refused categorically to work together with him. Stalin proposed then that this matter be left open and that it be solved in the process of the work itself. Two days later a decision was arrived at that Beria would receive the Party post and that Kartvelishvili would be deported from the Trans-Caucasus.

This fact can be confirmed by Comrades Mikoyan and Kaganovich who were present at that session.

The long unfriendly relations between Kartvelishvili and Beria were widely known; they date back to the time when Comrade Sergo [Ordzhonikidze] was active in the Trans-Caucasus; Kartvelishvili was the closest assistant of Sergo. The unfriendly relationship impelled Beria to fabricate a "case" against Kartvelishvili.

It is a characteristic thing that in this "case" Kartvelishvili was charged with a terroristic act against Beria.

The indictment in the Beria case contains a discussion of his crimes. Some things should, however, be recalled, especially since it is possible that not all delegates to the Congress have read this document. I wish to recall Beria's bestial disposition of the cases of Kedrov, Golubiev, and Golubiev's adopted mother, Baturina — persons who wished to inform the Central Committee concerning Beria's treacherous activity. They were shot without any trial and the sentence was passed ex-post facto, after the execution.

Here is what the old Communist, Comrade Kedrov, wrote to the Central Committee through Comrade Andreyev (Comrade Andreyev was then a Central Committee secretary):

> I am calling to you for help from a gloomy cell of the Lefortosky prison. Let my cry of horror reach your ears; do not remain deaf; take me under your protection; please, help remove the nightmare of interrogations and show that this is all a mistake.
>
> I suffer innocently. Please believe me. Time will testify to the truth. I am not an agent-provocateur of the Tsarist Okhrana; I am not a spy; I am not a member of an anti-Soviet organization of which I am being accused on the basis of denunciations. I am also not guilty of any other crimes against the Party and the government. I am an old Bolshevik, free of any stain; I have honestly

fought for almost 40 years in the ranks of the Party for the good and the prosperity of the nation. . . .

. . . Today, I, a 62-year-old man, am being threatened by the investigative judges with more severe, cruel and degrading methods of physical pressure. They [the judges] are no longer capable of becoming aware of their error and of recognizing that their handling of my case is illegal and impermissible. They try to justify their actions by picturing me as a hardened and raving enemy and are demanding increased repressions. But let the Party know that I am innocent and that there is nothing which can turn a loyal son of the Party into an enemy, even right up to his last dying breath.

But I have no way out. I cannot divert from myself the hastily approaching new and powerful blows.

Everything, however, has its limits. My torture has reached the extreme. My health is broken, my strength and my energy are waning, the end is drawing near. To die in a Soviet prison, branded as a vile traitor to the Fatherland — what can be more monstrous for an honest man. And how monstrous all this is! Unsurpassed bitterness and pain grips my heart. No! No! This will not happen; this cannot be — I cry. Neither the Party, nor the Soviet government, nor the People's Commissar, L. P. Beria, will permit this cruel irreparable injustice. I am firmly certain that given a quiet, objective examination, without any foul rantings, without any anger and without the fearful tortures, it would be easy to prove the baselessness of the charges. I believe deeply that truth and justice will triumph. I believe. I believe.

The old Bolshevik, Comrade Kedrov, was found innocent by the Military Collegium. But despite this, he was shot at Beria's order. (*Indignation in the hall.*)

Beria also handled cruelly the family of Comrade Ordzhonikidze. Why? Because Ordzhonikidze had tried to prevent Beria from realizing his shameful plans. Beria had cleared from his way all persons who could possibly interfere with him. Ordzhonikidze was always an opponent of Beria, which he told to Stalin. Instead of examining this affair and taking appropriate steps, Stalin allowed the liquidation of Ordzhonikidze's brother and brought Ordzhonikidze himself to such a state that he was forced to shoot himself. (*Indignation in the hall.*) Such was Beria.

Beria was unmasked by the Party's Central Committee shortly after Stalin's death. As a result of the particularly detailed legal proceedings it was established that Beria had committed monstrous crimes and Beria was shot.

The question arises why Beria, who had liquidated tens of thousands of Party and Soviet workers, was not unmasked during Stalin's life? He was not unmasked earlier because he had utilized very skillfully Stalin's weaknesses; feeding him with suspicions, he assisted Stalin in everything and acted with his support.

Comrades! The cult of the individual acquired such monstrous size chiefly because Stalin himself, using all conceivable methods, supported the glorification of his own person. This is supported by numerous facts. One of the most characteristic examples of Stalin's self-glorification and of his lack of even elementary modesty is the edition of his *Short Biography,* which was published in 1948.

This book is an expression of the most dissolute flattery, an example of making a man into a godhead, of transforming him into an infallible sage, "the greatest leader," "sublime strategist of all times and nations." Finally no other words could be found with which to lift Stalin up to the heavens.

We need not give here examples of the loathsome adulation filling this book. All we need to add is that they all were approved and edited by Stalin personally and some of them were added in his own handwriting to the draft text of the book.

What did Stalin consider essential to write into this book? Did he want to cool the ardor of his flatterers who were composing his *Short Biography?* No! He marked the very places where he thought that the praise of his services was insufficient.

Here are some examples characterizing Stalin's activity, added in Stalin's own hand:

> In this fight against the skeptics and capitulators, the Trotskyites, Zinovievites, Bukharinites and Kamenevites, there was definitely welded together, after Lenin's death, that leading core of the Party . . . that upheld the great banner of Lenin, rallied the Party behind Lenin's behests, and brought the Soviet people into the broad road of industrializing the country and collectivizing the rural economy. The leader of this core and the guiding force of the Party and the State was Comrade Stalin.

Thus writes Stalin himself! Then he adds:

> Although he performed his task of leader of the Party and the people with consummate skill and enjoyed the unreserved support of the entire Soviet people, Stalin never allowed his work to be marred by the slightest hint of vanity, conceit or self-adulation.

Where and when could a leader so praise himself? Is this worthy of a leader of the Marxist-Leninist type? No. Precisely against this did Marx and Engels take such a strong position. This also was always sharply condemned by Vladimir Ilyich Lenin.

In the draft text of his book appeared the following sentence: "Stalin is the Lenin of today." This sentence appeared to Stalin to be too weak, so in his own handwriting he changed it to read: "Stalin is the worthy continuer of Lenin's work, or, as it is said in our Party, Stalin is the Lenin of today." You see how well it is said, not by the nation but by Stalin himself.

It is possible to give many such self-praising appraisals written into the draft text of that book in Stalin's hand. Especially generously does he endow himself with praises pertaining to his military genius, to his talent for strategy.

I will cite one more insertion made by Stalin concerning the theme of the Stalinist military genius.

"The advanced Soviet science of war received further development," he writes,

> at Comrade Stalin's hands. Comrade Stalin elaborated the theory of the permanently operating factors that decide the issue of wars, of active defense and the laws of counter-offensive and offensive, of the co-operation of all services and arms in modern warfare, of the role of big tank masses and air forces in modern war, and of the artillery as the most formidable of the armed services. At the various stages of the war Stalin's genius found the correct solutions that took account of all the circumstances of the situation.

(*Movement in the hall.*) And further, writes Stalin:

> Stalin's military mastership was displayed both in defense and offense. Comrade Stalin's genius enabled him to divine the enemy's plans and defeat them. The battles in which Comrade Stalin di-

rected the Soviet armies are brilliant examples of operational military skill.

In this manner was Stalin praised as a strategist. Who did this? Stalin himself, not in his role as a strategist but in the role of an author-editor, one of the main creators of his self-adulatory biography.

Such, comrades, are the facts. We should rather say shameful facts.

And one additional fact from the same *Short Biography* of Stalin. As is known, *The Short Course of the History of the All-Union Communist Party (Bolsheviks)* was written by a commission of the Party Central Committee.

This book, parenthetically, was also permeated with the cult of the individual and was written by a designated group of authors. This fact was reflected in the following formulation on the proof copy of the *Short Biography* of Stalin:

A commission of the Central Committee, All-Union Communist Party (Bolsheviks), under the direction of Comrade Stalin and with his most active personal participation, has prepared a *Short Course of the History of the All-Union Communist Party (Bolsheviks)*.

But even this phrase did not satisfy Stalin; the following sentence replaced it in the final version of the *Short Biography:*

"In 1938 appeared the book, *History of the All-Union Communist Party (Bolsheviks)*, *Short Course*, written by Comrade Stalin and approved by a commission of the Central Committee, All Union Communist Party (Bolsheviks)." Can one add anything more? (*Animation in the hall.*)

As you see, a surprising metamorphosis changed the work created by a group into a book written by Stalin. It is not necessary to state how and why this metamorphosis took place.

A pertinent question comes to our mind: If Stalin is the author of this book, why did he need to praise the person of Stalin so much and to transform the whole post-October historical period of our glorious Communist Party solely into an action of "the Stalin genius"?

Did this book properly reflect the efforts of the Party in the socialist transformation of the country, in the construction of socialist society, in the industrialization and collectivization of the country, and also other steps taken by the Party which undeviatingly traveled the path outlined by Lenin? This book speaks principally about Stalin, about his speeches, about his reports. Everything without the smallest exception is tied to his name.

And when Stalin himself asserts that he himself wrote the *Short Course of the History of the All-Union Communist Party (Bolsheviks)*, this calls at least for amazement. Can a Marxist-Leninist thus write about himself, praising his own person to the heavens?

Or let us take the matter of the Stalin Prizes. (*Movement in the hall.*) Not even the tsars created prizes which they named after themselves.

Stalin recognized as the best a text of the national anthem of the Soviet Union which contains not a word about the Communist Party; it contains, however, the following unprecedented praise of Stalin:

> *Stalin brought us up in loyalty to the people,*
> *He inspired us to great toil and acts.*

In these lines of the anthem is the whole educational, directional and inspirational activity of the great Leninist Party ascribed to Stalin. This is, of course, a clear deviation from Marxism-Leninism, a clear debasing and belittling of the role of the Party. We should add for your information that the Presidium of the Central Committee has already passed a resolution concerning the composition of a new text of the anthem, which will reflect the role of the people, and the role of the Party. (*Loud, prolonged applause.*)

And was it without Stalin's knowledge that many of the largest enterprises and towns were named after him? Was it without his knowledge that Stalin monuments were erected in the whole country — these "memorials to the living"? It is a fact that Stalin himself had signed on July 2, 1951, a resolution of the USSR Council of Ministers concerning the erection on the Volga-Don Canal of an impressive monument to Stalin; on September 4 of the same year he issued an order making 33 tons of copper available for the construction of this impressive monument. Anyone who has visited the Stalingrad area must have seen the huge statue which is being built there, and that on a site which hardly any people frequent. Huge sums were spent to build it at a time when people of this area had lived since the war in huts. Consider yourself, was Stalin right when he wrote in his biography that ". . . he did not allow in himself . . . even a shadow of conceit, pride, or self-adoration"?

At the same time Stalin gave proofs of his lack of respect for Lenin's memory. It is not a coincidence that, despite the decision taken over 30 years ago to build a Palace of Soviets as a monument to Vladimir Il-yich, this Palace was not built, its construction was always postponed, and the project allowed to lapse.

We cannot forget to recall the Soviet government resolution of August 14, 1925, concerning "the founding of Lenin prizes for educational work." This resolution was published in the press, but until this day there are no Lenin prizes. This, too, should be corrected. (*Tumultuous, prolonged applause.*)

During Stalin's life, thanks to known methods which I have mentioned, and quoting facts, for instance, from the *Short Biography* of Stalin — all events were explained as if Lenin played only a secondary role, even during the October Socialist Revolution. In many films and in many literary works, the figure of Lenin was incorrectly presented and inadmissibly depreciated.

Stalin loved to see the film "The Unforgettable Year of 1919," in which he was shown on the steps of an armored train and where he was practically vanquishing the foe with his own saber. Let Kliment Yefremovich, our dear friend, find the necessary courage and write the truth about Stalin; after all, he knows how Stalin had fought. It will be difficult for Comrade Voroshilov to undertake this, but it would be good if he did it. Everyone will approve of it, both the people and the Party. Even his grandsons will thank him. (*Prolonged applause.*)

In speaking about the events of the October Revolution and about the Civil War, the impression was created that Stalin always played the main role, as if everywhere and always Stalin had suggested to Lenin what to do and how to do it. However, this is slander of Lenin. (*Prolonged applause.*)

I will probably not sin against the truth when I say that 99 percent of the persons present here heard and knew very little about Stalin before the year 1924, while Lenin was known to all; he was known to the whole Party, to the whole nation, from the children up to the gray-beards. (*Tumultuous, prolonged applause.*)

All this has to be thoroughly revised, so that history, literature, and the fine arts properly reflect V. I. Lenin's role and the great deeds of our Communist Party and of the Soviet people — the creative people. (*Applause.*)

Comrades! The cult of the individual has caused the employment of faulty principles in Party work and in economic activity; it brought about rude violation of internal Party and Soviet democracy, sterile administration, deviations of all sorts, covering up of shortcomings and varnishing of reality. Our nation gave birth to many flatterers and specialists in false optimism and deceit.

We should also not forget that due to the numerous arrests of Party, Soviet and economic leaders, many workers began to work uncertainly, showed over-cautiousness, feared all which was new, feared their own shadows and began to show less initiative in their work.

Take, for instance, Party and Soviet resolutions. They were prepared in a routine manner often without considering the concrete situation. This went so far that Party workers, even during the smallest sessions, read their speeches. All this produced the danger of formalizing the Party and Soviet work and of bureaucratizing the whole apparatus.

Stalin's reluctance to consider life's realities and the fact that he was not aware of the real state of affairs in the provinces can be illustrated by his direction of agriculture.

All those who interested themselves even a little in the national situation saw the difficult situation in agriculture, but Stalin never even noted it. Did we tell Stalin about this? Yes, we told him, but he did not support us. Why? Because Stalin never traveled anywhere, did not meet city and kolkhoz workers; he did not know the actual situation in the provinces.

He knew the country and agriculture only from films. And these films had dressed up and beautified the existing situation in agriculture.

Many films so pictured kolkhoz life that the tables were bending from the weight of turkeys and geese. Evidently Stalin thought that it was actually so.

Vladimir Ilyich Lenin looked at life differently; he was always close to the people; he used to receive peasant delegates, and often spoke at factory gatherings; he used to visit villages and talk with the peasants.

Stalin separated himself from the people and never went anyhere. This lasted tens of years. The last time he visited a village was in January 1928 when he visited Siberia in connection with grain deliveries. How then could he have known the situation in the provinces?

And when he was once told during a discussion that our situation on the land was a difficult one and that the situation of cattle breeding and meat production was especially bad, a commission was formed which was charged with the preparation of a resolution called, "Means toward further development of animal breeding in kolkhozes and sovkhozes." We worked out this project.

Of course, our propositions of that time did not contain all possibilities, but we did charter ways in which animal breeding on the kolkhozes and sovkhozes would be raised. We had proposed then to raise the prices of such products in order to create material incentives for the kolkhoz, MTS and sovkhoz workers in the development of cattle breeding. But our project was not accepted and in February 1953 was laid aside entirely.

What is more, while reviewing this project Stalin proposed that the taxes paid by the kolkhozes and by the kolkhoz workers should be raised by 40 billion rubles; according to him the peasants are well off and the kolkhoz worker would need to sell only one more chicken to pay his tax in full.

Imagine what this meant. Certainly 40 billion rubles is a sum which the kolkhoz workers did not realize for all the products which they sold to the government. In 1952, for instance, the kolkhozes and the kolkhoz workers received 26,280 million rubles for all their products delivered and sold to the government.

Did Stalin's position then rest on data of any sort whatever? Of course not.

In such cases facts and figures did not interest him. If Stalin said anything, it meant it was so — after all, he was a "genius" and a genius does not need to count, he only needs to look and can immediately tell how it should be. When he expresses his opinion, everyone has to repeat it and to admire his wisdom.

But how much wisdom was contained in the proposal to raise the agricultural tax by 40 billion rubles? None, absolutely none, because the proposal was not based on an actual assessment of the situation but on the fantastic ideas of a person divorced from reality. We are currently beginning slowly to work our way out of a difficult agricultural situation. The speeches of the delegates to the XXth Congress please us all; we are glad that many delegates deliver speeches, that there are conditions for the fulfillment of the Sixth Five-Year Plan for animal husbandry, not during the period of five years, but within two to three years. We are certain that the commitments of the new Five-Year Plan will be accomplished successfully. (*Prolonged applause.*)

Comrades! If we sharply criticize today the cult of the individual which was so widespread during Stalin's life and if we speak about the many negative phenomena generated by this cult which is so alien to the spirit of Marxism-Leninism, various persons may ask: How could it be? Stalin headed the Party and the country for 30 years and many victories were gained during his lifetime. Can we deny this? In my opinion, the question can be asked in this manner only by those who are blinded and hopelessly hypnotized by the cult of the individual, only by those who do not understand the essence of the revolution and of the Soviet state, only by those who do not understand, in a Leninist manner, the role of the Party and of the nation in the development of the Soviet society.

The socialist revolution was attained by the working class and by the poor peasantry with the partial support of middle-class peasants. It was attained by the people under the leadership of the Bolshevik Party. Lenin's great service consisted of the fact that he created a militant Party of the working class, but he was armed with Marxist understanding of the laws of social development and with the science of proletarian victory in the fight with capitalism, and he steeled this Party in the crucible of revolutionary struggle of the masses of the people. During this fight the Party consistently defended the interests of the people, became its experienced leader, and led the working masses to power, to the creation of the first socialist state.

You remember well the wise words of Lenin that the Soviet state is strong because of the awareness of the masses that history is created by the millions and tens of millions of people.

Our historical victories were attained thanks to the organizational work of the Party, to the many provincial organizations, and to the self-sacrificing work of our great nation. These victories are the result of the great drive and activity of the nation and of the Party as a whole; they are not at all the fruit of the leadership of Stalin, as the situation was pictured during the period of the cult of the individual.

If we are to consider this matter as Marxists and as Leninists, then we have to state unequivocally that the leadership practice which came into being during the last years of Stalin's life became a serious obstacle in the path of Soviet social development.

Stalin often failed for months to take up some unusually important problems concerning the life of the Party and of the state whose solution could not be postponed. During Stalin's leadership our peaceful relations with other nations were often threatened, because one-man decisions could cause and often did cause great complications.

In the last years, when we managed to free ourselves of the harmful practice of the cult of the individual and took several proper steps in the sphere of internal and external policies, everyone saw how activity grew before their very eyes, how the creative activity of the broad working masses developed, how favorably all this acted upon the development of economy and of culture. (*Applause.*)

Some comrades may ask us: Where were the members of the Political Bureau of the Central Committee? Why did they not assert themselves against the cult of the individual in time? And why is this being done only now?

First of all we have to consider the fact that the members of the Political Bureau viewed these matters in a different way at different times. Initially, many of them backed Stalin actively because Stalin was one of the strongest Marxists and his logic, his strength and his will greatly influenced the cadres and Party work.

It is known that Stalin, after Lenin's death, especially during the first years, actively fought for Leninism against the enemies of Leninist theory and against those who deviated. Beginning with Leninist theory, the Party, with its Central Committee at the head, started on a great scale the work of socialist industrialization of the country, agricultural collectivization and the cultural revolution. At that time Stalin gained great popularity, sympathy and support. The Party had to fight those who attempted to lead the country away from the correct Leninist path; it had to fight Trotskyites, Zinovievites and rightists, and the bourgeois nationalists. This fight was indispensable. Later, however, Stalin, abusing his power more and more, began to fight eminent Party and government leaders and to use terroristic methods against honest Soviet people. As we have already shown, Stalin thus handled such eminent Party and government leaders as Kossior, Rudzutak, Eikhe, Postyshev and many others.

Attempts to oppose groundless suspicions and charges resulted in the opponent falling victim of the repression. This characterized the fall of Comrade Postyshev.

In one of his speeches Stalin expressed his dissatisfaction with Postyshev and asked him, "What are you actually?"

Postyshev answered clearly, "I am a Bolshevik, Comrade Stalin, a Bolshevik."

This assertion was at first considered to show a lack of respect for Stalin; later it was considered a harmful act and consequently resulted in Postyshev's annihilation and branding without any reason as a "people's enemy."

In the situation which then prevailed I have talked often with Nikolai Alexandrovich Bulganin; once when we two were traveling in a car, he said, "It has happened sometimes that a man goes to Stalin on his invitation as a friend. And when he sits with Stalin, he does not know where he will be sent next, home or to jail."

It is clear that such conditions put every member of the Political Bureau in a very difficult situation. And when we also consider the fact that in the last years the Central Committee plenary sessions were not convened and that the sessions of the Political Bureau occurred only occasionally, from time to time, then we will understand how difficult it was for any member of the Political Bureau to take a stand against one or another injust or improper procedure, against serious errors and shortcomings in the practices of leadership.

As we have already shown, many decisions were taken either by one person or in a roundabout way, without collective discussions. The sad fate of Political Bureau member, Comrade Voznesensky, who fell victim to Stalin's repressions, is known to all. It is a characteristic thing that the decision to remove him from the Political Bureau was never discussed but was reached in a devious fashion. In the same way came the decision concerning the removal of Kuznetsov and Rodionov from their posts.

The importance of the Central Committee's Political Bureau was reduced and its work was disorganized by the creation within the Political Bureau of various commissions — the so-called "quintets," "sextets," "septets" and "novenaries." Here is, for instance, a resolution of the Political Bureau of October 3, 1946.

Stalin's Proposal:

1. The Political Bureau Commission for Foreign Affairs ("Sextet") is to concern itself in the future, in addition to foreign affairs, also with matters of internal construction and domestic policy.

2. The Sextet is to add to its roster the Chairman of the State Commission of Economic Planning of the USSR, Comrade Voznesensky, and is to be known as a Septet.

Signed: Secretary of the Central Committee, J. Stalin.

What a terminology of a card player! (*Laughter in the hall.*) It is clear that the creation within the Political Bureau of this type of commission — "quintets," "sextets," "septets," and "novenaries" — was against the principle of collective leadership. The result of this was that some members of the Political Bureau were in this way kept away from participation in reaching the most important state matters.

One of the oldest members of our Party, Kliment Yefremovich Voroshilov, found himself in an almost impossible situation. For several years he was actually deprived of the right of participation in Political Bureau sessions. Stalin forbade him to attend the Political Bureau sessions and to receive documents. When the Political Bureau was in session and Comrade Voroshilov heard about it, he telephoned each time and asked whether he would be allowed to attend. Sometimes Stalin permitted it, but always showed his dissatisfaction. Because of his extreme suspicion, Stalin toyed also with the absurd and ridiculous suspicion that Voroshilov was an English agent. (*Laughter in the hall.*) It's true — an English agent. A special tapping device was installed in his home to listen to what was said there. (*Indignation in the hall.*)

By unilateral decision Stalin had also separated one other man from the work of the Political Bureau — Andrei Andreyevich Andreyev. This was one of the most unbridled acts of willfulness.

Let us consider the first Central Committee Plenum after the XIXth Party Congress when Stalin, in his talk at the Plenum, characterized Vyacheslav Mikhailovich Molotov and Anastas Ivanovich Mikoyan and suggested that these old workers of our Party were guilty of some baseless charges. It is not excluded that had Stalin remained at the helm for another several months, Comrades Molotov and Mikoyan would probably have not delivered any speeches at this Congress.

Stalin evidently had plans to finish off the old members of the Political Bureau. He often stated that Political Bureau members should be replaced by new ones.

His proposal, after the XIXth Congress concerning the selection of 25 persons to the Central Committee Presidium, was aimed at the removal of the old Political Bureau members and the bringing in of less experienced persons so that these would extol him in all sorts of ways.

We can assume that this was also a design for the future annihilation of the old Political Bureau members and in this way a cover for all shameful acts of Stalin, acts which we are now considering.

Comrades! In order not to repeat errors of the past, the Central Committee has declared itself resolutely against the cult of the individual. We consider that Stalin was excessively extolled. However, in the past Stalin doubtless performed great services to the Party, to the working class, and to the international workers' movement.

This question is complicated by the fact that all this which we have just discussed was done during Stalin's life under his leadership and with his concurrence; here Stalin was convinced that this was necessary for the defense of the interests of the working classes against the plotting of the enemies and against the attack of the imperialist camp. He saw this from the position of the interest of the working class, of the interest of the laboring people, of the interest of the victory of socialism and Communism. We cannot say that these were the deeds of a giddy despot. He considered that this should be done in the interest of the Party; of the working masses, in the name of the defense of the revolution's gains. In this lies the whole tragedy!

Comrades! Lenin had often stressed that modesty is an absolutely integral part of a real Bolshevik. Lenin himself was the living personification of the greatest modesty. We cannot say that we have been following this Leninist example in all respects. It is enough to point out that many towns, factories and industrial enterprises, kolkhozes and sovkhozes, Soviet institutions and cultural institutions have been referred to by us with a title — if I may express it so — of private property of the names of these or those government or Party leaders who were still active and in good health. Many of us participated in the action of assigning our names to various towns, rayons, undertakings and kolkhozes. We must correct this. (*Applause.*)

But this should be done calmly and slowly. The Central Committee will discuss this matter and consider it carefully in order to prevent errors and excesses. I can remember how the Ukraine learned about Kossior's arrest. The Kiev radio used to start its programs thus: "This is radio [in the name of] Kossior." When one day the programs began without naming Kossior, everyone was quite certain that something had happened to Kossior, that he probably had been arrested.

Thus, if today we begin to remove the signs everywhere and to change names, people will think that these comrades in whose honor the given enterprises, kolkhozes or cities are named also met some bad fate and that they have also been arrested. (*Animation in the hall.*)

How is the authority and the importance of this or that leader judged? On the basis of how many towns, industrial enterprises and factories, kolkhozes and sovkhozes carry his name. Is it not about time

that we eliminate this "private property" and "nationalize" the factories, the industrial enterprises, the kolkhozes and the sovkhozes?
(*Laughter, applause, voices: "That is right."*) This will benefit our
cause. After all the cult of the individual is manifested also in this way.

We should in all seriousness consider the question of the cult of the
individual. We cannot let this matter get out of the Party, especially
not to the press. It is for this reason that we are considering it here at
a closed Congress session. We should know the limits; we should not
give ammunition to the enemy; we should not wash our dirty linen before their eyes. I think that the delegates to the Congress will understand and assess properly all these proposals. (*Tumultuous applause.*)

Comrades: We must abolish the cult of the individual decisively,
once and for all; we must draw the proper conclusions concerning both
ideological-theoretical and practical work.

It is necessary for this purpose:

First, in a Bolshevik manner to condemn and to eradicate the cult of
the individual as alien to Marxism-Leninism and not consonant with
the principles of Party leadership and the norms of Party life, and to
fight inexorably all attempts at bringing back this practice in one form
or another.

To return to and actually practice in all our ideological work the
most important theses of Marxist-Leninist science about the people as
the creator of history and as the creator of all material and spiritual
good of humanity, about the decisive role of the Marxist Party in the
revolutionary fight for the transformation of society, about the victory
of Communism.

In this connection we will be forced to do much work in order to examine critically from the Marxist-Leninist viewpoint and to correct the
widely spread erroneous views connected with the cult of the individual in the sphere of history, philosophy, economy and of other sciences,
as well as in literature and the fine arts. It is especially necessary that
in the immediate future we compile a serious textbook of the history of
our Party which will be edited in accordance with scientific Marxist
objectivism, a textbook of the history of Soviet society, a book pertaining to the events of the Civil War and the Great Patriotic War.

Secondly, to continue systematically and consistently the work done
by the Party's Central Committee during the last years, a work characterized by minute observation in all Party organizations, from the bot-

tom to the top, of the Leninist principles of Party leadership, characterized, above all, by the main principle of collective leadership, characterized by the observation of the norms of Party life described in the Statutes of our Party, and finally, characterized by the wide practice of criticism and self-criticism.

Thirdly, to restore completely the Leninist principles of Soviet socialist democracy, expressed in the Constitution of the Soviet Union, to fight willfulness of individuals abusing their power. The evil caused by acts violating revolutionary socialist legality which have accumulated during a long time as a result of the negative influence of the cult of the individual has to be completely corrected. Comrades! The XXth Congress of the Communist Party of the Soviet Union has manifested with a new strength the unshakable unity of our Party, its cohesiveness around the Central Committee, its resolute will to accomplish the great task of building Communism. (*Tumultuous applause.*) And the fact that we present in all their ramifications the basic problems of overcoming the cult of the individual which is alien to Marxism-Leninism, as well as the problem of liquidating its burdensome consequences, is an evidence of the great moral and political strength of our Party. (*Prolonged applause.*)

We are absolutely certain that our Party, armed with the historical resolutions of the XXth Congress, will lead the Soviet people along the Leninist path to new successes, to new victories. (*Tumultuous, prolonged applause.*)

Long live the victorious banner of our Party — Leninism! (*Tumultuous, prolonged applause ending in ovation. All rise.*)

Index